Yeah!

by Peter Bagge and Gilbert Hernandez

FANTAGRAPHICS BOOKS

Fantagraphics Books, 7563 Lake City Way NE, Seattle WA 98115 | This material was previously published by DC Comics as a series of nine comic books in 1999 and 2000. | All contents © 2011 Peter Bagge. This edition is copyright © 2011 Fantagraphics Books, Inc. All rights reserved. Permission to quote or reproduce material for reviews or notices must be obtained from Fantagraphics Books, in writing, at 7563 Lake City Way NE, Seattle, WA 98115. | Distributed in the U.S. (bookstores) by W.W. Norton and Company, Inc. (212-354-4830) | Distributed in the U.S. (comics shops) by Diamond Comic Distributors, Inc. (800-452-6642 x 215) | Distributed in Canada by Canadian Manda Group (800-452-6642 x 862) | Distributed in the United Kingdom by Turnaround Distribution (208-829-3009) | First edition: May, 2011. Printed in Hong Kong. | ISBN: 978-1-60699-412-2

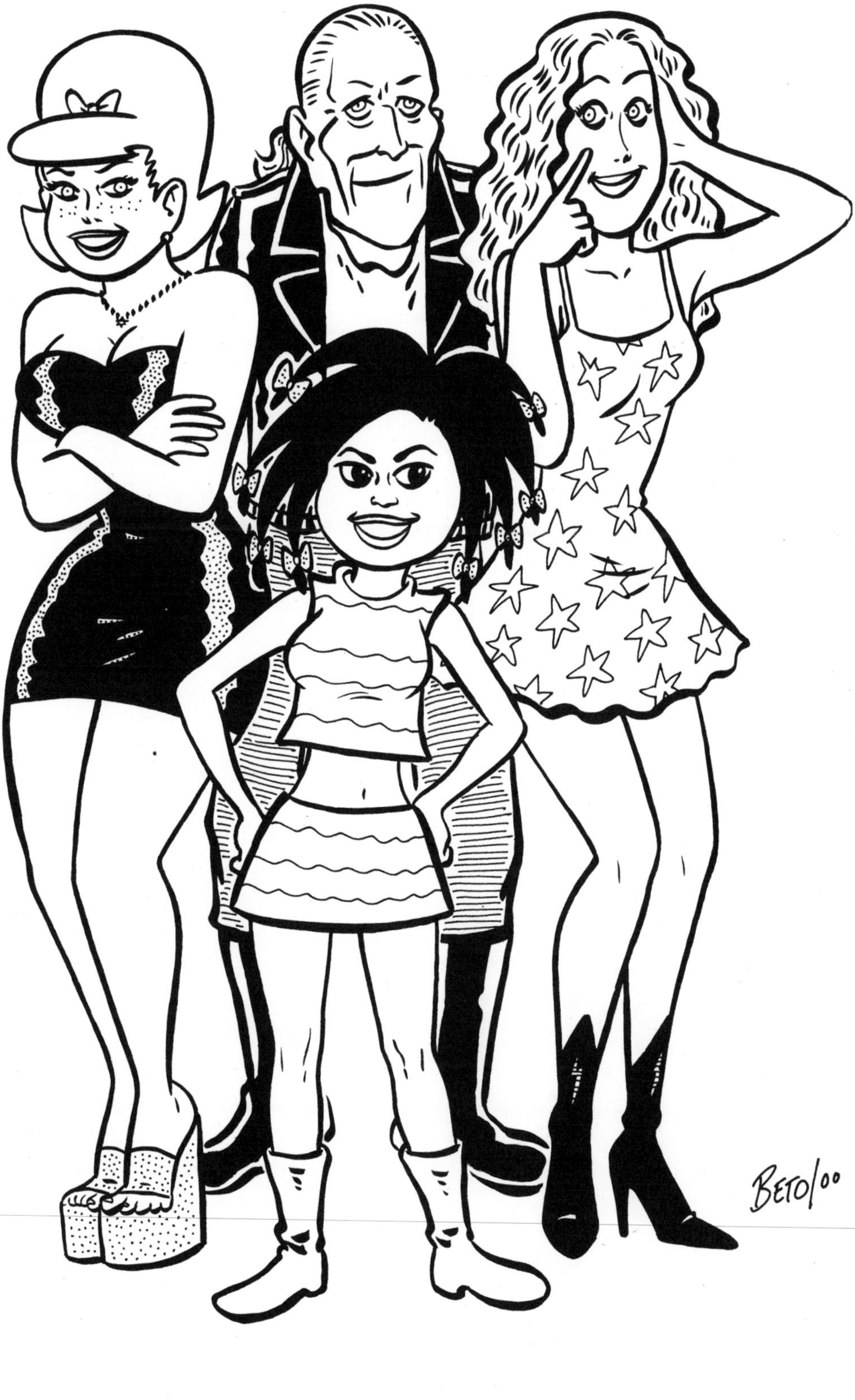
BETO/00

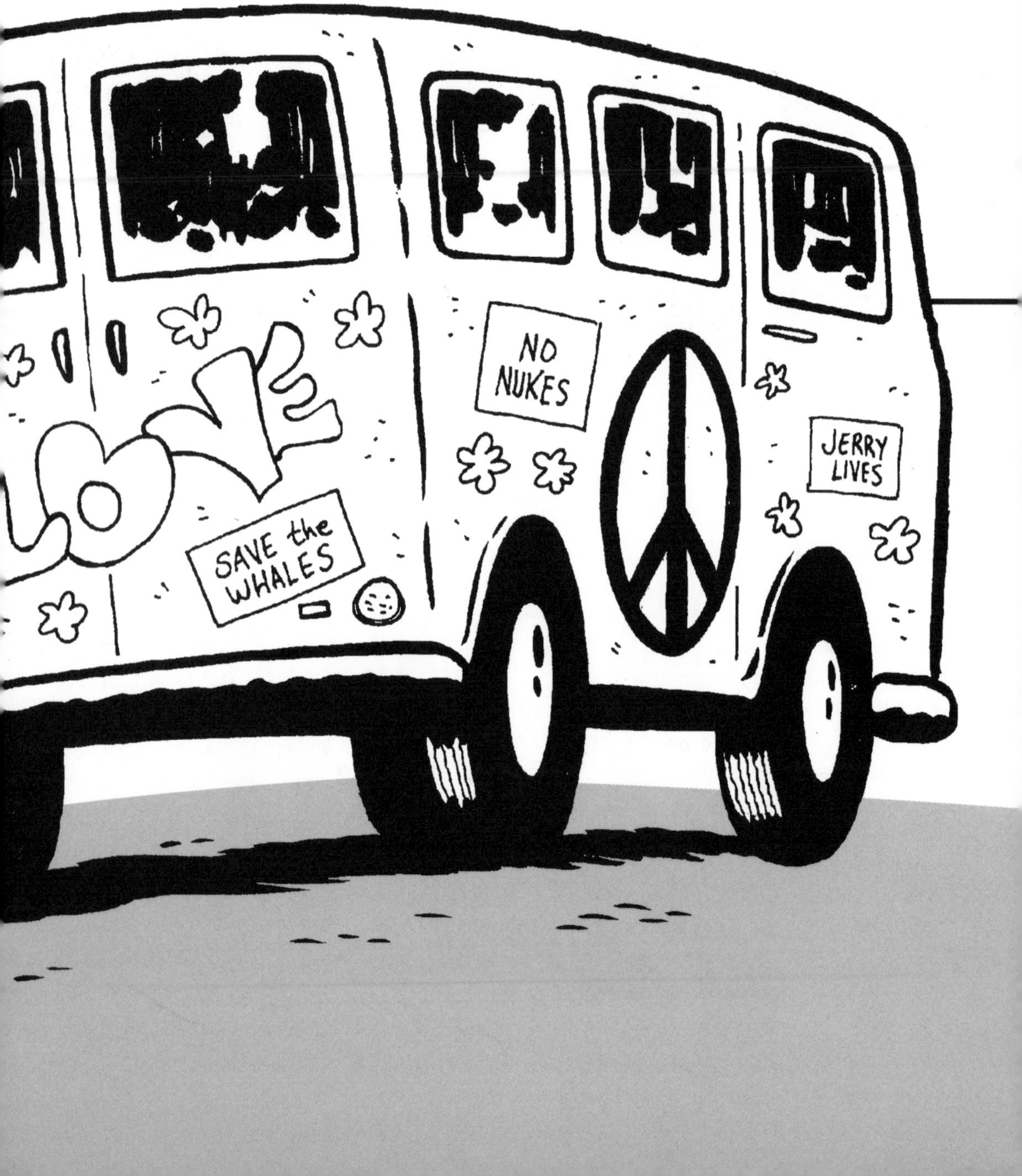

NO NUKES
JERRY LIVES
SAVE the WHALES

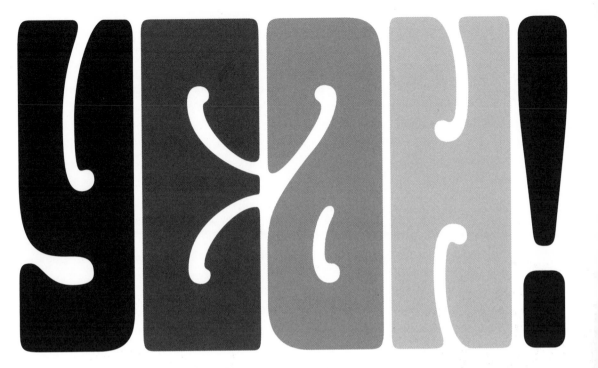

— An Explainer by Peter Bagge —

By the end of the last millennium, I had almost entirely devoted the last 10 years of my life not only to producing so-called alternative comics, but to producing one title in particular: HATE. As the title suggests, HATE was quite "edgy" — it followed the foibles of a semi-autobiographical character and his nihilistic, no-account friends in a rather uncensored, warts-and-all manner. The end results were hardly for everyone, but the people who did enjoy it were overwhelmingly of a certain type: urban-dwelling 20-somethings who were eager to embrace anything that wasn't mainstream or easily accessible. *You know, hipsters.*

When you consider who my hard-earned fan base was, you would think that suddenly creating a squeaky clean all-ages comic book for some huge corporate outfit would be the worst career move I could have possibly made, yet that's exactly what I did. Hey, I was bored! Though I also was quite eager to attempt

something radically different at that time, when an opportunity presented itself to do just that.

A long-time editor at DC/Vertigo named Shelly Roeberg (now Shelly Bond) called me and asked if I'd like to develop title a monthly for Vertigo – the only catch being that I'd only be able to write it and not draw it, which was fine with me since writing had always come a bit easier to me anyway. My biggest problem was coming up with something suitable for the Vertigo line, which relied on genres — i.e.: gothic romance, post-apocalyptic sci-fi, etc. — that I'd no experience working in or even much interest in in general. It didn't look like a good fit, in other words.

Meanwhile, being the father of a then 8-year-old girl, I suddenly found myself neck deep in "girl" pop culture, and found myself getting into some of the pop music I was hearing through her. I especially enjoyed the Spice Girls, whom I found to be wildly funny and entertaining. It also revived my interest in various kinds of teenybopper or "bubblegum" music from my own past, and found myself enjoying all of it more than ever, coming at it as I was from a much less self-conscious angle.

So, figuring it was a long shot I pro-posed an all-ages title that would be heavily inspired by the Spice Girls and Josie and the Pussycats, with some slightly ragged punk/DYI attitude thrown in for flavor. Much to my surprise, Shelly loved the idea, though she had to arrange for it to be released on a different imprint (DC/Homage), for it to happen. At my perverse insistence, the title would also be Comic Code approved, since I was curious to see if I was capable of writing scripts that would routinely meet with those anonymous censors' approval (and I succeeded! — as much as one could consider such a thing a "success," that is).

The next step was finding a suitable artist for the project, and after some arm-twisting Gilbert Hernandez of LOVE AND ROCKETS fame agreed to take on the project. I was quite thrilled about this, since not only is Gilbert one of my favorite artists ever, he also was able to recreate that Dan DeCarlo-esque '60s Archies look that I had in mind for the title. The main thing that concerned both of us was being able to meet a monthly deadline. We alternative cartoonist type are quite precious creatures who can only create when the stars are aligned and our jasmine tea is at just the right temperature, so having to play slave to a calendar was something new to us. Yet hack away we did! Like the late great Bill Finger, we never missed a deadline!

In spite of all this — AND in spite of the fact that the resulting title was everything I envisioned it to be and then some — YEAH! was a failure. My existing fan base didn't get it, for one thing. They kept looking for irony and satire when there wasn't any, so my intentions were both lost and wasted on them. It also failed in reaching what we hoped would be a big potential audience, namely pre-teen girls. Perhaps they couldn't find it or simply didn't like it — or maybe it was too old-fashioned looking to them, the product of a different era. Ironically, young females started reading more comics than anyone else shortly after YEAH! ended, though it would be those godawful "manga" comics that would draw them in, rather than my stupid slop.

So after 9 issues and ever-dwindling sales, YEAH! Was tragically yet mercifully brought to an end. Amazingly, this failed title came close to becoming a TV show shortly after its cancellation. I had a luc-rative development deal with an established production company behind it, but before I even started on a pilot script a feature film version of *Josie and the Pussycats* was released to empty theaters and horrendous reviews (I LOVED that flick, btw), which seemed to take all the wind out of the sails of my backers. So once again, that was that.

Until now that is. Now there's a book collection of the entire series that you're holding in your grubby mitts, thanks to the fine folks at Fantagraphic Books. SO here's hoping YEAH! finally finds its "audience" at last!

Best,
Peter Bagge

SEATTLE, WA | FEB. 3, 2011

ONE!

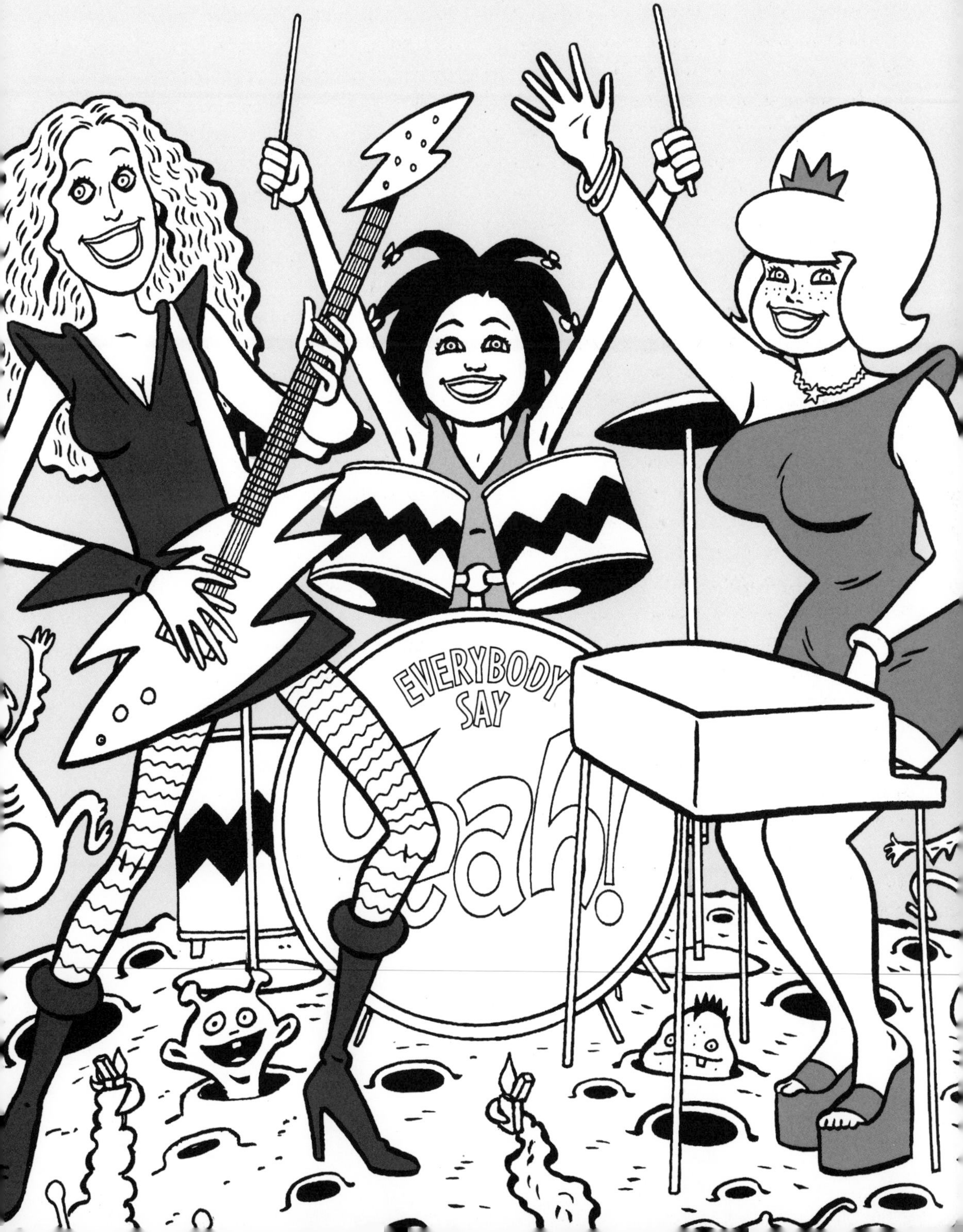
EVERYBODY SAY
Yeah!

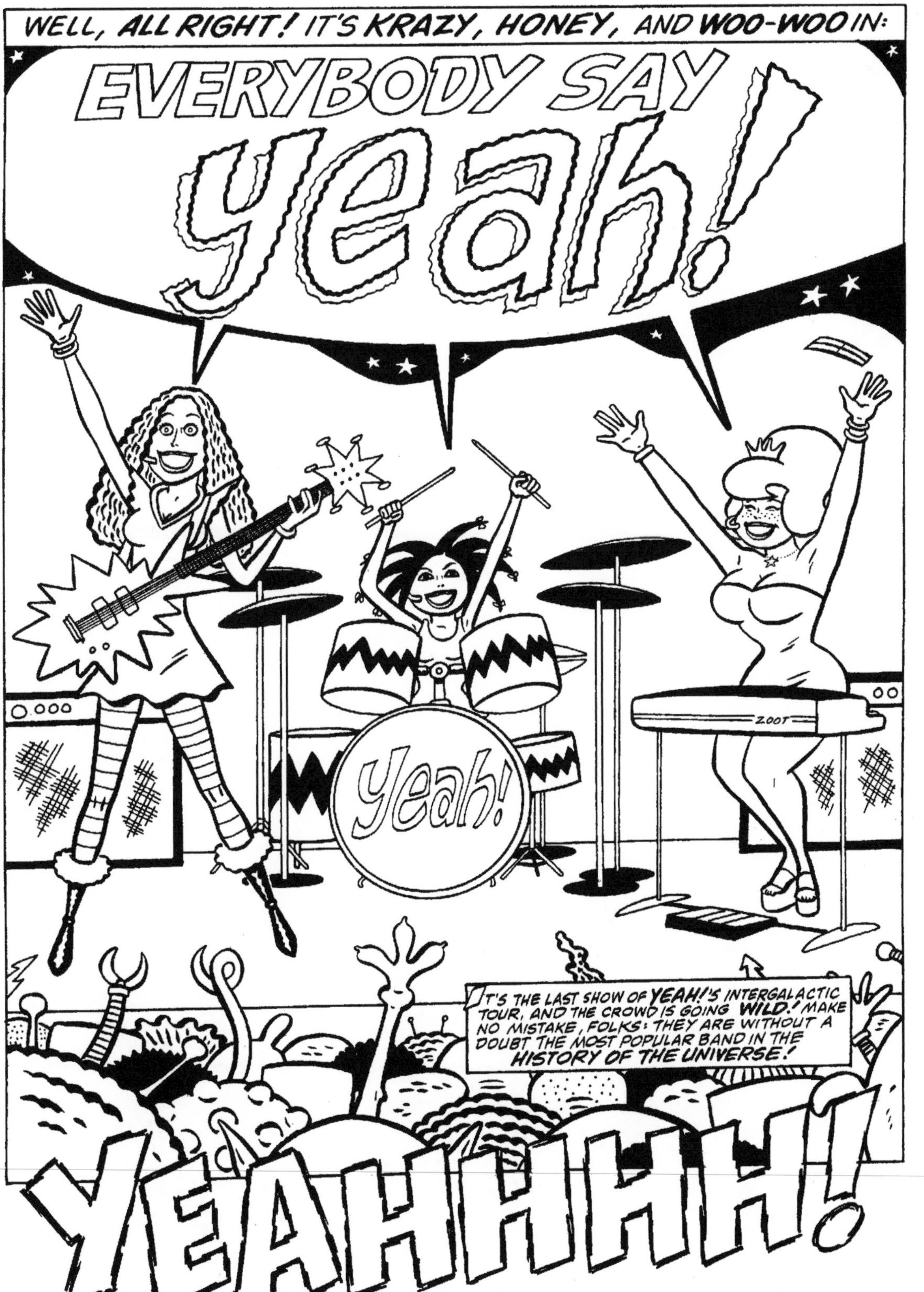

WELL, ALL RIGHT! IT'S KRAZY, HONEY, AND WOO-WOO IN:
EVERYBODY SAY yeah!
ZOOT
yeah!
IT'S THE LAST SHOW OF YEAH!'S INTERGALACTIC TOUR, AND THE CROWD IS GOING WILD! MAKE NO MISTAKE, FOLKS: THEY ARE WITHOUT A DOUBT THE MOST POPULAR BAND IN THE HISTORY OF THE UNIVERSE!
YEAHHHHH!

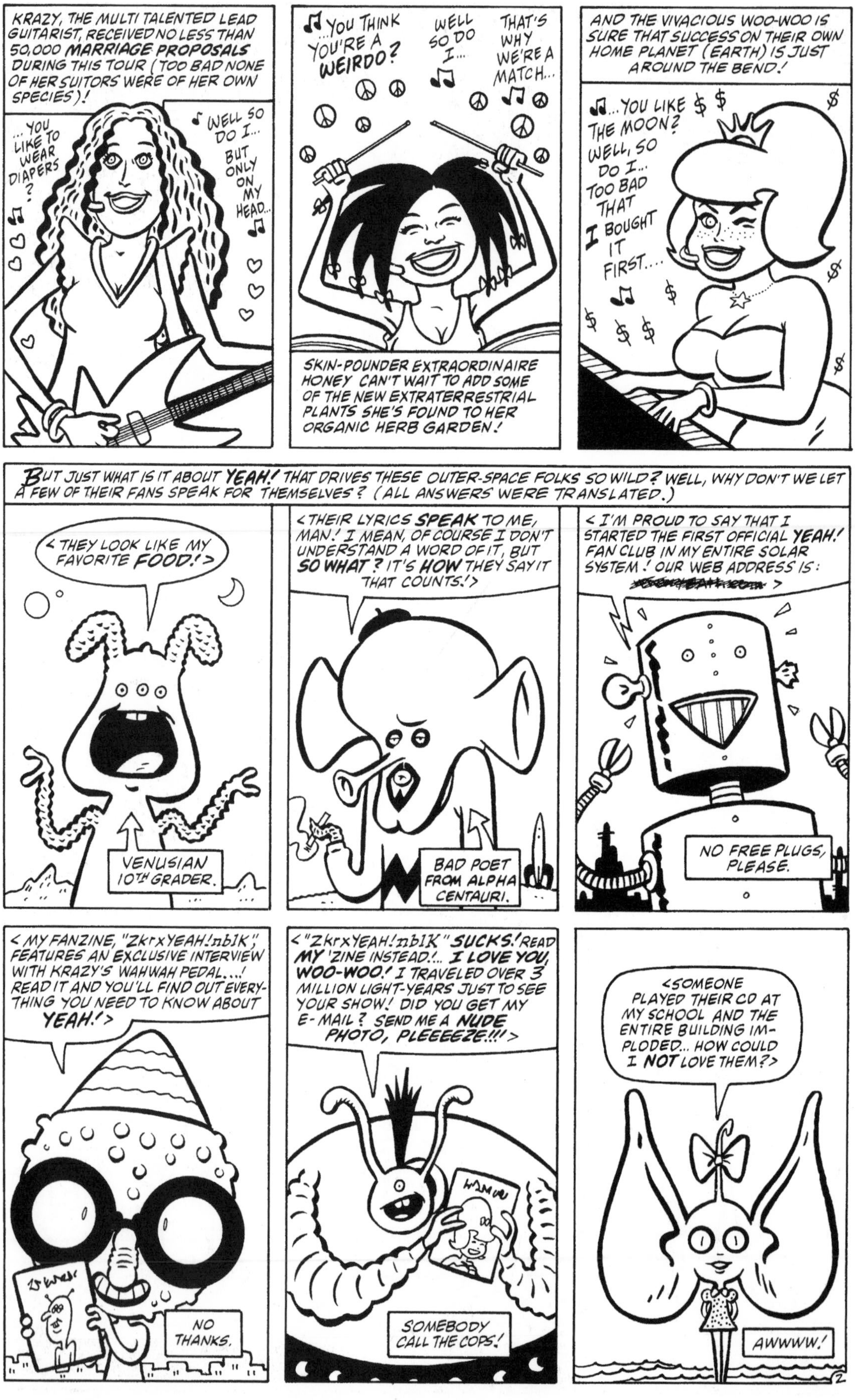
KRAZY, THE MULTI TALENTED LEAD GUITARIST, RECEIVED NO LESS THAN 50,000 MARRIAGE PROPOSALS DURING THIS TOUR (TOO BAD NONE OF HER SUITORS WERE OF HER OWN SPECIES)!
...YOU LIKE TO WEAR DIAPERS?
WELL SO DO I... BUT ONLY ON MY HEAD...
...YOU THINK YOU'RE A WEIRDO?
WELL SO DO I...
THAT'S WHY WE'RE A MATCH...
SKIN-POUNDER EXTRAORDINAIRE HONEY CAN'T WAIT TO ADD SOME OF THE NEW EXTRATERRESTRIAL PLANTS SHE'S FOUND TO HER ORGANIC HERB GARDEN!
AND THE VIVACIOUS WOO-WOO IS SURE THAT SUCCESS ON THEIR OWN HOME PLANET (EARTH) IS JUST AROUND THE BEND!
...YOU LIKE THE MOON? WELL, SO DO I... TOO BAD THAT I BOUGHT IT FIRST....
BUT JUST WHAT IS IT ABOUT YEAH! THAT DRIVES THESE OUTER-SPACE FOLKS SO WILD? WELL, WHY DON'T WE LET A FEW OF THEIR FANS SPEAK FOR THEMSELVES? (ALL ANSWERS WERE TRANSLATED.)
<THEY LOOK LIKE MY FAVORITE FOOD!>
VENUSIAN 10TH GRADER.
<THEIR LYRICS SPEAK TO ME, MAN! I MEAN, OF COURSE I DON'T UNDERSTAND A WORD OF IT, BUT SO WHAT? IT'S HOW THEY SAY IT THAT COUNTS!>
BAD POET FROM ALPHA CENTAURI.
<I'M PROUD TO SAY THAT I STARTED THE FIRST OFFICIAL YEAH! FAN CLUB IN MY ENTIRE SOLAR SYSTEM! OUR WEB ADDRESS IS: [redacted]>
NO FREE PLUGS, PLEASE.
<MY FANZINE, "ZkrxYEAH!nblK," FEATURES AN EXCLUSIVE INTERVIEW WITH KRAZY'S WAHWAH PEDAL....! READ IT AND YOU'LL FIND OUT EVERYTHING YOU NEED TO KNOW ABOUT YEAH!>
NO THANKS.
<"ZkrxYEAH!nblK" SUCKS! READ MY 'ZINE INSTEAD!... I LOVE YOU, WOO-WOO! I TRAVELED OVER 3 MILLION LIGHT-YEARS JUST TO SEE YOUR SHOW! DID YOU GET MY E-MAIL? SEND ME A NUDE PHOTO, PLEEEEZE!!!>
SOMEBODY CALL THE COPS!
<SOMEONE PLAYED THEIR CD AT MY SCHOOL AND THE ENTIRE BUILDING IMPLODED... HOW COULD I NOT LOVE THEM?>
AWWWW!

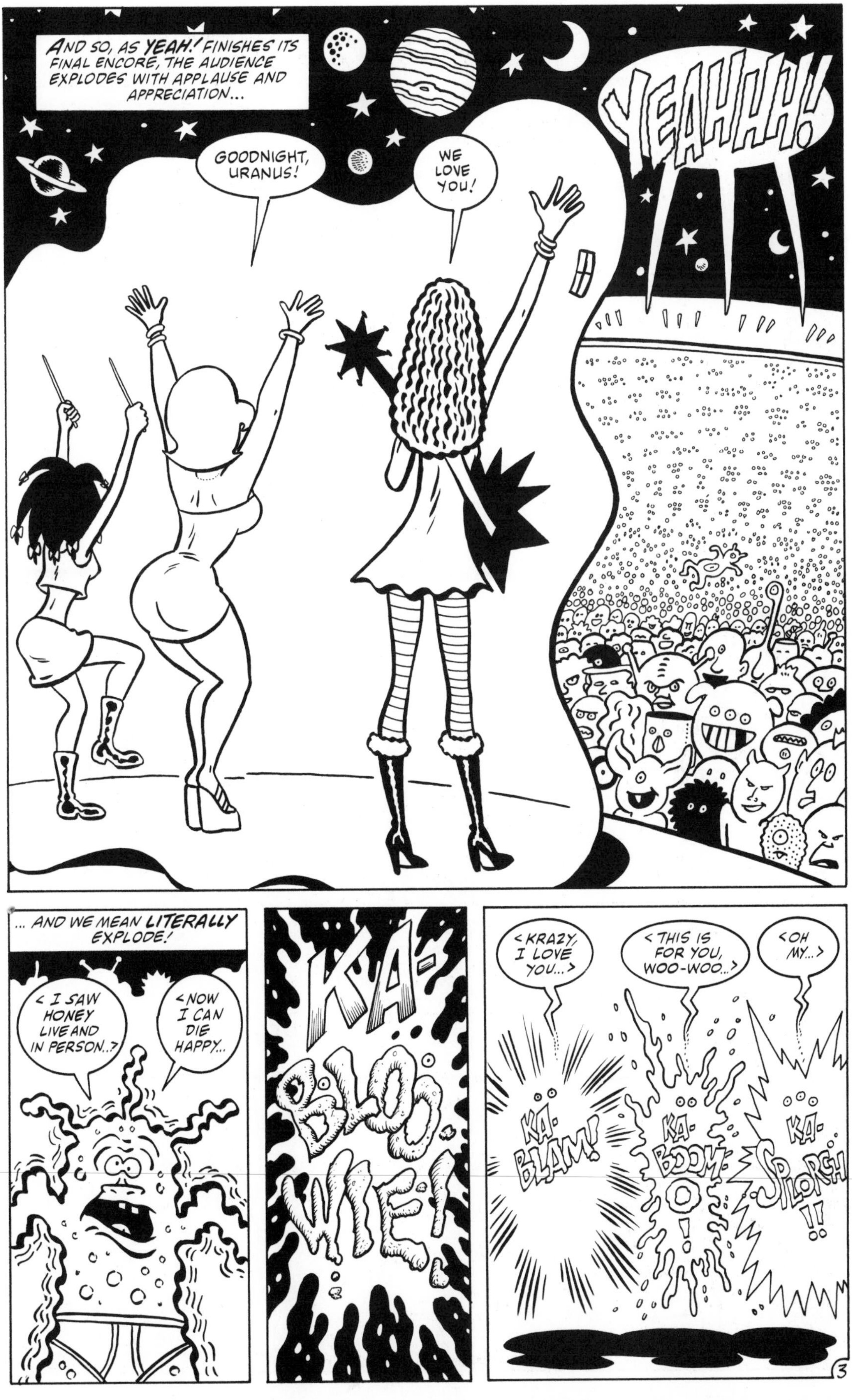
AND SO, AS YEAH! FINISHES ITS FINAL ENCORE, THE AUDIENCE EXPLODES WITH APPLAUSE AND APPRECIATION...
GOODNIGHT, URANUS!
WE LOVE YOU!
YEAHHH!
... AND WE MEAN LITERALLY EXPLODE!
< I SAW HONEY LIVE AND IN PERSON..>
<NOW I CAN DIE HAPPY...
KA-BLOOWIE!
<KRAZY, I LOVE YOU...>
< THIS IS FOR YOU, WOO-WOO...>
<OH MY...>
KA-BLAM!
KA-BOOM!
KA-SPLORCH!!

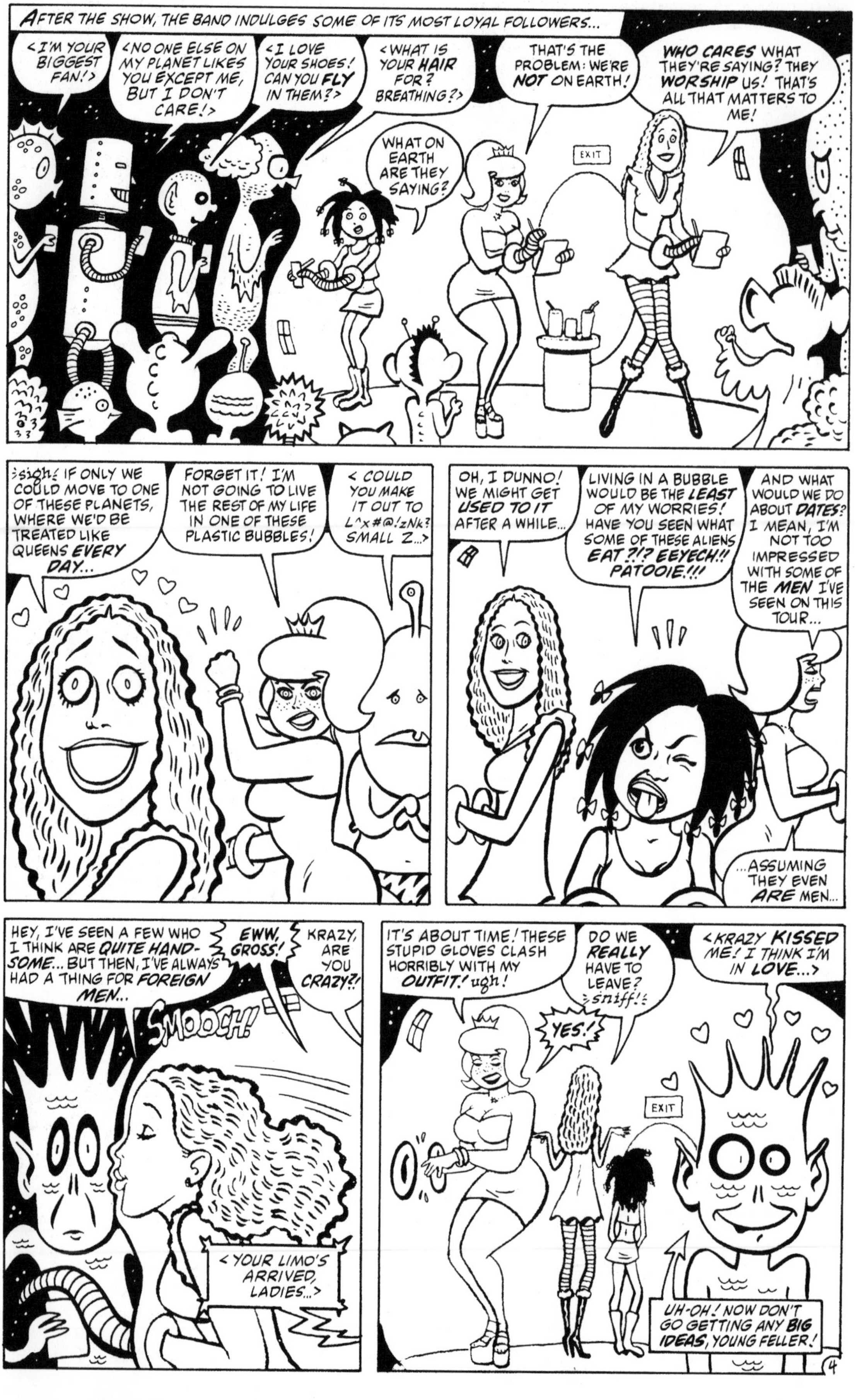

AFTER THE SHOW, THE BAND INDULGES SOME OF ITS MOST LOYAL FOLLOWERS...
<I'M YOUR BIGGEST FAN!>
<NO ONE ELSE ON MY PLANET LIKES YOU EXCEPT ME, BUT I DON'T CARE!>
<I LOVE YOUR SHOES! CAN YOU FLY IN THEM?>
<WHAT IS YOUR HAIR FOR? BREATHING?>
WHAT ON EARTH ARE THEY SAYING?
THAT'S THE PROBLEM: WE'RE NOT ON EARTH!
WHO CARES WHAT THEY'RE SAYING? THEY WORSHIP US! THAT'S ALL THAT MATTERS TO ME!
EXIT
:sigh: IF ONLY WE COULD MOVE TO ONE OF THESE PLANETS, WHERE WE'D BE TREATED LIKE QUEENS EVERY DAY...
FORGET IT! I'M NOT GOING TO LIVE THE REST OF MY LIFE IN ONE OF THESE PLASTIC BUBBLES!
< COULD YOU MAKE IT OUT TO L^x#@!zNk? SMALL Z...>
OH, I DUNNO! WE MIGHT GET USED TO IT AFTER A WHILE...
LIVING IN A BUBBLE WOULD BE THE LEAST OF MY WORRIES! HAVE YOU SEEN WHAT SOME OF THESE ALIENS EAT?!? EEYECH!! PATOOIE!!!
AND WHAT WOULD WE DO ABOUT DATES? I MEAN, I'M NOT TOO IMPRESSED WITH SOME OF THE MEN I'VE SEEN ON THIS TOUR...
...ASSUMING THEY EVEN ARE MEN...
HEY, I'VE SEEN A FEW WHO I THINK ARE QUITE HANDSOME... BUT THEN, I'VE ALWAYS HAD A THING FOR FOREIGN MEN...
EWW, GROSS!
KRAZY, ARE YOU CRAZY?!
SMOOCH!
<YOUR LIMO'S ARRIVED, LADIES...>
IT'S ABOUT TIME! THESE STUPID GLOVES CLASH HORRIBLY WITH MY OUTFIT! ugh!
DO WE REALLY HAVE TO LEAVE? :sniff!:
YES!
<KRAZY KISSED ME! I THINK I'M IN LOVE...>
EXIT
UH-OH! NOW DON'T GO GETTING ANY BIG IDEAS, YOUNG FELLER!

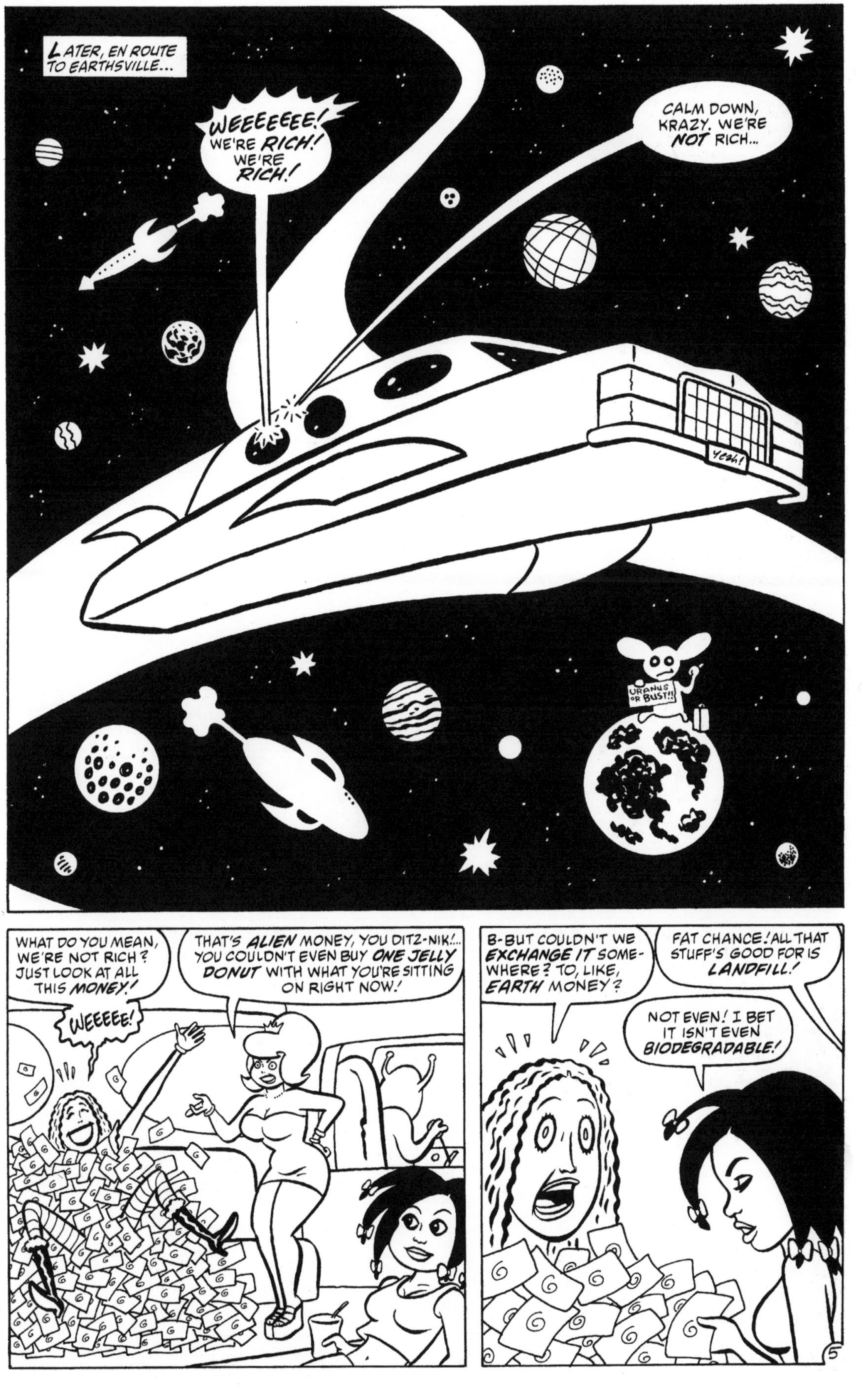
LATER, EN ROUTE TO EARTHSVILLE...
WEEEEEEE! WE'RE RICH! WE'RE RICH!
CALM DOWN, KRAZY. WE'RE NOT RICH...
Yeah!
URANUS OR BUST!!
WHAT DO YOU MEAN, WE'RE NOT RICH? JUST LOOK AT ALL THIS MONEY!
WEEEEE!
THAT'S ALIEN MONEY, YOU DITZ-NIK!... YOU COULDN'T EVEN BUY ONE JELLY DONUT WITH WHAT YOU'RE SITTING ON RIGHT NOW!
B-BUT COULDN'T WE EXCHANGE IT SOME-WHERE? TO, LIKE, EARTH MONEY?
FAT CHANCE! ALL THAT STUFF'S GOOD FOR IS LANDFILL!
NOT EVEN! I BET IT ISN'T EVEN BIODEGRADABLE!

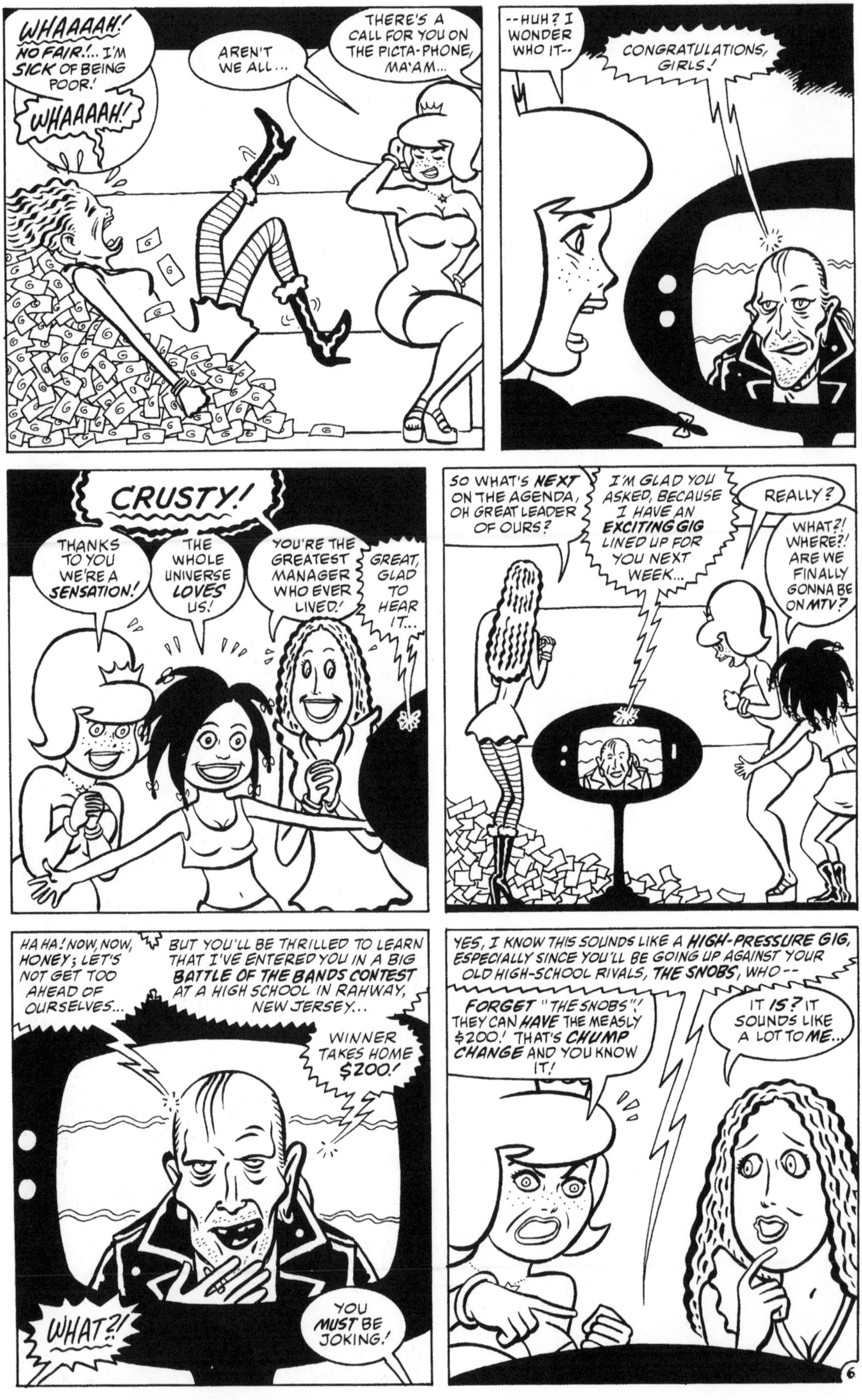
WHAAAAH! NO FAIR!.. I'M SICK OF BEING POOR!
WHAAAAH!
AREN'T WE ALL...
THERE'S A CALL FOR YOU ON THE PICTA-PHONE, MA'AM...
--HUH? I WONDER WHO IT--
CONGRATULATIONS, GIRLS!
CRUSTY!
THANKS TO YOU WE'RE A SENSATION!
THE WHOLE UNIVERSE LOVES US!
YOU'RE THE GREATEST MANAGER WHO EVER LIVED!
GREAT, GLAD TO HEAR IT...
SO WHAT'S NEXT ON THE AGENDA, OH GREAT LEADER OF OURS?
I'M GLAD YOU ASKED, BECAUSE I HAVE AN EXCITING GIG LINED UP FOR YOU NEXT WEEK...
REALLY?
WHAT?! WHERE?! ARE WE FINALLY GONNA BE ON MTV?
HA HA! NOW, NOW, HONEY; LET'S NOT GET TOO AHEAD OF OURSELVES...
BUT YOU'LL BE THRILLED TO LEARN THAT I'VE ENTERED YOU IN A BIG BATTLE OF THE BANDS CONTEST AT A HIGH SCHOOL IN RAHWAY, NEW JERSEY...
WINNER TAKES HOME $200!
WHAT?!
YOU MUST BE JOKING!
YES, I KNOW THIS SOUNDS LIKE A HIGH-PRESSURE GIG, ESPECIALLY SINCE YOU'LL BE GOING UP AGAINST YOUR OLD HIGH-SCHOOL RIVALS, THE SNOBS, WHO--
FORGET "THE SNOBS"! THEY CAN HAVE THE MEASLY $200! THAT'S CHUMP CHANGE AND YOU KNOW IT!
IT IS? IT SOUNDS LIKE A LOT TO ME...

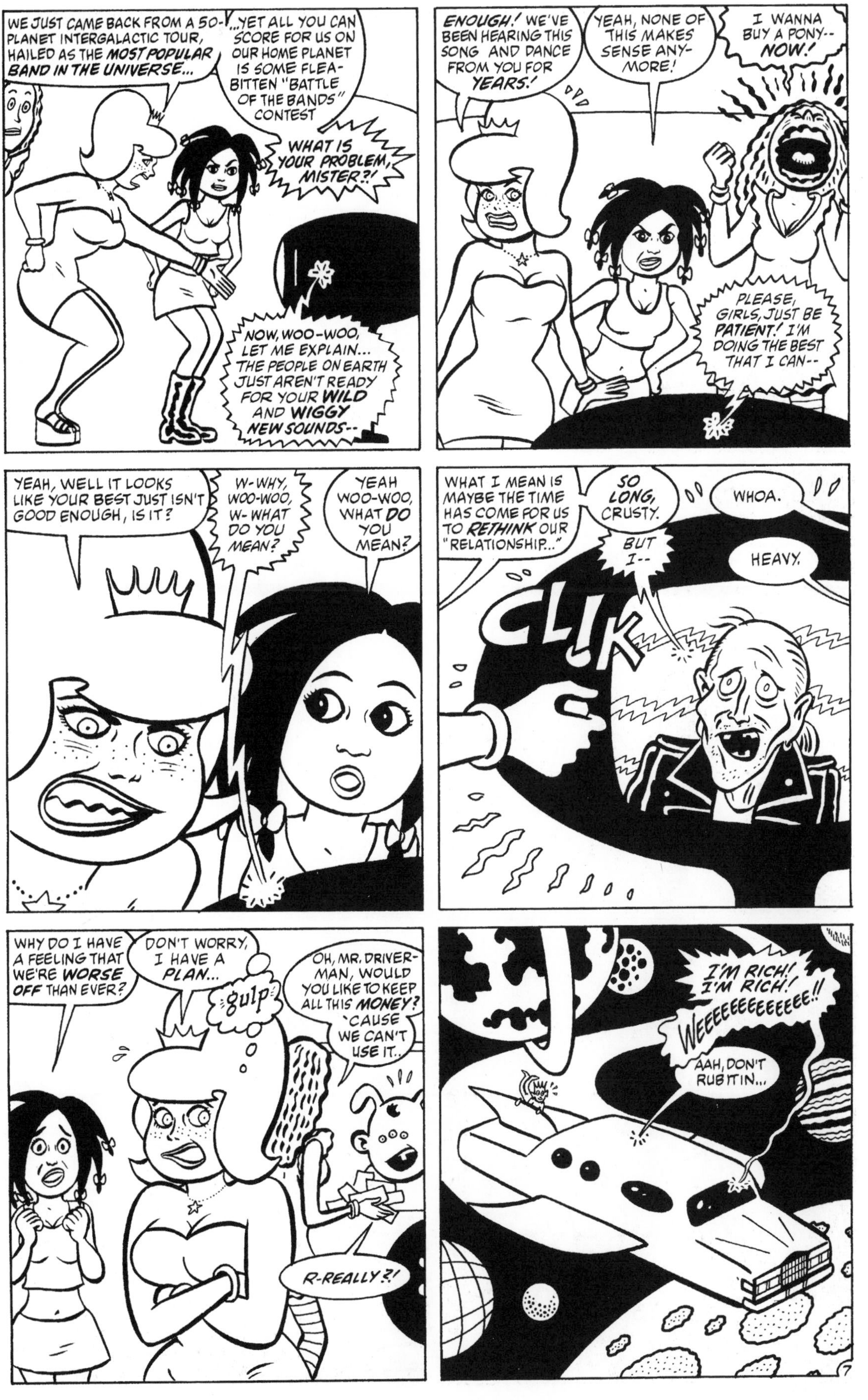
WE JUST CAME BACK FROM A 50-PLANET INTERGALACTIC TOUR, HAILED AS THE MOST POPULAR BAND IN THE UNIVERSE...
...YET ALL YOU CAN SCORE FOR US ON OUR HOME PLANET IS SOME FLEA-BITTEN "BATTLE OF THE BANDS" CONTEST
WHAT IS YOUR PROBLEM, MISTER?!
NOW, WOO-WOO, LET ME EXPLAIN... THE PEOPLE ON EARTH JUST AREN'T READY FOR YOUR WILD AND WIGGY NEW SOUNDS--
ENOUGH! WE'VE BEEN HEARING THIS SONG AND DANCE FROM YOU FOR YEARS!
YEAH, NONE OF THIS MAKES SENSE ANYMORE!
I WANNA BUY A PONY-- NOW!
PLEASE, GIRLS, JUST BE PATIENT! I'M DOING THE BEST THAT I CAN--
YEAH, WELL IT LOOKS LIKE YOUR BEST JUST ISN'T GOOD ENOUGH, IS IT?
W-WHY, WOO-WOO, W-WHAT DO YOU MEAN?
YEAH WOO-WOO, WHAT DO YOU MEAN?
WHAT I MEAN IS MAYBE THE TIME HAS COME FOR US TO RETHINK OUR "RELATIONSHIP..."
SO LONG, CRUSTY.
BUT I--
CLIK
WHOA.
HEAVY.
WHY DO I HAVE A FEELING THAT WE'RE WORSE OFF THAN EVER?
DON'T WORRY, I HAVE A PLAN...
gulp
OH, MR. DRIVER-MAN, WOULD YOU LIKE TO KEEP ALL THIS MONEY? 'CAUSE WE CAN'T USE IT..
R-REALLY?!
I'M RICH! I'M RICH!
WEEEEEEEEEEEEE!!
AAH, DON'T RUB IT IN...

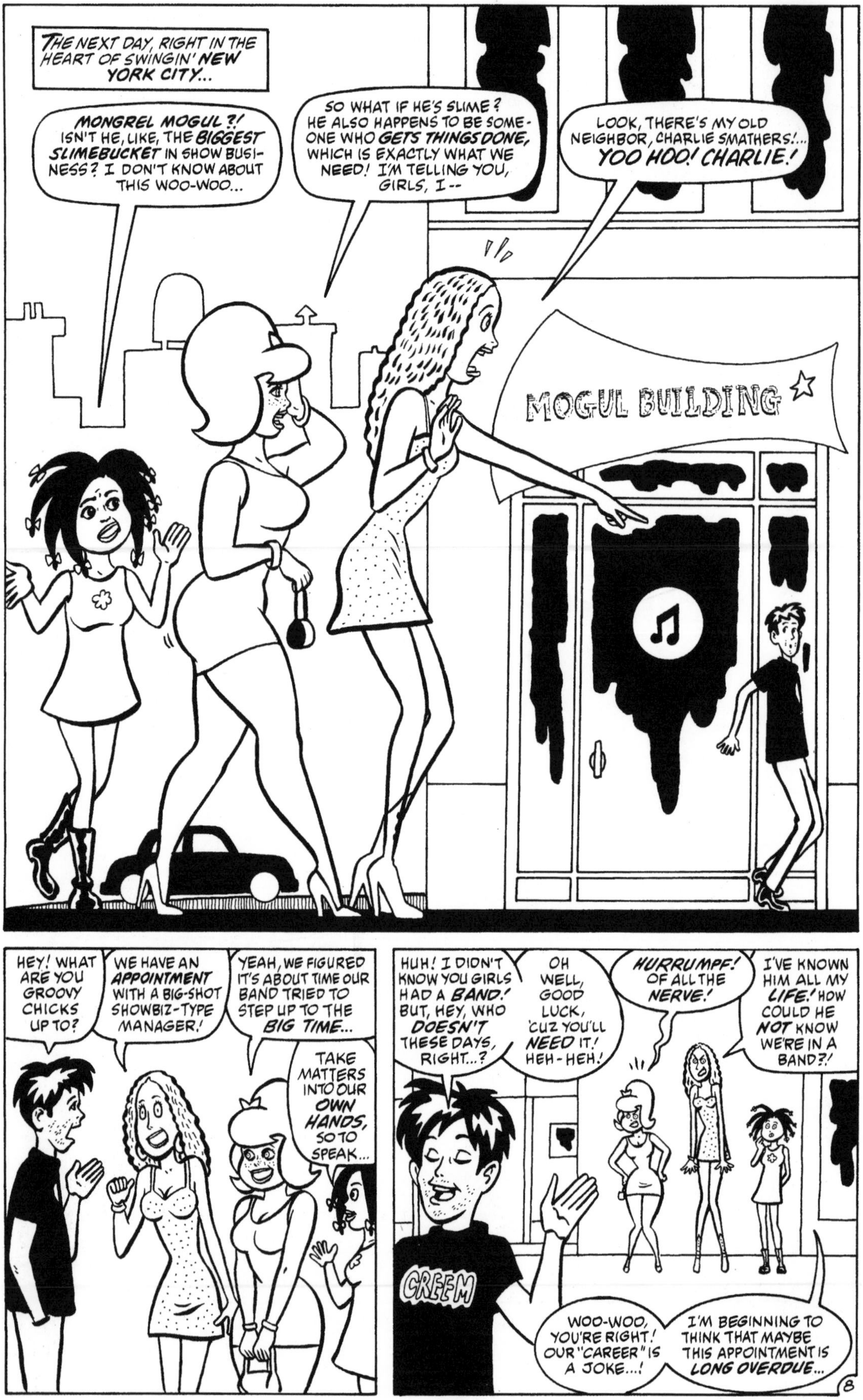
THE NEXT DAY, RIGHT IN THE HEART OF SWINGIN' NEW YORK CITY...
MONGREL MOGUL?! ISN'T HE, LIKE, THE BIGGEST SLIMEBUCKET IN SHOW BUSINESS? I DON'T KNOW ABOUT THIS WOO-WOO...
SO WHAT IF HE'S SLIME? HE ALSO HAPPENS TO BE SOMEONE WHO GETS THINGS DONE, WHICH IS EXACTLY WHAT WE NEED! I'M TELLING YOU, GIRLS, I--
LOOK, THERE'S MY OLD NEIGHBOR, CHARLIE SMATHERS!... YOO HOO! CHARLIE!
MOGUL BUILDING
HEY! WHAT ARE YOU GROOVY CHICKS UP TO?
WE HAVE AN APPOINTMENT WITH A BIG-SHOT SHOWBIZ-TYPE MANAGER!
YEAH, WE FIGURED IT'S ABOUT TIME OUR BAND TRIED TO STEP UP TO THE BIG TIME...
TAKE MATTERS INTO OUR OWN HANDS, SO TO SPEAK...
HUH! I DIDN'T KNOW YOU GIRLS HAD A BAND! BUT, HEY, WHO DOESN'T THESE DAYS, RIGHT...?
OH WELL, GOOD LUCK, 'CUZ YOU'LL NEED IT! HEH-HEH!
HURRUMPF! OF ALL THE NERVE!
I'VE KNOWN HIM ALL MY LIFE! HOW COULD HE NOT KNOW WE'RE IN A BAND?!
CREEM
WOO-WOO, YOU'RE RIGHT! OUR "CAREER" IS A JOKE...!
I'M BEGINNING TO THINK THAT MAYBE THIS APPOINTMENT IS LONG OVERDUE...

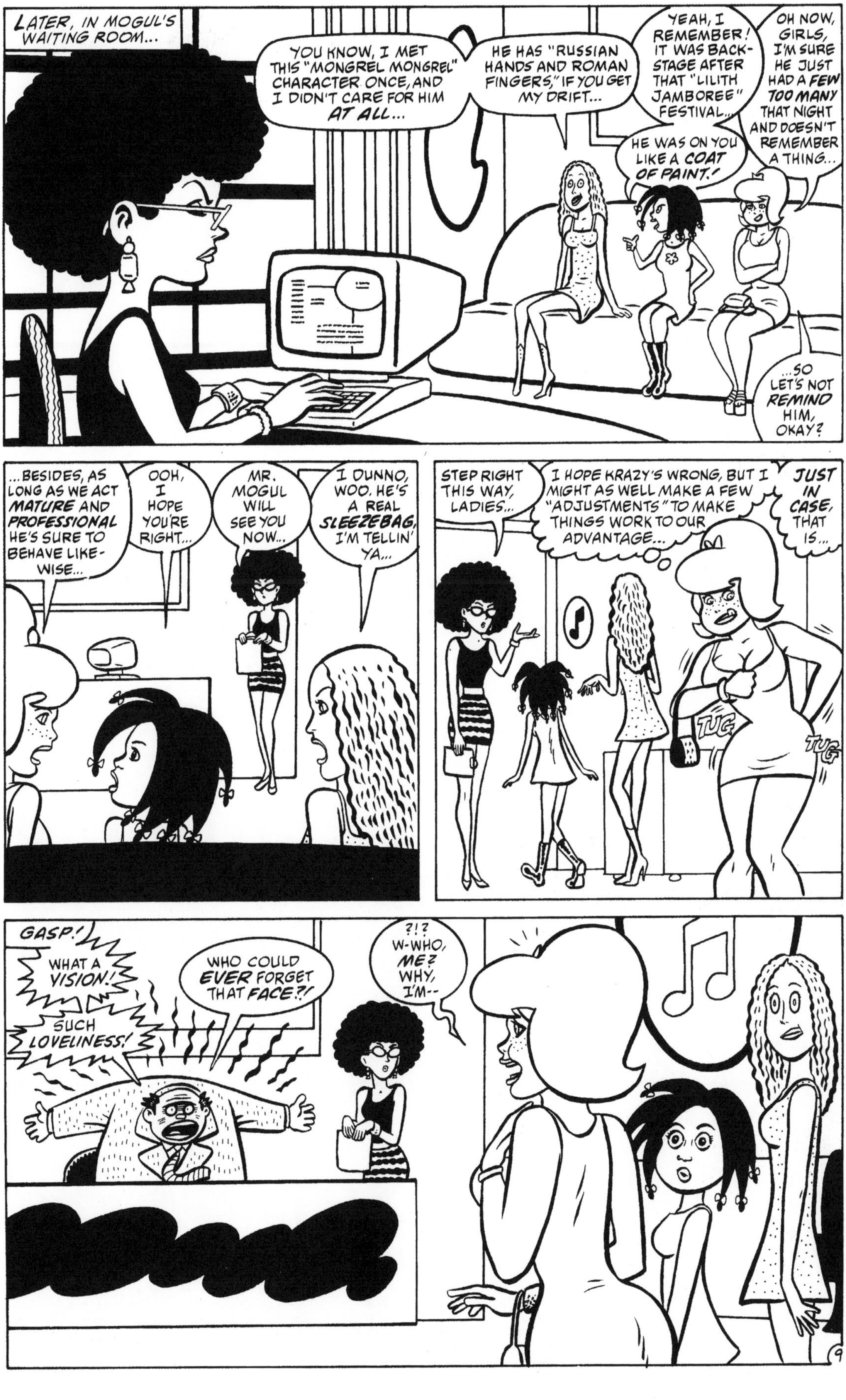
LATER, IN MOGUL'S WAITING ROOM...
YOU KNOW, I MET THIS "MONGREL MONGREL" CHARACTER ONCE, AND I DIDN'T CARE FOR HIM AT ALL...
HE HAS "RUSSIAN HANDS AND ROMAN FINGERS," IF YOU GET MY DRIFT...
YEAH, I REMEMBER! IT WAS BACK-STAGE AFTER THAT "LILITH JAMBOREE" FESTIVAL...
HE WAS ON YOU LIKE A COAT OF PAINT!
OH NOW, GIRLS, I'M SURE HE JUST HAD A FEW TOO MANY THAT NIGHT AND DOESN'T REMEMBER A THING...
...SO LET'S NOT REMIND HIM, OKAY?
...BESIDES, AS LONG AS WE ACT MATURE AND PROFESSIONAL HE'S SURE TO BEHAVE LIKE-WISE...
OOH, I HOPE YOU'RE RIGHT...
MR. MOGUL WILL SEE YOU NOW...
I DUNNO, WOO. HE'S A REAL SLEEZEBAG, I'M TELLIN' YA...
STEP RIGHT THIS WAY, LADIES...
I HOPE KRAZY'S WRONG, BUT I MIGHT AS WELL MAKE A FEW "ADJUSTMENTS" TO MAKE THINGS WORK TO OUR ADVANTAGE...
JUST IN CASE, THAT IS...
TUG
TUG
GASP!
WHAT A VISION!
SUCH LOVELINESS!
WHO COULD EVER FORGET THAT FACE?!
?!?
W-WHO, ME? WHY, I'M--
9

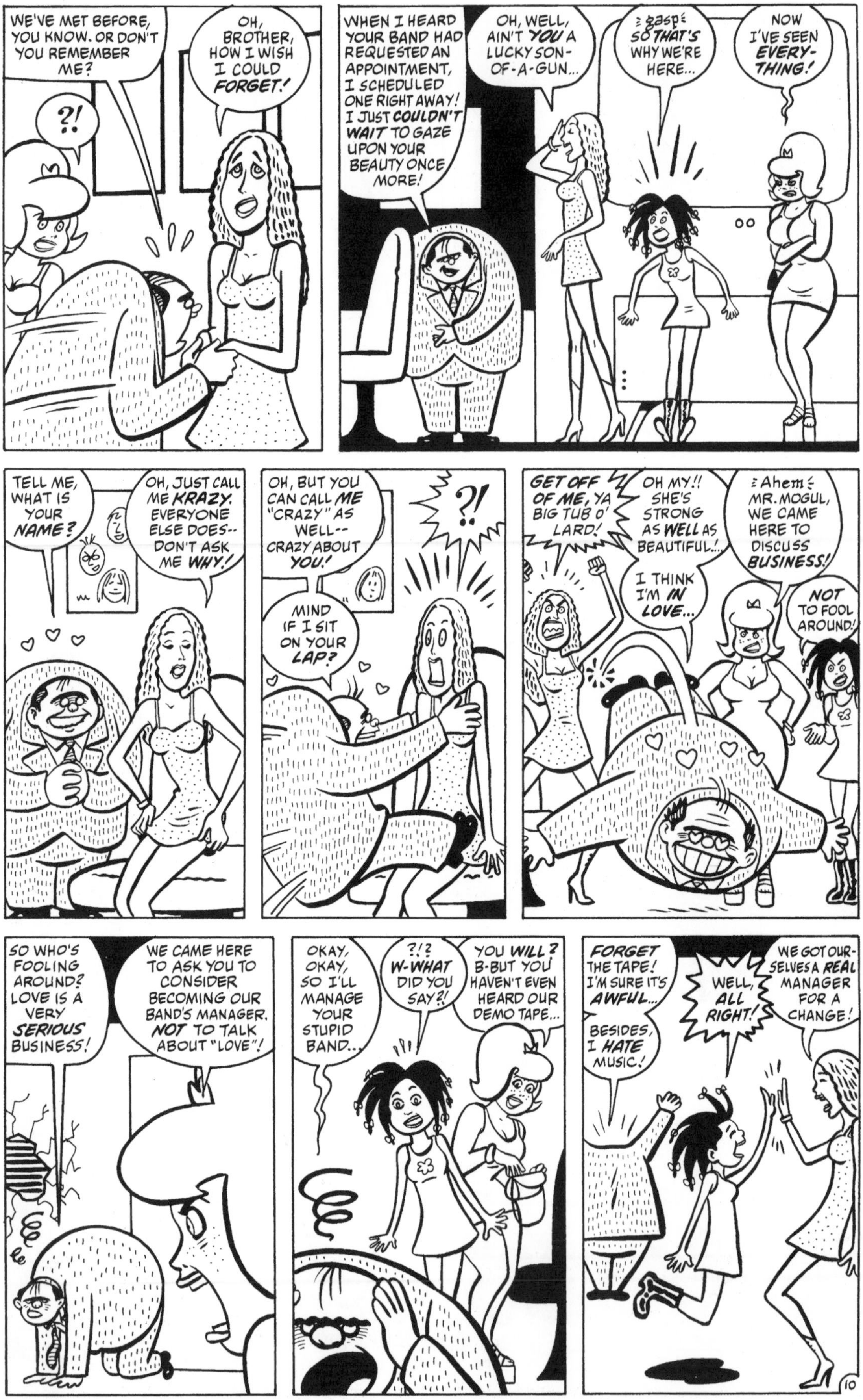
WE'VE MET BEFORE, YOU KNOW. OR DON'T YOU REMEMBER ME?
?!
OH, BROTHER, HOW I WISH I COULD FORGET!
WHEN I HEARD YOUR BAND HAD REQUESTED AN APPOINTMENT, I SCHEDULED ONE RIGHT AWAY! I JUST COULDN'T WAIT TO GAZE UPON YOUR BEAUTY ONCE MORE!
OH, WELL, AIN'T YOU A LUCKY SON-OF-A-GUN...
gasp SO THAT'S WHY WE'RE HERE...
NOW I'VE SEEN EVERYTHING!
TELL ME, WHAT IS YOUR NAME?
OH, JUST CALL ME KRAZY. EVERYONE ELSE DOES-- DON'T ASK ME WHY!
OH, BUT YOU CAN CALL ME "CRAZY" AS WELL-- CRAZY ABOUT YOU!
MIND IF I SIT ON YOUR LAP?
?!
GET OFF OF ME, YA BIG TUB O' LARD!
OH MY!! SHE'S STRONG AS WELL AS BEAUTIFUL!...
I THINK I'M IN LOVE...
Ahem MR. MOGUL, WE CAME HERE TO DISCUSS BUSINESS!
NOT TO FOOL AROUND!
SO WHO'S FOOLING AROUND? LOVE IS A VERY SERIOUS BUSINESS!
WE CAME HERE TO ASK YOU TO CONSIDER BECOMING OUR BAND'S MANAGER, NOT TO TALK ABOUT "LOVE"!
OKAY, OKAY, SO I'LL MANAGE YOUR STUPID BAND...
?!? W-WHAT DID YOU SAY?!
YOU WILL? B-BUT YOU HAVEN'T EVEN HEARD OUR DEMO TAPE...
FORGET THE TAPE! I'M SURE IT'S AWFUL...
BESIDES, I HATE MUSIC!
WELL, ALL RIGHT!
WE GOT OURSELVES A REAL MANAGER FOR A CHANGE!

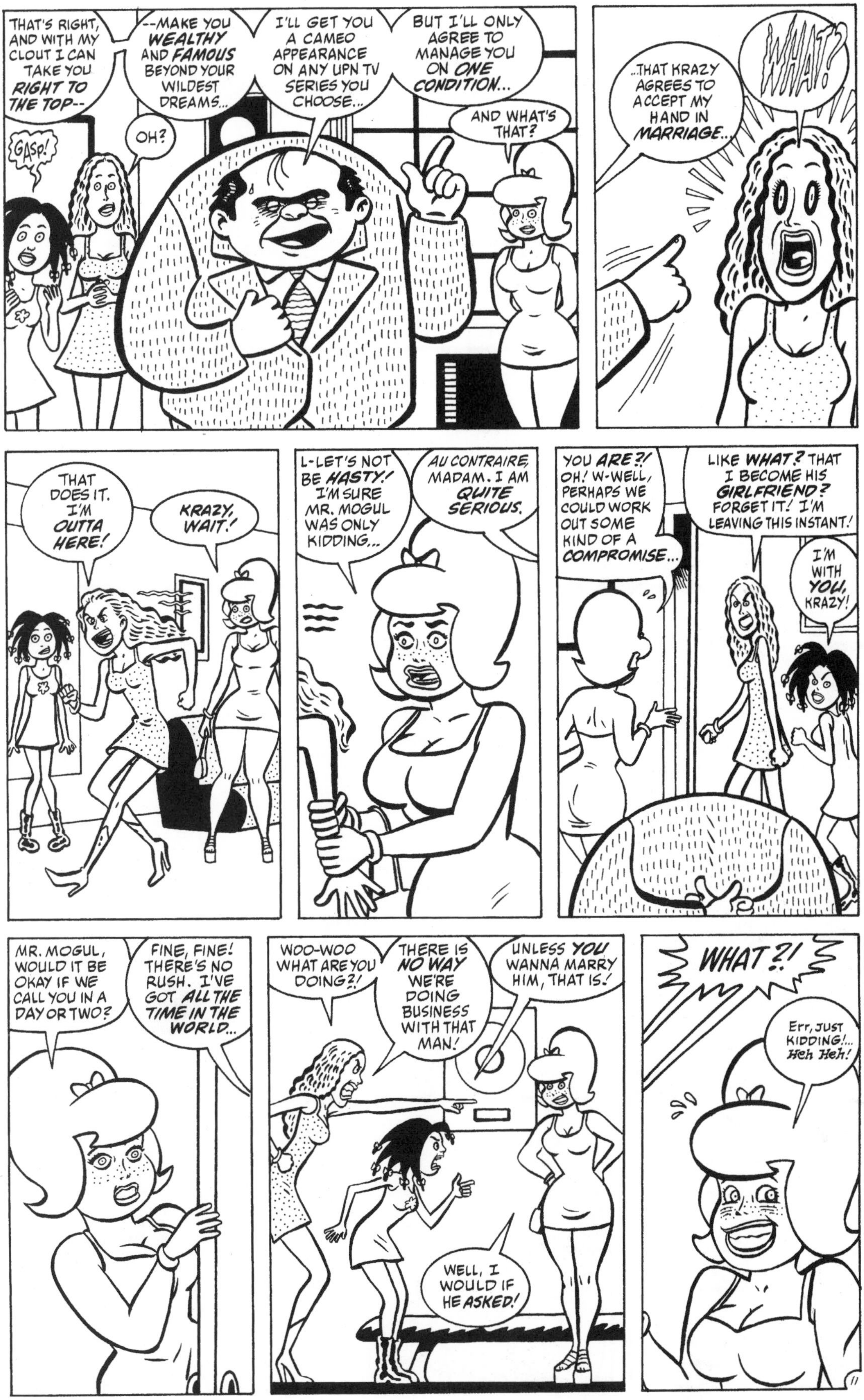
THAT'S RIGHT, AND WITH MY CLOUT I CAN TAKE YOU RIGHT TO THE TOP--
--MAKE YOU WEALTHY AND FAMOUS BEYOND YOUR WILDEST DREAMS...
GASP!
OH?
I'LL GET YOU A CAMEO APPEARANCE ON ANY UPN TV SERIES YOU CHOOSE...
BUT I'LL ONLY AGREE TO MANAGE YOU ON ONE CONDITION...
AND WHAT'S THAT?
..THAT KRAZY AGREES TO ACCEPT MY HAND IN MARRIAGE...
WHAT?
THAT DOES IT. I'M OUTTA HERE!
KRAZY, WAIT!
L-LET'S NOT BE HASTY! I'M SURE MR. MOGUL WAS ONLY KIDDING...
AU CONTRAIRE, MADAM. I AM QUITE SERIOUS.
YOU ARE?! OH! W-WELL, PERHAPS WE COULD WORK OUT SOME KIND OF A COMPROMISE...
LIKE WHAT? THAT I BECOME HIS GIRLFRIEND? FORGET IT! I'M LEAVING THIS INSTANT!
I'M WITH YOU, KRAZY!
MR. MOGUL, WOULD IT BE OKAY IF WE CALL YOU IN A DAY OR TWO?
FINE, FINE! THERE'S NO RUSH. I'VE GOT ALL THE TIME IN THE WORLD...
WOO-WOO WHAT ARE YOU DOING?!
THERE IS NO WAY WE'RE DOING BUSINESS WITH THAT MAN!
UNLESS YOU WANNA MARRY HIM, THAT IS!
WELL, I WOULD IF HE ASKED!
WHAT?!
Err, JUST KIDDING!... Heh Heh!

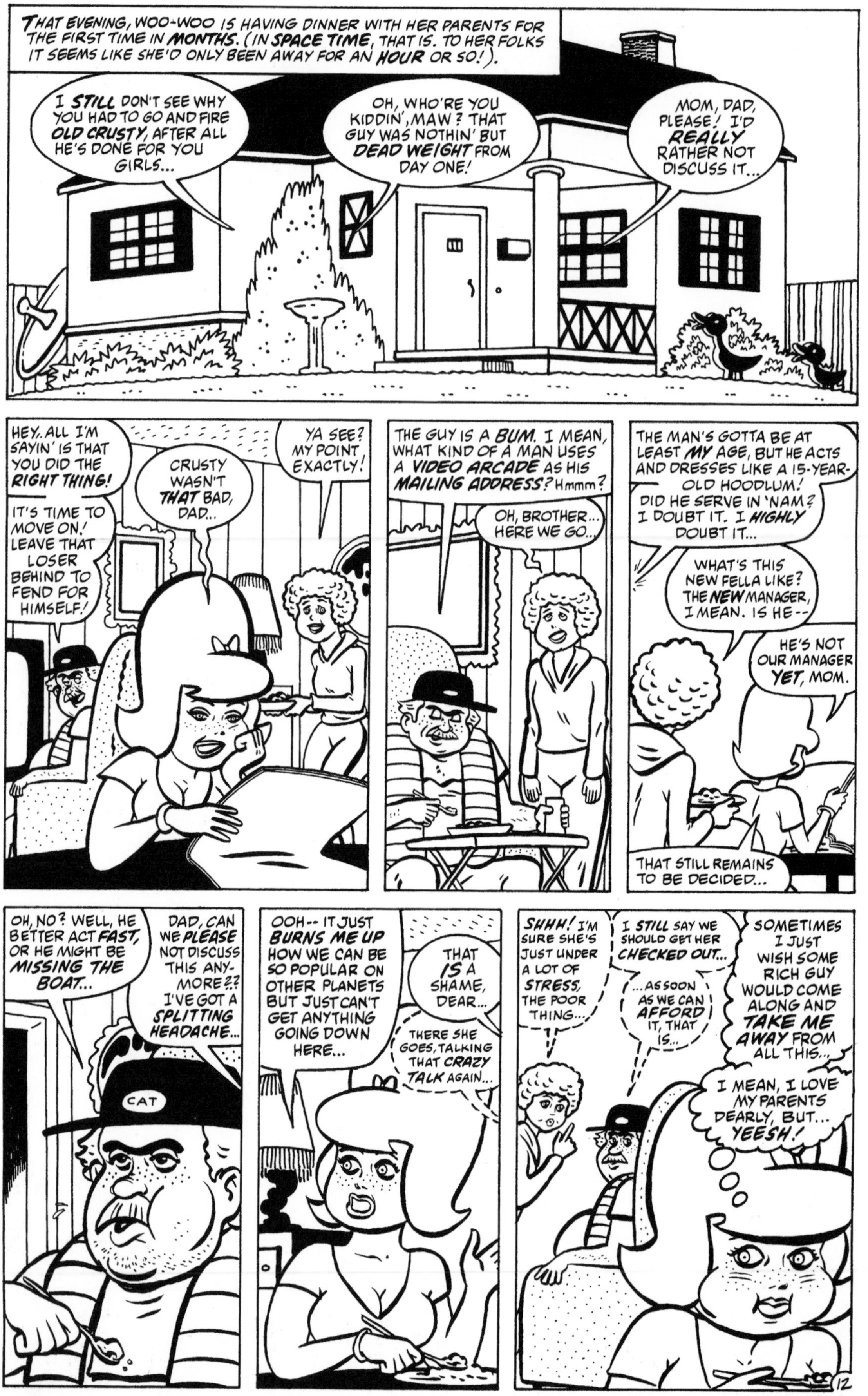
THAT EVENING, WOO-WOO IS HAVING DINNER WITH HER PARENTS FOR THE FIRST TIME IN MONTHS. (IN SPACE TIME, THAT IS. TO HER FOLKS IT SEEMS LIKE SHE'D ONLY BEEN AWAY FOR AN HOUR OR SO!).
I STILL DON'T SEE WHY YOU HAD TO GO AND FIRE OLD CRUSTY, AFTER ALL HE'S DONE FOR YOU GIRLS...
OH, WHO'RE YOU KIDDIN', MAW? THAT GUY WAS NOTHIN' BUT DEAD WEIGHT FROM DAY ONE!
MOM, DAD, PLEASE! I'D REALLY RATHER NOT DISCUSS IT...
HEY, ALL I'M SAYIN' IS THAT YOU DID THE RIGHT THING!
IT'S TIME TO MOVE ON! LEAVE THAT LOSER BEHIND TO FEND FOR HIMSELF!
CRUSTY WASN'T THAT BAD, DAD...
YA SEE? MY POINT EXACTLY!
THE GUY IS A BUM. I MEAN, WHAT KIND OF A MAN USES A VIDEO ARCADE AS HIS MAILING ADDRESS? Hmmm?
OH, BROTHER... HERE WE GO...
THE MAN'S GOTTA BE AT LEAST MY AGE, BUT HE ACTS AND DRESSES LIKE A 15-YEAR-OLD HOODLUM! DID HE SERVE IN 'NAM? I DOUBT IT. I HIGHLY DOUBT IT...
WHAT'S THIS NEW FELLA LIKE? THE NEW MANAGER, I MEAN. IS HE --
HE'S NOT OUR MANAGER YET, MOM.
THAT STILL REMAINS TO BE DECIDED...
OH, NO? WELL, HE BETTER ACT FAST, OR HE MIGHT BE MISSING THE BOAT...
DAD, CAN WE PLEASE NOT DISCUSS THIS ANYMORE?? I'VE GOT A SPLITTING HEADACHE...
CAT
OOH -- IT JUST BURNS ME UP HOW WE CAN BE SO POPULAR ON OTHER PLANETS BUT JUST CAN'T GET ANYTHING GOING DOWN HERE...
THAT IS A SHAME, DEAR...
THERE SHE GOES, TALKING THAT CRAZY TALK AGAIN...
SHHH! I'M SURE SHE'S JUST UNDER A LOT OF STRESS, THE POOR THING...
I STILL SAY WE SHOULD GET HER CHECKED OUT...
...AS SOON AS WE CAN AFFORD IT, THAT IS...
SOMETIMES I JUST WISH SOME RICH GUY WOULD COME ALONG AND TAKE ME AWAY FROM ALL THIS...
I MEAN, I LOVE MY PARENTS DEARLY, BUT... YEESH!

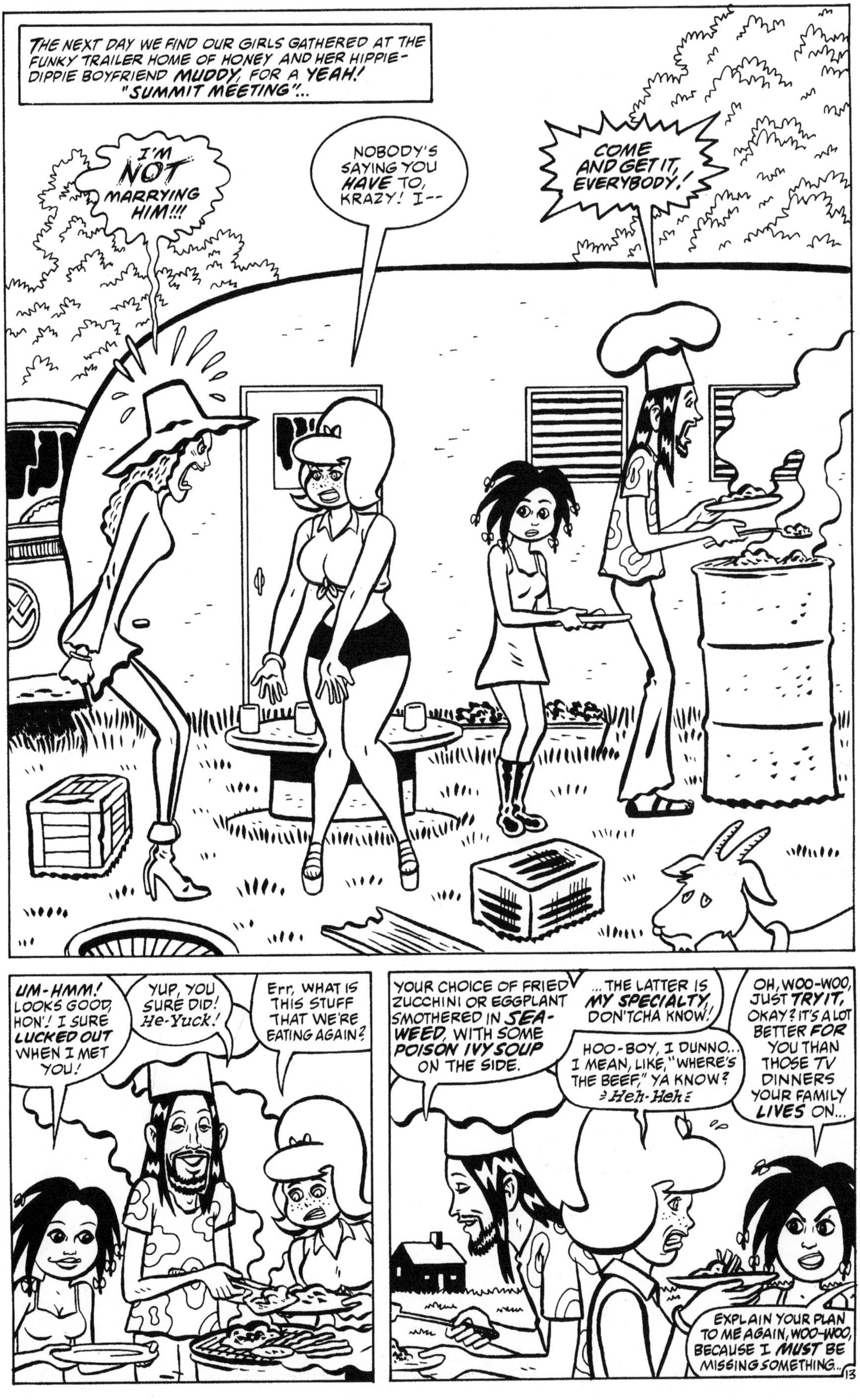
THE NEXT DAY WE FIND OUR GIRLS GATHERED AT THE FUNKY TRAILER HOME OF HONEY AND HER HIPPIE-DIPPIE BOYFRIEND MUDDY, FOR A YEAH! "SUMMIT MEETING"...
I'M NOT MARRYING HIM!!!
NOBODY'S SAYING YOU HAVE TO, KRAZY! I--
COME AND GET IT, EVERYBODY!
UM-HMM! LOOKS GOOD, HON'! I SURE LUCKED OUT WHEN I MET YOU!
YUP, YOU SURE DID! He-Yuck!
Err, WHAT IS THIS STUFF THAT WE'RE EATING AGAIN?
YOUR CHOICE OF FRIED ZUCCHINI OR EGGPLANT SMOTHERED IN SEA-WEED, WITH SOME POISON IVY SOUP ON THE SIDE.
...THE LATTER IS MY SPECIALTY, DON'TCHA KNOW!
HOO-BOY, I DUNNO... I MEAN, LIKE, "WHERE'S THE BEEF," YA KNOW? Heh-Heh
OH, WOO-WOO, JUST TRY IT, OKAY? IT'S A LOT BETTER FOR YOU THAN THOSE TV DINNERS YOUR FAMILY LIVES ON...
EXPLAIN YOUR PLAN TO ME AGAIN, WOO-WOO, BECAUSE I MUST BE MISSING SOMETHING...

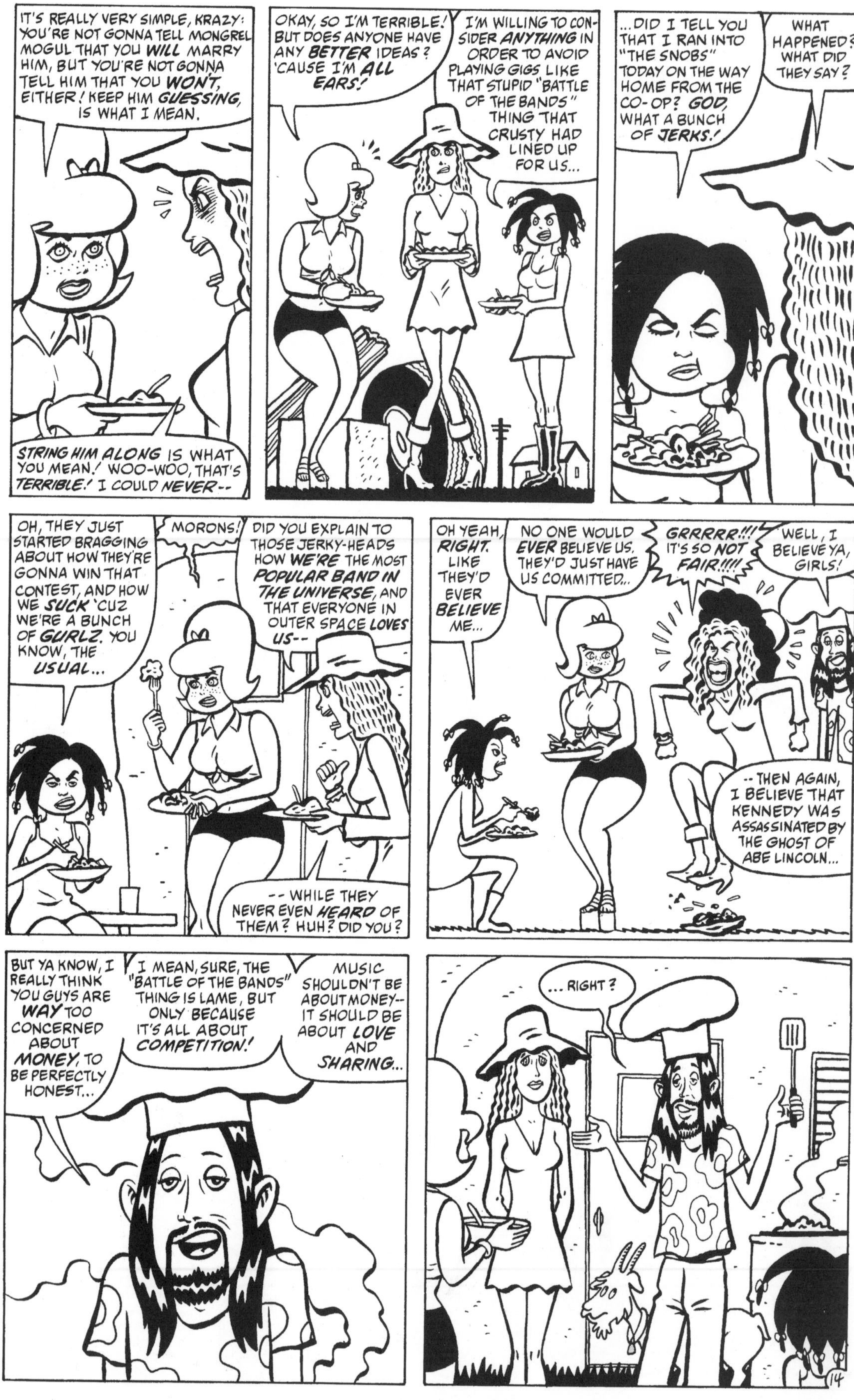

IT'S REALLY VERY SIMPLE, KRAZY: YOU'RE NOT GONNA TELL MONGREL MOGUL THAT YOU WILL MARRY HIM, BUT YOU'RE NOT GONNA TELL HIM THAT YOU WON'T, EITHER! KEEP HIM GUESSING, IS WHAT I MEAN.
STRING HIM ALONG IS WHAT YOU MEAN! WOO-WOO, THAT'S TERRIBLE! I COULD NEVER--
OKAY, SO I'M TERRIBLE! BUT DOES ANYONE HAVE ANY BETTER IDEAS? 'CAUSE I'M ALL EARS!
I'M WILLING TO CONSIDER ANYTHING IN ORDER TO AVOID PLAYING GIGS LIKE THAT STUPID "BATTLE OF THE BANDS" THING THAT CRUSTY HAD LINED UP FOR US...
...DID I TELL YOU THAT I RAN INTO "THE SNOBS" TODAY ON THE WAY HOME FROM THE CO-OP? GOD, WHAT A BUNCH OF JERKS!
WHAT HAPPENED? WHAT DID THEY SAY?
OH, THEY JUST STARTED BRAGGING ABOUT HOW THEY'RE GONNA WIN THAT CONTEST, AND HOW WE SUCK 'CUZ WE'RE A BUNCH OF GURLZ. YOU KNOW, THE USUAL...
MORONS!
DID YOU EXPLAIN TO THOSE JERKY-HEADS HOW WE'RE THE MOST POPULAR BAND IN THE UNIVERSE, AND THAT EVERYONE IN OUTER SPACE LOVES US--
-- WHILE THEY NEVER EVEN HEARD OF THEM? HUH? DID YOU?
OH YEAH, RIGHT. LIKE THEY'D EVER BELIEVE ME...
NO ONE WOULD EVER BELIEVE US. THEY'D JUST HAVE US COMMITTED...
GRRRRR!!! IT'S SO NOT FAIR!!!!
WELL, I BELIEVE YA, GIRLS!
-- THEN AGAIN, I BELIEVE THAT KENNEDY WAS ASSASSINATED BY THE GHOST OF ABE LINCOLN...
BUT YA KNOW, I REALLY THINK YOU GUYS ARE WAY TOO CONCERNED ABOUT MONEY, TO BE PERFECTLY HONEST...
I MEAN, SURE, THE "BATTLE OF THE BANDS" THING IS LAME, BUT ONLY BECAUSE IT'S ALL ABOUT COMPETITION!
MUSIC SHOULDN'T BE ABOUT MONEY-- IT SHOULD BE ABOUT LOVE AND SHARING...
... RIGHT?

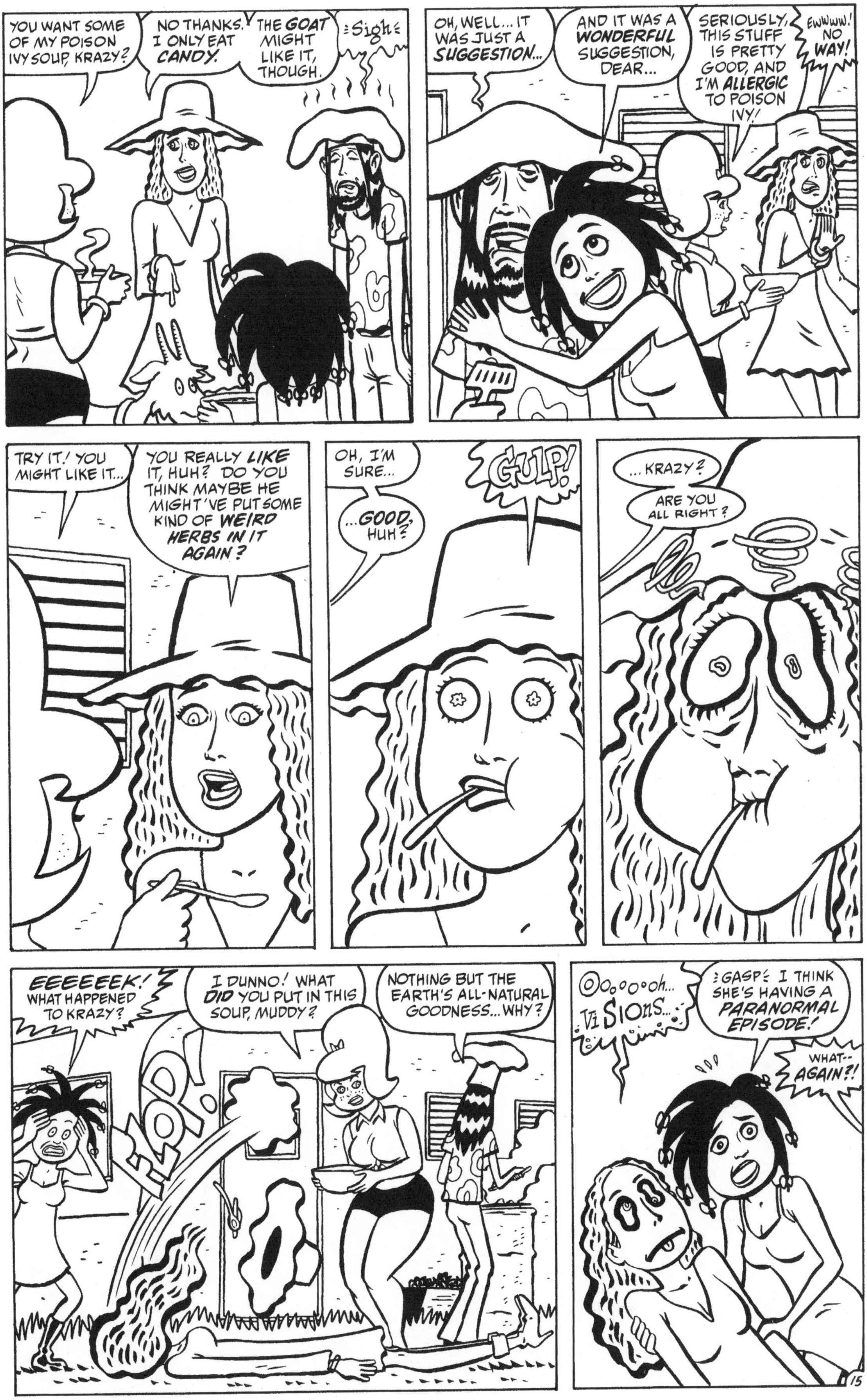

YOU WANT SOME OF MY POISON IVY SOUP, KRAZY?
NO THANKS. I ONLY EAT CANDY.
THE GOAT MIGHT LIKE IT, THOUGH.
Sigh
OH, WELL... IT WAS JUST A SUGGESTION...
AND IT WAS A WONDERFUL SUGGESTION, DEAR...
SERIOUSLY, THIS STUFF IS PRETTY GOOD, AND I'M ALLERGIC TO POISON IVY!
EWWWW! NO WAY!
TRY IT! YOU MIGHT LIKE IT...
YOU REALLY LIKE IT, HUH? DO YOU THINK MAYBE HE MIGHT'VE PUT SOME KIND OF WEIRD HERBS IN IT AGAIN?
OH, I'M SURE...
...GOOD, HUH?
GULP!
...KRAZY?
ARE YOU ALL RIGHT?
EEEEEEK! WHAT HAPPENED TO KRAZY?
I DUNNO! WHAT DID YOU PUT IN THIS SOUP, MUDDY?
NOTHING BUT THE EARTH'S ALL-NATURAL GOODNESS... WHY?
FLOP!
Oooooh... ViSions...
GASP! I THINK SHE'S HAVING A PARANORMAL EPISODE!
WHAT-- AGAIN?!

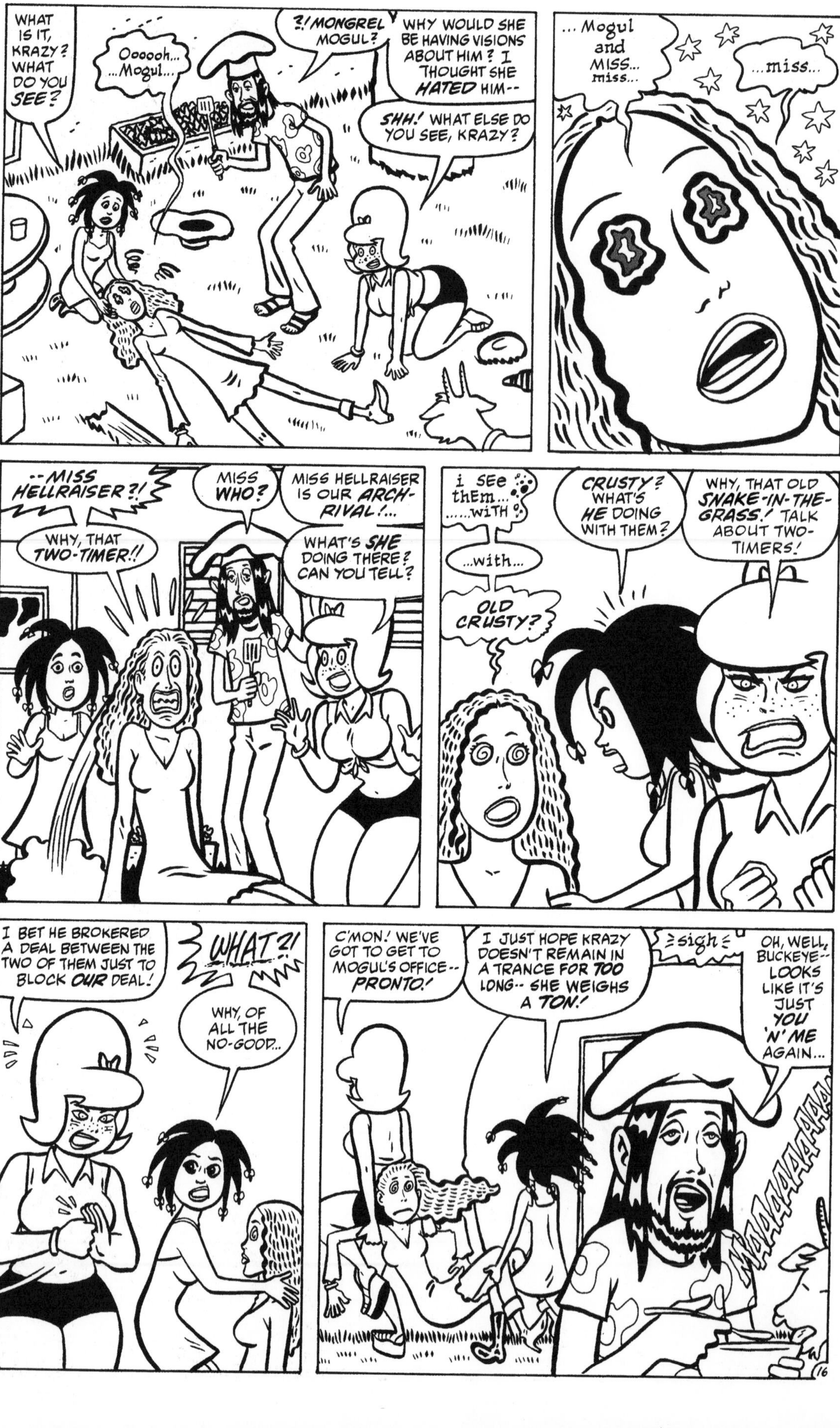

WHAT IS IT, KRAZY? WHAT DO YOU SEE?
Oooooh... ...Mogul...
?! MONGREL MOGUL?
WHY WOULD SHE BE HAVING VISIONS ABOUT HIM? I THOUGHT SHE HATED HIM--
SHH! WHAT ELSE DO YOU SEE, KRAZY?
... Mogul and MISS... miss...
...miss...
--MISS HELLRAISER?!
WHY, THAT TWO-TIMER!!
MISS WHO?
MISS HELLRAISER IS OUR ARCH-RIVAL!...
WHAT'S SHE DOING THERE? CAN YOU TELL?
i see them... ......with
...with...
OLD CRUSTY?
CRUSTY? WHAT'S HE DOING WITH THEM?
WHY, THAT OLD SNAKE-IN-THE-GRASS! TALK ABOUT TWO-TIMERS!
I BET HE BROKERED A DEAL BETWEEN THE TWO OF THEM JUST TO BLOCK OUR DEAL!
WHAT?!
WHY, OF ALL THE NO-GOOD...
C'MON! WE'VE GOT TO GET TO MOGUL'S OFFICE--PRONTO!
I JUST HOPE KRAZY DOESN'T REMAIN IN A TRANCE FOR TOO LONG-- SHE WEIGHS A TON!
sigh
OH, WELL, BUCKEYE-- LOOKS LIKE IT'S JUST YOU 'N' ME AGAIN...

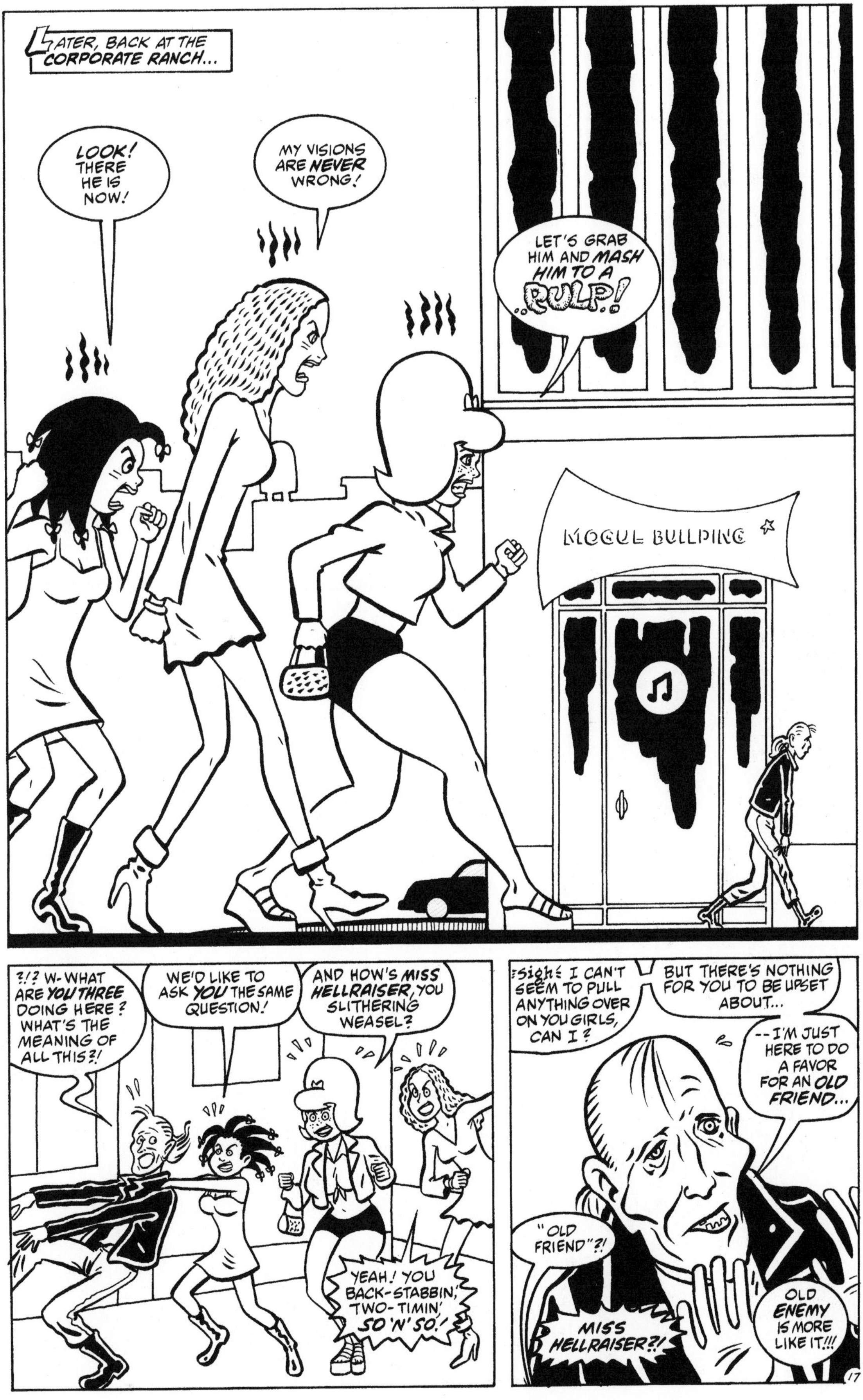
LATER, BACK AT THE CORPORATE RANCH...
LOOK! THERE HE IS NOW!
MY VISIONS ARE NEVER WRONG!
LET'S GRAB HIM AND MASH HIM TO A PULP!
MOGUL BUILDING
?!? W-WHAT ARE YOU THREE DOING HERE? WHAT'S THE MEANING OF ALL THIS?!
WE'D LIKE TO ASK YOU THE SAME QUESTION!
AND HOW'S MISS HELLRAISER, YOU SLITHERING WEASEL?
YEAH! YOU BACK-STABBIN', TWO-TIMIN' SO 'N' SO!
SIGH I CAN'T SEEM TO PULL ANYTHING OVER ON YOU GIRLS, CAN I?
BUT THERE'S NOTHING FOR YOU TO BE UPSET ABOUT...
--I'M JUST HERE TO DO A FAVOR FOR AN OLD FRIEND...
"OLD FRIEND"?!
MISS HELLRAISER?!
OLD ENEMY IS MORE LIKE IT!!!

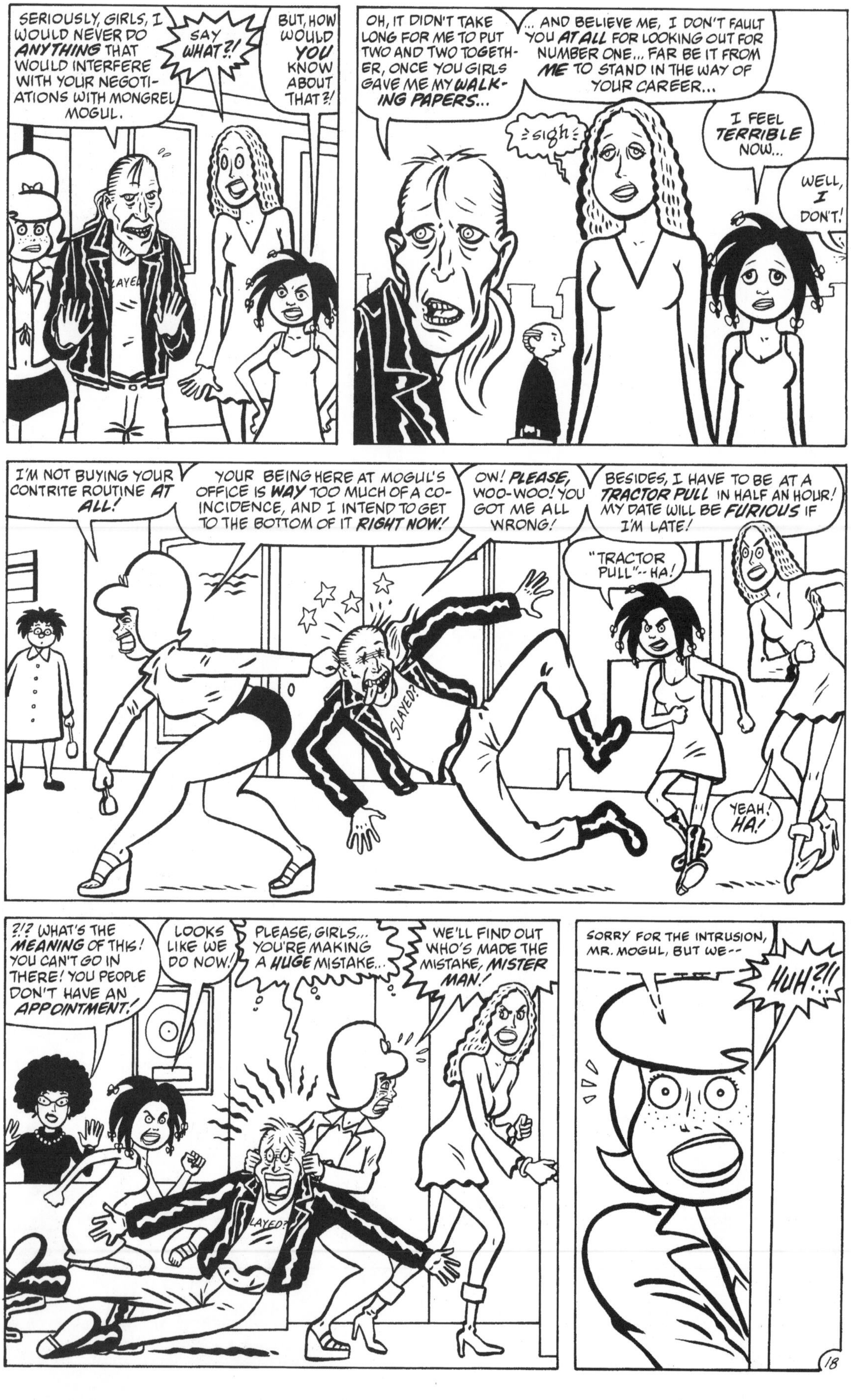
SERIOUSLY, GIRLS, I WOULD NEVER DO ANYTHING THAT WOULD INTERFERE WITH YOUR NEGOTIATIONS WITH MONGREL MOGUL.
SAY WHAT?!
BUT, HOW WOULD YOU KNOW ABOUT THAT?!
SLAYED
OH, IT DIDN'T TAKE LONG FOR ME TO PUT TWO AND TWO TOGETHER, ONCE YOU GIRLS GAVE ME MY WALKING PAPERS...
... AND BELIEVE ME, I DON'T FAULT YOU AT ALL FOR LOOKING OUT FOR NUMBER ONE... FAR BE IT FROM ME TO STAND IN THE WAY OF YOUR CAREER...
sigh
I FEEL TERRIBLE NOW...
WELL, I DON'T!
I'M NOT BUYING YOUR CONTRITE ROUTINE AT ALL!
YOUR BEING HERE AT MOGUL'S OFFICE IS WAY TOO MUCH OF A COINCIDENCE, AND I INTEND TO GET TO THE BOTTOM OF IT RIGHT NOW!
OW! PLEASE, WOO-WOO! YOU GOT ME ALL WRONG!
BESIDES, I HAVE TO BE AT A TRACTOR PULL IN HALF AN HOUR! MY DATE WILL BE FURIOUS IF I'M LATE!
"TRACTOR PULL"-- HA!
SLAYED?
YEAH! HA!
?!? WHAT'S THE MEANING OF THIS! YOU CAN'T GO IN THERE! YOU PEOPLE DON'T HAVE AN APPOINTMENT!
LOOKS LIKE WE DO NOW!
PLEASE, GIRLS... YOU'RE MAKING A HUGE MISTAKE...
WE'LL FIND OUT WHO'S MADE THE MISTAKE, MISTER MAN!
LAYED?
SORRY FOR THE INTRUSION, MR. MOGUL, BUT WE--
HUH?!!

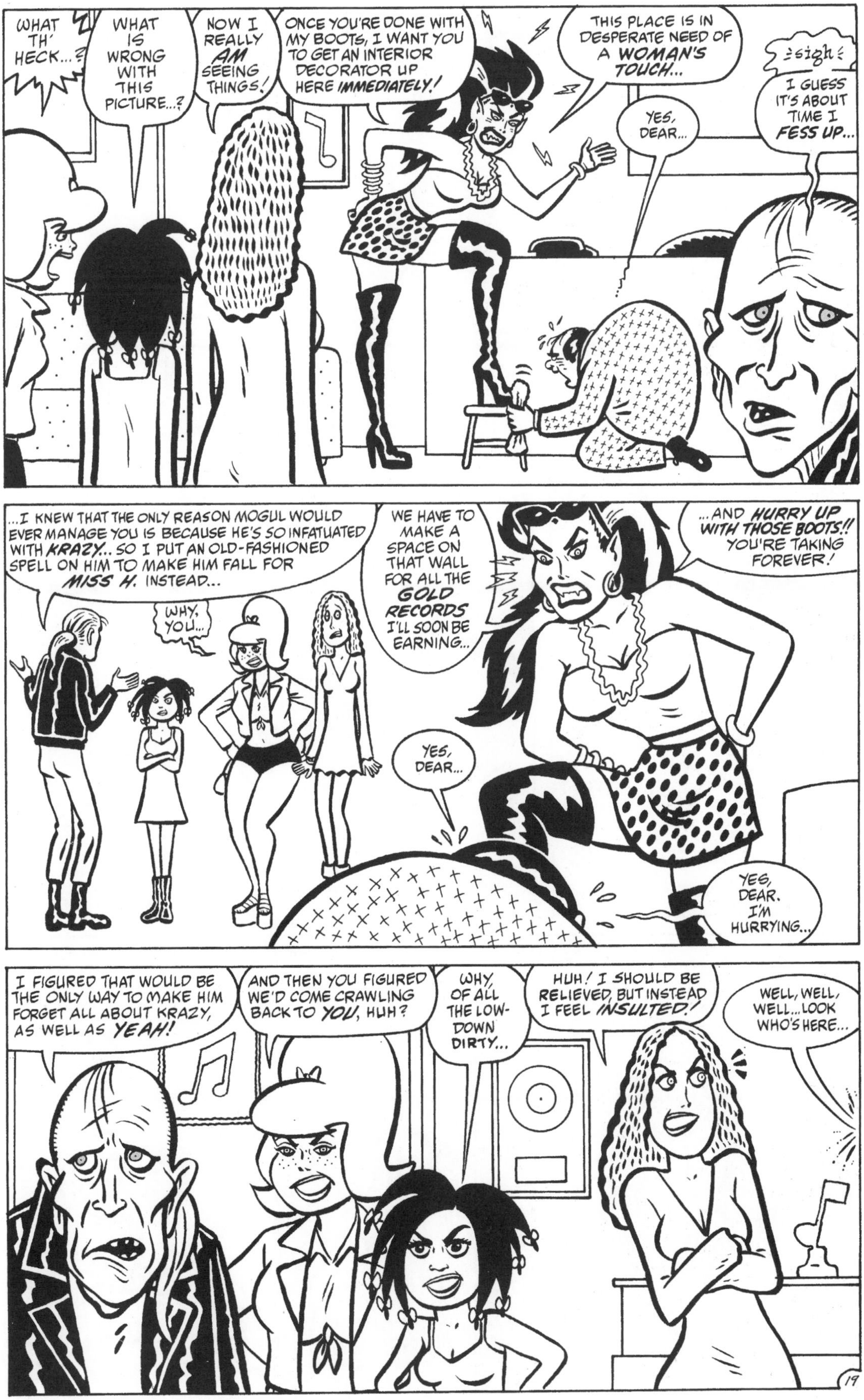
WHAT TH' HECK...?
WHAT IS WRONG WITH THIS PICTURE...?
NOW I REALLY AM SEEING THINGS!
ONCE YOU'RE DONE WITH MY BOOTS, I WANT YOU TO GET AN INTERIOR DECORATOR UP HERE IMMEDIATELY!
THIS PLACE IS IN DESPERATE NEED OF A WOMAN'S TOUCH...
YES, DEAR...
:sigh:
I GUESS IT'S ABOUT TIME I FESS UP...
...I KNEW THAT THE ONLY REASON MOGUL WOULD EVER MANAGE YOU IS BECAUSE HE'S SO INFATUATED WITH KRAZY... SO I PUT AN OLD-FASHIONED SPELL ON HIM TO MAKE HIM FALL FOR MISS H. INSTEAD...
WHY, YOU...
WE HAVE TO MAKE A SPACE ON THAT WALL FOR ALL THE GOLD RECORDS I'LL SOON BE EARNING...
...AND HURRY UP WITH THOSE BOOTS!! YOU'RE TAKING FOREVER!
YES, DEAR...
YES, DEAR. I'M HURRYING...
I FIGURED THAT WOULD BE THE ONLY WAY TO MAKE HIM FORGET ALL ABOUT KRAZY, AS WELL AS YEAH!
AND THEN YOU FIGURED WE'D COME CRAWLING BACK TO YOU, HUH?
WHY, OF ALL THE LOW-DOWN DIRTY...
HUH! I SHOULD BE RELIEVED, BUT INSTEAD I FEEL INSULTED!
WELL, WELL, WELL... LOOK WHO'S HERE...

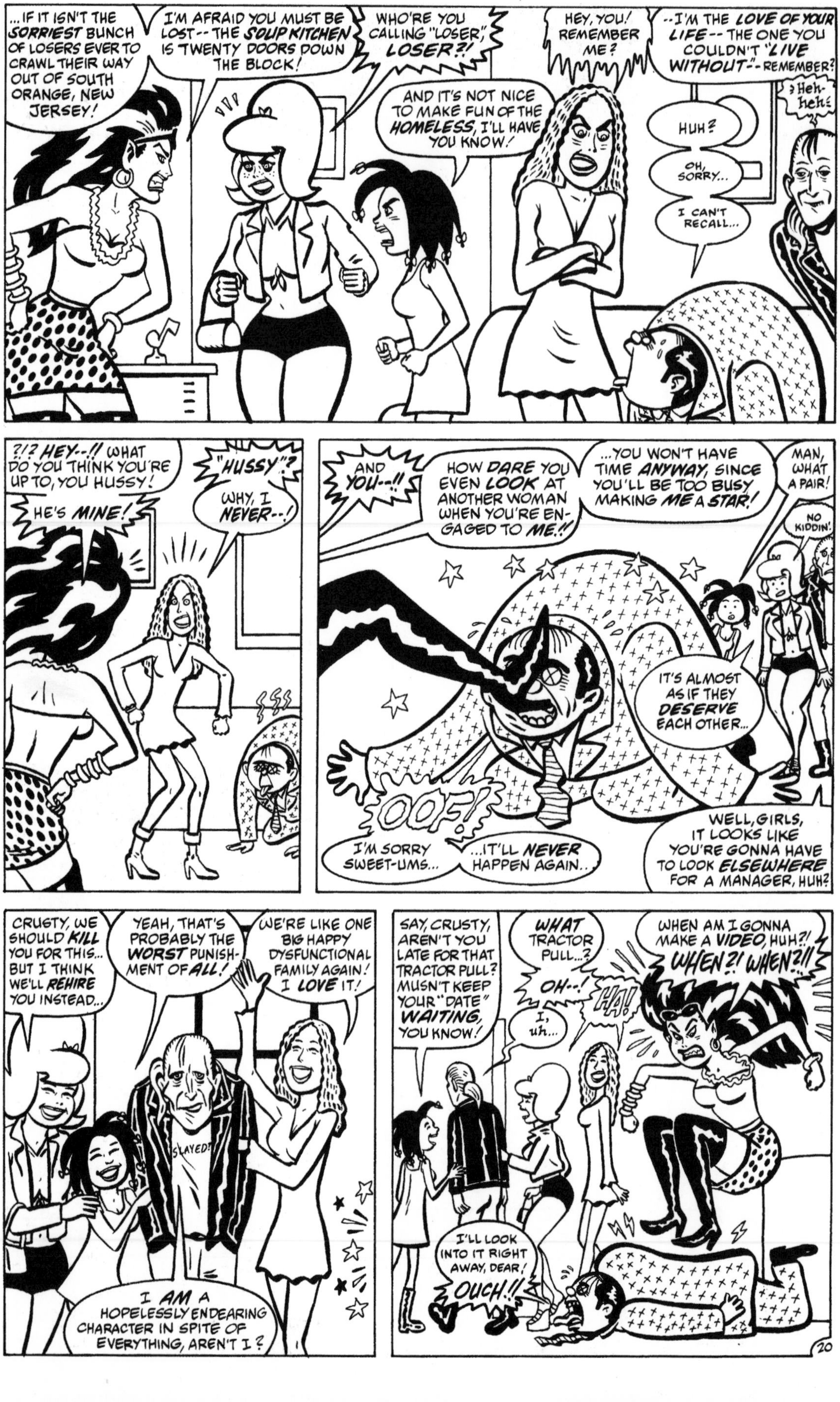

...IF IT ISN'T THE SORRIEST BUNCH OF LOSERS EVER TO CRAWL THEIR WAY OUT OF SOUTH ORANGE, NEW JERSEY!
I'M AFRAID YOU MUST BE LOST-- THE SOUP KITCHEN IS TWENTY DOORS DOWN THE BLOCK!
WHO'RE YOU CALLING "LOSER," LOSER?!
AND IT'S NOT NICE TO MAKE FUN OF THE HOMELESS, I'LL HAVE YOU KNOW!
HEY, YOU! REMEMBER ME?
--I'M THE LOVE OF YOUR LIFE -- THE ONE YOU COULDN'T "LIVE WITHOUT"-- REMEMBER?
Heh-heh
HUH?
OH, SORRY...
I CAN'T RECALL...
?!? HEY--!! WHAT DO YOU THINK YOU'RE UP TO, YOU HUSSY!
HE'S MINE!
"HUSSY"?
WHY, I NEVER--!
AND YOU--!!
HOW DARE YOU EVEN LOOK AT ANOTHER WOMAN WHEN YOU'RE ENGAGED TO ME!!
...YOU WON'T HAVE TIME ANYWAY, SINCE YOU'LL BE TOO BUSY MAKING ME A STAR!
MAN, WHAT A PAIR!
NO KIDDIN'.
IT'S ALMOST AS IF THEY DESERVE EACH OTHER...
OOF!
I'M SORRY SWEET-UMS...
...IT'LL NEVER HAPPEN AGAIN...
WELL, GIRLS, IT LOOKS LIKE YOU'RE GONNA HAVE TO LOOK ELSEWHERE FOR A MANAGER, HUH?
CRUSTY, WE SHOULD KILL YOU FOR THIS... BUT I THINK WE'LL REHIRE YOU INSTEAD...
YEAH, THAT'S PROBABLY THE WORST PUNISHMENT OF ALL!
WE'RE LIKE ONE BIG HAPPY DYSFUNCTIONAL FAMILY AGAIN! I LOVE IT!
SLAYED!
I AM A HOPELESSLY ENDEARING CHARACTER IN SPITE OF EVERYTHING, AREN'T I?
SAY, CRUSTY, AREN'T YOU LATE FOR THAT TRACTOR PULL? MUSN'T KEEP YOUR "DATE" WAITING, YOU KNOW!
WHAT TRACTOR PULL...?
OH--!
I, uh...
HA!
WHEN AM I GONNA MAKE A VIDEO, HUH?! WHEN?! WHEN?!!
I'LL LOOK INTO IT RIGHT AWAY, DEAR!
OUCH!!

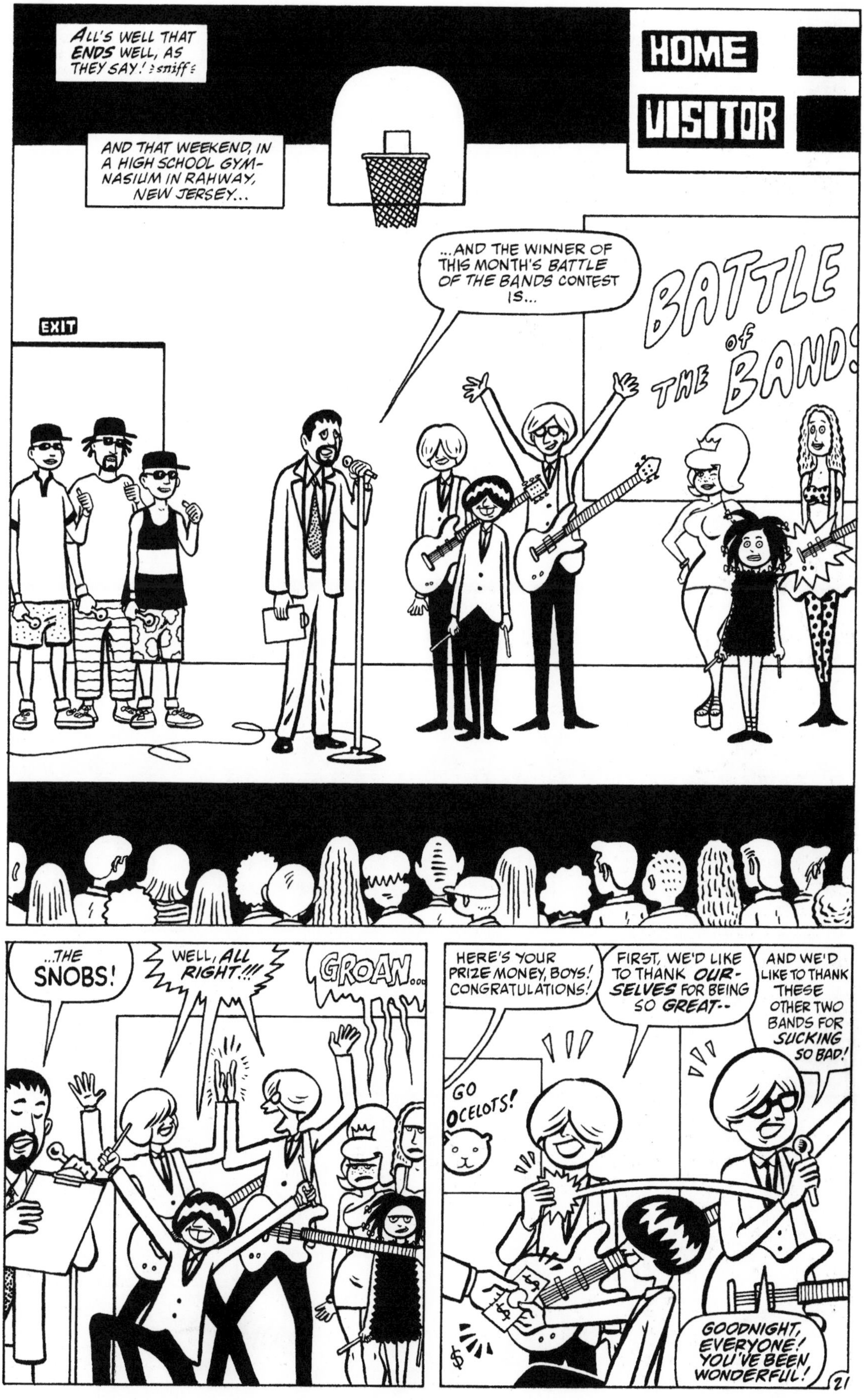
ALL'S WELL THAT ENDS WELL, AS THEY SAY! sniff
HOME
VISITOR
AND THAT WEEKEND, IN A HIGH SCHOOL GYMNASIUM IN RAHWAY, NEW JERSEY...
EXIT
...AND THE WINNER OF THIS MONTH'S BATTLE OF THE BANDS CONTEST IS...
BATTLE of THE BANDS
...THE SNOBS!
WELL, ALL RIGHT!!!
GROAN...
HERE'S YOUR PRIZE MONEY, BOYS! CONGRATULATIONS!
GO OCELOTS!
FIRST, WE'D LIKE TO THANK OURSELVES FOR BEING SO GREAT--
AND WE'D LIKE TO THANK THESE OTHER TWO BANDS FOR SUCKING SO BAD!
GOODNIGHT, EVERYONE! YOU'VE BEEN WONDERFUL!

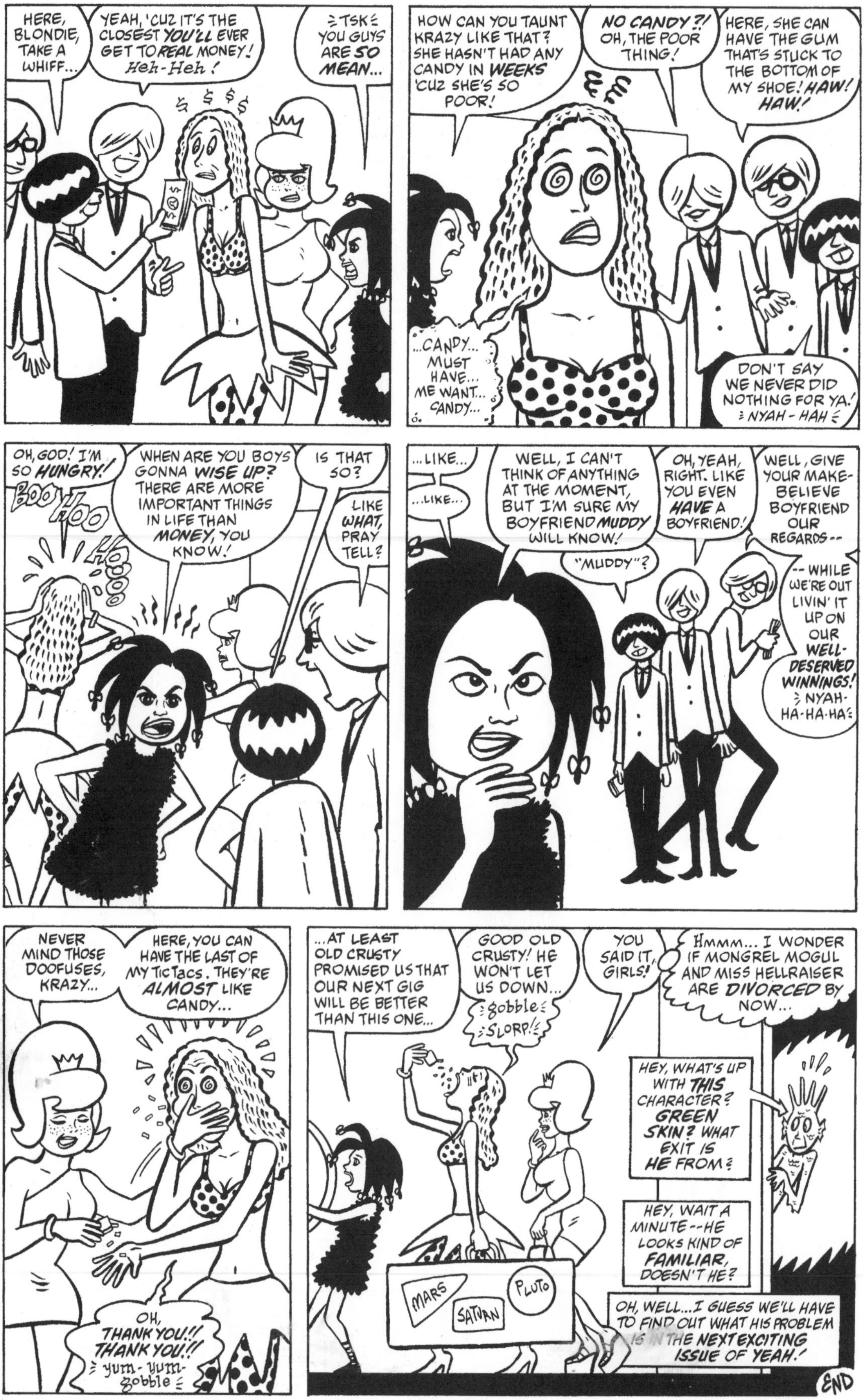
HERE, BLONDIE, TAKE A WHIFF...
YEAH, 'CUZ IT'S THE CLOSEST YOU'LL EVER GET TO REAL MONEY! Heh-Heh!
TSK YOU GUYS ARE SO MEAN...
HOW CAN YOU TAUNT KRAZY LIKE THAT? SHE HASN'T HAD ANY CANDY IN WEEKS 'CUZ SHE'S SO POOR!
NO CANDY?! OH, THE POOR THING!
HERE, SHE CAN HAVE THE GUM THAT'S STUCK TO THE BOTTOM OF MY SHOE! HAW! HAW!
...CANDY... MUST HAVE... ME WANT... CANDY...
DON'T SAY WE NEVER DID NOTHING FOR YA! NYAH-HAH
OH, GOD! I'M SO HUNGRY!
BOO HOO HOOOO
WHEN ARE YOU BOYS GONNA WISE UP? THERE ARE MORE IMPORTANT THINGS IN LIFE THAN MONEY, YOU KNOW!
IS THAT SO?
LIKE WHAT, PRAY TELL?
...LIKE...
...LIKE...
WELL, I CAN'T THINK OF ANYTHING AT THE MOMENT, BUT I'M SURE MY BOYFRIEND MUDDY WILL KNOW!
"MUDDY"?
OH, YEAH, RIGHT. LIKE YOU EVEN HAVE A BOYFRIEND!
WELL, GIVE YOUR MAKE-BELIEVE BOYFRIEND OUR REGARDS--
--WHILE WE'RE OUT LIVIN' IT UP ON OUR WELL-DESERVED WINNINGS! NYAH-HA-HA-HA
NEVER MIND THOSE DOOFUSES, KRAZY...
HERE, YOU CAN HAVE THE LAST OF MY TicTacs. THEY'RE ALMOST LIKE CANDY...
OH, THANK YOU!! THANK YOU!! yum-yum-gobble
...AT LEAST OLD CRUSTY PROMISED US THAT OUR NEXT GIG WILL BE BETTER THAN THIS ONE...
GOOD OLD CRUSTY! HE WON'T LET US DOWN...
gobble SLORP!
YOU SAID IT, GIRLS!
Hmmm... I WONDER IF MONGREL MOGUL AND MISS HELLRAISER ARE DIVORCED BY NOW...
HEY, WHAT'S UP WITH THIS CHARACTER? GREEN SKIN? WHAT EXIT IS HE FROM?
HEY, WAIT A MINUTE--HE LOOKS KIND OF FAMILIAR, DOESN'T HE?
MARS
SATURN
PLUTO
OH, WELL...I GUESS WE'LL HAVE TO FIND OUT WHAT HIS PROBLEM IS IN THE NEXT EXCITING ISSUE OF YEAH!
END

TWO!

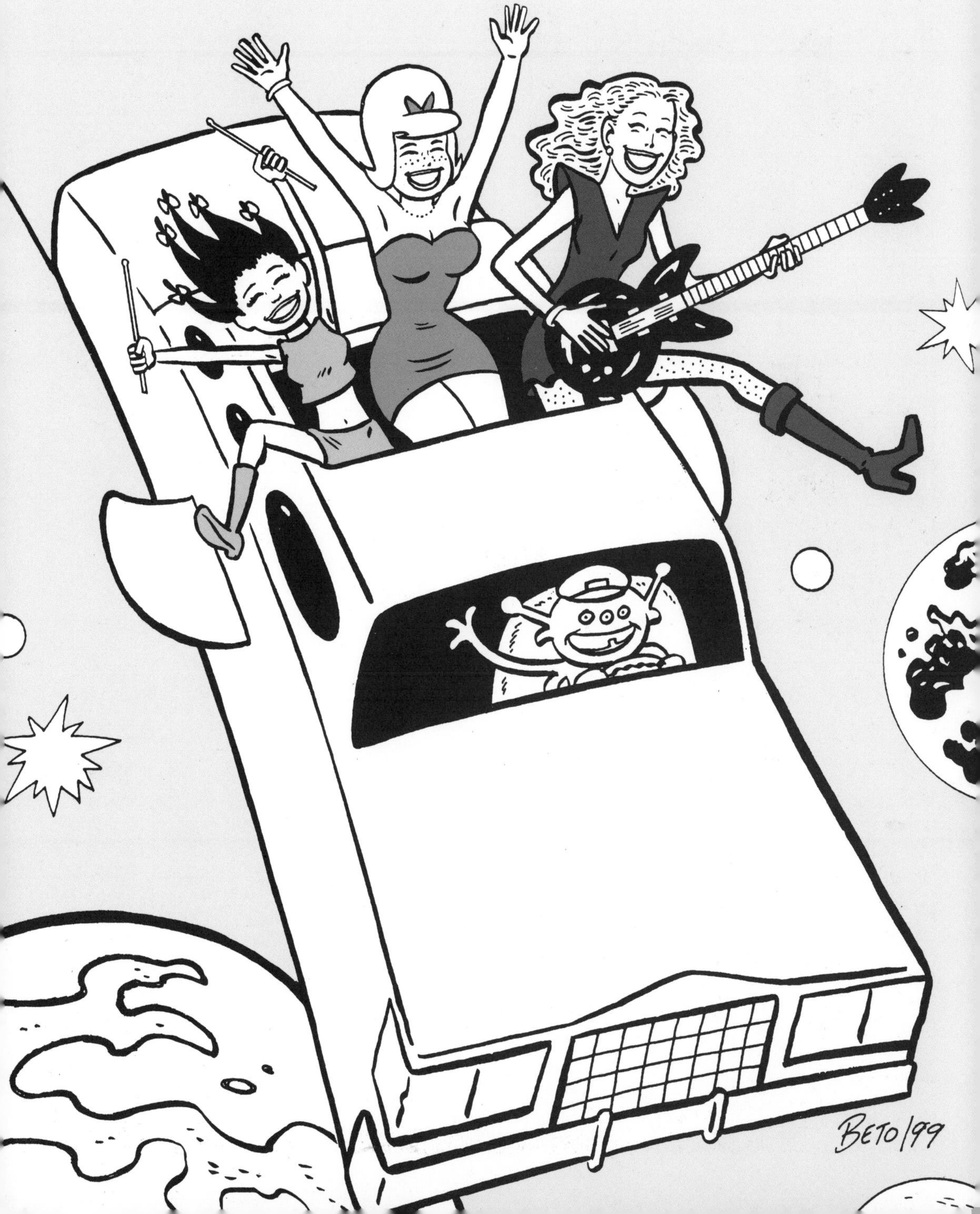
BETO/99

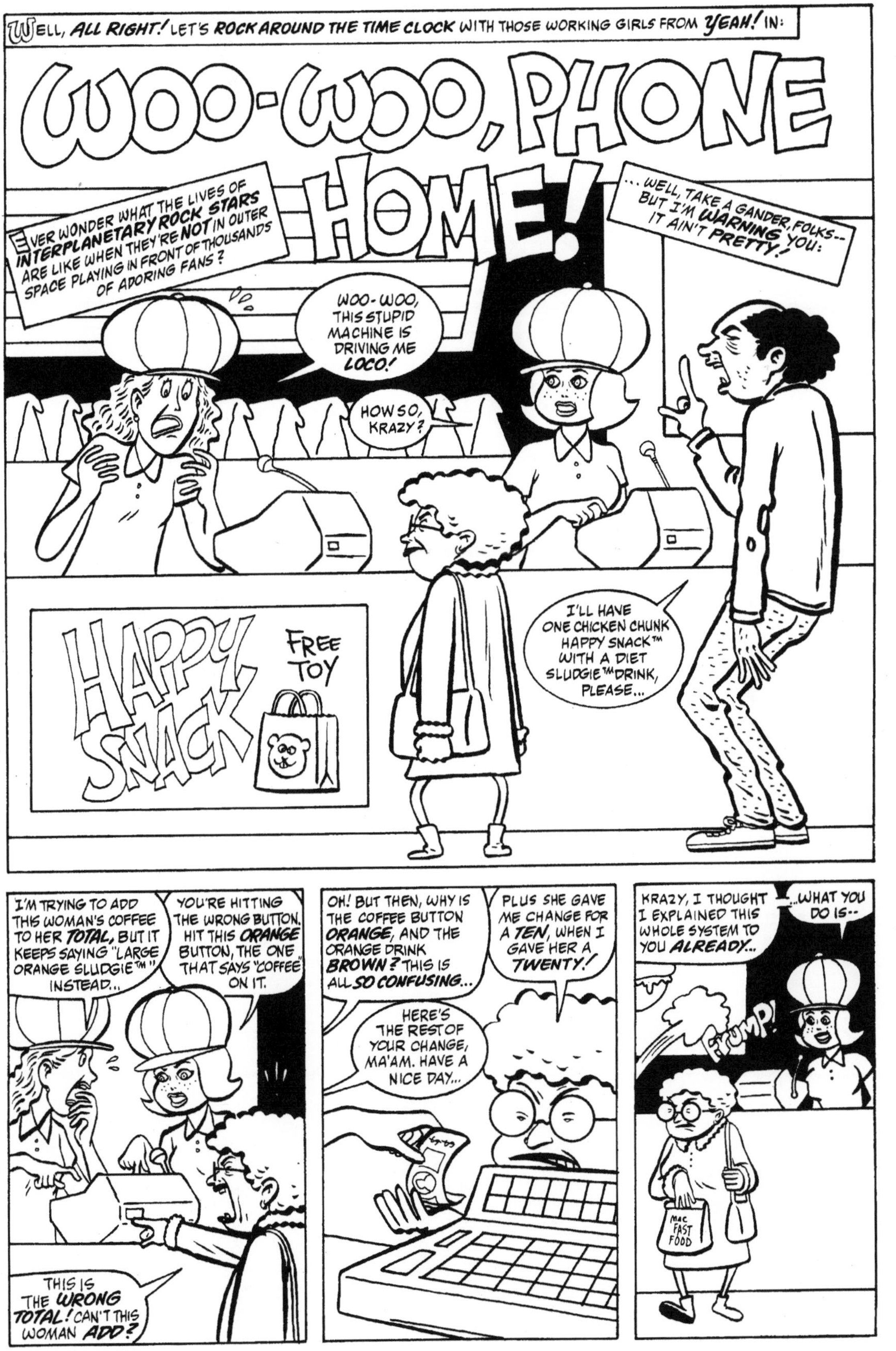
WELL, ALL RIGHT! LET'S ROCK AROUND THE TIME CLOCK WITH THOSE WORKING GIRLS FROM YEAH! IN:
WOO-WOO, PHONE HOME!
EVER WONDER WHAT THE LIVES OF INTERPLANETARY ROCK STARS ARE LIKE WHEN THEY'RE NOT IN OUTER SPACE PLAYING IN FRONT OF THOUSANDS OF ADORING FANS?
...WELL, TAKE A GANDER, FOLKS-- BUT I'M WARNING YOU: IT AIN'T PRETTY!
WOO-WOO, THIS STUPID MACHINE IS DRIVING ME LOCO!
HOW SO, KRAZY?
I'LL HAVE ONE CHICKEN CHUNK HAPPY SNACK™ WITH A DIET SLUDGIE™ DRINK, PLEASE...
HAPPY SNACK
FREE TOY
I'M TRYING TO ADD THIS WOMAN'S COFFEE TO HER TOTAL, BUT IT KEEPS SAYING "LARGE ORANGE SLUDGIE™" INSTEAD...
YOU'RE HITTING THE WRONG BUTTON. HIT THIS ORANGE BUTTON, THE ONE THAT SAYS "COFFEE" ON IT.
THIS IS THE WRONG TOTAL! CAN'T THIS WOMAN ADD?
OH! BUT THEN, WHY IS THE COFFEE BUTTON ORANGE, AND THE ORANGE DRINK BROWN? THIS IS ALL SO CONFUSING...
PLUS SHE GAVE ME CHANGE FOR A TEN, WHEN I GAVE HER A TWENTY!
HERE'S THE REST OF YOUR CHANGE, MA'AM. HAVE A NICE DAY...
KRAZY, I THOUGHT I EXPLAINED THIS WHOLE SYSTEM TO YOU ALREADY...
...WHAT YOU DO IS--
FRUMP!
MAC FAST FOOD

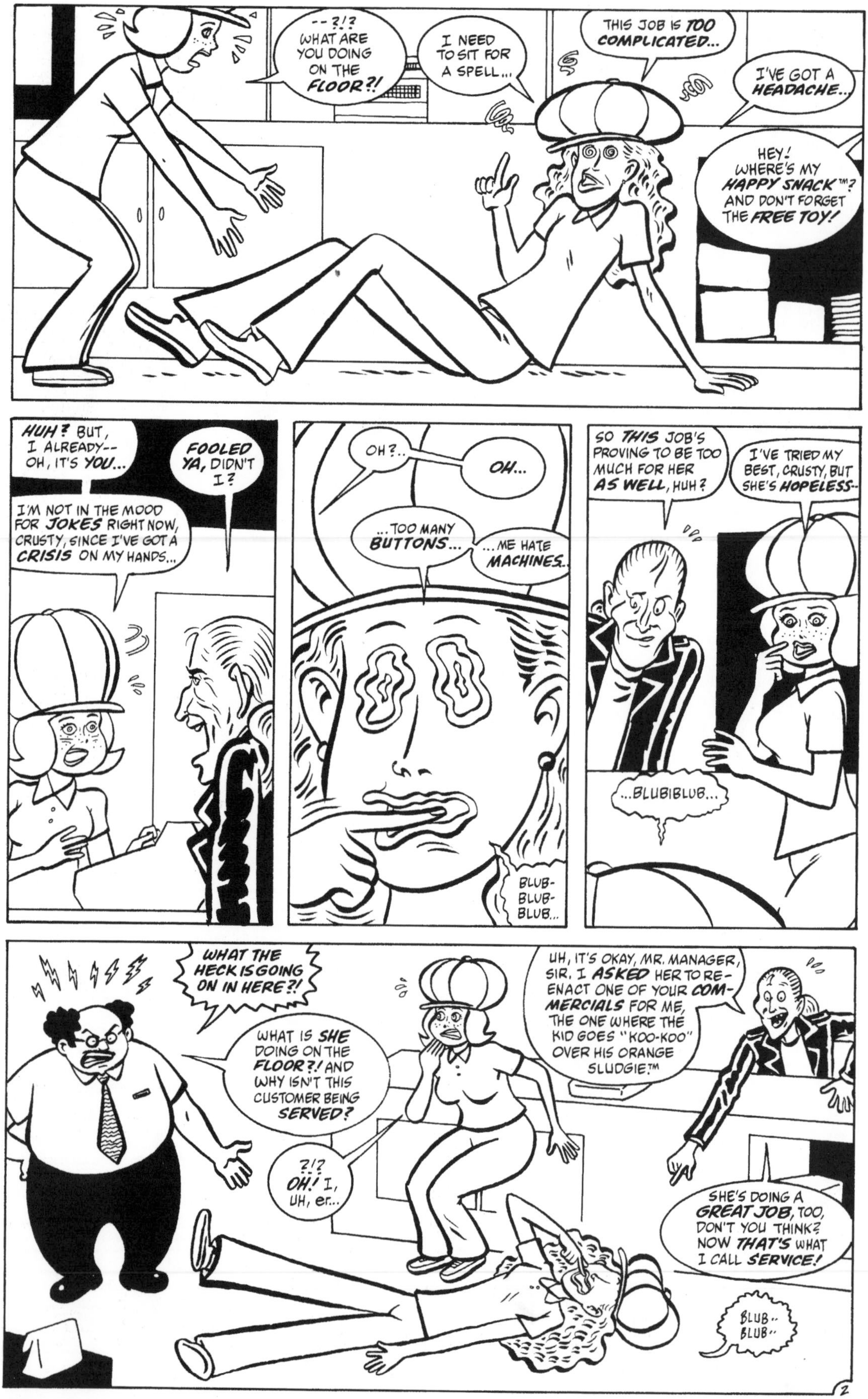
--?!?
WHAT ARE YOU DOING ON THE FLOOR?!
I NEED TO SIT FOR A SPELL...
THIS JOB IS TOO COMPLICATED...
I'VE GOT A HEADACHE...
HEY! WHERE'S MY HAPPY SNACK™? AND DON'T FORGET THE FREE TOY!
HUH? BUT, I ALREADY-- OH, IT'S YOU...
FOOLED YA, DIDN'T I?
I'M NOT IN THE MOOD FOR JOKES RIGHT NOW, CRUSTY, SINCE I'VE GOT A CRISIS ON MY HANDS...
OH?..
OH...
...TOO MANY BUTTONS...
...ME HATE MACHINES...
BLUB-BLUB-BLUB...
SO THIS JOB'S PROVING TO BE TOO MUCH FOR HER AS WELL, HUH?
I'VE TRIED MY BEST, CRUSTY, BUT SHE'S HOPELESS--
...BLUBIBLUB...
WHAT THE HECK IS GOING ON IN HERE?!
WHAT IS SHE DOING ON THE FLOOR?! AND WHY ISN'T THIS CUSTOMER BEING SERVED?
?!? OH! I, UH, er...
UH, IT'S OKAY, MR. MANAGER, SIR. I ASKED HER TO RE-ENACT ONE OF YOUR COMMERCIALS FOR ME, THE ONE WHERE THE KID GOES "KOO-KOO" OVER HIS ORANGE SLUDGIE™
SHE'S DOING A GREAT JOB, TOO, DON'T YOU THINK? NOW THAT'S WHAT I CALL SERVICE!
BLUB.. BLUB..

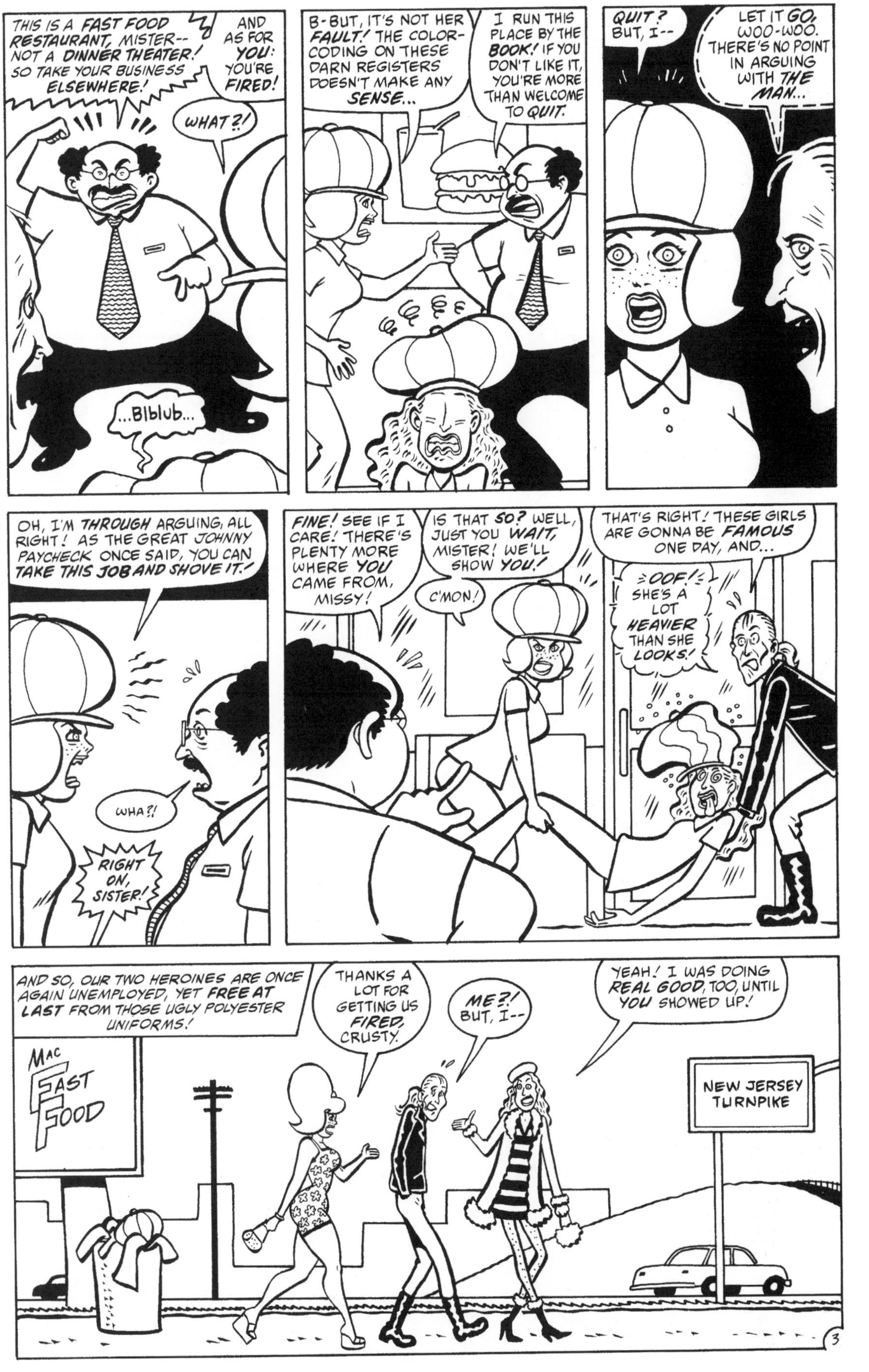

THIS IS A FAST FOOD RESTAURANT, MISTER-- NOT A DINNER THEATER! SO TAKE YOUR BUSINESS ELSEWHERE!
AND AS FOR YOU: YOU'RE FIRED!
WHAT?!
...Blblub...
B-BUT, IT'S NOT HER FAULT! THE COLOR-CODING ON THESE DARN REGISTERS DOESN'T MAKE ANY SENSE...
I RUN THIS PLACE BY THE BOOK! IF YOU DON'T LIKE IT, YOU'RE MORE THAN WELCOME TO QUIT.
QUIT? BUT, I--
LET IT GO, WOO-WOO. THERE'S NO POINT IN ARGUING WITH THE MAN...
OH, I'M THROUGH ARGUING, ALL RIGHT! AS THE GREAT JOHNNY PAYCHECK ONCE SAID, YOU CAN TAKE THIS JOB AND SHOVE IT!
WHA?!
RIGHT ON, SISTER!
FINE! SEE IF I CARE! THERE'S PLENTY MORE WHERE YOU CAME FROM, MISSY!
IS THAT SO? WELL, JUST YOU WAIT, MISTER! WE'LL SHOW YOU!
C'MON!
THAT'S RIGHT! THESE GIRLS ARE GONNA BE FAMOUS ONE DAY, AND...
OOF! SHE'S A LOT HEAVIER THAN SHE LOOKS!
AND SO, OUR TWO HEROINES ARE ONCE AGAIN UNEMPLOYED, YET FREE AT LAST FROM THOSE UGLY POLYESTER UNIFORMS!
THANKS A LOT FOR GETTING US FIRED, CRUSTY.
ME?! BUT, I--
YEAH! I WAS DOING REAL GOOD, TOO, UNTIL YOU SHOWED UP!
MAC FAST FOOD
NEW JERSEY TURNPIKE

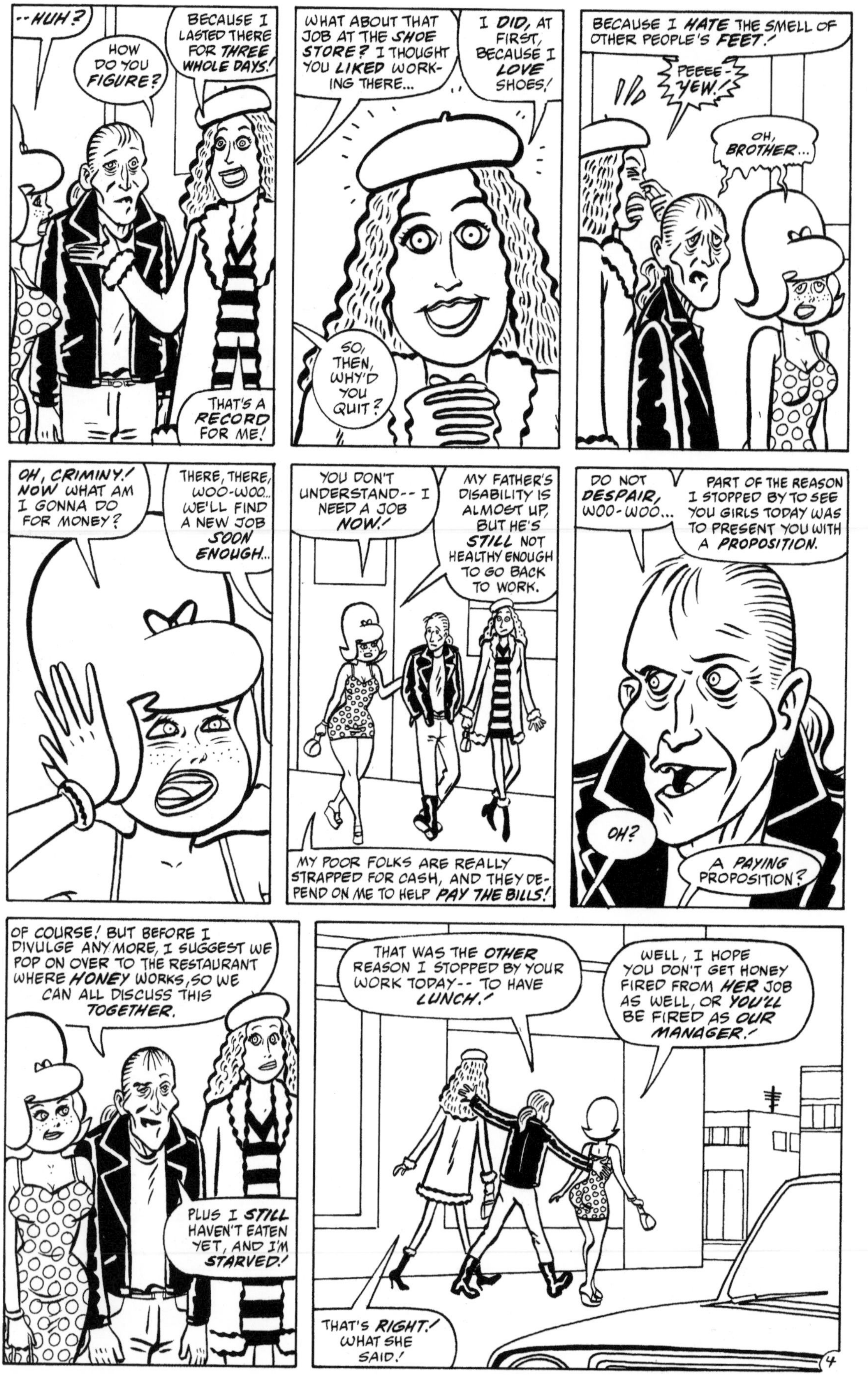

--HUH?
HOW DO YOU FIGURE?
BECAUSE I LASTED THERE FOR THREE WHOLE DAYS!
THAT'S A RECORD FOR ME!
WHAT ABOUT THAT JOB AT THE SHOE STORE? I THOUGHT YOU LIKED WORKING THERE...
I DID, AT FIRST, BECAUSE I LOVE SHOES!
SO, THEN, WHY'D YOU QUIT?
BECAUSE I HATE THE SMELL OF OTHER PEOPLE'S FEET!
PEEEE-YEW!
OH, BROTHER...
OH, CRIMINY! NOW WHAT AM I GONNA DO FOR MONEY?
THERE, THERE, WOO-WOO... WE'LL FIND A NEW JOB SOON ENOUGH...
YOU DON'T UNDERSTAND-- I NEED A JOB NOW!
MY FATHER'S DISABILITY IS ALMOST UP, BUT HE'S STILL NOT HEALTHY ENOUGH TO GO BACK TO WORK.
MY POOR FOLKS ARE REALLY STRAPPED FOR CASH, AND THEY DEPEND ON ME TO HELP PAY THE BILLS!
DO NOT DESPAIR, WOO-WOO...
PART OF THE REASON I STOPPED BY TO SEE YOU GIRLS TODAY WAS TO PRESENT YOU WITH A PROPOSITION.
OH?
A PAYING PROPOSITION?
OF COURSE! BUT BEFORE I DIVULGE ANY MORE, I SUGGEST WE POP ON OVER TO THE RESTAURANT WHERE HONEY WORKS, SO WE CAN ALL DISCUSS THIS TOGETHER.
PLUS I STILL HAVEN'T EATEN YET, AND I'M STARVED!
THAT WAS THE OTHER REASON I STOPPED BY YOUR WORK TODAY-- TO HAVE LUNCH!
WELL, I HOPE YOU DON'T GET HONEY FIRED FROM HER JOB AS WELL, OR YOU'LL BE FIRED AS OUR MANAGER!
THAT'S RIGHT! WHAT SHE SAID!

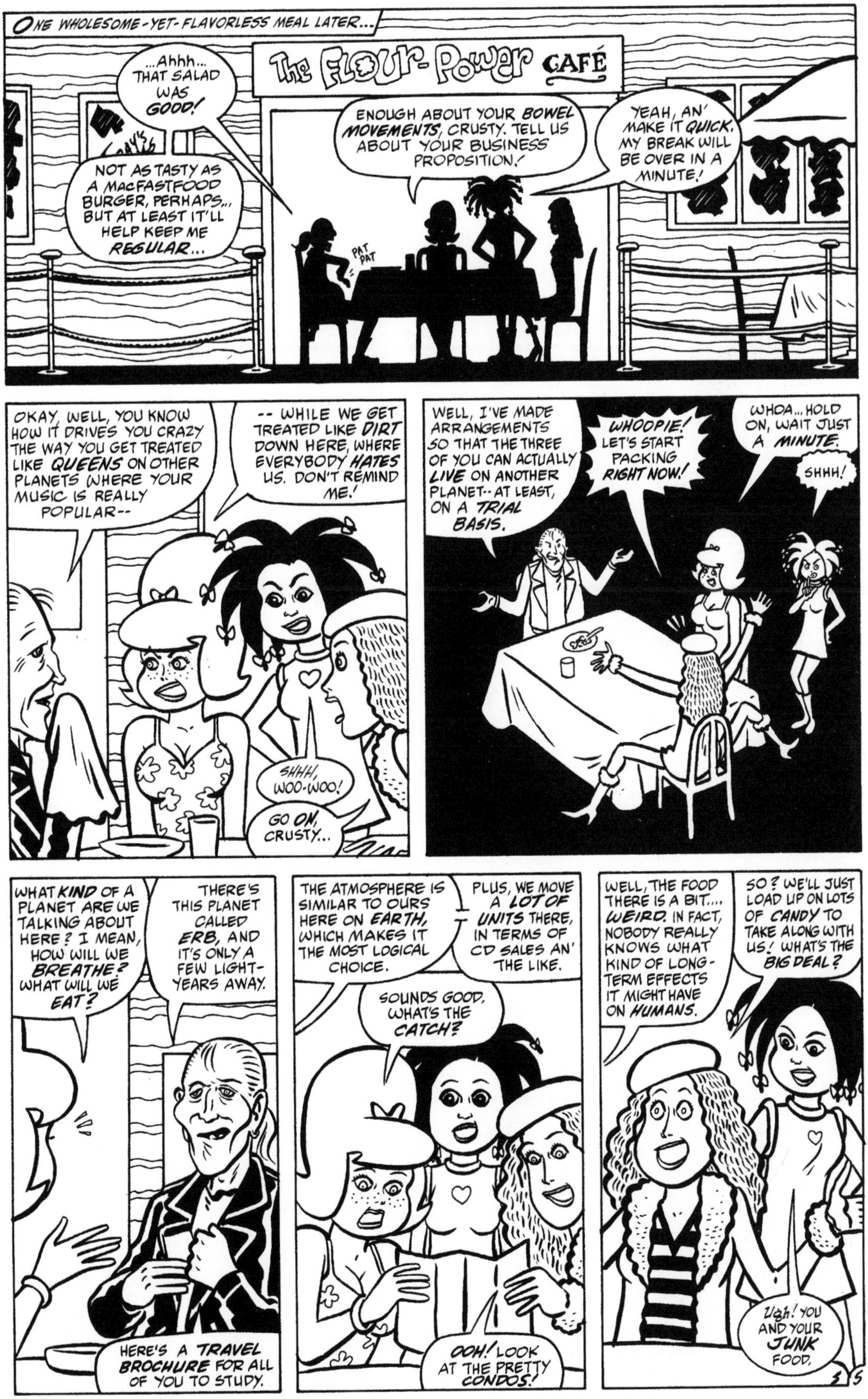

ONE WHOLESOME-YET-FLAVORLESS MEAL LATER...
The FLOUR-POWER CAFÉ
...Ahhh... THAT SALAD WAS GOOD!
NOT AS TASTY AS A MacFASTFOOD BURGER, PERHAPS... BUT AT LEAST IT'LL HELP KEEP ME REGULAR...
PAT PAT
ENOUGH ABOUT YOUR BOWEL MOVEMENTS, CRUSTY. TELL US ABOUT YOUR BUSINESS PROPOSITION!
YEAH, AN' MAKE IT QUICK. MY BREAK WILL BE OVER IN A MINUTE!
OKAY, WELL, YOU KNOW HOW IT DRIVES YOU CRAZY THE WAY YOU GET TREATED LIKE QUEENS ON OTHER PLANETS WHERE YOUR MUSIC IS REALLY POPULAR--
-- WHILE WE GET TREATED LIKE DIRT DOWN HERE, WHERE EVERYBODY HATES US. DON'T REMIND ME!
SHHH, WOO-WOO!
GO ON, CRUSTY...
WELL, I'VE MADE ARRANGEMENTS SO THAT THE THREE OF YOU CAN ACTUALLY LIVE ON ANOTHER PLANET-- AT LEAST, ON A TRIAL BASIS.
WHOOPIE! LET'S START PACKING RIGHT NOW!
WHOA... HOLD ON, WAIT JUST A MINUTE.
SHHH!
WHAT KIND OF A PLANET ARE WE TALKING ABOUT HERE? I MEAN, HOW WILL WE BREATHE? WHAT WILL WE EAT?
THERE'S THIS PLANET CALLED ERB, AND IT'S ONLY A FEW LIGHT-YEARS AWAY.
HERE'S A TRAVEL BROCHURE FOR ALL OF YOU TO STUDY.
THE ATMOSPHERE IS SIMILAR TO OURS HERE ON EARTH, WHICH MAKES IT THE MOST LOGICAL CHOICE.
PLUS, WE MOVE A LOT OF UNITS THERE, IN TERMS OF CD SALES AN' THE LIKE.
SOUNDS GOOD. WHAT'S THE CATCH?
OOH! LOOK AT THE PRETTY CONDOS!
WELL, THE FOOD THERE IS A BIT.... WEIRD. IN FACT, NOBODY REALLY KNOWS WHAT KIND OF LONG-TERM EFFECTS IT MIGHT HAVE ON HUMANS.
SO? WE'LL JUST LOAD UP ON LOTS OF CANDY TO TAKE ALONG WITH US! WHAT'S THE BIG DEAL?
Ugh! YOU AND YOUR JUNK FOOD.

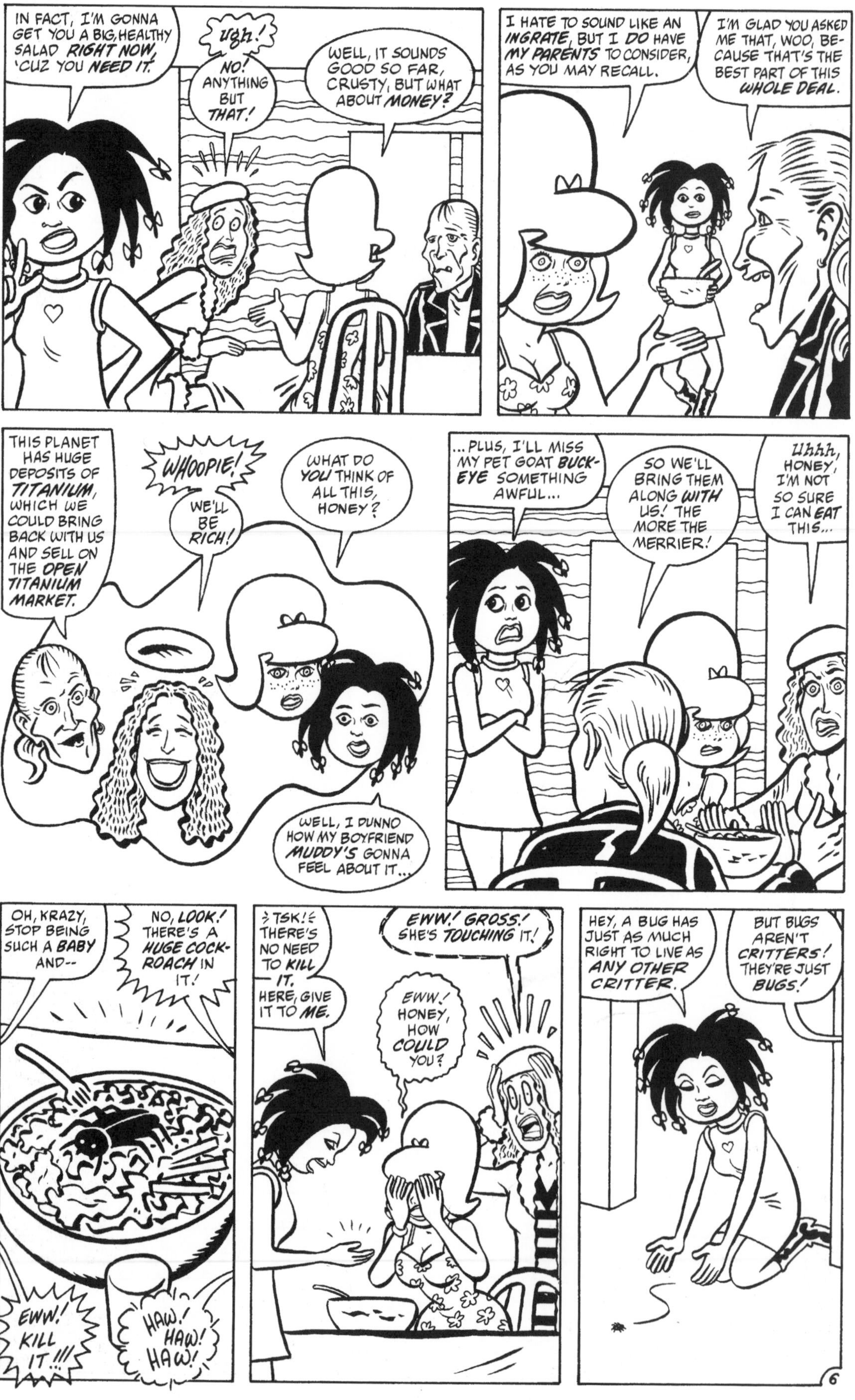
IN FACT, I'M GONNA GET YOU A BIG, HEALTHY SALAD RIGHT NOW, 'CUZ YOU NEED IT.
Ugh!
NO! ANYTHING BUT THAT!
WELL, IT SOUNDS GOOD SO FAR, CRUSTY, BUT WHAT ABOUT MONEY?
I HATE TO SOUND LIKE AN INGRATE, BUT I DO HAVE MY PARENTS TO CONSIDER, AS YOU MAY RECALL.
I'M GLAD YOU ASKED ME THAT, WOO, BECAUSE THAT'S THE BEST PART OF THIS WHOLE DEAL.
THIS PLANET HAS HUGE DEPOSITS OF TITANIUM, WHICH WE COULD BRING BACK WITH US AND SELL ON THE OPEN TITANIUM MARKET.
WHOOPIE!
WE'LL BE RICH!
WHAT DO YOU THINK OF ALL THIS, HONEY?
WELL, I DUNNO HOW MY BOYFRIEND MUDDY'S GONNA FEEL ABOUT IT...
...PLUS, I'LL MISS MY PET GOAT BUCKEYE SOMETHING AWFUL...
SO WE'LL BRING THEM ALONG WITH US! THE MORE THE MERRIER!
Uhhh, HONEY, I'M NOT SO SURE I CAN EAT THIS...
OH, KRAZY, STOP BEING SUCH A BABY AND--
NO, LOOK! THERE'S A HUGE COCKROACH IN IT!
EWW! KILL IT!!!
HAW! HAW! HAW!
TSK! THERE'S NO NEED TO KILL IT. HERE, GIVE IT TO ME.
EWW! GROSS! SHE'S TOUCHING IT!
EWW! HONEY, HOW COULD YOU?
HEY, A BUG HAS JUST AS MUCH RIGHT TO LIVE AS ANY OTHER CRITTER.
BUT BUGS AREN'T CRITTERS! THEY'RE JUST BUGS!

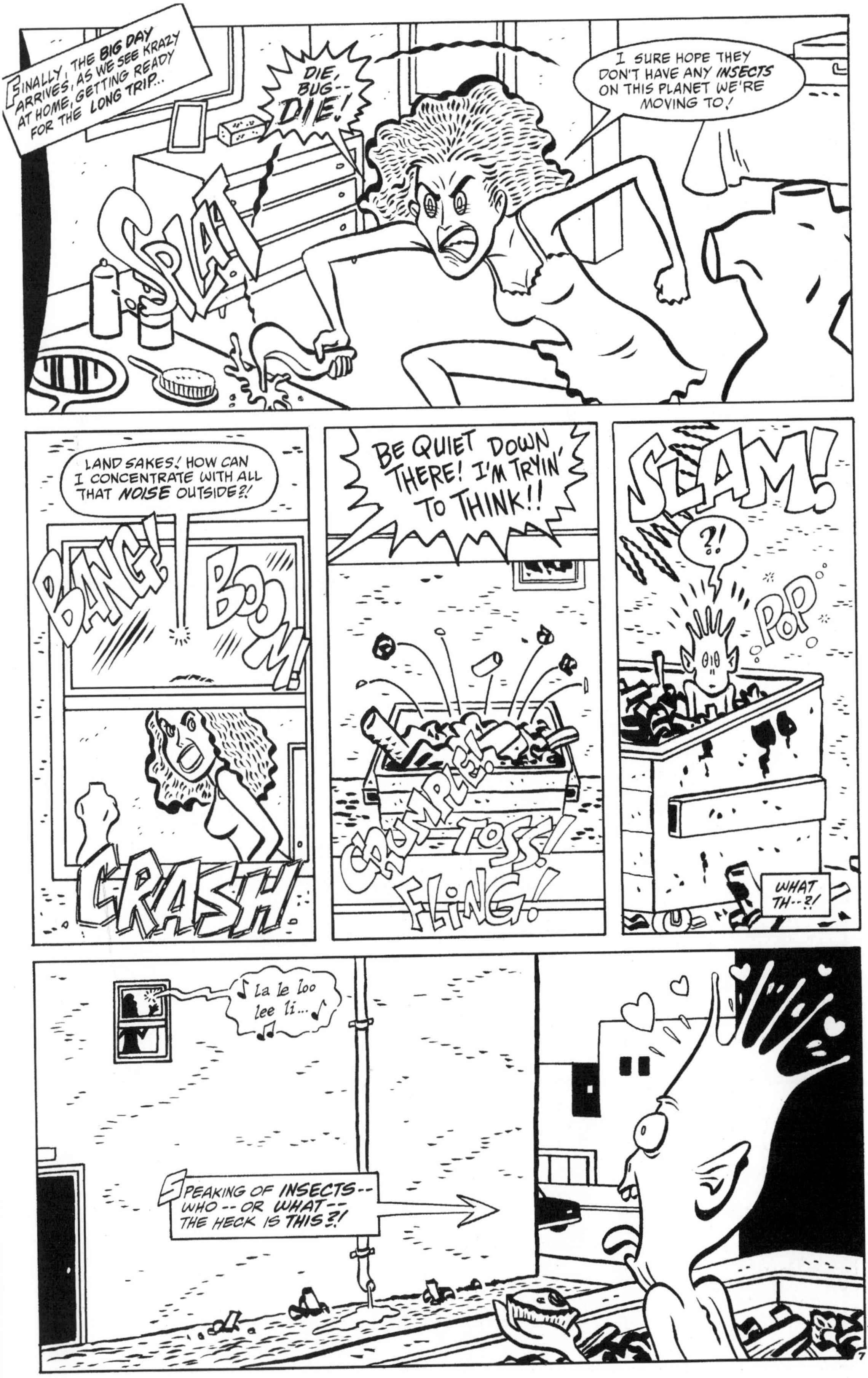
FINALLY, THE BIG DAY ARRIVES, AS WE SEE KRAZY AT HOME, GETTING READY FOR THE LONG TRIP...
DIE, BUG-- DIE!
I SURE HOPE THEY DON'T HAVE ANY INSECTS ON THIS PLANET WE'RE MOVING TO!
SPLAT
LAND SAKES! HOW CAN I CONCENTRATE WITH ALL THAT NOISE OUTSIDE?!
BANG!
BOOM!
CRASH
BE QUIET DOWN THERE! I'M TRYIN' TO THINK!!
CRUMPLE! TOSS! FLING!
SLAM!
?!
POP
WHAT TH--?!
La le loo lee li...
SPEAKING OF INSECTS-- WHO -- OR WHAT -- THE HECK IS THIS?!

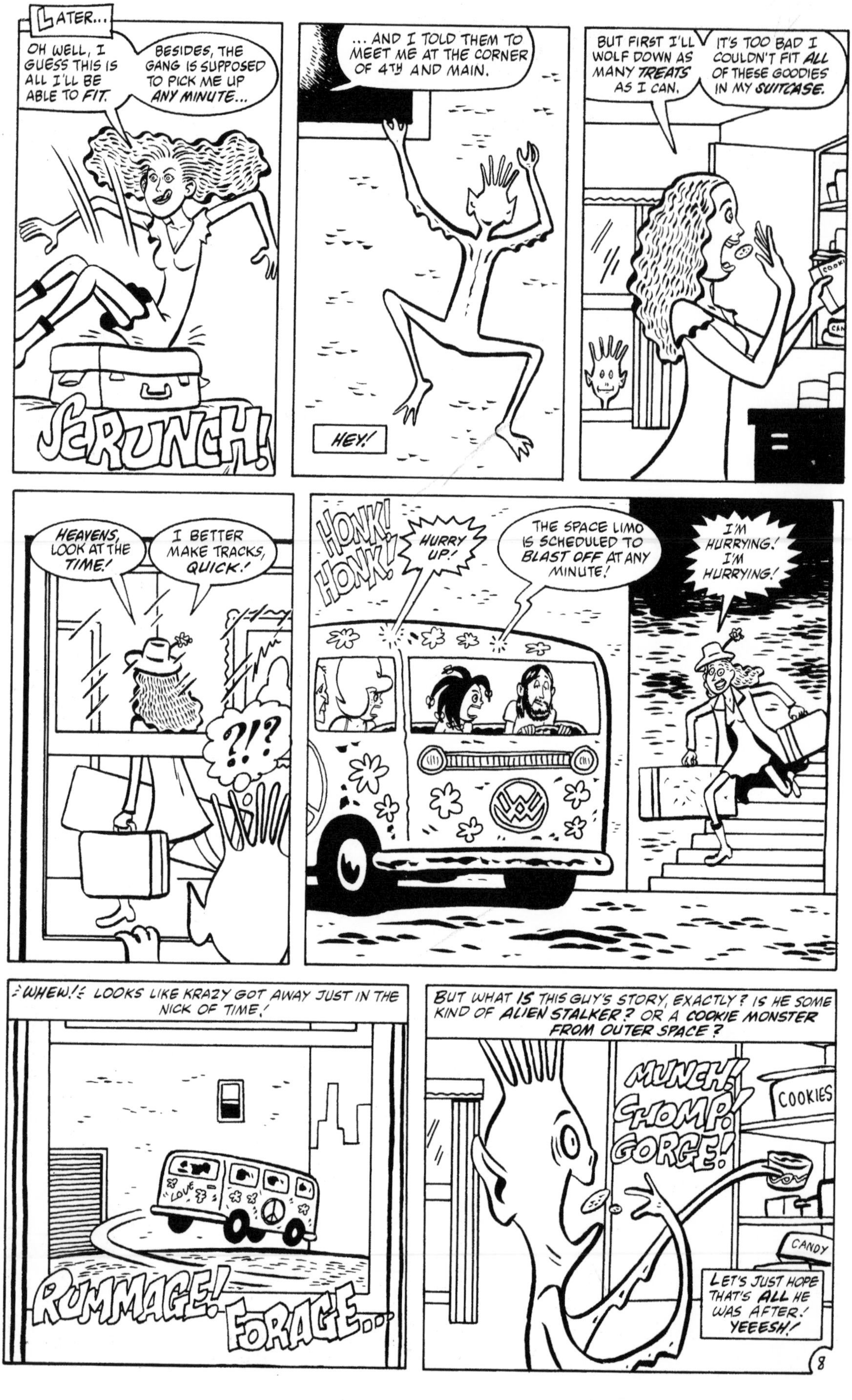
LATER...
OH WELL, I GUESS THIS IS ALL I'LL BE ABLE TO FIT.
BESIDES, THE GANG IS SUPPOSED TO PICK ME UP ANY MINUTE...
SCRUNCH!
... AND I TOLD THEM TO MEET ME AT THE CORNER OF 4TH AND MAIN.
HEY!
BUT FIRST I'LL WOLF DOWN AS MANY TREATS AS I CAN.
IT'S TOO BAD I COULDN'T FIT ALL OF THESE GOODIES IN MY SUITCASE.
HEAVENS, LOOK AT THE TIME!
I BETTER MAKE TRACKS, QUICK!
?!?
HONK! HONK!
HURRY UP!
THE SPACE LIMO IS SCHEDULED TO BLAST OFF AT ANY MINUTE!
I'M HURRYING! I'M HURRYING!
WHEW! LOOKS LIKE KRAZY GOT AWAY JUST IN THE NICK OF TIME!
LOVE
RUMMAGE! FORAGE...
BUT WHAT IS THIS GUY'S STORY, EXACTLY? IS HE SOME KIND OF ALIEN STALKER? OR A COOKIE MONSTER FROM OUTER SPACE?
MUNCH! CHOMP! GORGE!
COOKIES
CANDY
LET'S JUST HOPE THAT'S ALL HE WAS AFTER! YEEESH!

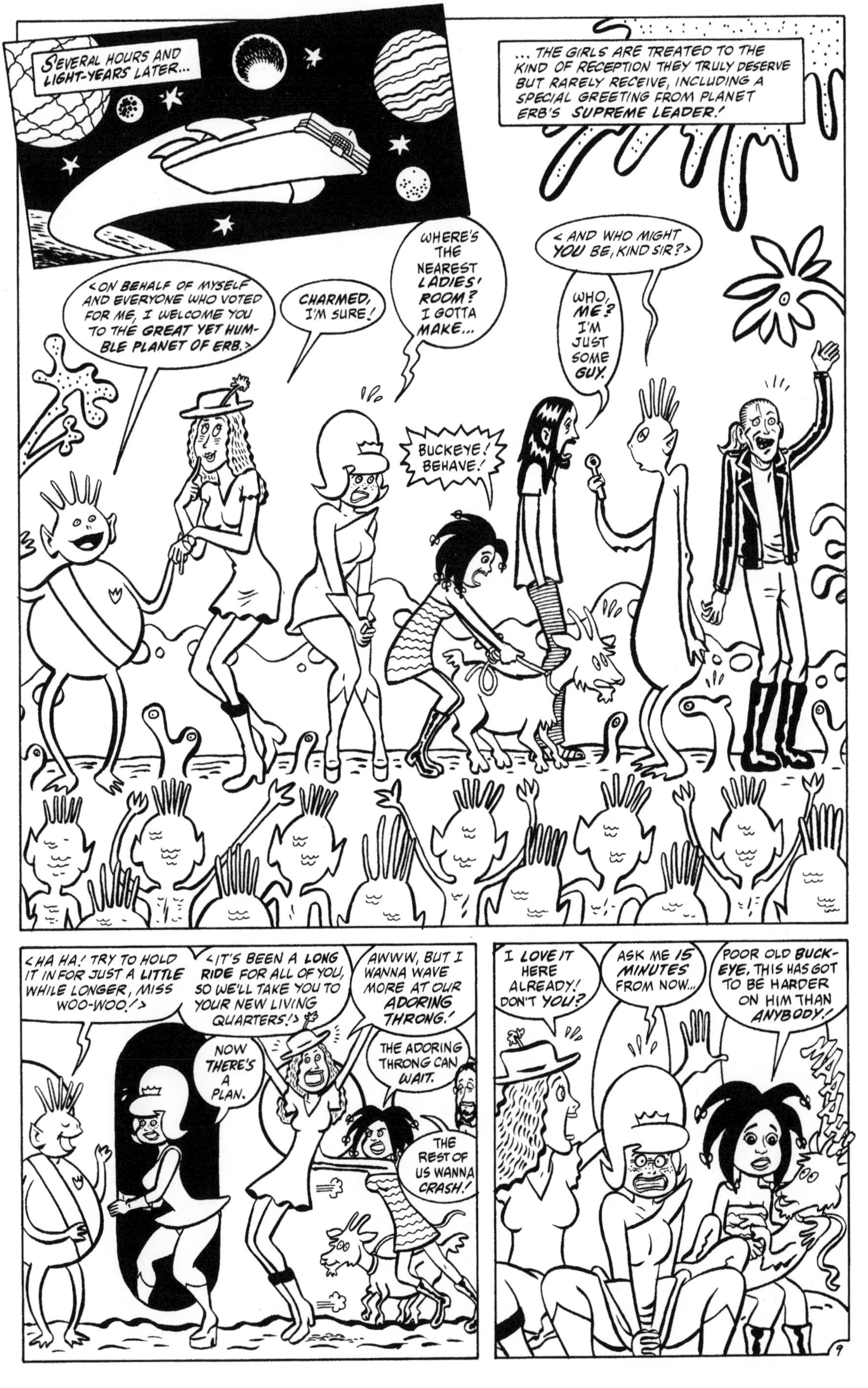
SEVERAL HOURS AND LIGHT-YEARS LATER...
... THE GIRLS ARE TREATED TO THE KIND OF RECEPTION THEY TRULY DESERVE BUT RARELY RECEIVE, INCLUDING A SPECIAL GREETING FROM PLANET ERB'S SUPREME LEADER!
< ON BEHALF OF MYSELF AND EVERYONE WHO VOTED FOR ME, I WELCOME YOU TO THE GREAT YET HUMBLE PLANET OF ERB. >
CHARMED, I'M SURE!
WHERE'S THE NEAREST LADIES' ROOM? I GOTTA MAKE...
BUCKEYE! BEHAVE!
< AND WHO MIGHT YOU BE, KIND SIR? >
WHO, ME? I'M JUST SOME GUY.
< HA HA! TRY TO HOLD IT IN FOR JUST A LITTLE WHILE LONGER, MISS WOO-WOO! >
< IT'S BEEN A LONG RIDE FOR ALL OF YOU, SO WE'LL TAKE YOU TO YOUR NEW LIVING QUARTERS! >
NOW THERE'S A PLAN.
AWWW, BUT I WANNA WAVE MORE AT OUR ADORING THRONG!
THE ADORING THRONG CAN WAIT.
THE REST OF US WANNA CRASH!
I LOVE IT HERE ALREADY! DON'T YOU?
ASK ME 15 MINUTES FROM NOW...
POOR OLD BUCKEYE. THIS HAS GOT TO BE HARDER ON HIM THAN ANYBODY!
MAAAH!

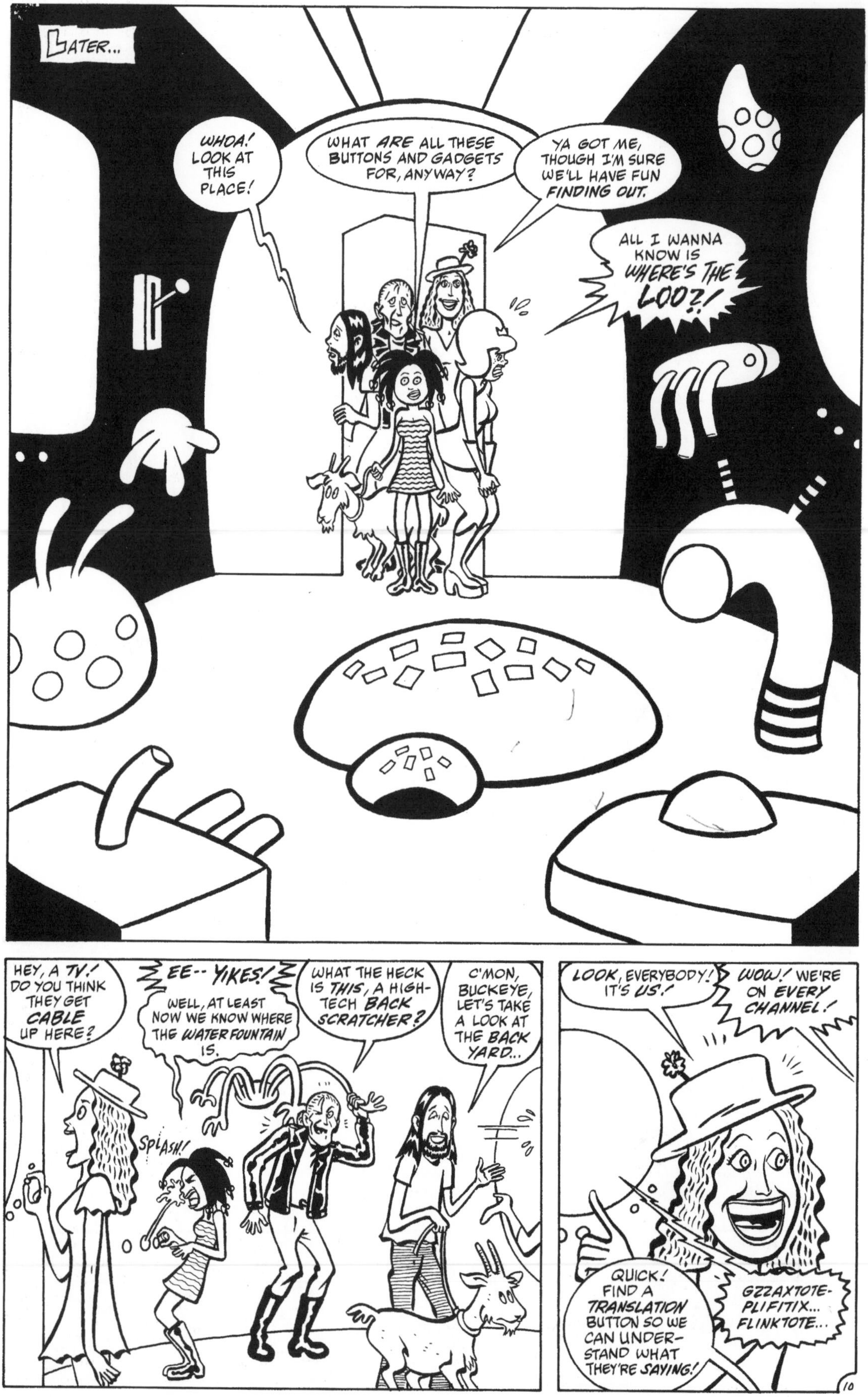
LATER...
WHOA! LOOK AT THIS PLACE!
WHAT ARE ALL THESE BUTTONS AND GADGETS FOR, ANYWAY?
YA GOT ME, THOUGH I'M SURE WE'LL HAVE FUN FINDING OUT.
ALL I WANNA KNOW IS WHERE'S THE LOO?!
HEY, A TV! DO YOU THINK THEY GET CABLE UP HERE?
EE-- YIKES!
SPLASH!
WELL, AT LEAST NOW WE KNOW WHERE THE WATER FOUNTAIN IS.
WHAT THE HECK IS THIS, A HIGH-TECH BACK SCRATCHER?
C'MON, BUCKEYE, LET'S TAKE A LOOK AT THE BACK YARD...
LOOK, EVERYBODY! IT'S US!
WOW! WE'RE ON EVERY CHANNEL!
QUICK! FIND A TRANSLATION BUTTON SO WE CAN UNDERSTAND WHAT THEY'RE SAYING!
GZZAXTOTE-PLIFITIX... FLINKTOTE...

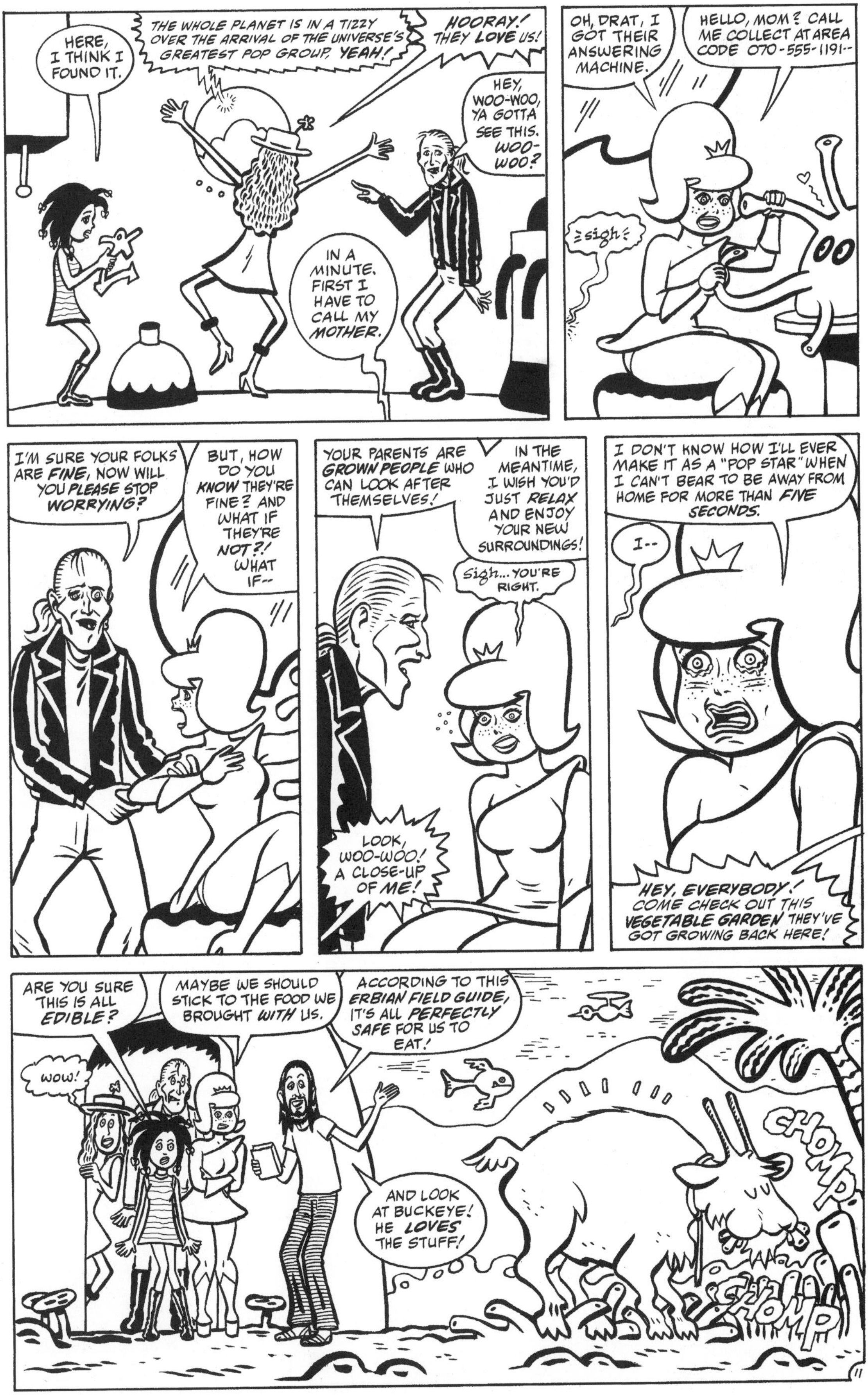
HERE, I THINK I FOUND IT.
THE WHOLE PLANET IS IN A TIZZY OVER THE ARRIVAL OF THE UNIVERSE'S GREATEST POP GROUP, YEAH!
HOORAY! THEY LOVE US!
HEY, WOO-WOO, YA GOTTA SEE THIS. WOO-WOO?
IN A MINUTE. FIRST I HAVE TO CALL MY MOTHER.
OH, DRAT, I GOT THEIR ANSWERING MACHINE.
HELLO, MOM? CALL ME COLLECT AT AREA CODE 070-555-1191--
sigh
I'M SURE YOUR FOLKS ARE FINE, NOW WILL YOU PLEASE STOP WORRYING?
BUT, HOW DO YOU KNOW THEY'RE FINE? AND WHAT IF THEY'RE NOT?! WHAT IF--
YOUR PARENTS ARE GROWN PEOPLE WHO CAN LOOK AFTER THEMSELVES!
IN THE MEANTIME, I WISH YOU'D JUST RELAX AND ENJOY YOUR NEW SURROUNDINGS!
sigh... YOU'RE RIGHT.
LOOK, WOO-WOO! A CLOSE-UP OF ME!
I DON'T KNOW HOW I'LL EVER MAKE IT AS A "POP STAR" WHEN I CAN'T BEAR TO BE AWAY FROM HOME FOR MORE THAN FIVE SECONDS.
I--
HEY, EVERYBODY! COME CHECK OUT THIS VEGETABLE GARDEN THEY'VE GOT GROWING BACK HERE!
ARE YOU SURE THIS IS ALL EDIBLE?
MAYBE WE SHOULD STICK TO THE FOOD WE BROUGHT WITH US.
ACCORDING TO THIS ERBIAN FIELD GUIDE, IT'S ALL PERFECTLY SAFE FOR US TO EAT!
WOW!
AND LOOK AT BUCKEYE! HE LOVES THE STUFF!
CHOMP!
CHOMP
CHOMP

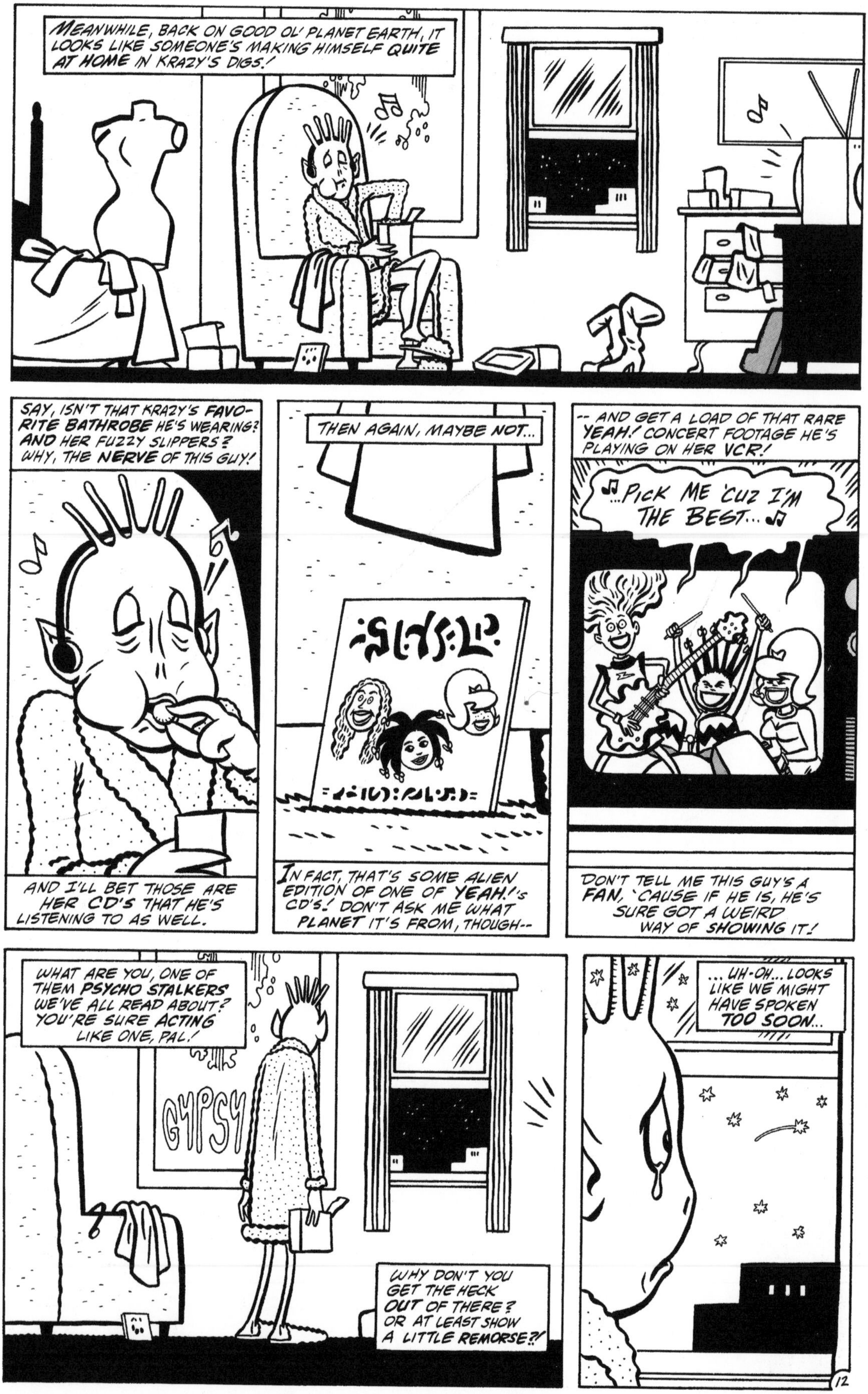
MEANWHILE, BACK ON GOOD OL' PLANET EARTH, IT LOOKS LIKE SOMEONE'S MAKING HIMSELF QUITE AT HOME IN KRAZY'S DIGS!
SAY, ISN'T THAT KRAZY'S FAVORITE BATHROBE HE'S WEARING? AND HER FUZZY SLIPPERS? WHY, THE NERVE OF THIS GUY!
AND I'LL BET THOSE ARE HER CD'S THAT HE'S LISTENING TO AS WELL.
THEN AGAIN, MAYBE NOT...
IN FACT, THAT'S SOME ALIEN EDITION OF ONE OF YEAH!'s CD'S! DON'T ASK ME WHAT PLANET IT'S FROM, THOUGH--
-- AND GET A LOAD OF THAT RARE YEAH! CONCERT FOOTAGE HE'S PLAYING ON HER VCR!
...PICK ME 'CUZ I'M THE BEST...
DON'T TELL ME THIS GUY'S A FAN, 'CAUSE IF HE IS, HE'S SURE GOT A WEIRD WAY OF SHOWING IT!
WHAT ARE YOU, ONE OF THEM PSYCHO STALKERS WE'VE ALL READ ABOUT? YOU'RE SURE ACTING LIKE ONE, PAL!
GYPSY
WHY DON'T YOU GET THE HECK OUT OF THERE? OR AT LEAST SHOW A LITTLE REMORSE?!
...UH-OH... LOOKS LIKE WE MIGHT HAVE SPOKEN TOO SOON...

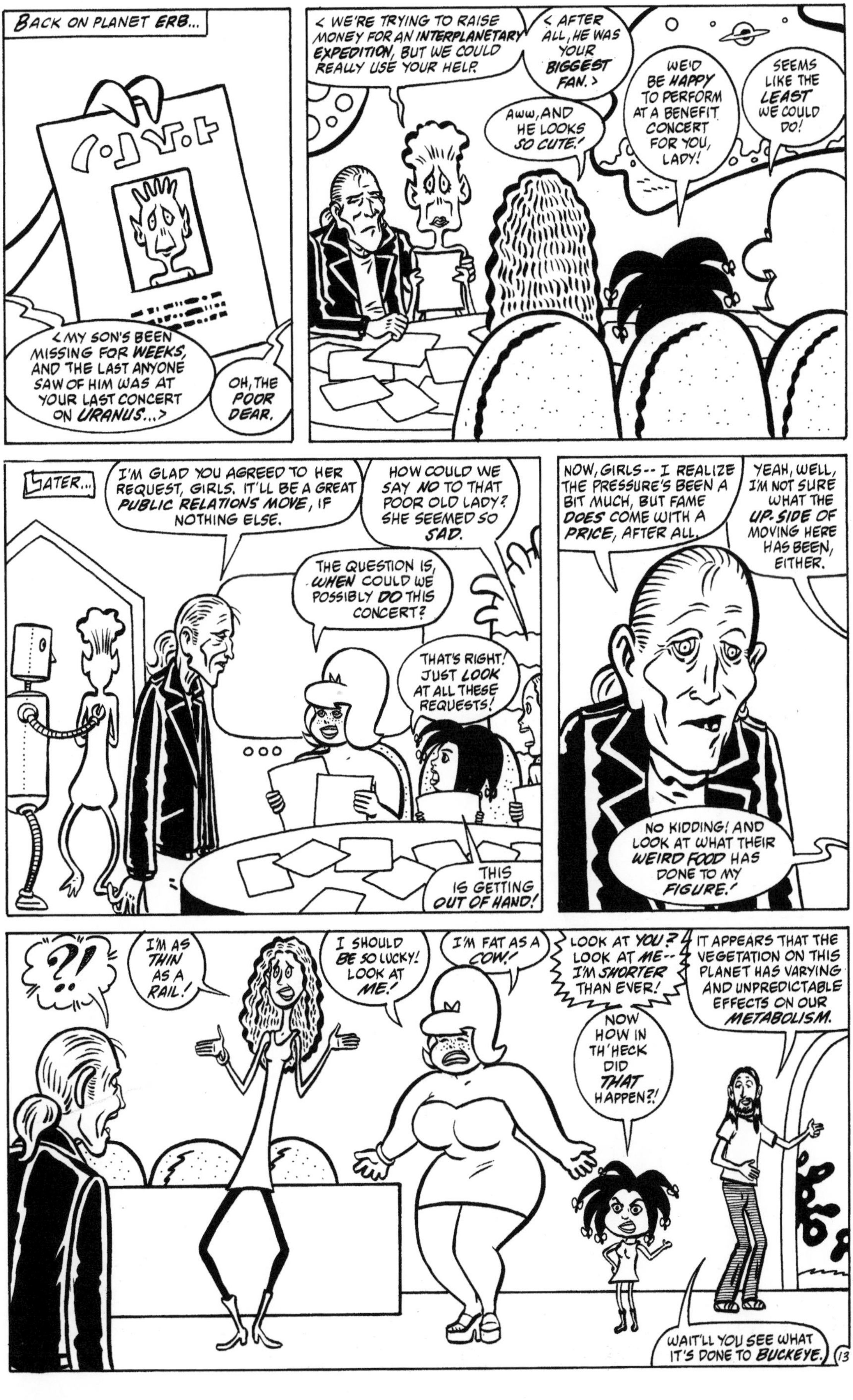
BACK ON PLANET ERB...
< MY SON'S BEEN MISSING FOR WEEKS, AND THE LAST ANYONE SAW OF HIM WAS AT YOUR LAST CONCERT ON URANUS...>
OH, THE POOR DEAR.
< WE'RE TRYING TO RAISE MONEY FOR AN INTERPLANETARY EXPEDITION, BUT WE COULD REALLY USE YOUR HELP.
< AFTER ALL, HE WAS YOUR BIGGEST FAN. >
AWW, AND HE LOOKS SO CUTE!
WE'D BE HAPPY TO PERFORM AT A BENEFIT CONCERT FOR YOU, LADY!
SEEMS LIKE THE LEAST WE COULD DO!
LATER...
I'M GLAD YOU AGREED TO HER REQUEST, GIRLS. IT'LL BE A GREAT PUBLIC RELATIONS MOVE, IF NOTHING ELSE.
HOW COULD WE SAY NO TO THAT POOR OLD LADY? SHE SEEMED SO SAD.
THE QUESTION IS, WHEN COULD WE POSSIBLY DO THIS CONCERT?
THAT'S RIGHT! JUST LOOK AT ALL THESE REQUESTS!
...
THIS IS GETTING OUT OF HAND!
NOW, GIRLS-- I REALIZE THE PRESSURE'S BEEN A BIT MUCH, BUT FAME DOES COME WITH A PRICE, AFTER ALL.
YEAH, WELL, I'M NOT SURE WHAT THE UP-SIDE OF MOVING HERE HAS BEEN, EITHER.
NO KIDDING! AND LOOK AT WHAT THEIR WEIRD FOOD HAS DONE TO MY FIGURE!
?!
I'M AS THIN AS A RAIL!
I SHOULD BE SO LUCKY! LOOK AT ME!
I'M FAT AS A COW!
LOOK AT YOU? LOOK AT ME-- I'M SHORTER THAN EVER!
NOW HOW IN TH'HECK DID THAT HAPPEN?!
IT APPEARS THAT THE VEGETATION ON THIS PLANET HAS VARYING AND UNPREDICTABLE EFFECTS ON OUR METABOLISM.
WAIT'LL YOU SEE WHAT IT'S DONE TO BUCKEYE.

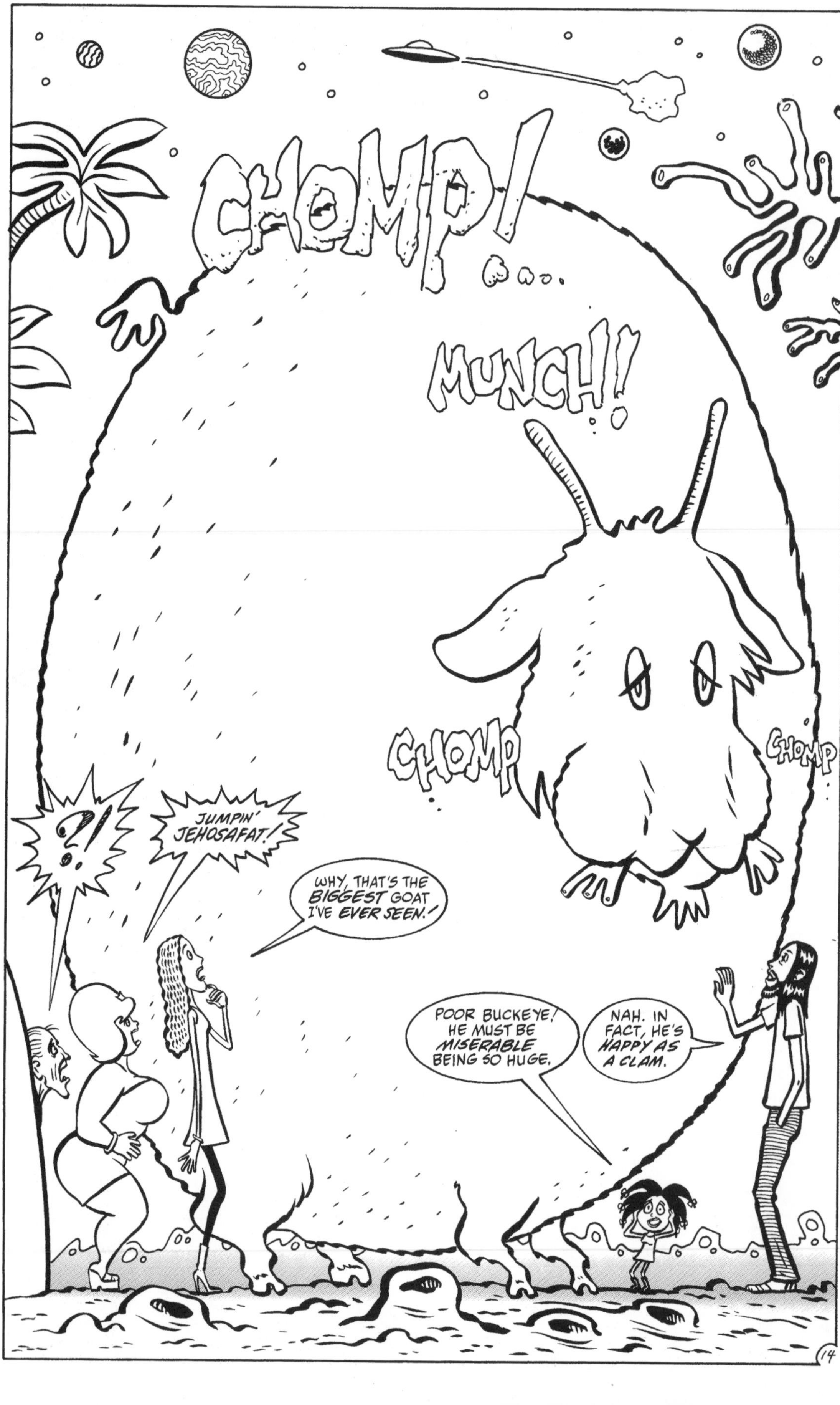
CHOMP!
MUNCH!
CHOMP
CHOMP
?!
JUMPIN' JEHOSAFAT!
WHY, THAT'S THE BIGGEST GOAT I'VE EVER SEEN!
POOR BUCKEYE! HE MUST BE MISERABLE BEING SO HUGE.
NAH. IN FACT, HE'S HAPPY AS A CLAM.

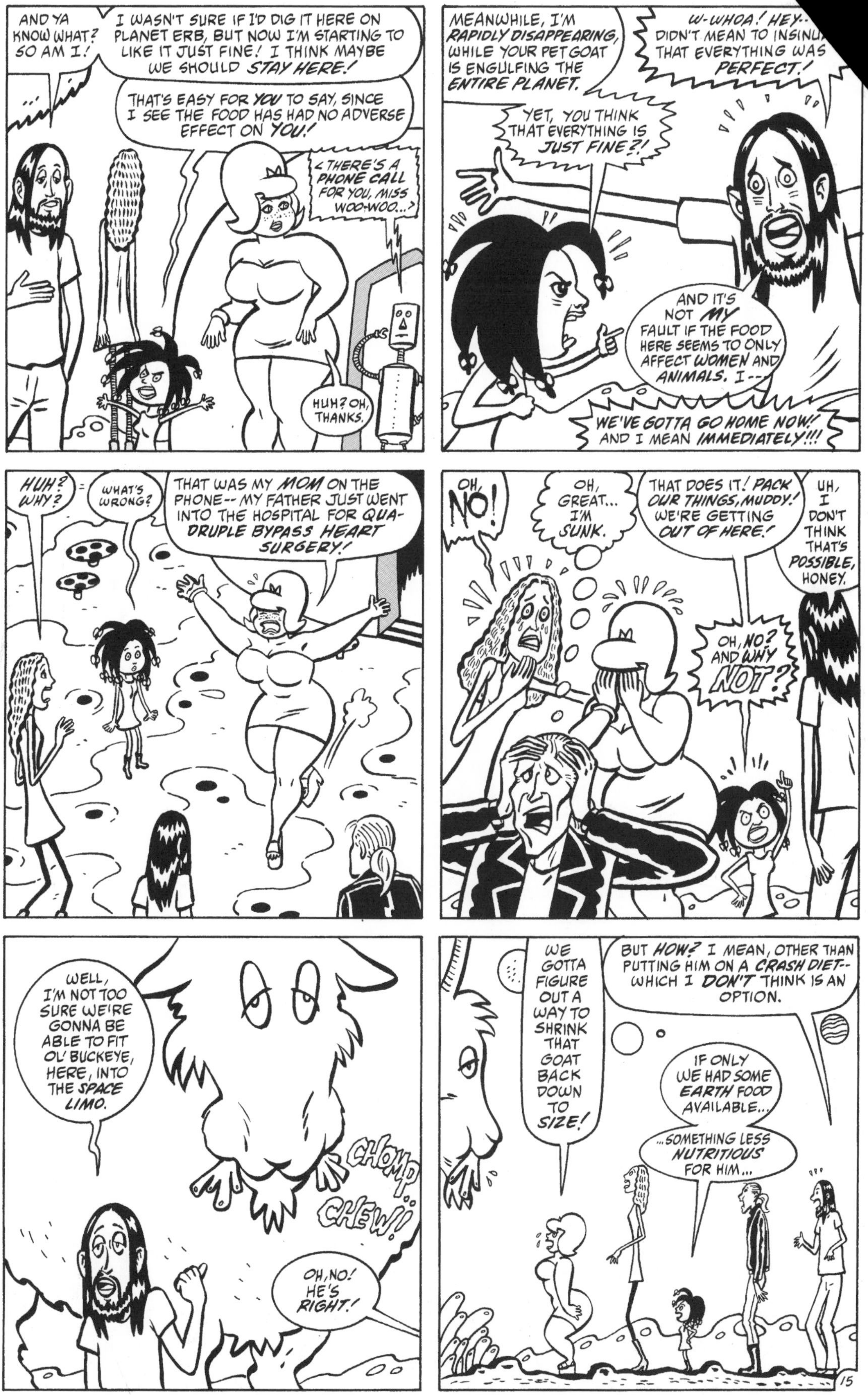
AND YA KNOW WHAT? SO AM I!
I WASN'T SURE IF I'D DIG IT HERE ON PLANET ERB, BUT NOW I'M STARTING TO LIKE IT JUST FINE! I THINK MAYBE WE SHOULD STAY HERE!
...
THAT'S EASY FOR YOU TO SAY, SINCE I SEE THE FOOD HAS HAD NO ADVERSE EFFECT ON YOU!
<THERE'S A PHONE CALL FOR YOU, MISS WOO-WOO...>
HUH? OH, THANKS.
MEANWHILE, I'M RAPIDLY DISAPPEARING, WHILE YOUR PET GOAT IS ENGULFING THE ENTIRE PLANET.
YET, YOU THINK THAT EVERYTHING IS JUST FINE?!
W-WHOA! HEY-- DIDN'T MEAN TO INSINU THAT EVERYTHING WAS PERFECT!
AND IT'S NOT MY FAULT IF THE FOOD HERE SEEMS TO ONLY AFFECT WOMEN AND ANIMALS. I---
WE'VE GOTTA GO HOME NOW! AND I MEAN IMMEDIATELY!!!
HUH? WHY?
WHAT'S WRONG?
THAT WAS MY MOM ON THE PHONE-- MY FATHER JUST WENT INTO THE HOSPITAL FOR QUADRUPLE BYPASS HEART SURGERY!
OH, NO!
OH, GREAT... I'M SUNK.
THAT DOES IT! PACK OUR THINGS, MUDDY! WE'RE GETTING OUT OF HERE!
UH, I DON'T THINK THAT'S POSSIBLE, HONEY.
OH, NO? AND WHY NOT?
WELL, I'M NOT TOO SURE WE'RE GONNA BE ABLE TO FIT OL' BUCKEYE, HERE, INTO THE SPACE LIMO.
CHOMP.. CHEW!!
OH, NO! HE'S RIGHT!
WE GOTTA FIGURE OUT A WAY TO SHRINK THAT GOAT BACK DOWN TO SIZE!
BUT HOW? I MEAN, OTHER THAN PUTTING HIM ON A CRASH DIET-- WHICH I DON'T THINK IS AN OPTION.
IF ONLY WE HAD SOME EARTH FOOD AVAILABLE...
...SOMETHING LESS NUTRITIOUS FOR HIM...

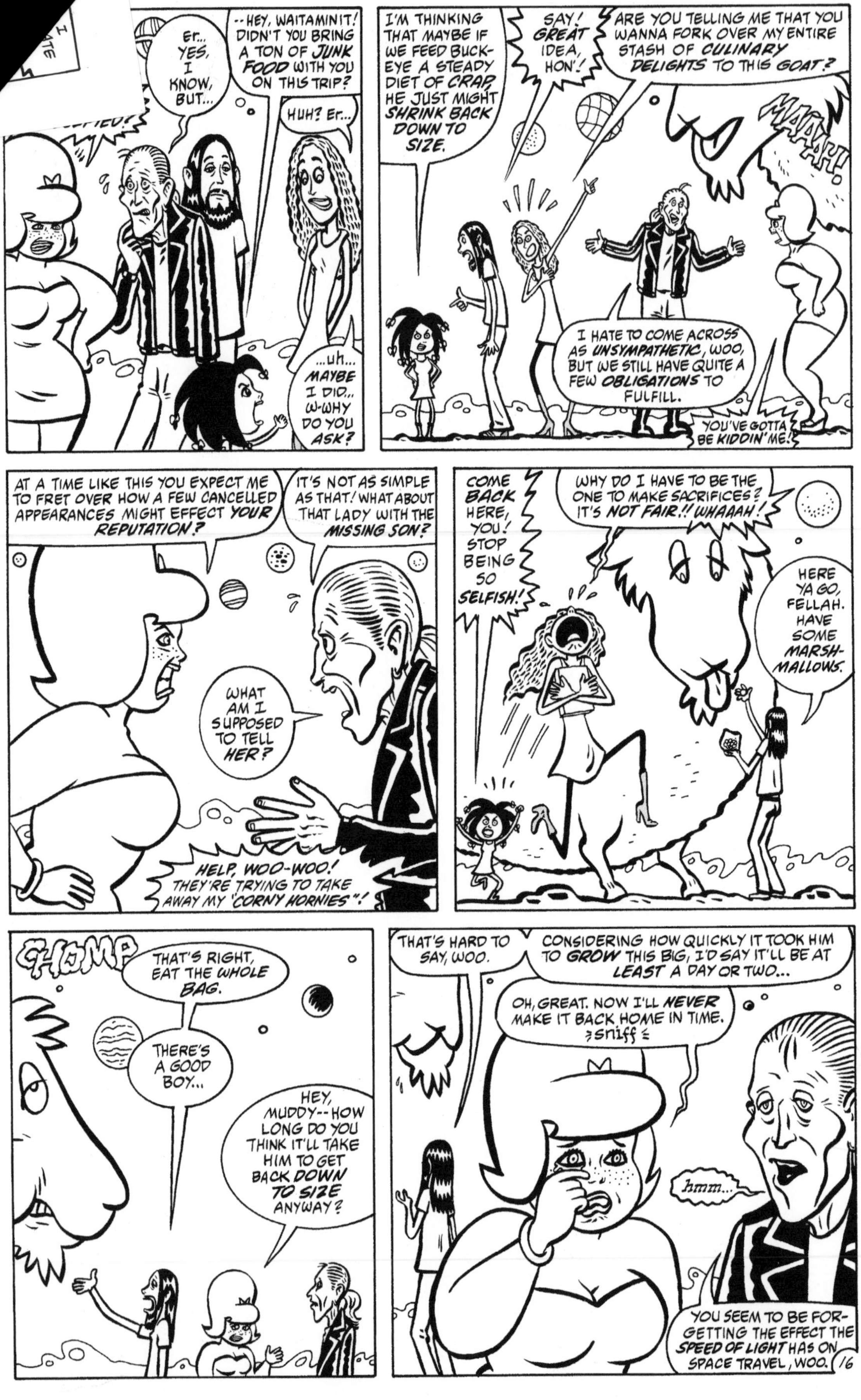
Er... YES, I KNOW, BUT...
--HEY, WAITAMINIT! DIDN'T YOU BRING A TON OF JUNK FOOD WITH YOU ON THIS TRIP?
HUH? Er...
...uh... MAYBE I DID... W-WHY DO YOU ASK?
I'M THINKING THAT MAYBE IF WE FEED BUCK-EYE A STEADY DIET OF CRAP, HE JUST MIGHT SHRINK BACK DOWN TO SIZE.
SAY! GREAT IDEA, HON'!
ARE YOU TELLING ME THAT YOU WANNA FORK OVER MY ENTIRE STASH OF CULINARY DELIGHTS TO THIS GOAT?
MAAAH!
I HATE TO COME ACROSS AS UNSYMPATHETIC, WOO, BUT WE STILL HAVE QUITE A FEW OBLIGATIONS TO FULFILL.
YOU'VE GOTTA BE KIDDIN' ME!
AT A TIME LIKE THIS YOU EXPECT ME TO FRET OVER HOW A FEW CANCELLED APPEARANCES MIGHT EFFECT YOUR REPUTATION?
IT'S NOT AS SIMPLE AS THAT! WHAT ABOUT THAT LADY WITH THE MISSING SON?
WHAT AM I SUPPOSED TO TELL HER?
HELP, WOO-WOO! THEY'RE TRYING TO TAKE AWAY MY "CORNY HORNIES"!
COME BACK HERE, YOU! STOP BEING SO SELFISH!
WHY DO I HAVE TO BE THE ONE TO MAKE SACRIFICES? IT'S NOT FAIR!! WHAAAH!
HERE YA GO, FELLAH. HAVE SOME MARSH-MALLOWS.
CHOMP
THAT'S RIGHT, EAT THE WHOLE BAG.
THERE'S A GOOD BOY...
HEY, MUDDY--HOW LONG DO YOU THINK IT'LL TAKE HIM TO GET BACK DOWN TO SIZE ANYWAY?
THAT'S HARD TO SAY, WOO.
CONSIDERING HOW QUICKLY IT TOOK HIM TO GROW THIS BIG, I'D SAY IT'LL BE AT LEAST A DAY OR TWO...
OH, GREAT. NOW I'LL NEVER MAKE IT BACK HOME IN TIME. sniff
hmm...
YOU SEEM TO BE FOR-GETTING THE EFFECT THE SPEED OF LIGHT HAS ON SPACE TRAVEL, WOO.

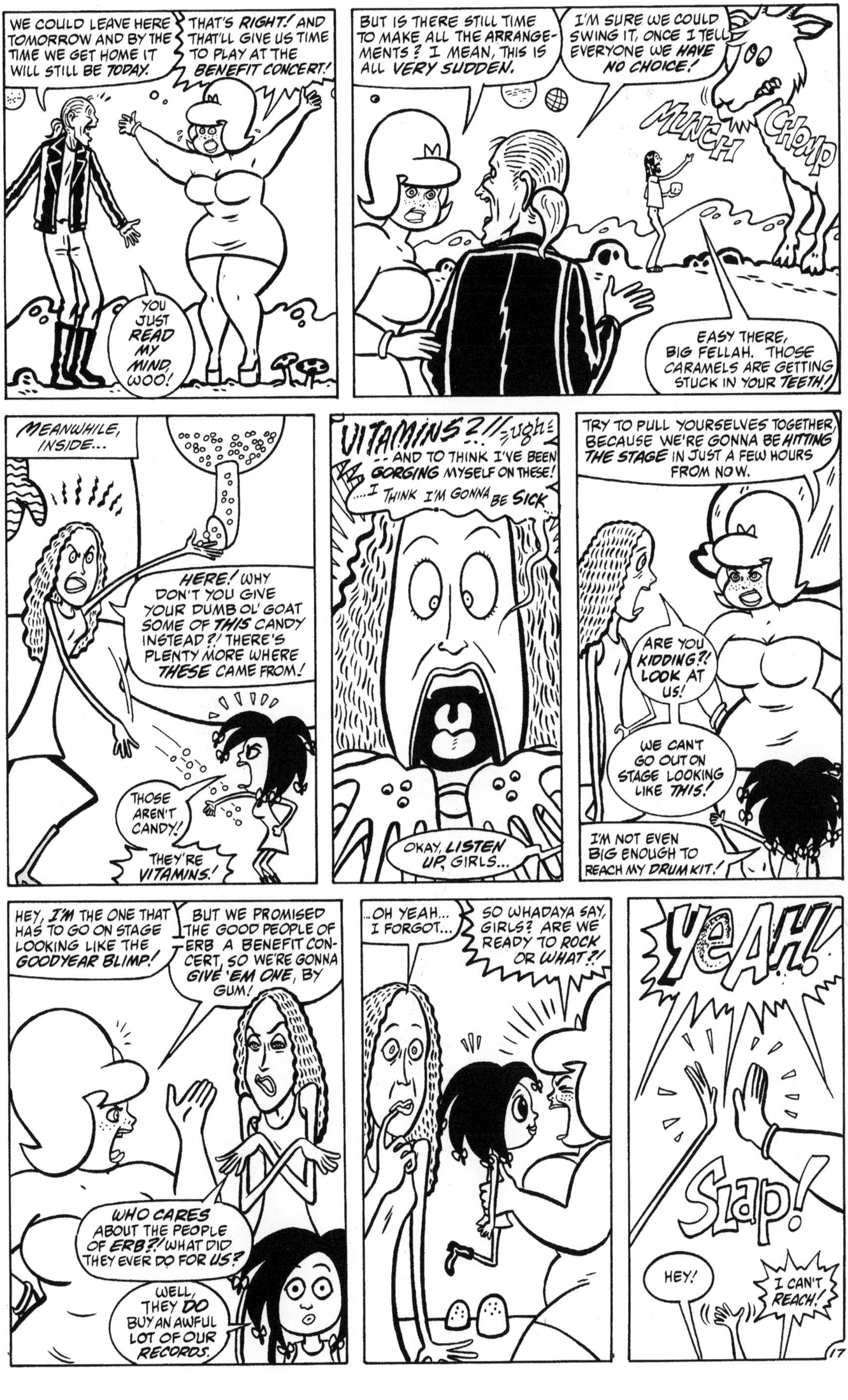
WE COULD LEAVE HERE TOMORROW AND BY THE TIME WE GET HOME IT WILL STILL BE TODAY.
THAT'S RIGHT! AND THAT'LL GIVE US TIME TO PLAY AT THE BENEFIT CONCERT!
YOU JUST READ MY MIND, WOO!
BUT IS THERE STILL TIME TO MAKE ALL THE ARRANGEMENTS? I MEAN, THIS IS ALL VERY SUDDEN.
I'M SURE WE COULD SWING IT, ONCE I TELL EVERYONE WE HAVE NO CHOICE!
MUNCH
CHOMP
EASY THERE, BIG FELLAH. THOSE CARAMELS ARE GETTING STUCK IN YOUR TEETH!
MEANWHILE, INSIDE...
HERE! WHY DON'T YOU GIVE YOUR DUMB OL' GOAT SOME OF THIS CANDY INSTEAD?! THERE'S PLENTY MORE WHERE THESE CAME FROM!
THOSE AREN'T CANDY!
THEY'RE VITAMINS!
VITAMINS?!
ugh
--AND TO THINK I'VE BEEN GORGING MYSELF ON THESE!
...I THINK I'M GONNA BE SICK...
OKAY, LISTEN UP, GIRLS...
TRY TO PULL YOURSELVES TOGETHER, BECAUSE WE'RE GONNA BE HITTING THE STAGE IN JUST A FEW HOURS FROM NOW.
ARE YOU KIDDING?! LOOK AT US!
WE CAN'T GO OUT ON STAGE LOOKING LIKE THIS!
I'M NOT EVEN BIG ENOUGH TO REACH MY DRUM KIT!
HEY, I'M THE ONE THAT HAS TO GO ON STAGE LOOKING LIKE THE GOODYEAR BLIMP!
BUT WE PROMISED THE GOOD PEOPLE OF ERB A BENEFIT CONCERT, SO WE'RE GONNA GIVE 'EM ONE, BY GUM!
WHO CARES ABOUT THE PEOPLE OF ERB?! WHAT DID THEY EVER DO FOR US?
WELL, THEY DO BUY AN AWFUL LOT OF OUR RECORDS.
...OH YEAH... I FORGOT...
SO WHADAYA SAY, GIRLS? ARE WE READY TO ROCK OR WHAT?!
YEAH!
SLAP!
HEY!
I CAN'T REACH!

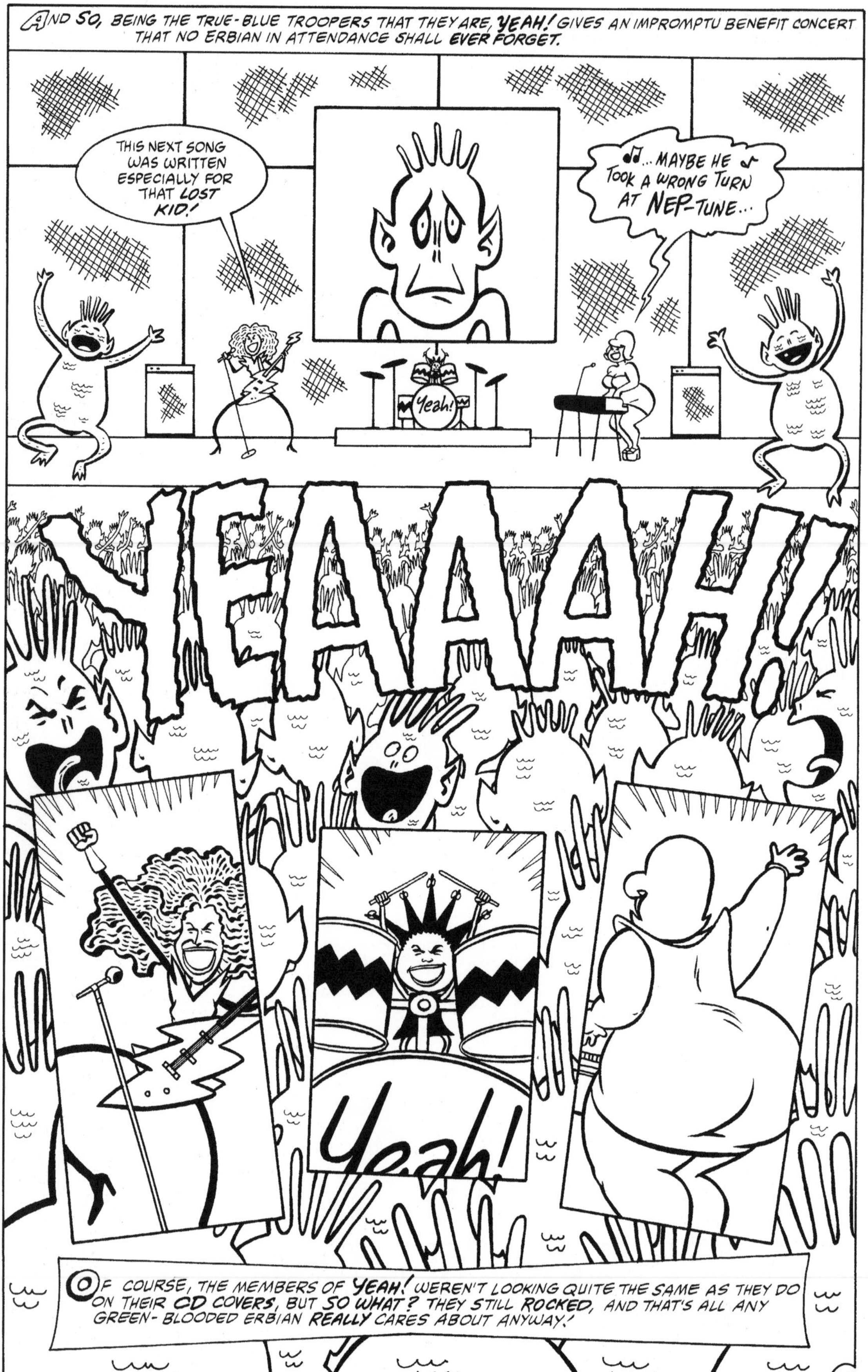
AND SO, BEING THE TRUE-BLUE TROOPERS THAT THEY ARE, YEAH! GIVES AN IMPROMPTU BENEFIT CONCERT THAT NO ERBIAN IN ATTENDANCE SHALL EVER FORGET.
THIS NEXT SONG WAS WRITTEN ESPECIALLY FOR THAT LOST KID!
... MAYBE HE TOOK A WRONG TURN AT NEP-TUNE...
Yeah!
YEAAAH!
Yeah!
OF COURSE, THE MEMBERS OF YEAH! WEREN'T LOOKING QUITE THE SAME AS THEY DO ON THEIR CD COVERS, BUT SO WHAT? THEY STILL ROCKED, AND THAT'S ALL ANY GREEN-BLOODED ERBIAN REALLY CARES ABOUT ANYWAY!

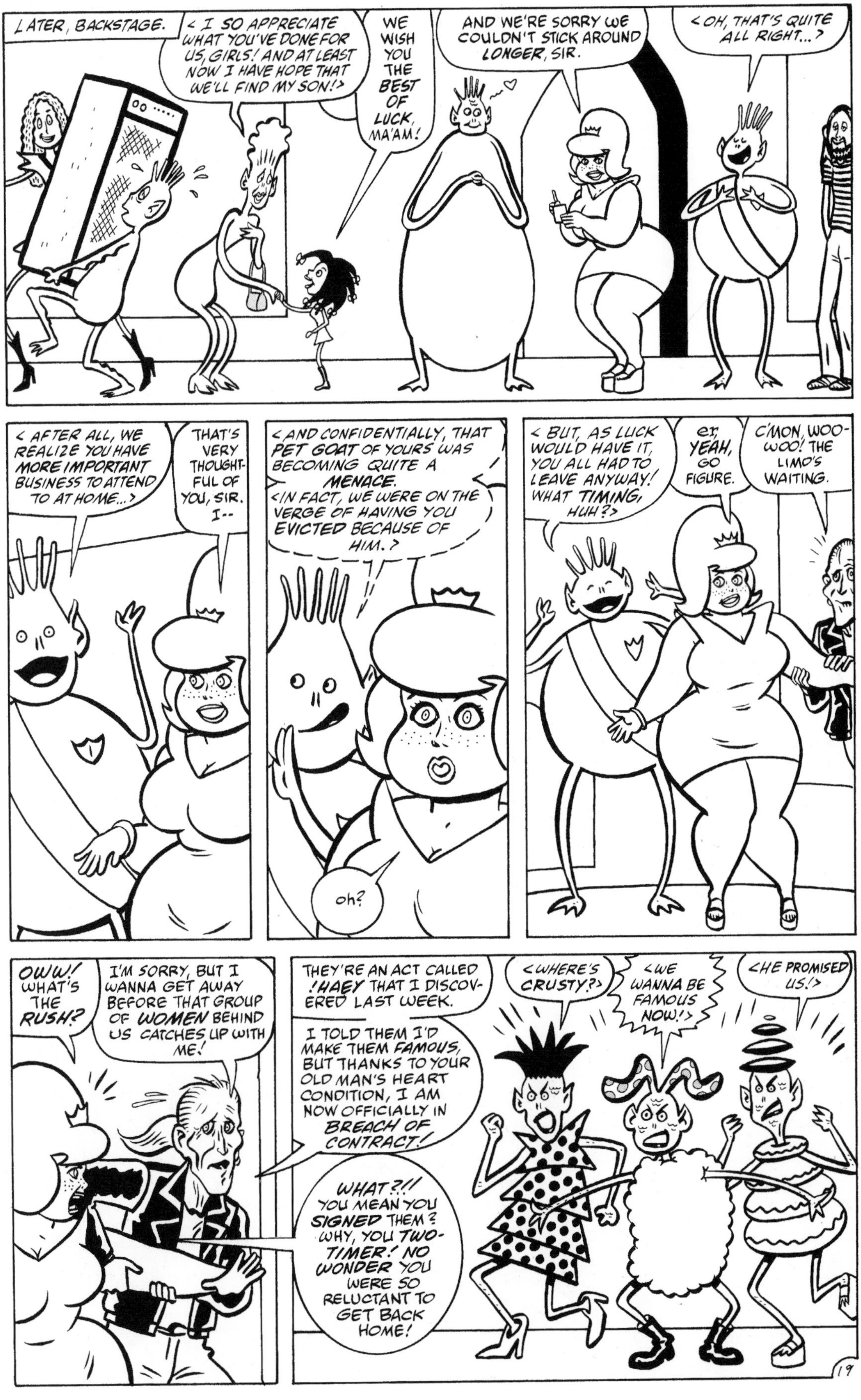
LATER, BACKSTAGE.
< I SO APPRECIATE WHAT YOU'VE DONE FOR US, GIRLS! AND AT LEAST NOW I HAVE HOPE THAT WE'LL FIND MY SON!>
WE WISH YOU THE BEST OF LUCK, MA'AM!
AND WE'RE SORRY WE COULDN'T STICK AROUND LONGER, SIR.
<OH, THAT'S QUITE ALL RIGHT...>
< AFTER ALL, WE REALIZE YOU HAVE MORE IMPORTANT BUSINESS TO ATTEND TO AT HOME...>
THAT'S VERY THOUGHTFUL OF YOU, SIR. I--
<AND CONFIDENTIALLY, THAT PET GOAT OF YOURS WAS BECOMING QUITE A MENACE.
<IN FACT, WE WERE ON THE VERGE OF HAVING YOU EVICTED BECAUSE OF HIM.>
oh?
< BUT, AS LUCK WOULD HAVE IT, YOU ALL HAD TO LEAVE ANYWAY! WHAT TIMING, HUH?>
er, YEAH, GO FIGURE.
C'MON, WOO-WOO! THE LIMO'S WAITING.
OWW! WHAT'S THE RUSH?
I'M SORRY, BUT I WANNA GET AWAY BEFORE THAT GROUP OF WOMEN BEHIND US CATCHES UP WITH ME!
THEY'RE AN ACT CALLED !HAEY THAT I DISCOVERED LAST WEEK.
I TOLD THEM I'D MAKE THEM FAMOUS, BUT THANKS TO YOUR OLD MAN'S HEART CONDITION, I AM NOW OFFICIALLY IN BREACH OF CONTRACT!
WHAT?!! YOU MEAN YOU SIGNED THEM? WHY, YOU TWO-TIMER! NO WONDER YOU WERE SO RELUCTANT TO GET BACK HOME!
<WHERE'S CRUSTY?>
<WE WANNA BE FAMOUS NOW!>
<HE PROMISED US!>

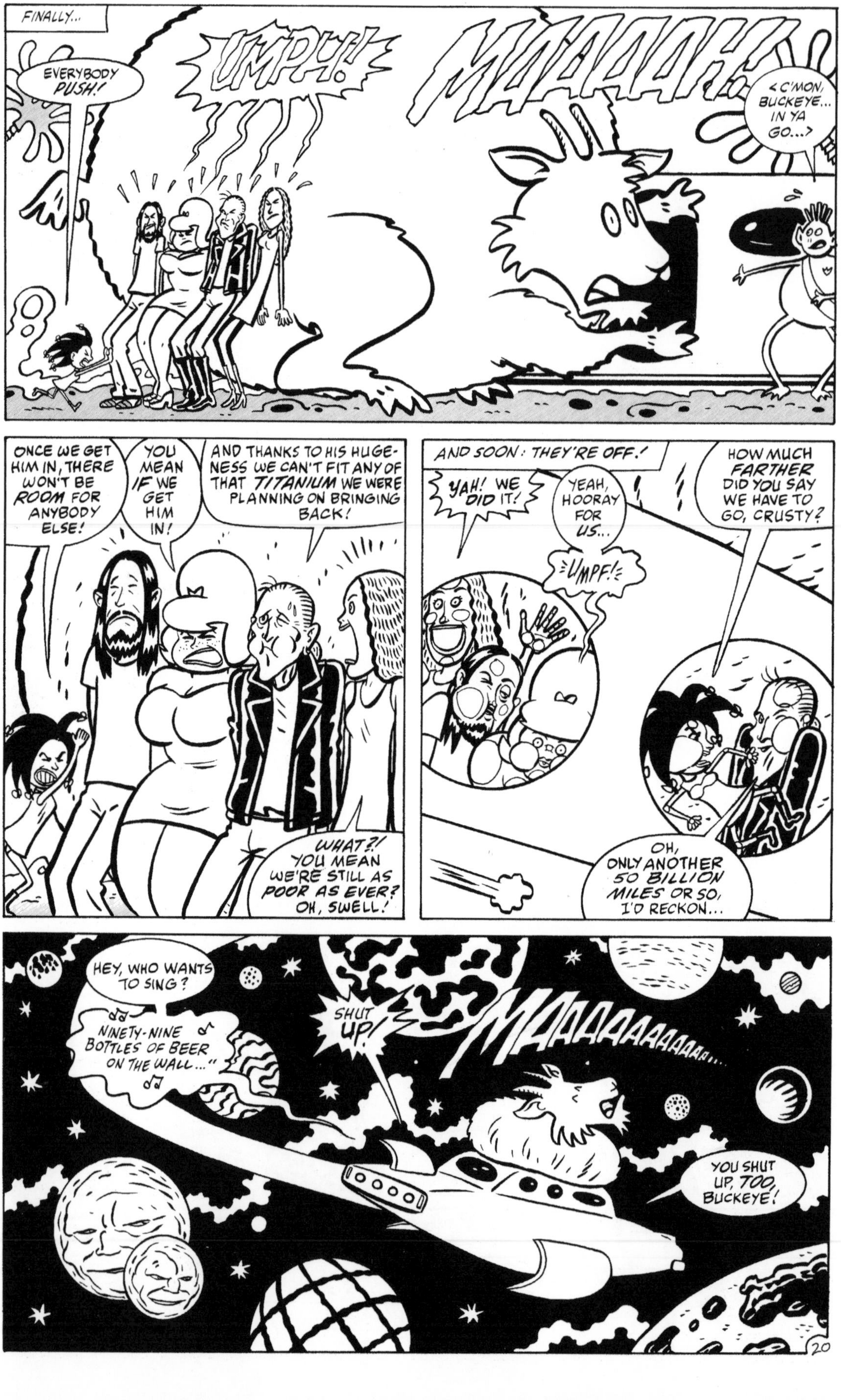

FINALLY...
EVERYBODY PUSH!
UMPH!
MAAAAAH!
<C'MON, BUCKEYE... IN YA GO...>
ONCE WE GET HIM IN, THERE WON'T BE ROOM FOR ANYBODY ELSE!
YOU MEAN IF WE GET HIM IN!
AND THANKS TO HIS HUGENESS WE CAN'T FIT ANY OF THAT TITANIUM WE WERE PLANNING ON BRINGING BACK!
WHAT?! YOU MEAN WE'RE STILL AS POOR AS EVER? OH, SWELL!
AND SOON: THEY'RE OFF!
YAH! WE DID IT!
YEAH, HOORAY FOR US...
UMPF!
HOW MUCH FARTHER DID YOU SAY WE HAVE TO GO, CRUSTY?
OH, ONLY ANOTHER 50 BILLION MILES OR SO, I'D RECKON...
HEY, WHO WANTS TO SING?
"NINETY-NINE BOTTLES OF BEER ON THE WALL..."
SHUT UP!
MAAAAAAAAAAA...
YOU SHUT UP, TOO, BUCKEYE!

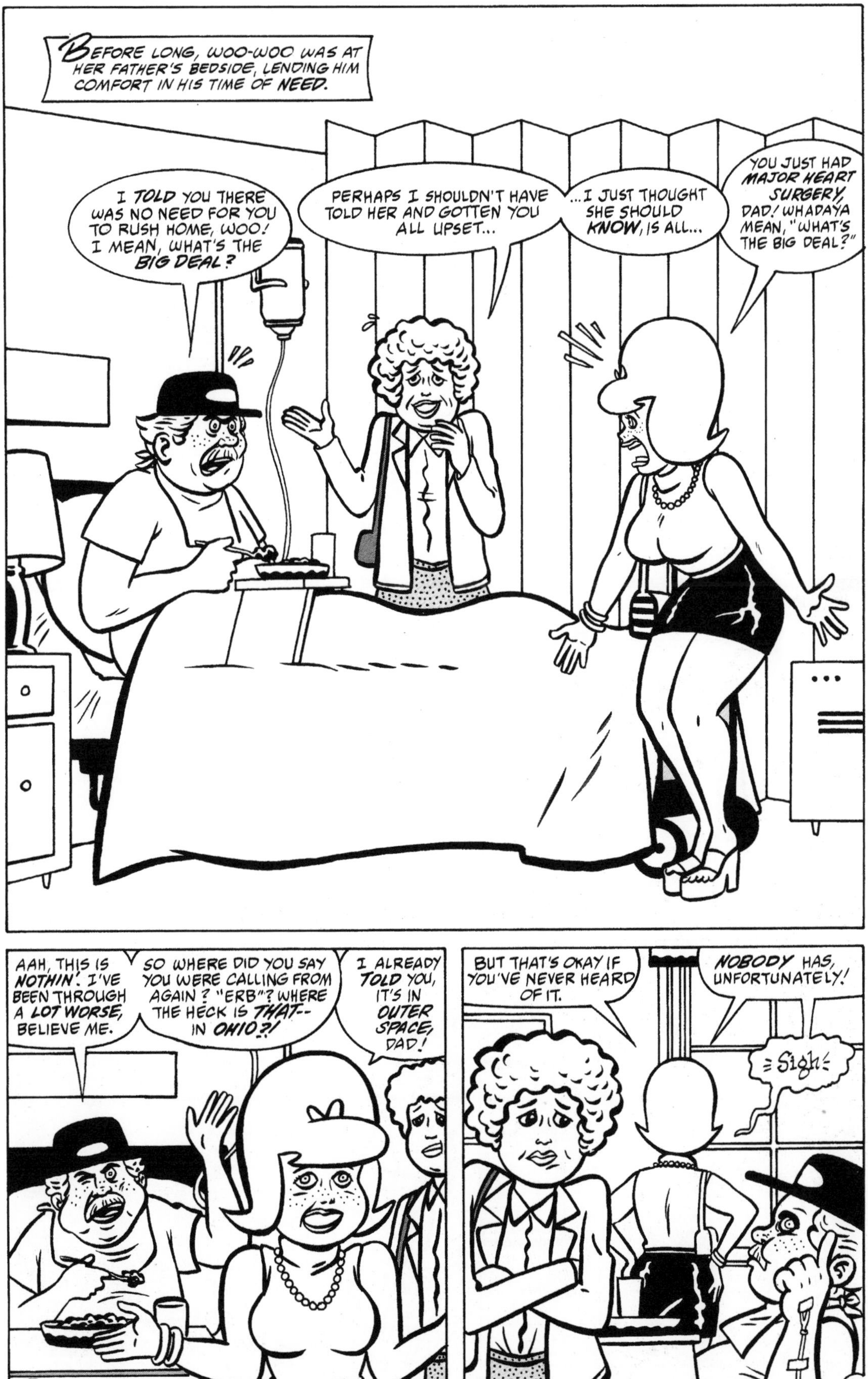
BEFORE LONG, WOO-WOO WAS AT HER FATHER'S BEDSIDE, LENDING HIM COMFORT IN HIS TIME OF NEED.
I TOLD YOU THERE WAS NO NEED FOR YOU TO RUSH HOME, WOO! I MEAN, WHAT'S THE BIG DEAL?
PERHAPS I SHOULDN'T HAVE TOLD HER AND GOTTEN YOU ALL UPSET...
...I JUST THOUGHT SHE SHOULD KNOW, IS ALL...
YOU JUST HAD MAJOR HEART SURGERY, DAD! WHADAYA MEAN, "WHAT'S THE BIG DEAL?"
AAH, THIS IS NOTHIN'. I'VE BEEN THROUGH A LOT WORSE, BELIEVE ME.
SO WHERE DID YOU SAY YOU WERE CALLING FROM AGAIN? "ERB"? WHERE THE HECK IS THAT-- IN OHIO?!
I ALREADY TOLD YOU, IT'S IN OUTER SPACE, DAD!
BUT THAT'S OKAY IF YOU'VE NEVER HEARD OF IT.
NOBODY HAS, UNFORTUNATELY!
Sigh

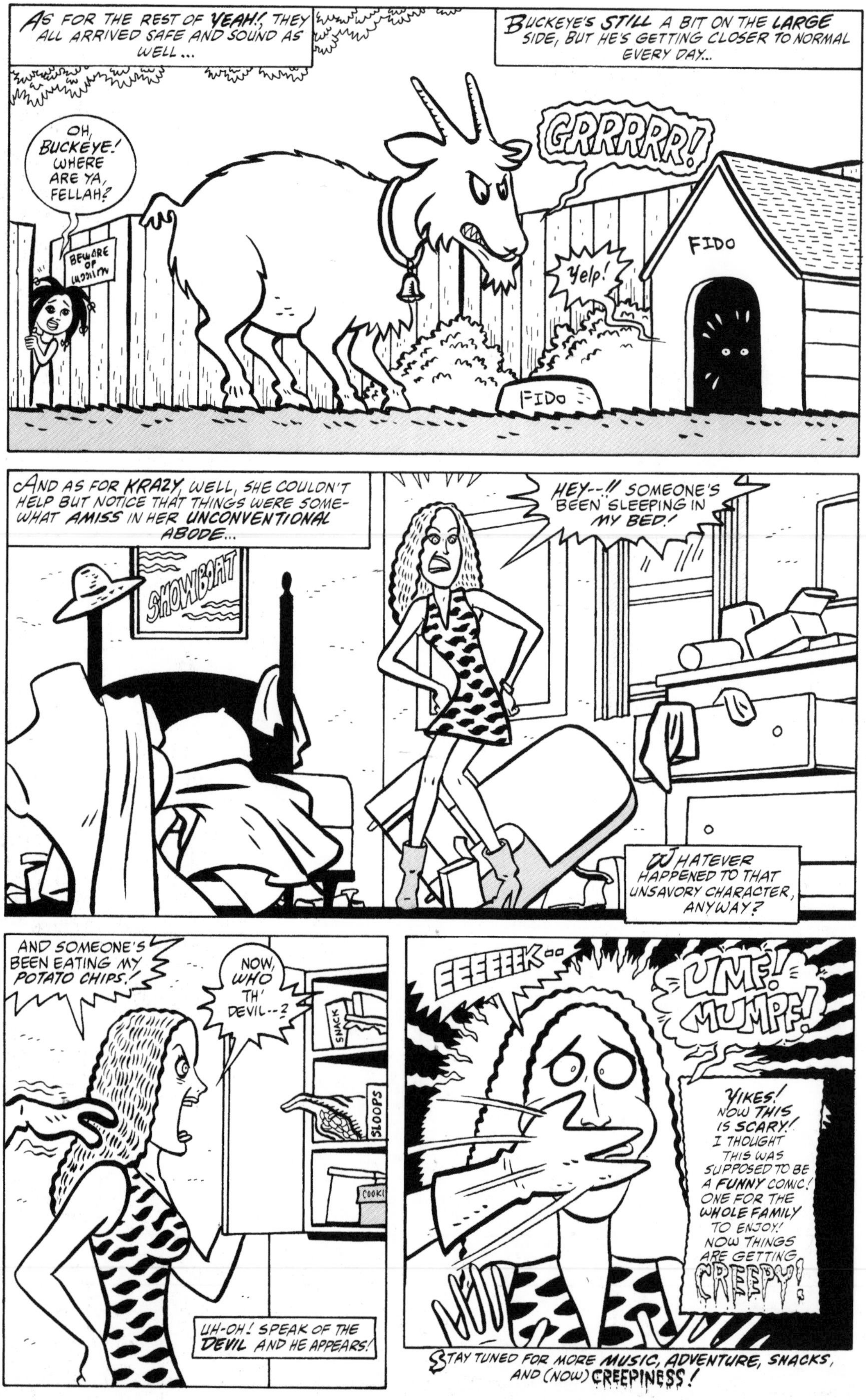
AS FOR THE REST OF YEAH!, THEY ALL ARRIVED SAFE AND SOUND AS WELL...
BUCKEYE'S STILL A BIT ON THE LARGE SIDE, BUT HE'S GETTING CLOSER TO NORMAL EVERY DAY...
OH, BUCKEYE! WHERE ARE YA, FELLAH?
BEWARE OF
GRRRRRR!
FIDO
Yelp!
FIDO
AND AS FOR KRAZY, WELL, SHE COULDN'T HELP BUT NOTICE THAT THINGS WERE SOMEWHAT AMISS IN HER UNCONVENTIONAL ABODE...
SHOWBOAT
HEY--!! SOMEONE'S BEEN SLEEPING IN MY BED!
WHATEVER HAPPENED TO THAT UNSAVORY CHARACTER, ANYWAY?
AND SOMEONE'S BEEN EATING MY POTATO CHIPS!
NOW, WHO TH' DEVIL--?
SNACK
SLOOPS
COOKI
UH-OH! SPEAK OF THE DEVIL AND HE APPEARS!
EEEEEEK--
UMF! MUMPF!
YIKES! NOW THIS IS SCARY! I THOUGHT THIS WAS SUPPOSED TO BE A FUNNY COMIC! ONE FOR THE WHOLE FAMILY TO ENJOY! NOW THINGS ARE GETTING CREEPY!
STAY TUNED FOR MORE MUSIC, ADVENTURE, SNACKS, AND (NOW) CREEPINESS!

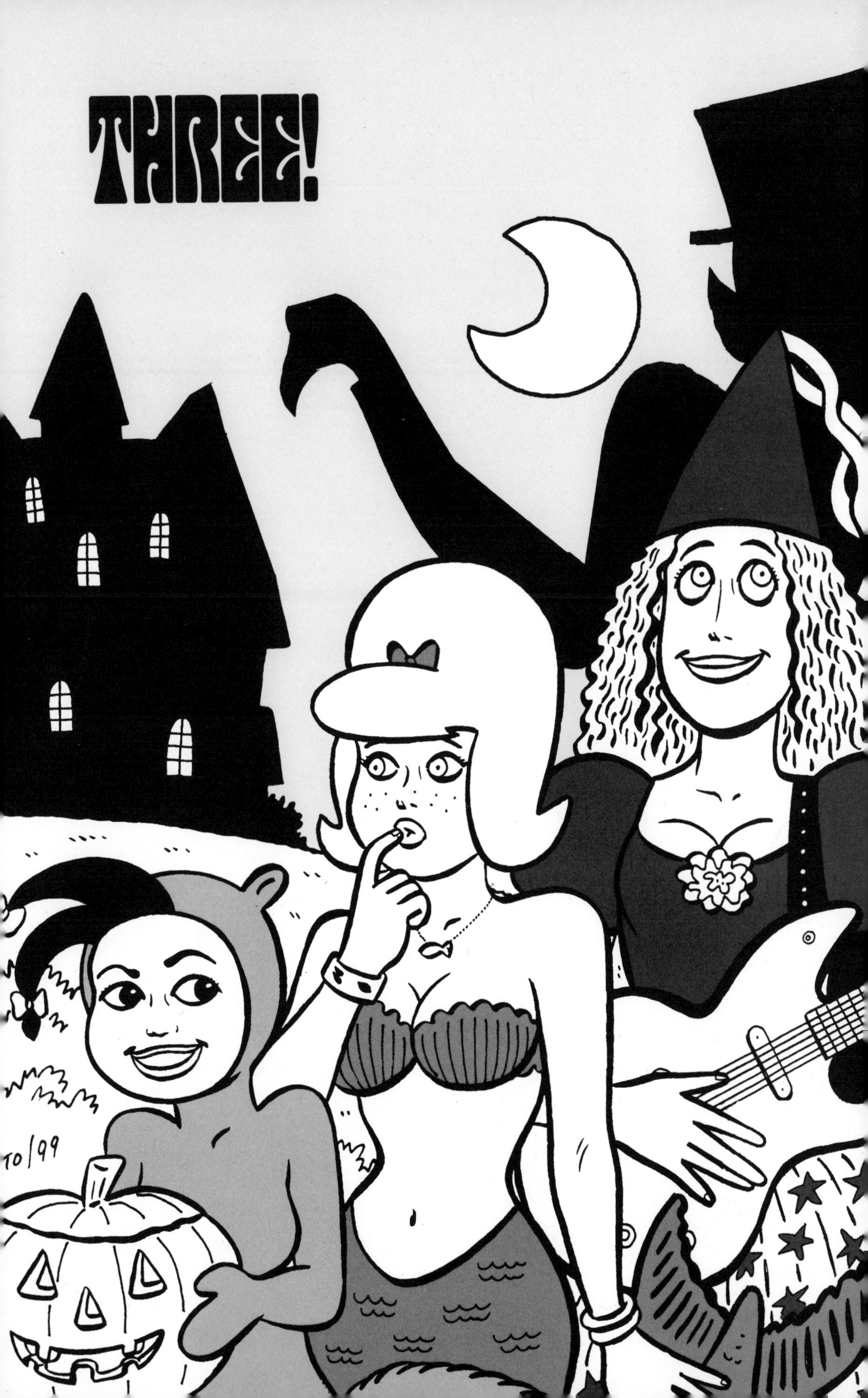
THREE!
10/99

'Stalky'

IN CLASSIC CLIFFHANGER FASHION, WE LAST LEFT KRAZY TO FEND FOR HERSELF WHILE A *GLOVED INTRUDER* ATTEMPTS TO MUFFLE HER SCREAMS.

=MMPf

PETER BAGGE / GILBERT HERNANDEZ / RICK PARKER / JOANNE BAGGE
WRITER / ARTIST / LETTERING / COLORIST

umph!

WHEN SUDDENLY...

CHOMP

YEEOWWCH!

WHO ARE-- EEEEKKK!

GEE WHIZ, KRAZY! WHAT DID YA BITE ME FOR?

WHAT TH--?!

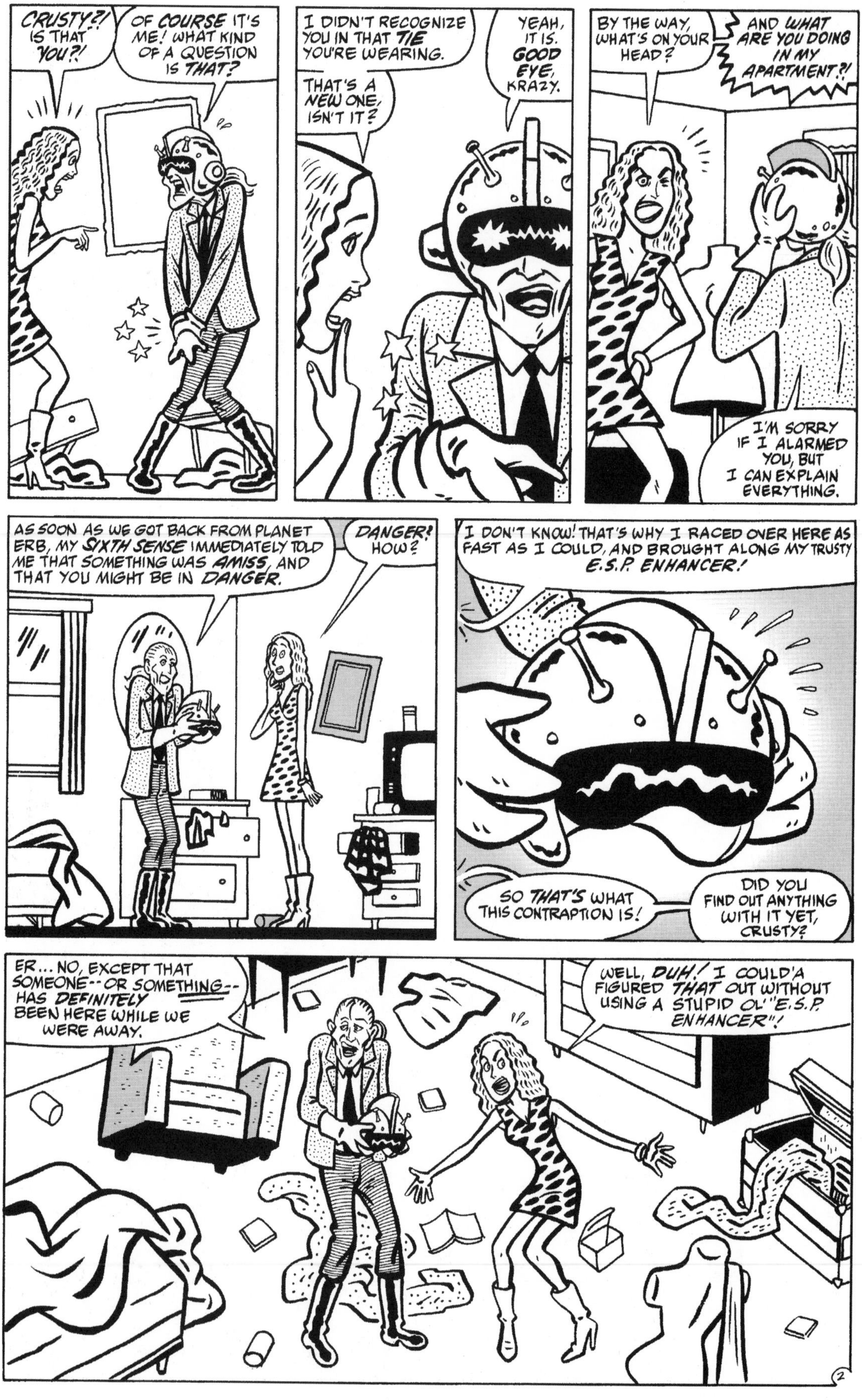
CRUSTY?! IS THAT YOU?!
OF COURSE IT'S ME! WHAT KIND OF A QUESTION IS THAT?
I DIDN'T RECOGNIZE YOU IN THAT TIE YOU'RE WEARING.
THAT'S A NEW ONE, ISN'T IT?
YEAH, IT IS. GOOD EYE, KRAZY.
BY THE WAY, WHAT'S ON YOUR HEAD?
AND WHAT ARE YOU DOING IN MY APARTMENT?!
I'M SORRY IF I ALARMED YOU, BUT I CAN EXPLAIN EVERYTHING.
AS SOON AS WE GOT BACK FROM PLANET ERB, MY SIXTH SENSE IMMEDIATELY TOLD ME THAT SOMETHING WAS AMISS, AND THAT YOU MIGHT BE IN DANGER.
DANGER! HOW?
I DON'T KNOW! THAT'S WHY I RACED OVER HERE AS FAST AS I COULD, AND BROUGHT ALONG MY TRUSTY E.S.P. ENHANCER!
SO THAT'S WHAT THIS CONTRAPTION IS!
DID YOU FIND OUT ANYTHING WITH IT YET, CRUSTY?
ER... NO, EXCEPT THAT SOMEONE--OR SOMETHING--HAS DEFINITELY BEEN HERE WHILE WE WERE AWAY.
WELL, DUH! I COULD'A FIGURED THAT OUT WITHOUT USING A STUPID OL' "E.S.P. ENHANCER"!
2

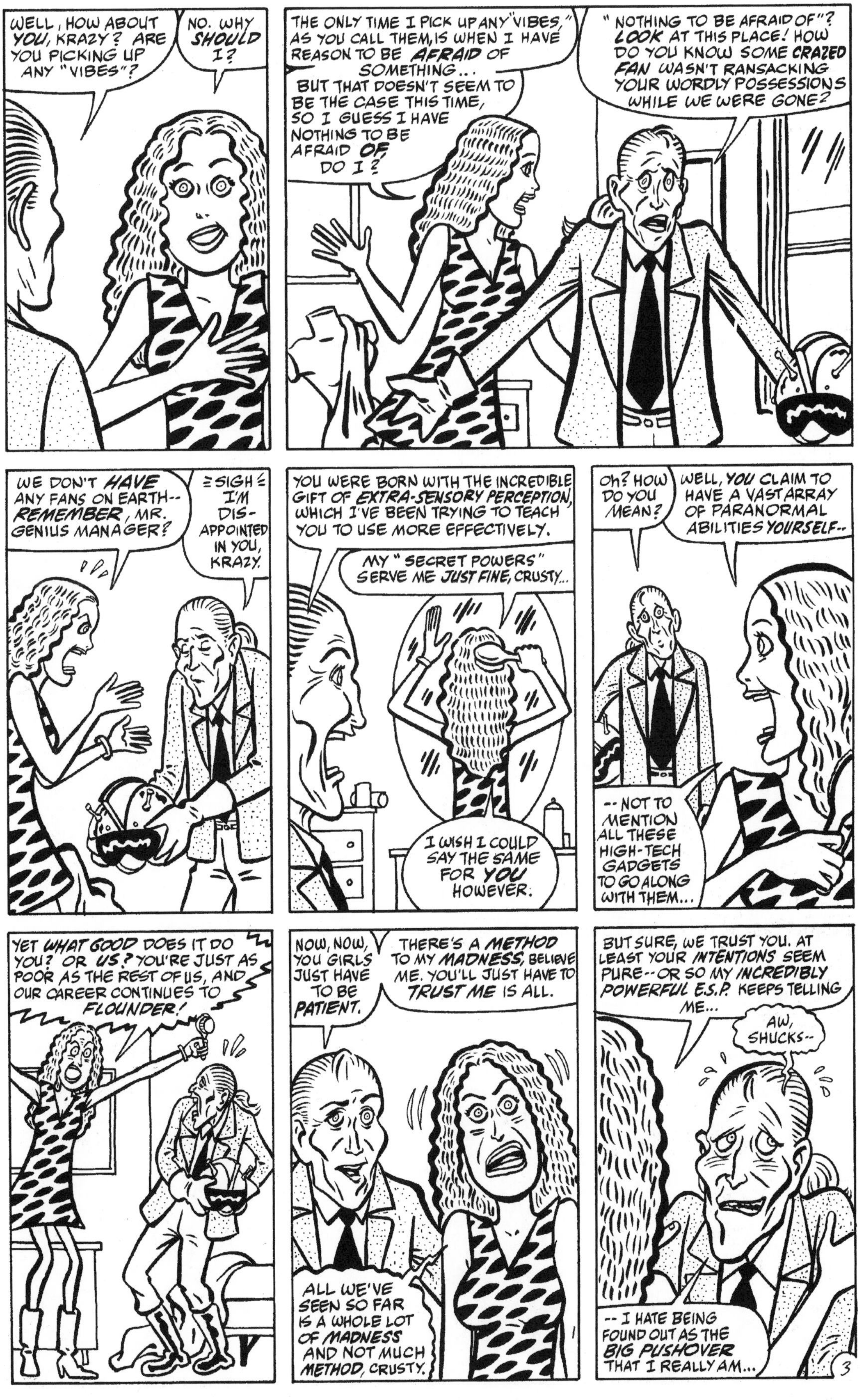

WELL, HOW ABOUT YOU, KRAZY? ARE YOU PICKING UP ANY "VIBES"?
NO. WHY SHOULD I?
THE ONLY TIME I PICK UP ANY "VIBES," AS YOU CALL THEM, IS WHEN I HAVE REASON TO BE AFRAID OF SOMETHING...
BUT THAT DOESN'T SEEM TO BE THE CASE THIS TIME, SO I GUESS I HAVE NOTHING TO BE AFRAID OF, DO I?
"NOTHING TO BE AFRAID OF"? LOOK AT THIS PLACE! HOW DO YOU KNOW SOME CRAZED FAN WASN'T RANSACKING YOUR WORDLY POSSESSIONS WHILE WE WERE GONE?
WE DON'T HAVE ANY FANS ON EARTH-- REMEMBER, MR. GENIUS MANAGER?
SIGH I'M DIS-APPOINTED IN YOU, KRAZY.
YOU WERE BORN WITH THE INCREDIBLE GIFT OF EXTRA-SENSORY PERCEPTION, WHICH I'VE BEEN TRYING TO TEACH YOU TO USE MORE EFFECTIVELY.
MY "SECRET POWERS" SERVE ME JUST FINE, CRUSTY...
I WISH I COULD SAY THE SAME FOR YOU HOWEVER.
OH? HOW DO YOU MEAN?
WELL, YOU CLAIM TO HAVE A VAST ARRAY OF PARANORMAL ABILITIES YOURSELF--
--NOT TO MENTION ALL THESE HIGH-TECH GADGETS TO GO ALONG WITH THEM...
YET WHAT GOOD DOES IT DO YOU? OR US? YOU'RE JUST AS POOR AS THE REST OF US, AND OUR CAREER CONTINUES TO FLOUNDER!
NOW, NOW, YOU GIRLS JUST HAVE TO BE PATIENT.
THERE'S A METHOD TO MY MADNESS, BELIEVE ME. YOU'LL JUST HAVE TO TRUST ME IS ALL.
ALL WE'VE SEEN SO FAR IS A WHOLE LOT OF MADNESS AND NOT MUCH METHOD, CRUSTY.
BUT SURE, WE TRUST YOU. AT LEAST YOUR INTENTIONS SEEM PURE--OR SO MY INCREDIBLY POWERFUL E.S.P. KEEPS TELLING ME...
AW, SHUCKS--
--I HATE BEING FOUND OUT AS THE BIG PUSHOVER THAT I REALLY AM...

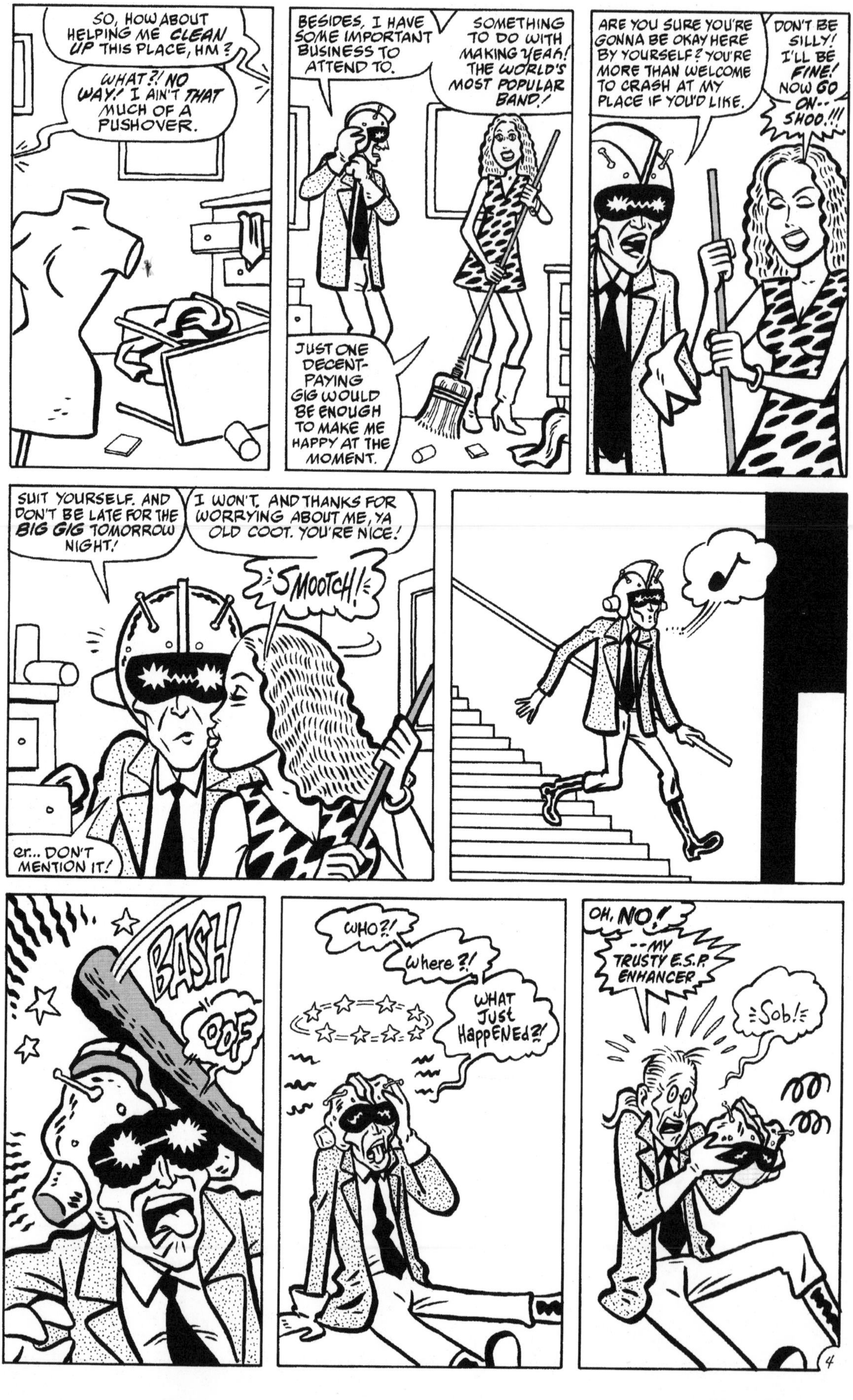
SO, HOW ABOUT HELPING ME CLEAN UP THIS PLACE, HM?
WHAT?! NO WAY! I AIN'T THAT MUCH OF A PUSHOVER.
BESIDES, I HAVE SOME IMPORTANT BUSINESS TO ATTEND TO.
SOMETHING TO DO WITH MAKING YEAH! THE WORLD'S MOST POPULAR BAND!
JUST ONE DECENT-PAYING GIG WOULD BE ENOUGH TO MAKE ME HAPPY AT THE MOMENT.
ARE YOU SURE YOU'RE GONNA BE OKAY HERE BY YOURSELF? YOU'RE MORE THAN WELCOME TO CRASH AT MY PLACE IF YOU'D LIKE.
DON'T BE SILLY! I'LL BE FINE! NOW GO ON.. SHOO!!!
SUIT YOURSELF. AND DON'T BE LATE FOR THE BIG GIG TOMORROW NIGHT!
I WON'T. AND THANKS FOR WORRYING ABOUT ME, YA OLD COOT. YOU'RE NICE!
SMOOTCH!
er... DON'T MENTION IT!
BASH
OOF
WHO?!
Where?!
WHAT Just HappENEd?!
OH, NO! --MY TRUSTY E.S.P. ENHANCER
Sob!
4

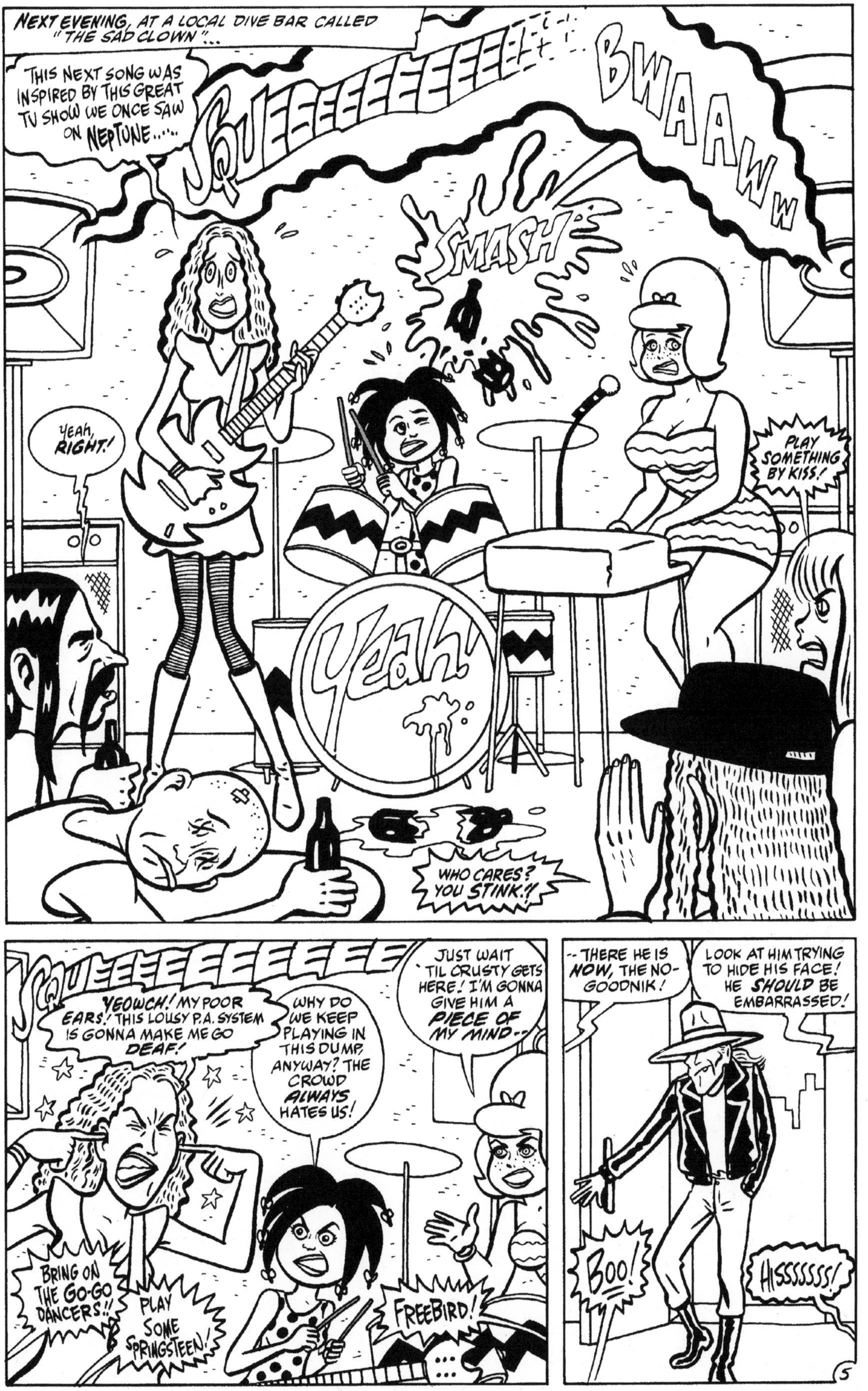
NEXT EVENING, AT A LOCAL DIVE BAR CALLED "THE SAD CLOWN"...
THIS NEXT SONG WAS INSPIRED BY THIS GREAT TV SHOW WE ONCE SAW ON NEPTUNE.....
SQUEEEEEEEEEEEE
BWAAAWw
SMASH
YEAH, RIGHT!
PLAY SOMETHING BY KISS!
YEAH!
WHO CARES? YOU STINK.!!
SQUEEEEEEEEEEEE
YEOWCH! MY POOR EARS! THIS LOUSY P.A. SYSTEM IS GONNA MAKE ME GO DEAF!
WHY DO WE KEEP PLAYING IN THIS DUMP, ANYWAY? THE CROWD ALWAYS HATES US!
JUST WAIT 'TIL CRUSTY GETS HERE! I'M GONNA GIVE HIM A PIECE OF MY MIND--
BRING ON THE GO-GO DANCERS!!
PLAY SOME SPRINGSTEEN!
FREEBIRD!
--THERE HE IS NOW, THE NO-GOODNIK!
LOOK AT HIM TRYING TO HIDE HIS FACE! HE SHOULD BE EMBARRASSED!
BOO!
HISSSSSSS!

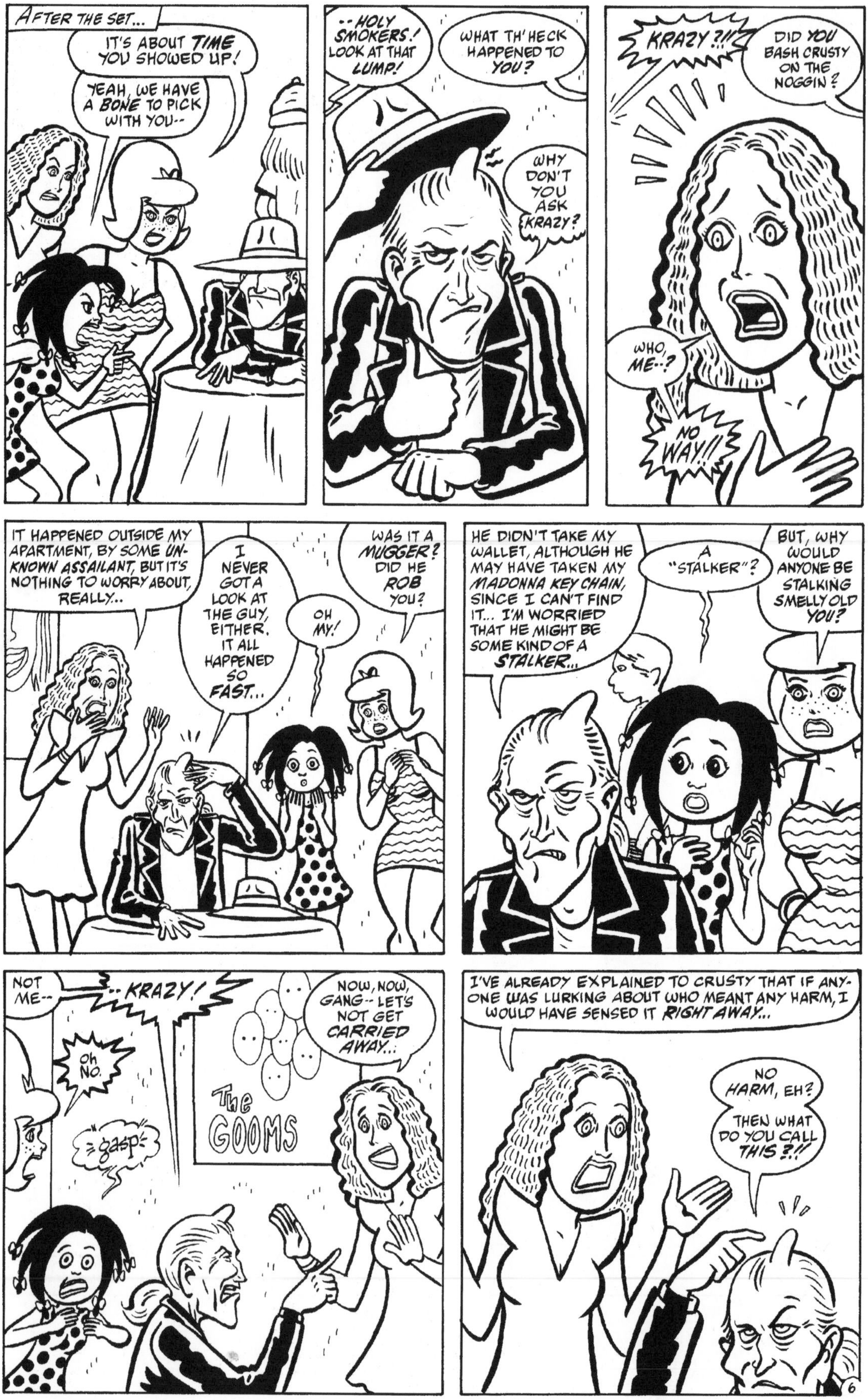
AFTER THE SET...
IT'S ABOUT TIME YOU SHOWED UP!
YEAH, WE HAVE A BONE TO PICK WITH YOU--
--HOLY SMOKERS! LOOK AT THAT LUMP!
WHAT TH' HECK HAPPENED TO YOU?
WHY DON'T YOU ASK KRAZY?
KRAZY?!!
DID YOU BASH CRUSTY ON THE NOGGIN?
WHO, ME--?
NO WAY!!
IT HAPPENED OUTSIDE MY APARTMENT, BY SOME UNKNOWN ASSAILANT, BUT IT'S NOTHING TO WORRY ABOUT, REALLY...
I NEVER GOT A LOOK AT THE GUY, EITHER. IT ALL HAPPENED SO FAST...
OH MY!
WAS IT A MUGGER? DID HE ROB YOU?
HE DIDN'T TAKE MY WALLET, ALTHOUGH HE MAY HAVE TAKEN MY MADONNA KEY CHAIN, SINCE I CAN'T FIND IT... I'M WORRIED THAT HE MIGHT BE SOME KIND OF A STALKER...
A "STALKER"?
BUT, WHY WOULD ANYONE BE STALKING SMELLY OLD YOU?
NOT ME--
--KRAZY!
Oh NO.
gasp
NOW, NOW, GANG-- LET'S NOT GET CARRIED AWAY...
The GOOMS
I'VE ALREADY EXPLAINED TO CRUSTY THAT IF ANYONE WAS LURKING ABOUT WHO MEANT ANY HARM, I WOULD HAVE SENSED IT RIGHT AWAY...
NO HARM, EH?
THEN WHAT DO YOU CALL THIS?!!

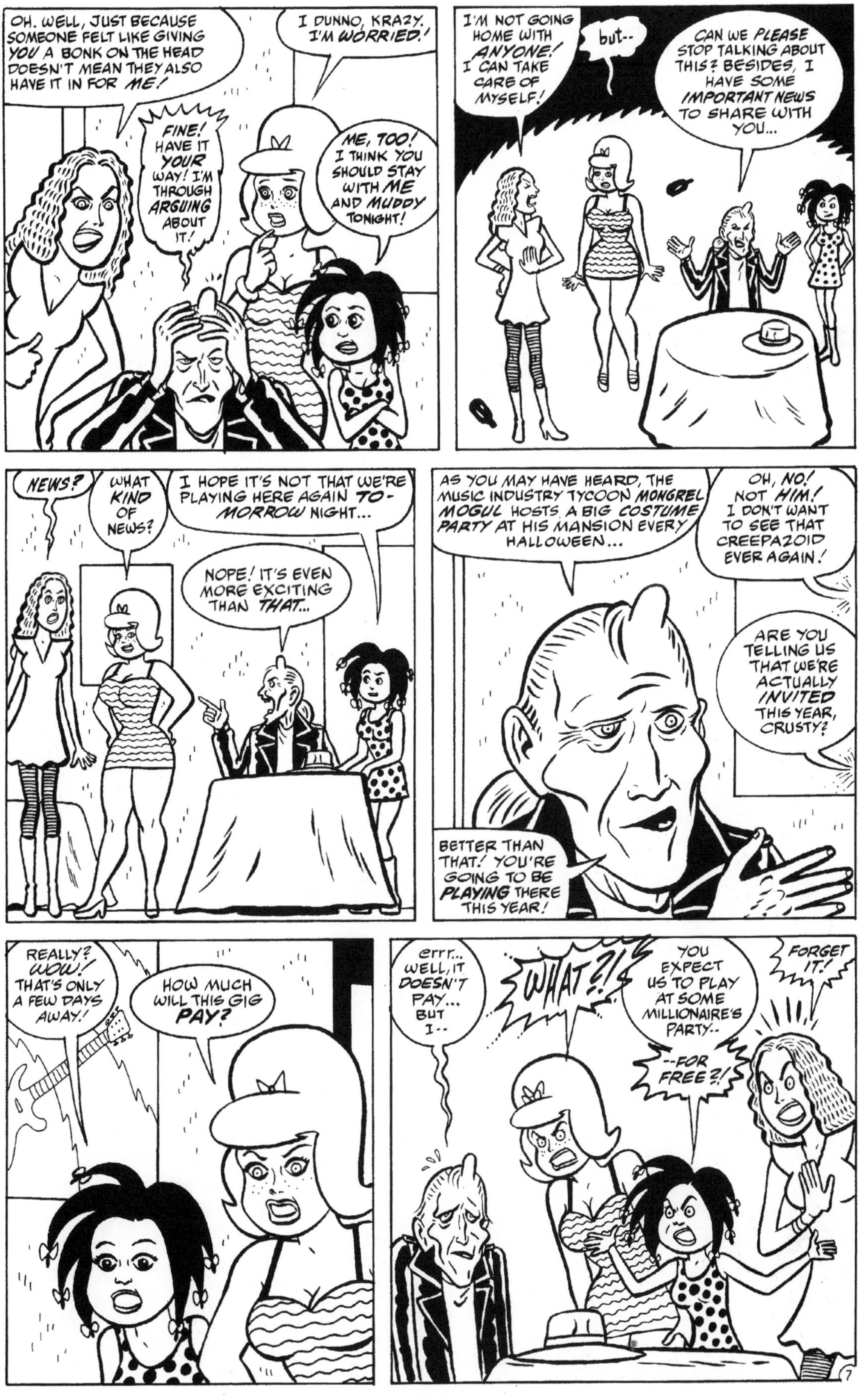
OH. WELL, JUST BECAUSE SOMEONE FELT LIKE GIVING YOU A BONK ON THE HEAD DOESN'T MEAN THEY ALSO HAVE IT IN FOR ME!
I DUNNO, KRAZY. I'M WORRIED!
FINE! HAVE IT YOUR WAY! I'M THROUGH ARGUING ABOUT IT!
ME, TOO! I THINK YOU SHOULD STAY WITH ME AND MUDDY TONIGHT!
I'M NOT GOING HOME WITH ANYONE! I CAN TAKE CARE OF MYSELF!
but--
CAN WE PLEASE STOP TALKING ABOUT THIS? BESIDES, I HAVE SOME IMPORTANT NEWS TO SHARE WITH YOU...
NEWS?
WHAT KIND OF NEWS?
I HOPE IT'S NOT THAT WE'RE PLAYING HERE AGAIN TO-MORROW NIGHT...
NOPE! IT'S EVEN MORE EXCITING THAN THAT...
AS YOU MAY HAVE HEARD, THE MUSIC INDUSTRY TYCOON MONGREL MOGUL HOSTS A BIG COSTUME PARTY AT HIS MANSION EVERY HALLOWEEN...
OH, NO! NOT HIM! I DON'T WANT TO SEE THAT CREEPAZOID EVER AGAIN!
ARE YOU TELLING US THAT WE'RE ACTUALLY INVITED THIS YEAR, CRUSTY?
BETTER THAN THAT! YOU'RE GOING TO BE PLAYING THERE THIS YEAR!
REALLY? WOW! THAT'S ONLY A FEW DAYS AWAY!
HOW MUCH WILL THIS GIG PAY?
errr... WELL, IT DOESN'T PAY... BUT I--
WHAT?!
YOU EXPECT US TO PLAY AT SOME MILLIONAIRE'S PARTY..
--FOR FREE?!
FORGET IT!

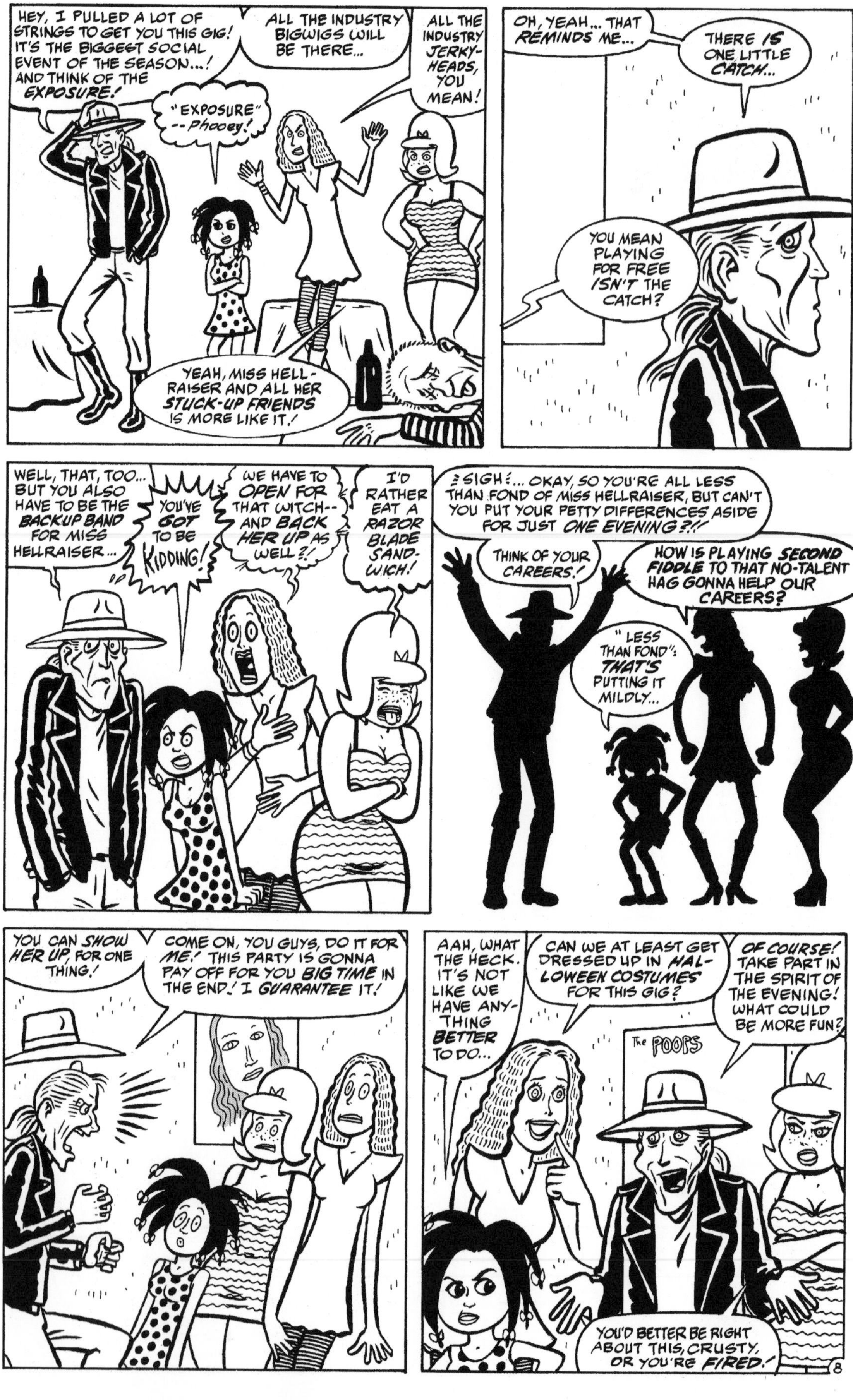
HEY, I PULLED A LOT OF STRINGS TO GET YOU THIS GIG! IT'S THE BIGGEST SOCIAL EVENT OF THE SEASON...! AND THINK OF THE EXPOSURE!
ALL THE INDUSTRY BIGWIGS WILL BE THERE...
ALL THE INDUSTRY JERKY-HEADS, YOU MEAN!
"EXPOSURE" --Phooey!
YEAH, MISS HELL-RAISER AND ALL HER STUCK-UP FRIENDS IS MORE LIKE IT!
OH, YEAH... THAT REMINDS ME...
THERE IS ONE LITTLE CATCH...
YOU MEAN PLAYING FOR FREE ISN'T THE CATCH?
WELL, THAT, TOO... BUT YOU ALSO HAVE TO BE THE BACKUP BAND FOR MISS HELLRAISER...
YOU'VE GOT TO BE KIDDING!
WE HAVE TO OPEN FOR THAT WITCH-- AND BACK HER UP AS WELL?!
I'D RATHER EAT A RAZOR BLADE SAND-WICH!
≷SIGH≶... OKAY, SO YOU'RE ALL LESS THAN FOND OF MISS HELLRAISER, BUT CAN'T YOU PUT YOUR PETTY DIFFERENCES ASIDE FOR JUST ONE EVENING?!!
THINK OF YOUR CAREERS!
HOW IS PLAYING SECOND FIDDLE TO THAT NO-TALENT HAG GONNA HELP OUR CAREERS?
"LESS THAN FOND": THAT'S PUTTING IT MILDLY...
YOU CAN SHOW HER UP, FOR ONE THING!
COME ON, YOU GUYS, DO IT FOR ME! THIS PARTY IS GONNA PAY OFF FOR YOU BIG TIME IN THE END! I GUARANTEE IT!
AAH, WHAT THE HECK. IT'S NOT LIKE WE HAVE ANY-THING BETTER TO DO...
CAN WE AT LEAST GET DRESSED UP IN HAL-LOWEEN COSTUMES FOR THIS GIG?
OF COURSE! TAKE PART IN THE SPIRIT OF THE EVENING! WHAT COULD BE MORE FUN?
The POOPS
YOU'D BETTER BE RIGHT ABOUT THIS, CRUSTY, OR YOU'RE FIRED!

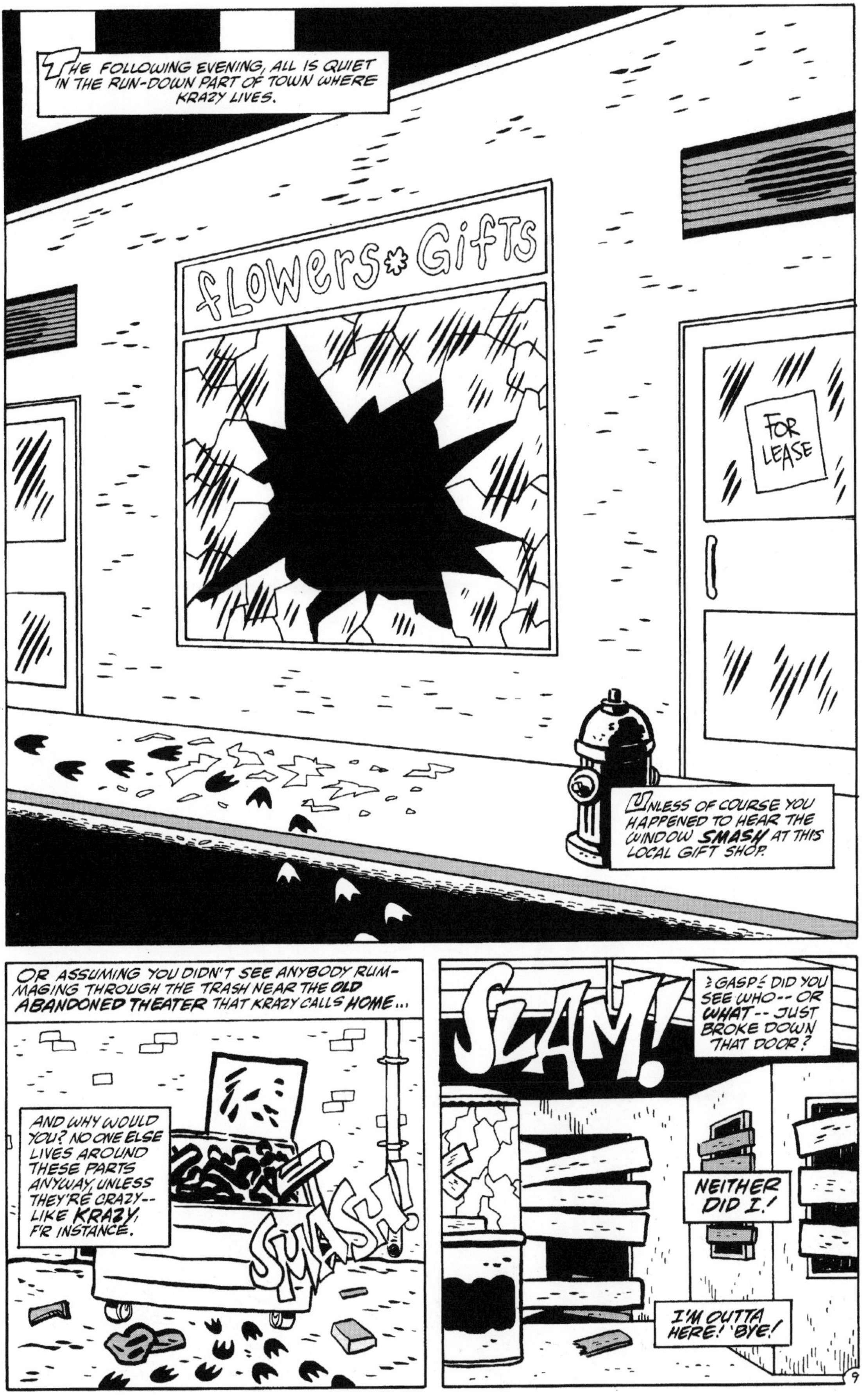
THE FOLLOWING EVENING, ALL IS QUIET IN THE RUN-DOWN PART OF TOWN WHERE KRAZY LIVES.
flowers * Gifts
FOR LEASE
UNLESS OF COURSE YOU HAPPENED TO HEAR THE WINDOW SMASH AT THIS LOCAL GIFT SHOP.
OR ASSUMING YOU DIDN'T SEE ANYBODY RUM-MAGING THROUGH THE TRASH NEAR THE OLD ABANDONED THEATER THAT KRAZY CALLS HOME...
AND WHY WOULD YOU? NO ONE ELSE LIVES AROUND THESE PARTS ANYWAY, UNLESS THEY'RE CRAZY-- LIKE KRAZY, F'R INSTANCE.
SMASH!
SLAM!
GASP! DID YOU SEE WHO-- OR WHAT-- JUST BROKE DOWN THAT DOOR?
NEITHER DID I!
I'M OUTTA HERE! 'BYE!

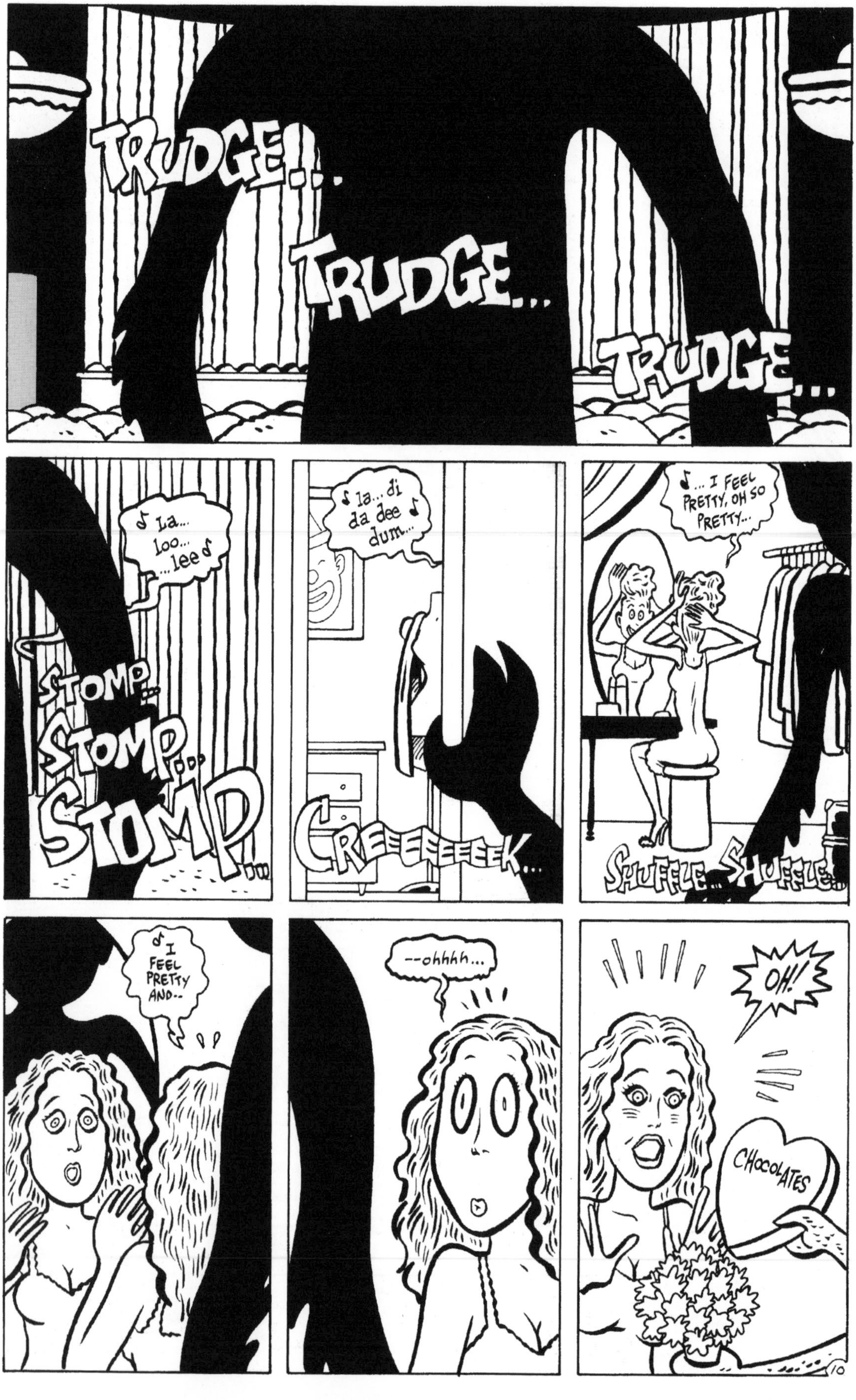
TRUDGE...
TRUDGE...
TRUDGE...
♪ La... loo... ...lee ♪
STOMP...
STOMP...
STOMP...
♪ la... di da dee dum...
CREEEEEEEK...
♪... I FEEL PRETTY, OH SO PRETTY...
SHUFFLE... SHUFFLE...
♪ I FEEL PRETTY AND--
--ohhhh...
OH!
CHOCOLATES

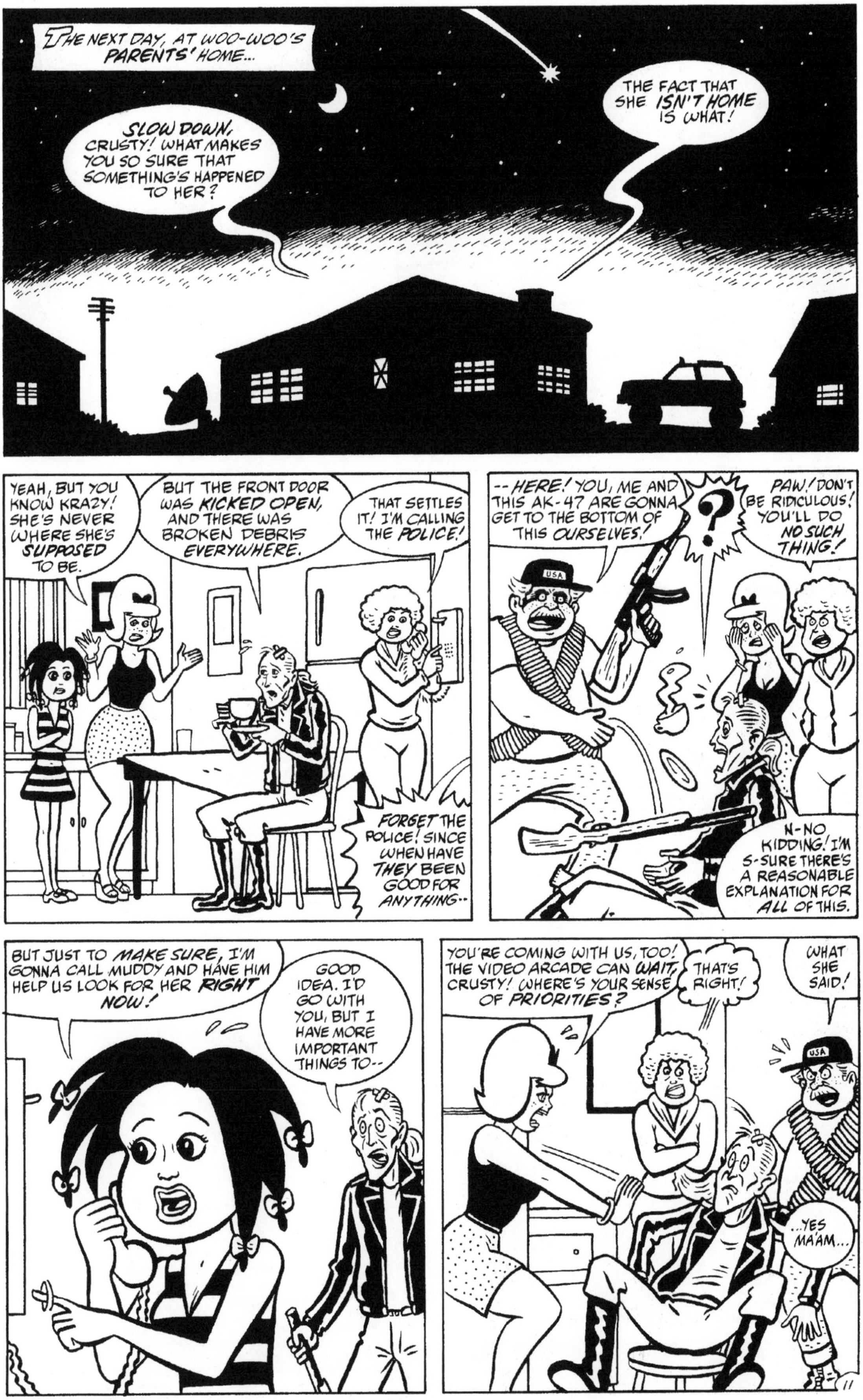
THE NEXT DAY, AT WOO-WOO'S PARENTS' HOME...
SLOW DOWN, CRUSTY! WHAT MAKES YOU SO SURE THAT SOMETHING'S HAPPENED TO HER?
THE FACT THAT SHE ISN'T HOME IS WHAT!
YEAH, BUT YOU KNOW KRAZY! SHE'S NEVER WHERE SHE'S SUPPOSED TO BE.
BUT THE FRONT DOOR WAS KICKED OPEN, AND THERE WAS BROKEN DEBRIS EVERYWHERE.
THAT SETTLES IT! I'M CALLING THE POLICE!
FORGET THE POLICE! SINCE WHEN HAVE THEY BEEN GOOD FOR ANYTHING--
--HERE! YOU, ME AND THIS AK-47 ARE GONNA GET TO THE BOTTOM OF THIS OURSELVES!
?
PAW! DON'T BE RIDICULOUS! YOU'LL DO NO SUCH THING!
N-NO KIDDING! I'M S-SURE THERE'S A REASONABLE EXPLANATION FOR ALL OF THIS.
BUT JUST TO MAKE SURE, I'M GONNA CALL MUDDY AND HAVE HIM HELP US LOOK FOR HER RIGHT NOW!
GOOD IDEA. I'D GO WITH YOU, BUT I HAVE MORE IMPORTANT THINGS TO--
YOU'RE COMING WITH US, TOO! THE VIDEO ARCADE CAN WAIT, CRUSTY! WHERE'S YOUR SENSE OF PRIORITIES?
THAT'S RIGHT!
WHAT SHE SAID!
...YES MA'AM...

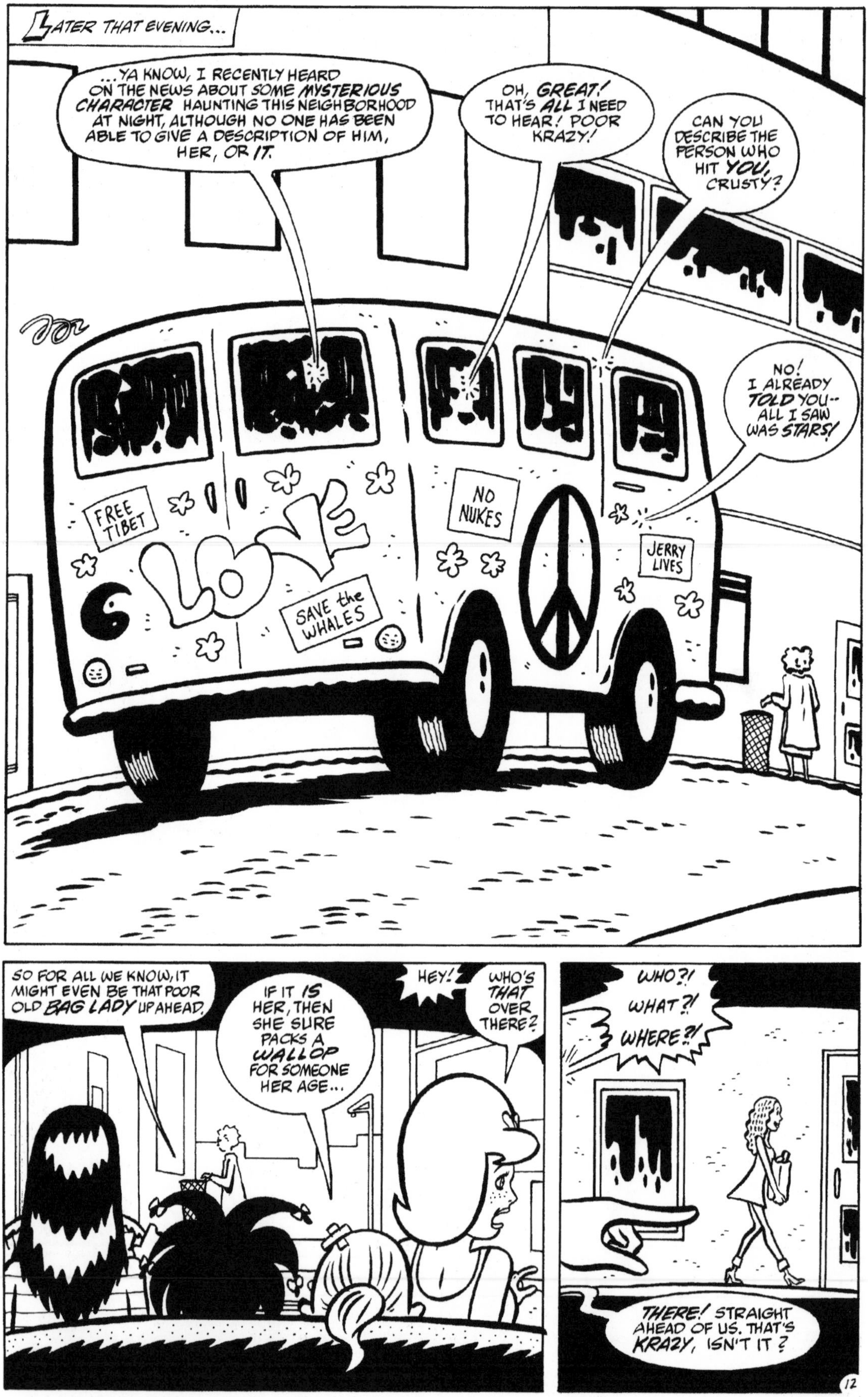
LATER THAT EVENING...
...YA KNOW, I RECENTLY HEARD ON THE NEWS ABOUT SOME MYSTERIOUS CHARACTER HAUNTING THIS NEIGHBORHOOD AT NIGHT, ALTHOUGH NO ONE HAS BEEN ABLE TO GIVE A DESCRIPTION OF HIM, HER, OR IT.
OH, GREAT! THAT'S ALL I NEED TO HEAR! POOR KRAZY!
CAN YOU DESCRIBE THE PERSON WHO HIT YOU, CRUSTY?
NO! I ALREADY TOLD YOU-- ALL I SAW WAS STARS!
FREE TIBET
LOVE
SAVE the WHALES
NO NUKES
JERRY LIVES
SO FOR ALL WE KNOW, IT MIGHT EVEN BE THAT POOR OLD BAG LADY UP AHEAD.
IF IT IS HER, THEN SHE SURE PACKS A WALLOP FOR SOMEONE HER AGE...
HEY!
WHO'S THAT OVER THERE?
WHO?! WHAT?! WHERE?!
THERE! STRAIGHT AHEAD OF US. THAT'S KRAZY, ISN'T IT?

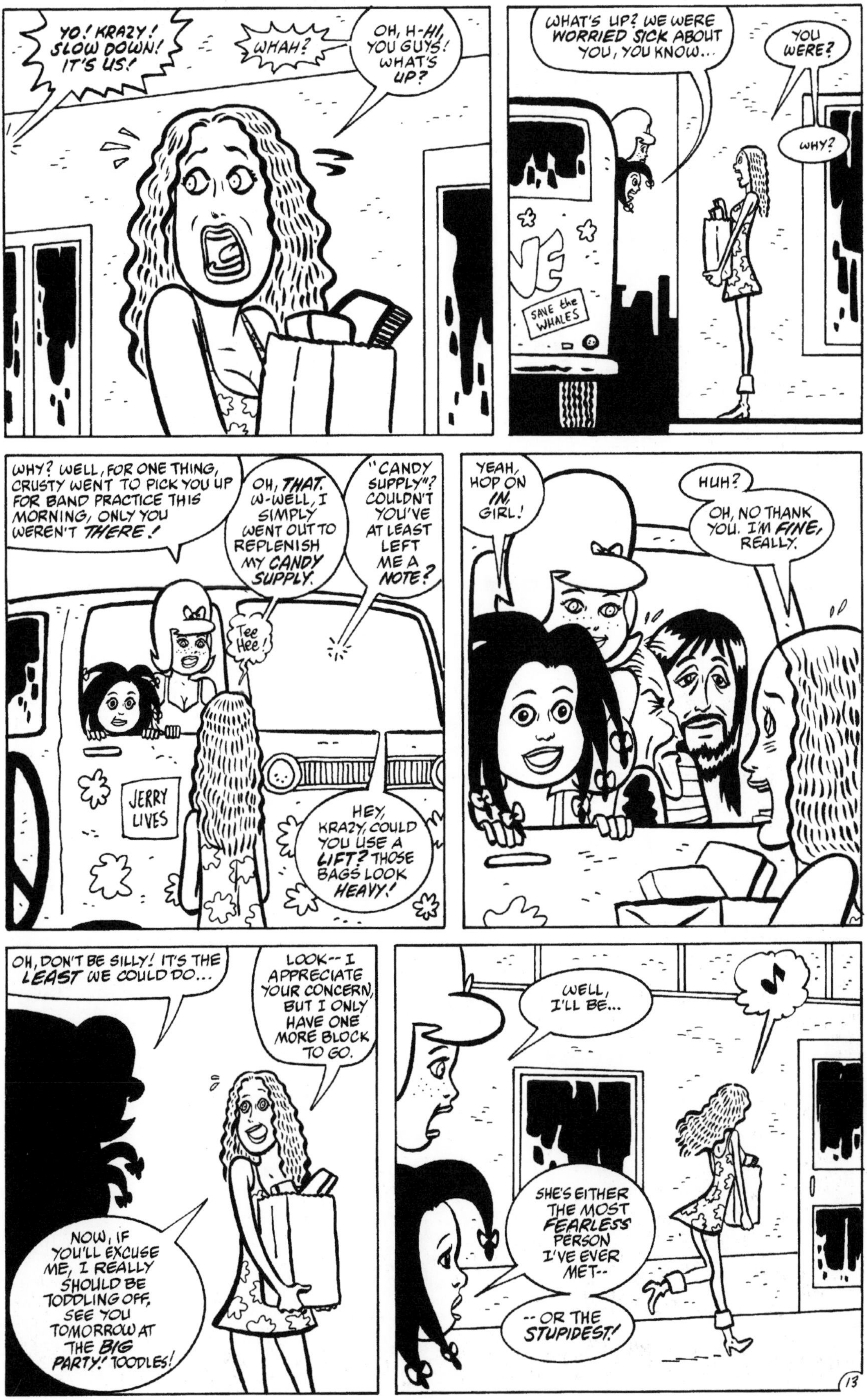
YO! KRAZY! SLOW DOWN! IT'S US!
WHAH?
OH, H-HI, YOU GUYS! WHAT'S UP?
WHAT'S UP? WE WERE WORRIED SICK ABOUT YOU, YOU KNOW...
YOU WERE?
WHY?
SAVE the WHALES
WHY? WELL, FOR ONE THING, CRUSTY WENT TO PICK YOU UP FOR BAND PRACTICE THIS MORNING, ONLY YOU WEREN'T THERE!
OH, THAT. W-WELL, I SIMPLY WENT OUT TO REPLENISH MY CANDY SUPPLY.
"CANDY SUPPLY"? COULDN'T YOU'VE AT LEAST LEFT ME A NOTE?
Tee Hee!
JERRY LIVES
HEY, KRAZY, COULD YOU USE A LIFT? THOSE BAGS LOOK HEAVY!
YEAH, HOP ON IN, GIRL!
HUH?
OH, NO THANK YOU. I'M FINE, REALLY.
OH, DON'T BE SILLY! IT'S THE LEAST WE COULD DO...
LOOK-- I APPRECIATE YOUR CONCERN, BUT I ONLY HAVE ONE MORE BLOCK TO GO.
NOW, IF YOU'LL EXCUSE ME, I REALLY SHOULD BE TODDLING OFF, SEE YOU TOMORROW AT THE BIG PARTY! TOODLES!
WELL, I'LL BE...
SHE'S EITHER THE MOST FEARLESS PERSON I'VE EVER MET--
-- OR THE STUPIDEST!
13

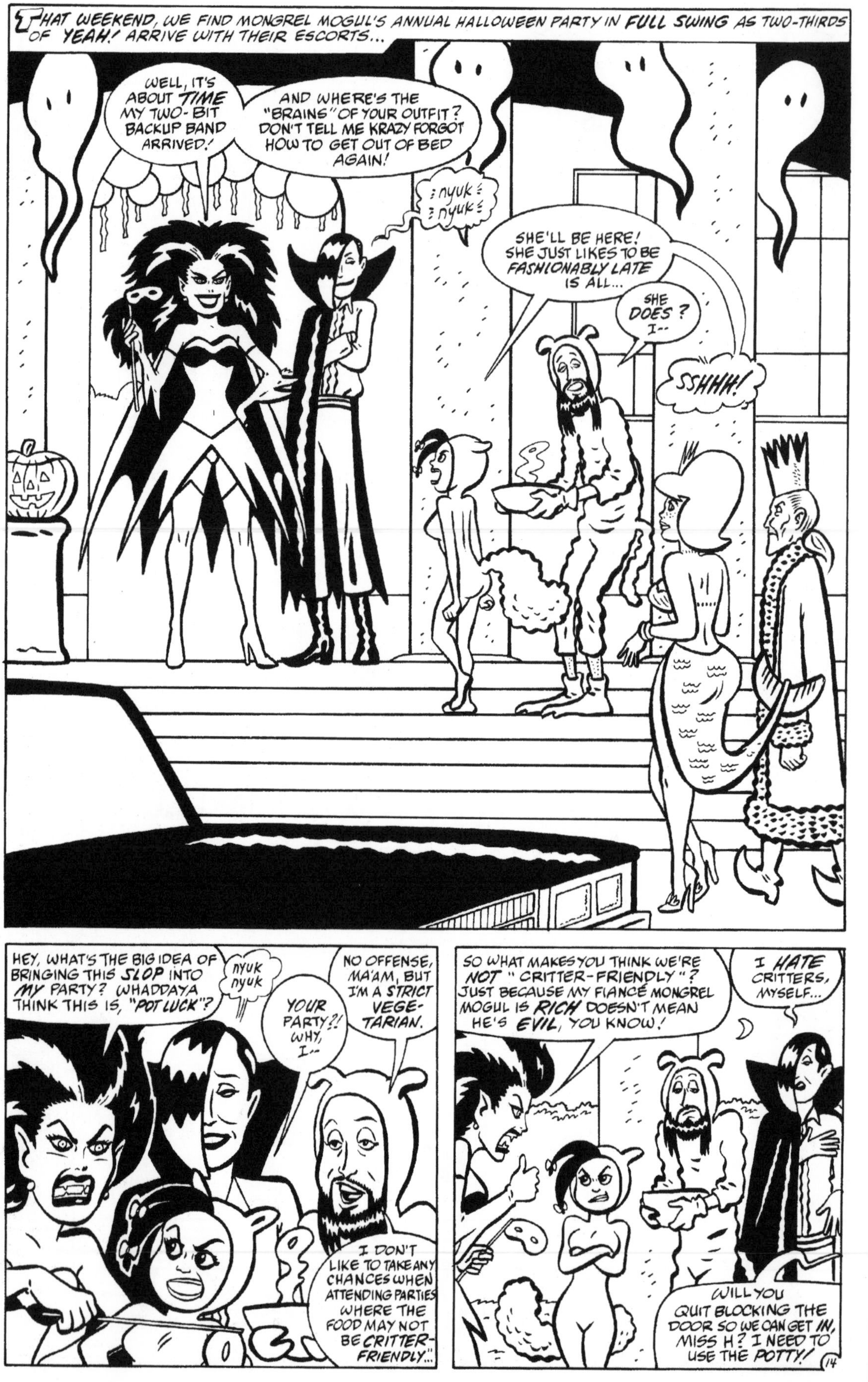
THAT WEEKEND, WE FIND MONGREL MOGUL'S ANNUAL HALLOWEEN PARTY IN FULL SWING AS TWO-THIRDS OF YEAH! ARRIVE WITH THEIR ESCORTS...
WELL, IT'S ABOUT TIME MY TWO-BIT BACKUP BAND ARRIVED!
AND WHERE'S THE "BRAINS" OF YOUR OUTFIT? DON'T TELL ME KRAZY FORGOT HOW TO GET OUT OF BED AGAIN!
nyuk nyuk
SHE'LL BE HERE! SHE JUST LIKES TO BE FASHIONABLY LATE IS ALL...
SHE DOES? I--
SSHHH!
HEY, WHAT'S THE BIG IDEA OF BRINGING THIS SLOP INTO MY PARTY? WHADDAYA THINK THIS IS, "POT LUCK"?
nyuk nyuk
YOUR PARTY?! WHY, I--
NO OFFENSE, MA'AM, BUT I'M A STRICT VEGE-TARIAN.
I DON'T LIKE TO TAKE ANY CHANCES WHEN ATTENDING PARTIES WHERE THE FOOD MAY NOT BE CRITTER-FRIENDLY...
SO WHAT MAKES YOU THINK WE'RE NOT "CRITTER-FRIENDLY"? JUST BECAUSE MY FIANCÉ MONGREL MOGUL IS RICH DOESN'T MEAN HE'S EVIL, YOU KNOW!
I HATE CRITTERS, MYSELF...
WILL YOU QUIT BLOCKING THE DOOR SO WE CAN GET IN, MISS H? I NEED TO USE THE POTTY!

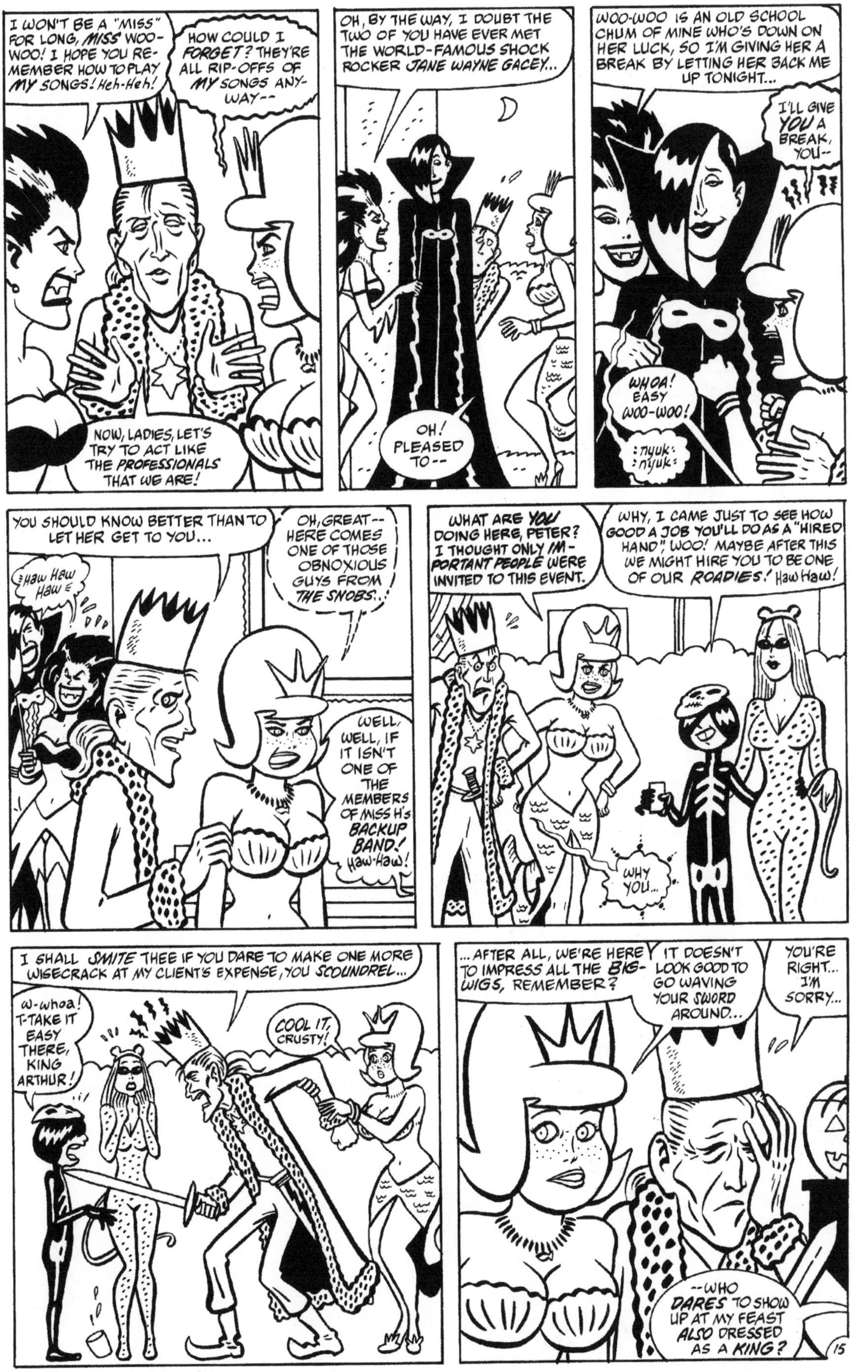
I WON'T BE A "MISS" FOR LONG, MISS WOO-WOO! I HOPE YOU REMEMBER HOW TO PLAY MY SONGS! Heh-Heh!
HOW COULD I FORGET? THEY'RE ALL RIP-OFFS OF MY SONGS ANYWAY--
NOW, LADIES, LET'S TRY TO ACT LIKE THE PROFESSIONALS THAT WE ARE!
OH, BY THE WAY, I DOUBT THE TWO OF YOU HAVE EVER MET THE WORLD-FAMOUS SHOCK ROCKER JANE WAYNE GACEY...
OH! PLEASED TO--
WOO-WOO IS AN OLD SCHOOL CHUM OF MINE WHO'S DOWN ON HER LUCK, SO I'M GIVING HER A BREAK BY LETTING HER BACK ME UP TONIGHT...
I'LL GIVE YOU A BREAK, YOU--
WHOA! EASY WOO-WOO!
nyuk nyuk
YOU SHOULD KNOW BETTER THAN TO LET HER GET TO YOU...
Haw Haw Haw
OH, GREAT-- HERE COMES ONE OF THOSE OBNOXIOUS GUYS FROM THE SNOBS...
WELL, WELL, IF IT ISN'T ONE OF THE MEMBERS OF MISS H's BACKUP BAND! Haw-Haw!
WHAT ARE YOU DOING HERE, PETER? I THOUGHT ONLY IMPORTANT PEOPLE WERE INVITED TO THIS EVENT.
WHY, I CAME JUST TO SEE HOW GOOD A JOB YOU'LL DO AS A "HIRED HAND", WOO! MAYBE AFTER THIS WE MIGHT HIRE YOU TO BE ONE OF OUR ROADIES! Haw Haw!
WHY YOU...
I SHALL SMITE THEE IF YOU DARE TO MAKE ONE MORE WISECRACK AT MY CLIENT'S EXPENSE, YOU SCOUNDREL...
W-WHOA! T-TAKE IT EASY THERE, KING ARTHUR!
COOL IT, CRUSTY!
...AFTER ALL, WE'RE HERE TO IMPRESS ALL THE BIG-WIGS, REMEMBER?
IT DOESN'T LOOK GOOD TO GO WAVING YOUR SWORD AROUND...
YOU'RE RIGHT... I'M SORRY...
--WHO DARES TO SHOW UP AT MY FEAST ALSO DRESSED AS A KING?

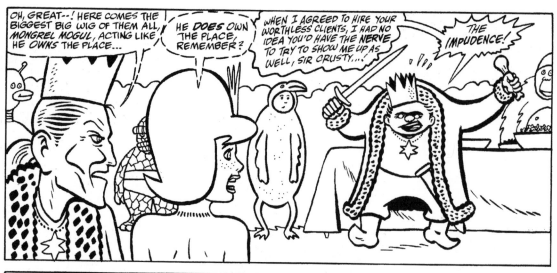

OH, GREAT--! HERE COMES THE BIGGEST BIG WIG OF THEM ALL, MONGREL MOGUL, ACTING LIKE HE OWNS THE PLACE...

HE *DOES* OWN THE PLACE, REMEMBER?

WHEN I AGREED TO HIRE YOUR WORTHLESS CLIENTS, I HAD NO IDEA YOU'D HAVE THE *NERVE* TO TRY TO SHOW ME UP AS WELL, SIR CRUSTY...

THE *IMPUDENCE!*

METHINKS THY COSTUME-- AS WELL AS THY *INFLATED INCOME*-- HAS GONE TO THY *FAT HEAD,* SIR MOGUL!

AND I SUSPECT THAT *THOU* ART IN NEED OF A LESSON ON HOW TO SUCK UP TO THY *BETTERS...*

PREPARE TO EAT CARDBOARD, KNAVE!

PSSSST! WOO-WOO!

CAN'T IT *WAIT,* HONEY? I WANNA *SEE* THIS!

NO, IT *CAN'T* WAIT!

KRAZY SAYS SHE NEEDS OUR HELP, *NOW!*

KRAZY? WHERE IS SHE?

OVER THERE, AND SHE'S IN A PANIC OVER *SOMETHING...*

OH, BROTHER... SHE'S *SUCH* A DRAMA QUEEN...

:sigh: WHAT IS IT *NOW,* KRAZY-- WHOA!

YOU GUYS HAVE TO COME OUTSIDE WITH ME *THIS INSTANT!*

OUTSIDE...

KRAZY-- DO YOU MIND EXPLA--

THERE'S NO *TIME* TO EXPLAIN! JUST PROMISE ME THAT YOU WON'T *FREAK OUT,* OKAY?

WE PROMISE! WE PROMISE! BUT THIS BETTER BE GOOD...

16

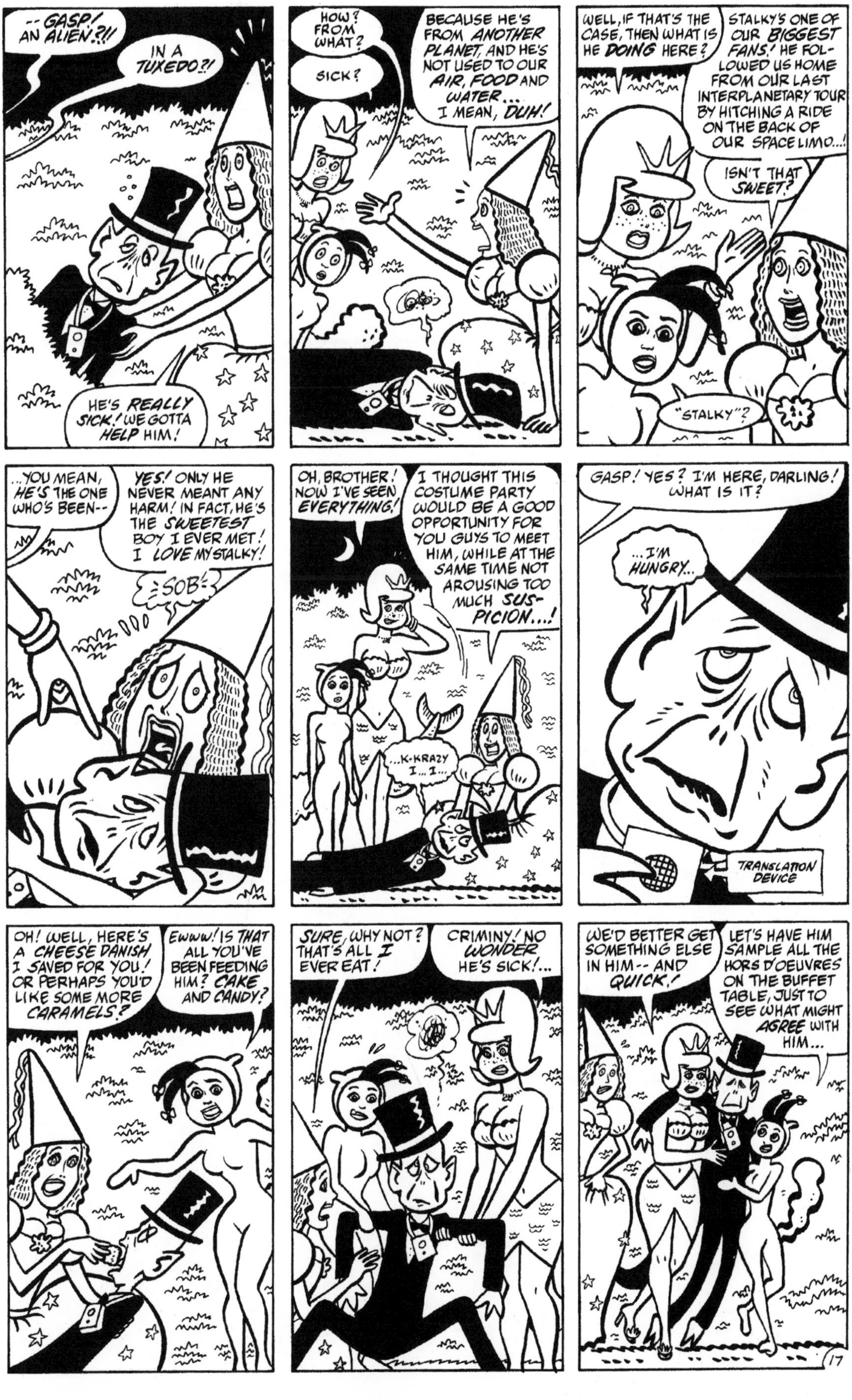
-- GASP! AN ALIEN?!!
IN A TUXEDO?!
HE'S REALLY SICK! WE GOTTA HELP HIM!
HOW? FROM WHAT?
SICK?
BECAUSE HE'S FROM ANOTHER PLANET, AND HE'S NOT USED TO OUR AIR, FOOD AND WATER... I MEAN, DUH!
WELL, IF THAT'S THE CASE, THEN WHAT IS HE DOING HERE?
STALKY'S ONE OF OUR BIGGEST FANS! HE FOLLOWED US HOME FROM OUR LAST INTERPLANETARY TOUR BY HITCHING A RIDE ON THE BACK OF OUR SPACE LIMO...!
ISN'T THAT SWEET?
"STALKY"?
...YOU MEAN, HE'S THE ONE WHO'S BEEN--
YES! ONLY HE NEVER MEANT ANY HARM! IN FACT, HE'S THE SWEETEST BOY I EVER MET! I LOVE MY STALKY!
SOB
OH, BROTHER! NOW I'VE SEEN EVERYTHING!
I THOUGHT THIS COSTUME PARTY WOULD BE A GOOD OPPORTUNITY FOR YOU GUYS TO MEET HIM, WHILE AT THE SAME TIME NOT AROUSING TOO MUCH SUSPICION...!
...K-KRAZY I... I...
GASP! YES? I'M HERE, DARLING! WHAT IS IT?
...I'M HUNGRY...
TRANSLATION DEVICE
OH! WELL, HERE'S A CHEESE DANISH I SAVED FOR YOU! OR PERHAPS YOU'D LIKE SOME MORE CARAMELS?
EWWW! IS THAT ALL YOU'VE BEEN FEEDING HIM? CAKE AND CANDY?
SURE, WHY NOT? THAT'S ALL I EVER EAT!
CRIMINY! NO WONDER HE'S SICK!...
WE'D BETTER GET SOMETHING ELSE IN HIM -- AND QUICK!
LET'S HAVE HIM SAMPLE ALL THE HORS D'OEUVRES ON THE BUFFET TABLE, JUST TO SEE WHAT MIGHT AGREE WITH HIM...

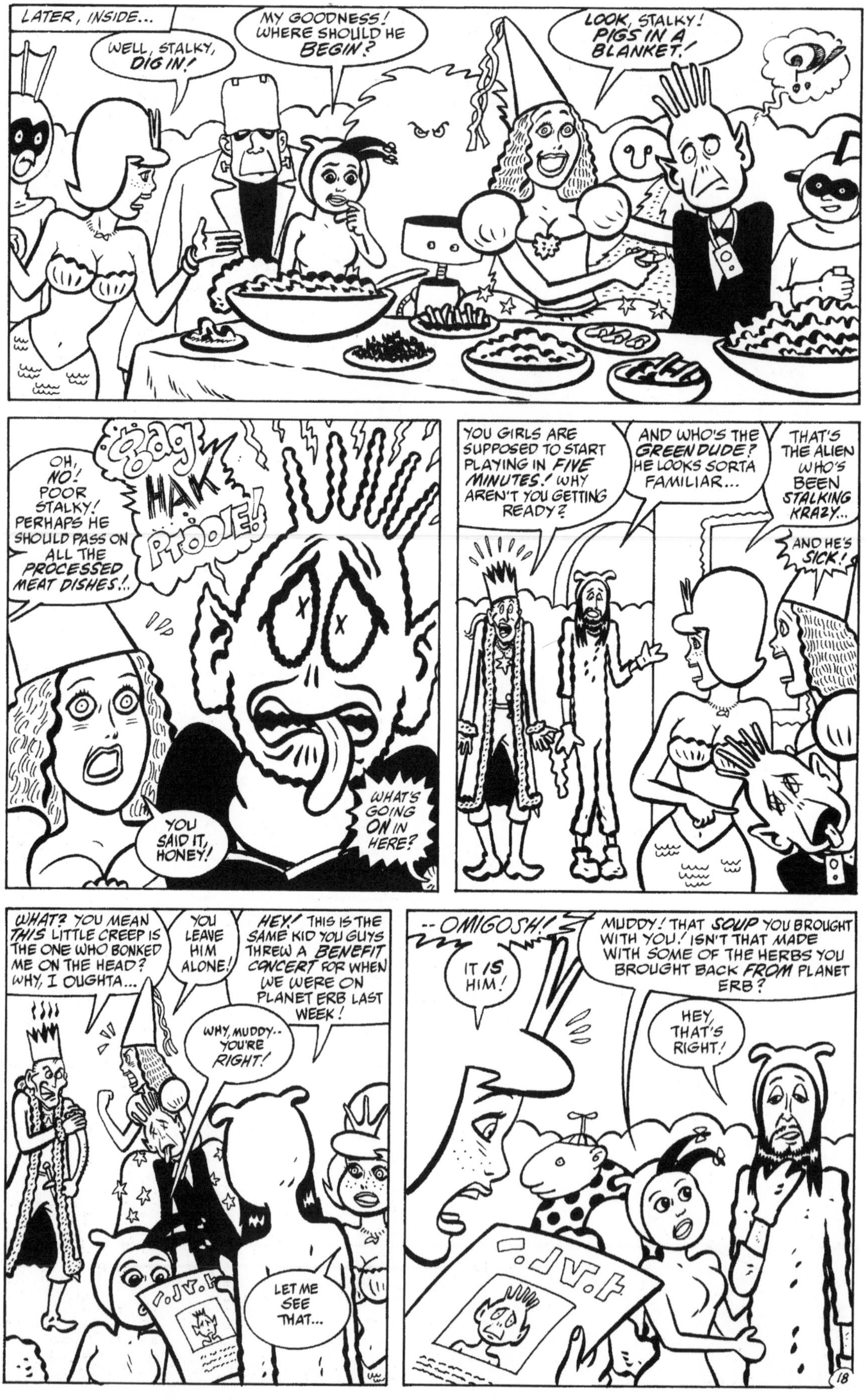
LATER, INSIDE...
WELL, STALKY, DIG IN!
MY GOODNESS! WHERE SHOULD HE BEGIN?
LOOK, STALKY! PIGS IN A BLANKET!
?!
OH, NO! POOR STALKY! PERHAPS HE SHOULD PASS ON ALL THE PROCESSED MEAT DISHES!..
GAG HAK PTOOIE!
YOU SAID IT, HONEY!
WHAT'S GOING ON IN HERE?
YOU GIRLS ARE SUPPOSED TO START PLAYING IN FIVE MINUTES! WHY AREN'T YOU GETTING READY?
AND WHO'S THE GREEN DUDE? HE LOOKS SORTA FAMILIAR...
THAT'S THE ALIEN WHO'S BEEN STALKING KRAZY...
AND HE'S SICK!
WHAT? YOU MEAN THIS LITTLE CREEP IS THE ONE WHO BONKED ME ON THE HEAD? WHY, I OUGHTA...
YOU LEAVE HIM ALONE!
HEY! THIS IS THE SAME KID YOU GUYS THREW A BENEFIT CONCERT FOR WHEN WE WERE ON PLANET ERB LAST WEEK!
WHY, MUDDY.. YOU'RE RIGHT!
LET ME SEE THAT...
--OMIGOSH!
IT IS HIM!
MUDDY! THAT SOUP YOU BROUGHT WITH YOU! ISN'T THAT MADE WITH SOME OF THE HERBS YOU BROUGHT BACK FROM PLANET ERB?
HEY, THAT'S RIGHT!

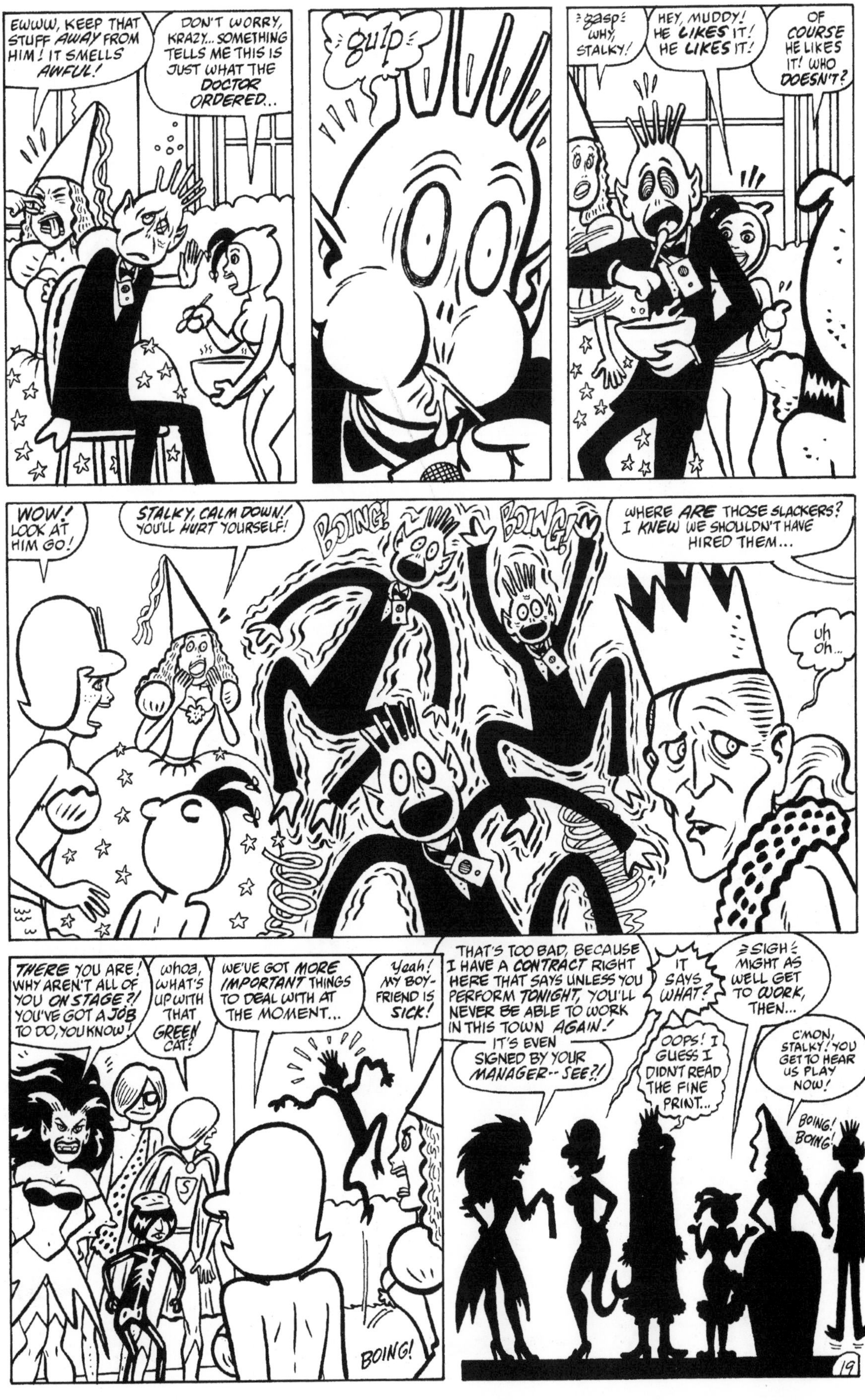

EWWW, KEEP THAT STUFF AWAY FROM HIM! IT SMELLS AWFUL!
DON'T WORRY, KRAZY... SOMETHING TELLS ME THIS IS JUST WHAT THE DOCTOR ORDERED...
gulp
gasp WHY, STALKY!
HEY, MUDDY! HE LIKES IT! HE LIKES IT!
OF COURSE HE LIKES IT! WHO DOESN'T?
WOW! LOOK AT HIM GO!
STALKY, CALM DOWN! YOU'LL HURT YOURSELF!
BOING!
BOING!
WHERE ARE THOSE SLACKERS? I KNEW WE SHOULDN'T HAVE HIRED THEM...
uh oh...
THERE YOU ARE! WHY AREN'T ALL OF YOU ON STAGE?! YOU'VE GOT A JOB TO DO, YOU KNOW!
whoa, WHAT'S UP WITH THAT GREEN CAT?
WE'VE GOT MORE IMPORTANT THINGS TO DEAL WITH AT THE MOMENT...
Yeah! MY BOY-FRIEND IS SICK!
BOING!
THAT'S TOO BAD, BECAUSE I HAVE A CONTRACT RIGHT HERE THAT SAYS UNLESS YOU PERFORM TONIGHT, YOU'LL NEVER BE ABLE TO WORK IN THIS TOWN AGAIN!
IT'S EVEN SIGNED BY YOUR MANAGER-- SEE?!
IT SAYS WHAT?
OOPS! I GUESS I DIDN'T READ THE FINE PRINT...
SIGH MIGHT AS WELL GET TO WORK, THEN...
C'MON, STALKY! YOU GET TO HEAR US PLAY NOW!
BOING! BOING!

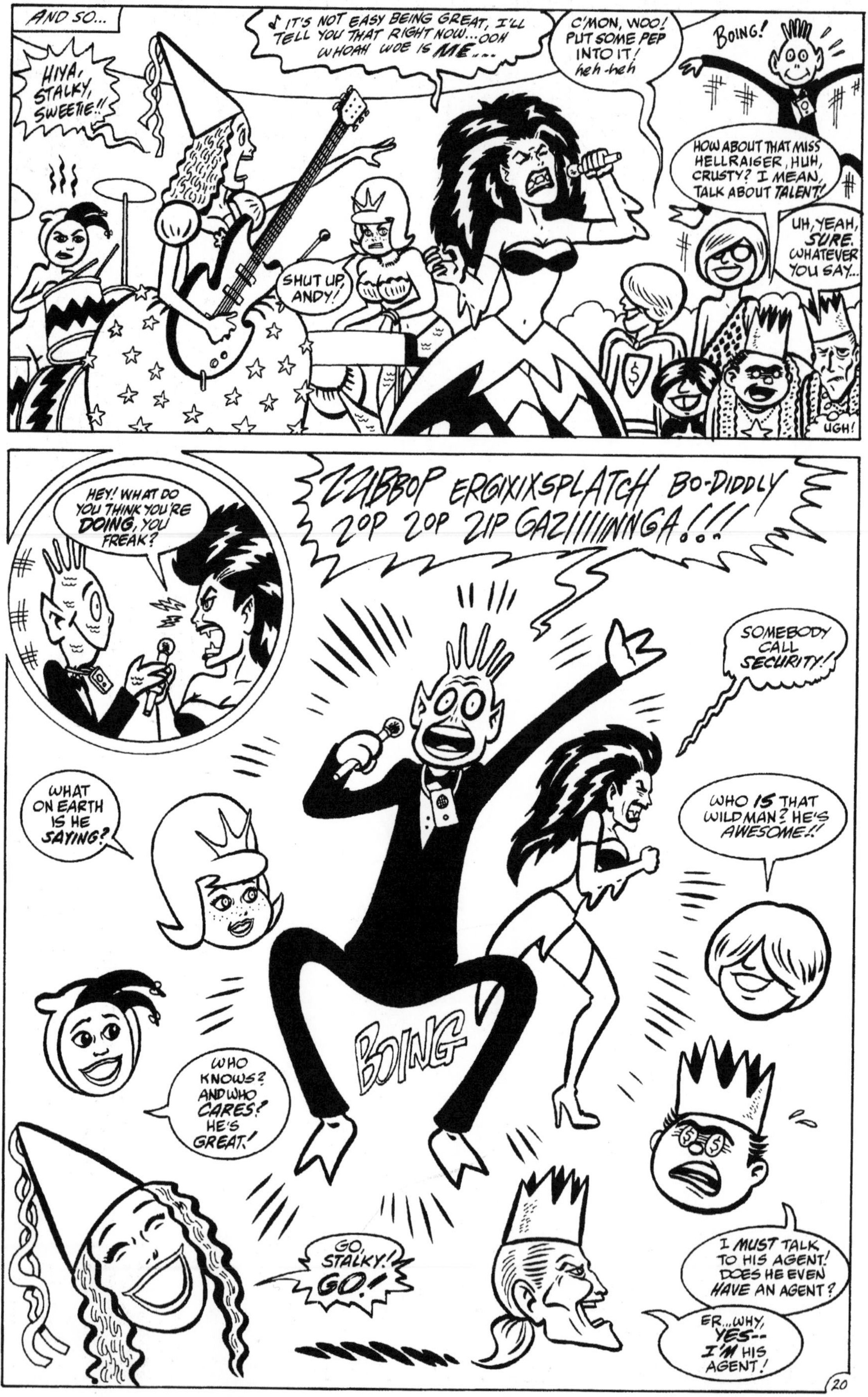
AND SO...
HIYA, STALKY, SWEETIE!!
♪ IT'S NOT EASY BEING GREAT, I'LL TELL YOU THAT RIGHT NOW...OOH WHOAH WOE IS ME...
C'MON, WOO! PUT SOME PEP INTO IT! heh-heh
BOING!
SHUT UP, ANDY!
HOW ABOUT THAT MISS HELLRAISER, HUH, CRUSTY? I MEAN, TALK ABOUT TALENT!
UH, YEAH, SURE. WHATEVER YOU SAY...
UGH!
HEY! WHAT DO YOU THINK YOU'RE DOING, YOU FREAK?
ZZIBBOP ERGIXIXSPLATCH BO-DIDDLY ZOP ZOP ZIP GAZIIIIINNGA!!!
SOMEBODY CALL SECURITY!
WHAT ON EARTH IS HE SAYING?
WHO IS THAT WILDMAN? HE'S AWESOME!!
BOING
WHO KNOWS? AND WHO CARES? HE'S GREAT!
GO, STALKY! GO!
I MUST TALK TO HIS AGENT! DOES HE EVEN HAVE AN AGENT?
ER...WHY, YES-- I'M HIS AGENT!

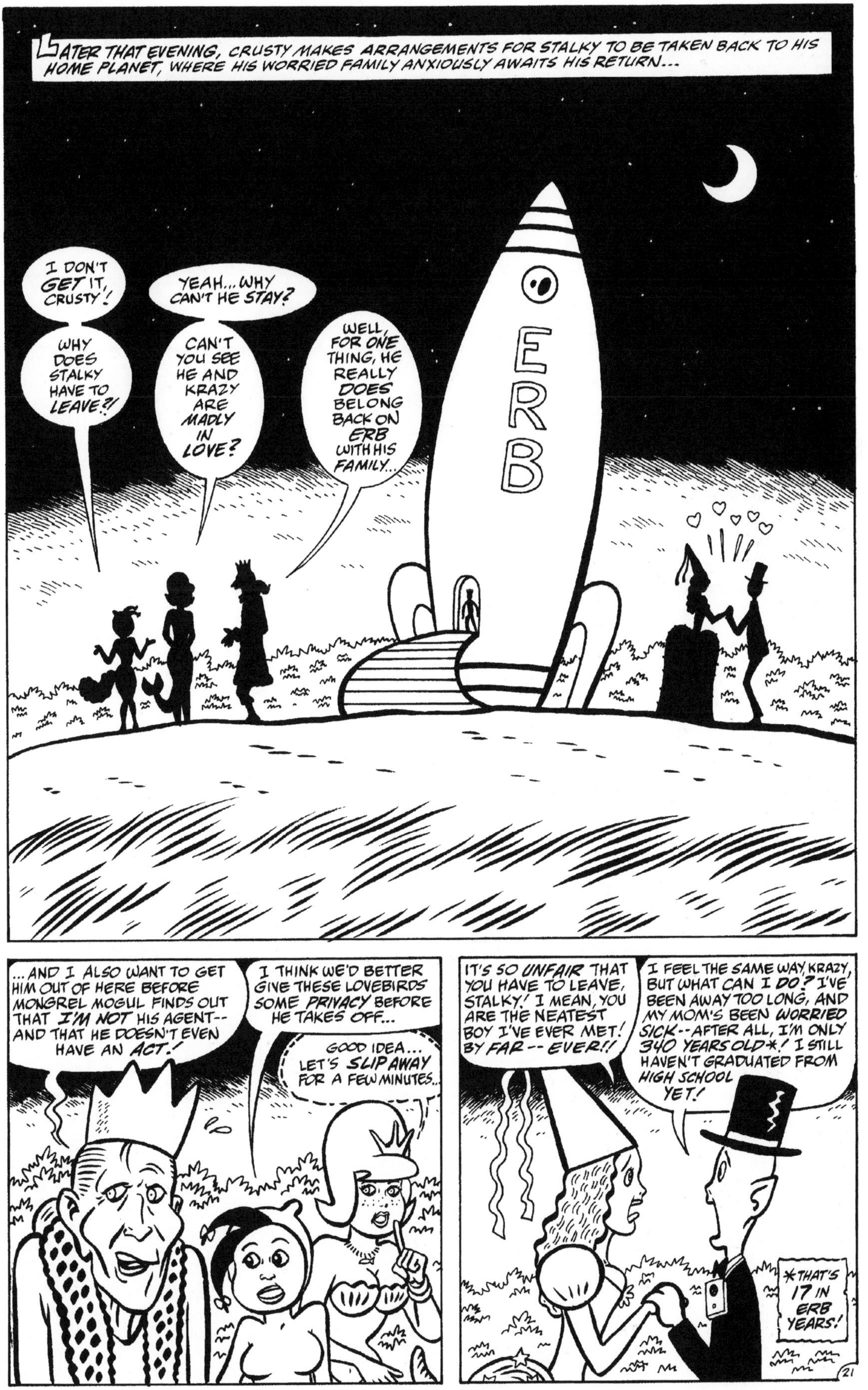
LATER THAT EVENING, CRUSTY MAKES ARRANGEMENTS FOR STALKY TO BE TAKEN BACK TO HIS HOME PLANET, WHERE HIS WORRIED FAMILY ANXIOUSLY AWAITS HIS RETURN...
I DON'T GET IT, CRUSTY!
WHY DOES STALKY HAVE TO LEAVE?!
YEAH... WHY CAN'T HE STAY?
CAN'T YOU SEE HE AND KRAZY ARE MADLY IN LOVE?
WELL, FOR ONE THING, HE REALLY DOES BELONG BACK ON ERB WITH HIS FAMILY...
ERB
...AND I ALSO WANT TO GET HIM OUT OF HERE BEFORE MONGREL MOGUL FINDS OUT THAT I'M NOT HIS AGENT-- AND THAT HE DOESN'T EVEN HAVE AN ACT!
I THINK WE'D BETTER GIVE THESE LOVEBIRDS SOME PRIVACY BEFORE HE TAKES OFF...
GOOD IDEA... LET'S SLIP AWAY FOR A FEW MINUTES...
IT'S SO UNFAIR THAT YOU HAVE TO LEAVE, STALKY! I MEAN, YOU ARE THE NEATEST BOY I'VE EVER MET! BY FAR -- EVER!!
I FEEL THE SAME WAY, KRAZY, BUT WHAT CAN I DO? I'VE BEEN AWAY TOO LONG, AND MY MOM'S BEEN WORRIED SICK -- AFTER ALL, I'M ONLY 340 YEARS OLD*! I STILL HAVEN'T GRADUATED FROM HIGH SCHOOL YET!
*THAT'S 17 IN ERB YEARS!

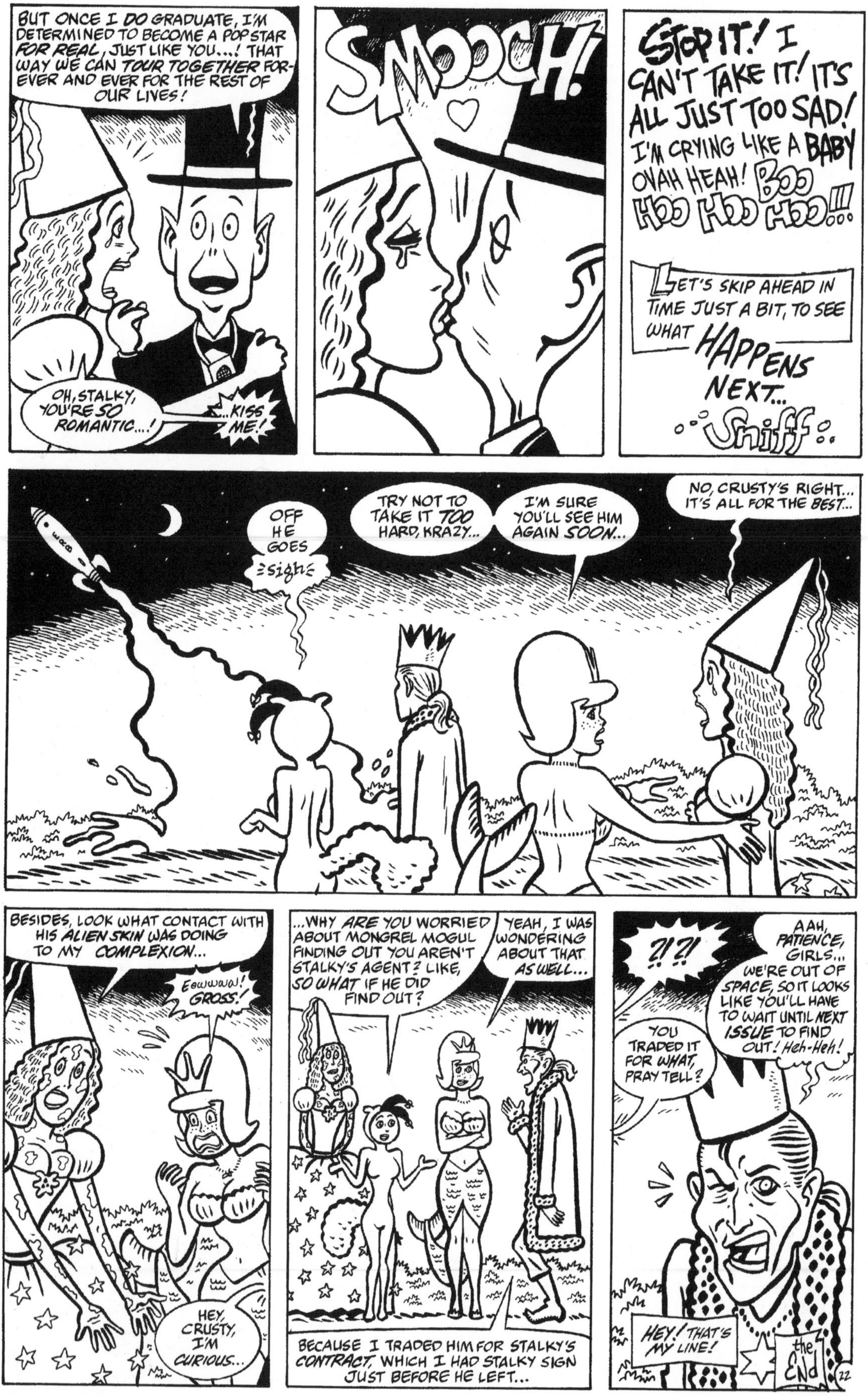
BUT ONCE I DO GRADUATE, I'M DETERMINED TO BECOME A POP STAR FOR REAL, JUST LIKE YOU...! THAT WAY WE CAN TOUR TOGETHER FOR-EVER AND EVER FOR THE REST OF OUR LIVES!
OH, STALKY, YOU'RE SO ROMANTIC...!
...KISS ME!
SMOOCH!
STOP IT! I CAN'T TAKE IT! IT'S ALL JUST TOO SAD! I'M CRYING LIKE A BABY OVAH HEAH! BOO HOO HOO HOO!!!
LET'S SKIP AHEAD IN TIME JUST A BIT, TO SEE WHAT HAPPENS NEXT...
Sniff
OFF HE GOES
sigh
TRY NOT TO TAKE IT TOO HARD, KRAZY...
I'M SURE YOU'LL SEE HIM AGAIN SOON...
NO, CRUSTY'S RIGHT... IT'S ALL FOR THE BEST...
BESIDES, LOOK WHAT CONTACT WITH HIS ALIEN SKIN WAS DOING TO MY COMPLEXION...
Eewwww! GROSS!
HEY, CRUSTY, I'M CURIOUS...
...WHY ARE YOU WORRIED ABOUT MONGREL MOGUL FINDING OUT YOU AREN'T STALKY'S AGENT? LIKE, SO WHAT IF HE DID FIND OUT?
YEAH, I WAS WONDERING ABOUT THAT AS WELL...
BECAUSE I TRADED HIM FOR STALKY'S CONTRACT, WHICH I HAD STALKY SIGN JUST BEFORE HE LEFT...
?!?!
AAH, PATIENCE, GIRLS... WE'RE OUT OF SPACE, SO IT LOOKS LIKE YOU'LL HAVE TO WAIT UNTIL NEXT ISSUE TO FIND OUT! Heh-Heh!
YOU TRADED IT FOR WHAT, PRAY TELL?
HEY! THAT'S MY LINE!
the End

FOUR!

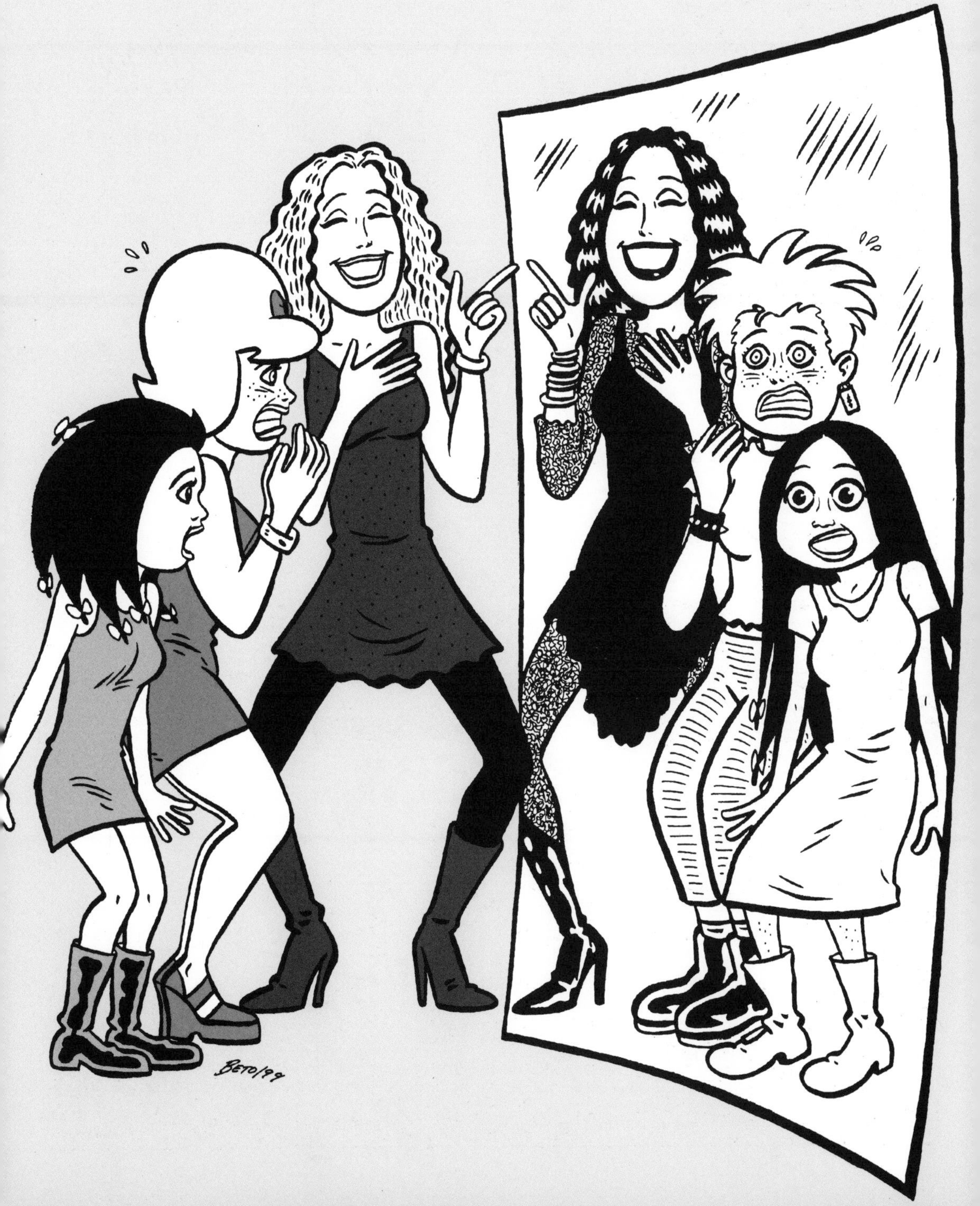
BETO/99

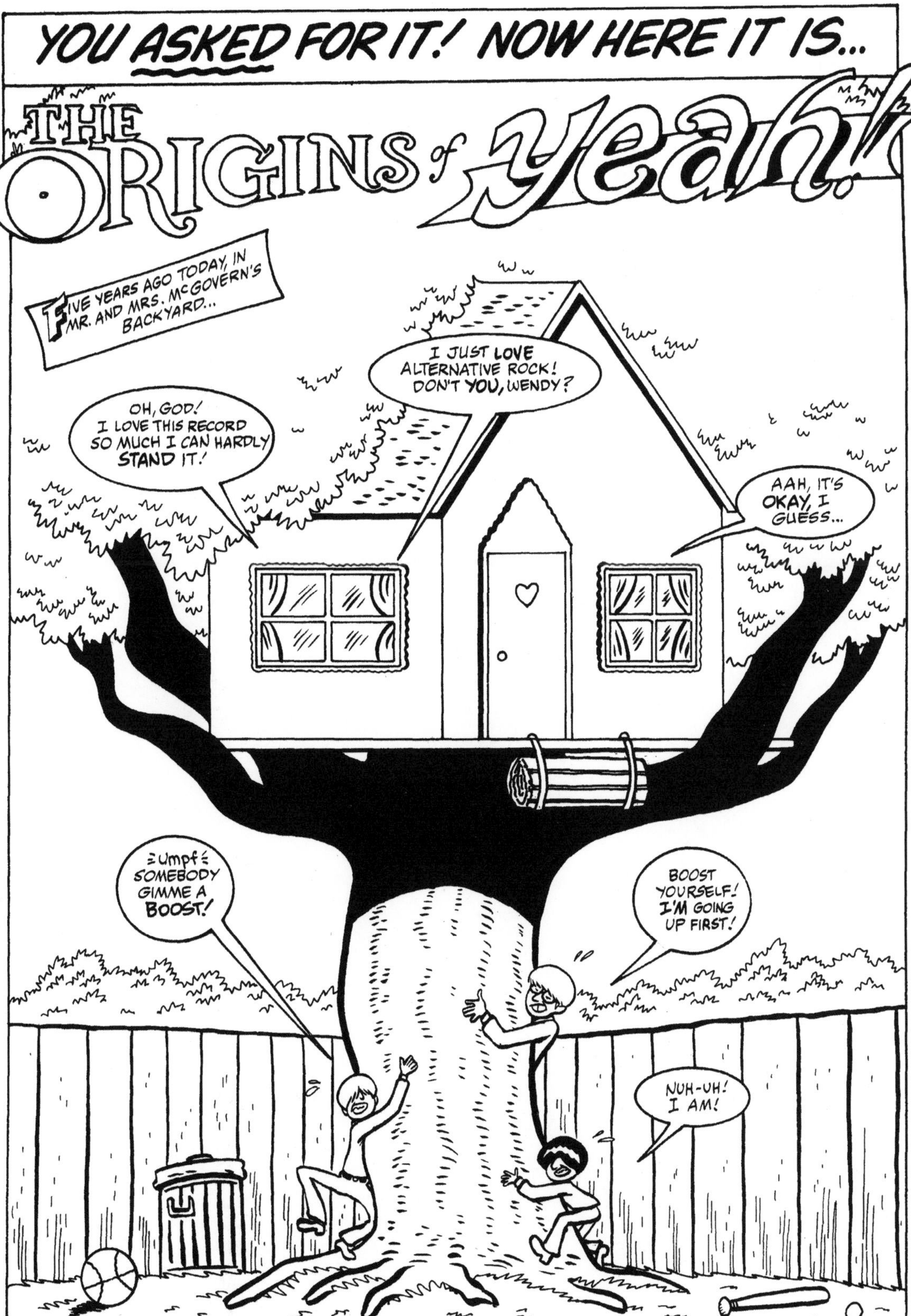
YOU ASKED FOR IT! NOW HERE IT IS...
THE ORIGINS of YEAH!
FIVE YEARS AGO TODAY, IN MR. AND MRS. McGOVERN'S BACKYARD...
OH, GOD! I LOVE THIS RECORD SO MUCH I CAN HARDLY STAND IT!
I JUST LOVE ALTERNATIVE ROCK! DON'T YOU, WENDY?
AAH, IT'S OKAY, I GUESS...
UMPF SOMEBODY GIMME A BOOST!
BOOST YOURSELF! I'M GOING UP FIRST!
NUH-UH! I AM!

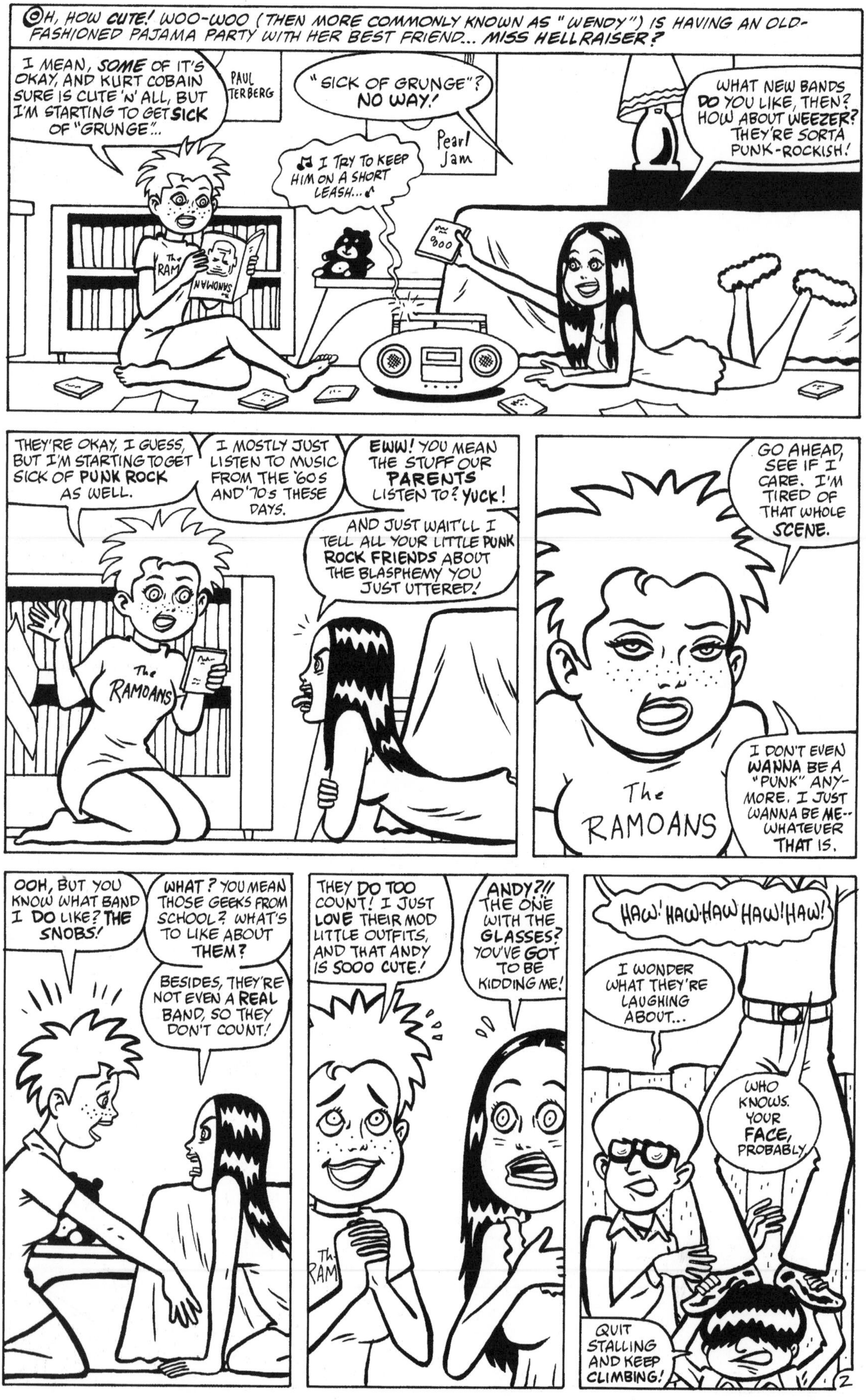
OH, HOW CUTE! WOO-WOO (THEN MORE COMMONLY KNOWN AS "WENDY") IS HAVING AN OLD-FASHIONED PAJAMA PARTY WITH HER BEST FRIEND... MISS HELLRAISER?
I MEAN, SOME OF IT'S OKAY, AND KURT COBAIN SURE IS CUTE 'N' ALL, BUT I'M STARTING TO GET SICK OF "GRUNGE"...
PAUL TERBERG
"SICK OF GRUNGE"? NO WAY!
Pearl Jam
♫ I TRY TO KEEP HIM ON A SHORT LEASH... ♪
WHAT NEW BANDS DO YOU LIKE, THEN? HOW ABOUT WEEZER? THEY'RE SORTA PUNK-ROCKISH!
The RAM
SANDMAN
THEY'RE OKAY, I GUESS, BUT I'M STARTING TO GET SICK OF PUNK ROCK AS WELL.
I MOSTLY JUST LISTEN TO MUSIC FROM THE '60S AND '70S THESE DAYS.
EWW! YOU MEAN THE STUFF OUR PARENTS LISTEN TO? YUCK!
AND JUST WAIT'LL I TELL ALL YOUR LITTLE PUNK ROCK FRIENDS ABOUT THE BLASPHEMY YOU JUST UTTERED!
The RAMOANS
GO AHEAD, SEE IF I CARE. I'M TIRED OF THAT WHOLE SCENE.
The RAMOANS
I DON'T EVEN WANNA BE A "PUNK" ANYMORE. I JUST WANNA BE ME-- WHATEVER THAT IS.
OOH, BUT YOU KNOW WHAT BAND I DO LIKE? THE SNOBS!
WHAT? YOU MEAN THOSE GEEKS FROM SCHOOL? WHAT'S TO LIKE ABOUT THEM?
BESIDES, THEY'RE NOT EVEN A REAL BAND, SO THEY DON'T COUNT!
THEY DO TOO COUNT! I JUST LOVE THEIR MOD LITTLE OUTFITS, AND THAT ANDY IS SOOO CUTE!
ANDY?!! THE ONE WITH THE GLASSES? YOU'VE GOT TO BE KIDDING ME!
HAW! HAW-HAW HAW! HAW!
I WONDER WHAT THEY'RE LAUGHING ABOUT...
WHO KNOWS. YOUR FACE, PROBABLY.
QUIT STALLING AND KEEP CLIMBING!

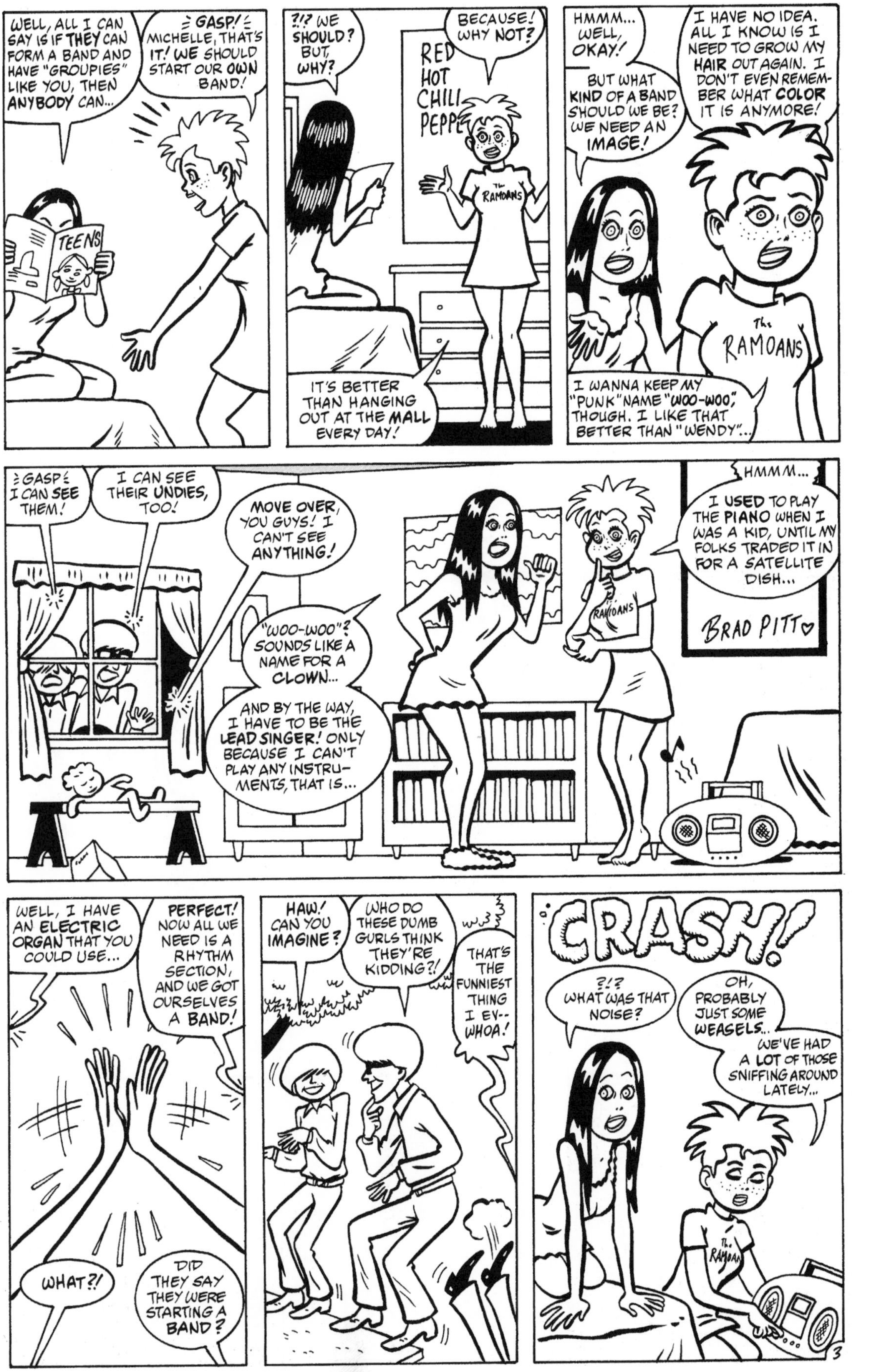
WELL, ALL I CAN SAY IS IF THEY CAN FORM A BAND AND HAVE "GROUPIES" LIKE YOU, THEN ANYBODY CAN...
GASP! MICHELLE, THAT'S IT! WE SHOULD START OUR OWN BAND!
TEENS
?!? WE SHOULD? BUT, WHY?
BECAUSE! WHY NOT?
RED HOT CHILI PEPPE
The RAMOANS
IT'S BETTER THAN HANGING OUT AT THE MALL EVERY DAY!
HMMM... WELL, OKAY!
BUT WHAT KIND OF A BAND SHOULD WE BE? WE NEED AN IMAGE!
I HAVE NO IDEA. ALL I KNOW IS I NEED TO GROW MY HAIR OUT AGAIN. I DON'T EVEN REMEMBER WHAT COLOR IT IS ANYMORE!
The RAMOANS
I WANNA KEEP MY "PUNK" NAME "WOO-WOO," THOUGH. I LIKE THAT BETTER THAN "WENDY"...
GASP I CAN SEE THEM!
I CAN SEE THEIR UNDIES, TOO!
MOVE OVER, YOU GUYS! I CAN'T SEE ANYTHING!
"WOO-WOO"? SOUNDS LIKE A NAME FOR A CLOWN...
AND BY THE WAY, I HAVE TO BE THE LEAD SINGER! ONLY BECAUSE I CAN'T PLAY ANY INSTRUMENTS, THAT IS...
RAMOANS
HMMM...
I USED TO PLAY THE PIANO WHEN I WAS A KID, UNTIL MY FOLKS TRADED IT IN FOR A SATELLITE DISH...
BRAD PITT♡
WELL, I HAVE AN ELECTRIC ORGAN THAT YOU COULD USE...
PERFECT! NOW ALL WE NEED IS A RHYTHM SECTION, AND WE GOT OURSELVES A BAND!
WHAT?!
DID THEY SAY THEY WERE STARTING A BAND?
HAW! CAN YOU IMAGINE?
WHO DO THESE DUMB GURLS THINK THEY'RE KIDDING?!
THAT'S THE FUNNIEST THING I EV-- WHOA!
CRASH!
?!? WHAT WAS THAT NOISE?
OH, PROBABLY JUST SOME WEASELS...
WE'VE HAD A LOT OF THOSE SNIFFING AROUND LATELY...
The RAMOANS

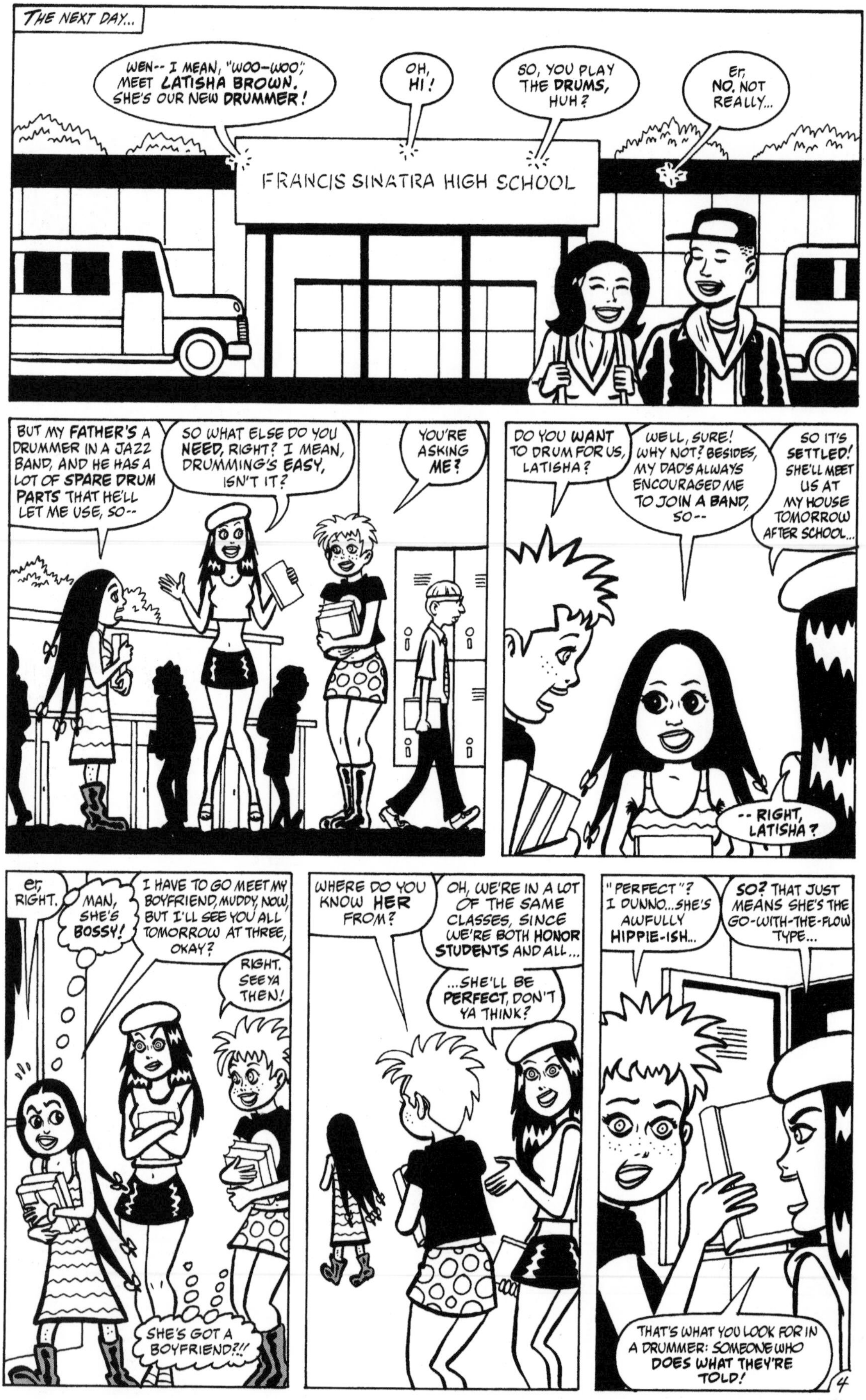
THE NEXT DAY...
WEN-- I MEAN, "WOO-WOO", MEET LATISHA BROWN. SHE'S OUR NEW DRUMMER!
OH, HI!
SO, YOU PLAY THE DRUMS, HUH?
Er, NO, NOT REALLY...
FRANCIS SINATRA HIGH SCHOOL
BUT MY FATHER'S A DRUMMER IN A JAZZ BAND, AND HE HAS A LOT OF SPARE DRUM PARTS THAT HE'LL LET ME USE, SO--
SO WHAT ELSE DO YOU NEED, RIGHT? I MEAN, DRUMMING'S EASY, ISN'T IT?
YOU'RE ASKING ME?
DO YOU WANT TO DRUM FOR US, LATISHA?
WELL, SURE! WHY NOT? BESIDES, MY DAD'S ALWAYS ENCOURAGED ME TO JOIN A BAND, SO--
SO IT'S SETTLED! SHE'LL MEET US AT MY HOUSE TOMORROW AFTER SCHOOL...
-- RIGHT, LATISHA?
er, RIGHT.
MAN, SHE'S BOSSY!
I HAVE TO GO MEET MY BOYFRIEND, MUDDY, NOW, BUT I'LL SEE YOU ALL TOMORROW AT THREE, OKAY?
RIGHT. SEE YA THEN!
SHE'S GOT A BOYFRIEND?!!
WHERE DO YOU KNOW HER FROM?
OH, WE'RE IN A LOT OF THE SAME CLASSES, SINCE WE'RE BOTH HONOR STUDENTS AND ALL...
...SHE'LL BE PERFECT, DON'T YA THINK?
"PERFECT"? I DUNNO...SHE'S AWFULLY HIPPIE-ISH...
SO? THAT JUST MEANS SHE'S THE GO-WITH-THE-FLOW TYPE...
THAT'S WHAT YOU LOOK FOR IN A DRUMMER: SOMEONE WHO DOES WHAT THEY'RE TOLD!

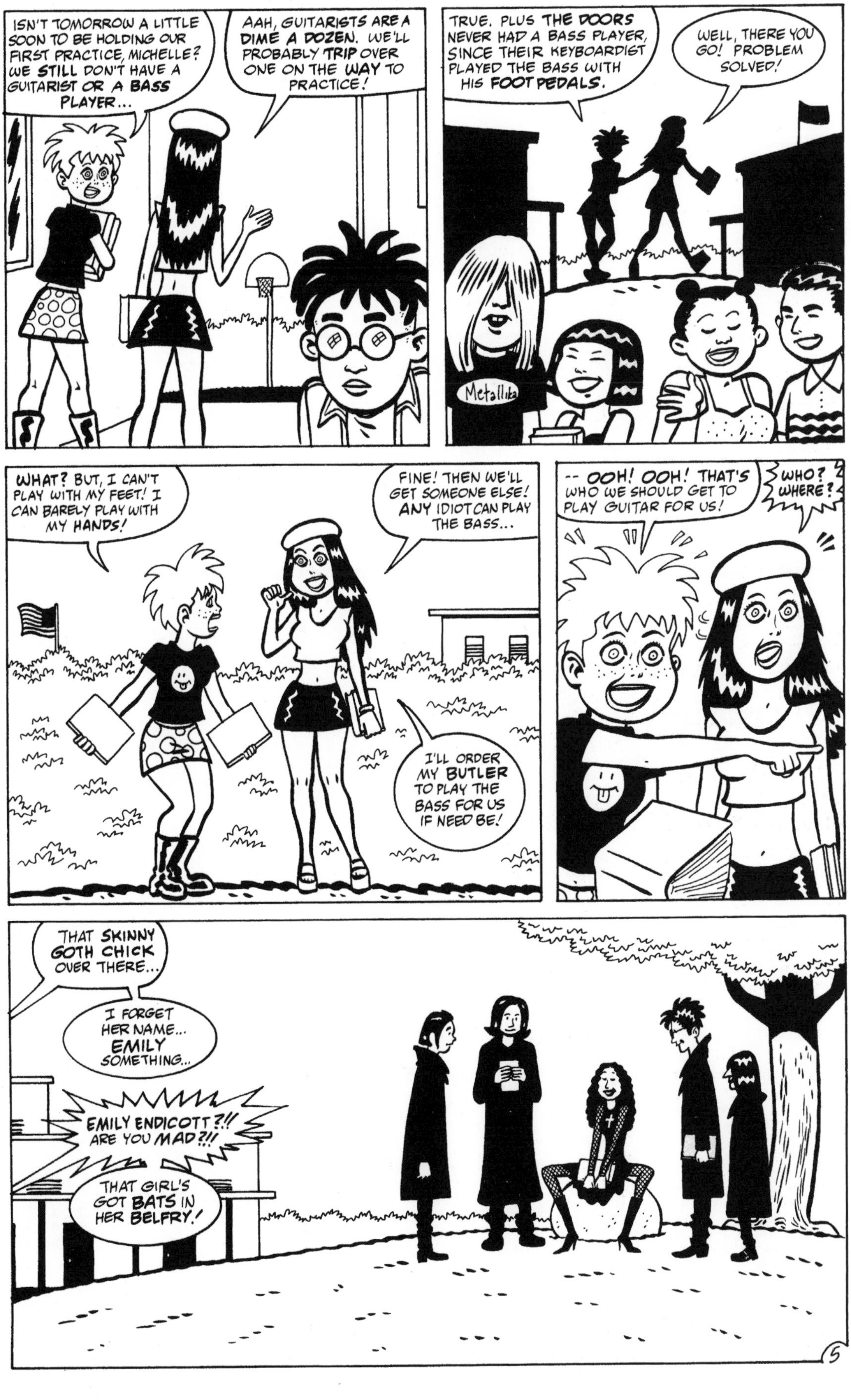

ISN'T TOMORROW A LITTLE SOON TO BE HOLDING OUR FIRST PRACTICE, MICHELLE? WE STILL DON'T HAVE A GUITARIST OR A BASS PLAYER...
AAH, GUITARISTS ARE A DIME A DOZEN. WE'LL PROBABLY TRIP OVER ONE ON THE WAY TO PRACTICE!
TRUE. PLUS THE DOORS NEVER HAD A BASS PLAYER, SINCE THEIR KEYBOARDIST PLAYED THE BASS WITH HIS FOOT PEDALS.
WELL, THERE YOU GO! PROBLEM SOLVED!
Metallika
WHAT? BUT, I CAN'T PLAY WITH MY FEET! I CAN BARELY PLAY WITH MY HANDS!
FINE! THEN WE'LL GET SOMEONE ELSE! ANY IDIOT CAN PLAY THE BASS...
I'LL ORDER MY BUTLER TO PLAY THE BASS FOR US IF NEED BE!
-- OOH! OOH! THAT'S WHO WE SHOULD GET TO PLAY GUITAR FOR US!
WHO? WHERE?
THAT SKINNY GOTH CHICK OVER THERE...
I FORGET HER NAME... EMILY SOMETHING...
EMILY ENDICOTT?!! ARE YOU MAD?!!
THAT GIRL'S GOT BATS IN HER BELFRY!

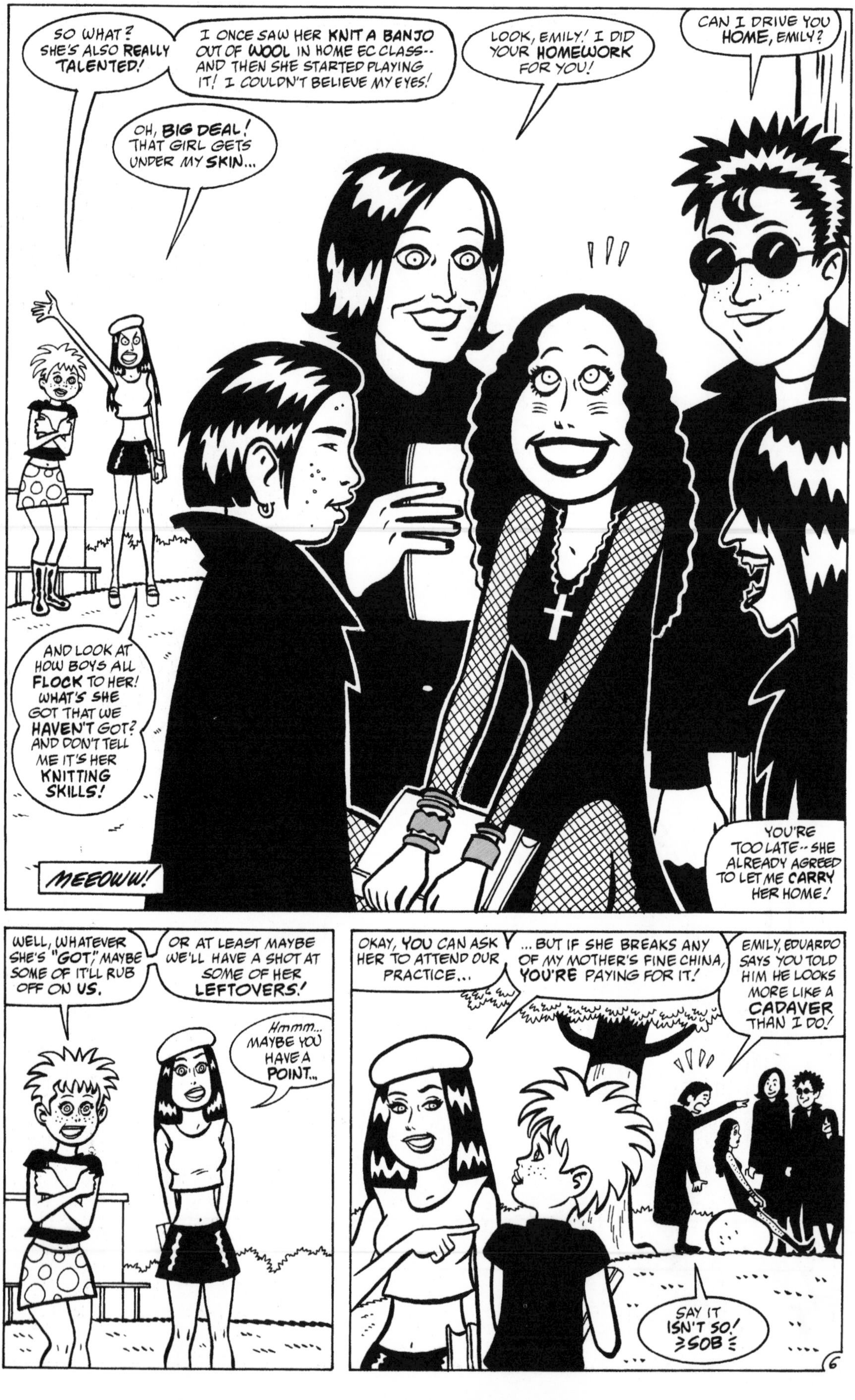

SO WHAT? SHE'S ALSO REALLY TALENTED!
I ONCE SAW HER KNIT A BANJO OUT OF WOOL IN HOME EC CLASS-- AND THEN SHE STARTED PLAYING IT! I COULDN'T BELIEVE MY EYES!
OH, BIG DEAL! THAT GIRL GETS UNDER MY SKIN...
LOOK, EMILY! I DID YOUR HOMEWORK FOR YOU!
CAN I DRIVE YOU HOME, EMILY?
AND LOOK AT HOW BOYS ALL FLOCK TO HER! WHAT'S SHE GOT THAT WE HAVEN'T GOT? AND DON'T TELL ME IT'S HER KNITTING SKILLS!
MEEOWW!
YOU'RE TOO LATE-- SHE ALREADY AGREED TO LET ME CARRY HER HOME!
WELL, WHATEVER SHE'S "GOT," MAYBE SOME OF IT'LL RUB OFF ON US.
OR AT LEAST MAYBE WE'LL HAVE A SHOT AT SOME OF HER LEFTOVERS!
Hmmm... MAYBE YOU HAVE A POINT...
OKAY, YOU CAN ASK HER TO ATTEND OUR PRACTICE...
... BUT IF SHE BREAKS ANY OF MY MOTHER'S FINE CHINA, YOU'RE PAYING FOR IT!
EMILY, EDUARDO SAYS YOU TOLD HIM HE LOOKS MORE LIKE A CADAVER THAN I DO!
SAY IT ISN'T SO! ≥SOB≤

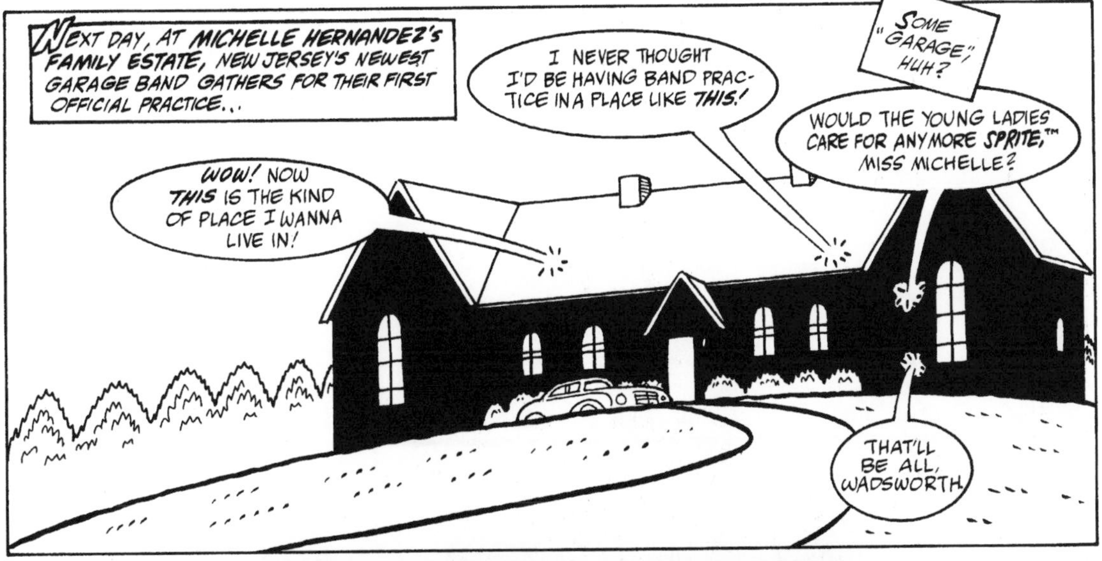
NEXT DAY, AT MICHELLE HERNANDEZ'S FAMILY ESTATE, NEW JERSEY'S NEWEST GARAGE BAND GATHERS FOR THEIR FIRST OFFICIAL PRACTICE...
WOW! NOW THIS IS THE KIND OF PLACE I WANNA LIVE IN!
I NEVER THOUGHT I'D BE HAVING BAND PRACTICE IN A PLACE LIKE THIS!
SOME "GARAGE," HUH?
WOULD THE YOUNG LADIES CARE FOR ANYMORE SPRITE,™ MISS MICHELLE?
THAT'LL BE ALL, WADSWORTH.

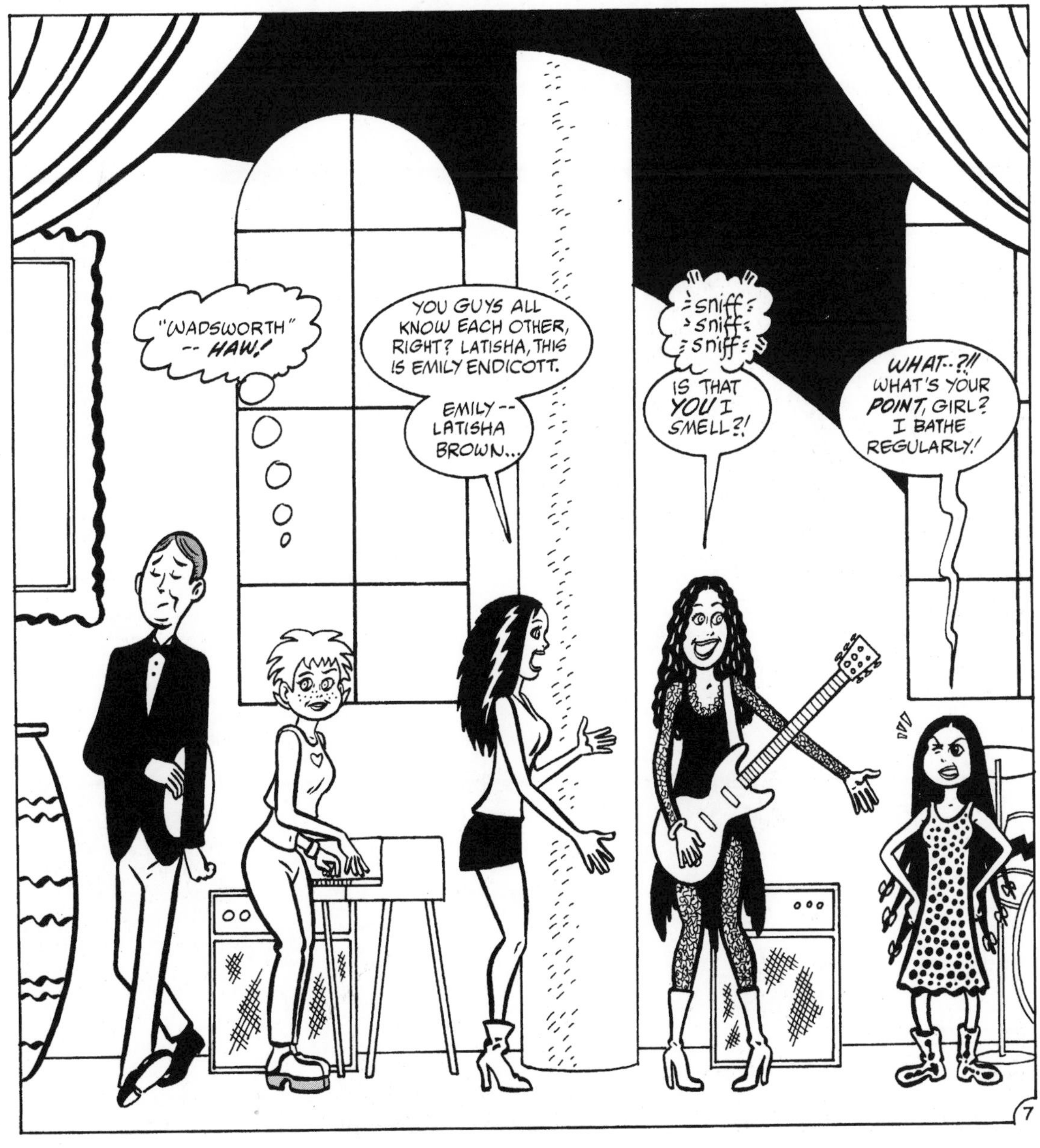
"WADSWORTH" -- HAW!
YOU GUYS ALL KNOW EACH OTHER, RIGHT? LATISHA, THIS IS EMILY ENDICOTT.
EMILY -- LATISHA BROWN...
sniff sniff sniff
IS THAT YOU I SMELL?!
WHAT--?!! WHAT'S YOUR POINT, GIRL? I BATHE REGULARLY!

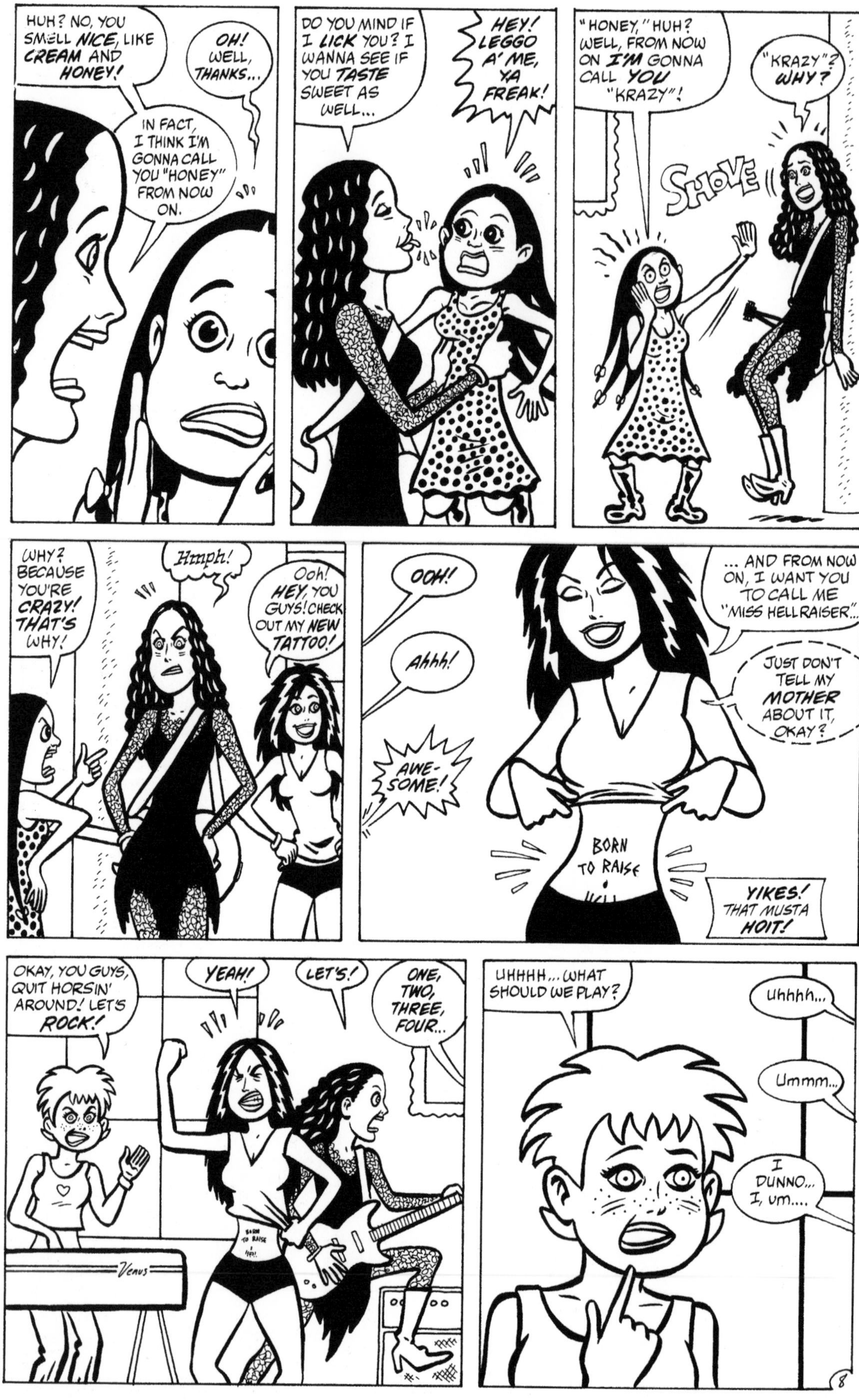
HUH? NO, YOU SMELL NICE, LIKE CREAM AND HONEY!
OH! WELL, THANKS...
IN FACT, I THINK I'M GONNA CALL YOU "HONEY" FROM NOW ON.
DO YOU MIND IF I LICK YOU? I WANNA SEE IF YOU TASTE SWEET AS WELL...
HEY! LEGGO A' ME, YA FREAK!
"HONEY," HUH? WELL, FROM NOW ON I'M GONNA CALL YOU "KRAZY"!
SHOVE
"KRAZY"? WHY?
WHY? BECAUSE YOU'RE CRAZY! THAT'S WHY!
Hmph!
Ooh! HEY, YOU GUYS! CHECK OUT MY NEW TATTOO!
OOH!
Ahhh!
AWESOME!
... AND FROM NOW ON, I WANT YOU TO CALL ME "MISS HELLRAISER"...
JUST DON'T TELL MY MOTHER ABOUT IT, OKAY?
BORN TO RAISE
YIKES! THAT MUSTA HOIT!
OKAY, YOU GUYS, QUIT HORSIN' AROUND! LET'S ROCK!
YEAH!
LET'S!
ONE, TWO, THREE, FOUR...
Venus
UHHHH... WHAT SHOULD WE PLAY?
Uhhhh...
Ummm...
I DUNNO... I, um....

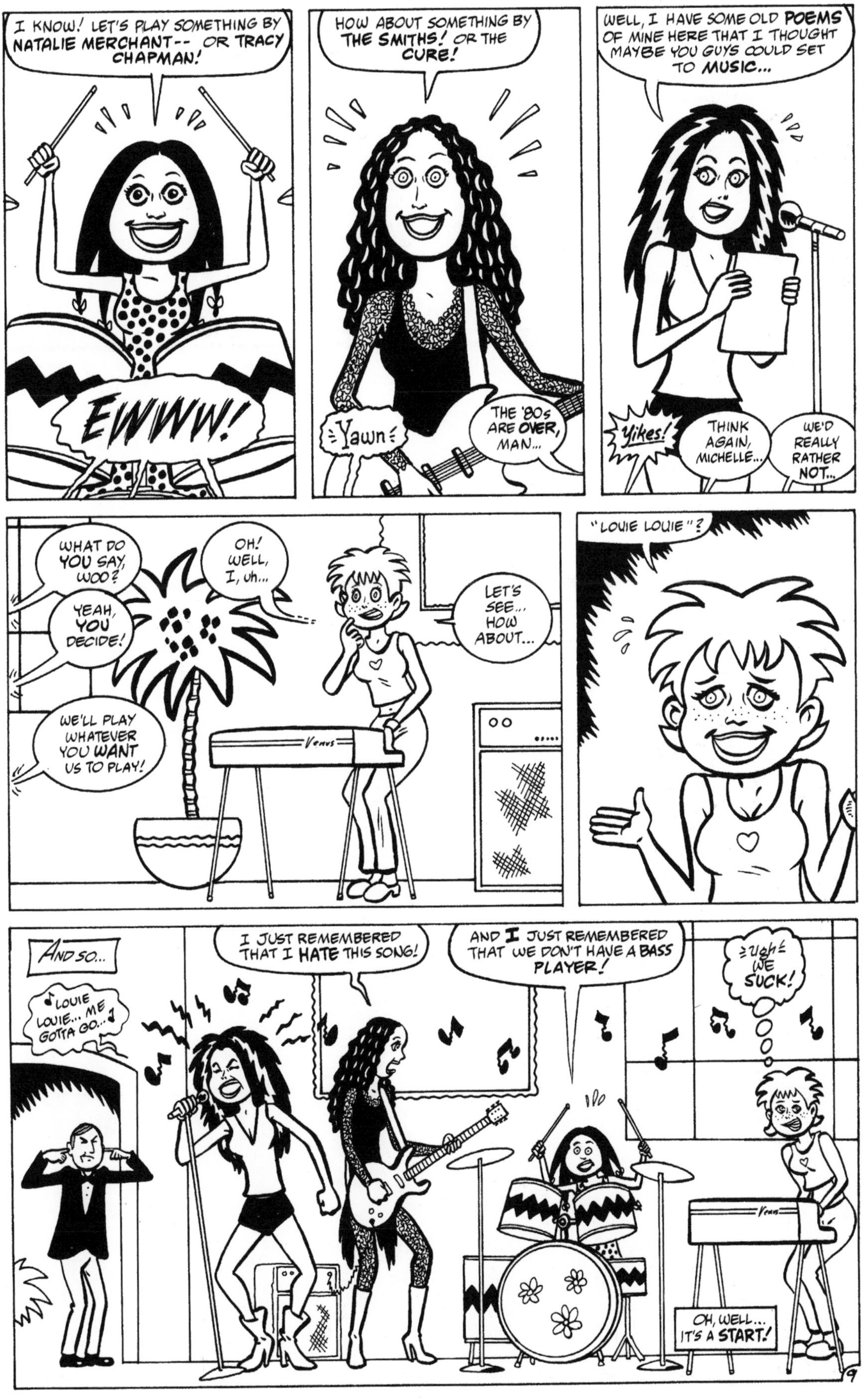
I KNOW! LET'S PLAY SOMETHING BY NATALIE MERCHANT-- OR TRACY CHAPMAN!
EWWW!
HOW ABOUT SOMETHING BY THE SMITHS! OR THE CURE!
Yawn
THE '80s ARE OVER, MAN...
WELL, I HAVE SOME OLD POEMS OF MINE HERE THAT I THOUGHT MAYBE YOU GUYS COULD SET TO MUSIC...
Yikes!
THINK AGAIN, MICHELLE...
WE'D REALLY RATHER NOT...
WHAT DO YOU SAY, WOO?
YEAH, YOU DECIDE!
WE'LL PLAY WHATEVER YOU WANT US TO PLAY!
OH! WELL, I, uh...
LET'S SEE... HOW ABOUT...
"LOUIE LOUIE"?
AND SO...
LOUIE LOUIE... ME GOTTA GO...
I JUST REMEMBERED THAT I HATE THIS SONG!
AND I JUST REMEMBERED THAT WE DON'T HAVE A BASS PLAYER!
Ugh WE SUCK!
OH, WELL... IT'S A START!

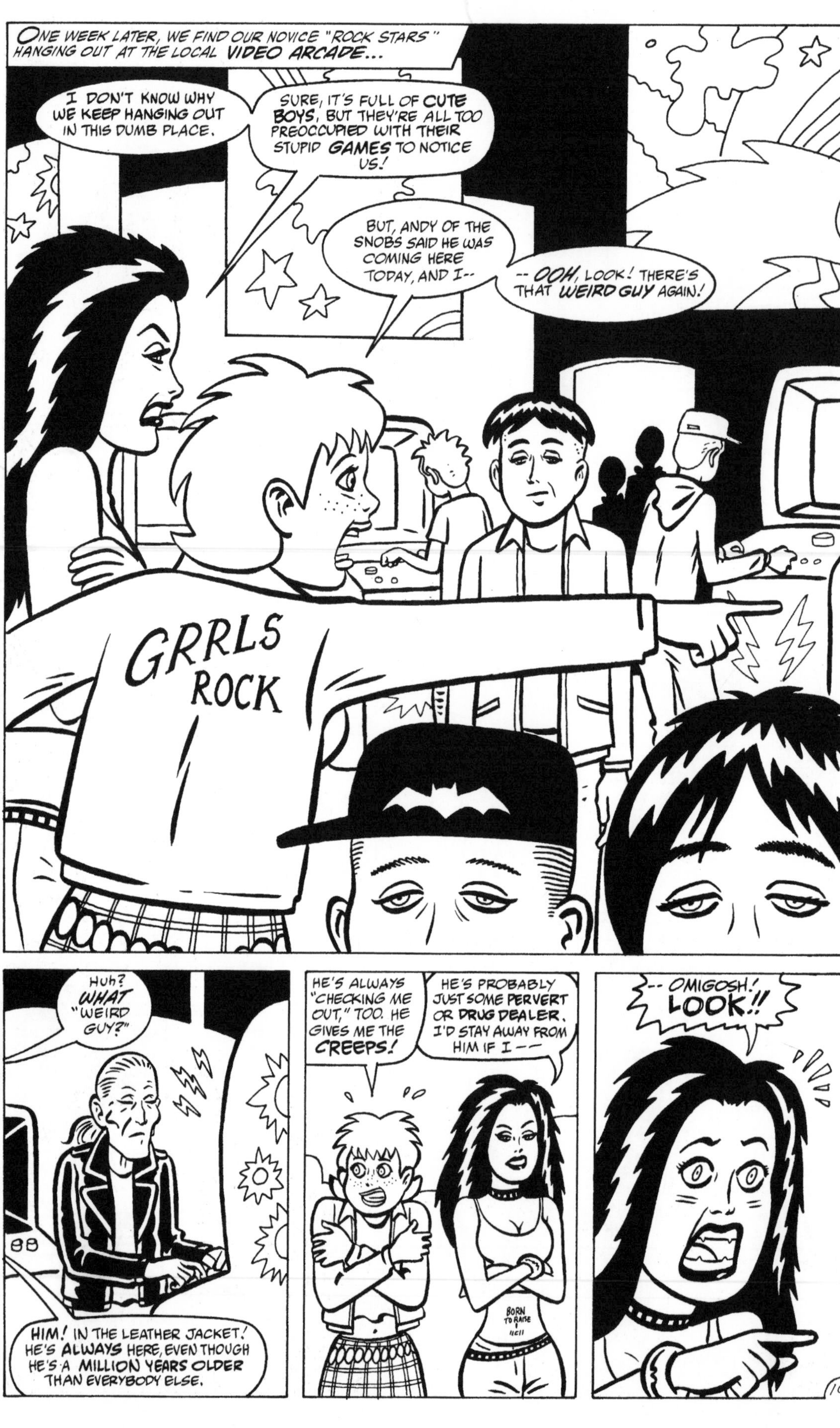
ONE WEEK LATER, WE FIND OUR NOVICE "ROCK STARS" HANGING OUT AT THE LOCAL VIDEO ARCADE...
I DON'T KNOW WHY WE KEEP HANGING OUT IN THIS DUMB PLACE.
SURE, IT'S FULL OF CUTE BOYS, BUT THEY'RE ALL TOO PREOCCUPIED WITH THEIR STUPID GAMES TO NOTICE US!
BUT, ANDY OF THE SNOBS SAID HE WAS COMING HERE TODAY, AND I--
-- OOH, LOOK! THERE'S THAT WEIRD GUY AGAIN!
GRRLS ROCK
HUH? WHAT "WEIRD GUY?"
HIM! IN THE LEATHER JACKET! HE'S ALWAYS HERE, EVEN THOUGH HE'S A MILLION YEARS OLDER THAN EVERYBODY ELSE.
HE'S ALWAYS "CHECKING ME OUT," TOO. HE GIVES ME THE CREEPS!
HE'S PROBABLY JUST SOME PERVERT OR DRUG DEALER. I'D STAY AWAY FROM HIM IF I --
BORN TO RAISE HELL
-- OMIGOSH! LOOK!!

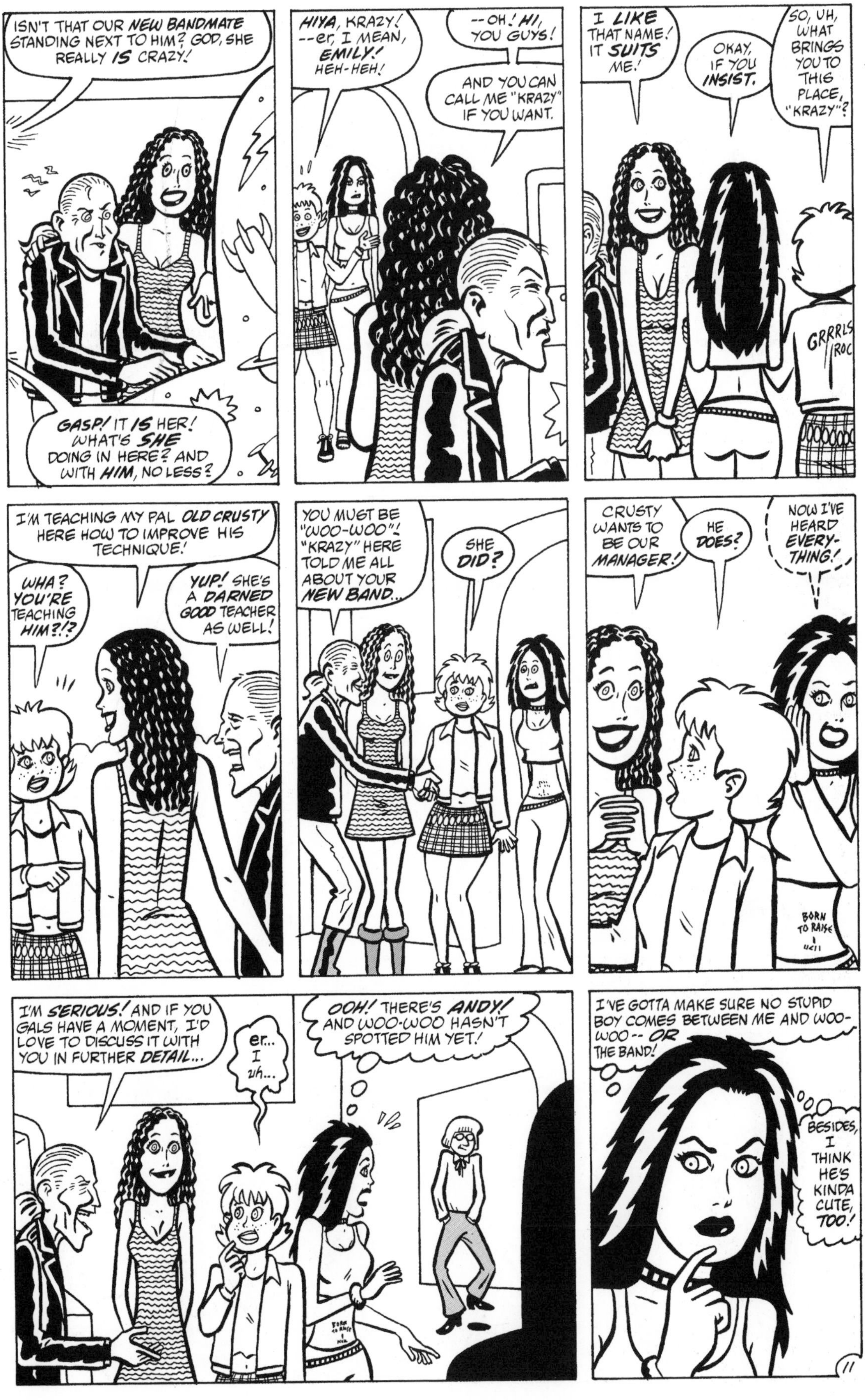

ISN'T THAT OUR NEW BANDMATE STANDING NEXT TO HIM? GOD, SHE REALLY IS CRAZY!
GASP! IT IS HER! WHAT'S SHE DOING IN HERE? AND WITH HIM, NO LESS?
HIYA, KRAZY! --er, I MEAN, EMILY! HEH-HEH!
--OH! HI, YOU GUYS!
AND YOU CAN CALL ME "KRAZY" IF YOU WANT.
I LIKE THAT NAME! IT SUITS ME!
OKAY, IF YOU INSIST.
SO, UH, WHAT BRINGS YOU TO THIS PLACE, "KRAZY"?
GRRRLS ROC
I'M TEACHING MY PAL OLD CRUSTY HERE HOW TO IMPROVE HIS TECHNIQUE!
WHA? YOU'RE TEACHING HIM?!?
YUP! SHE'S A DARNED GOOD TEACHER AS WELL!
YOU MUST BE "WOO-WOO"! "KRAZY" HERE TOLD ME ALL ABOUT YOUR NEW BAND...
SHE DID?
CRUSTY WANTS TO BE OUR MANAGER!
HE DOES?
NOW I'VE HEARD EVERYTHING!
BORN TO RAISE
I'M SERIOUS! AND IF YOU GALS HAVE A MOMENT, I'D LOVE TO DISCUSS IT WITH YOU IN FURTHER DETAIL...
er... I uh...
OOH! THERE'S ANDY! AND WOO-WOO HASN'T SPOTTED HIM YET!
I'VE GOTTA MAKE SURE NO STUPID BOY COMES BETWEEN ME AND WOO-WOO -- OR THE BAND!
BESIDES, I THINK HE'S KINDA CUTE, TOO!

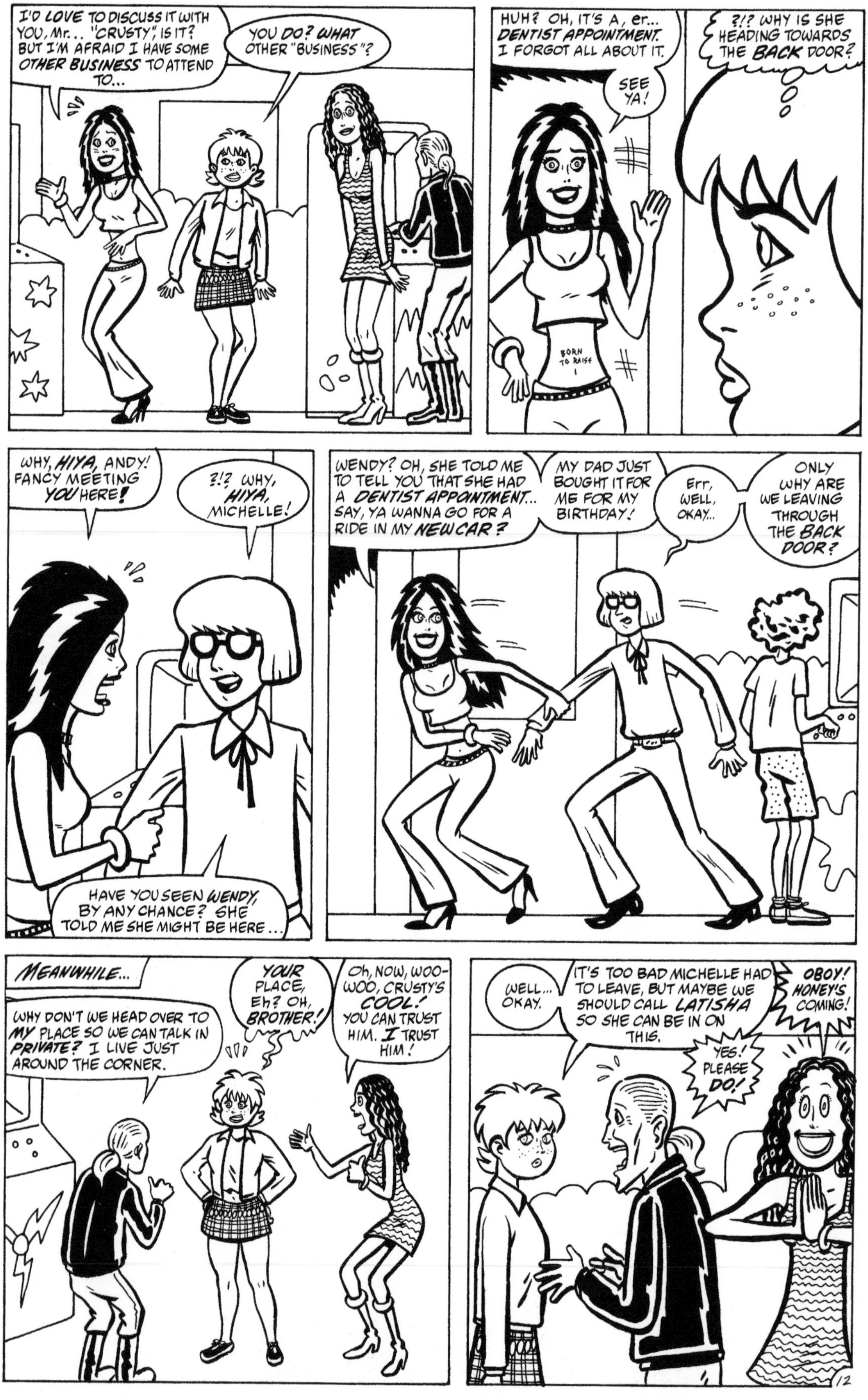

I'D LOVE TO DISCUSS IT WITH YOU, Mr... "CRUSTY", IS IT? BUT I'M AFRAID I HAVE SOME OTHER BUSINESS TO ATTEND TO...
YOU DO? WHAT OTHER "BUSINESS"?
HUH? OH, IT'S A, er... DENTIST APPOINTMENT. I FORGOT ALL ABOUT IT.
SEE YA!
BORN TO RAISE !
?!? WHY IS SHE HEADING TOWARDS THE BACK DOOR?
WHY, HIYA, ANDY! FANCY MEETING YOU HERE!
?!? WHY, HIYA, MICHELLE!
HAVE YOU SEEN WENDY, BY ANY CHANCE? SHE TOLD ME SHE MIGHT BE HERE...
WENDY? OH, SHE TOLD ME TO TELL YOU THAT SHE HAD A DENTIST APPOINTMENT... SAY, YA WANNA GO FOR A RIDE IN MY NEW CAR?
MY DAD JUST BOUGHT IT FOR ME FOR MY BIRTHDAY!
Err, WELL, OKAY...
ONLY WHY ARE WE LEAVING THROUGH THE BACK DOOR?
MEANWHILE...
WHY DON'T WE HEAD OVER TO MY PLACE SO WE CAN TALK IN PRIVATE? I LIVE JUST AROUND THE CORNER.
YOUR PLACE, Eh? OH, BROTHER!
Oh, NOW, WOO-WOO, CRUSTY'S COOL! YOU CAN TRUST HIM. I TRUST HIM!
WELL... OKAY.
IT'S TOO BAD MICHELLE HAD TO LEAVE, BUT MAYBE WE SHOULD CALL LATISHA SO SHE CAN BE IN ON THIS.
OBOY! HONEY'S COMING!
YES! PLEASE DO!
12

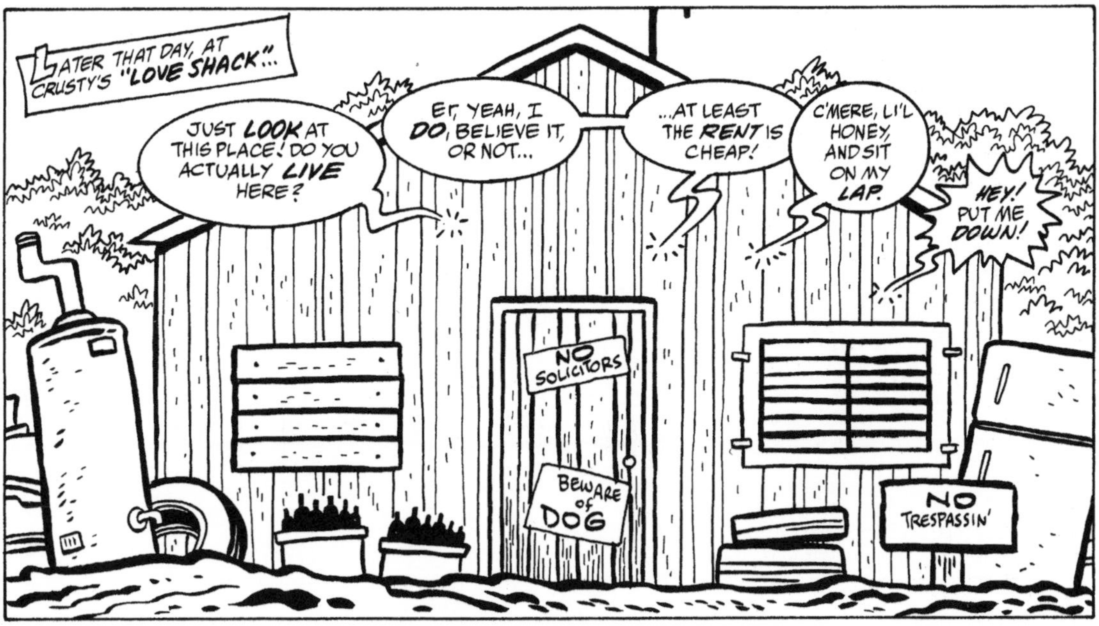
LATER THAT DAY, AT CRUSTY'S "LOVE SHACK"...
JUST LOOK AT THIS PLACE! DO YOU ACTUALLY LIVE HERE?
ER, YEAH, I DO, BELIEVE IT, OR NOT...
...AT LEAST THE RENT IS CHEAP!
C'MERE, LI'L HONEY, AND SIT ON MY LAP.
HEY! PUT ME DOWN!
NO SOLICITORS
BEWARE of DOG
NO TRESPASSIN'

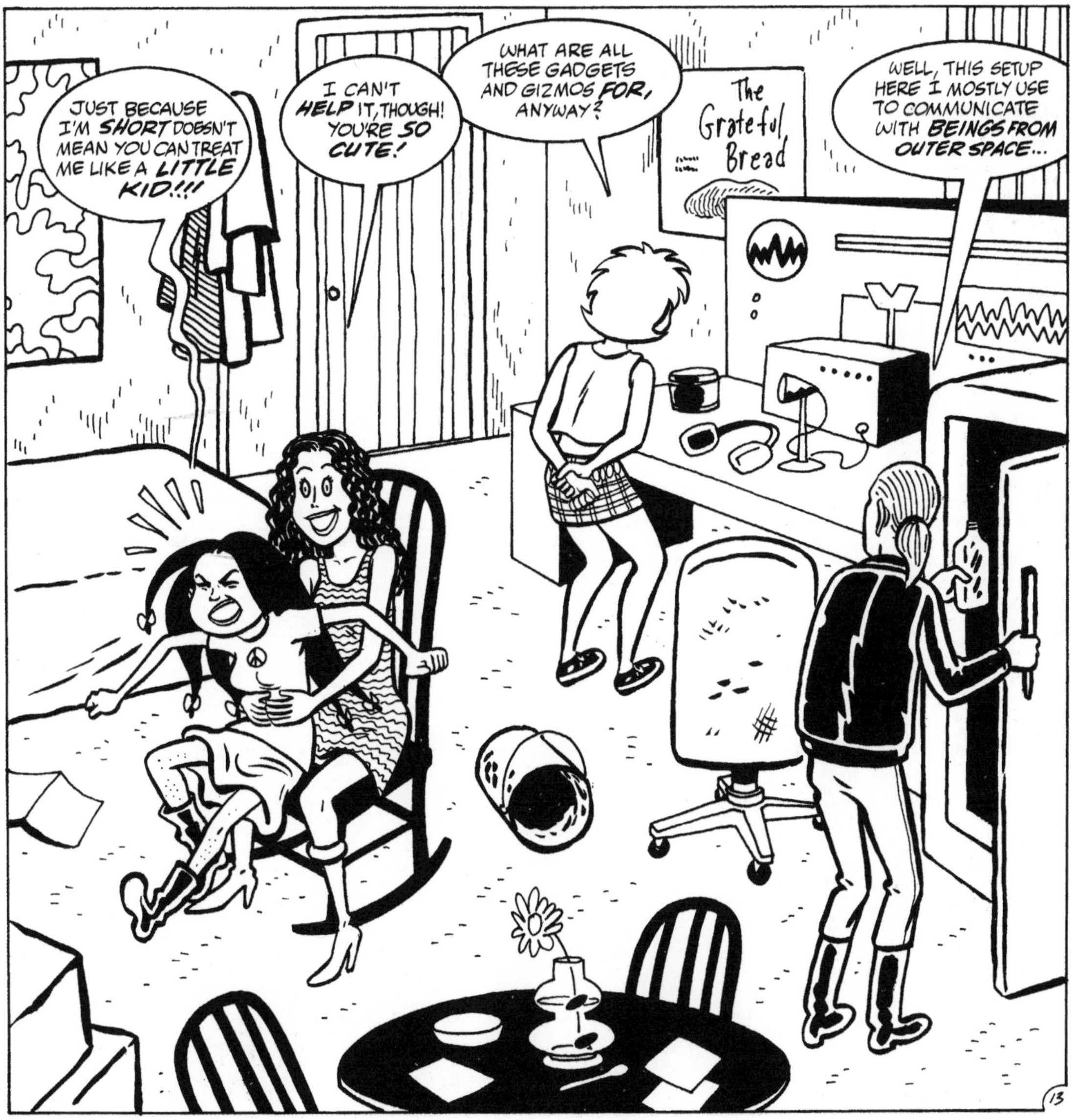
JUST BECAUSE I'M SHORT DOESN'T MEAN YOU CAN TREAT ME LIKE A LITTLE KID!!!
I CAN'T HELP IT, THOUGH! YOU'RE SO CUTE!
WHAT ARE ALL THESE GADGETS AND GIZMOS FOR, ANYWAY?
WELL, THIS SETUP HERE I MOSTLY USE TO COMMUNICATE WITH BEINGS FROM OUTER SPACE...
The Grateful Bread

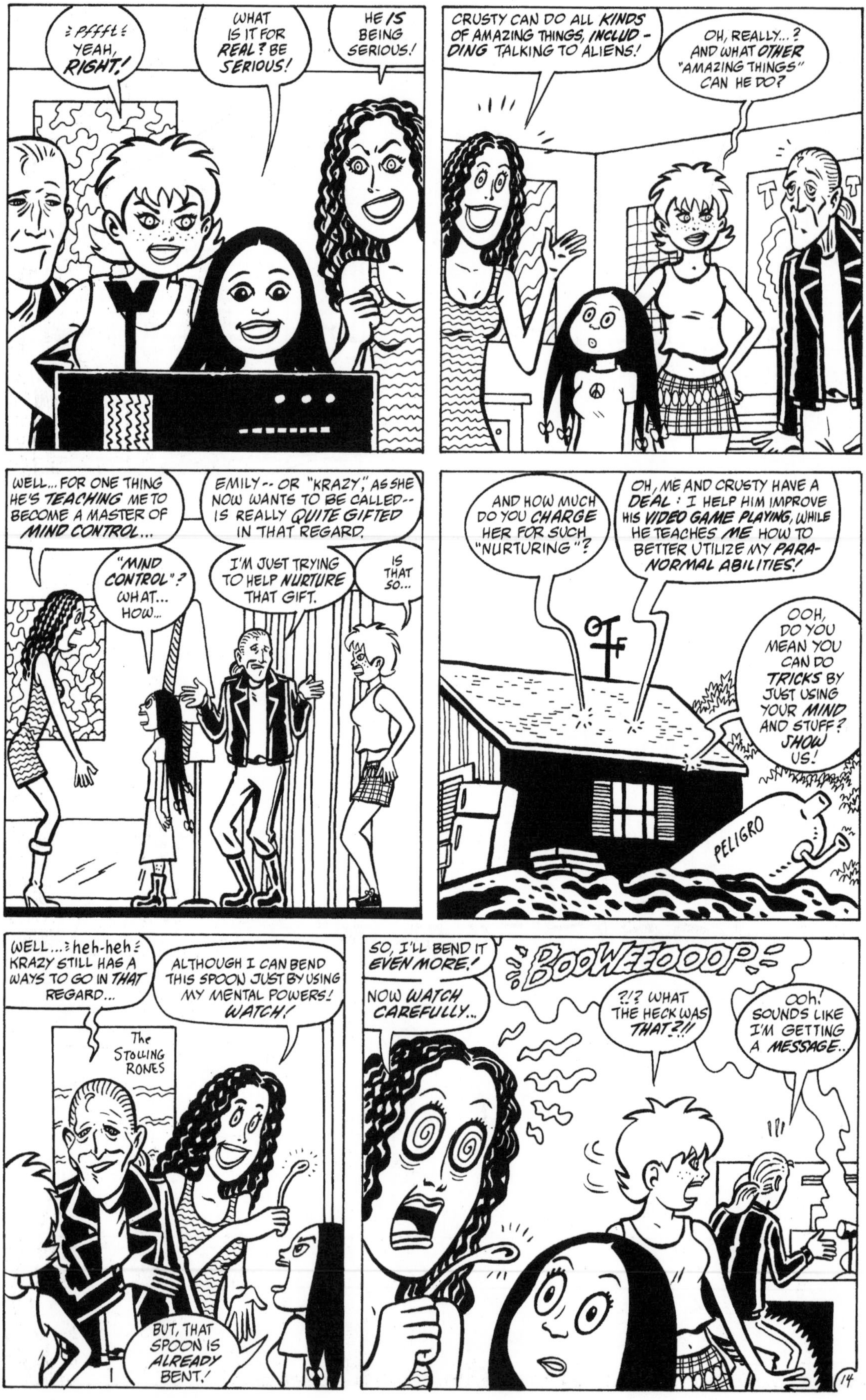

PFFFT YEAH, RIGHT!
WHAT IS IT FOR REAL? BE SERIOUS!
HE IS BEING SERIOUS!
CRUSTY CAN DO ALL KINDS OF AMAZING THINGS, INCLUDING TALKING TO ALIENS!
OH, REALLY...? AND WHAT OTHER "AMAZING THINGS" CAN HE DO?
WELL... FOR ONE THING HE'S TEACHING ME TO BECOME A MASTER OF MIND CONTROL...
"MIND CONTROL"? WHAT... HOW...
EMILY -- OR "KRAZY," AS SHE NOW WANTS TO BE CALLED -- IS REALLY QUITE GIFTED IN THAT REGARD.
I'M JUST TRYING TO HELP NURTURE THAT GIFT.
IS THAT SO...
AND HOW MUCH DO YOU CHARGE HER FOR SUCH "NURTURING"?
OH, ME AND CRUSTY HAVE A DEAL: I HELP HIM IMPROVE HIS VIDEO GAME PLAYING, WHILE HE TEACHES ME HOW TO BETTER UTILIZE MY PARANORMAL ABILITIES!
OOH, DO YOU MEAN YOU CAN DO TRICKS BY JUST USING YOUR MIND AND STUFF? SHOW US!
PELIGRO
WELL... heh-heh KRAZY STILL HAS A WAYS TO GO IN THAT REGARD...
ALTHOUGH I CAN BEND THIS SPOON JUST BY USING MY MENTAL POWERS! WATCH!
The STOLLING RONES
BUT, THAT SPOON IS ALREADY BENT!
SO, I'LL BEND IT EVEN MORE!
NOW WATCH CAREFULLY...
BOOWEEOOOP!
?!? WHAT THE HECK WAS THAT?!!
Ooh! SOUNDS LIKE I'M GETTING A MESSAGE...

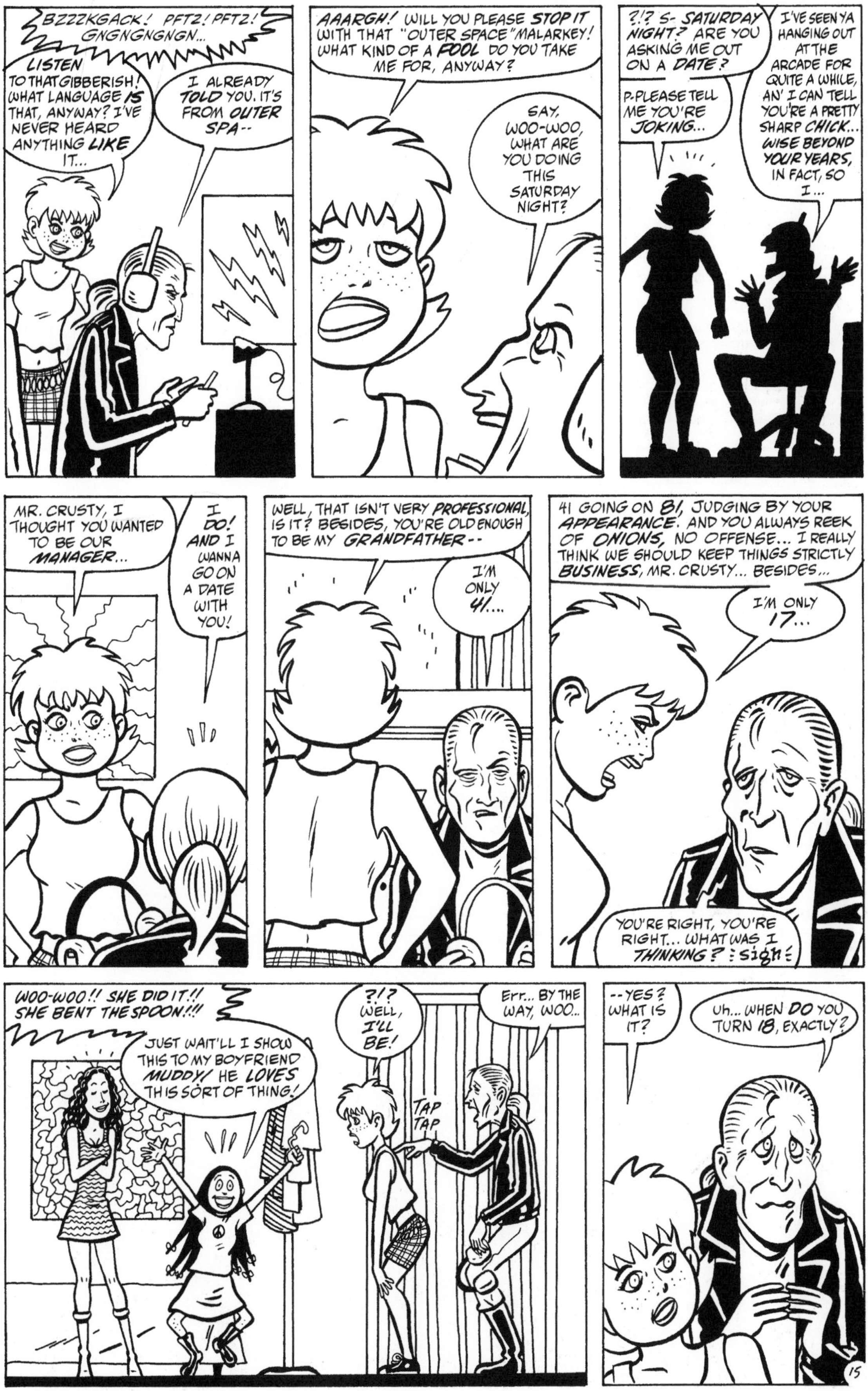
BZZZKGACK! PFTZ! PFTZ! GNGNGNGNGN...
LISTEN TO THAT GIBBERISH! WHAT LANGUAGE IS THAT, ANYWAY? I'VE NEVER HEARD ANYTHING LIKE IT...
I ALREADY TOLD YOU. IT'S FROM OUTER SPA--
AAARGH! WILL YOU PLEASE STOP IT WITH THAT "OUTER SPACE" MALARKEY! WHAT KIND OF A FOOL DO YOU TAKE ME FOR, ANYWAY?
SAY, WOO-WOO, WHAT ARE YOU DOING THIS SATURDAY NIGHT?
?!? S- SATURDAY NIGHT? ARE YOU ASKING ME OUT ON A DATE?
P-PLEASE TELL ME YOU'RE JOKING...
I'VE SEEN YA HANGING OUT AT THE ARCADE FOR QUITE A WHILE, AN' I CAN TELL YOU'RE A PRETTY SHARP CHICK... WISE BEYOND YOUR YEARS, IN FACT, SO I...
MR. CRUSTY, I THOUGHT YOU WANTED TO BE OUR MANAGER...
I DO! AND I WANNA GO ON A DATE WITH YOU!
WELL, THAT ISN'T VERY PROFESSIONAL, IS IT? BESIDES, YOU'RE OLD ENOUGH TO BE MY GRANDFATHER--
I'M ONLY 41....
41 GOING ON 81, JUDGING BY YOUR APPEARANCE. AND YOU ALWAYS REEK OF ONIONS, NO OFFENSE... I REALLY THINK WE SHOULD KEEP THINGS STRICTLY BUSINESS, MR. CRUSTY... BESIDES...
I'M ONLY 17...
YOU'RE RIGHT, YOU'RE RIGHT... WHAT WAS I THINKING? sigh
WOO-WOO!! SHE DID IT!! SHE BENT THE SPOON!!!
JUST WAIT'LL I SHOW THIS TO MY BOYFRIEND MUDDY! HE LOVES THIS SORT OF THING!
?!? WELL, I'LL BE!
Err... BY THE WAY, WOO...
TAP TAP
--YES? WHAT IS IT?
Uh... WHEN DO YOU TURN 18, EXACTLY?

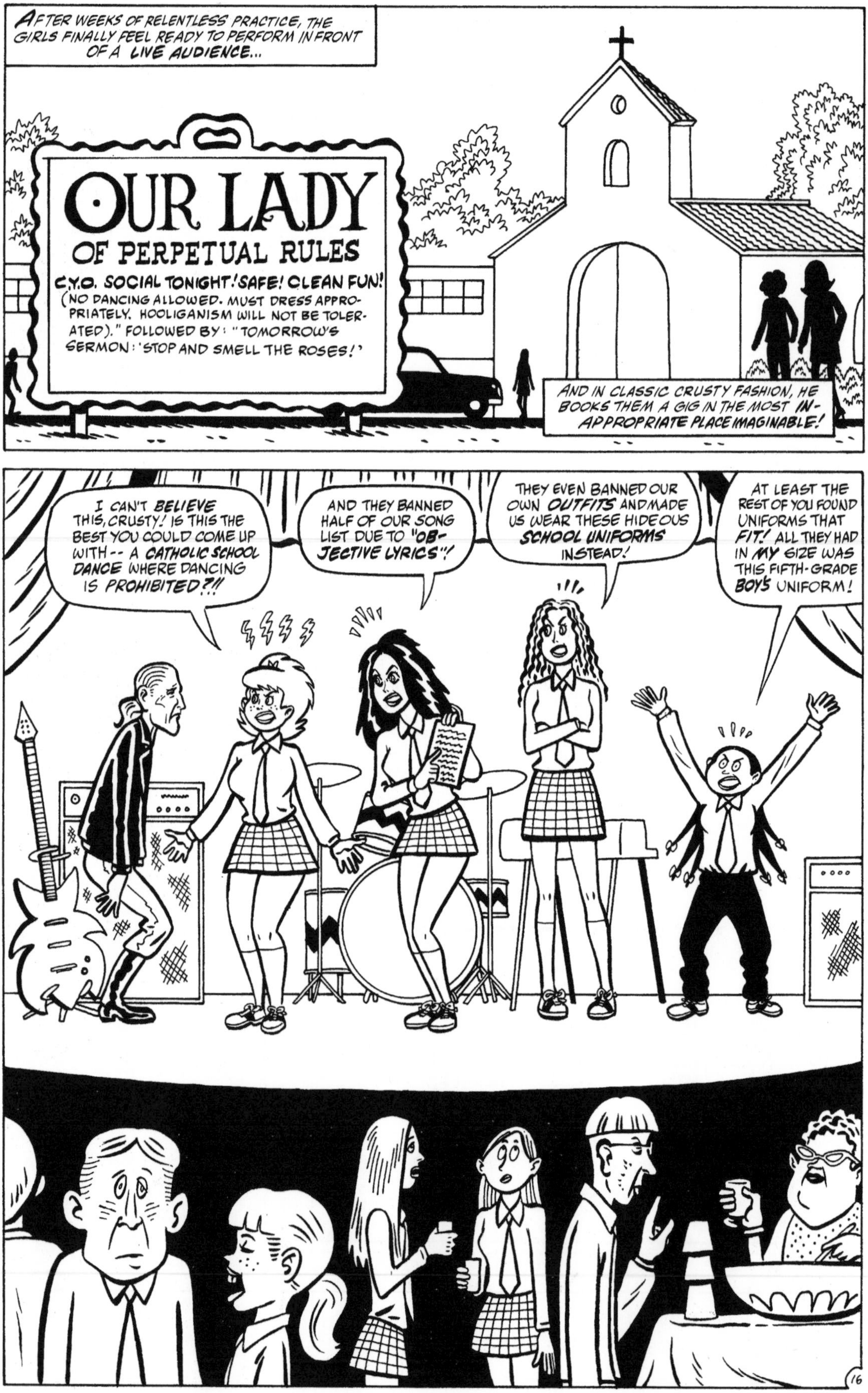
AFTER WEEKS OF RELENTLESS PRACTICE, THE GIRLS FINALLY FEEL READY TO PERFORM IN FRONT OF A LIVE AUDIENCE...
OUR LADY OF PERPETUAL RULES
C.Y.O. SOCIAL TONIGHT! SAFE! CLEAN FUN! (NO DANCING ALLOWED. MUST DRESS APPROPRIATELY. HOOLIGANISM WILL NOT BE TOLERATED)." FOLLOWED BY: "TOMORROW'S SERMON: 'STOP AND SMELL THE ROSES!'
AND IN CLASSIC CRUSTY FASHION, HE BOOKS THEM A GIG IN THE MOST INAPPROPRIATE PLACE IMAGINABLE!
I CAN'T BELIEVE THIS, CRUSTY! IS THIS THE BEST YOU COULD COME UP WITH -- A CATHOLIC SCHOOL DANCE WHERE DANCING IS PROHIBITED?!!
AND THEY BANNED HALF OF OUR SONG LIST DUE TO "OBJECTIVE LYRICS"!
THEY EVEN BANNED OUR OWN OUTFITS AND MADE US WEAR THESE HIDEOUS SCHOOL UNIFORMS INSTEAD!
AT LEAST THE REST OF YOU FOUND UNIFORMS THAT FIT! ALL THEY HAD IN MY SIZE WAS THIS FIFTH-GRADE BOY'S UNIFORM!

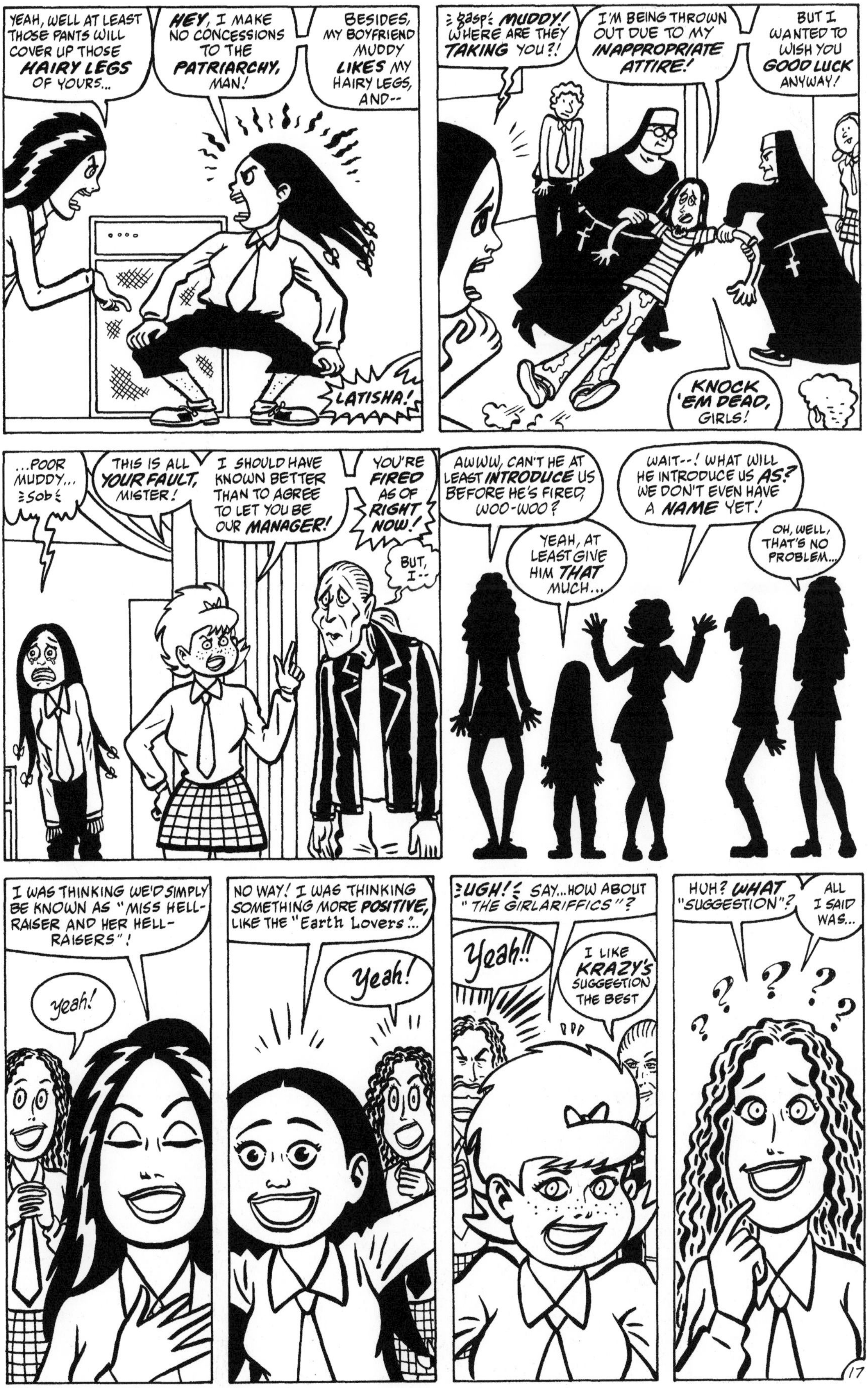
YEAH, WELL AT LEAST THOSE PANTS WILL COVER UP THOSE HAIRY LEGS OF YOURS...
HEY, I MAKE NO CONCESSIONS TO THE PATRIARCHY, MAN!
BESIDES, MY BOYFRIEND MUDDY LIKES MY HAIRY LEGS, AND--
LATISHA!
gasp MUDDY! WHERE ARE THEY TAKING YOU?!
I'M BEING THROWN OUT DUE TO MY INAPPROPRIATE ATTIRE!
BUT I WANTED TO WISH YOU GOOD LUCK ANYWAY!
KNOCK 'EM DEAD, GIRLS!
...POOR MUDDY... Sob
THIS IS ALL YOUR FAULT, MISTER!
I SHOULD HAVE KNOWN BETTER THAN TO AGREE TO LET YOU BE OUR MANAGER!
YOU'RE FIRED AS OF RIGHT NOW!
BUT, I--
AWWW, CAN'T HE AT LEAST INTRODUCE US BEFORE HE'S FIRED, WOO-WOO?
YEAH, AT LEAST GIVE HIM THAT MUCH...
WAIT--! WHAT WILL HE INTRODUCE US AS? WE DON'T EVEN HAVE A NAME YET!
OH, WELL, THAT'S NO PROBLEM...
I WAS THINKING WE'D SIMPLY BE KNOWN AS "MISS HELL-RAISER AND HER HELL-RAISERS"!
yeah!
NO WAY! I WAS THINKING SOMETHING MORE POSITIVE, LIKE THE "Earth Lovers"...
Yeah!
UGH! SAY...HOW ABOUT "THE GIRLARIFFICS"?
Yeah!!
I LIKE KRAZY'S SUGGESTION THE BEST
HUH? WHAT "SUGGESTION"?
ALL I SAID WAS...
? ? ? ? ?

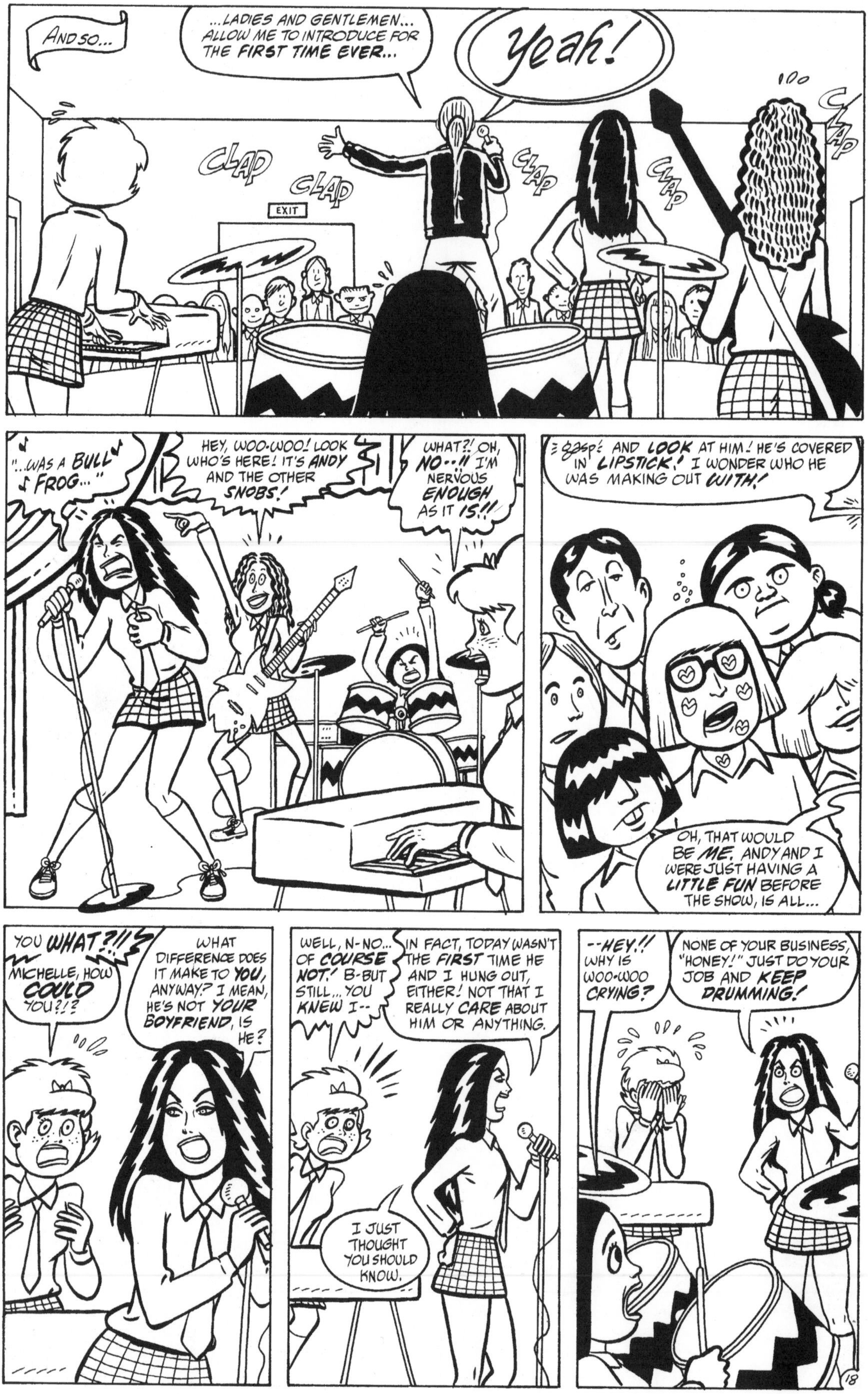
AND SO...
...LADIES AND GENTLEMEN... ALLOW ME TO INTRODUCE FOR THE FIRST TIME EVER...
yeah!
CLAP
CLAP
EXIT
CLAP
CLAP
CLAP
"...WAS A BULL FROG..."
HEY, WOO-WOO! LOOK WHO'S HERE! IT'S ANDY AND THE OTHER SNOBS!
WHAT?! OH, NO--!! I'M NERVOUS ENOUGH AS IT IS!!
gasp! AND LOOK AT HIM! HE'S COVERED IN LIPSTICK! I WONDER WHO HE WAS MAKING OUT WITH!
OH, THAT WOULD BE ME. ANDY AND I WERE JUST HAVING A LITTLE FUN BEFORE THE SHOW, IS ALL...
YOU WHAT?!!
MICHELLE, HOW COULD YOU?!?
WHAT DIFFERENCE DOES IT MAKE TO YOU, ANYWAY? I MEAN, HE'S NOT YOUR BOYFRIEND, IS HE?
WELL, N-NO... OF COURSE NOT! B-BUT STILL... YOU KNEW I--
IN FACT, TODAY WASN'T THE FIRST TIME HE AND I HUNG OUT, EITHER! NOT THAT I REALLY CARE ABOUT HIM OR ANYTHING.
I JUST THOUGHT YOU SHOULD KNOW.
--HEY!! WHY IS WOO-WOO CRYING?
NONE OF YOUR BUSINESS, "HONEY!" JUST DO YOUR JOB AND KEEP DRUMMING!

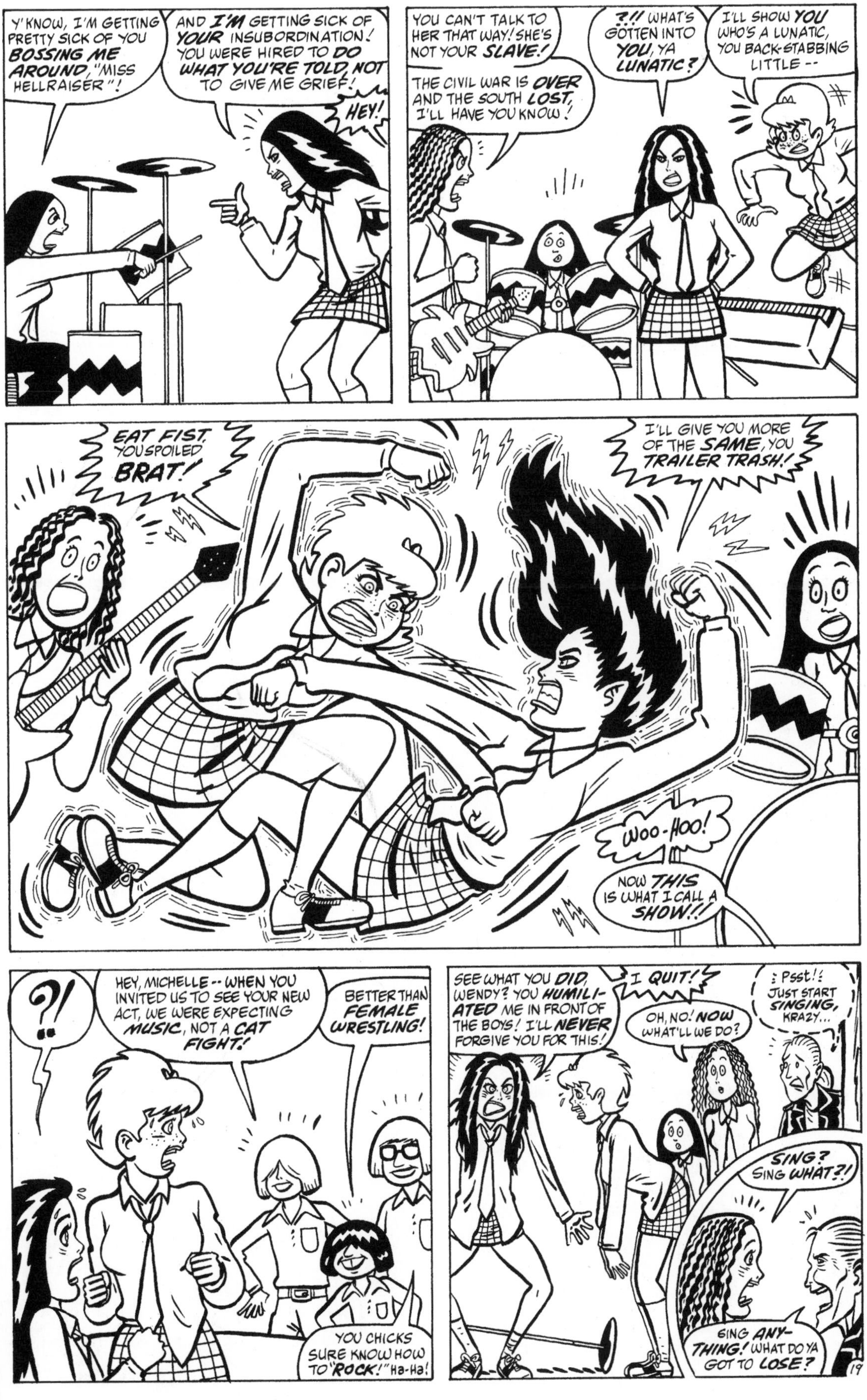

Y'KNOW, I'M GETTING PRETTY SICK OF YOU BOSSING ME AROUND, "MISS HELLRAISER"!
AND I'M GETTING SICK OF YOUR INSUBORDINATION! YOU WERE HIRED TO DO WHAT YOU'RE TOLD, NOT TO GIVE ME GRIEF!
HEY!
YOU CAN'T TALK TO HER THAT WAY! SHE'S NOT YOUR SLAVE!
THE CIVIL WAR IS OVER AND THE SOUTH LOST, I'LL HAVE YOU KNOW!
?!! WHAT'S GOTTEN INTO YOU, YA LUNATIC?
I'LL SHOW YOU WHO'S A LUNATIC, YOU BACK-STABBING LITTLE --
EAT FIST, YOU SPOILED BRAT!
I'LL GIVE YOU MORE OF THE SAME, YOU TRAILER TRASH!
WOO-HOO!
NOW THIS IS WHAT I CALL A SHOW!!
?!
HEY, MICHELLE -- WHEN YOU INVITED US TO SEE YOUR NEW ACT, WE WERE EXPECTING MUSIC, NOT A CAT FIGHT!
BETTER THAN FEMALE WRESTLING!
YOU CHICKS SURE KNOW HOW TO "ROCK!" Ha-Ha!
SEE WHAT YOU DID, WENDY? YOU HUMILIATED ME IN FRONT OF THE BOYS! I'LL NEVER FORGIVE YOU FOR THIS!
I QUIT!
OH, NO! NOW WHAT'LL WE DO?
Psst!! JUST START SINGING, KRAZY...
SING? SING WHAT?!
SING ANYTHING! WHAT DO YA GOT TO LOSE?

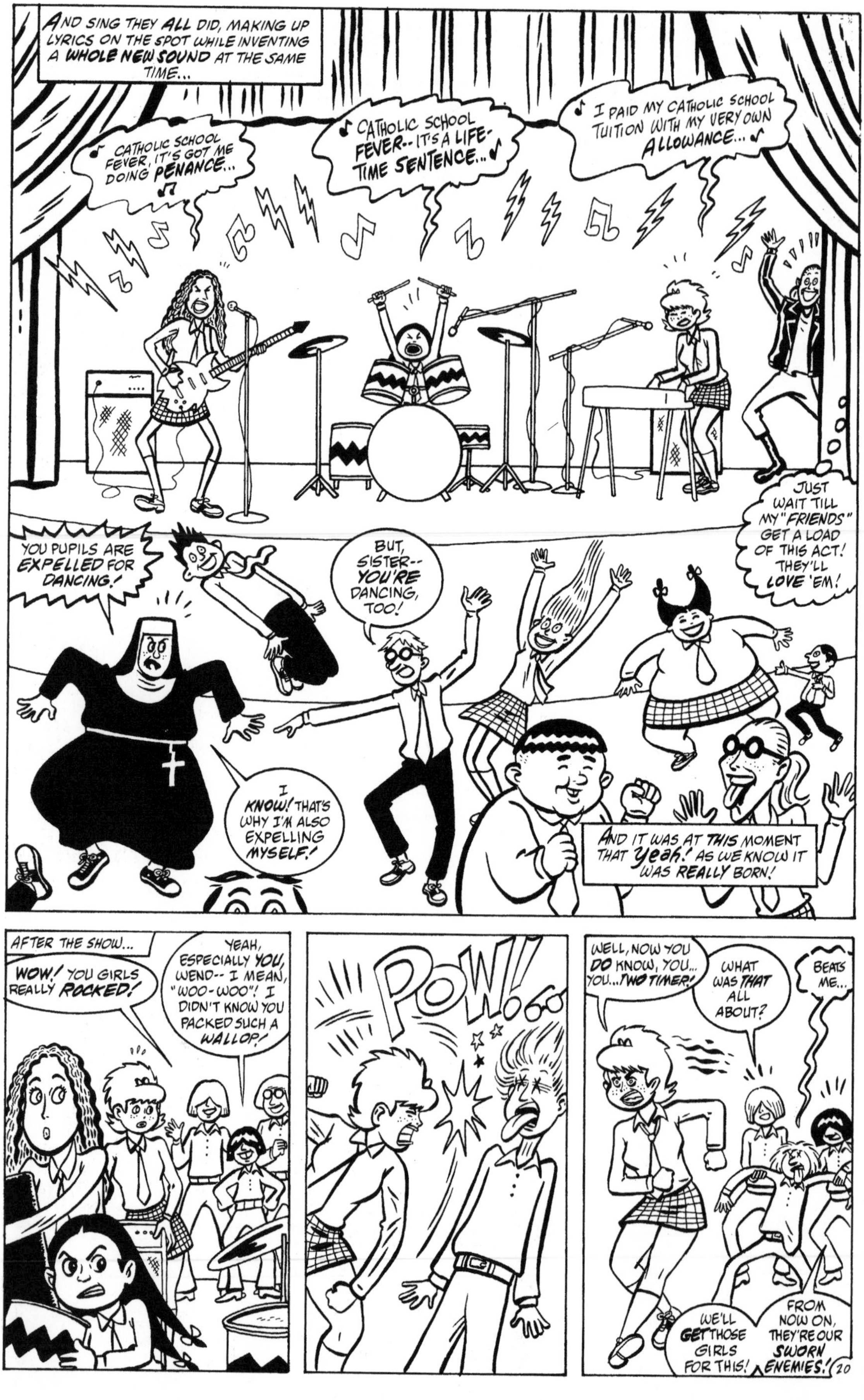
AND SING THEY ALL DID, MAKING UP LYRICS ON THE SPOT WHILE INVENTING A WHOLE NEW SOUND AT THE SAME TIME...
CATHOLIC SCHOOL FEVER, IT'S GOT ME DOING PENANCE...
CATHOLIC SCHOOL FEVER-- IT'S A LIFE-TIME SENTENCE...
I PAID MY CATHOLIC SCHOOL TUITION WITH MY VERY OWN ALLOWANCE...
YOU PUPILS ARE EXPELLED FOR DANCING!
BUT, SISTER-- YOU'RE DANCING, TOO!
JUST WAIT TILL MY "FRIENDS" GET A LOAD OF THIS ACT! THEY'LL LOVE 'EM!
I KNOW! THAT'S WHY I'M ALSO EXPELLING MYSELF!
AND IT WAS AT THIS MOMENT THAT YEAH! AS WE KNOW IT WAS REALLY BORN!
AFTER THE SHOW...
WOW! YOU GIRLS REALLY ROCKED!
YEAH, ESPECIALLY YOU, WEND-- I MEAN, "WOO-WOO"! I DIDN'T KNOW YOU PACKED SUCH A WALLOP!
POW!!
WELL, NOW YOU DO KNOW, YOU... YOU...TWO TIMER!
WHAT WAS THAT ALL ABOUT?
BEATS ME...
WE'LL GET THOSE GIRLS FOR THIS!
FROM NOW ON, THEY'RE OUR SWORN ENEMIES!

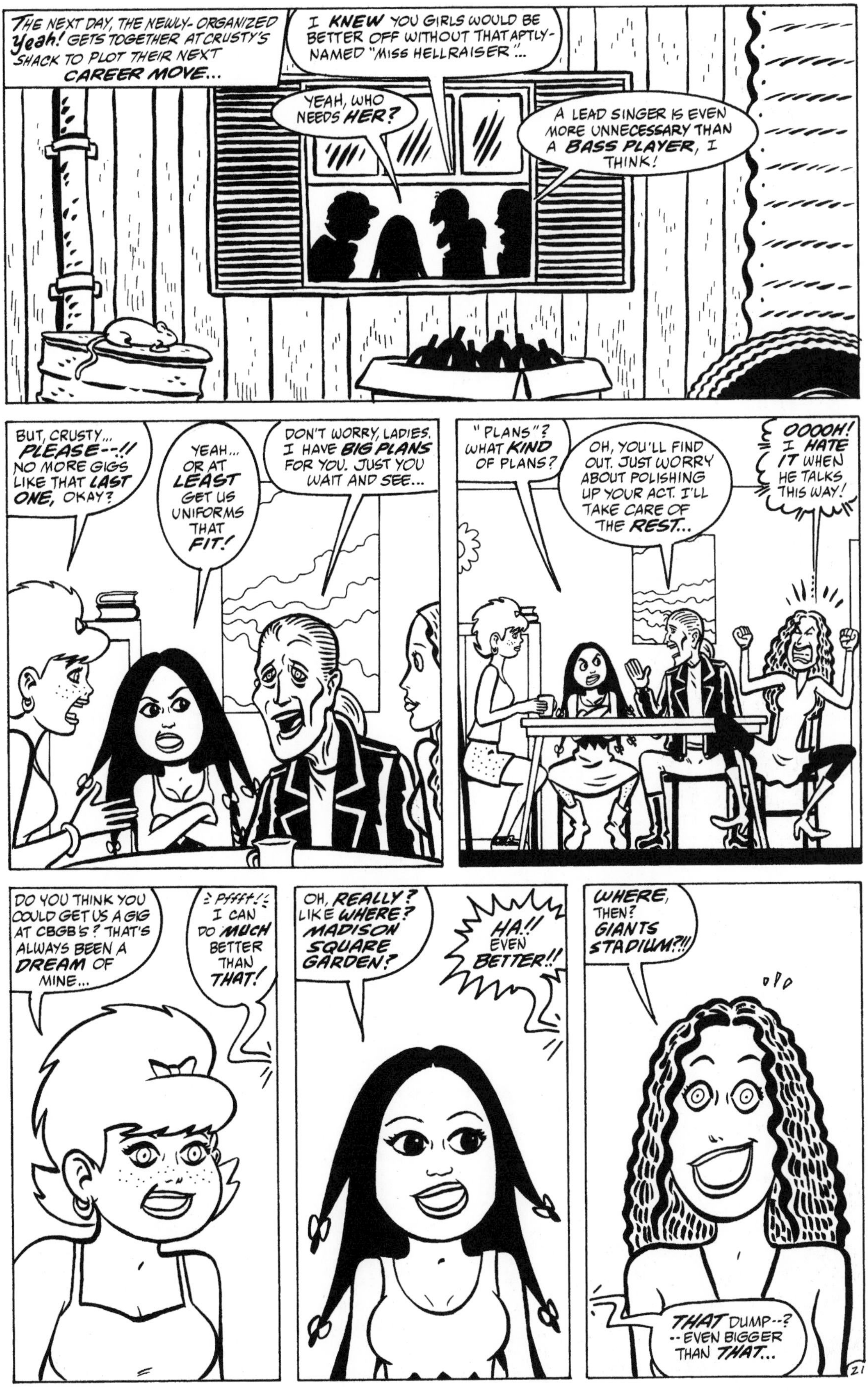
THE NEXT DAY, THE NEWLY-ORGANIZED Yeah! GETS TOGETHER AT CRUSTY'S SHACK TO PLOT THEIR NEXT CAREER MOVE...
I KNEW YOU GIRLS WOULD BE BETTER OFF WITHOUT THAT APTLY-NAMED "MISS HELLRAISER"...
YEAH, WHO NEEDS HER?
A LEAD SINGER IS EVEN MORE UNNECESSARY THAN A BASS PLAYER, I THINK!
BUT, CRUSTY... PLEASE--!! NO MORE GIGS LIKE THAT LAST ONE, OKAY?
YEAH... OR AT LEAST GET US UNIFORMS THAT FIT!
DON'T WORRY, LADIES. I HAVE BIG PLANS FOR YOU. JUST YOU WAIT AND SEE...
"PLANS"? WHAT KIND OF PLANS?
OH, YOU'LL FIND OUT. JUST WORRY ABOUT POLISHING UP YOUR ACT. I'LL TAKE CARE OF THE REST...
OOOOH! I HATE IT WHEN HE TALKS THIS WAY!
DO YOU THINK YOU COULD GET US A GIG AT CBGB'S? THAT'S ALWAYS BEEN A DREAM OF MINE...
Pfffft! I CAN DO MUCH BETTER THAN THAT!
OH, REALLY? LIKE WHERE? MADISON SQUARE GARDEN?
HA!! EVEN BETTER!!
WHERE, THEN? GIANTS STADIUM?!!
THAT DUMP--? --EVEN BIGGER THAN THAT...

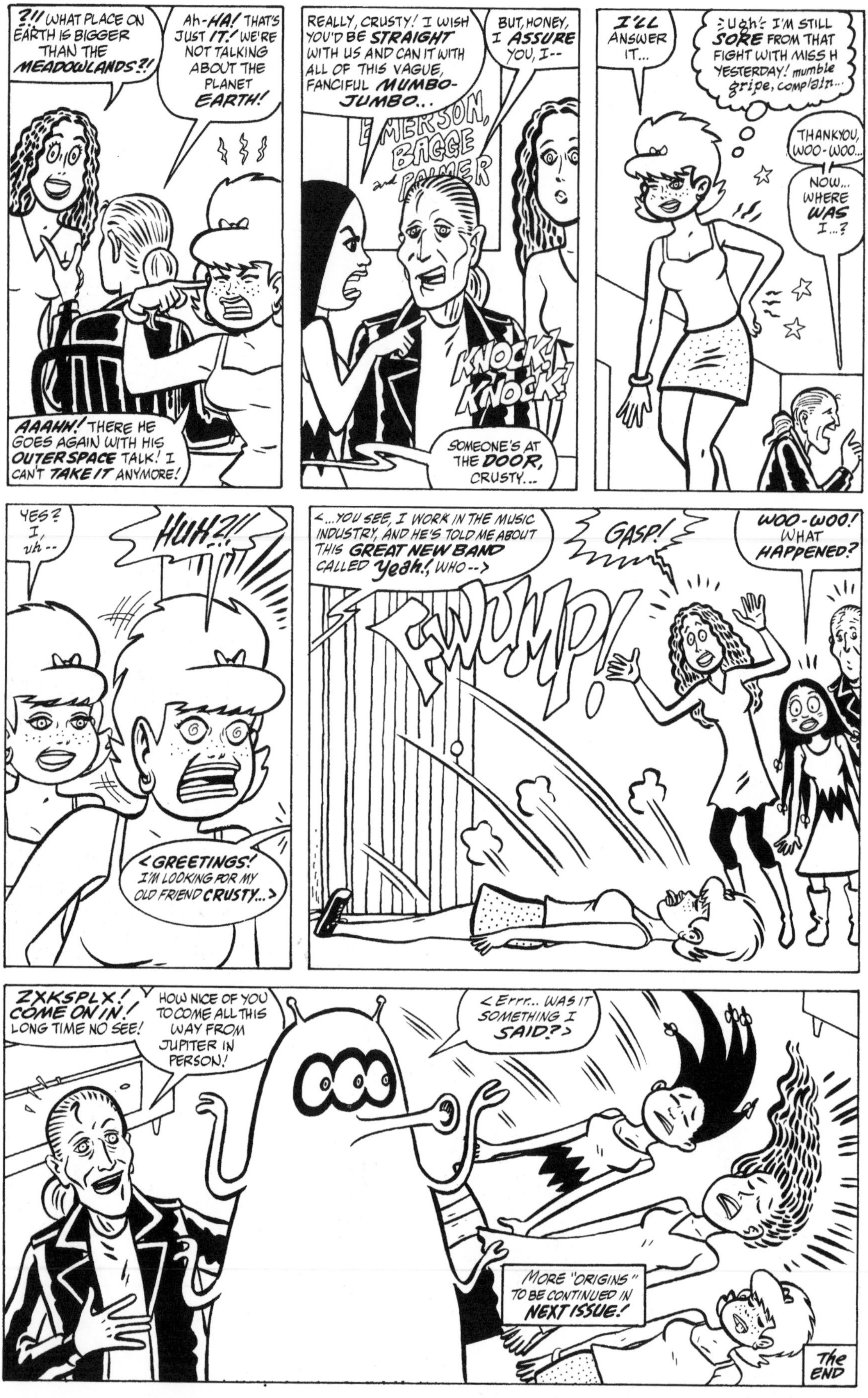
?!! WHAT PLACE ON EARTH IS BIGGER THAN THE MEADOWLANDS?!
Ah-HA! THAT'S JUST IT! WE'RE NOT TALKING ABOUT THE PLANET EARTH!
AAAHH! THERE HE GOES AGAIN WITH HIS OUTERSPACE TALK! I CAN'T TAKE IT ANYMORE!
REALLY, CRUSTY! I WISH YOU'D BE STRAIGHT WITH US AND CAN IT WITH ALL OF THIS VAGUE, FANCIFUL MUMBO-JUMBO...
BUT, HONEY, I ASSURE YOU, I--
EMERSON, BAGGE and PALMER
KNOCK, KNOCK!
SOMEONE'S AT THE DOOR, CRUSTY...
I'LL ANSWER IT...
Ugh! I'M STILL SORE FROM THAT FIGHT WITH MISS H YESTERDAY! mumble gripe, complain...
THANKYOU, WOO-WOO...
NOW... WHERE WAS I...?
YES? I, uh--
HUH?!!
<GREETINGS! I'M LOOKING FOR MY OLD FRIEND CRUSTY...>
<...YOU SEE, I WORK IN THE MUSIC INDUSTRY, AND HE'S TOLD ME ABOUT THIS GREAT NEW BAND CALLED Yeah!, WHO-->
FWUMP!
GASP!
WOO-WOO! WHAT HAPPENED?
ZXKSPLX! COME ON IN! LONG TIME NO SEE!
HOW NICE OF YOU TO COME ALL THIS WAY FROM JUPITER IN PERSON!
<Errr... WAS IT SOMETHING I SAID?>
MORE "ORIGINS" TO BE CONTINUED IN NEXT ISSUE!
The END

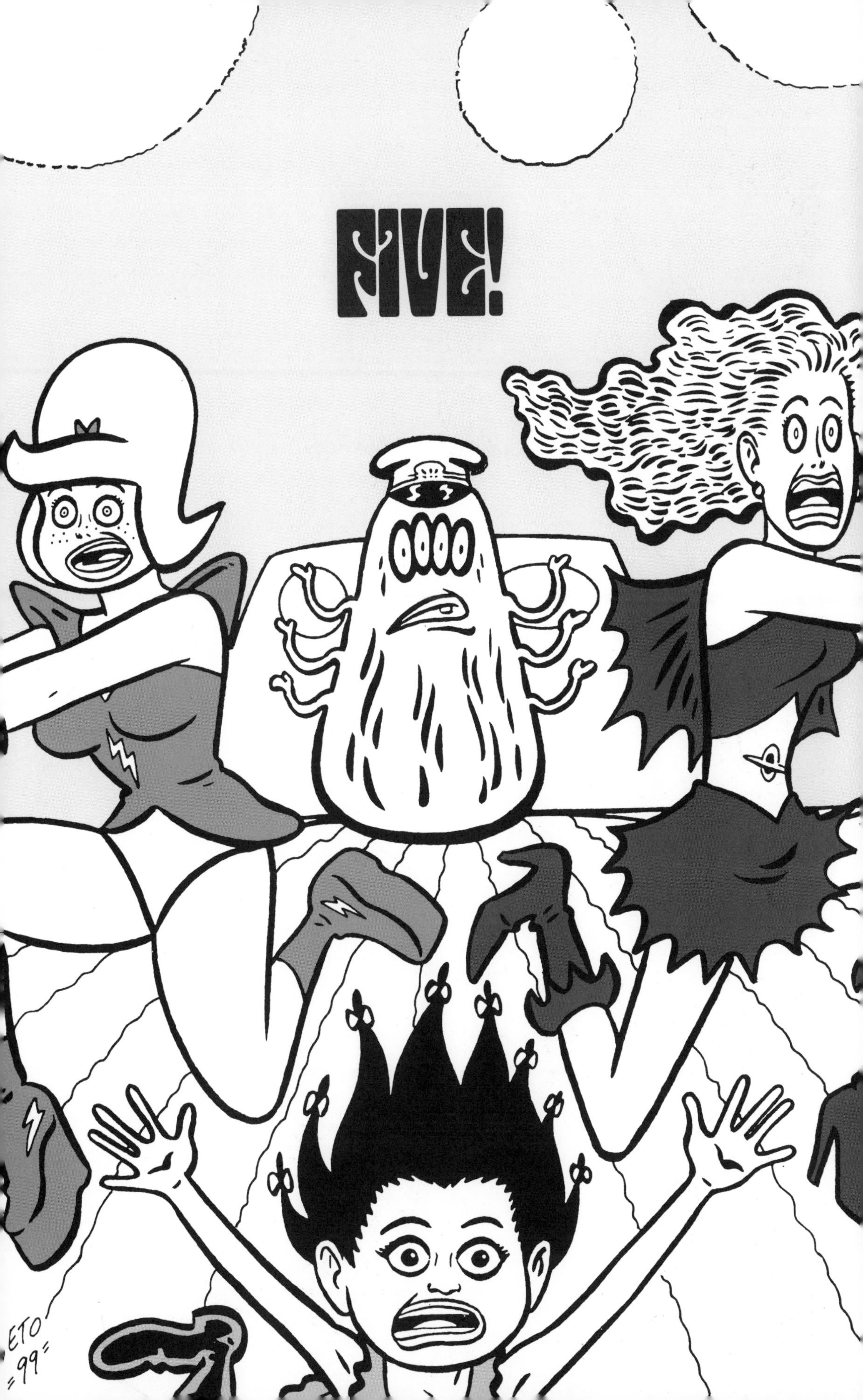
FIVE!
ETO
99

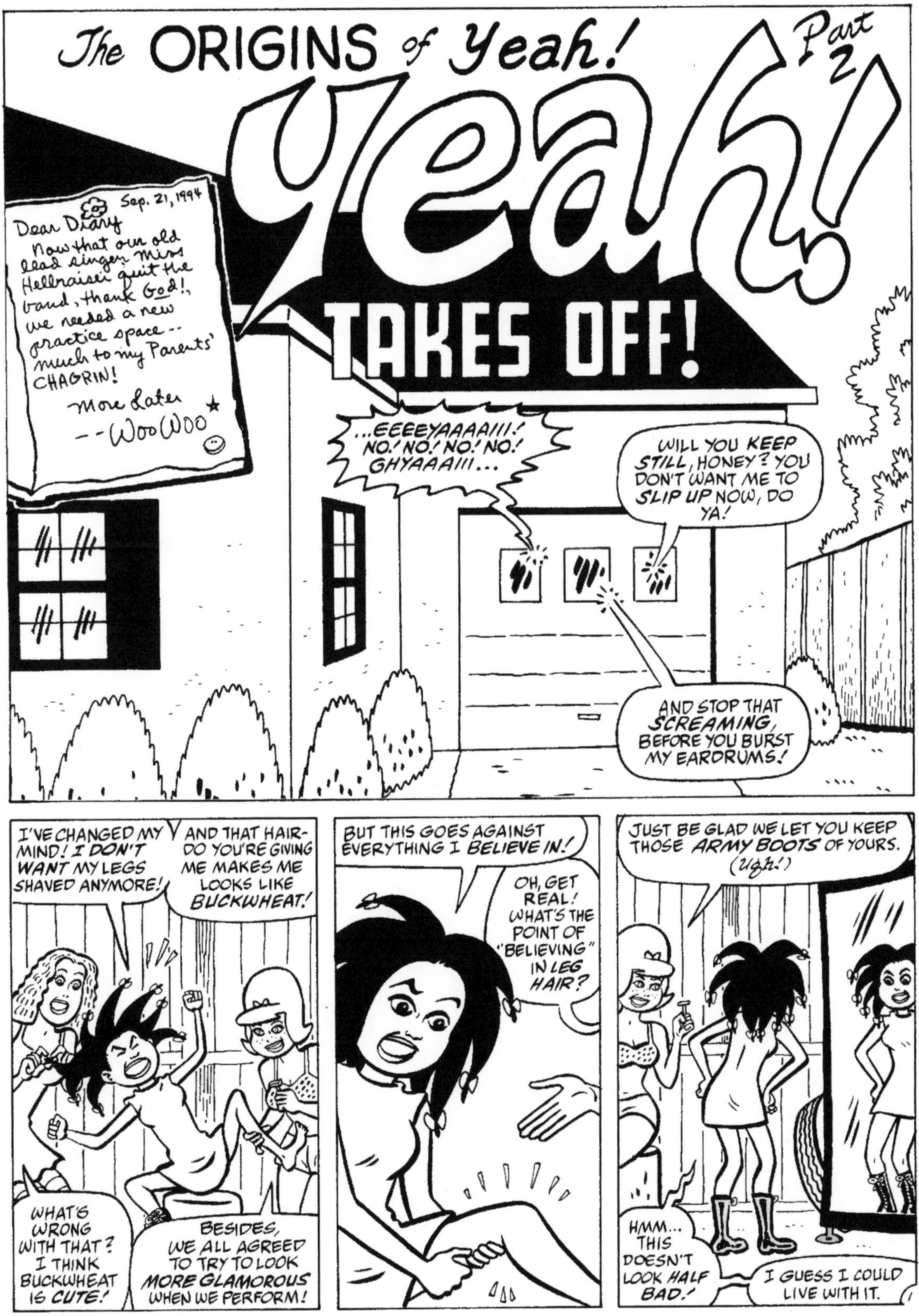
The ORIGINS of Yeah! Part 2
Yeah! TAKES OFF!
Sep. 21, 1994 Dear Diary Now that our old lead singer, Miss Hellraiser quit the band, thank God!, we needed a new practice space -- much to my Parents' CHAGRIN! More Later --WooWoo
...EEEEYAAAAIII! NO! NO! NO! NO! GHYAAAIII...
WILL YOU KEEP STILL, HONEY? YOU DON'T WANT ME TO SLIP UP NOW, DO YA!
AND STOP THAT SCREAMING, BEFORE YOU BURST MY EARDRUMS!
I'VE CHANGED MY MIND! I DON'T WANT MY LEGS SHAVED ANYMORE!
AND THAT HAIR-DO YOU'RE GIVING ME MAKES ME LOOKS LIKE BUCKWHEAT!
WHAT'S WRONG WITH THAT? I THINK BUCKWHEAT IS CUTE!
BESIDES, WE ALL AGREED TO TRY TO LOOK MORE GLAMOROUS WHEN WE PERFORM!
BUT THIS GOES AGAINST EVERYTHING I BELIEVE IN!
OH, GET REAL! WHAT'S THE POINT OF "BELIEVING" IN LEG HAIR?
JUST BE GLAD WE LET YOU KEEP THOSE ARMY BOOTS OF YOURS. (Ugh!)
HMM... THIS DOESN'T LOOK HALF BAD!
I GUESS I COULD LIVE WITH IT.

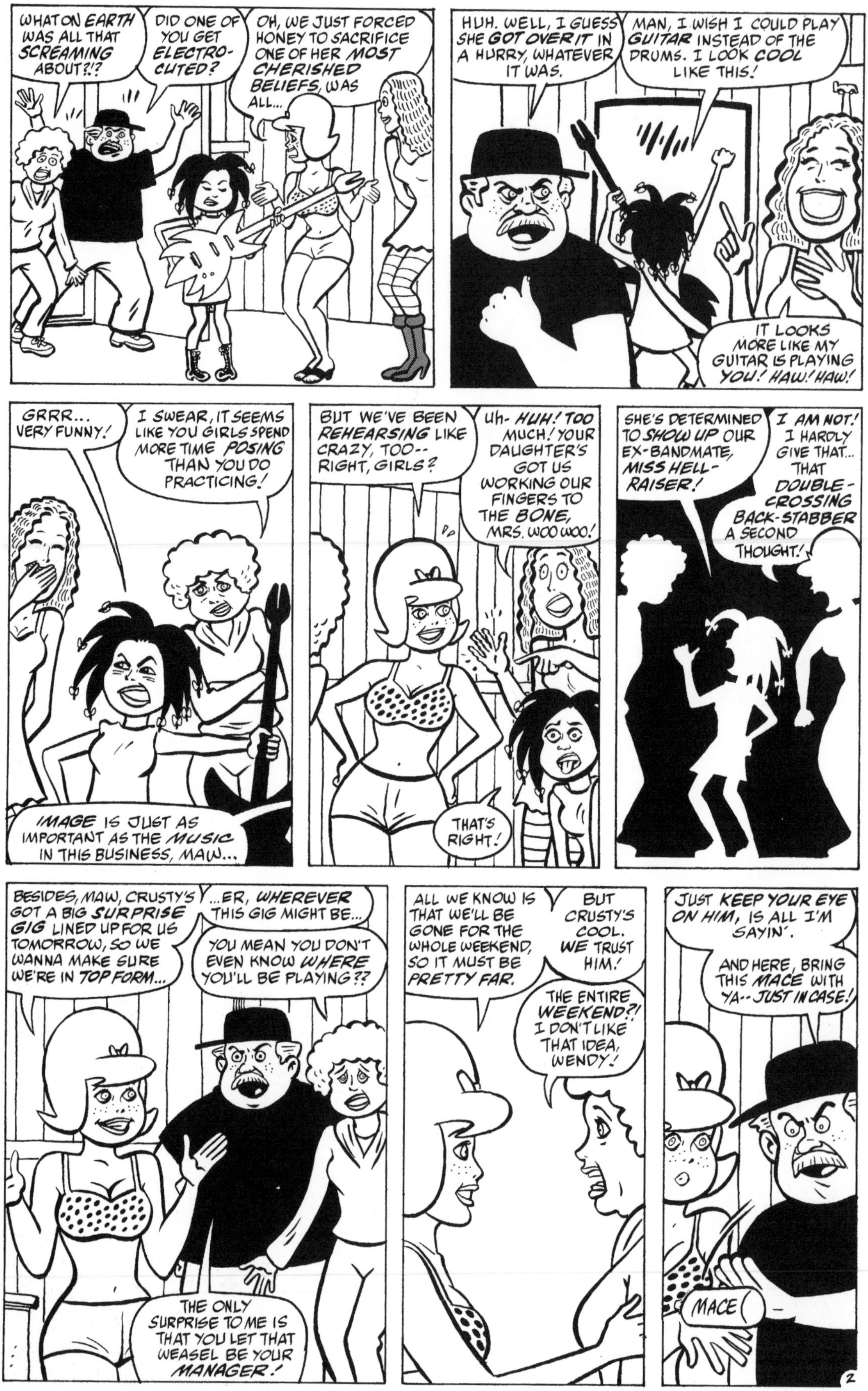
WHAT ON EARTH WAS ALL THAT SCREAMING ABOUT?!?
DID ONE OF YOU GET ELECTRO-CUTED?
OH, WE JUST FORCED HONEY TO SACRIFICE ONE OF HER MOST CHERISHED BELIEFS, WAS ALL...
HUH. WELL, I GUESS SHE GOT OVER IT IN A HURRY, WHATEVER IT WAS.
MAN, I WISH I COULD PLAY GUITAR INSTEAD OF THE DRUMS. I LOOK COOL LIKE THIS!
IT LOOKS MORE LIKE MY GUITAR IS PLAYING YOU! HAW! HAW!
GRRR... VERY FUNNY!
I SWEAR, IT SEEMS LIKE YOU GIRLS SPEND MORE TIME POSING THAN YOU DO PRACTICING!
IMAGE IS JUST AS IMPORTANT AS THE MUSIC IN THIS BUSINESS, MAW...
BUT WE'VE BEEN REHEARSING LIKE CRAZY, TOO-- RIGHT, GIRLS?
Uh-HUH! TOO MUCH! YOUR DAUGHTER'S GOT US WORKING OUR FINGERS TO THE BONE, MRS. WOO WOO!
THAT'S RIGHT!
SHE'S DETERMINED TO SHOW UP OUR EX-BANDMATE, MISS HELL-RAISER!
I AM NOT! I HARDLY GIVE THAT... THAT DOUBLE-CROSSING BACK-STABBER A SECOND THOUGHT!
BESIDES, MAW, CRUSTY'S GOT A BIG SURPRISE GIG LINED UP FOR US TOMORROW, SO WE WANNA MAKE SURE WE'RE IN TOP FORM...
...ER, WHEREVER THIS GIG MIGHT BE...
YOU MEAN YOU DON'T EVEN KNOW WHERE YOU'LL BE PLAYING??
THE ONLY SURPRISE TO ME IS THAT YOU LET THAT WEASEL BE YOUR MANAGER!
ALL WE KNOW IS THAT WE'LL BE GONE FOR THE WHOLE WEEKEND, SO IT MUST BE PRETTY FAR.
BUT CRUSTY'S COOL. WE TRUST HIM!
THE ENTIRE WEEKEND?! I DON'T LIKE THAT IDEA, WENDY!
JUST KEEP YOUR EYE ON HIM, IS ALL I'M SAYIN'.
AND HERE, BRING THIS MACE WITH YA-- JUST IN CASE!
MACE

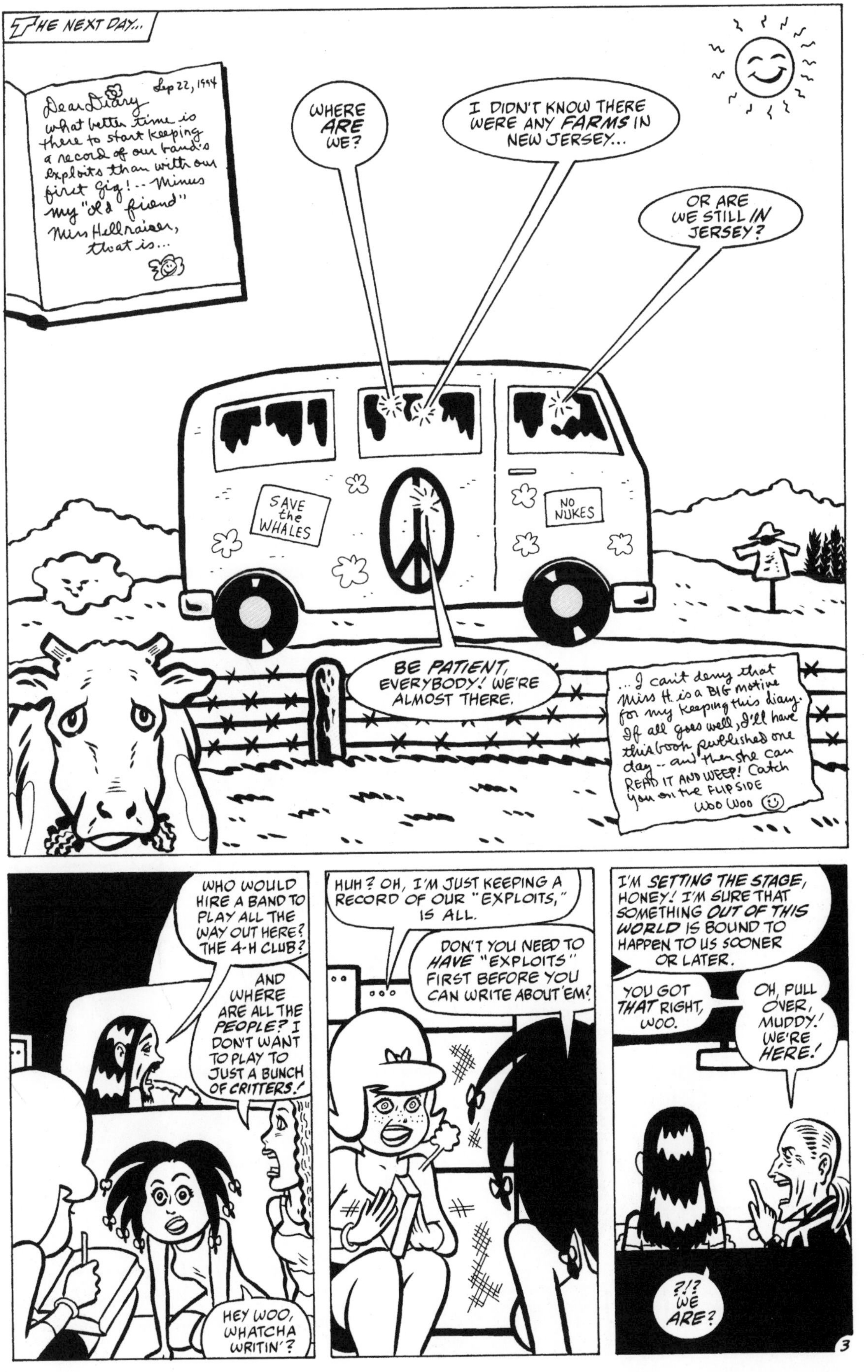
THE NEXT DAY...
Sep 22, 1994
Dear Diary
what better time is there to start keeping a record of our band's exploits than with our first gig! -- Minus my "old friend" Miss Hellraiser, that is...
WHERE ARE WE?
I DIDN'T KNOW THERE WERE ANY FARMS IN NEW JERSEY...
OR ARE WE STILL IN JERSEY?
SAVE the WHALES
NO NUKES
BE PATIENT, EVERYBODY! WE'RE ALMOST THERE.
...I can't deny that Miss H. is a BIG motive for my keeping this diary. If all goes well, I'll have this book published one day -- and then she can READ IT AND WEEP! Catch you on the FLIP SIDE
Woo Woo
WHO WOULD HIRE A BAND TO PLAY ALL THE WAY OUT HERE? THE 4-H CLUB?
AND WHERE ARE ALL THE PEOPLE? I DON'T WANT TO PLAY TO JUST A BUNCH OF CRITTERS!
HEY WOO, WHATCHA WRITIN'?
HUH? OH, I'M JUST KEEPING A RECORD OF OUR "EXPLOITS," IS ALL.
DON'T YOU NEED TO HAVE "EXPLOITS" FIRST BEFORE YOU CAN WRITE ABOUT 'EM?
I'M SETTING THE STAGE, HONEY! I'M SURE THAT SOMETHING OUT OF THIS WORLD IS BOUND TO HAPPEN TO US SOONER OR LATER.
YOU GOT THAT RIGHT, WOO.
OH, PULL OVER, MUDDY! WE'RE HERE!
?!? WE ARE?

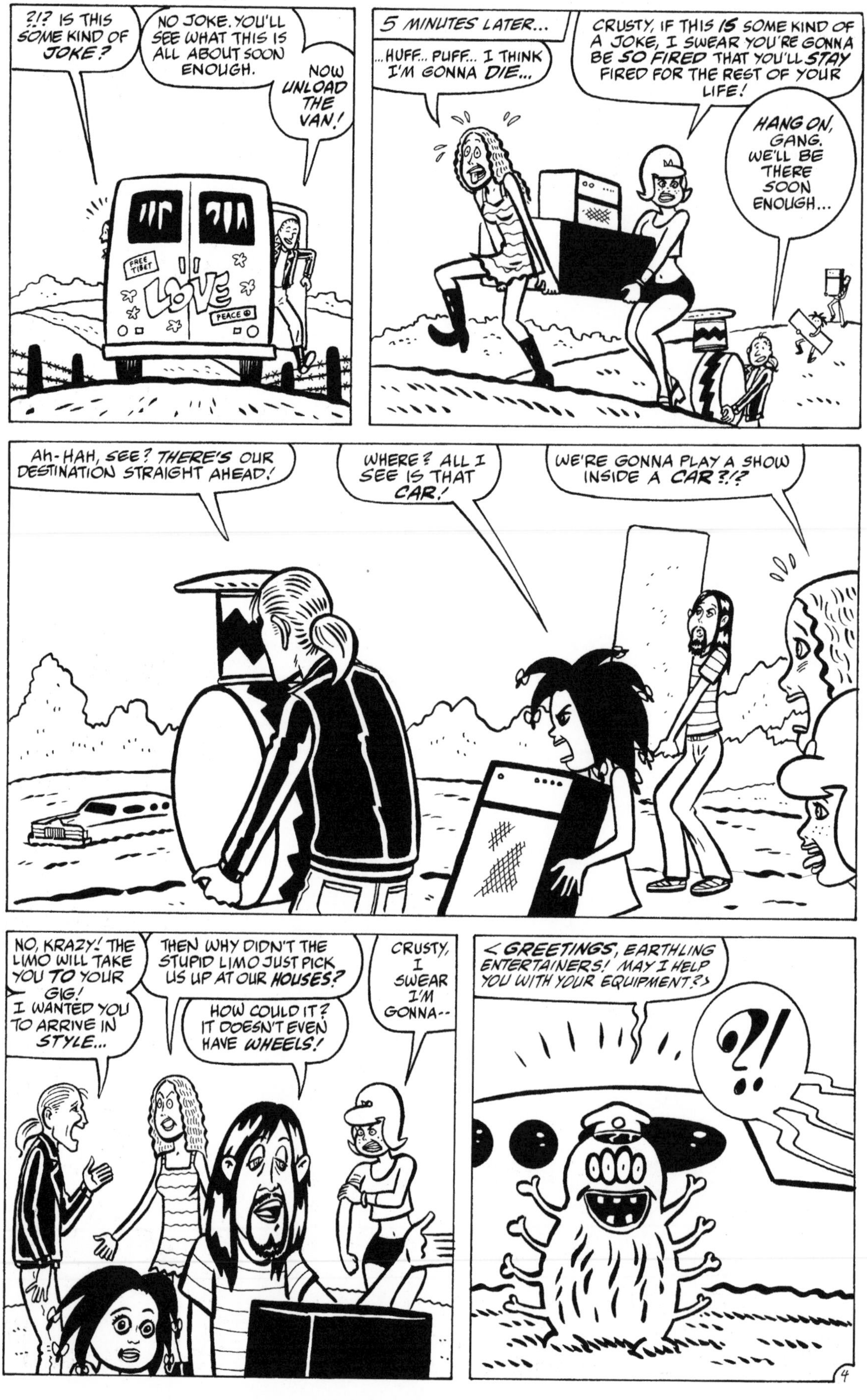
?!? IS THIS SOME KIND OF JOKE?
NO JOKE. YOU'LL SEE WHAT THIS IS ALL ABOUT SOON ENOUGH.
NOW UNLOAD THE VAN!
FREE TIBET
LOVE
PEACE
5 MINUTES LATER...
...HUFF... PUFF... I THINK I'M GONNA DIE...
CRUSTY, IF THIS IS SOME KIND OF A JOKE, I SWEAR YOU'RE GONNA BE SO FIRED THAT YOU'LL STAY FIRED FOR THE REST OF YOUR LIFE!
HANG ON, GANG. WE'LL BE THERE SOON ENOUGH...
Ah-HAH, SEE? THERE'S OUR DESTINATION STRAIGHT AHEAD!
WHERE? ALL I SEE IS THAT CAR!
WE'RE GONNA PLAY A SHOW INSIDE A CAR?!?
NO, KRAZY! THE LIMO WILL TAKE YOU TO YOUR GIG! I WANTED YOU TO ARRIVE IN STYLE...
THEN WHY DIDN'T THE STUPID LIMO JUST PICK US UP AT OUR HOUSES?
HOW COULD IT? IT DOESN'T EVEN HAVE WHEELS!
CRUSTY, I SWEAR I'M GONNA--
<GREETINGS, EARTHLING ENTERTAINERS! MAY I HELP YOU WITH YOUR EQUIPMENT?>
?!

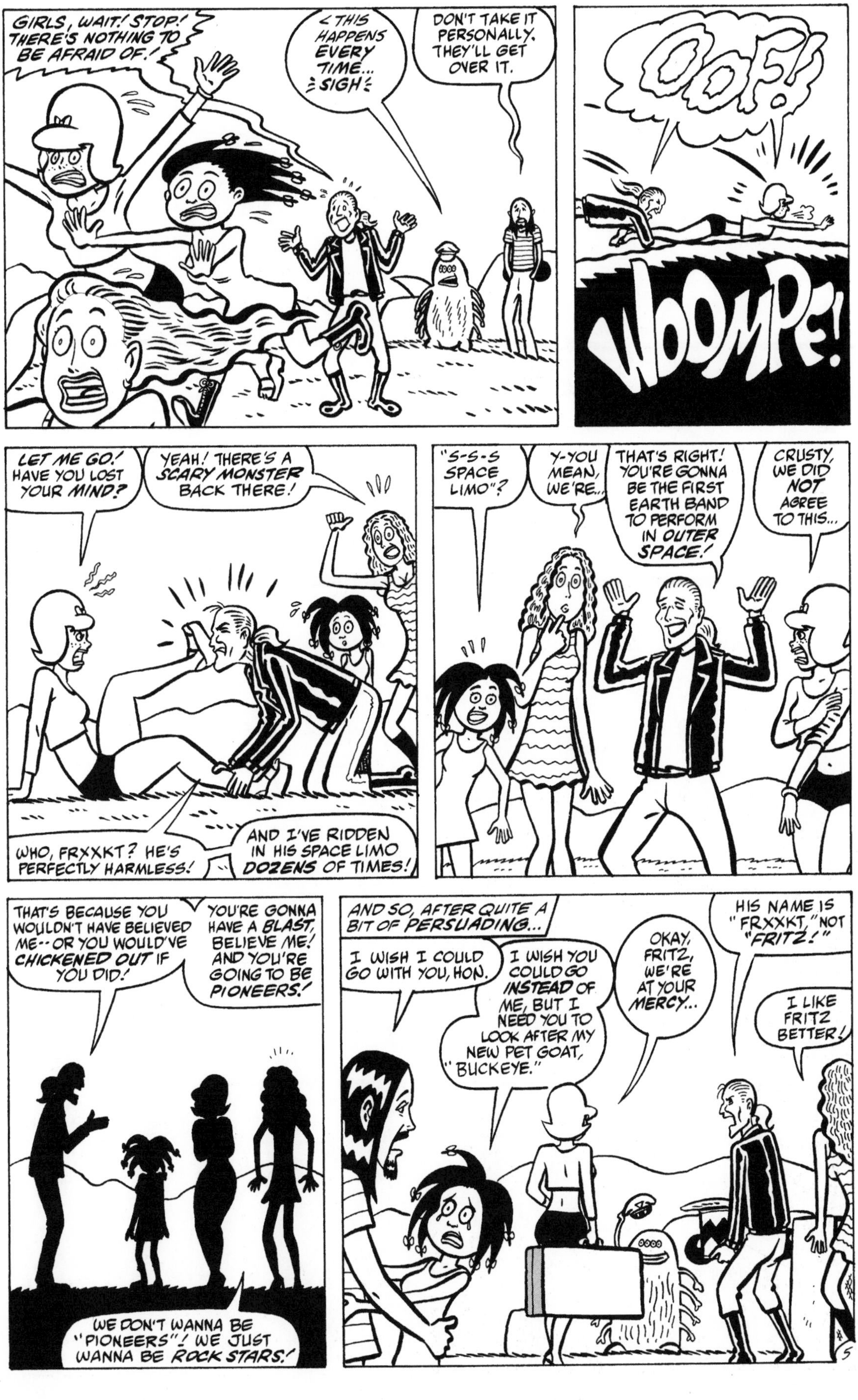
GIRLS, WAIT! STOP! THERE'S NOTHING TO BE AFRAID OF!
< THIS HAPPENS EVERY TIME... SIGH >
DON'T TAKE IT PERSONALLY. THEY'LL GET OVER IT.
OOF!!
WOOMPF!
LET ME GO! HAVE YOU LOST YOUR MIND?
YEAH! THERE'S A SCARY MONSTER BACK THERE!
WHO, FRXXKT? HE'S PERFECTLY HARMLESS!
AND I'VE RIDDEN IN HIS SPACE LIMO DOZENS OF TIMES!
"S-S-S SPACE LIMO"?
Y-YOU MEAN, WE'RE...
THAT'S RIGHT! YOU'RE GONNA BE THE FIRST EARTH BAND TO PERFORM IN OUTER SPACE!
CRUSTY, WE DID NOT AGREE TO THIS...
THAT'S BECAUSE YOU WOULDN'T HAVE BELIEVED ME-- OR YOU WOULD'VE CHICKENED OUT IF YOU DID!
YOU'RE GONNA HAVE A BLAST, BELIEVE ME! AND YOU'RE GOING TO BE PIONEERS!
WE DON'T WANNA BE "PIONEERS"! WE JUST WANNA BE ROCK STARS!
AND SO, AFTER QUITE A BIT OF PERSUADING...
I WISH I COULD GO WITH YOU, HON.
I WISH YOU COULD GO INSTEAD OF ME, BUT I NEED YOU TO LOOK AFTER MY NEW PET GOAT, "BUCKEYE."
OKAY, FRITZ, WE'RE AT YOUR MERCY...
HIS NAME IS "FRXXKT," NOT "FRITZ!"
I LIKE FRITZ BETTER!
5

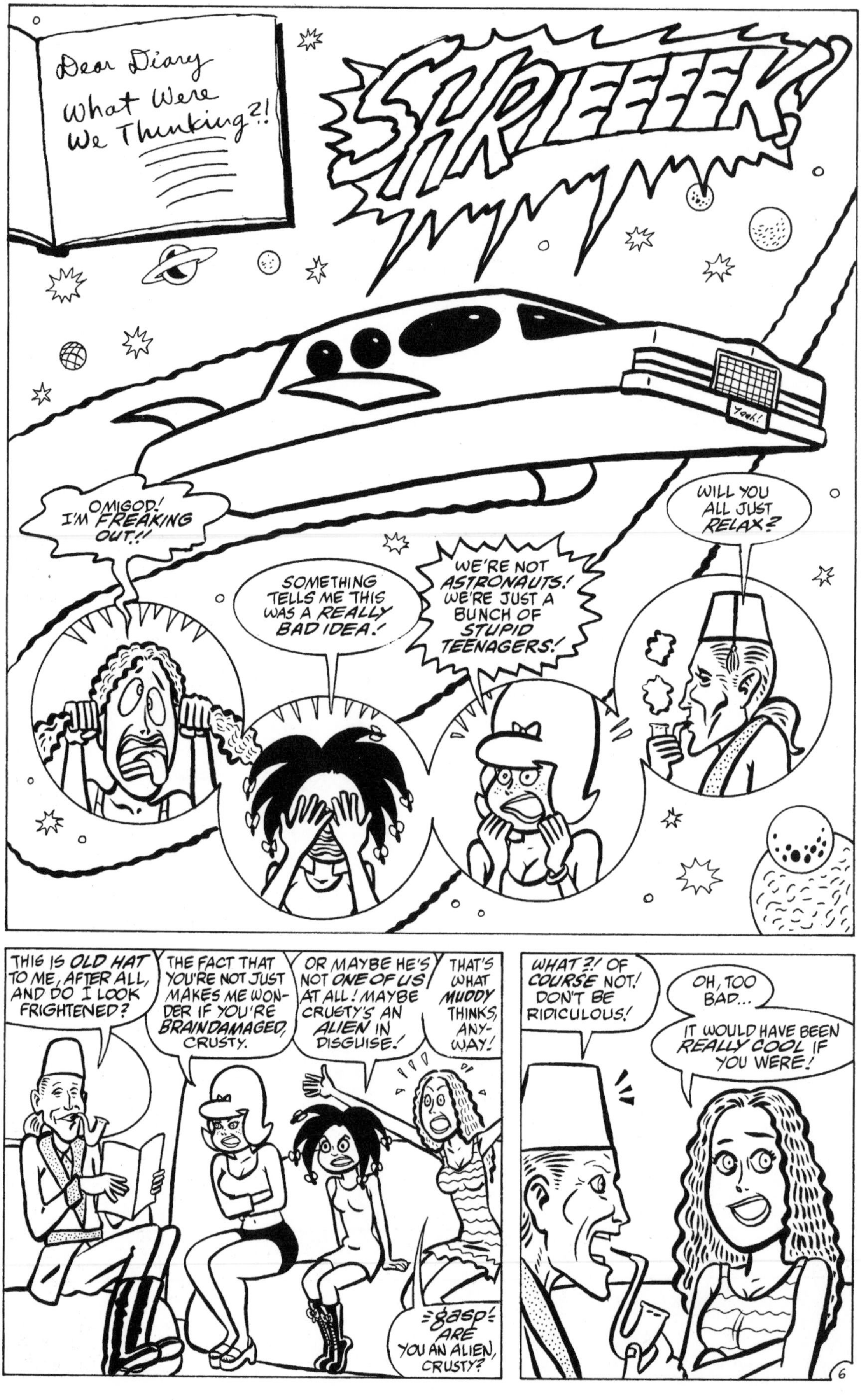

Dear Diary
What Were We Thinking?!
SHRIEEEEK!
Yeah!
OMIGOD! I'M FREAKING OUT!!
SOMETHING TELLS ME THIS WAS A REALLY BAD IDEA!
WE'RE NOT ASTRONAUTS! WE'RE JUST A BUNCH OF STUPID TEENAGERS!
WILL YOU ALL JUST RELAX?
THIS IS OLD HAT TO ME, AFTER ALL, AND DO I LOOK FRIGHTENED?
THE FACT THAT YOU'RE NOT JUST MAKES ME WONDER IF YOU'RE BRAINDAMAGED, CRUSTY.
OR MAYBE HE'S NOT ONE OF US AT ALL! MAYBE CRUSTY'S AN ALIEN IN DISGUISE!
THAT'S WHAT MUDDY THINKS, ANYWAY!
gasp ARE YOU AN ALIEN, CRUSTY?
WHAT?! OF COURSE NOT! DON'T BE RIDICULOUS!
OH, TOO BAD...
IT WOULD HAVE BEEN REALLY COOL IF YOU WERE!

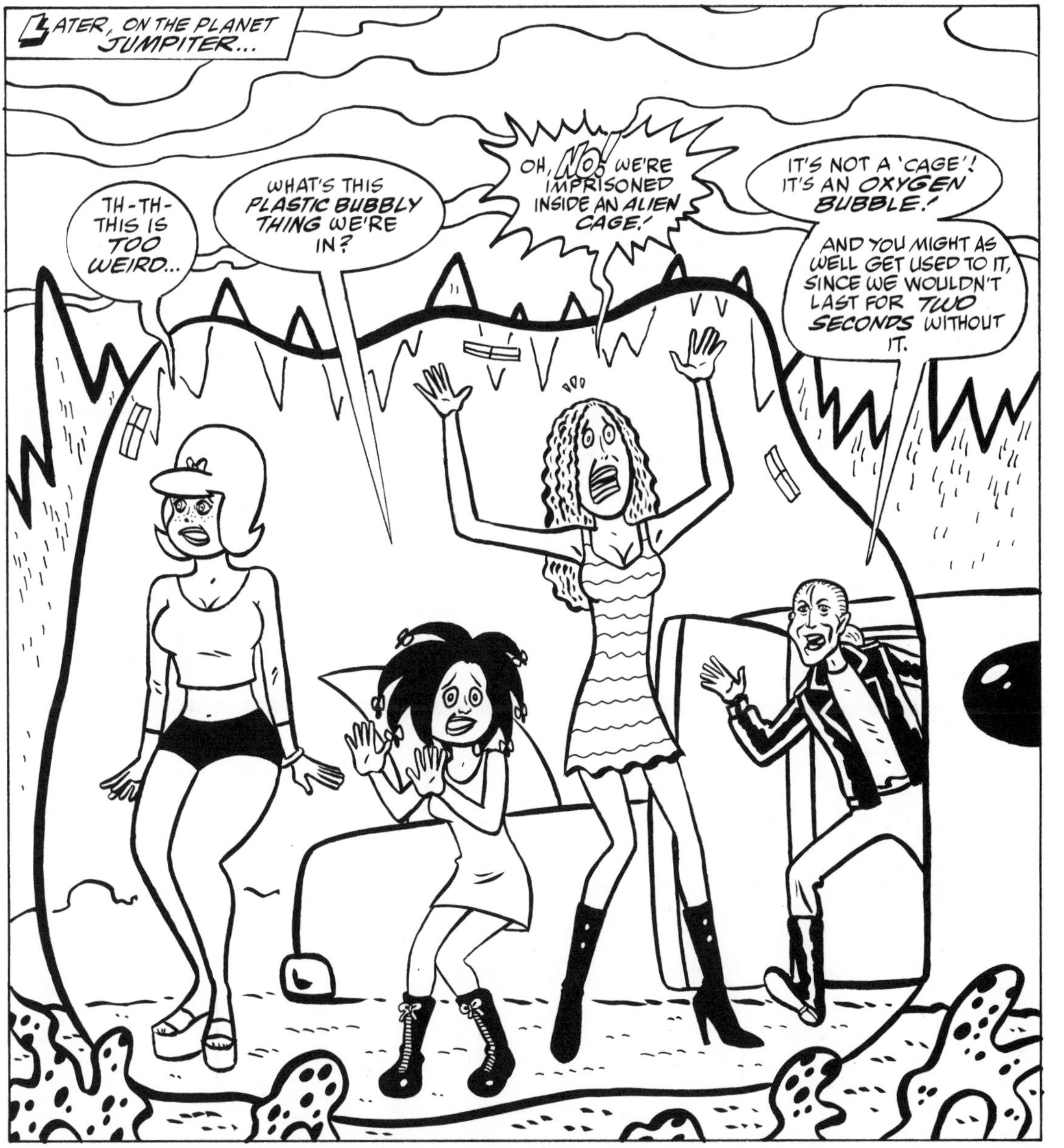
LATER, ON THE PLANET JUMPITER...
TH-TH-THIS IS TOO WEIRD...
WHAT'S THIS PLASTIC BUBBLY THING WE'RE IN?
OH, NO! WE'RE IMPRISONED INSIDE AN ALIEN CAGE!
IT'S NOT A 'CAGE'! IT'S AN OXYGEN BUBBLE!
AND YOU MIGHT AS WELL GET USED TO IT, SINCE WE WOULDN'T LAST FOR TWO SECONDS WITHOUT IT.

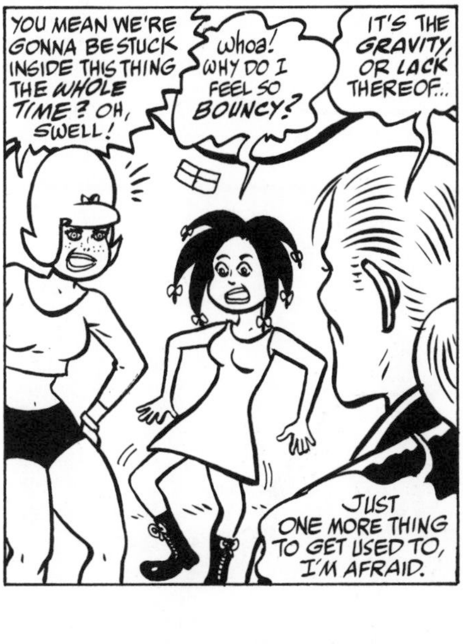
YOU MEAN WE'RE GONNA BE STUCK INSIDE THIS THING THE WHOLE TIME? OH, SWELL!
Whoa! WHY DO I FEEL SO BOUNCY?
IT'S THE GRAVITY, OR LACK THEREOF...
JUST ONE MORE THING TO GET USED TO, I'M AFRAID.

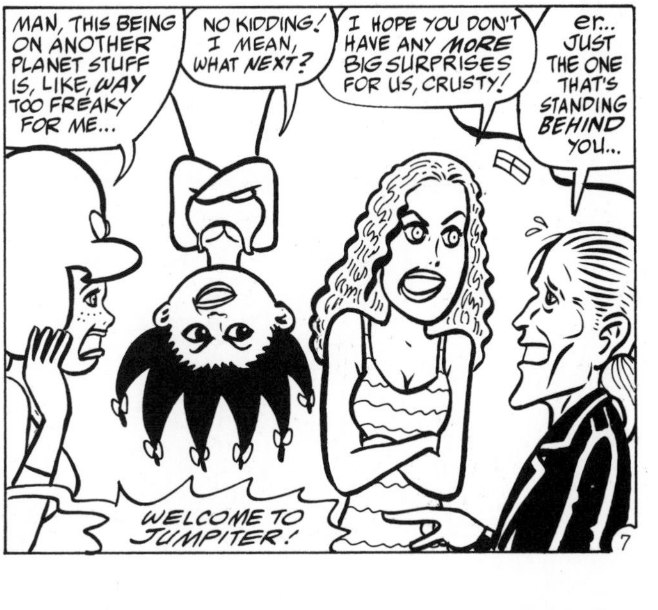
MAN, THIS BEING ON ANOTHER PLANET STUFF IS, LIKE, WAY TOO FREAKY FOR ME...
NO KIDDING! I MEAN, WHAT NEXT?
I HOPE YOU DON'T HAVE ANY MORE BIG SURPRISES FOR US, CRUSTY!
er... JUST THE ONE THAT'S STANDING BEHIND YOU...
WELCOME TO JUMPITER!

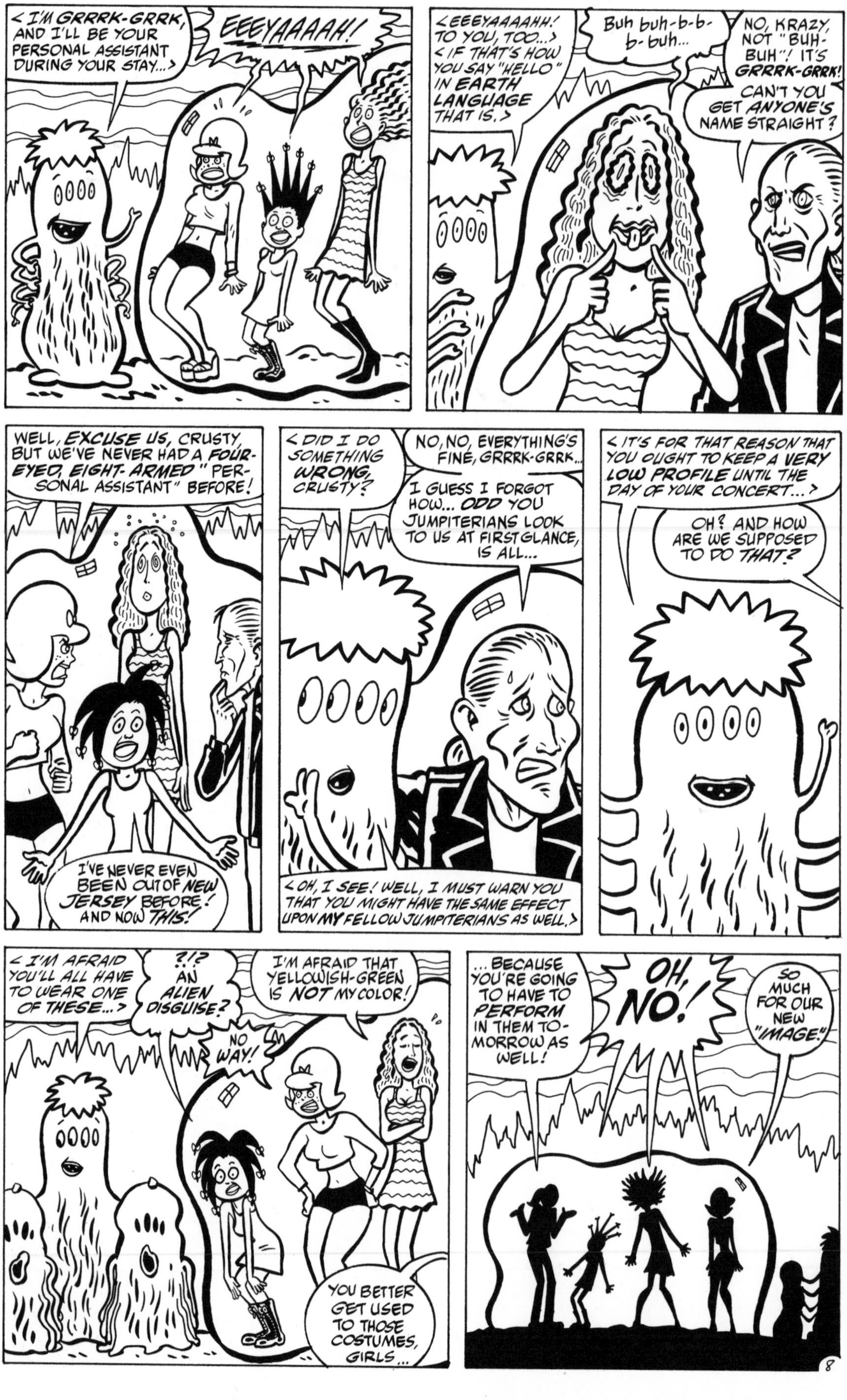
<I'M GRRRK-GRRK, AND I'LL BE YOUR PERSONAL ASSISTANT DURING YOUR STAY...>
EEEYAAAAAH!
<EEEYAAAAHH! TO YOU, TOO...> <IF THAT'S HOW YOU SAY "HELLO" IN EARTH LANGUAGE THAT IS.>
Buh buh-b-b-b-buh...
NO, KRAZY, NOT "BUH-BUH"! IT'S GRRRK-GRRK!
CAN'T YOU GET ANYONE'S NAME STRAIGHT?
WELL, EXCUSE US, CRUSTY, BUT WE'VE NEVER HAD A FOUR-EYED, EIGHT-ARMED "PERSONAL ASSISTANT" BEFORE!
I'VE NEVER EVEN BEEN OUT OF NEW JERSEY BEFORE! AND NOW THIS!
<DID I DO SOMETHING WRONG, CRUSTY?
NO, NO, EVERYTHING'S FINE, GRRRK-GRRK...
I GUESS I FORGOT HOW... ODD YOU JUMPITERIANS LOOK TO US AT FIRST GLANCE, IS ALL...
<OH, I SEE! WELL, I MUST WARN YOU THAT YOU MIGHT HAVE THE SAME EFFECT UPON MY FELLOW JUMPITERIANS AS WELL.>
<IT'S FOR THAT REASON THAT YOU OUGHT TO KEEP A VERY LOW PROFILE UNTIL THE DAY OF YOUR CONCERT...>
OH? AND HOW ARE WE SUPPOSED TO DO THAT?
<I'M AFRAID YOU'LL ALL HAVE TO WEAR ONE OF THESE...>
?!? AN ALIEN DISGUISE?
NO WAY!
I'M AFRAID THAT YELLOWISH-GREEN IS NOT MY COLOR!
YOU BETTER GET USED TO THOSE COSTUMES, GIRLS...
...BECAUSE YOU'RE GOING TO HAVE TO PERFORM IN THEM TO-MORROW AS WELL!
OH, NO!
SO MUCH FOR OUR NEW "IMAGE."

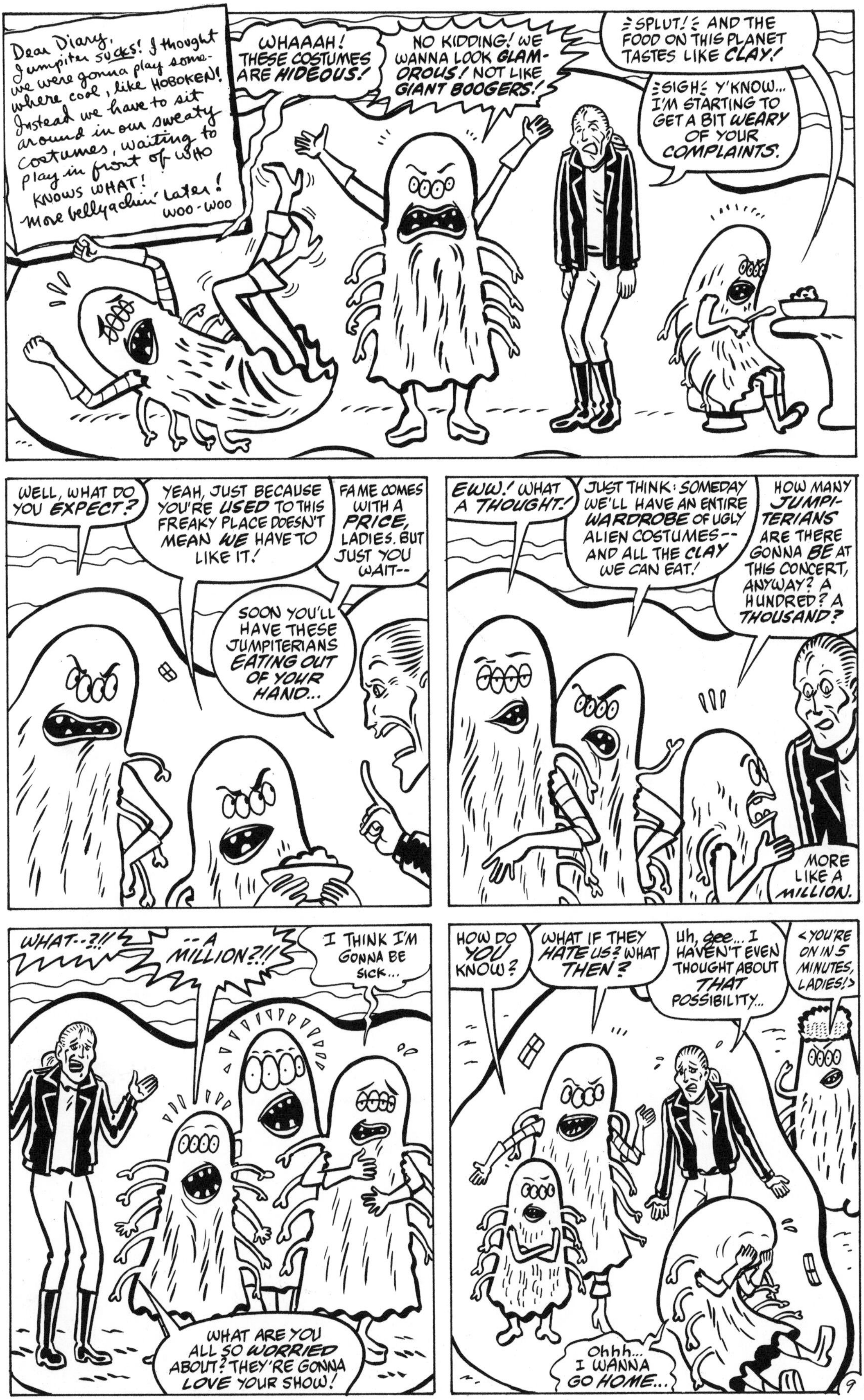
Dear Diary, Jumpiter SUCKS! I thought we were gonna play somewhere cool, like HOBOKEN! Instead we have to sit around in our sweaty costumes, waiting to play in front of WHO KNOWS WHAT! More bellyachin' later! WOO-WOO
WHAAAH! THESE COSTUMES ARE HIDEOUS!
NO KIDDING! WE WANNA LOOK GLAMOROUS! NOT LIKE GIANT BOOGERS!
SPLUT! AND THE FOOD ON THIS PLANET TASTES LIKE CLAY!
SIGH Y'KNOW... I'M STARTING TO GET A BIT WEARY OF YOUR COMPLAINTS.
WELL, WHAT DO YOU EXPECT?
YEAH, JUST BECAUSE YOU'RE USED TO THIS FREAKY PLACE DOESN'T MEAN WE HAVE TO LIKE IT!
FAME COMES WITH A PRICE, LADIES. BUT JUST YOU WAIT--
SOON YOU'LL HAVE THESE JUMPITERIANS EATING OUT OF YOUR HAND...
EWW! WHAT A THOUGHT!
JUST THINK: SOMEDAY WE'LL HAVE AN ENTIRE WARDROBE OF UGLY ALIEN COSTUMES-- AND ALL THE CLAY WE CAN EAT!
HOW MANY JUMPITERIANS ARE THERE GONNA BE AT THIS CONCERT, ANYWAY? A HUNDRED? A THOUSAND?
MORE LIKE A MILLION.
WHAT--?!!
--A MILLION?!!
I THINK I'M GONNA BE SICK...
WHAT ARE YOU ALL SO WORRIED ABOUT? THEY'RE GONNA LOVE YOUR SHOW!
HOW DO YOU KNOW?
WHAT IF THEY HATE US? WHAT THEN?
UH, GEE... I HAVEN'T EVEN THOUGHT ABOUT THAT POSSIBILITY...
<YOU'RE ON IN 5 MINUTES, LADIES!>
Ohhh... I WANNA GO HOME...

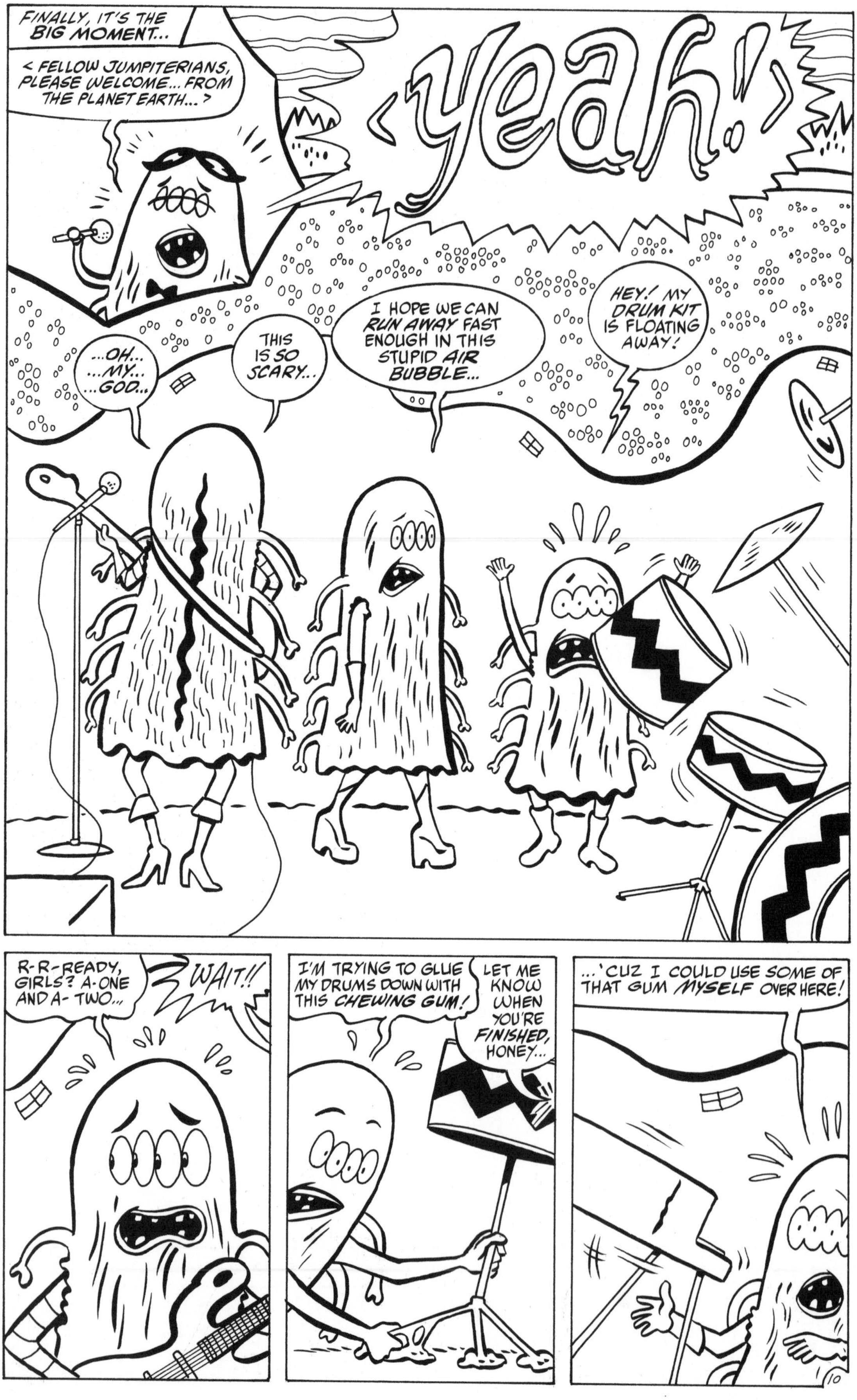

FINALLY, IT'S THE BIG MOMENT...
< FELLOW JUMPITERIANS, PLEASE WELCOME... FROM THE PLANET EARTH... >
‹YEAH!›
...OH... ...MY... ...GOD...
THIS IS SO SCARY...
I HOPE WE CAN RUN AWAY FAST ENOUGH IN THIS STUPID AIR BUBBLE...
HEY! MY DRUM KIT IS FLOATING AWAY!
R-R-READY, GIRLS? A-ONE AND A- TWO...
WAIT!!
I'M TRYING TO GLUE MY DRUMS DOWN WITH THIS CHEWING GUM!
LET ME KNOW WHEN YOU'RE FINISHED, HONEY...
...'CUZ I COULD USE SOME OF THAT GUM MYSELF OVER HERE!
10

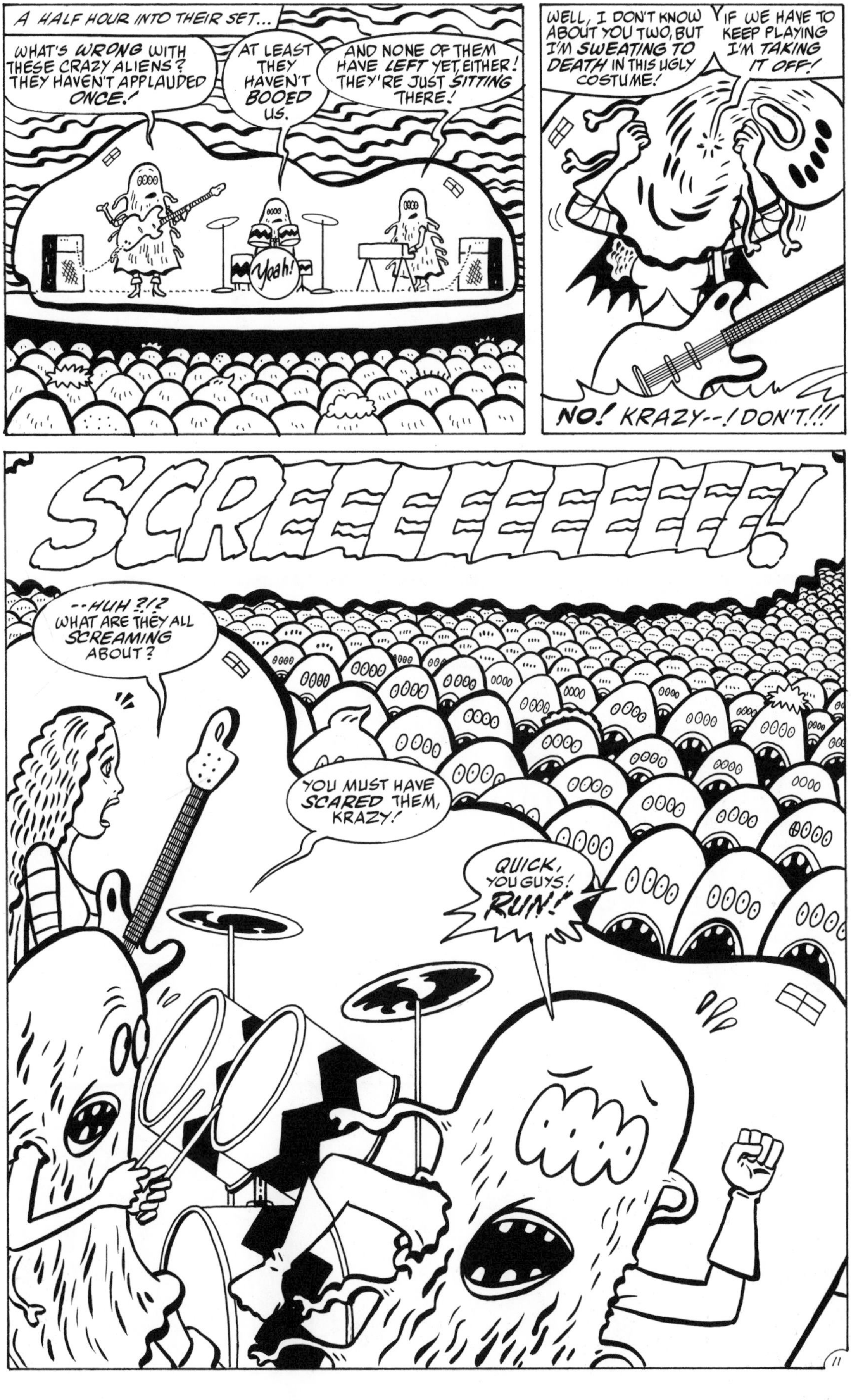
A HALF HOUR INTO THEIR SET...
WHAT'S WRONG WITH THESE CRAZY ALIENS? THEY HAVEN'T APPLAUDED ONCE!
AT LEAST THEY HAVEN'T BOOED US.
AND NONE OF THEM HAVE LEFT YET, EITHER! THEY'RE JUST SITTING THERE!
Yeah!
WELL, I DON'T KNOW ABOUT YOU TWO, BUT I'M SWEATING TO DEATH IN THIS UGLY COSTUME!
IF WE HAVE TO KEEP PLAYING I'M TAKING IT OFF!
NO! KRAZY--! DON'T!!!
SCREEEEEEEEEEEE!
--HUH?!? WHAT ARE THEY ALL SCREAMING ABOUT?
YOU MUST HAVE SCARED THEM, KRAZY!
QUICK, YOU GUYS! RUN!

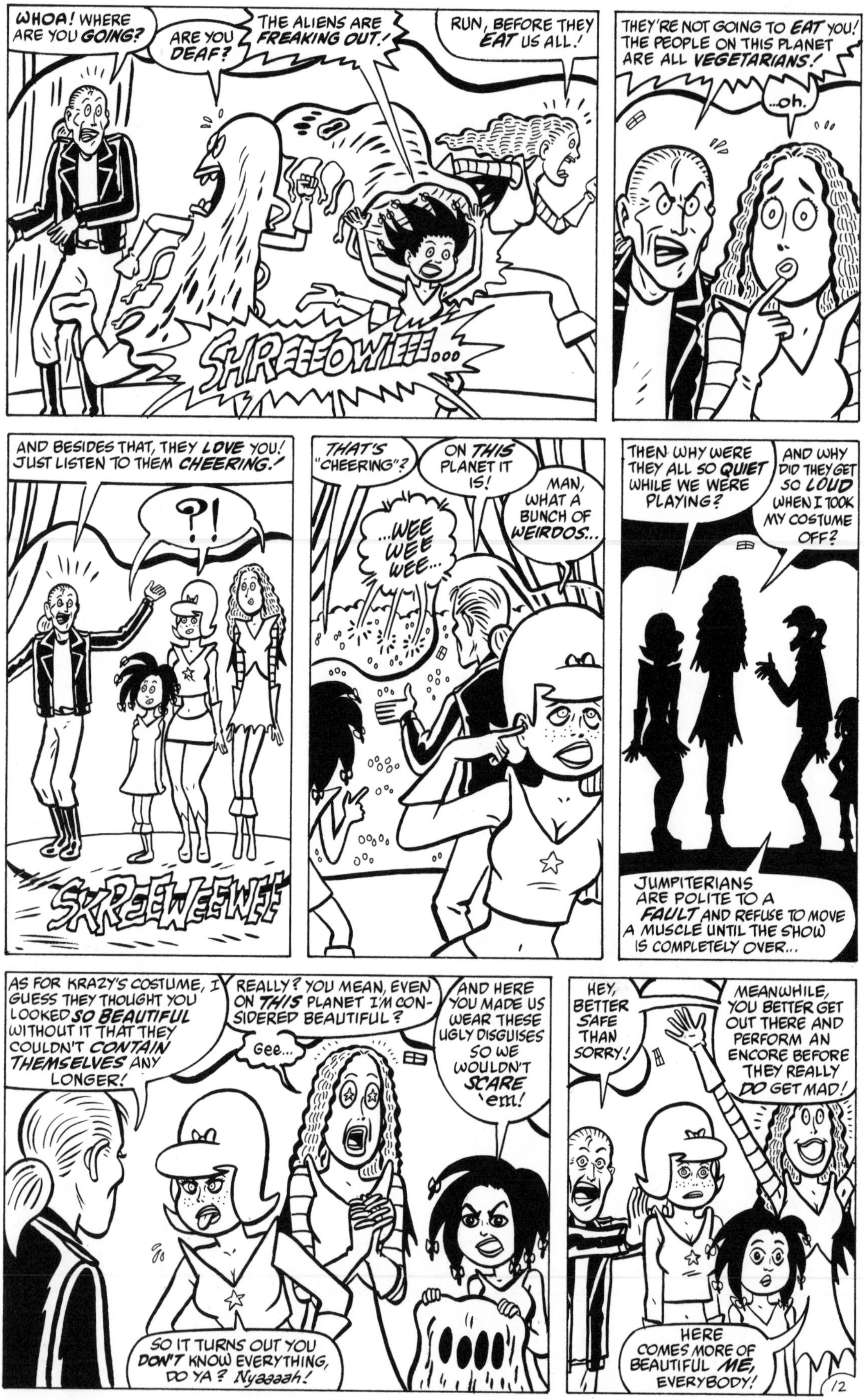
WHOA! WHERE ARE YOU GOING?
ARE YOU DEAF?
THE ALIENS ARE FREAKING OUT!
RUN, BEFORE THEY EAT US ALL!
SHREEEOWIEEE...
THEY'RE NOT GOING TO EAT YOU! THE PEOPLE ON THIS PLANET ARE ALL VEGETARIANS!
...oh.
AND BESIDES THAT, THEY LOVE YOU! JUST LISTEN TO THEM CHEERING!
?!
SKREEWEEWEE
THAT'S "CHEERING"?
ON THIS PLANET IT IS!
...WEE WEE WEE...
MAN, WHAT A BUNCH OF WEIRDOS...
THEN WHY WERE THEY ALL SO QUIET WHILE WE WERE PLAYING?
AND WHY DID THEY GET SO LOUD WHEN I TOOK MY COSTUME OFF?
JUMPITERIANS ARE POLITE TO A FAULT AND REFUSE TO MOVE A MUSCLE UNTIL THE SHOW IS COMPLETELY OVER...
AS FOR KRAZY'S COSTUME, I GUESS THEY THOUGHT YOU LOOKED SO BEAUTIFUL WITHOUT IT THAT THEY COULDN'T CONTAIN THEMSELVES ANY LONGER!
REALLY? YOU MEAN, EVEN ON THIS PLANET I'M CONSIDERED BEAUTIFUL?
Gee...
AND HERE YOU MADE US WEAR THESE UGLY DISGUISES SO WE WOULDN'T SCARE 'em!
SO IT TURNS OUT YOU DON'T KNOW EVERYTHING, DO YA? Nyaaaah!
HEY, BETTER SAFE THAN SORRY!
MEANWHILE, YOU BETTER GET OUT THERE AND PERFORM AN ENCORE BEFORE THEY REALLY DO GET MAD!
HERE COMES MORE OF BEAUTIFUL ME, EVERYBODY!

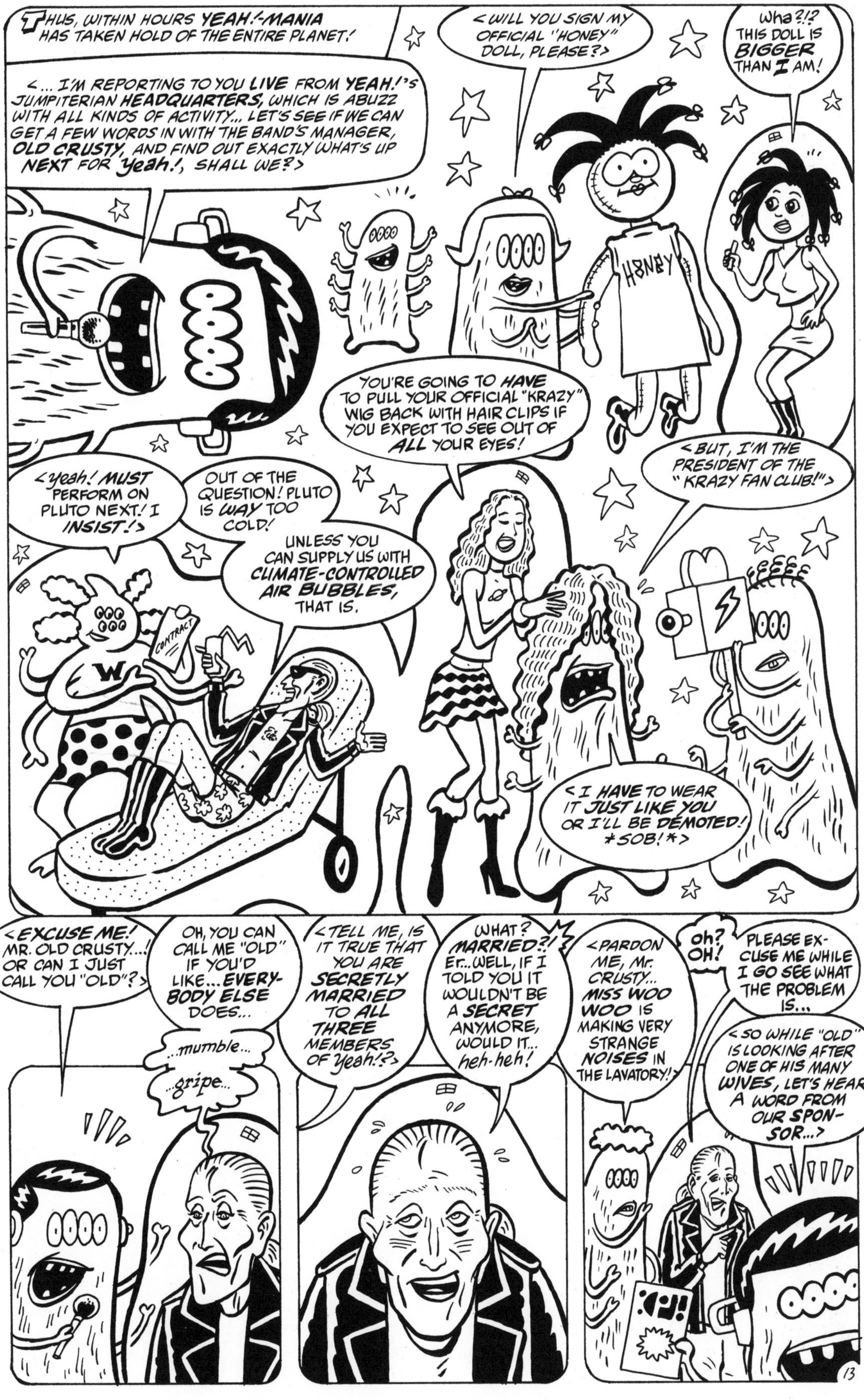
THUS, WITHIN HOURS YEAH!-MANIA HAS TAKEN HOLD OF THE ENTIRE PLANET!
<... I'M REPORTING TO YOU LIVE FROM YEAH!'S JUMPITERIAN HEADQUARTERS, WHICH IS ABUZZ WITH ALL KINDS OF ACTIVITY... LET'S SEE IF WE CAN GET A FEW WORDS IN WITH THE BAND'S MANAGER, OLD CRUSTY, AND FIND OUT EXACTLY WHAT'S UP NEXT FOR Yeah!, SHALL WE?>
<WILL YOU SIGN MY OFFICIAL "HONEY" DOLL, PLEASE?>
Wha?!? THIS DOLL IS BIGGER THAN I AM!
HONEY
YOU'RE GOING TO HAVE TO PULL YOUR OFFICIAL "KRAZY" WIG BACK WITH HAIR CLIPS IF YOU EXPECT TO SEE OUT OF ALL YOUR EYES!
<BUT, I'M THE PRESIDENT OF THE "KRAZY FAN CLUB!">
<Yeah! MUST PERFORM ON PLUTO NEXT! I INSIST!>
OUT OF THE QUESTION! PLUTO IS WAY TOO COLD!
UNLESS YOU CAN SUPPLY US WITH CLIMATE-CONTROLLED AIR BUBBLES, THAT IS.
CONTRACT
<I HAVE TO WEAR IT JUST LIKE YOU OR I'LL BE DEMOTED! *SOB!*>
<EXCUSE ME! MR. OLD CRUSTY...! OR CAN I JUST CALL YOU "OLD"?>
OH, YOU CAN CALL ME "OLD" IF YOU'D LIKE... EVERYBODY ELSE DOES...
...mumble...
...gripe...
<TELL ME, IS IT TRUE THAT YOU ARE SECRETLY MARRIED TO ALL THREE MEMBERS OF Yeah!?>
WHAT? MARRIED?! Er... WELL, IF I TOLD YOU IT WOULDN'T BE A SECRET ANYMORE, WOULD IT... heh-heh!
<PARDON ME, Mr. CRUSTY... MISS WOO WOO IS MAKING VERY STRANGE NOISES IN THE LAVATORY!>
Oh? OH!
PLEASE EXCUSE ME WHILE I GO SEE WHAT THE PROBLEM IS...
<SO WHILE "OLD" IS LOOKING AFTER ONE OF HIS MANY WIVES, LET'S HEAR A WORD FROM OUR SPONSOR...>

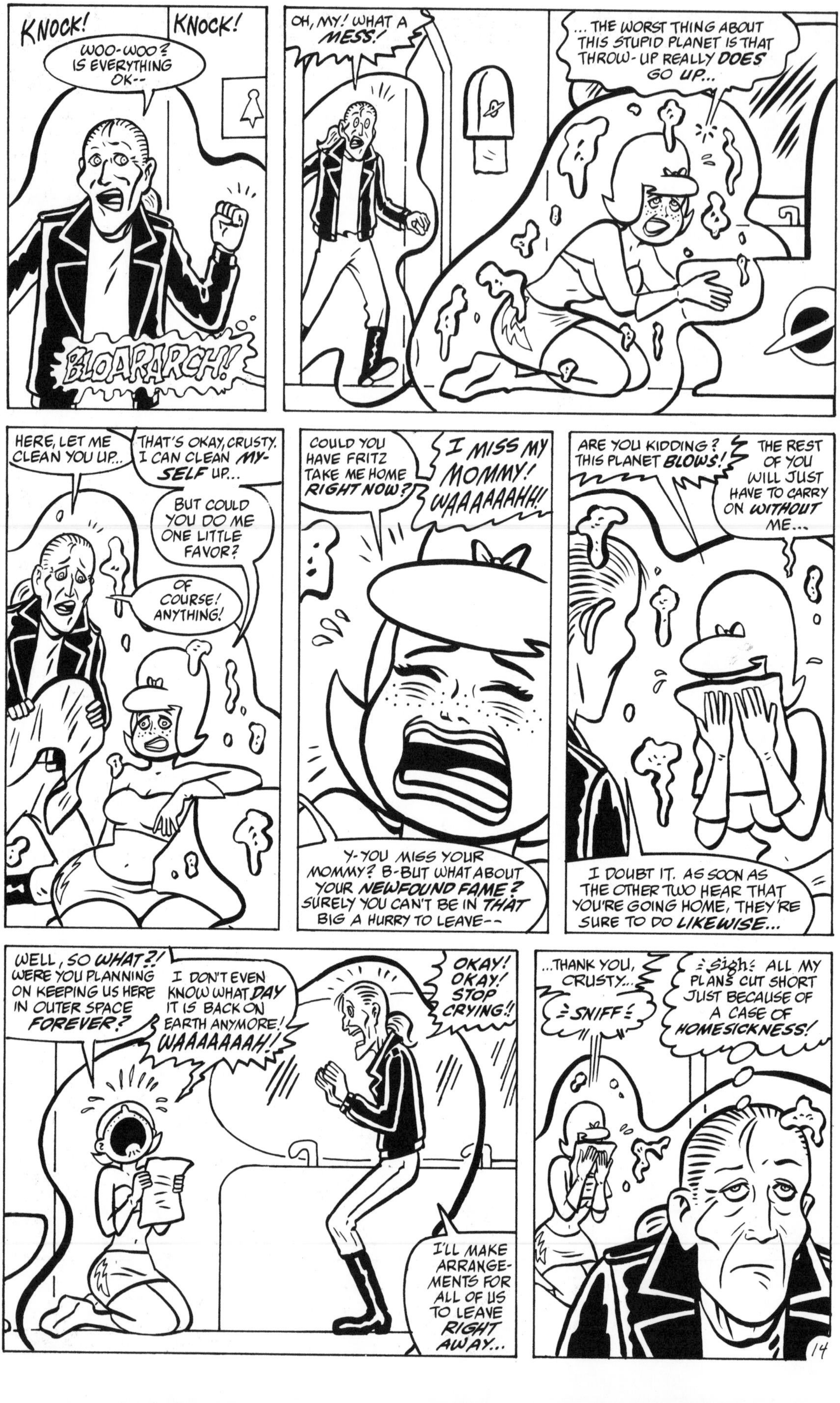
KNOCK!
KNOCK!
WOO-WOO? IS EVERYTHING OK--
BLOARARCH!
OH, MY! WHAT A MESS!
...THE WORST THING ABOUT THIS STUPID PLANET IS THAT THROW-UP REALLY DOES GO UP...
HERE, LET ME CLEAN YOU UP...
THAT'S OKAY, CRUSTY. I CAN CLEAN MYSELF UP...
BUT COULD YOU DO ME ONE LITTLE FAVOR?
OF COURSE! ANYTHING!
COULD YOU HAVE FRITZ TAKE ME HOME RIGHT NOW?
I MISS MY MOMMY! WAAAAAAHH!
Y-YOU MISS YOUR MOMMY? B-BUT WHAT ABOUT YOUR NEWFOUND FAME? SURELY YOU CAN'T BE IN THAT BIG A HURRY TO LEAVE--
ARE YOU KIDDING? THIS PLANET BLOWS!
THE REST OF YOU WILL JUST HAVE TO CARRY ON WITHOUT ME...
I DOUBT IT. AS SOON AS THE OTHER TWO HEAR THAT YOU'RE GOING HOME, THEY'RE SURE TO DO LIKEWISE...
WELL, SO WHAT?! WERE YOU PLANNING ON KEEPING US HERE IN OUTER SPACE FOREVER?
I DON'T EVEN KNOW WHAT DAY IT IS BACK ON EARTH ANYMORE! WAAAAAAAH!
OKAY! OKAY! STOP CRYING!!
I'LL MAKE ARRANGEMENTS FOR ALL OF US TO LEAVE RIGHT AWAY...
...THANK YOU, CRUSTY...
SNIFF
SIGH ALL MY PLANS CUT SHORT JUST BECAUSE OF A CASE OF HOMESICKNESS!

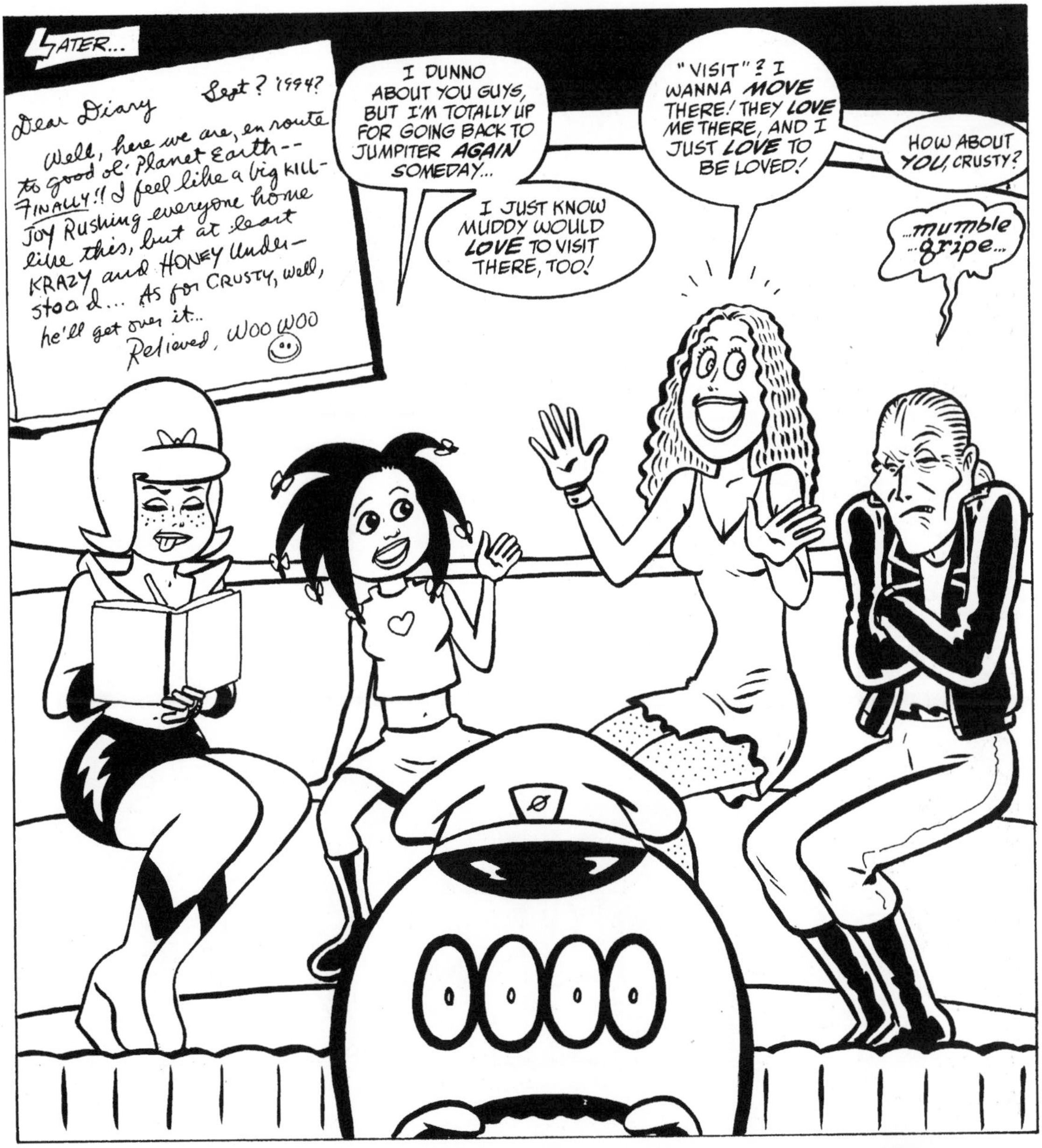
LATER...
Dear Diary Sept? 1994?
Well, here we are, en route to good ol' Planet Earth-- FINALLY!! I feel like a big KILL-JOY Rushing everyone home like this, but at least KRAZY and HONEY Understood... As for CRUSTY, well, he'll get over it...
Relieved, WOO WOO
I DUNNO ABOUT YOU GUYS, BUT I'M TOTALLY UP FOR GOING BACK TO JUMPITER AGAIN SOMEDAY...
I JUST KNOW MUDDY WOULD LOVE TO VISIT THERE, TOO!
"VISIT"?! I WANNA MOVE THERE! THEY LOVE ME THERE, AND I JUST LOVE TO BE LOVED!
HOW ABOUT YOU, CRUSTY?
...mumble ...gripe...

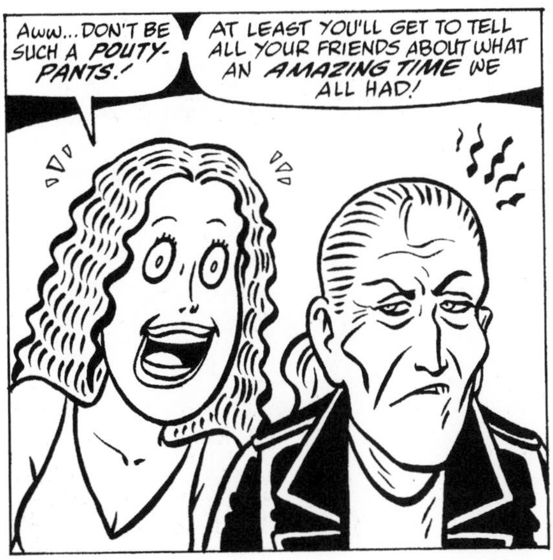
AWW... DON'T BE SUCH A POUTY-PANTS!
AT LEAST YOU'LL GET TO TELL ALL YOUR FRIENDS ABOUT WHAT AN AMAZING TIME WE ALL HAD!

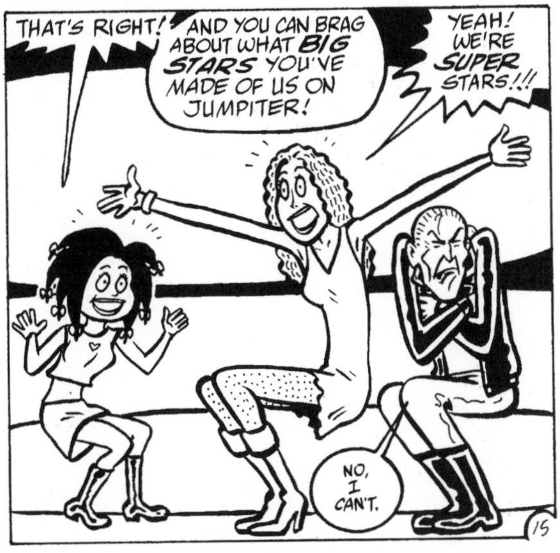
THAT'S RIGHT!
AND YOU CAN BRAG ABOUT WHAT BIG STARS YOU'VE MADE OF US ON JUMPITER!
YEAH! WE'RE SUPER STARS!!!
NO, I CAN'T.

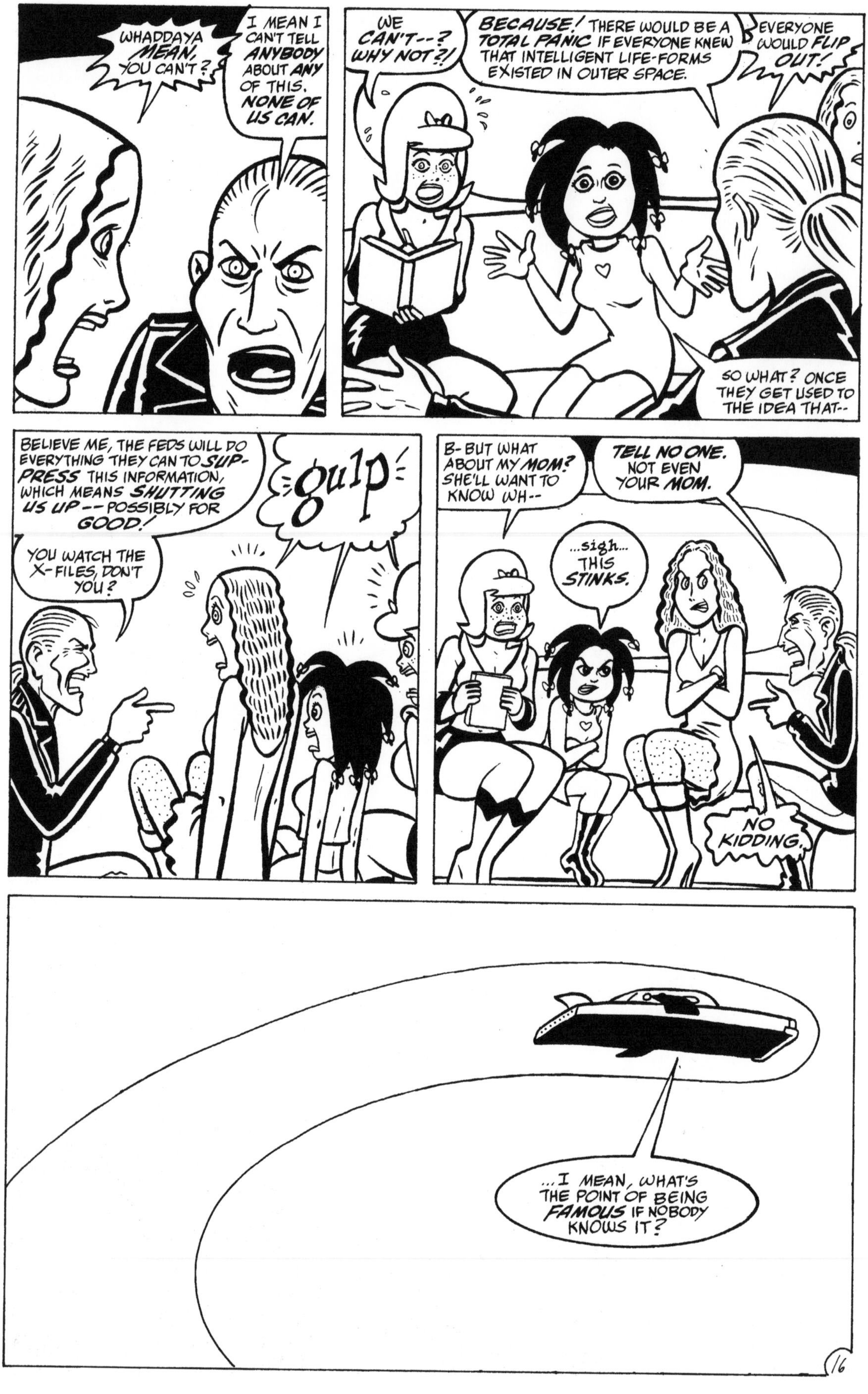
WHADDAYA MEAN, YOU CAN'T?
I MEAN I CAN'T TELL ANYBODY ABOUT ANY OF THIS. NONE OF US CAN.
WE CAN'T--? WHY NOT?!
BECAUSE! THERE WOULD BE A TOTAL PANIC IF EVERYONE KNEW THAT INTELLIGENT LIFE-FORMS EXISTED IN OUTER SPACE.
EVERYONE WOULD FLIP OUT!
SO WHAT? ONCE THEY GET USED TO THE IDEA THAT--
BELIEVE ME, THE FEDS WILL DO EVERYTHING THEY CAN TO SUPPRESS THIS INFORMATION, WHICH MEANS SHUTTING US UP -- POSSIBLY FOR GOOD!
YOU WATCH THE X-FILES, DON'T YOU?
gulp
B-BUT WHAT ABOUT MY MOM? SHE'LL WANT TO KNOW WH--
TELL NO ONE. NOT EVEN YOUR MOM.
...sigh... THIS STINKS.
NO KIDDING.
...I MEAN, WHAT'S THE POINT OF BEING FAMOUS IF NOBODY KNOWS IT?

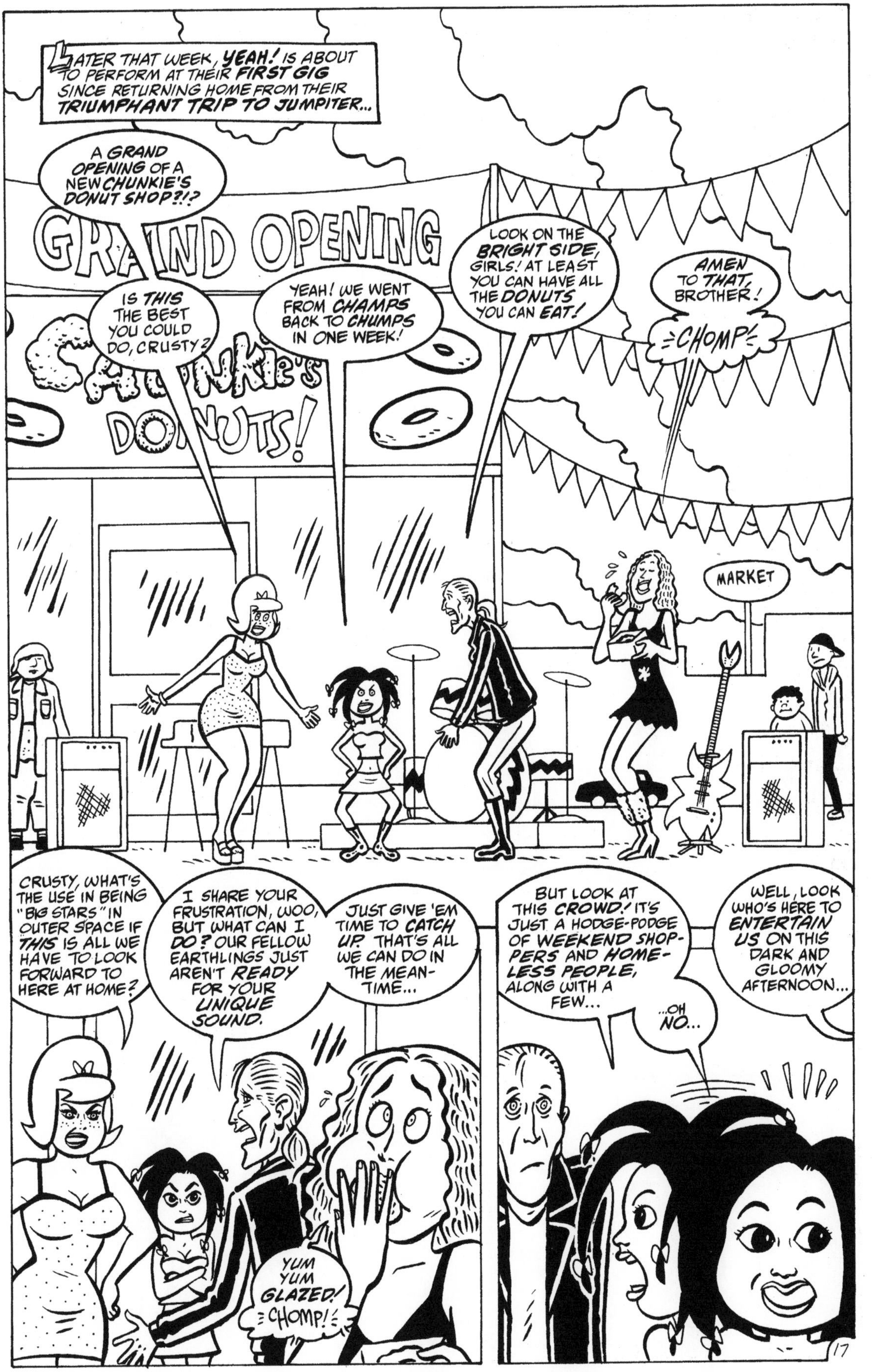
LATER THAT WEEK, YEAH! IS ABOUT TO PERFORM AT THEIR FIRST GIG SINCE RETURNING HOME FROM THEIR TRIUMPHANT TRIP TO JUMPITER...
A GRAND OPENING OF A NEW CHUNKIE'S DONUT SHOP?!?
GRAND OPENING
CHUNKIE'S DONUTS!
IS THIS THE BEST YOU COULD DO, CRUSTY?
YEAH! WE WENT FROM CHAMPS BACK TO CHUMPS IN ONE WEEK!
LOOK ON THE BRIGHT SIDE, GIRLS! AT LEAST YOU CAN HAVE ALL THE DONUTS YOU CAN EAT!
AMEN TO THAT, BROTHER!
CHOMP!
MARKET
CRUSTY, WHAT'S THE USE IN BEING "BIG STARS" IN OUTER SPACE IF THIS IS ALL WE HAVE TO LOOK FORWARD TO HERE AT HOME?
I SHARE YOUR FRUSTRATION, WOO, BUT WHAT CAN I DO? OUR FELLOW EARTHLINGS JUST AREN'T READY FOR YOUR UNIQUE SOUND.
JUST GIVE 'EM TIME TO CATCH UP. THAT'S ALL WE CAN DO IN THE MEAN-TIME...
YUM YUM GLAZED! CHOMP!
BUT LOOK AT THIS CROWD! IT'S JUST A HODGE-PODGE OF WEEKEND SHOP-PERS AND HOME-LESS PEOPLE, ALONG WITH A FEW...
...OH NO...
WELL, LOOK WHO'S HERE TO ENTERTAIN US ON THIS DARK AND GLOOMY AFTERNOON...

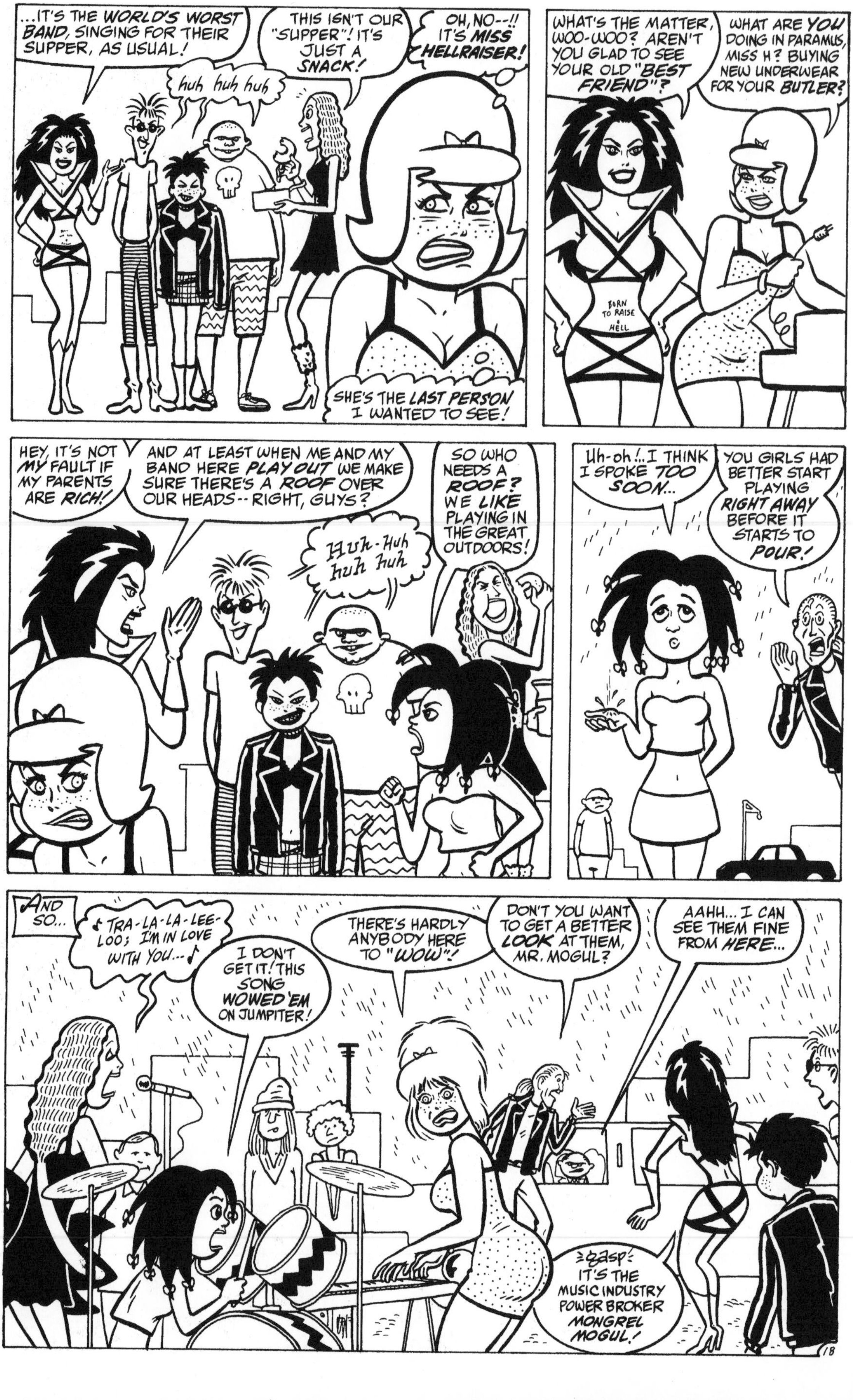
...IT'S THE WORLD'S WORST BAND, SINGING FOR THEIR SUPPER, AS USUAL!
THIS ISN'T OUR "SUPPER"! IT'S JUST A SNACK!
huh huh huh
OH, NO--!! IT'S MISS HELLRAISER!
SHE'S THE LAST PERSON I WANTED TO SEE!
WHAT'S THE MATTER, WOO-WOO? AREN'T YOU GLAD TO SEE YOUR OLD "BEST FRIEND"?
WHAT ARE YOU DOING IN PARAMUS, MISS H? BUYING NEW UNDERWEAR FOR YOUR BUTLER?
BORN TO RAISE HELL
HEY, IT'S NOT MY FAULT IF MY PARENTS ARE RICH!
AND AT LEAST WHEN ME AND MY BAND HERE PLAY OUT WE MAKE SURE THERE'S A ROOF OVER OUR HEADS-- RIGHT, GUYS?
Huh-Huh huh huh
SO WHO NEEDS A ROOF? WE LIKE PLAYING IN THE GREAT OUTDOORS!
Uh-oh!...I THINK I SPOKE TOO SOON...
YOU GIRLS HAD BETTER START PLAYING RIGHT AWAY BEFORE IT STARTS TO POUR!
AND SO...
TRA-LA-LA-LEE-LOO; I'M IN LOVE WITH YOU...
I DON'T GET IT! THIS SONG WOWED 'EM ON JUMPITER!
THERE'S HARDLY ANYBODY HERE TO "WOW"!
DON'T YOU WANT TO GET A BETTER LOOK AT THEM, MR. MOGUL?
AAHH... I CAN SEE THEM FINE FROM HERE...
gasp! IT'S THE MUSIC INDUSTRY POWER BROKER MONGREL MOGUL!

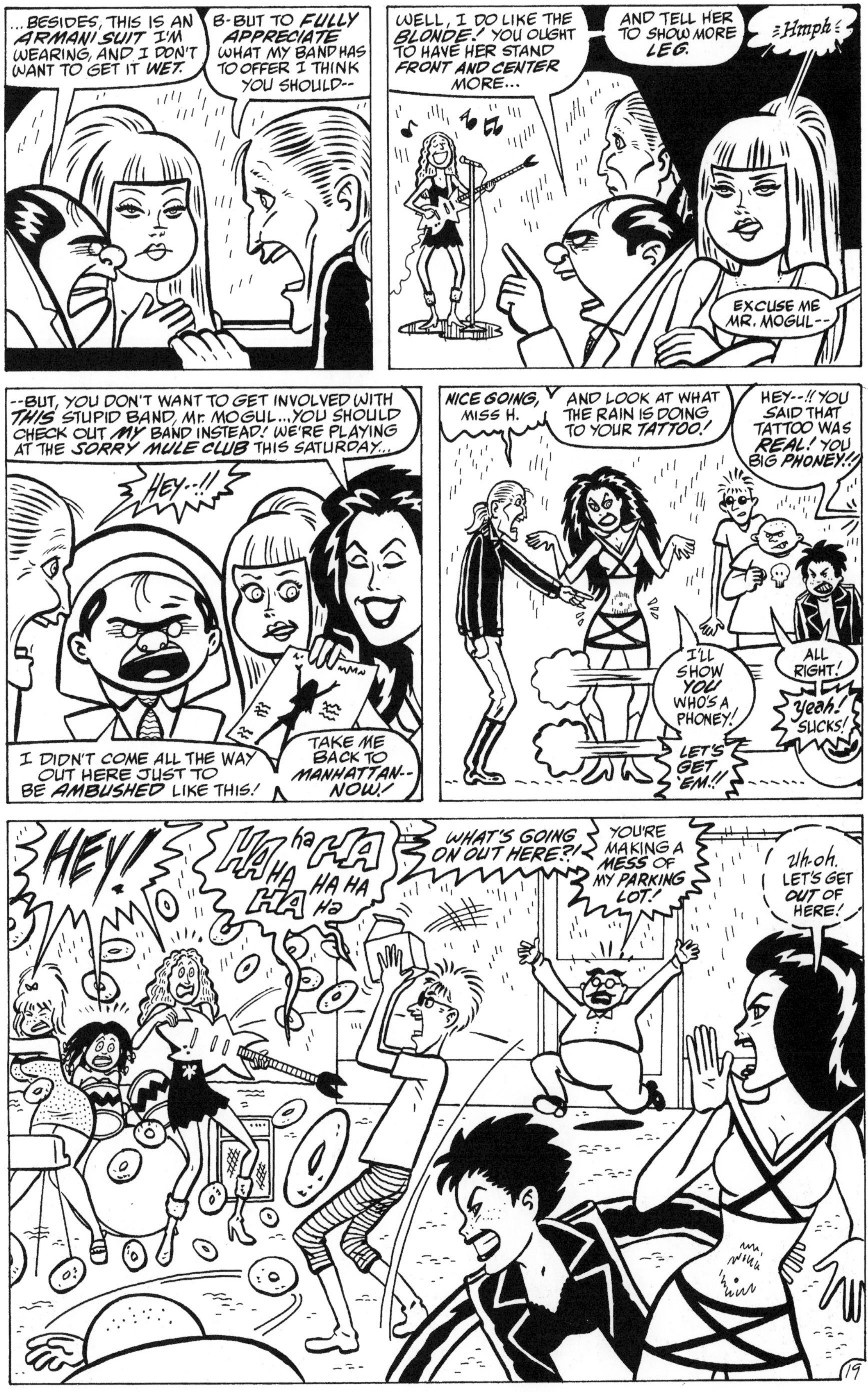
...BESIDES, THIS IS AN ARMANI SUIT I'M WEARING, AND I DON'T WANT TO GET IT WET.
B-BUT TO FULLY APPRECIATE WHAT MY BAND HAS TO OFFER I THINK YOU SHOULD--
WELL, I DO LIKE THE BLONDE! YOU OUGHT TO HAVE HER STAND FRONT AND CENTER MORE...
AND TELL HER TO SHOW MORE LEG.
Hmph!
EXCUSE ME MR. MOGUL--
--BUT, YOU DON'T WANT TO GET INVOLVED WITH THIS STUPID BAND, Mr. MOGUL...YOU SHOULD CHECK OUT MY BAND INSTEAD! WE'RE PLAYING AT THE SORRY MULE CLUB THIS SATURDAY...
HEY--!!
I DIDN'T COME ALL THE WAY OUT HERE JUST TO BE AMBUSHED LIKE THIS!
TAKE ME BACK TO MANHATTAN--NOW!
NICE GOING, MISS H.
AND LOOK AT WHAT THE RAIN IS DOING TO YOUR TATTOO!
HEY--!! YOU SAID THAT TATTOO WAS REAL! YOU BIG PHONEY!!
I'LL SHOW YOU WHO'S A PHONEY!
ALL RIGHT!
yeah! SUCKS!
LET'S GET 'EM!!
HEY!
HA ha HA HA HA HA HA HA ha
WHAT'S GOING ON OUT HERE?!
YOU'RE MAKING A MESS OF MY PARKING LOT!
uh-oh. LET'S GET OUT OF HERE!

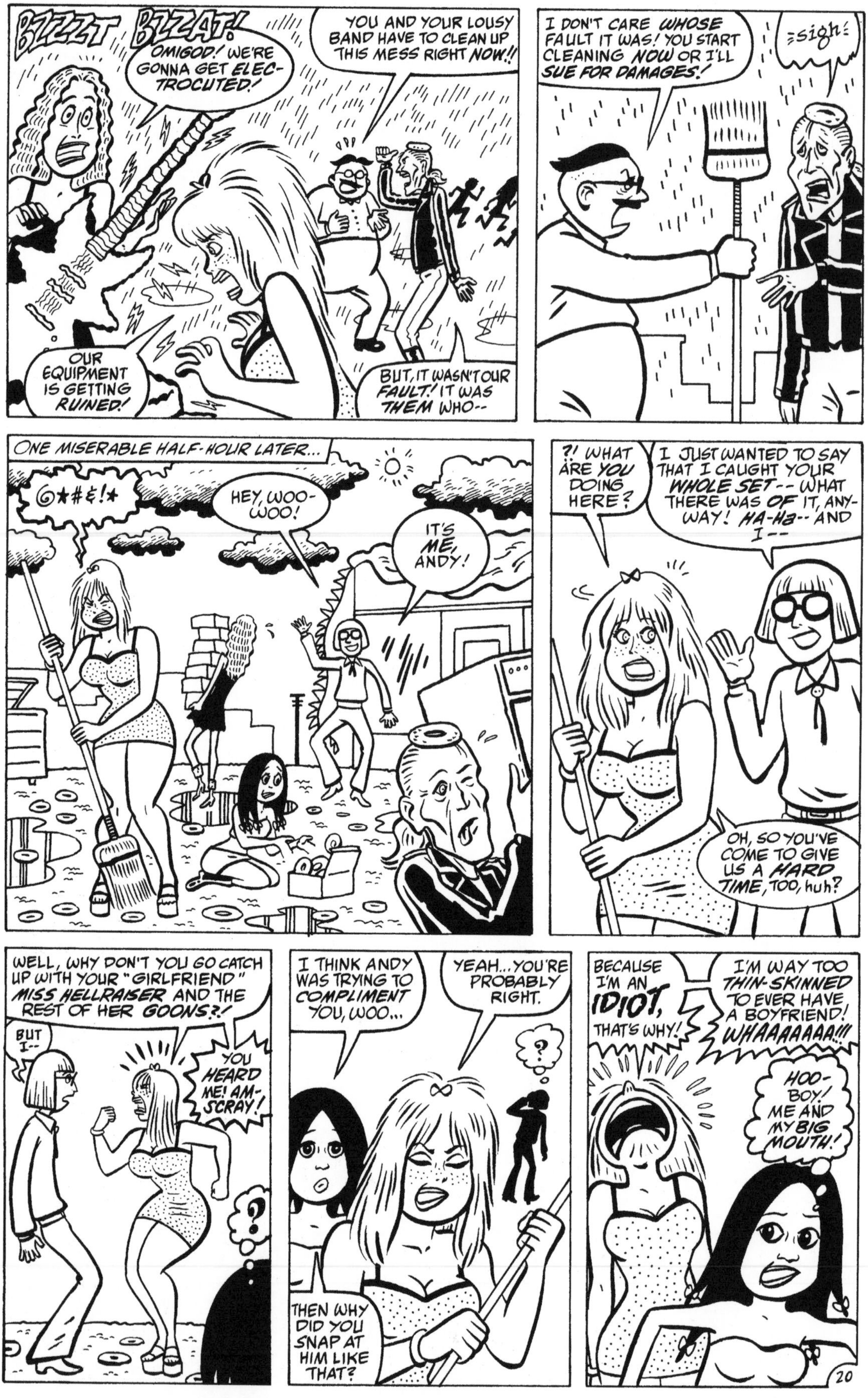
BZZZT BZZAT!
OMIGOD! WE'RE GONNA GET ELEC-TROCUTED!
YOU AND YOUR LOUSY BAND HAVE TO CLEAN UP THIS MESS RIGHT NOW!!
OUR EQUIPMENT IS GETTING RUINED!
BUT, IT WASN'T OUR FAULT! IT WAS THEM WHO--
I DON'T CARE WHOSE FAULT IT WAS! YOU START CLEANING NOW OR I'LL SUE FOR DAMAGES!
sigh
ONE MISERABLE HALF-HOUR LATER...
6★#&!★
HEY, WOO-WOO!
IT'S ME, ANDY!
?! WHAT ARE YOU DOING HERE?
I JUST WANTED TO SAY THAT I CAUGHT YOUR WHOLE SET-- WHAT THERE WAS OF IT, ANY-WAY! HA-Ha-- AND I--
OH, SO YOU'VE COME TO GIVE US A HARD TIME, TOO, huh?
WELL, WHY DON'T YOU GO CATCH UP WITH YOUR "GIRLFRIEND" MISS HELLRAISER AND THE REST OF HER GOONS?!
BUT I--
YOU HEARD ME! AM-SCRAY!
?
I THINK ANDY WAS TRYING TO COMPLIMENT YOU, WOO...
YEAH... YOU'RE PROBABLY RIGHT.
?
THEN WHY DID YOU SNAP AT HIM LIKE THAT?
BECAUSE I'M AN IDIOT, THAT'S WHY!
I'M WAY TOO THIN-SKINNED TO EVER HAVE A BOYFRIEND! WHAAAAAAA!!!
HOO-BOY! ME AND MY BIG MOUTH!

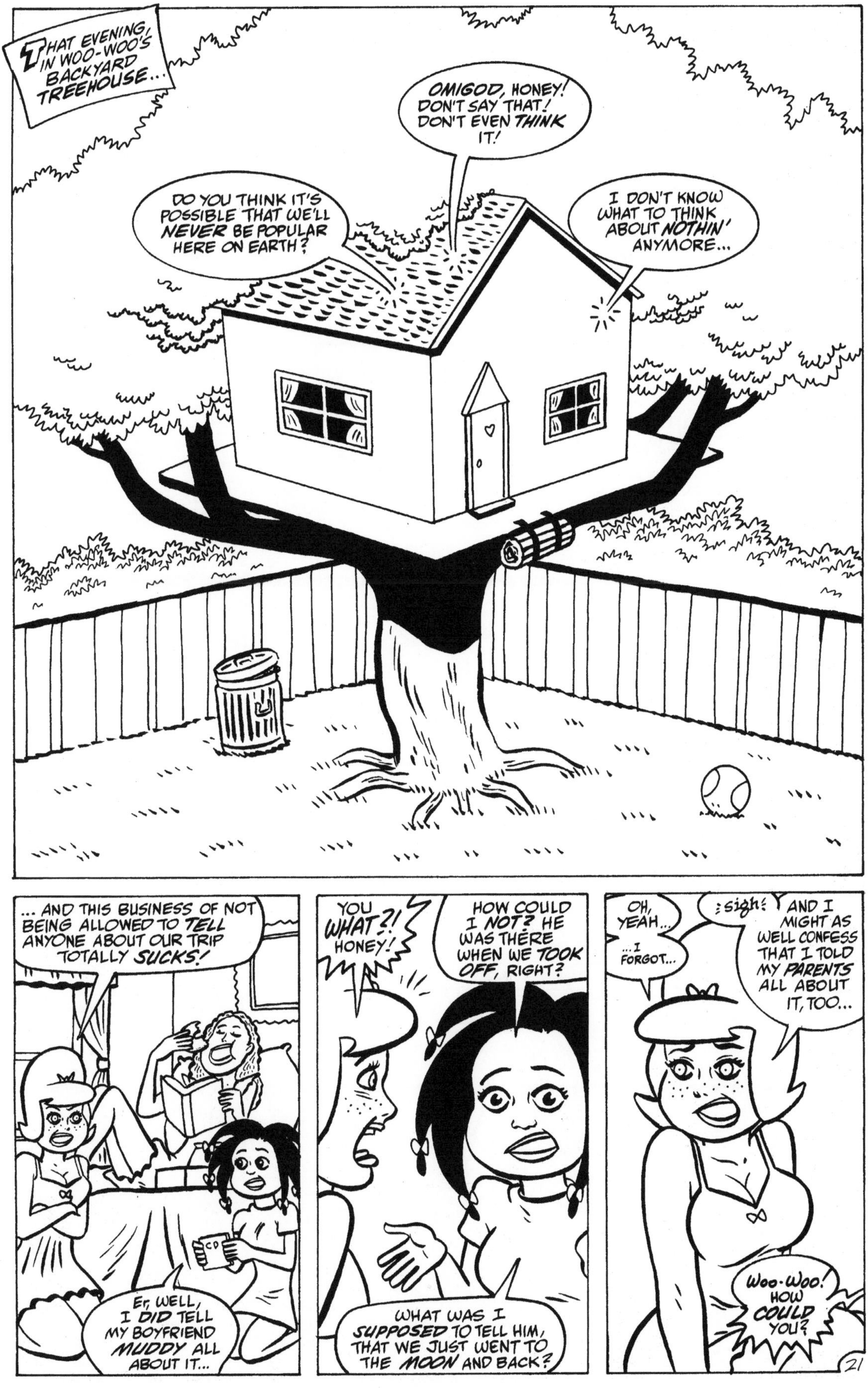
THAT EVENING, IN WOO-WOO'S BACKYARD TREEHOUSE...
DO YOU THINK IT'S POSSIBLE THAT WE'LL NEVER BE POPULAR HERE ON EARTH?
OMIGOD, HONEY! DON'T SAY THAT! DON'T EVEN THINK IT!
I DON'T KNOW WHAT TO THINK ABOUT NOTHIN' ANYMORE...
... AND THIS BUSINESS OF NOT BEING ALLOWED TO TELL ANYONE ABOUT OUR TRIP TOTALLY SUCKS!
Er, WELL, I DID TELL MY BOYFRIEND MUDDY ALL ABOUT IT...
YOU WHAT?! HONEY!
HOW COULD I NOT? HE WAS THERE WHEN WE TOOK OFF, RIGHT?
WHAT WAS I SUPPOSED TO TELL HIM, THAT WE JUST WENT TO THE MOON AND BACK?
OH, YEAH...
...I FORGOT...
:sigh:
AND I MIGHT AS WELL CONFESS THAT I TOLD MY PARENTS ALL ABOUT IT, TOO...
Woo-Woo! HOW COULD YOU?
21

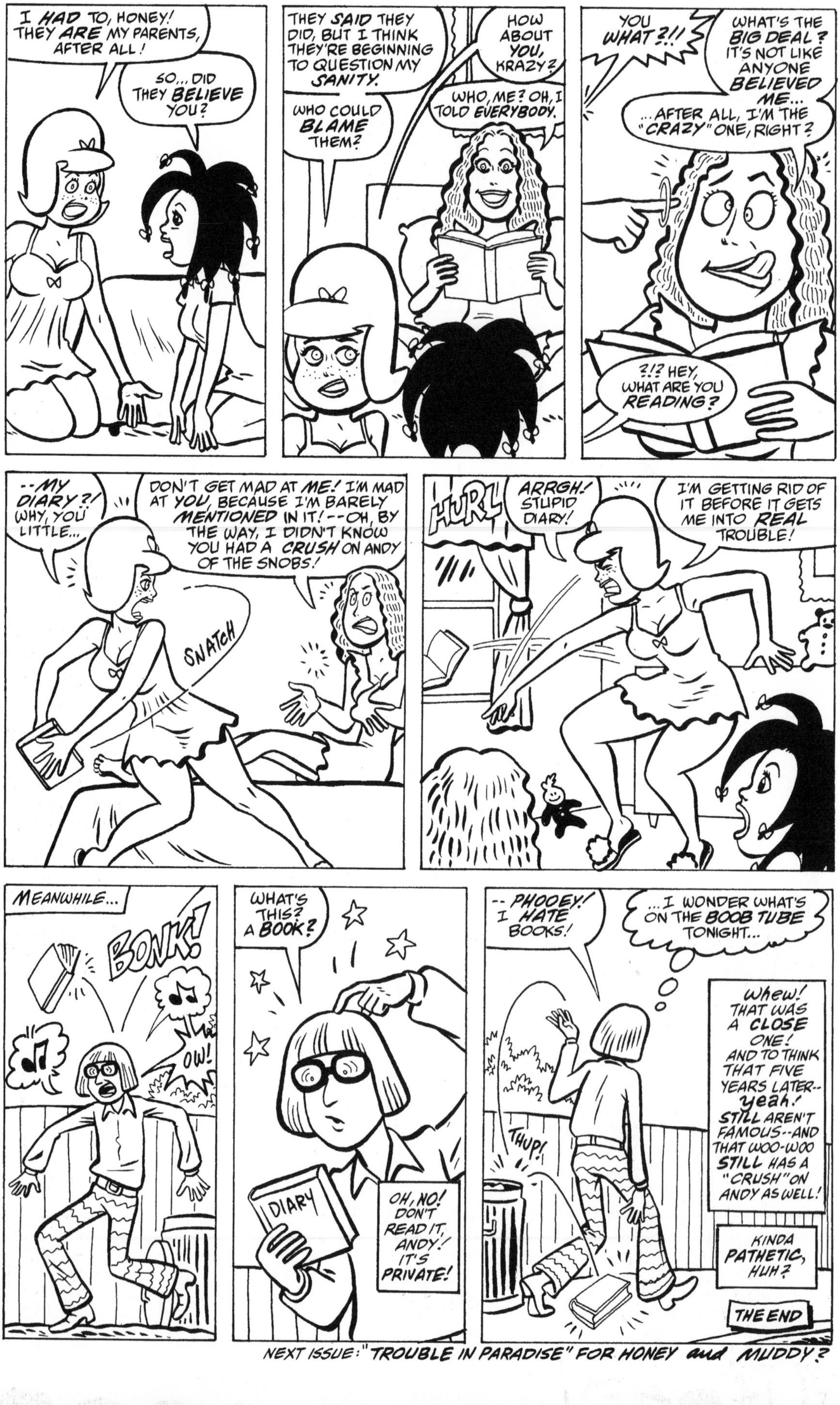
I HAD TO, HONEY! THEY ARE MY PARENTS, AFTER ALL!
SO... DID THEY BELIEVE YOU?
THEY SAID THEY DID, BUT I THINK THEY'RE BEGINNING TO QUESTION MY SANITY.
WHO COULD BLAME THEM?
HOW ABOUT YOU, KRAZY?
WHO, ME? OH, I TOLD EVERYBODY.
YOU WHAT?!!
WHAT'S THE BIG DEAL? IT'S NOT LIKE ANYONE BELIEVED ME...
...AFTER ALL, I'M THE "CRAZY" ONE, RIGHT?
?!? HEY, WHAT ARE YOU READING?
--MY DIARY?! WHY, YOU LITTLE...
DON'T GET MAD AT ME! I'M MAD AT YOU, BECAUSE I'M BARELY MENTIONED IN IT! --OH, BY THE WAY, I DIDN'T KNOW YOU HAD A CRUSH ON ANDY OF THE SNOBS!
SNATCH
HURL
ARRGH! STUPID DIARY!
I'M GETTING RID OF IT BEFORE IT GETS ME INTO REAL TROUBLE!
MEANWHILE...
BONK!
OW!
WHAT'S THIS? A BOOK?
DIARY
OH, NO! DON'T READ IT, ANDY! IT'S PRIVATE!
--PHOOEY! I HATE BOOKS!
...I WONDER WHAT'S ON THE BOOB TUBE TONIGHT...
THUP!
WHEW! THAT WAS A CLOSE ONE! AND TO THINK THAT FIVE YEARS LATER--YEAH! STILL AREN'T FAMOUS--AND THAT WOO-WOO STILL HAS A "CRUSH" ON ANDY AS WELL!
KINDA PATHETIC, HUH?
THE END

NEXT ISSUE: "TROUBLE IN PARADISE" FOR HONEY and MUDDY?

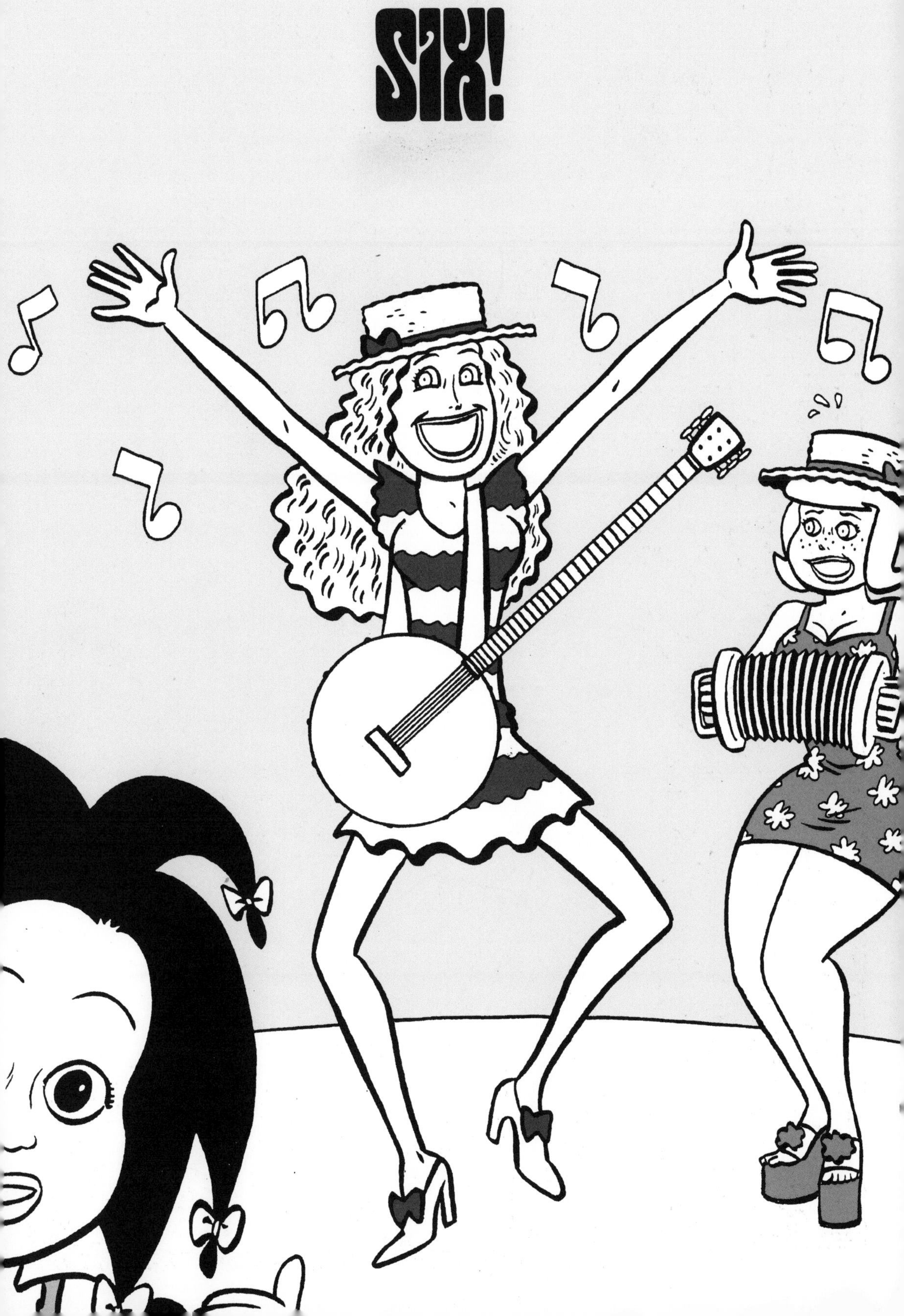
SIX!

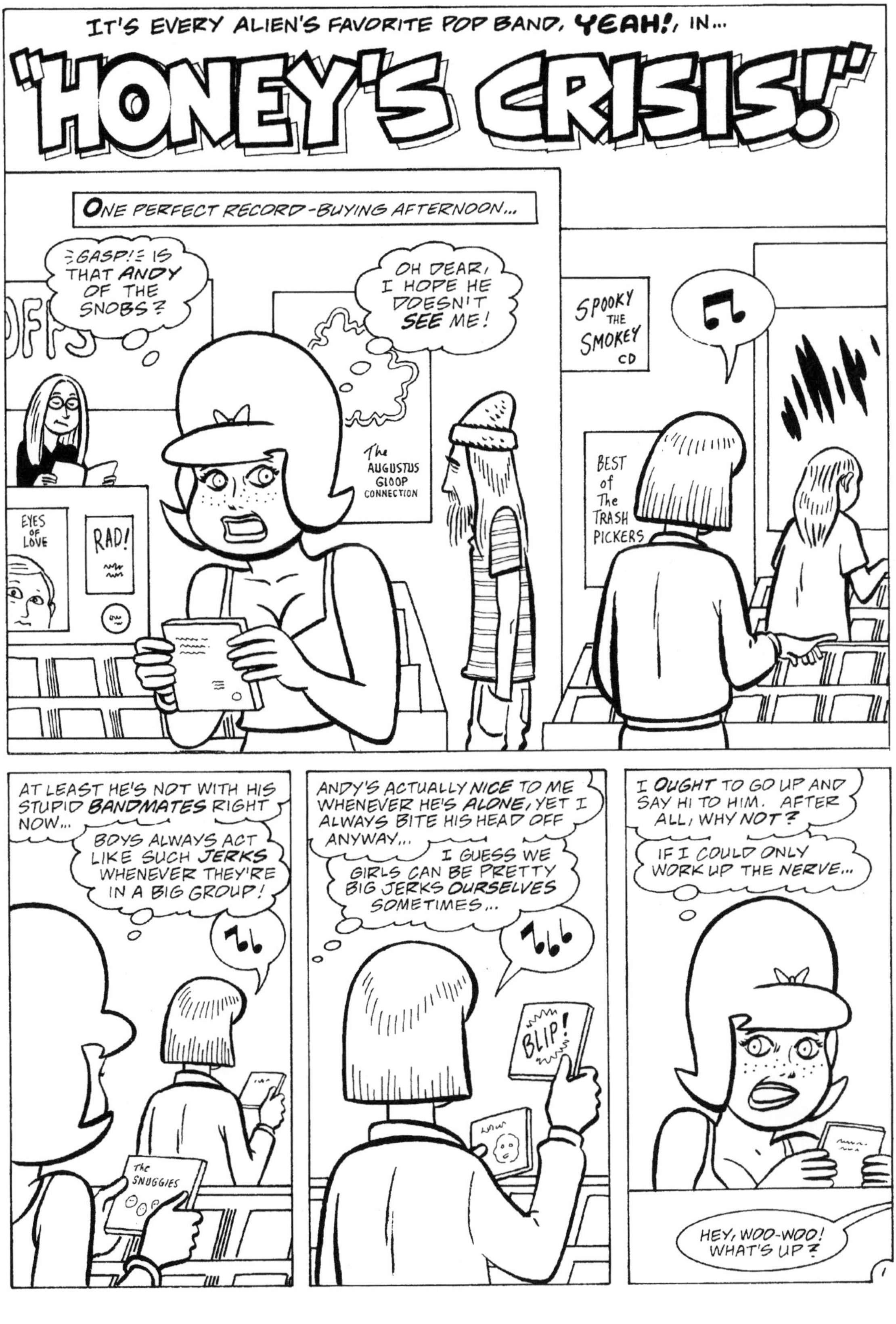
IT'S EVERY ALIEN'S FAVORITE POP BAND, YEAH!, IN...
"HONEY'S CRISIS!"
ONE PERFECT RECORD-BUYING AFTERNOON...
GASP! IS THAT ANDY OF THE SNOBS?
OH DEAR, I HOPE HE DOESN'T SEE ME!
SPOOKY THE SMOKEY CD
The AUGUSTUS GLOOP CONNECTION
BEST of The TRASH PICKERS
EYES OF LOVE
RAD!
AT LEAST HE'S NOT WITH HIS STUPID BANDMATES RIGHT NOW...
BOYS ALWAYS ACT LIKE SUCH JERKS WHENEVER THEY'RE IN A BIG GROUP!
The SNUGGIES
ANDY'S ACTUALLY NICE TO ME WHENEVER HE'S ALONE, YET I ALWAYS BITE HIS HEAD OFF ANYWAY...
I GUESS WE GIRLS CAN BE PRETTY BIG JERKS OURSELVES SOMETIMES...
BLIP!
I OUGHT TO GO UP AND SAY HI TO HIM. AFTER ALL, WHY NOT?
IF I COULD ONLY WORK UP THE NERVE...
HEY, WOO-WOO! WHAT'S UP?

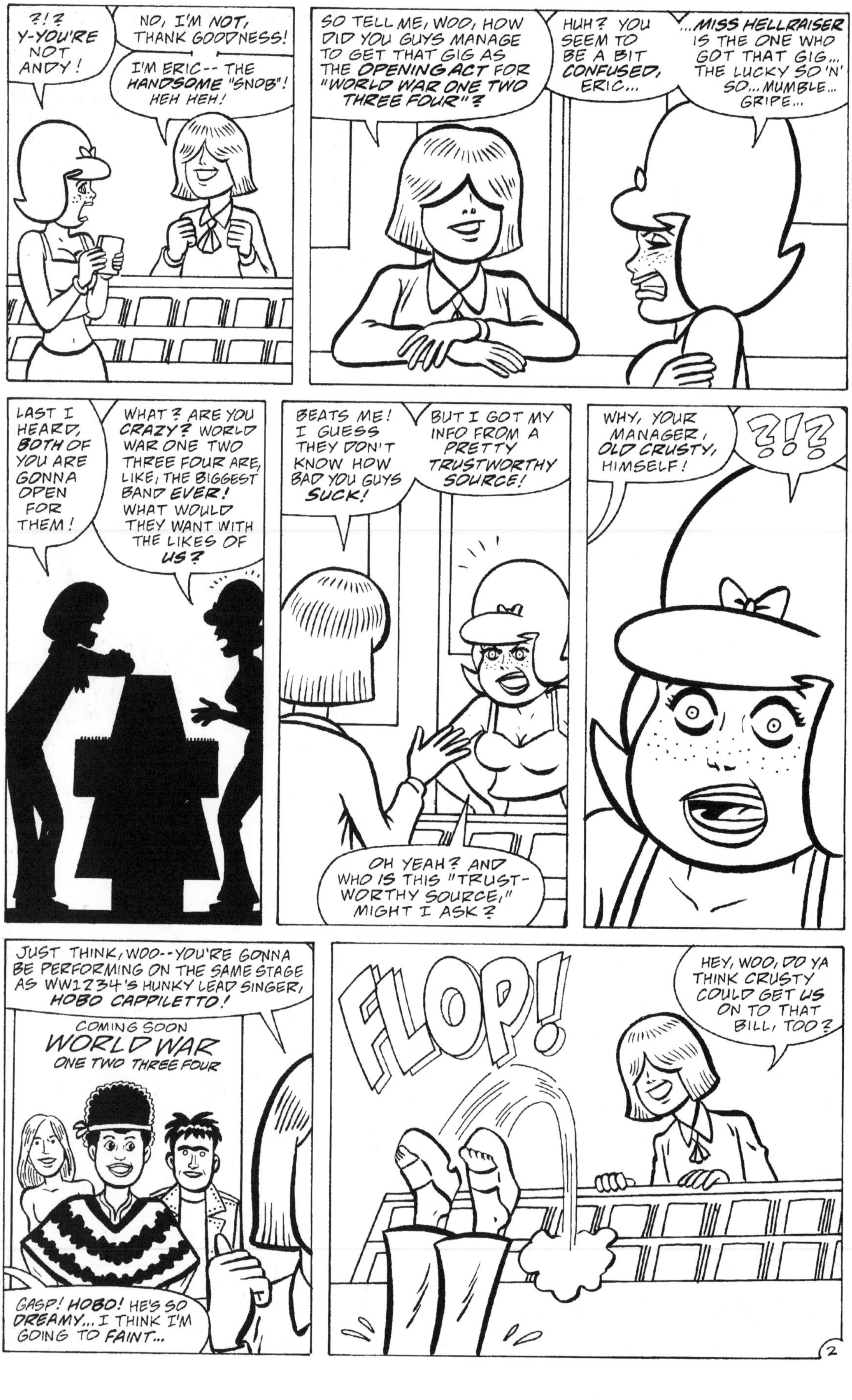
?!? Y-YOU'RE NOT ANDY!
NO, I'M NOT, THANK GOODNESS!
I'M ERIC-- THE HANDSOME "SNOB"! HEH HEH!
SO TELL ME, WOO, HOW DID YOU GUYS MANAGE TO GET THAT GIG AS THE OPENING ACT FOR "WORLD WAR ONE TWO THREE FOUR"?
HUH? YOU SEEM TO BE A BIT CONFUSED, ERIC...
...MISS HELLRAISER IS THE ONE WHO GOT THAT GIG... THE LUCKY SO 'N' SO... MUMBLE... GRIPE...
LAST I HEARD, BOTH OF YOU ARE GONNA OPEN FOR THEM!
WHAT? ARE YOU CRAZY? WORLD WAR ONE TWO THREE FOUR ARE, LIKE, THE BIGGEST BAND EVER! WHAT WOULD THEY WANT WITH THE LIKES OF US?
BEATS ME! I GUESS THEY DON'T KNOW HOW BAD YOU GUYS SUCK!
BUT I GOT MY INFO FROM A PRETTY TRUSTWORTHY SOURCE!
OH YEAH? AND WHO IS THIS "TRUST-WORTHY SOURCE," MIGHT I ASK?
WHY, YOUR MANAGER, OLD CRUSTY, HIMSELF!
?!?
JUST THINK, WOO--YOU'RE GONNA BE PERFORMING ON THE SAME STAGE AS WW1234'S HUNKY LEAD SINGER, HOBO CAPPILETTO!
COMING SOON
WORLD WAR
ONE TWO THREE FOUR
GASP! HOBO! HE'S SO DREAMY... I THINK I'M GOING TO FAINT...
FLOP!
HEY, WOO, DO YA THINK CRUSTY COULD GET US ON TO THAT BILL, TOO?

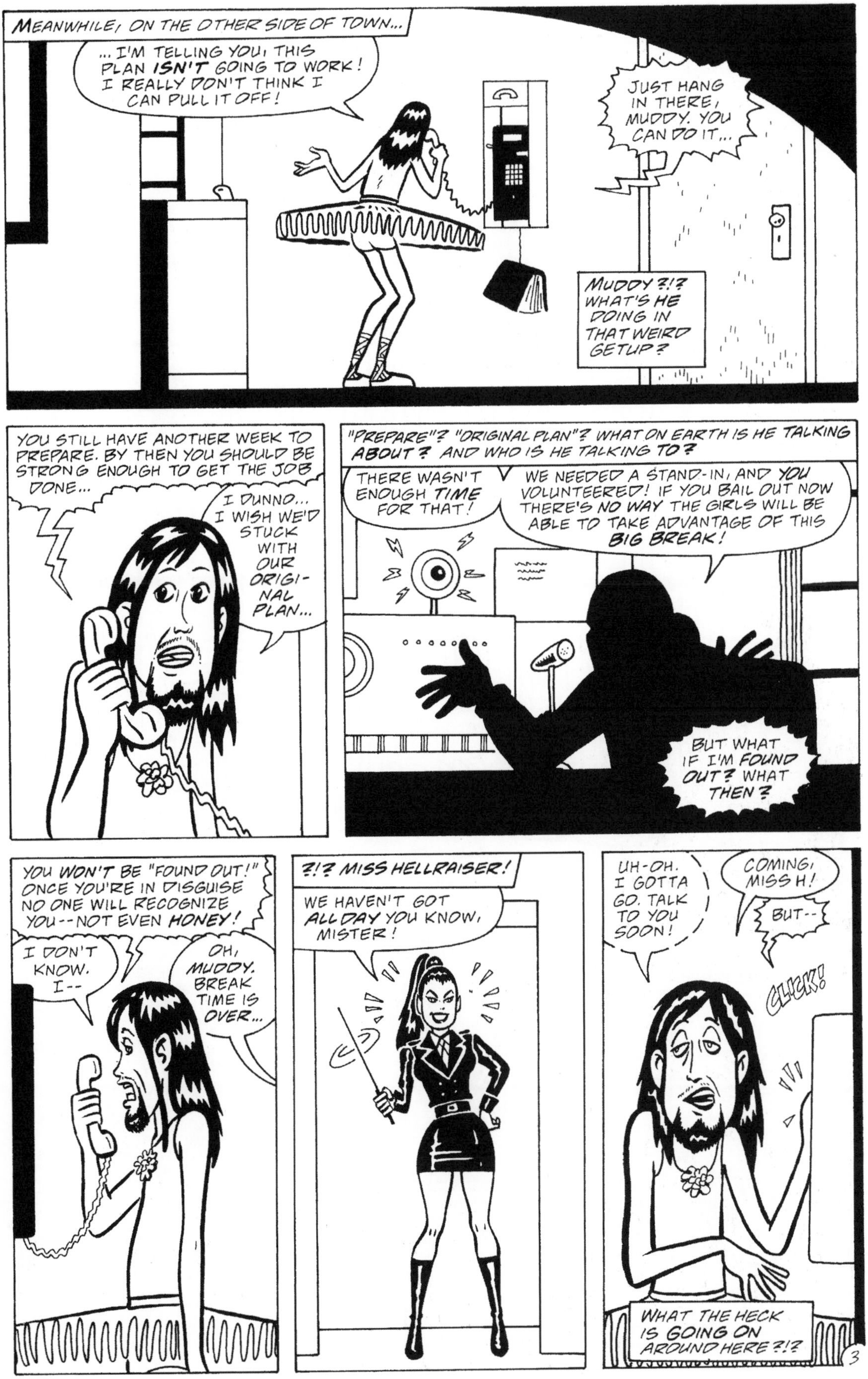

MEANWHILE, ON THE OTHER SIDE OF TOWN...
... I'M TELLING YOU, THIS PLAN ISN'T GOING TO WORK! I REALLY DON'T THINK I CAN PULL IT OFF!
JUST HANG IN THERE, MUDDY. YOU CAN DO IT...
MUDDY?!? WHAT'S HE DOING IN THAT WEIRD GETUP?
YOU STILL HAVE ANOTHER WEEK TO PREPARE. BY THEN YOU SHOULD BE STRONG ENOUGH TO GET THE JOB DONE...
I DUNNO... I WISH WE'D STUCK WITH OUR ORIGINAL PLAN...
"PREPARE"? "ORIGINAL PLAN"? WHAT ON EARTH IS HE TALKING ABOUT? AND WHO IS HE TALKING TO?
THERE WASN'T ENOUGH TIME FOR THAT!
WE NEEDED A STAND-IN, AND YOU VOLUNTEERED! IF YOU BAIL OUT NOW THERE'S NO WAY THE GIRLS WILL BE ABLE TO TAKE ADVANTAGE OF THIS BIG BREAK!
BUT WHAT IF I'M FOUND OUT? WHAT THEN?
YOU WON'T BE "FOUND OUT!" ONCE YOU'RE IN DISGUISE NO ONE WILL RECOGNIZE YOU--NOT EVEN HONEY!
I DON'T KNOW. I--
OH, MUDDY. BREAK TIME IS OVER...
?!? MISS HELLRAISER!
WE HAVEN'T GOT ALL DAY YOU KNOW, MISTER!
UH-OH. I GOTTA GO. TALK TO YOU SOON!
COMING, MISS H!
BUT--
CLICK!
WHAT THE HECK IS GOING ON AROUND HERE?!?

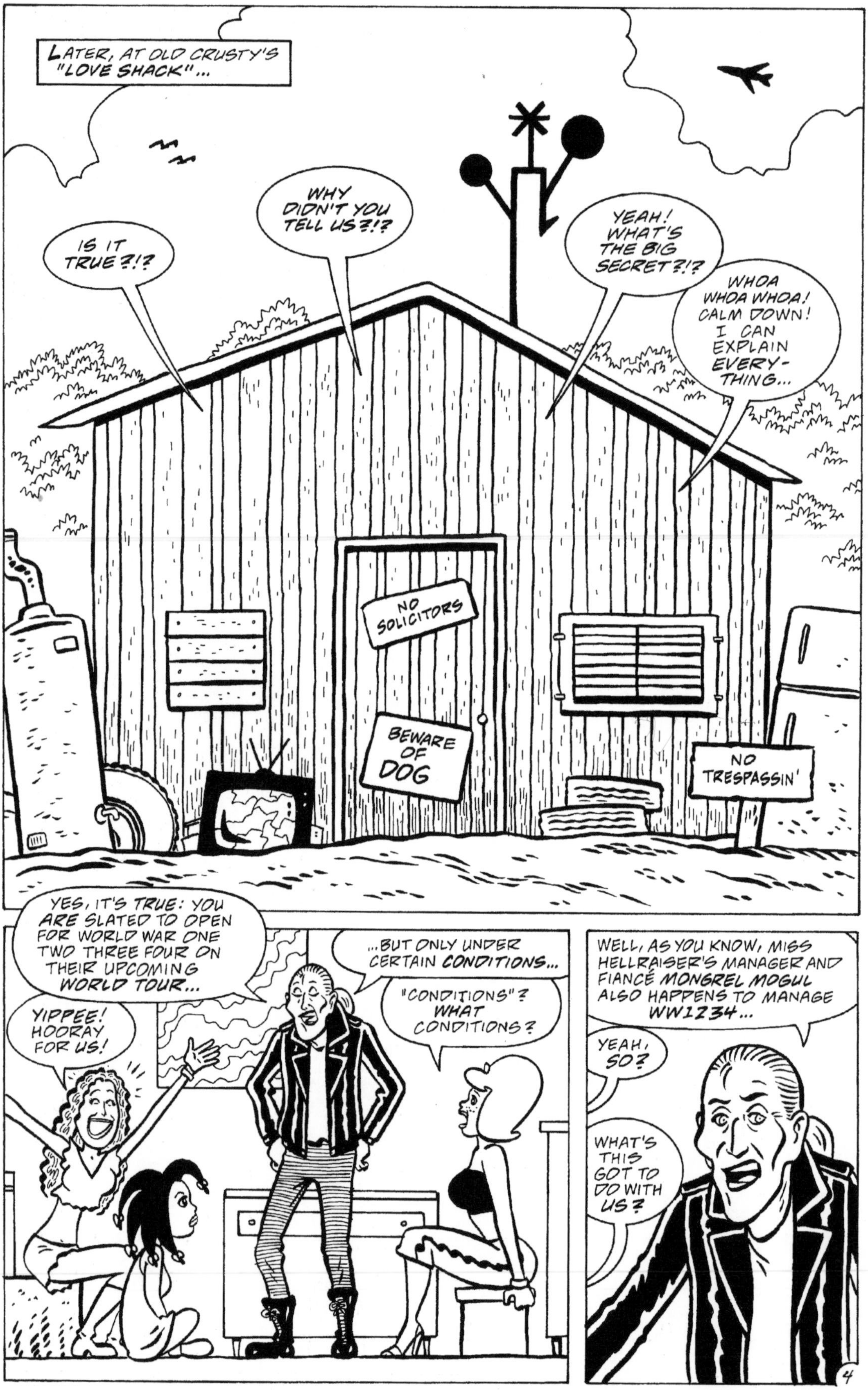
LATER, AT OLD CRUSTY'S "LOVE SHACK"...
IS IT TRUE?!?
WHY DIDN'T YOU TELL US?!?
YEAH! WHAT'S THE BIG SECRET?!?
WHOA WHOA WHOA! CALM DOWN! I CAN EXPLAIN EVERY-THING...
NO SOLICITORS
BEWARE OF DOG
NO TRESPASSIN'
YES, IT'S TRUE: YOU ARE SLATED TO OPEN FOR WORLD WAR ONE TWO THREE FOUR ON THEIR UPCOMING WORLD TOUR...
YIPPEE! HOORAY FOR US!
...BUT ONLY UNDER CERTAIN CONDITIONS...
"CONDITIONS"? WHAT CONDITIONS?
WELL, AS YOU KNOW, MISS HELLRAISER'S MANAGER AND FIANCÉ MONGREL MOGUL ALSO HAPPENS TO MANAGE WW1234...
YEAH, SO?
WHAT'S THIS GOT TO DO WITH US?

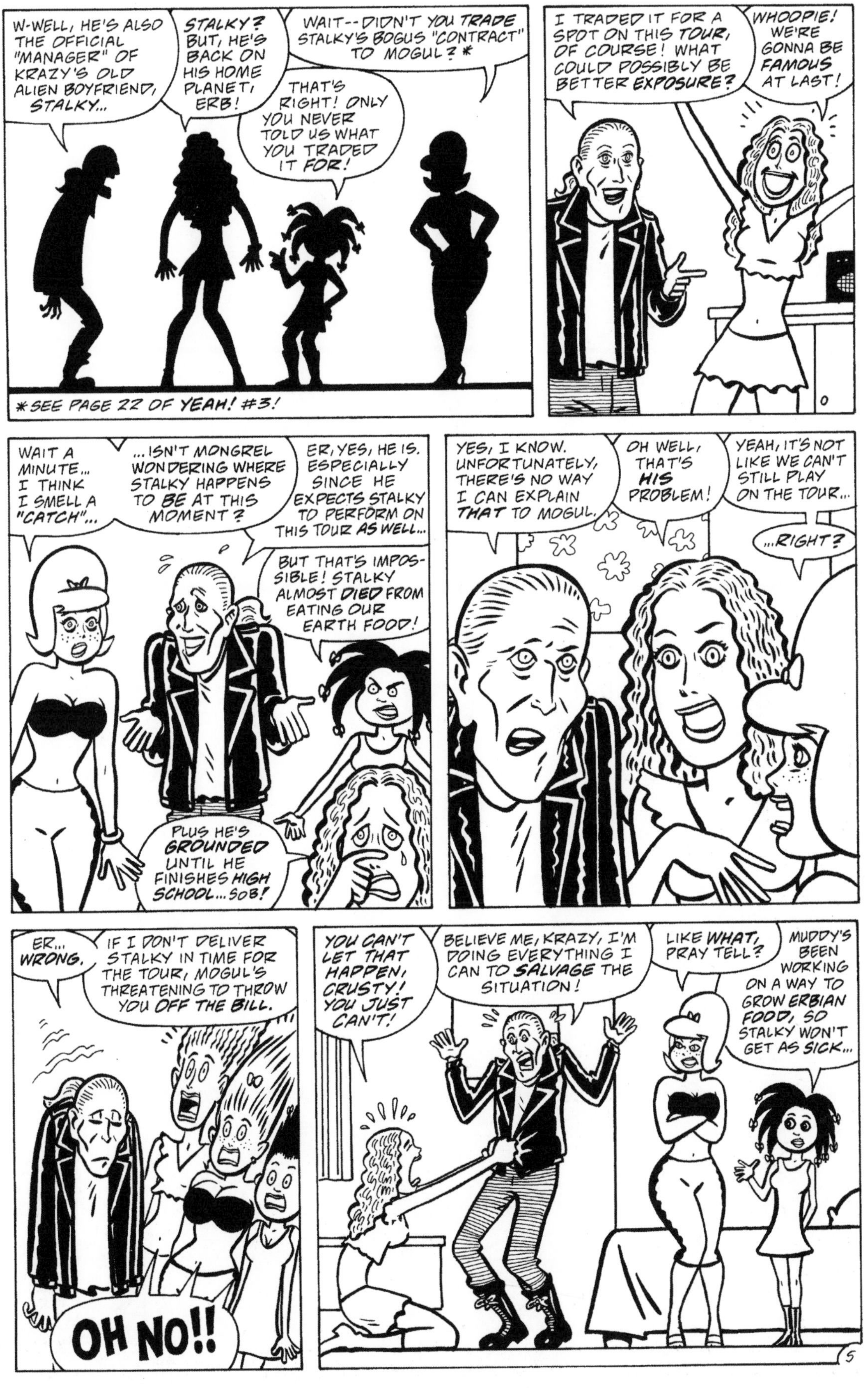
W-WELL, HE'S ALSO THE OFFICIAL "MANAGER" OF KRAZY'S OLD ALIEN BOYFRIEND, STALKY...
STALKY? BUT, HE'S BACK ON HIS HOME PLANET, ERB!
WAIT--DIDN'T YOU TRADE STALKY'S BOGUS "CONTRACT" TO MOGUL? *
THAT'S RIGHT! ONLY YOU NEVER TOLD US WHAT YOU TRADED IT FOR!
* SEE PAGE 22 OF YEAH! #3!
I TRADED IT FOR A SPOT ON THIS TOUR, OF COURSE! WHAT COULD POSSIBLY BE BETTER EXPOSURE?
WHOOPIE! WE'RE GONNA BE FAMOUS AT LAST!
WAIT A MINUTE... I THINK I SMELL A "CATCH"...
...ISN'T MONGREL WONDERING WHERE STALKY HAPPENS TO BE AT THIS MOMENT?
ER, YES, HE IS. ESPECIALLY SINCE HE EXPECTS STALKY TO PERFORM ON THIS TOUR AS WELL...
BUT THAT'S IMPOSSIBLE! STALKY ALMOST DIED FROM EATING OUR EARTH FOOD!
PLUS HE'S GROUNDED UNTIL HE FINISHES HIGH SCHOOL... SOB!
YES, I KNOW. UNFORTUNATELY, THERE'S NO WAY I CAN EXPLAIN THAT TO MOGUL.
OH WELL, THAT'S HIS PROBLEM!
YEAH, IT'S NOT LIKE WE CAN'T STILL PLAY ON THE TOUR...
...RIGHT?
ER... WRONG.
IF I DON'T DELIVER STALKY IN TIME FOR THE TOUR, MOGUL'S THREATENING TO THROW YOU OFF THE BILL.
OH NO!!
YOU CAN'T LET THAT HAPPEN, CRUSTY! YOU JUST CAN'T!
BELIEVE ME, KRAZY, I'M DOING EVERYTHING I CAN TO SALVAGE THE SITUATION!
LIKE WHAT, PRAY TELL?
MUDDY'S BEEN WORKING ON A WAY TO GROW ERBIAN FOOD, SO STALKY WON'T GET AS SICK...

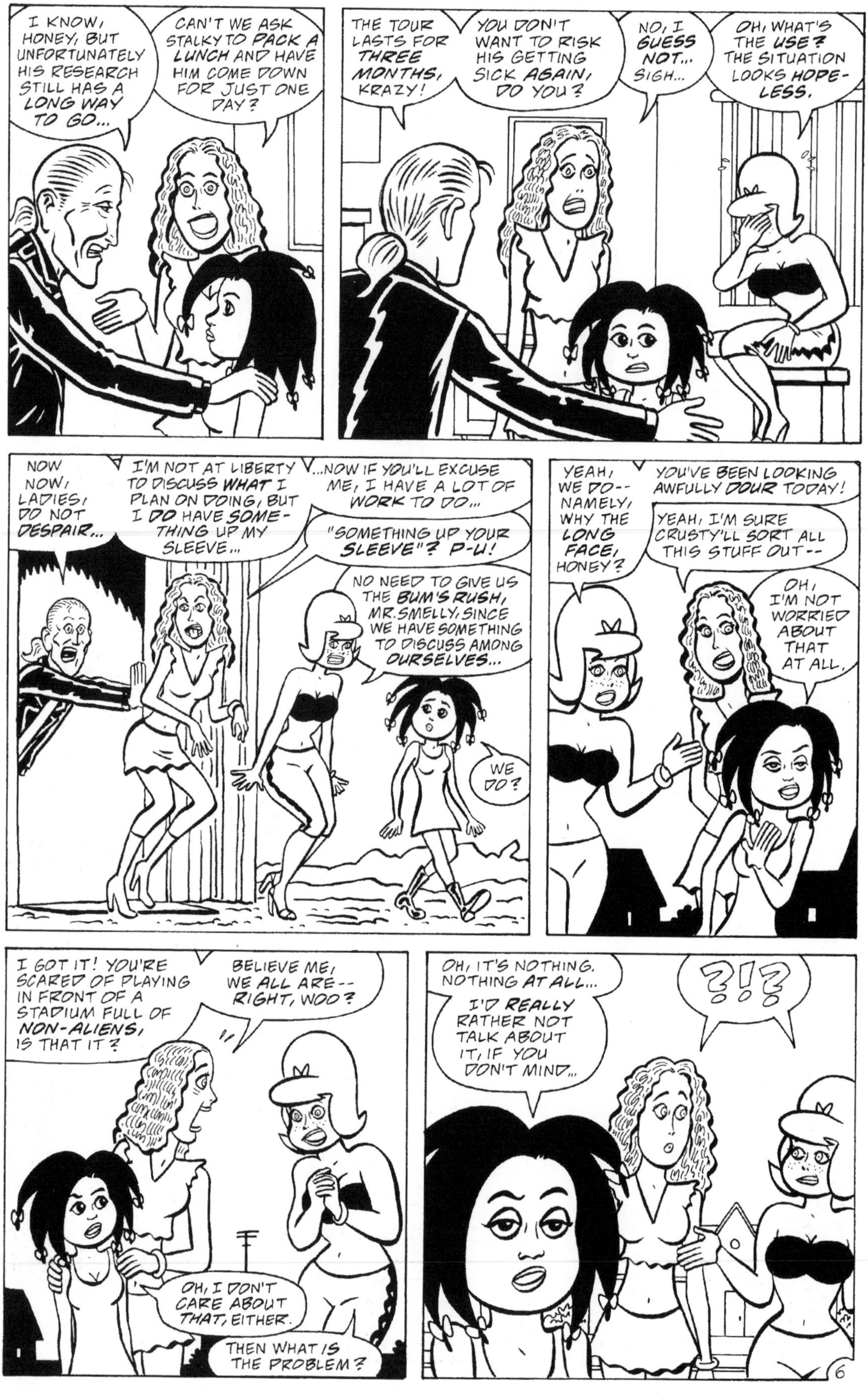

I KNOW, HONEY, BUT UNFORTUNATELY HIS RESEARCH STILL HAS A LONG WAY TO GO...
CAN'T WE ASK STALKY TO PACK A LUNCH AND HAVE HIM COME DOWN FOR JUST ONE DAY?
THE TOUR LASTS FOR THREE MONTHS, KRAZY!
YOU DON'T WANT TO RISK HIS GETTING SICK AGAIN, DO YOU?
NO, I GUESS NOT... SIGH...
OH, WHAT'S THE USE? THE SITUATION LOOKS HOPELESS.
NOW NOW, LADIES, DO NOT DESPAIR...
I'M NOT AT LIBERTY TO DISCUSS WHAT I PLAN ON DOING, BUT I DO HAVE SOMETHING UP MY SLEEVE...
...NOW IF YOU'LL EXCUSE ME, I HAVE A LOT OF WORK TO DO...
"SOMETHING UP YOUR SLEEVE"? P-U!
NO NEED TO GIVE US THE BUM'S RUSH, MR. SMELLY, SINCE WE HAVE SOMETHING TO DISCUSS AMONG OURSELVES...
WE DO?
YEAH, WE DO-- NAMELY, WHY THE LONG FACE, HONEY?
YOU'VE BEEN LOOKING AWFULLY DOUR TODAY!
YEAH, I'M SURE CRUSTY'LL SORT ALL THIS STUFF OUT--
OH, I'M NOT WORRIED ABOUT THAT AT ALL.
I GOT IT! YOU'RE SCARED OF PLAYING IN FRONT OF A STADIUM FULL OF NON-ALIENS, IS THAT IT?
BELIEVE ME, WE ALL ARE-- RIGHT, WOO?
OH, I DON'T CARE ABOUT THAT, EITHER.
THEN WHAT IS THE PROBLEM?
OH, IT'S NOTHING. NOTHING AT ALL...
I'D REALLY RATHER NOT TALK ABOUT IT, IF YOU DON'T MIND...
?!?

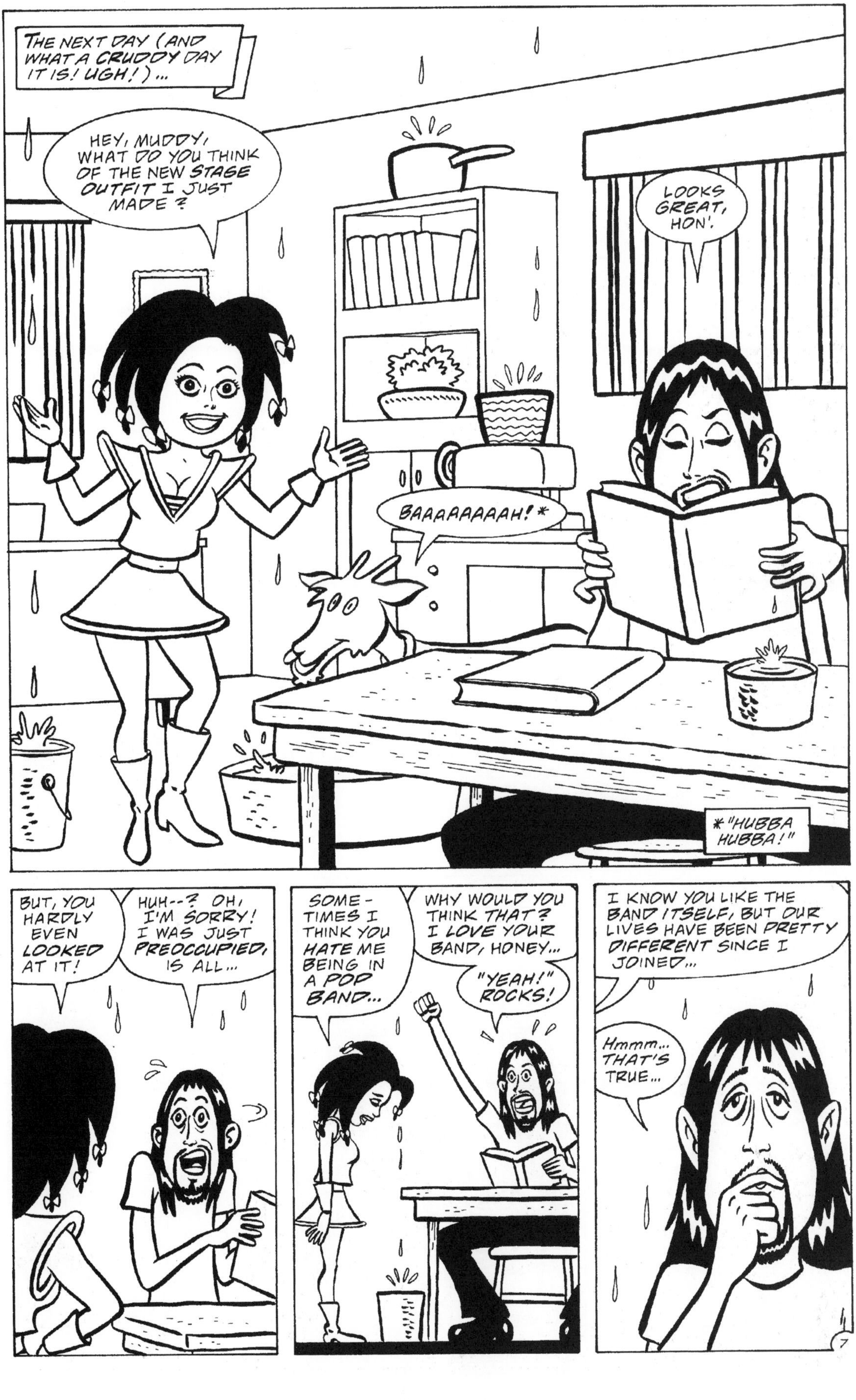
THE NEXT DAY (AND WHAT A CRUDDY DAY IT IS! UGH!)...
HEY, MUDDY, WHAT DO YOU THINK OF THE NEW STAGE OUTFIT I JUST MADE?
LOOKS GREAT, HON'.
BAAAAAAAAH!*
*"HUBBA HUBBA!"
BUT, YOU HARDLY EVEN LOOKED AT IT!
HUH--? OH, I'M SORRY! I WAS JUST PREOCCUPIED, IS ALL...
SOMETIMES I THINK YOU HATE ME BEING IN A POP BAND...
WHY WOULD YOU THINK THAT? I LOVE YOUR BAND, HONEY...
"YEAH!" ROCKS!
I KNOW YOU LIKE THE BAND ITSELF, BUT OUR LIVES HAVE BEEN PRETTY DIFFERENT SINCE I JOINED...
Hmmm... THAT'S TRUE...

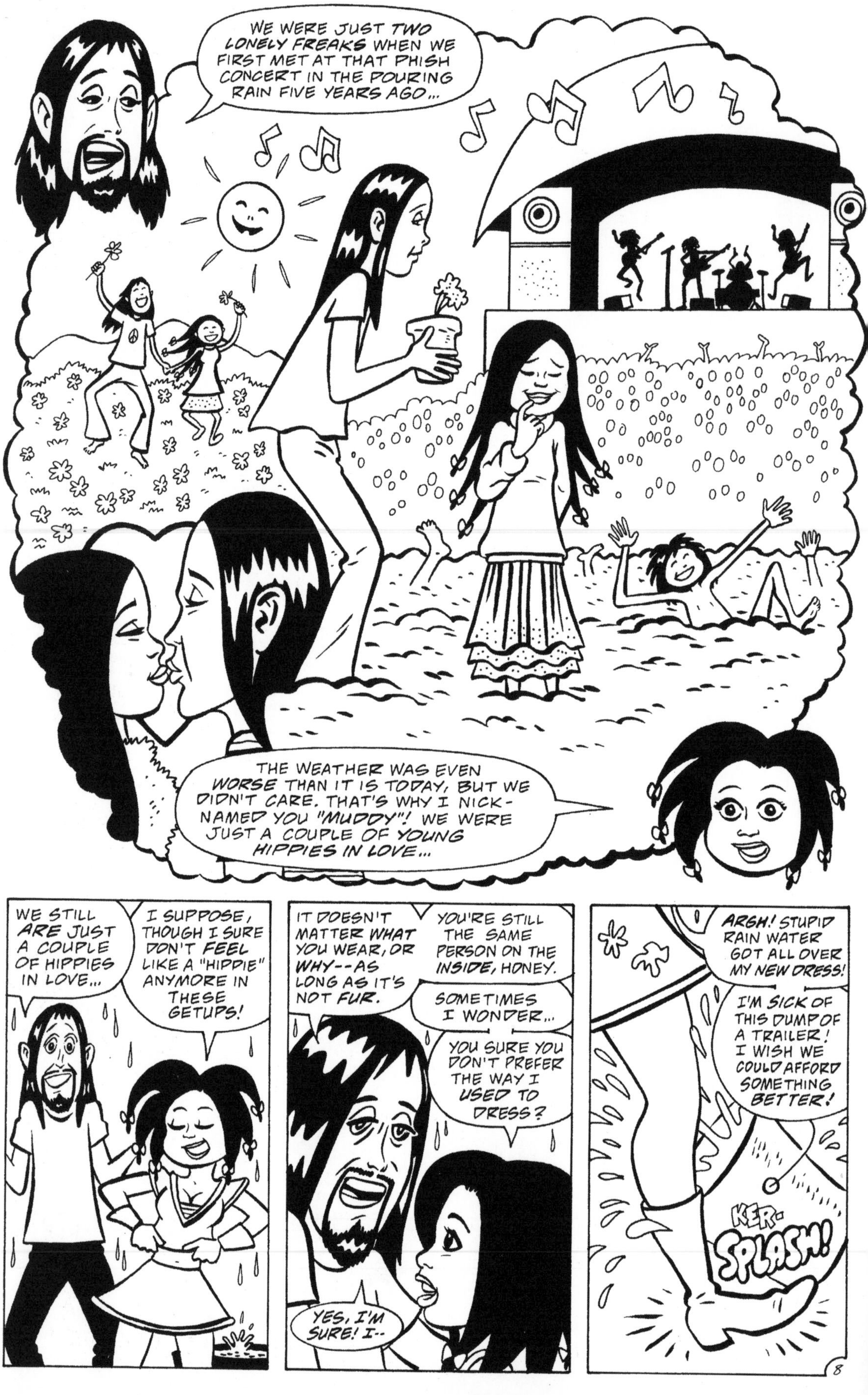

WE WERE JUST TWO LONELY FREAKS WHEN WE FIRST MET AT THAT PHISH CONCERT IN THE POURING RAIN FIVE YEARS AGO...
THE WEATHER WAS EVEN WORSE THAN IT IS TODAY, BUT WE DIDN'T CARE. THAT'S WHY I NICK-NAMED YOU "MUDDY"! WE WERE JUST A COUPLE OF YOUNG HIPPIES IN LOVE...
WE STILL ARE JUST A COUPLE OF HIPPIES IN LOVE...
I SUPPOSE, THOUGH I SURE DON'T FEEL LIKE A "HIPPIE" ANYMORE IN THESE GETUPS!
IT DOESN'T MATTER WHAT YOU WEAR, OR WHY--AS LONG AS IT'S NOT FUR.
YOU'RE STILL THE SAME PERSON ON THE INSIDE, HONEY.
SOMETIMES I WONDER...
YOU SURE YOU DON'T PREFER THE WAY I USED TO DRESS?
YES, I'M SURE! I--
ARGH! STUPID RAIN WATER GOT ALL OVER MY NEW DRESS!
I'M SICK OF THIS DUMP OF A TRAILER! I WISH WE COULD AFFORD SOMETHING BETTER!
KER-SPLASH!

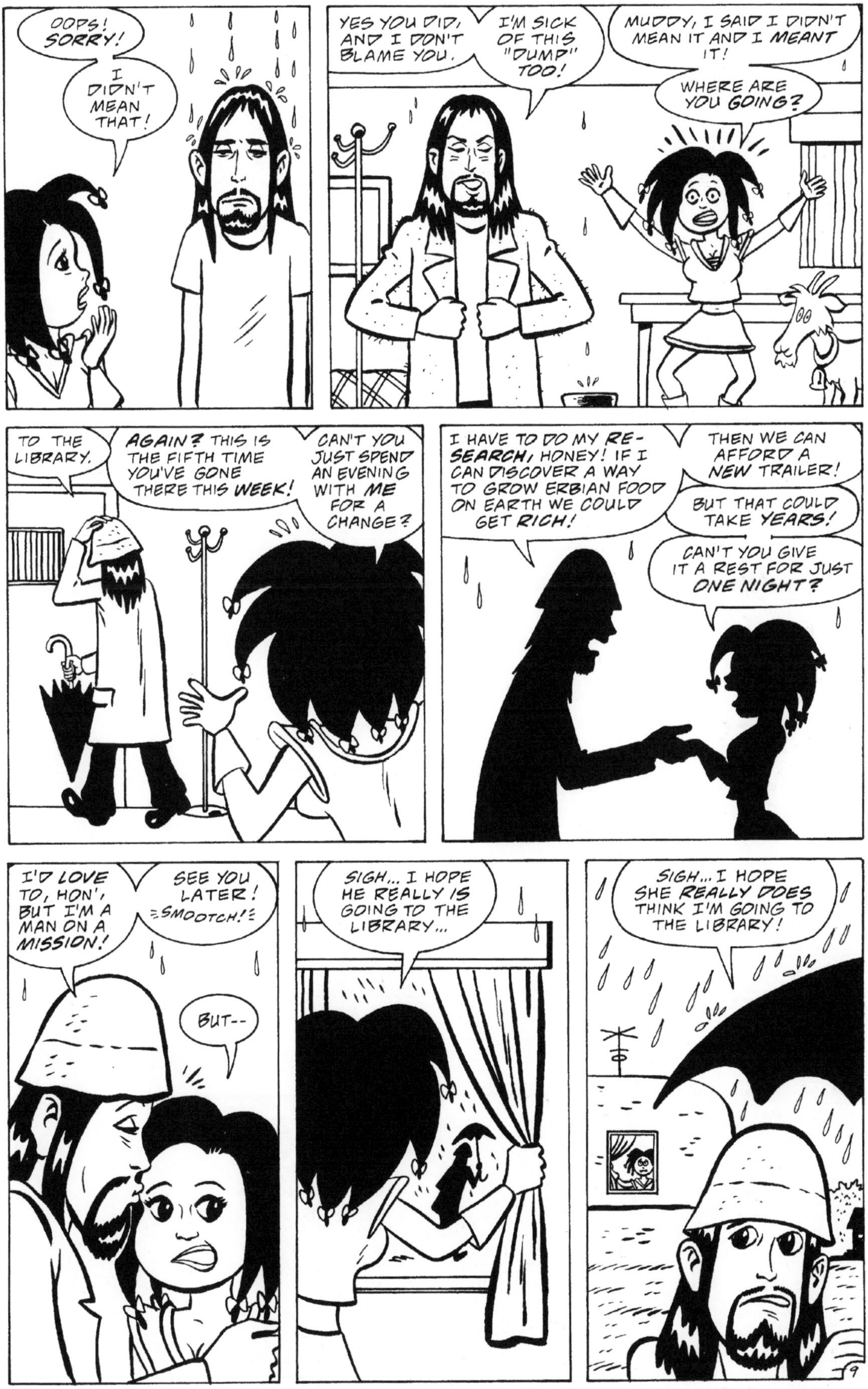
OOPS! SORRY!
I DIDN'T MEAN THAT!
YES YOU DID, AND I DON'T BLAME YOU.
I'M SICK OF THIS "DUMP" TOO!
MUDDY, I SAID I DIDN'T MEAN IT AND I MEANT IT!
WHERE ARE YOU GOING?
TO THE LIBRARY.
AGAIN? THIS IS THE FIFTH TIME YOU'VE GONE THERE THIS WEEK!
CAN'T YOU JUST SPEND AN EVENING WITH ME FOR A CHANGE?
I HAVE TO DO MY RESEARCH, HONEY! IF I CAN DISCOVER A WAY TO GROW ERBIAN FOOD ON EARTH WE COULD GET RICH!
THEN WE CAN AFFORD A NEW TRAILER!
BUT THAT COULD TAKE YEARS!
CAN'T YOU GIVE IT A REST FOR JUST ONE NIGHT?
I'D LOVE TO, HON', BUT I'M A MAN ON A MISSION!
SEE YOU LATER! SMOOTCH!
BUT--
SIGH... I HOPE HE REALLY IS GOING TO THE LIBRARY...
SIGH... I HOPE SHE REALLY DOES THINK I'M GOING TO THE LIBRARY!

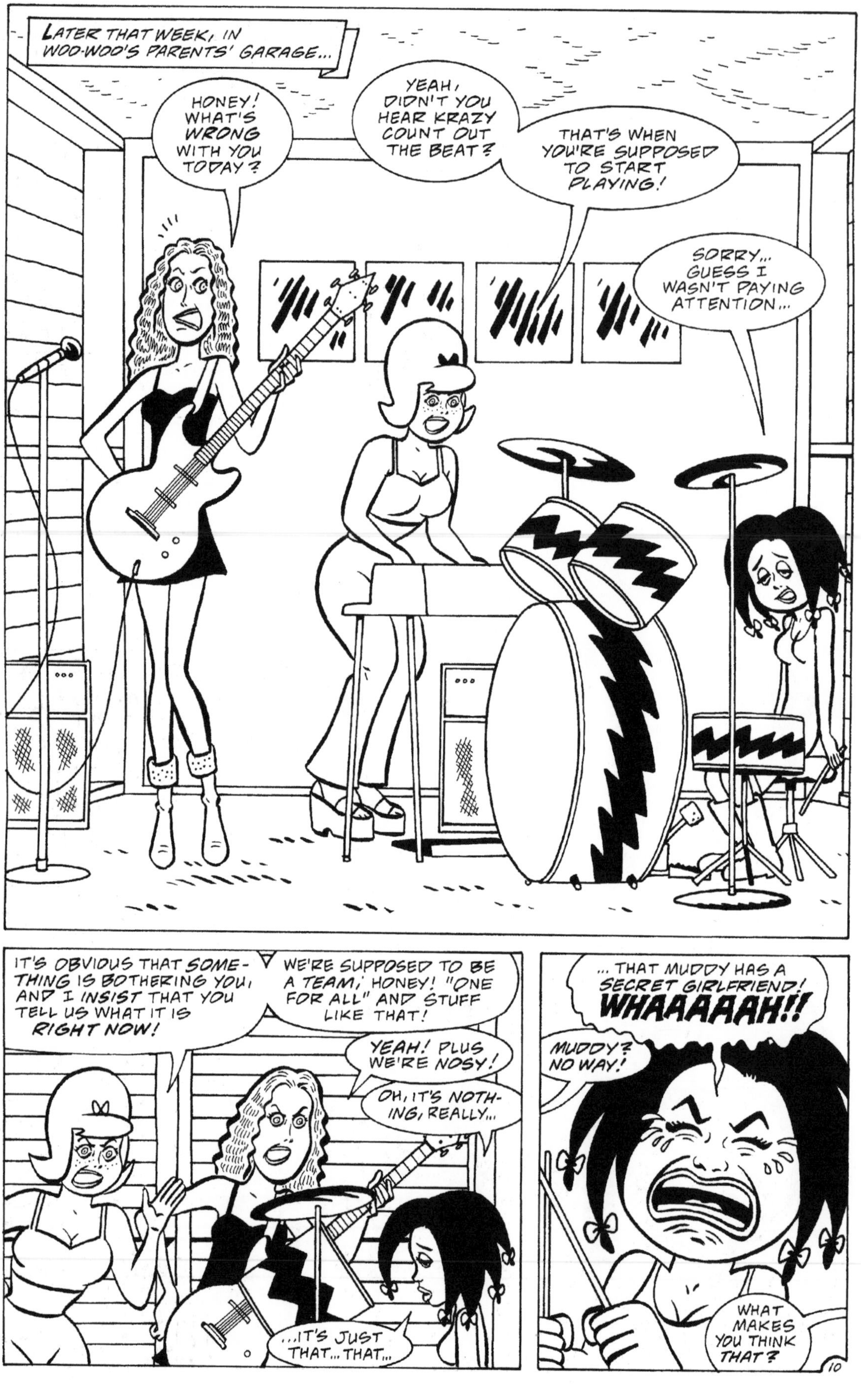
LATER THAT WEEK, IN WOO-WOO'S PARENTS' GARAGE...
HONEY! WHAT'S WRONG WITH YOU TODAY?
YEAH, DIDN'T YOU HEAR KRAZY COUNT OUT THE BEAT?
THAT'S WHEN YOU'RE SUPPOSED TO START PLAYING!
SORRY... GUESS I WASN'T PAYING ATTENTION...
IT'S OBVIOUS THAT SOMETHING IS BOTHERING YOU, AND I INSIST THAT YOU TELL US WHAT IT IS RIGHT NOW!
WE'RE SUPPOSED TO BE A TEAM, HONEY! "ONE FOR ALL" AND STUFF LIKE THAT!
YEAH! PLUS WE'RE NOSY!
OH, IT'S NOTHING, REALLY...
...IT'S JUST THAT... THAT...
...THAT MUDDY HAS A SECRET GIRLFRIEND! WHAAAAAH!!
MUDDY? NO WAY!
WHAT MAKES YOU THINK THAT?

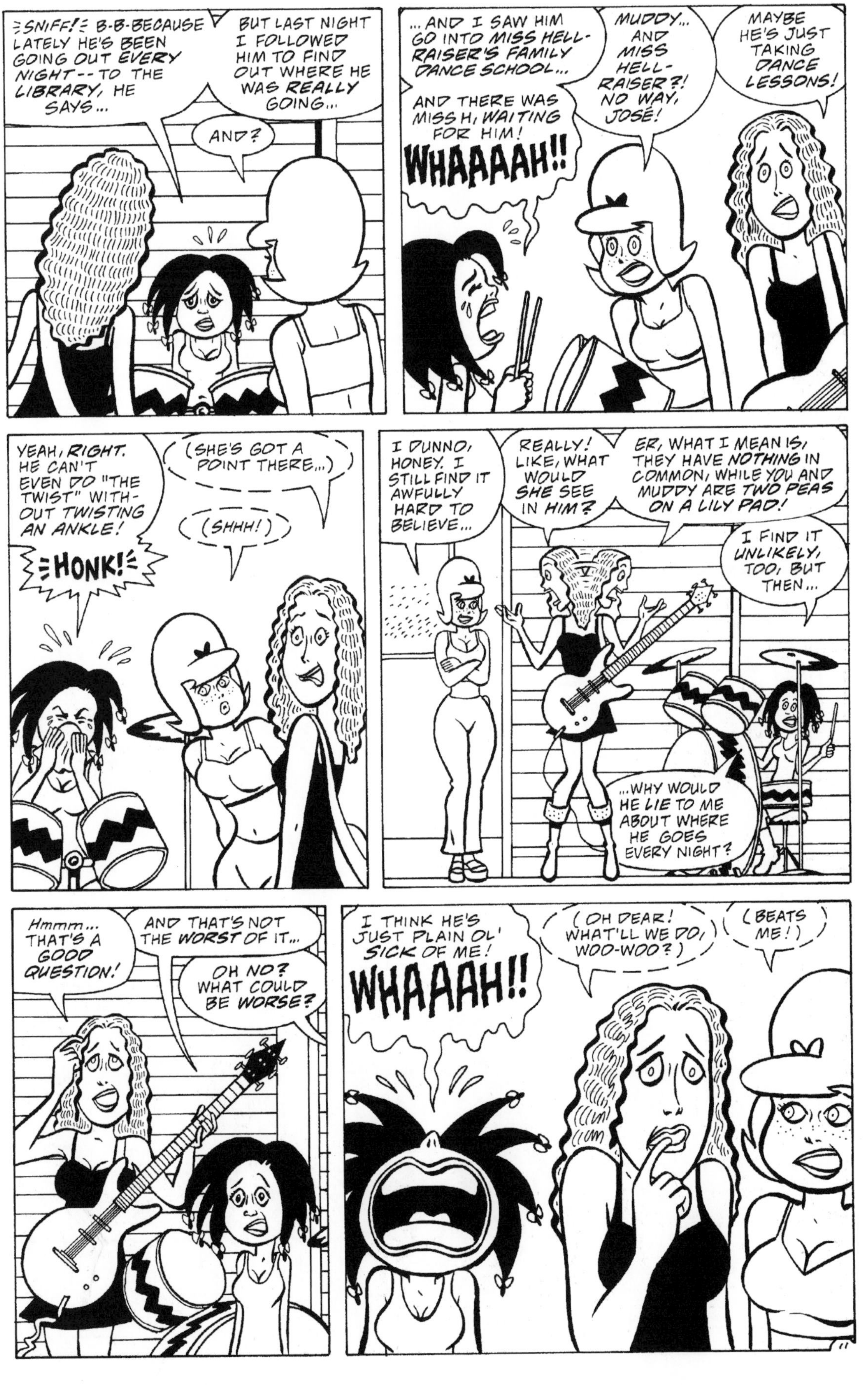

SNIFF! B-B-BECAUSE LATELY HE'S BEEN GOING OUT EVERY NIGHT -- TO THE LIBRARY, HE SAYS...
BUT LAST NIGHT I FOLLOWED HIM TO FIND OUT WHERE HE WAS REALLY GOING...
AND?
...AND I SAW HIM GO INTO MISS HELL-RAISER'S FAMILY DANCE SCHOOL...
AND THERE WAS MISS H, WAITING FOR HIM!
WHAAAAH!!
MUDDY... AND MISS HELL-RAISER?! NO WAY, JOSÉ!
MAYBE HE'S JUST TAKING DANCE LESSONS!
YEAH, RIGHT. HE CAN'T EVEN DO "THE TWIST" WITH-OUT TWISTING AN ANKLE!
HONK!
(SHE'S GOT A POINT THERE...)
(SHHH!)
I DUNNO, HONEY. I STILL FIND IT AWFULLY HARD TO BELIEVE...
REALLY! LIKE, WHAT WOULD SHE SEE IN HIM?
ER, WHAT I MEAN IS, THEY HAVE NOTHING IN COMMON, WHILE YOU AND MUDDY ARE TWO PEAS ON A LILY PAD!
I FIND IT UNLIKELY, TOO, BUT THEN...
...WHY WOULD HE LIE TO ME ABOUT WHERE HE GOES EVERY NIGHT?
Hmmm... THAT'S A GOOD QUESTION!
AND THAT'S NOT THE WORST OF IT...
OH NO? WHAT COULD BE WORSE?
I THINK HE'S JUST PLAIN OL' SICK OF ME!
WHAAAH!!
(OH DEAR! WHAT'LL WE DO, WOO-WOO?)
(BEATS ME!)

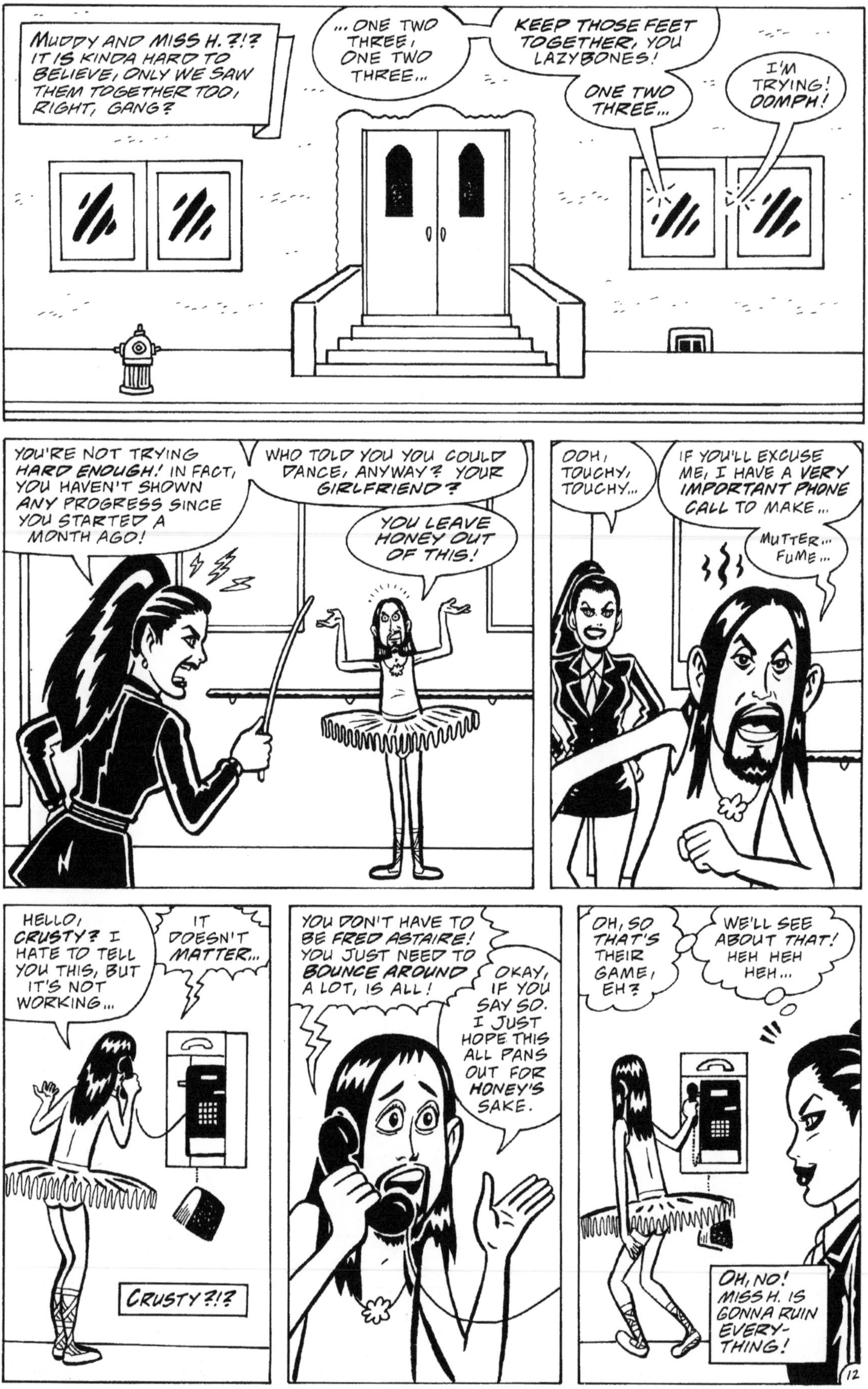
MUDDY AND MISS H.?!? IT IS KINDA HARD TO BELIEVE, ONLY WE SAW THEM TOGETHER TOO, RIGHT, GANG?
...ONE TWO THREE, ONE TWO THREE...
KEEP THOSE FEET TOGETHER, YOU LAZYBONES!
ONE TWO THREE...
I'M TRYING! OOMPH!
YOU'RE NOT TRYING HARD ENOUGH! IN FACT, YOU HAVEN'T SHOWN ANY PROGRESS SINCE YOU STARTED A MONTH AGO!
WHO TOLD YOU YOU COULD DANCE, ANYWAY? YOUR GIRLFRIEND?
YOU LEAVE HONEY OUT OF THIS!
OOH, TOUCHY, TOUCHY...
IF YOU'LL EXCUSE ME, I HAVE A VERY IMPORTANT PHONE CALL TO MAKE...
MUTTER... FUME...
HELLO, CRUSTY? I HATE TO TELL YOU THIS, BUT IT'S NOT WORKING...
IT DOESN'T MATTER...
CRUSTY?!?
YOU DON'T HAVE TO BE FRED ASTAIRE! YOU JUST NEED TO BOUNCE AROUND A LOT, IS ALL!
OKAY, IF YOU SAY SO. I JUST HOPE THIS ALL PANS OUT FOR HONEY'S SAKE.
OH, SO THAT'S THEIR GAME, EH?
WE'LL SEE ABOUT THAT! HEH HEH HEH...
OH, NO! MISS H. IS GONNA RUIN EVERY-THING!

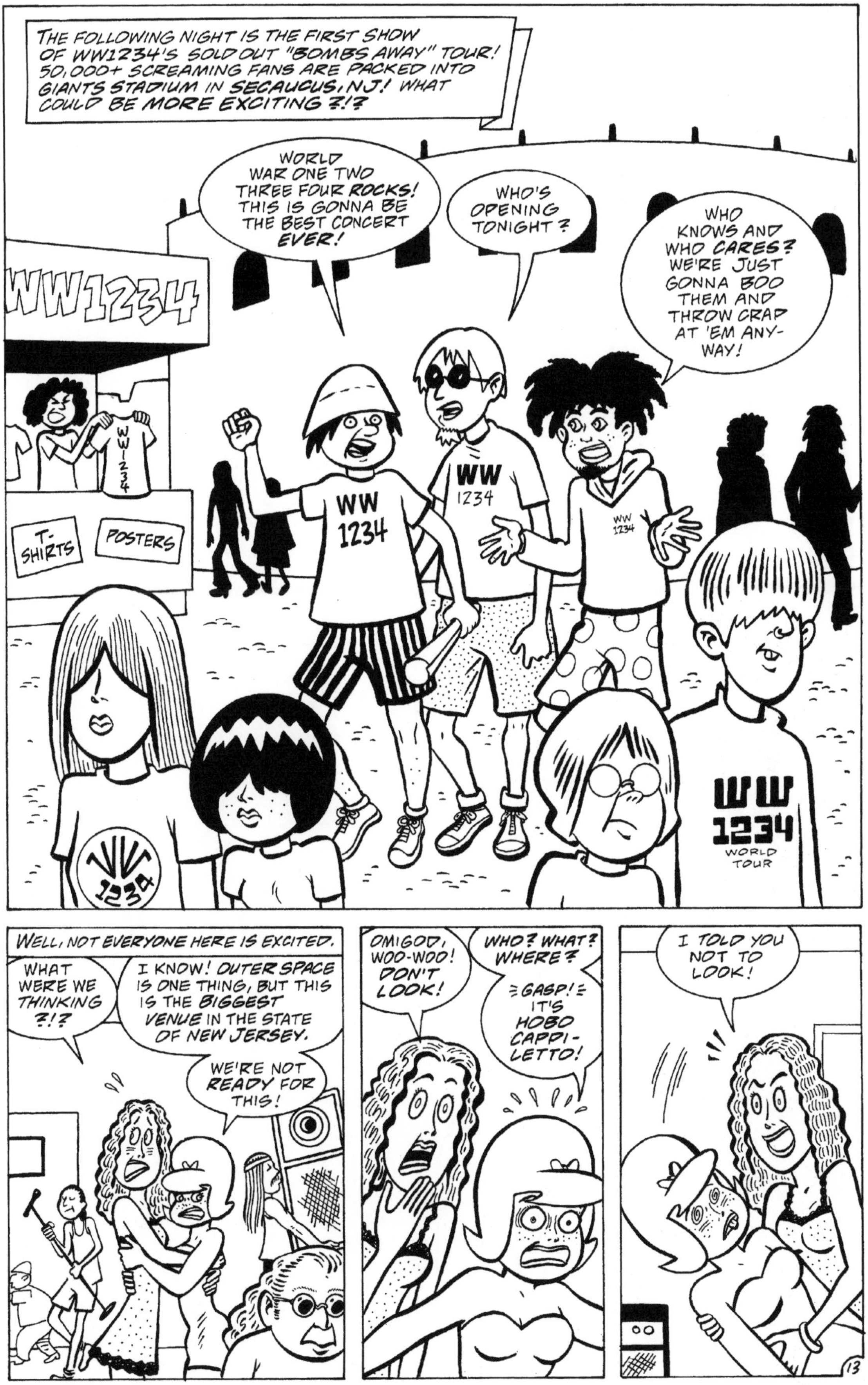
THE FOLLOWING NIGHT IS THE FIRST SHOW OF WW1234'S SOLD OUT "BOMBS AWAY" TOUR! 50,000+ SCREAMING FANS ARE PACKED INTO GIANTS STADIUM IN SECAUCUS, NJ! WHAT COULD BE MORE EXCITING ?!?
WW1234
WORLD WAR ONE TWO THREE FOUR ROCKS! THIS IS GONNA BE THE BEST CONCERT EVER!
WHO'S OPENING TONIGHT?
WHO KNOWS AND WHO CARES? WE'RE JUST GONNA BOO THEM AND THROW CRAP AT 'EM ANYWAY!
WW1234
WW 1234
WW 1234
WW 1234
T-SHIRTS
POSTERS
WW 1234
WW 1234 WORLD TOUR
WELL, NOT EVERYONE HERE IS EXCITED.
WHAT WERE WE THINKING ?!?
I KNOW! OUTER SPACE IS ONE THING, BUT THIS IS THE BIGGEST VENUE IN THE STATE OF NEW JERSEY.
WE'RE NOT READY FOR THIS!
OMIGOD, WOO-WOO! DON'T LOOK!
WHO? WHAT? WHERE?
GASP! IT'S HOBO CAPPILETTO!
I TOLD YOU NOT TO LOOK!

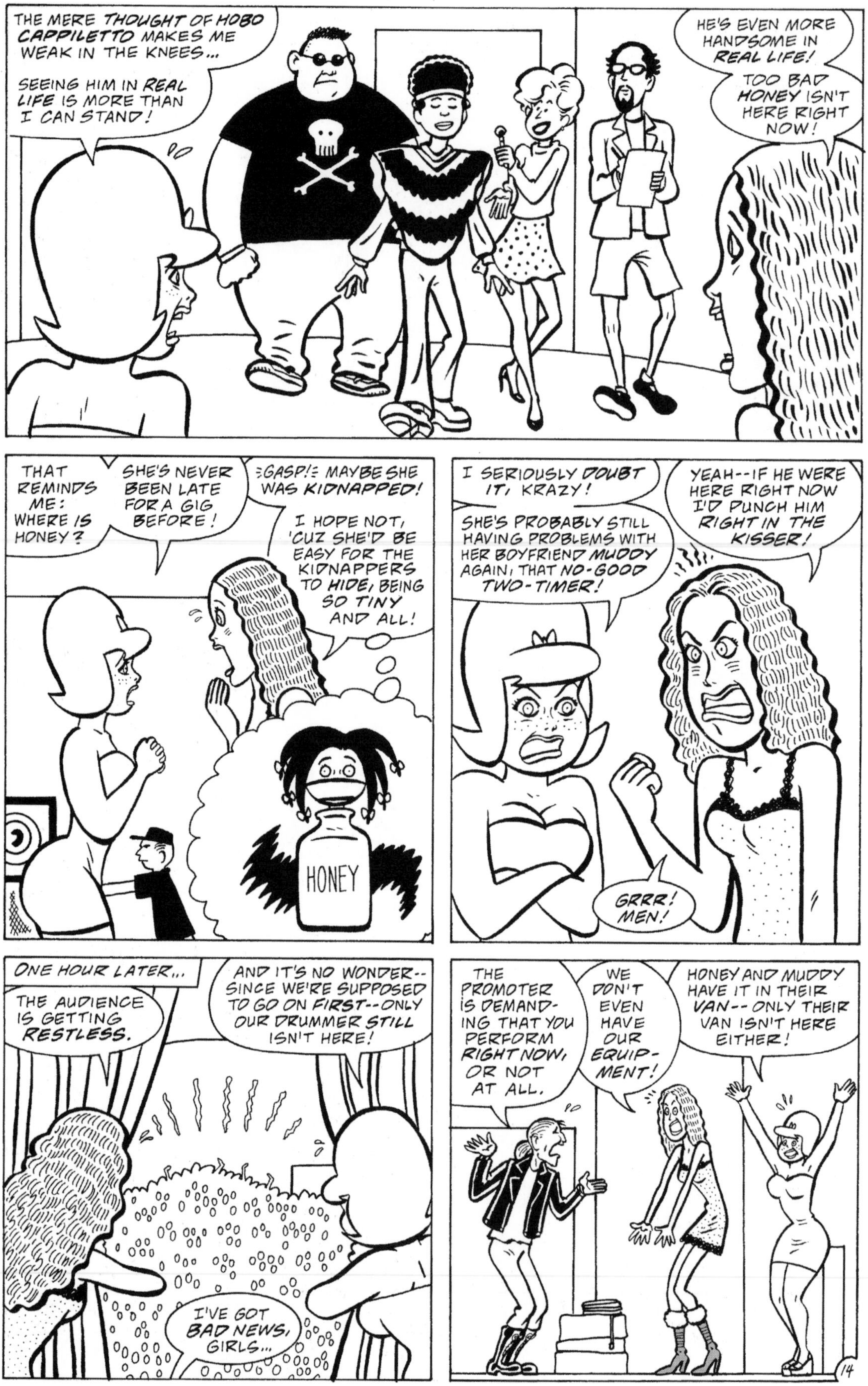
THE MERE THOUGHT OF HOBO CAPPILETTO MAKES ME WEAK IN THE KNEES...
SEEING HIM IN REAL LIFE IS MORE THAN I CAN STAND!
HE'S EVEN MORE HANDSOME IN REAL LIFE!
TOO BAD HONEY ISN'T HERE RIGHT NOW!
THAT REMINDS ME: WHERE IS HONEY?
SHE'S NEVER BEEN LATE FOR A GIG BEFORE!
=GASP!= MAYBE SHE WAS KIDNAPPED!
I HOPE NOT, 'CUZ SHE'D BE EASY FOR THE KIDNAPPERS TO HIDE, BEING SO TINY AND ALL!
HONEY
I SERIOUSLY DOUBT IT, KRAZY!
SHE'S PROBABLY STILL HAVING PROBLEMS WITH HER BOYFRIEND MUDDY AGAIN, THAT NO-GOOD TWO-TIMER!
YEAH--IF HE WERE HERE RIGHT NOW I'D PUNCH HIM RIGHT IN THE KISSER!
GRRR! MEN!
ONE HOUR LATER...
THE AUDIENCE IS GETTING RESTLESS.
AND IT'S NO WONDER--SINCE WE'RE SUPPOSED TO GO ON FIRST--ONLY OUR DRUMMER STILL ISN'T HERE!
I'VE GOT BAD NEWS, GIRLS...
THE PROMOTER IS DEMANDING THAT YOU PERFORM RIGHT NOW, OR NOT AT ALL.
WE DON'T EVEN HAVE OUR EQUIPMENT!
HONEY AND MUDDY HAVE IT IN THEIR VAN--ONLY THEIR VAN ISN'T HERE EITHER!
14

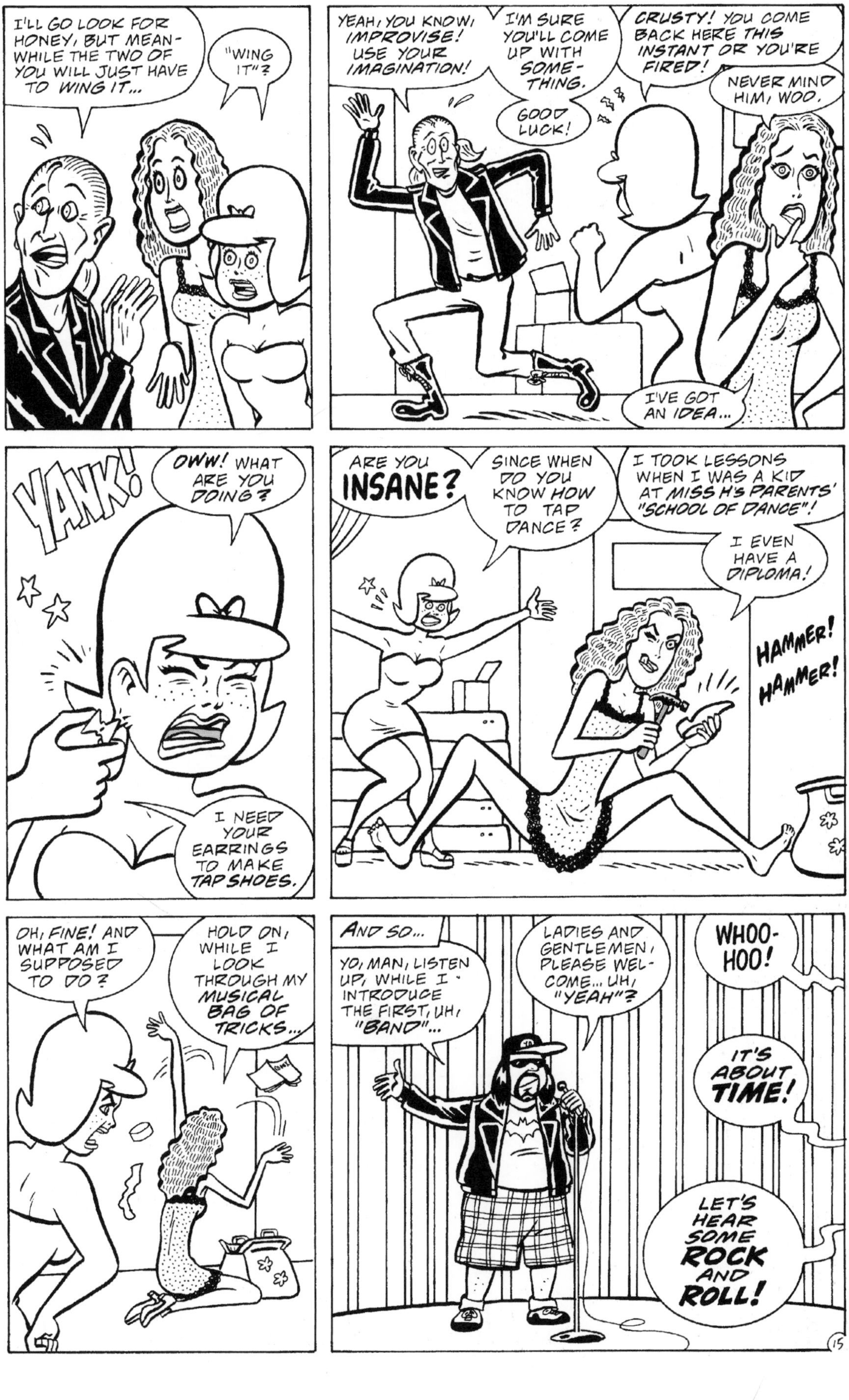
I'LL GO LOOK FOR HONEY, BUT MEAN-WHILE THE TWO OF YOU WILL JUST HAVE TO WING IT...
"WING IT"?
YEAH, YOU KNOW, IMPROVISE! USE YOUR IMAGINATION!
I'M SURE YOU'LL COME UP WITH SOME-THING.
GOOD LUCK!
CRUSTY! YOU COME BACK HERE THIS INSTANT OR YOU'RE FIRED!
NEVER MIND HIM, WOO.
I'VE GOT AN IDEA...
YANK!
OWW! WHAT ARE YOU DOING?
I NEED YOUR EARRINGS TO MAKE TAP SHOES.
ARE YOU INSANE?
SINCE WHEN DO YOU KNOW HOW TO TAP DANCE?
I TOOK LESSONS WHEN I WAS A KID AT MISS H's PARENTS' "SCHOOL OF DANCE"!
I EVEN HAVE A DIPLOMA!
HAMMER! HAMMER!
OH, FINE! AND WHAT AM I SUPPOSED TO DO?
HOLD ON, WHILE I LOOK THROUGH MY MUSICAL BAG OF TRICKS...
AND SO...
YO, MAN, LISTEN UP, WHILE I INTRODUCE THE FIRST, UH, "BAND"...
LADIES AND GENTLEMEN, PLEASE WEL-COME... UH, "YEAH"?
WHOO-HOO!
IT'S ABOUT TIME!
LET'S HEAR SOME ROCK AND ROLL!

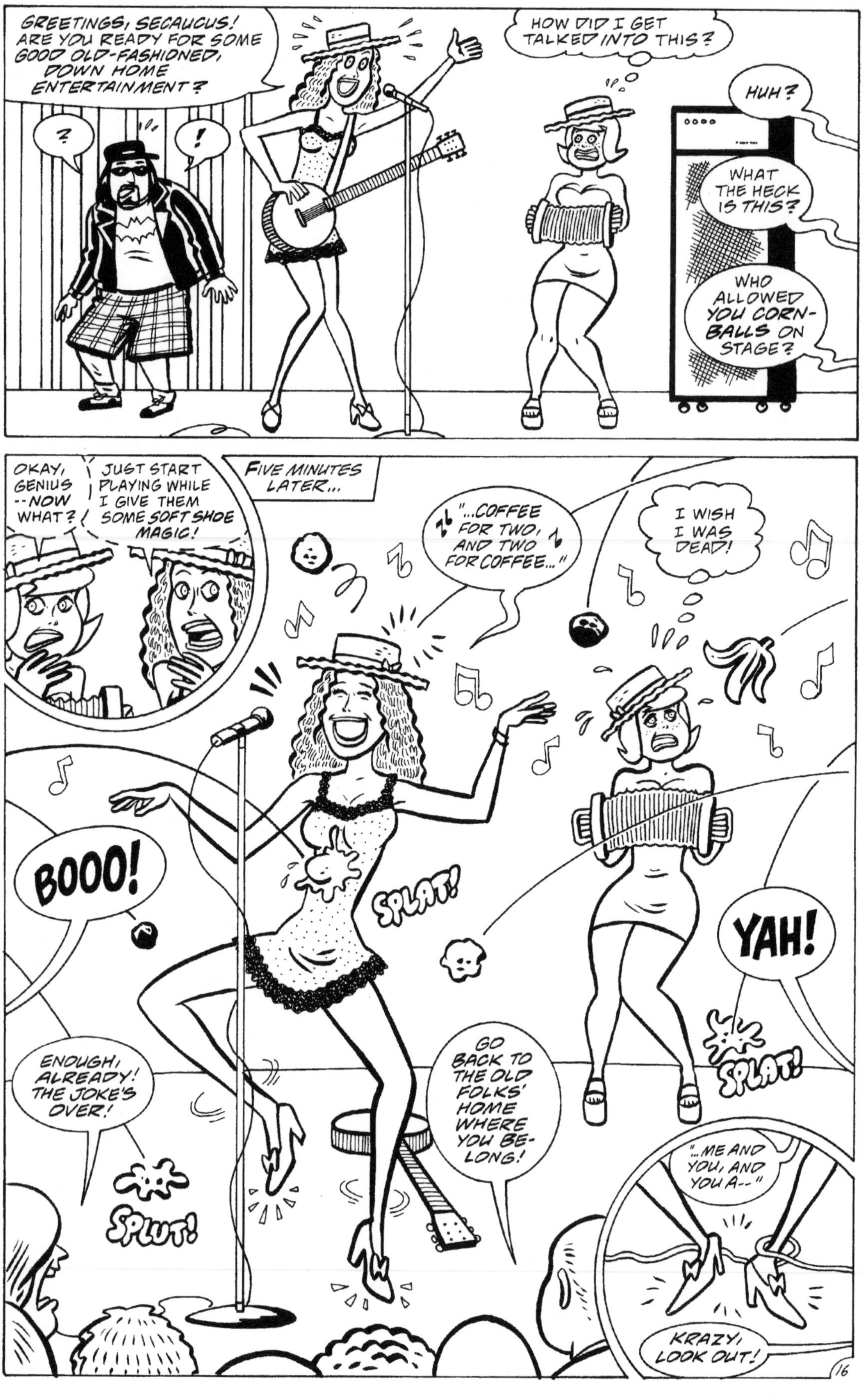
GREETINGS, SECAUCUS! ARE YOU READY FOR SOME GOOD OLD-FASHIONED, DOWN HOME ENTERTAINMENT?
HOW DID I GET TALKED INTO THIS?
?
!
HUH?
WHAT THE HECK IS THIS?
WHO ALLOWED YOU CORN-BALLS ON STAGE?
OKAY, GENIUS --NOW WHAT?
JUST START PLAYING WHILE I GIVE THEM SOME SOFT SHOE MAGIC!
FIVE MINUTES LATER...
"...COFFEE FOR TWO, AND TWO FOR COFFEE..."
I WISH I WAS DEAD!
BOOO!
SPLAT!
YAH!
ENOUGH, ALREADY! THE JOKE'S OVER!
GO BACK TO THE OLD FOLKS' HOME WHERE YOU BE-LONG!
SPLAT!
SPLUT!
"...ME AND YOU, AND YOU A--"
KRAZY, LOOK OUT!

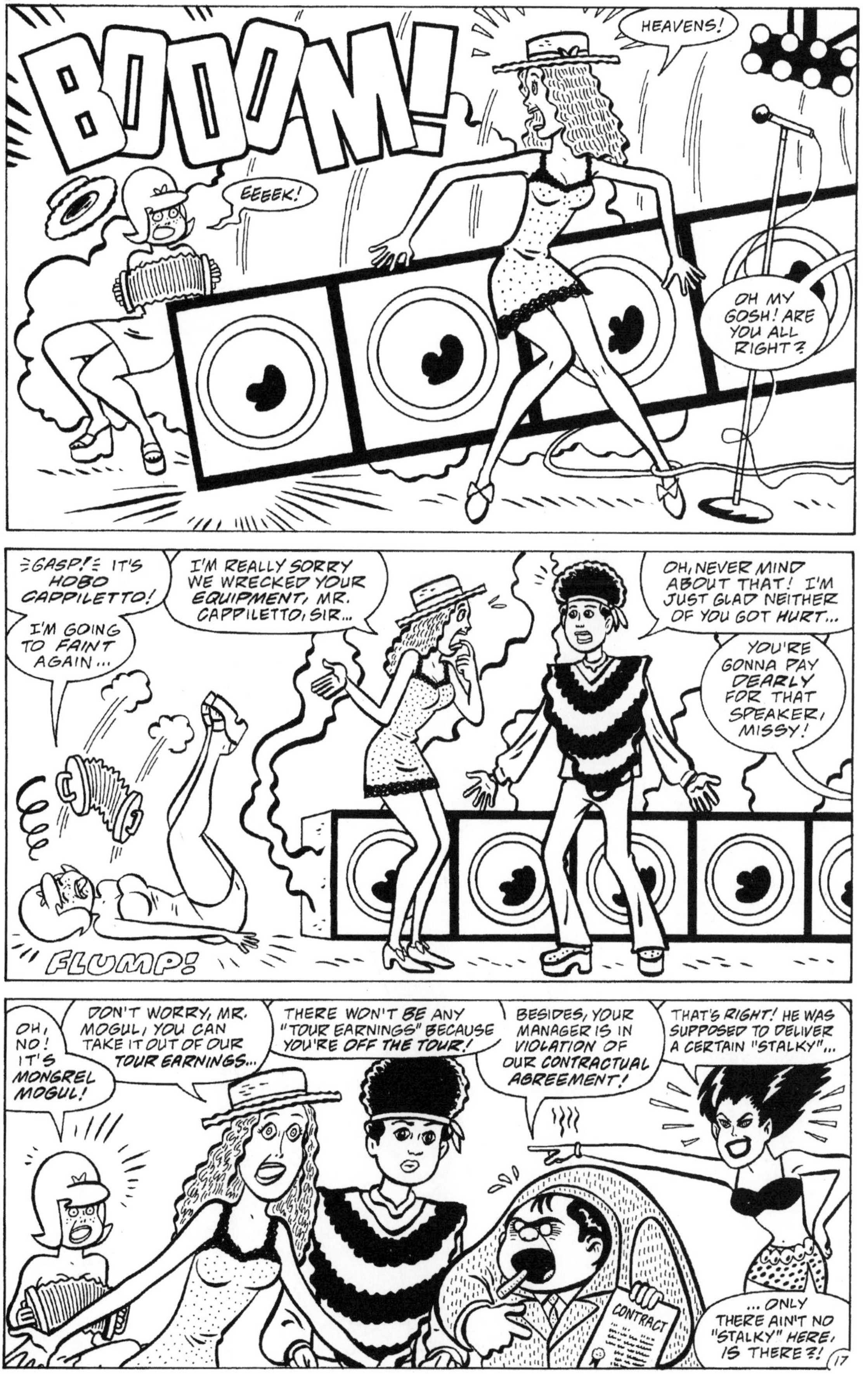
BOOOM!
HEAVENS!
EEEEK!
OH MY GOSH! ARE YOU ALL RIGHT?
≡GASP!≡ IT'S HOBO CAPPILETTO!
I'M GOING TO FAINT AGAIN...
I'M REALLY SORRY WE WRECKED YOUR EQUIPMENT, MR. CAPPILETTO, SIR...
OH, NEVER MIND ABOUT THAT! I'M JUST GLAD NEITHER OF YOU GOT HURT...
YOU'RE GONNA PAY DEARLY FOR THAT SPEAKER, MISSY!
FLUMP!
OH, NO! IT'S MONGREL MOGUL!
DON'T WORRY, MR. MOGUL, YOU CAN TAKE IT OUT OF OUR TOUR EARNINGS...
THERE WON'T BE ANY "TOUR EARNINGS" BECAUSE YOU'RE OFF THE TOUR!
BESIDES, YOUR MANAGER IS IN VIOLATION OF OUR CONTRACTUAL AGREEMENT!
THAT'S RIGHT! HE WAS SUPPOSED TO DELIVER A CERTAIN "STALKY"...
CONTRACT
... ONLY THERE AIN'T NO "STALKY" HERE, IS THERE?!

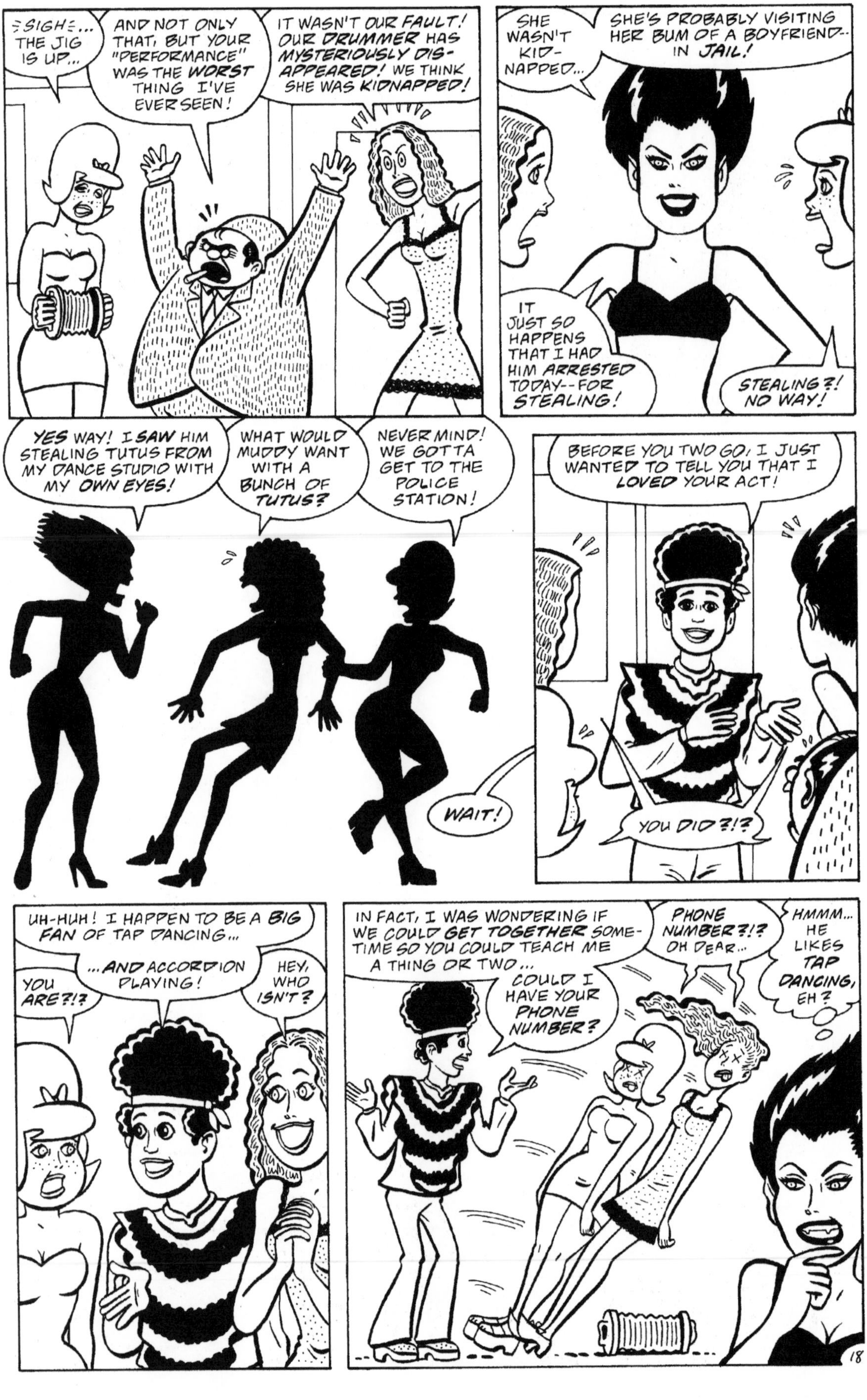
SIGH... THE JIG IS UP...
AND NOT ONLY THAT, BUT YOUR "PERFORMANCE" WAS THE WORST THING I'VE EVER SEEN!
IT WASN'T OUR FAULT! OUR DRUMMER HAS MYSTERIOUSLY DIS-APPEARED! WE THINK SHE WAS KIDNAPPED!
SHE WASN'T KID-NAPPED...
SHE'S PROBABLY VISITING HER BUM OF A BOYFRIEND-- IN JAIL!
IT JUST SO HAPPENS THAT I HAD HIM ARRESTED TODAY--FOR STEALING!
STEALING?! NO WAY!
YES WAY! I SAW HIM STEALING TUTUS FROM MY DANCE STUDIO WITH MY OWN EYES!
WHAT WOULD MUDDY WANT WITH A BUNCH OF TUTUS?
NEVER MIND! WE GOTTA GET TO THE POLICE STATION!
WAIT!
BEFORE YOU TWO GO, I JUST WANTED TO TELL YOU THAT I LOVED YOUR ACT!
YOU DID?!?
UH-HUH! I HAPPEN TO BE A BIG FAN OF TAP DANCING...
...AND ACCORDION PLAYING!
YOU ARE?!?
HEY, WHO ISN'T?
IN FACT, I WAS WONDERING IF WE COULD GET TOGETHER SOME-TIME SO YOU COULD TEACH ME A THING OR TWO...
COULD I HAVE YOUR PHONE NUMBER?
PHONE NUMBER?!? OH DEAR...
HMMM... HE LIKES TAP DANCING, EH?

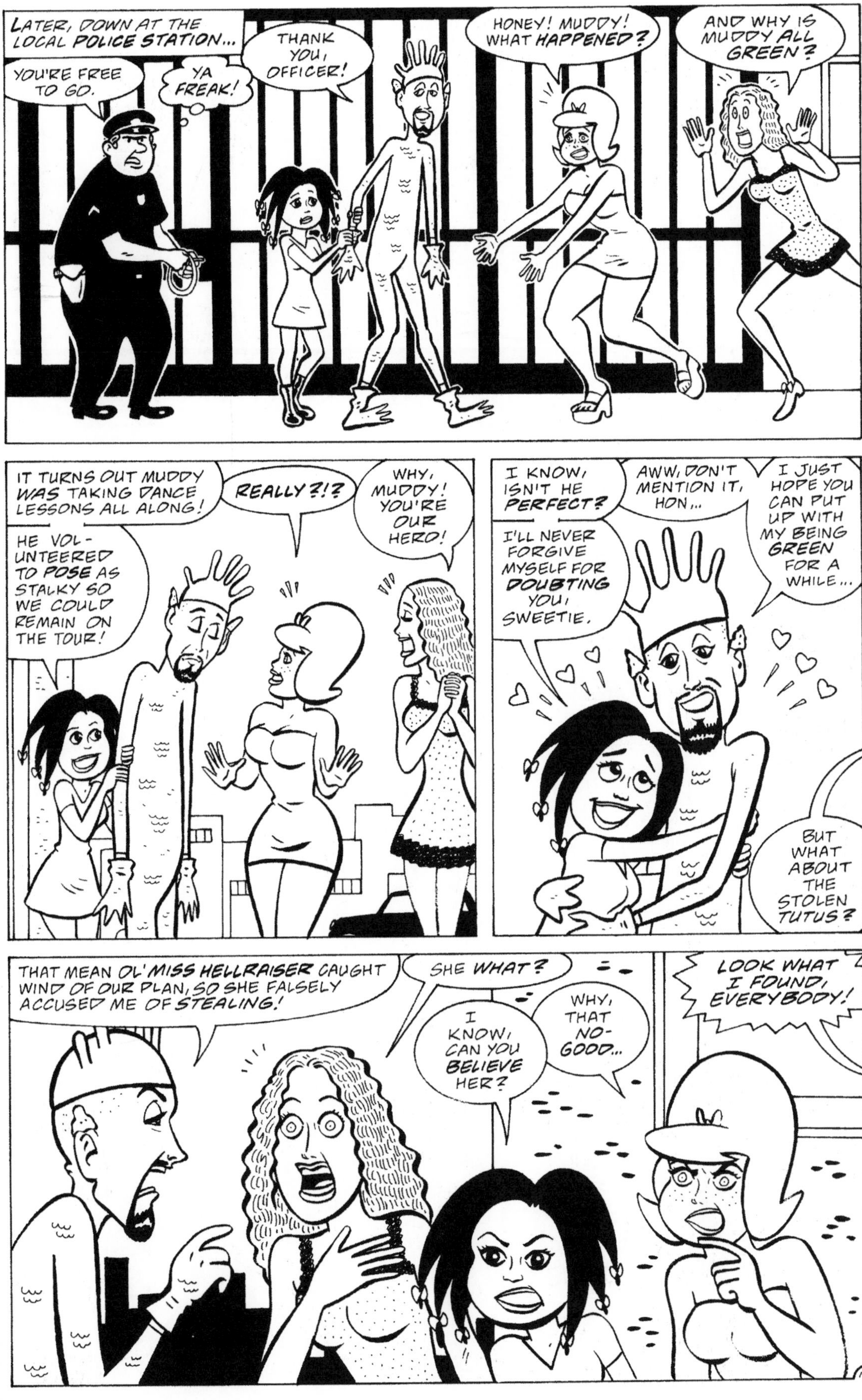
LATER, DOWN AT THE LOCAL POLICE STATION...
YOU'RE FREE TO GO.
YA FREAK!
THANK YOU, OFFICER!
HONEY! MUDDY! WHAT HAPPENED?
AND WHY IS MUDDY ALL GREEN?
IT TURNS OUT MUDDY WAS TAKING DANCE LESSONS ALL ALONG!
HE VOLUNTEERED TO POSE AS STALKY SO WE COULD REMAIN ON THE TOUR!
REALLY?!?
WHY, MUDDY! YOU'RE OUR HERO!
I KNOW, ISN'T HE PERFECT?
I'LL NEVER FORGIVE MYSELF FOR DOUBTING YOU, SWEETIE.
AWW, DON'T MENTION IT, HON...
I JUST HOPE YOU CAN PUT UP WITH MY BEING GREEN FOR A WHILE...
BUT WHAT ABOUT THE STOLEN TUTUS?
THAT MEAN OL' MISS HELLRAISER CAUGHT WIND OF OUR PLAN, SO SHE FALSELY ACCUSED ME OF STEALING!
SHE WHAT?
I KNOW, CAN YOU BELIEVE HER?
WHY, THAT NO-GOOD...
LOOK WHAT I FOUND, EVERYBODY!

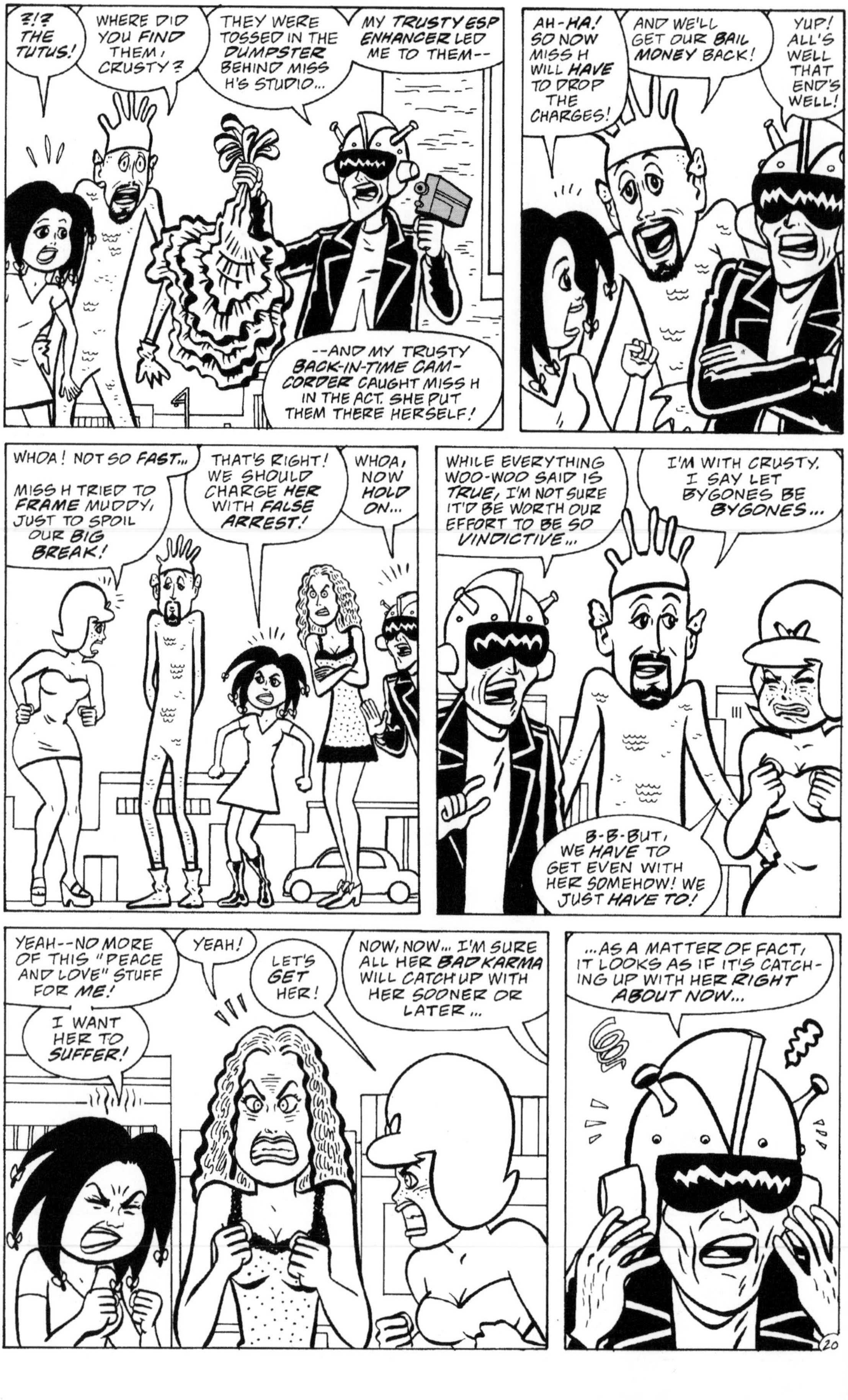
?!? THE TUTUS!
WHERE DID YOU FIND THEM, CRUSTY?
THEY WERE TOSSED IN THE DUMPSTER BEHIND MISS H'S STUDIO...
MY TRUSTY ESP ENHANCER LED ME TO THEM--
--AND MY TRUSTY BACK-IN-TIME CAM-CORDER CAUGHT MISS H IN THE ACT. SHE PUT THEM THERE HERSELF!
AH-HA! SO NOW MISS H WILL HAVE TO DROP THE CHARGES!
AND WE'LL GET OUR BAIL MONEY BACK!
YUP! ALL'S WELL THAT END'S WELL!
WHOA! NOT SO FAST...
MISS H TRIED TO FRAME MUDDY, JUST TO SPOIL OUR BIG BREAK!
THAT'S RIGHT! WE SHOULD CHARGE HER WITH FALSE ARREST!
WHOA, NOW HOLD ON...
WHILE EVERYTHING WOO-WOO SAID IS TRUE, I'M NOT SURE IT'D BE WORTH OUR EFFORT TO BE SO VINDICTIVE...
I'M WITH CRUSTY. I SAY LET BYGONES BE BYGONES...
B-B-BUT, WE HAVE TO GET EVEN WITH HER SOMEHOW! WE JUST HAVE TO!
YEAH--NO MORE OF THIS "PEACE AND LOVE" STUFF FOR ME!
I WANT HER TO SUFFER!
YEAH!
LET'S GET HER!
NOW, NOW... I'M SURE ALL HER BAD KARMA WILL CATCH UP WITH HER SOONER OR LATER...
...AS A MATTER OF FACT, IT LOOKS AS IF IT'S CATCH-ING UP WITH HER RIGHT ABOUT NOW...

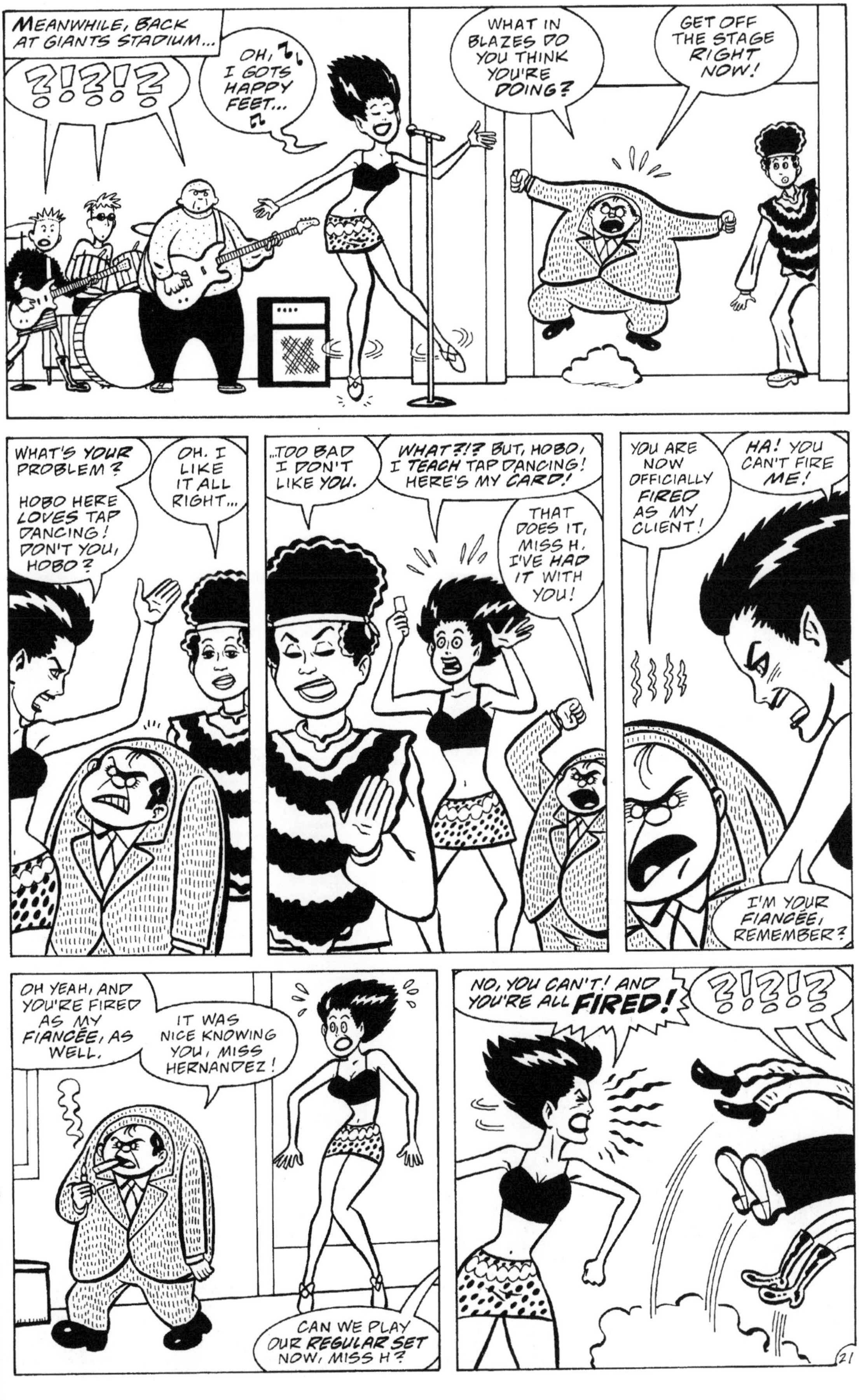
MEANWHILE, BACK AT GIANTS STADIUM...
?!?!?
OH, I GOTS HAPPY FEET...
WHAT IN BLAZES DO YOU THINK YOU'RE DOING?
GET OFF THE STAGE RIGHT NOW!
WHAT'S YOUR PROBLEM?
HOBO HERE LOVES TAP DANCING! DON'T YOU, HOBO?
OH. I LIKE IT ALL RIGHT...
...TOO BAD I DON'T LIKE YOU.
WHAT?!? BUT, HOBO, I TEACH TAP DANCING! HERE'S MY CARD!
THAT DOES IT, MISS H. I'VE HAD IT WITH YOU!
YOU ARE NOW OFFICIALLY FIRED AS MY CLIENT!
HA! YOU CAN'T FIRE ME!
I'M YOUR FIANCÉE, REMEMBER?
OH YEAH, AND YOU'RE FIRED AS MY FIANCÉE, AS WELL.
IT WAS NICE KNOWING YOU, MISS HERNANDEZ!
CAN WE PLAY OUR REGULAR SET NOW, MISS H?
NO, YOU CAN'T! AND YOU'RE ALL FIRED!
?!?!?

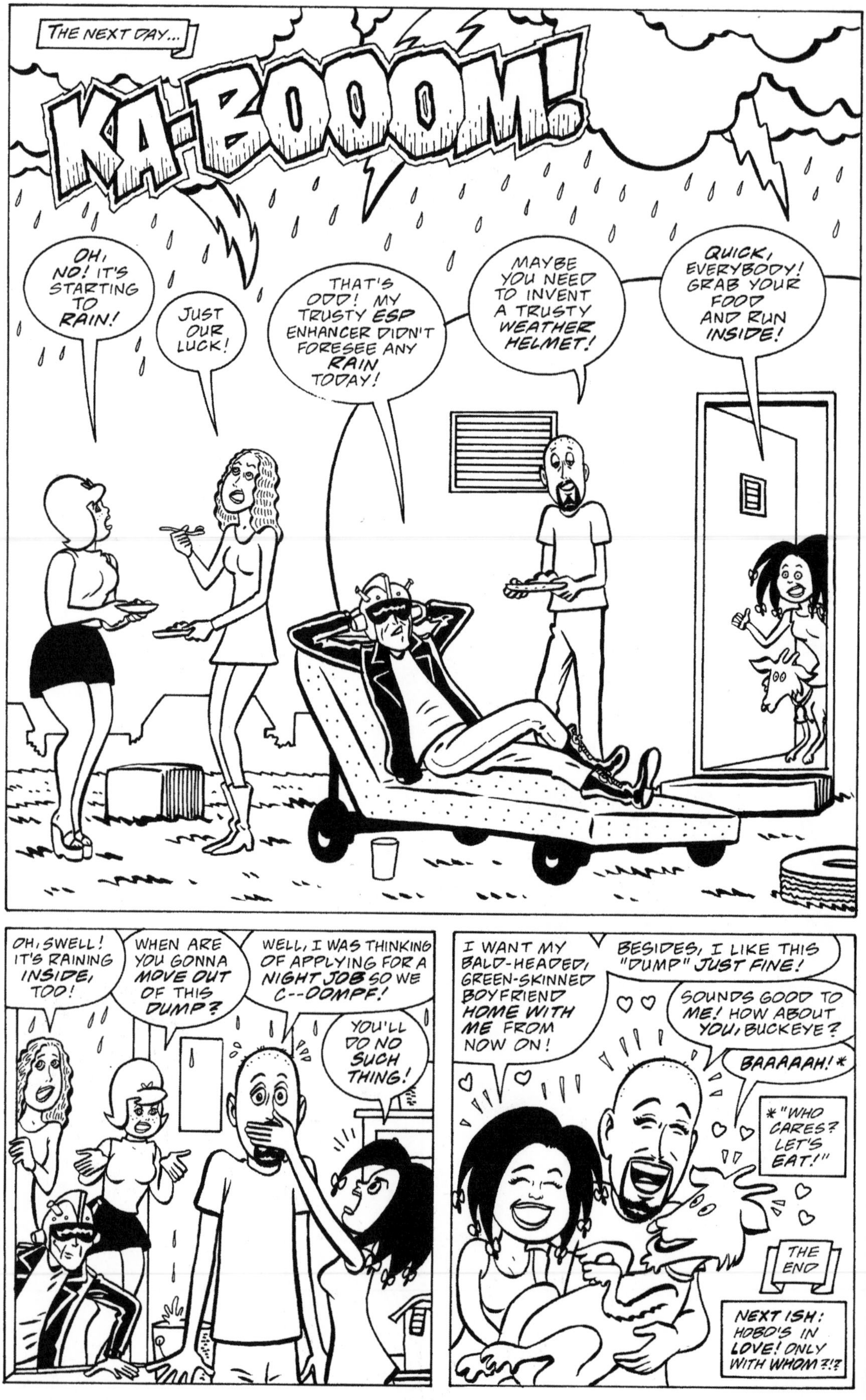
THE NEXT DAY...
KA-BOOOM!
OH, NO! IT'S STARTING TO RAIN!
JUST OUR LUCK!
THAT'S ODD! MY TRUSTY ESP ENHANCER DIDN'T FORESEE ANY RAIN TODAY!
MAYBE YOU NEED TO INVENT A TRUSTY WEATHER HELMET!
QUICK, EVERYBODY! GRAB YOUR FOOD AND RUN INSIDE!
OH, SWELL! IT'S RAINING INSIDE, TOO!
WHEN ARE YOU GONNA MOVE OUT OF THIS DUMP?
WELL, I WAS THINKING OF APPLYING FOR A NIGHT JOB SO WE C--OOMPF!
YOU'LL DO NO SUCH THING!
I WANT MY BALD-HEADED, GREEN-SKINNED BOYFRIEND HOME WITH ME FROM NOW ON!
BESIDES, I LIKE THIS "DUMP" JUST FINE!
SOUNDS GOOD TO ME! HOW ABOUT YOU, BUCKEYE?
BAAAAAH!*
*"WHO CARES? LET'S EAT!"
THE END
NEXT ISH: HOBO'S IN LOVE! ONLY WITH WHOM?!?

SEVEN!

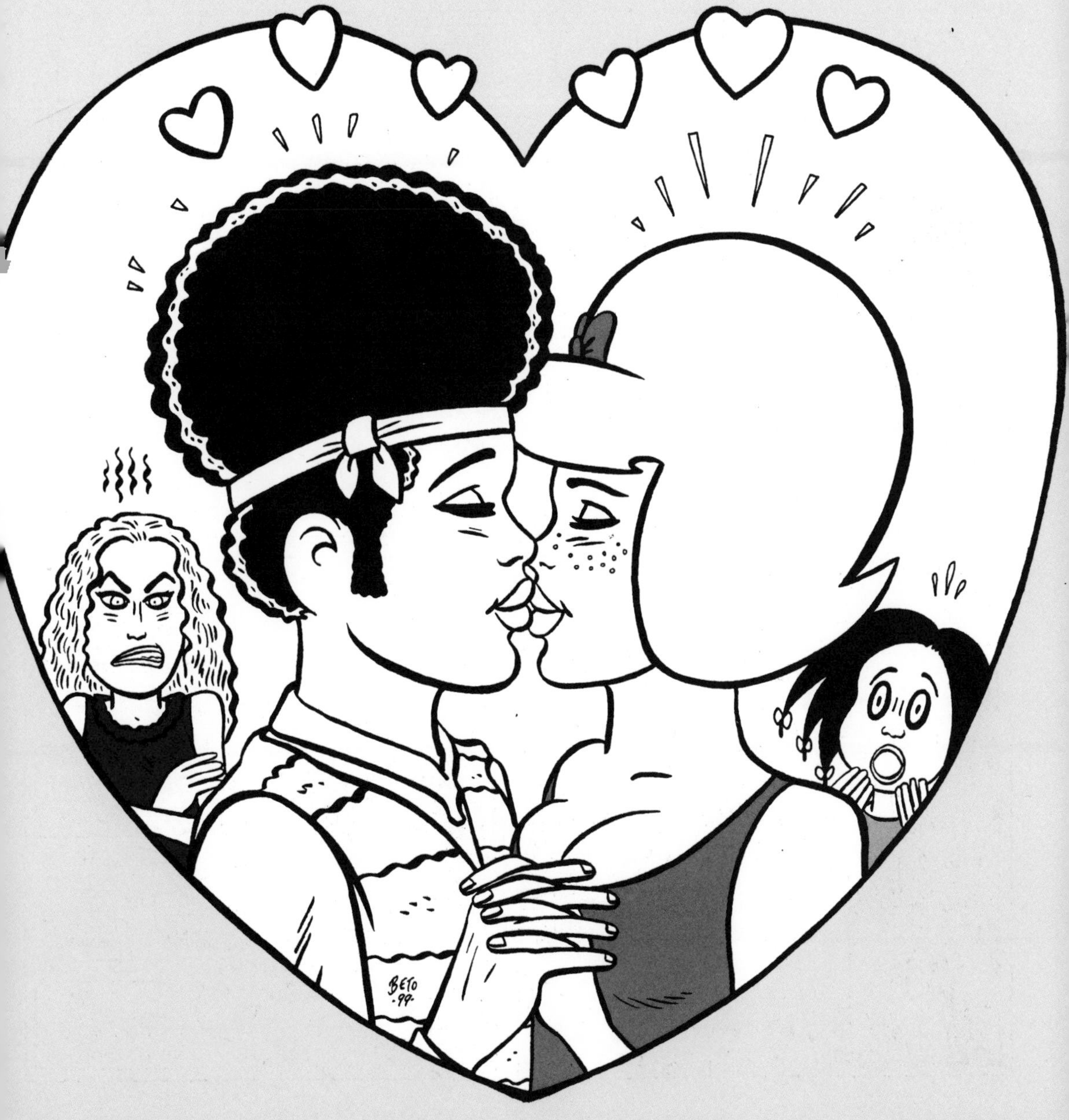
BETO ·99·

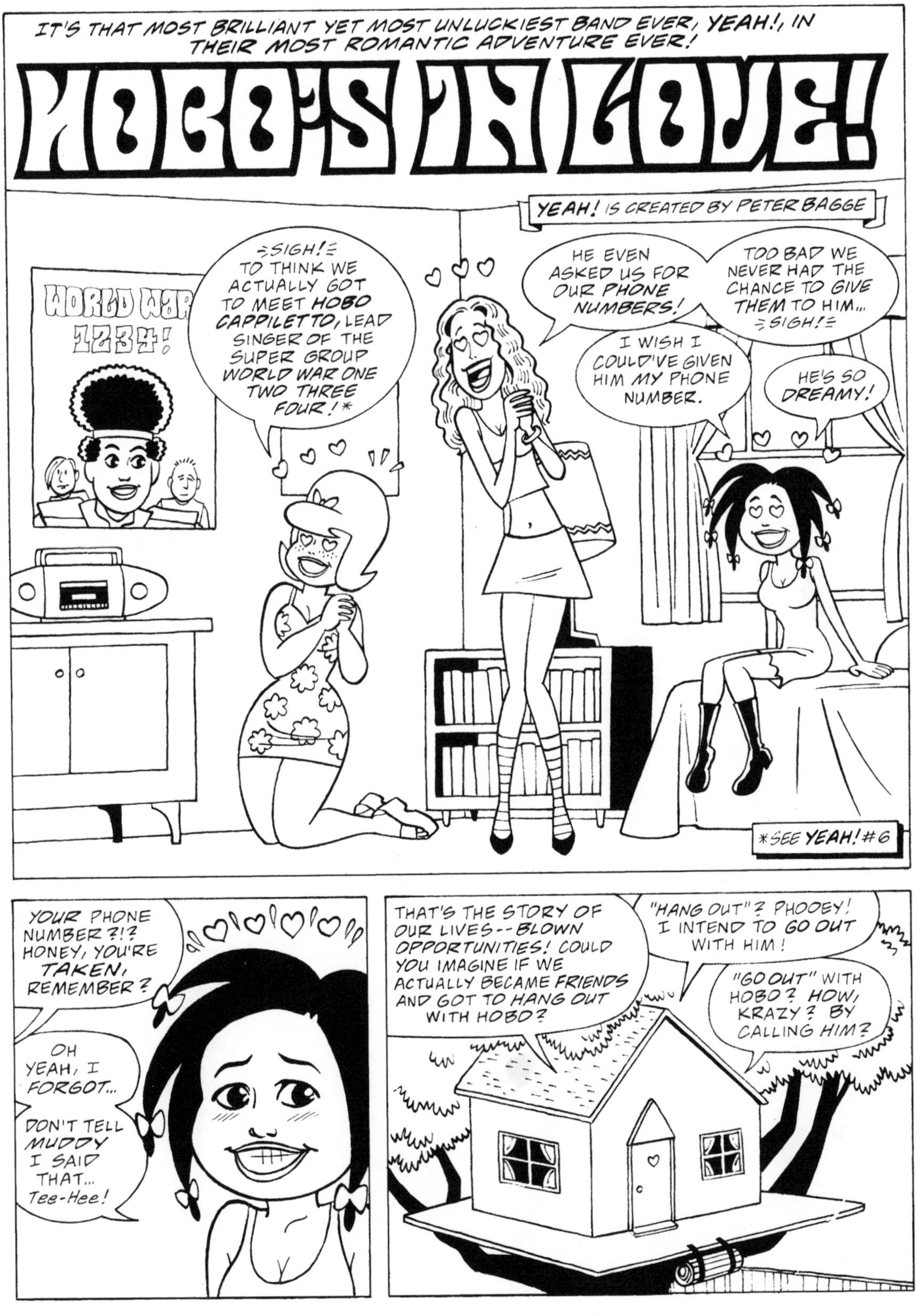
IT'S THAT MOST BRILLIANT YET MOST UNLUCKIEST BAND EVER, YEAH!, IN THEIR MOST ROMANTIC ADVENTURE EVER!
HOBO'S IN LOVE!
YEAH! IS CREATED BY PETER BAGGE
WORLD WAR 1234!
=SIGH!= TO THINK WE ACTUALLY GOT TO MEET HOBO CAPPILETTO, LEAD SINGER OF THE SUPER GROUP WORLD WAR ONE TWO THREE FOUR! *
HE EVEN ASKED US FOR OUR PHONE NUMBERS!
TOO BAD WE NEVER HAD THE CHANCE TO GIVE THEM TO HIM... =SIGH!=
I WISH I COULD'VE GIVEN HIM MY PHONE NUMBER.
HE'S SO DREAMY!
* SEE YEAH! #6
YOUR PHONE NUMBER?!? HONEY, YOU'RE TAKEN, REMEMBER?
OH YEAH, I FORGOT...
DON'T TELL MUDDY I SAID THAT... Tee-Hee!
THAT'S THE STORY OF OUR LIVES--BLOWN OPPORTUNITIES! COULD YOU IMAGINE IF WE ACTUALLY BECAME FRIENDS AND GOT TO HANG OUT WITH HOBO?
"HANG OUT"? PHOOEY! I INTEND TO GO OUT WITH HIM!
"GO OUT" WITH HOBO? HOW, KRAZY? BY CALLING HIM?

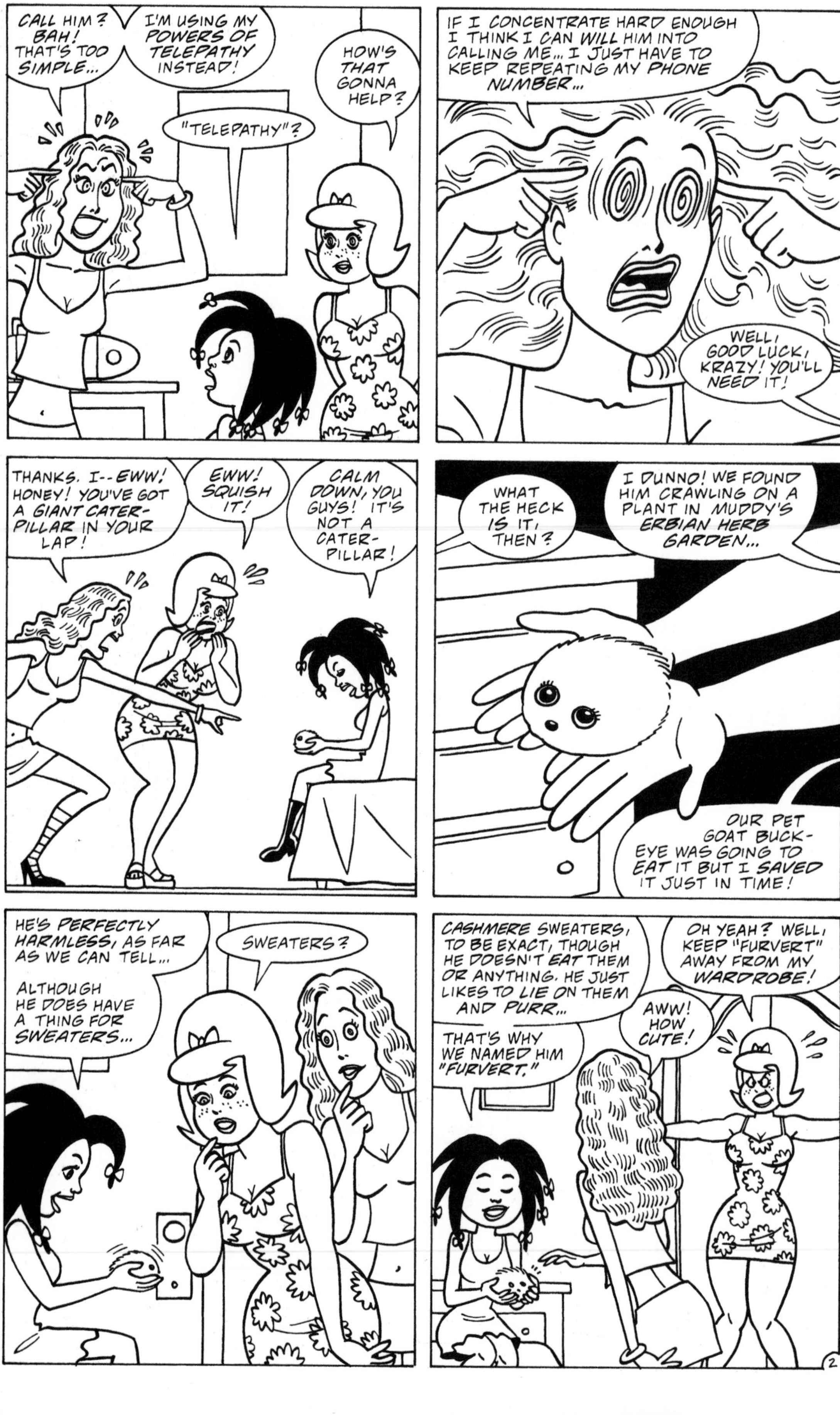
CALL HIM? BAH! THAT'S TOO SIMPLE...
I'M USING MY POWERS OF TELEPATHY INSTEAD!
"TELEPATHY"?
HOW'S THAT GONNA HELP?
IF I CONCENTRATE HARD ENOUGH I THINK I CAN WILL HIM INTO CALLING ME... I JUST HAVE TO KEEP REPEATING MY PHONE NUMBER...
WELL, GOOD LUCK, KRAZY! YOU'LL NEED IT!
THANKS. I--EWW! HONEY! YOU'VE GOT A GIANT CATER-PILLAR IN YOUR LAP!
EWW! SQUISH IT!
CALM DOWN, YOU GUYS! IT'S NOT A CATER-PILLAR!
WHAT THE HECK IS IT, THEN?
I DUNNO! WE FOUND HIM CRAWLING ON A PLANT IN MUDDY'S ERBIAN HERB GARDEN...
OUR PET GOAT BUCK-EYE WAS GOING TO EAT IT BUT I SAVED IT JUST IN TIME!
HE'S PERFECTLY HARMLESS, AS FAR AS WE CAN TELL...
ALTHOUGH HE DOES HAVE A THING FOR SWEATERS...
SWEATERS?
CASHMERE SWEATERS, TO BE EXACT, THOUGH HE DOESN'T EAT THEM OR ANYTHING. HE JUST LIKES TO LIE ON THEM AND PURR...
THAT'S WHY WE NAMED HIM "FURVERT."
AWW! HOW CUTE!
OH YEAH? WELL, KEEP "FURVERT" AWAY FROM MY WARDROBE!
2

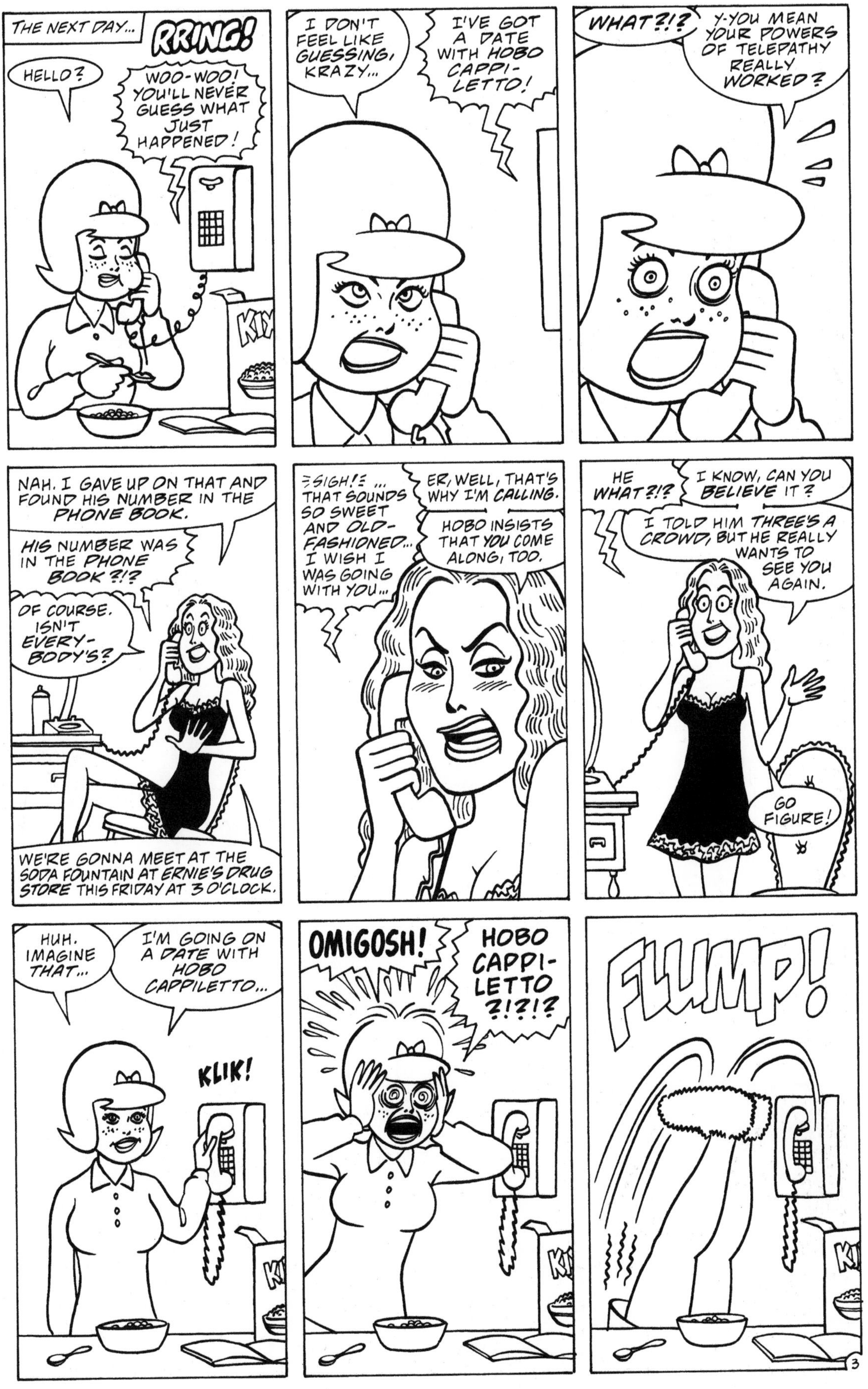
THE NEXT DAY...
RRING!
HELLO?
WOO-WOO! YOU'LL NEVER GUESS WHAT JUST HAPPENED!
KIX
I DON'T FEEL LIKE GUESSING, KRAZY...
I'VE GOT A DATE WITH HOBO CAPPI-LETTO!
WHAT?!?
Y-YOU MEAN YOUR POWERS OF TELEPATHY REALLY WORKED?
NAH. I GAVE UP ON THAT AND FOUND HIS NUMBER IN THE PHONE BOOK.
HIS NUMBER WAS IN THE PHONE BOOK?!?
OF COURSE. ISN'T EVERY-BODY'S?
WE'RE GONNA MEET AT THE SODA FOUNTAIN AT ERNIE'S DRUG STORE THIS FRIDAY AT 3 O'CLOCK.
SIGH! ... THAT SOUNDS SO SWEET AND OLD-FASHIONED... I WISH I WAS GOING WITH YOU...
ER, WELL, THAT'S WHY I'M CALLING.
HOBO INSISTS THAT YOU COME ALONG, TOO.
HE WHAT?!?
I KNOW, CAN YOU BELIEVE IT?
I TOLD HIM THREE'S A CROWD, BUT HE REALLY WANTS TO SEE YOU AGAIN.
GO FIGURE!
HUH. IMAGINE THAT...
I'M GOING ON A DATE WITH HOBO CAPPILETTO...
KLIK!
OMIGOSH!
HOBO CAPPI-LETTO ?!?!?
FLUMP!

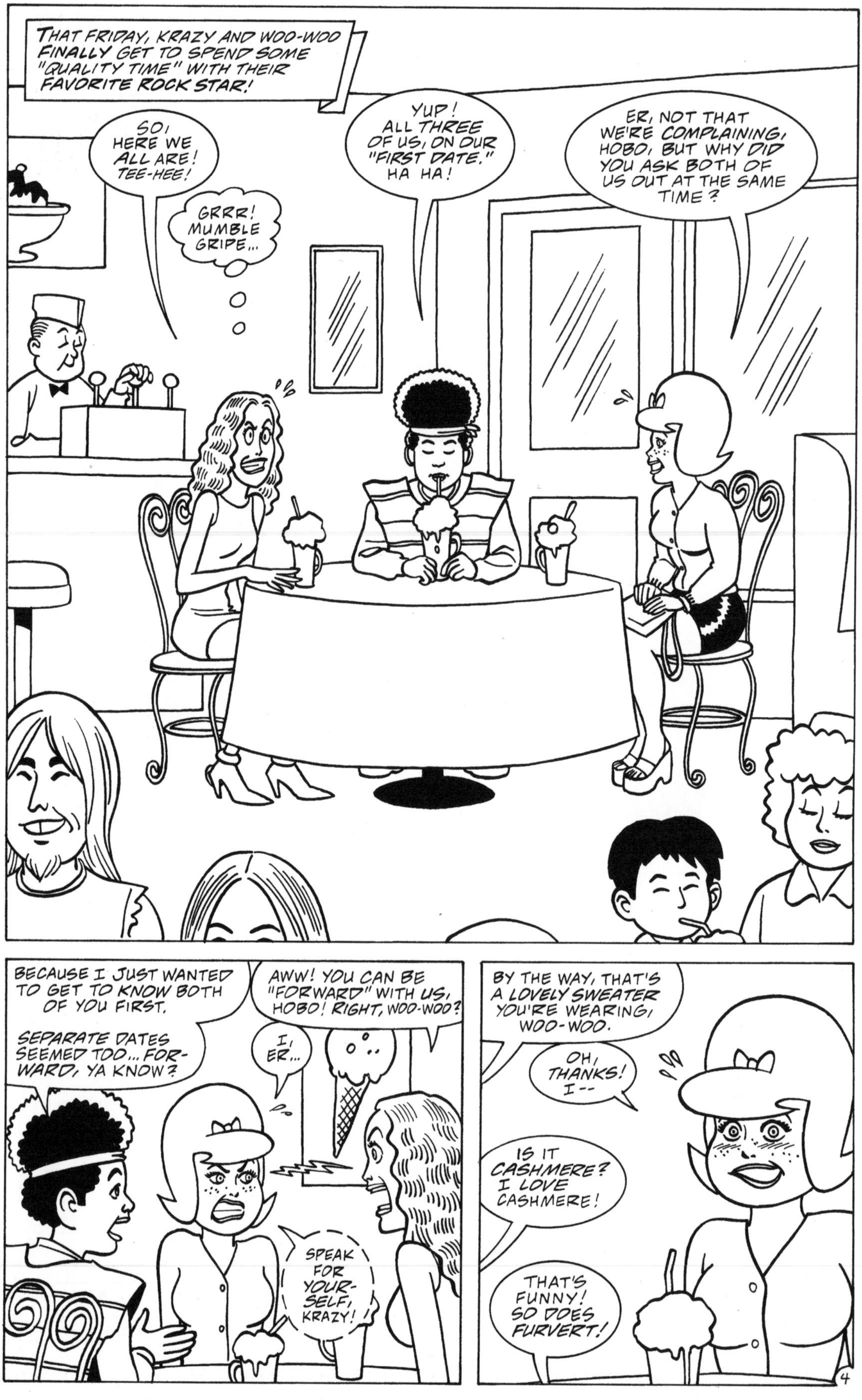
THAT FRIDAY, KRAZY AND WOO-WOO FINALLY GET TO SPEND SOME "QUALITY TIME" WITH THEIR FAVORITE ROCK STAR!
SO, HERE WE ALL ARE! TEE-HEE!
GRRR! MUMBLE GRIPE...
YUP! ALL THREE OF US, ON OUR "FIRST DATE." HA HA!
ER, NOT THAT WE'RE COMPLAINING, HOBO, BUT WHY DID YOU ASK BOTH OF US OUT AT THE SAME TIME?
BECAUSE I JUST WANTED TO GET TO KNOW BOTH OF YOU FIRST.
SEPARATE DATES SEEMED TOO... FOR-WARD, YA KNOW?
AWW! YOU CAN BE "FORWARD" WITH US, HOBO! RIGHT, WOO-WOO?
I, ER...
SPEAK FOR YOUR-SELF, KRAZY!
BY THE WAY, THAT'S A LOVELY SWEATER YOU'RE WEARING, WOO-WOO.
OH, THANKS! I--
IS IT CASHMERE? I LOVE CASHMERE!
THAT'S FUNNY! SO DOES FURVERT!

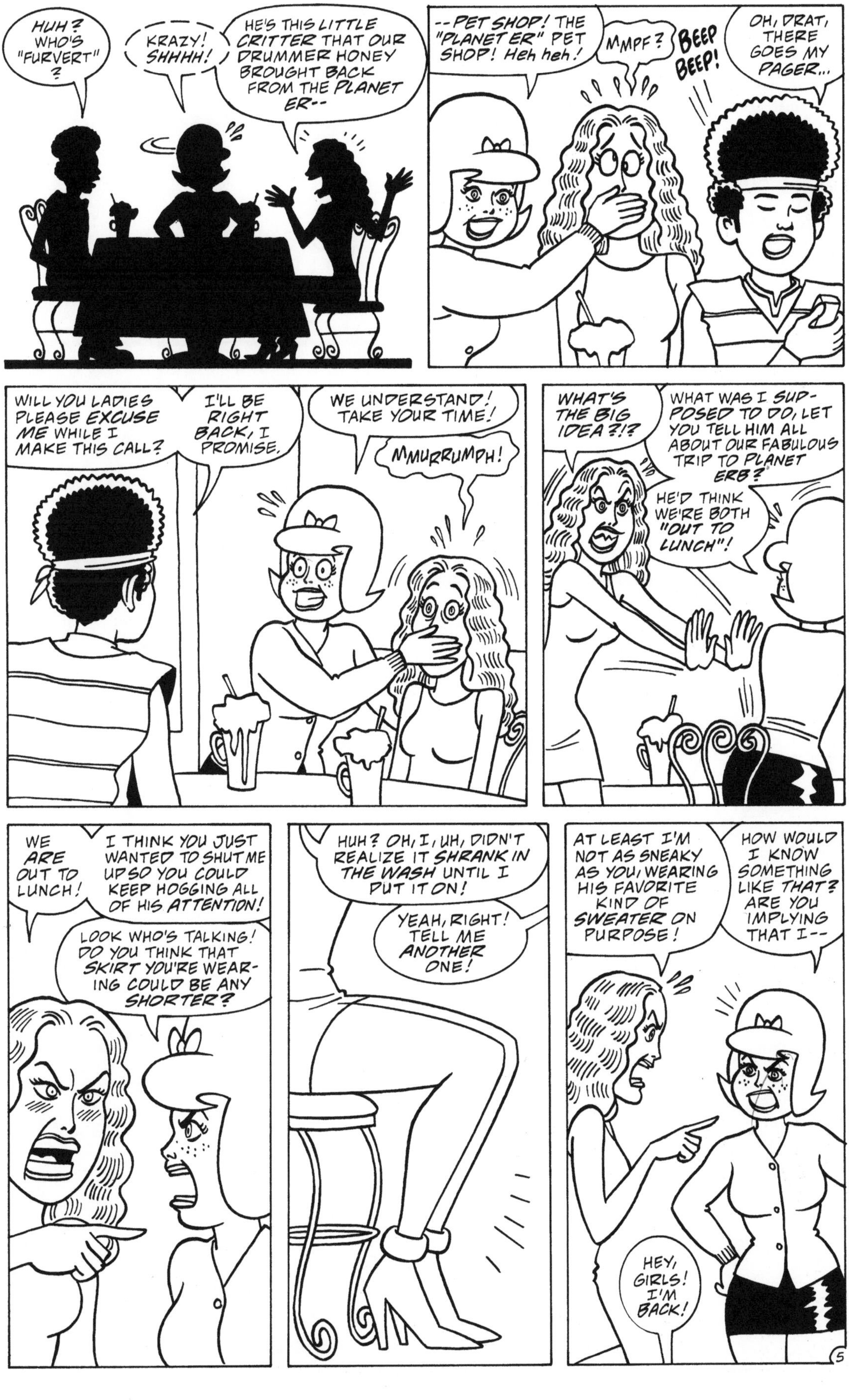
HUH? WHO'S "FURVERT"?
KRAZY! SHHHH!
HE'S THIS LITTLE CRITTER THAT OUR DRUMMER HONEY BROUGHT BACK FROM THE PLANET ER--
--PET SHOP! THE "PLANET ER" PET SHOP! Heh heh!
MMPF?
BEEP BEEP!
OH, DRAT, THERE GOES MY PAGER...
WILL YOU LADIES PLEASE EXCUSE ME WHILE I MAKE THIS CALL?
I'LL BE RIGHT BACK, I PROMISE.
WE UNDERSTAND! TAKE YOUR TIME!
MMURRUMPH!
WHAT'S THE BIG IDEA?!?
WHAT WAS I SUPPOSED TO DO, LET YOU TELL HIM ALL ABOUT OUR FABULOUS TRIP TO PLANET ERB?
HE'D THINK WE'RE BOTH "OUT TO LUNCH"!
WE ARE OUT TO LUNCH!
I THINK YOU JUST WANTED TO SHUT ME UP SO YOU COULD KEEP HOGGING ALL OF HIS ATTENTION!
LOOK WHO'S TALKING! DO YOU THINK THAT SKIRT YOU'RE WEARING COULD BE ANY SHORTER?
HUH? OH, I, UH, DIDN'T REALIZE IT SHRANK IN THE WASH UNTIL I PUT IT ON!
YEAH, RIGHT! TELL ME ANOTHER ONE!
AT LEAST I'M NOT AS SNEAKY AS YOU, WEARING HIS FAVORITE KIND OF SWEATER ON PURPOSE!
HOW WOULD I KNOW SOMETHING LIKE THAT? ARE YOU IMPLYING THAT I--
HEY, GIRLS! I'M BACK!

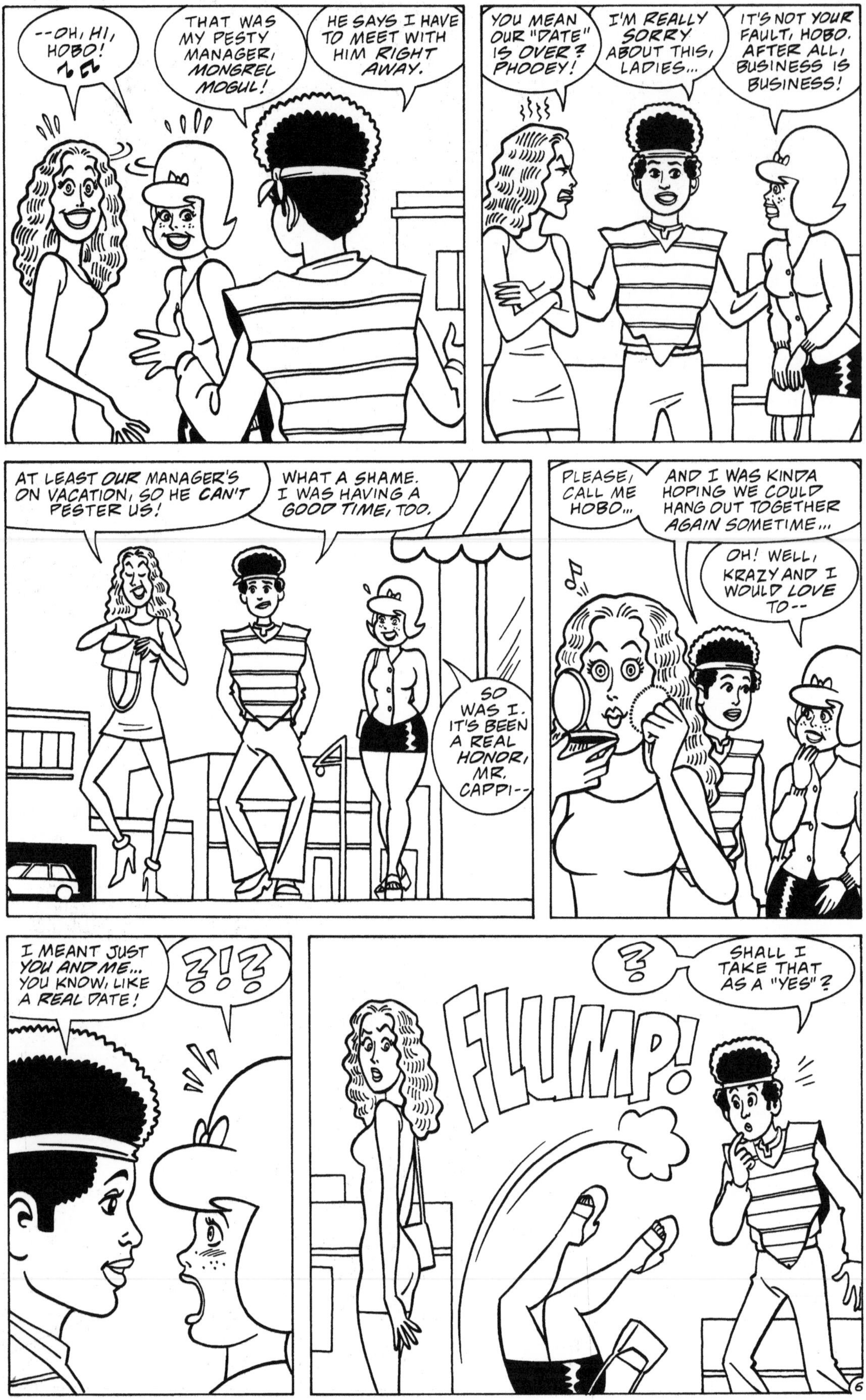
--OH, HI, HOBO!
THAT WAS MY PESTY MANAGER, MONGREL MOGUL!
HE SAYS I HAVE TO MEET WITH HIM RIGHT AWAY.
YOU MEAN OUR "DATE" IS OVER? PHOOEY!
I'M REALLY SORRY ABOUT THIS, LADIES...
IT'S NOT YOUR FAULT, HOBO. AFTER ALL, BUSINESS IS BUSINESS!
AT LEAST OUR MANAGER'S ON VACATION, SO HE CAN'T PESTER US!
WHAT A SHAME. I WAS HAVING A GOOD TIME, TOO.
SO WAS I. IT'S BEEN A REAL HONOR, MR. CAPPI--
PLEASE, CALL ME HOBO...
AND I WAS KINDA HOPING WE COULD HANG OUT TOGETHER AGAIN SOMETIME...
OH! WELL, KRAZY AND I WOULD LOVE TO--
I MEANT JUST YOU AND ME... YOU KNOW, LIKE A REAL DATE!
?!?
?
SHALL I TAKE THAT AS A "YES"?
FLUMP!
6

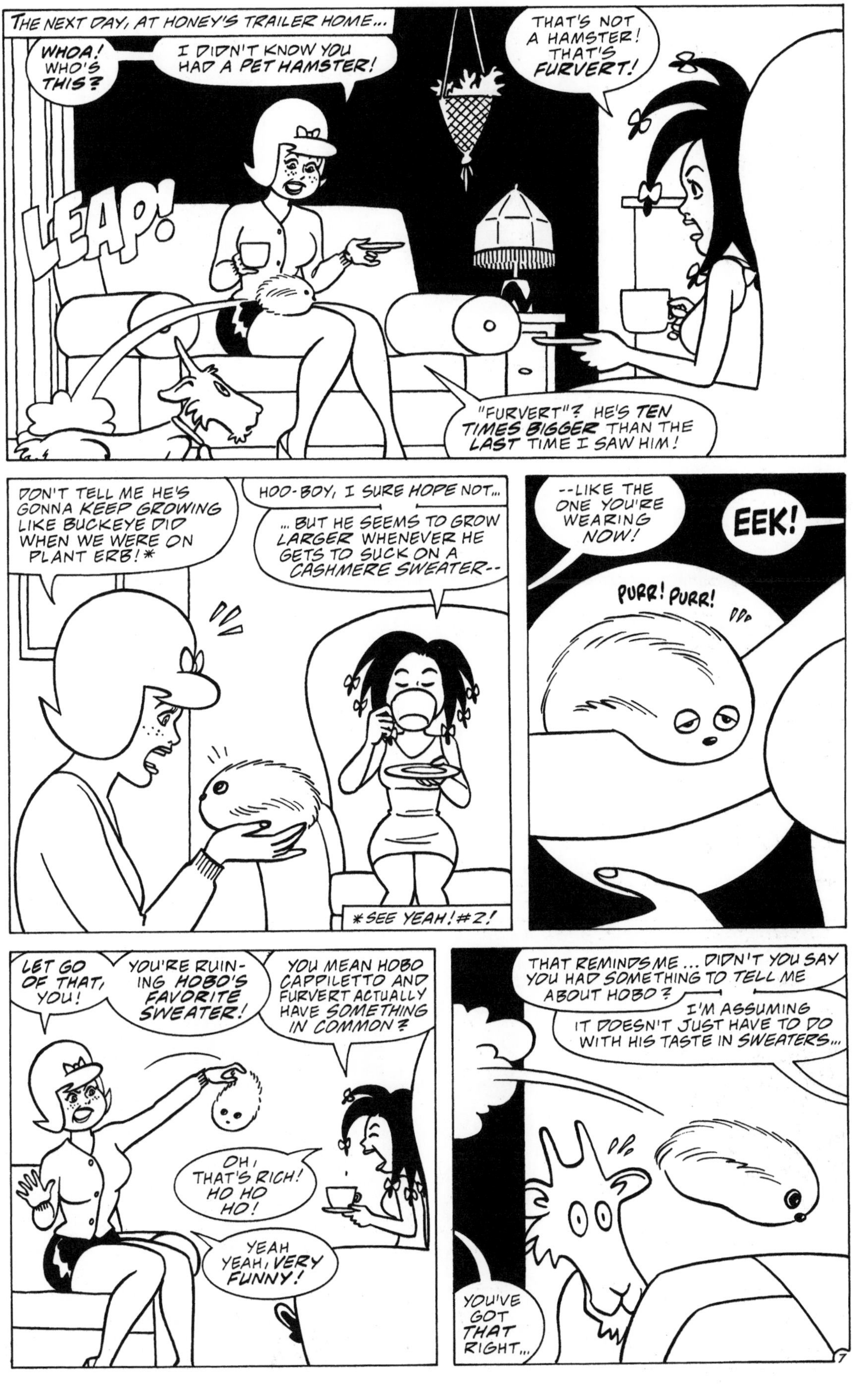
THE NEXT DAY, AT HONEY'S TRAILER HOME...
WHOA! WHO'S THIS?
I DIDN'T KNOW YOU HAD A PET HAMSTER!
THAT'S NOT A HAMSTER! THAT'S FURVERT!
LEAP!
"FURVERT"? HE'S TEN TIMES BIGGER THAN THE LAST TIME I SAW HIM!
DON'T TELL ME HE'S GONNA KEEP GROWING LIKE BUCKEYE DID WHEN WE WERE ON PLANT ERB!*
HOO-BOY, I SURE HOPE NOT...
...BUT HE SEEMS TO GROW LARGER WHENEVER HE GETS TO SUCK ON A CASHMERE SWEATER--
*SEE YEAH! #2!
--LIKE THE ONE YOU'RE WEARING NOW!
EEK!
PURR! PURR!
LET GO OF THAT, YOU!
YOU'RE RUIN-ING HOBO'S FAVORITE SWEATER!
YOU MEAN HOBO CAPPILETTO AND FURVERT ACTUALLY HAVE SOMETHING IN COMMON?
OH, THAT'S RICH! HO HO HO!
YEAH YEAH, VERY FUNNY!
THAT REMINDS ME... DIDN'T YOU SAY YOU HAD SOMETHING TO TELL ME ABOUT HOBO?
I'M ASSUMING IT DOESN'T JUST HAVE TO DO WITH HIS TASTE IN SWEATERS...
YOU'VE GOT THAT RIGHT...

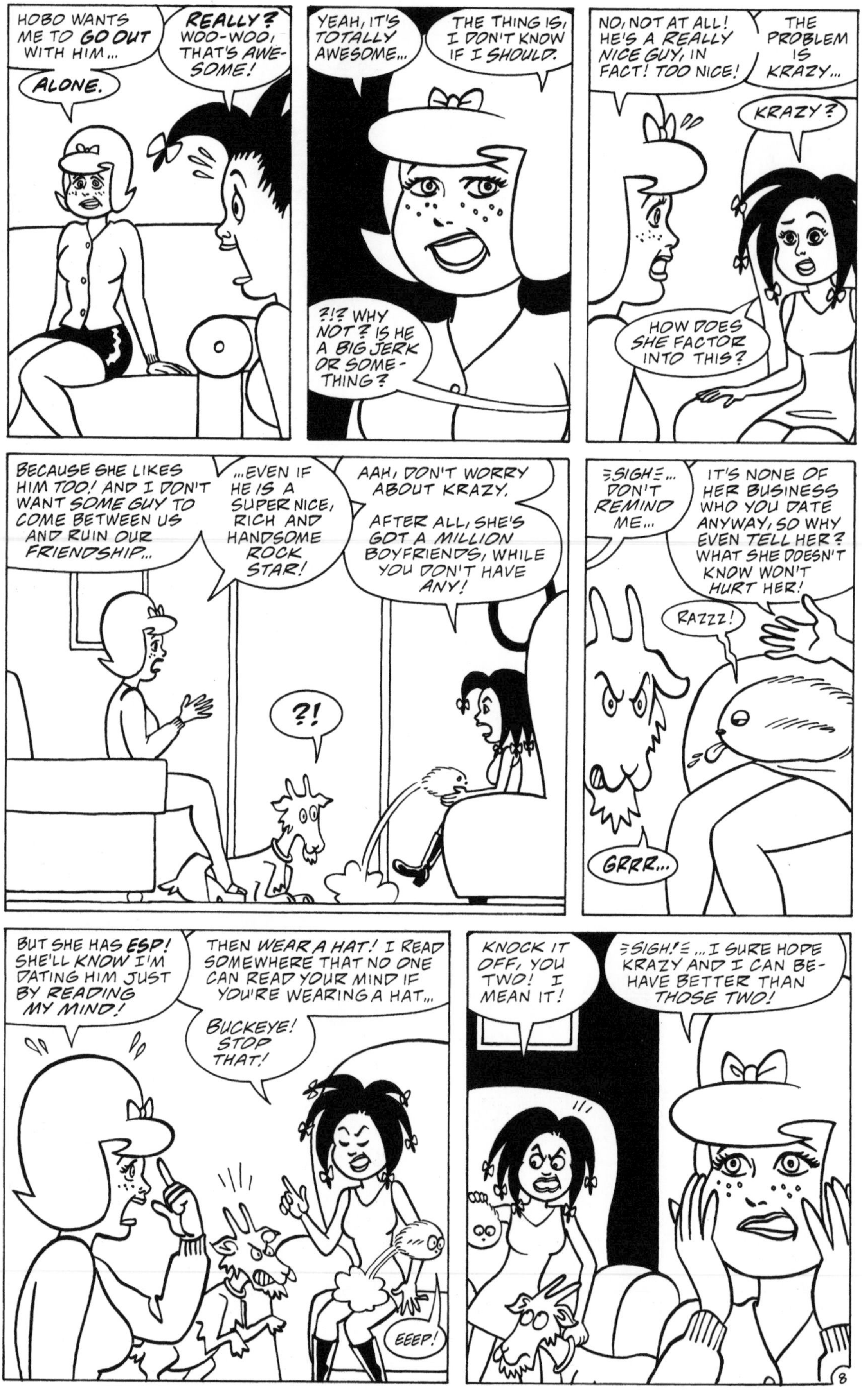
HOBO WANTS ME TO GO OUT WITH HIM...
ALONE.
REALLY? WOO-WOO, THAT'S AWE-SOME!
YEAH, IT'S TOTALLY AWESOME...
THE THING IS, I DON'T KNOW IF I SHOULD.
?!? WHY NOT? IS HE A BIG JERK OR SOME-THING?
NO, NOT AT ALL! HE'S A REALLY NICE GUY, IN FACT! TOO NICE!
THE PROBLEM IS KRAZY...
KRAZY?
HOW DOES SHE FACTOR INTO THIS?
BECAUSE SHE LIKES HIM TOO! AND I DON'T WANT SOME GUY TO COME BETWEEN US AND RUIN OUR FRIENDSHIP...
...EVEN IF HE IS A SUPER NICE, RICH AND HANDSOME ROCK STAR!
AAH, DON'T WORRY ABOUT KRAZY.
AFTER ALL, SHE'S GOT A MILLION BOYFRIENDS, WHILE YOU DON'T HAVE ANY!
?!
≡SIGH≡... DON'T REMIND ME...
IT'S NONE OF HER BUSINESS WHO YOU DATE ANYWAY, SO WHY EVEN TELL HER? WHAT SHE DOESN'T KNOW WON'T HURT HER!
RAZZZ!
GRRR...
BUT SHE HAS ESP! SHE'LL KNOW I'M DATING HIM JUST BY READING MY MIND!
THEN WEAR A HAT! I READ SOMEWHERE THAT NO ONE CAN READ YOUR MIND IF YOU'RE WEARING A HAT...
BUCKEYE! STOP THAT!
EEEP!
KNOCK IT OFF, YOU TWO! I MEAN IT!
≡SIGH!≡ ...I SURE HOPE KRAZY AND I CAN BE-HAVE BETTER THAN THOSE TWO!

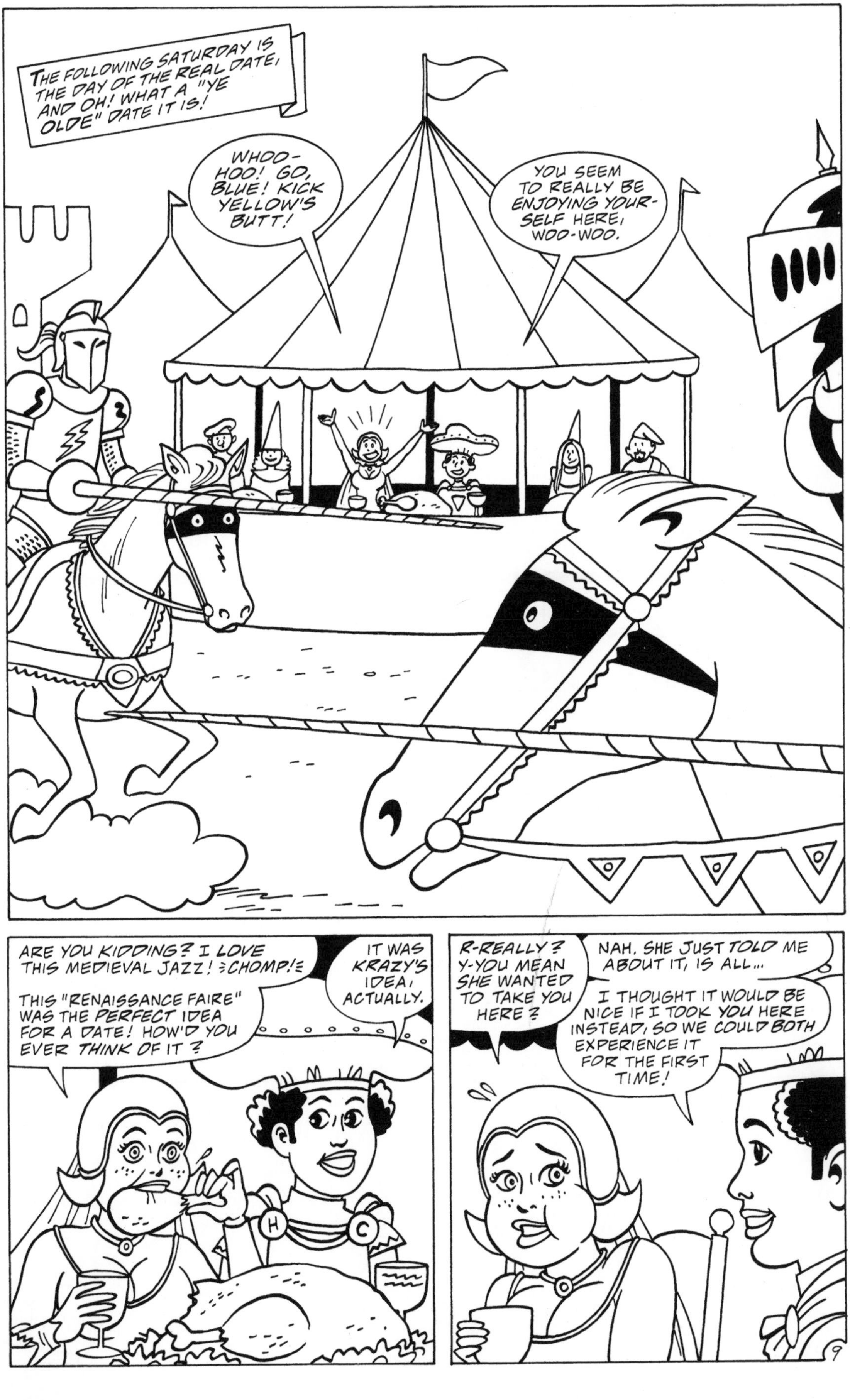
THE FOLLOWING SATURDAY IS THE DAY OF THE REAL DATE, AND OH! WHAT A "YE OLDE" DATE IT IS!
WHOO-HOO! GO, BLUE! KICK YELLOW'S BUTT!
YOU SEEM TO REALLY BE ENJOYING YOURSELF HERE, WOO-WOO.
ARE YOU KIDDING? I LOVE THIS MEDIEVAL JAZZ! CHOMP!
THIS "RENAISSANCE FAIRE" WAS THE PERFECT IDEA FOR A DATE! HOW'D YOU EVER THINK OF IT?
IT WAS KRAZY'S IDEA, ACTUALLY.
H
C
R-REALLY? Y-YOU MEAN SHE WANTED TO TAKE YOU HERE?
NAH, SHE JUST TOLD ME ABOUT IT, IS ALL...
I THOUGHT IT WOULD BE NICE IF I TOOK YOU HERE INSTEAD, SO WE COULD BOTH EXPERIENCE IT FOR THE FIRST TIME!

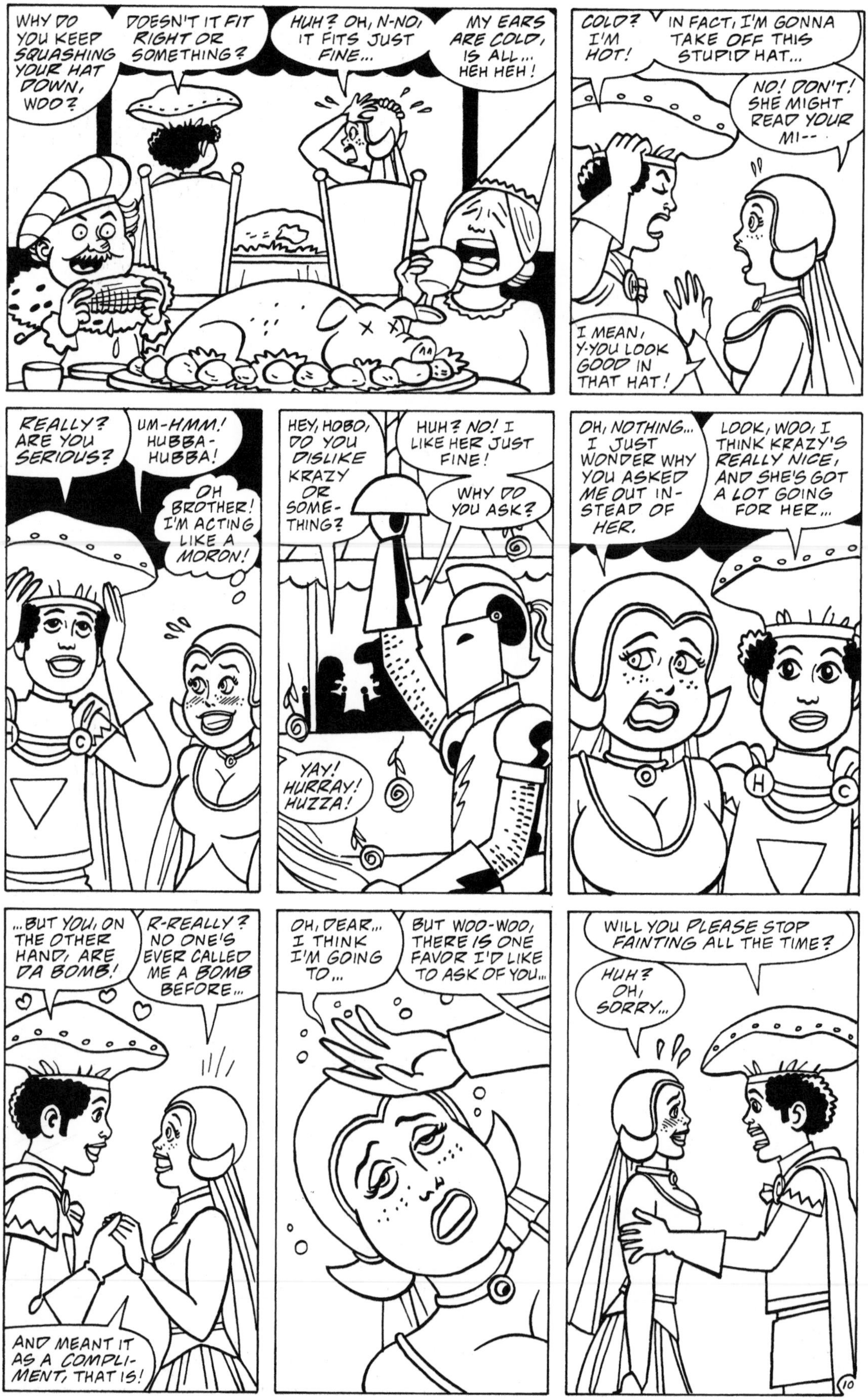
WHY DO YOU KEEP SQUASHING YOUR HAT DOWN, WOO?
DOESN'T IT FIT RIGHT OR SOMETHING?
HUH? OH, N-NO, IT FITS JUST FINE...
MY EARS ARE COLD, IS ALL... HEH HEH!
COLD? I'M HOT!
IN FACT, I'M GONNA TAKE OFF THIS STUPID HAT...
NO! DON'T! SHE MIGHT READ YOUR MI--
I MEAN, Y-YOU LOOK GOOD IN THAT HAT!
REALLY? ARE YOU SERIOUS?
UM-HMM! HUBBA-HUBBA!
OH BROTHER! I'M ACTING LIKE A MORON!
HEY, HOBO, DO YOU DISLIKE KRAZY OR SOME-THING?
HUH? NO! I LIKE HER JUST FINE!
WHY DO YOU ASK?
YAY! HURRAY! HUZZA!
OH, NOTHING... I JUST WONDER WHY YOU ASKED ME OUT IN-STEAD OF HER.
LOOK, WOO, I THINK KRAZY'S REALLY NICE, AND SHE'S GOT A LOT GOING FOR HER...
...BUT YOU, ON THE OTHER HAND, ARE DA BOMB!
R-REALLY? NO ONE'S EVER CALLED ME A BOMB BEFORE...
AND MEANT IT AS A COMPLI-MENT, THAT IS!
OH, DEAR... I THINK I'M GOING TO...
BUT WOO-WOO, THERE IS ONE FAVOR I'D LIKE TO ASK OF YOU...
WILL YOU PLEASE STOP FAINTING ALL THE TIME?
HUH? OH, SORRY...

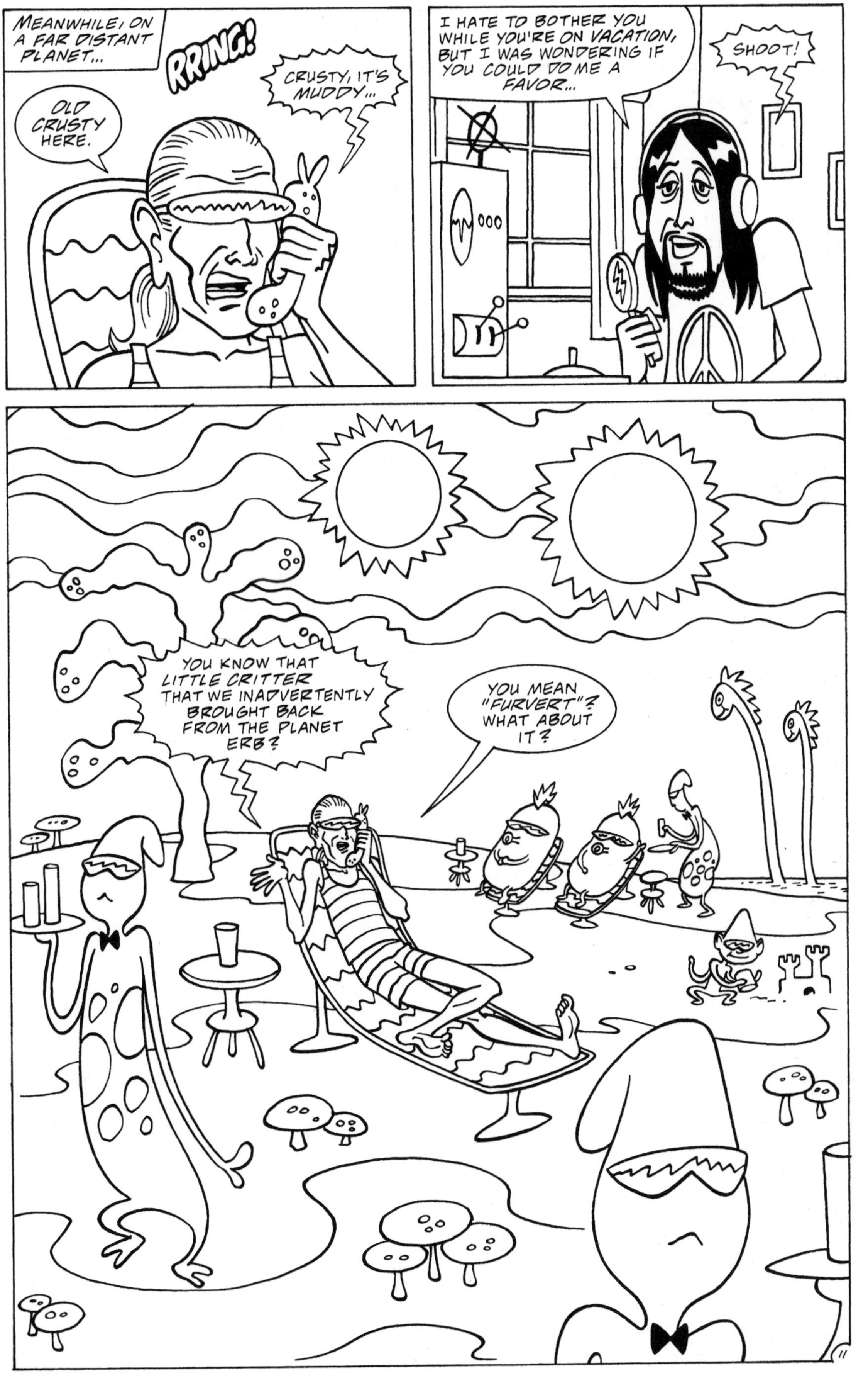
MEANWHILE, ON A FAR DISTANT PLANET...
RRING!
OLD CRUSTY HERE.
CRUSTY, IT'S MUDDY...
I HATE TO BOTHER YOU WHILE YOU'RE ON VACATION, BUT I WAS WONDERING IF YOU COULD DO ME A FAVOR...
SHOOT!
YOU KNOW THAT LITTLE CRITTER THAT WE INADVERTENTLY BROUGHT BACK FROM THE PLANET ERB?
YOU MEAN "FURVERT"? WHAT ABOUT IT?

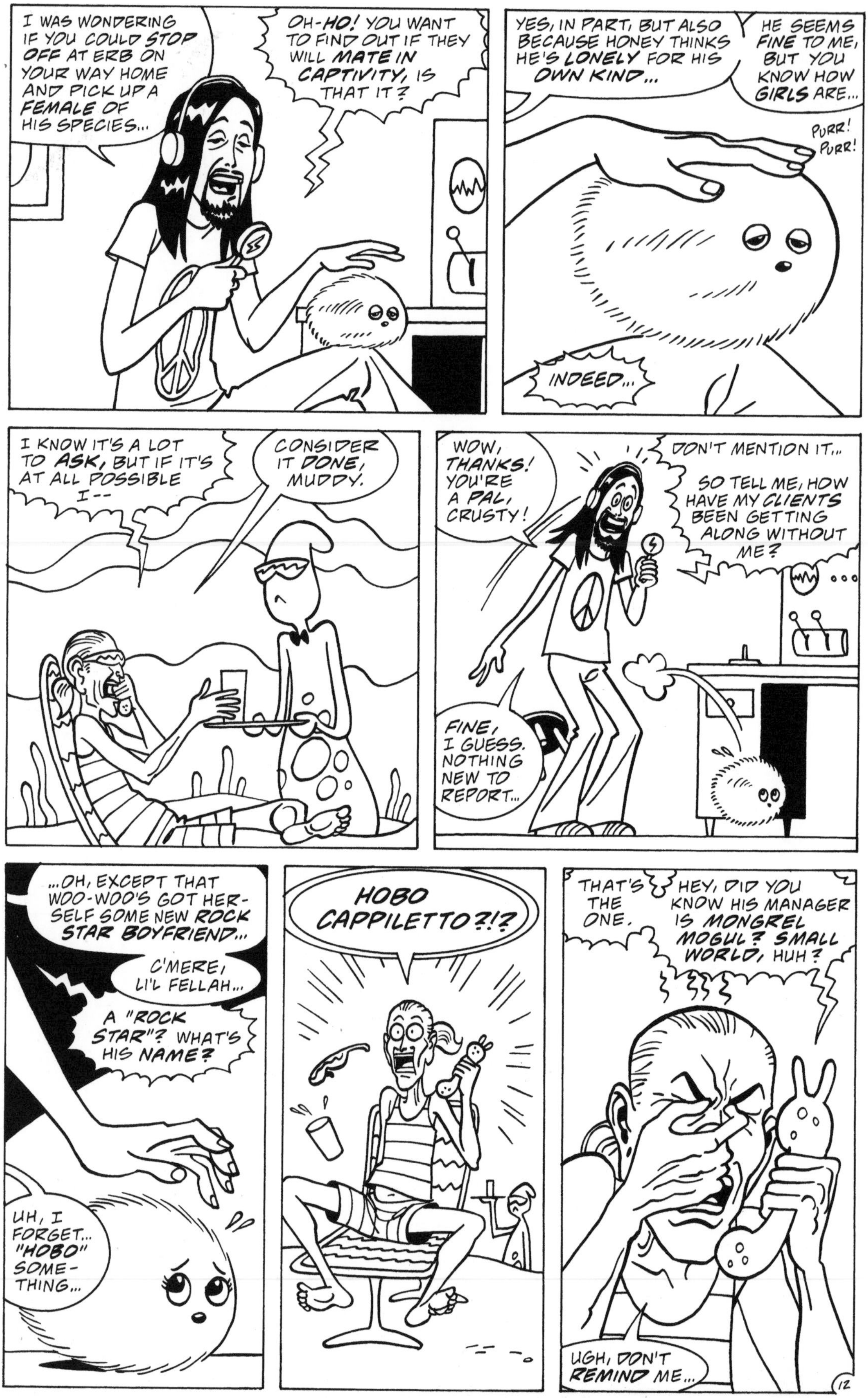
I WAS WONDERING IF YOU COULD STOP OFF AT ERB ON YOUR WAY HOME AND PICK UP A FEMALE OF HIS SPECIES...
OH-HO! YOU WANT TO FIND OUT IF THEY WILL MATE IN CAPTIVITY, IS THAT IT?
YES, IN PART, BUT ALSO BECAUSE HONEY THINKS HE'S LONELY FOR HIS OWN KIND...
HE SEEMS FINE TO ME, BUT YOU KNOW HOW GIRLS ARE...
PURR! PURR!
INDEED...
I KNOW IT'S A LOT TO ASK, BUT IF IT'S AT ALL POSSIBLE I--
CONSIDER IT DONE, MUDDY.
WOW, THANKS! YOU'RE A PAL, CRUSTY!
DON'T MENTION IT...
SO TELL ME, HOW HAVE MY CLIENTS BEEN GETTING ALONG WITHOUT ME?
FINE, I GUESS. NOTHING NEW TO REPORT...
...OH, EXCEPT THAT WOO-WOO'S GOT HER-SELF SOME NEW ROCK STAR BOYFRIEND...
C'MERE, LI'L FELLAH...
A "ROCK STAR"? WHAT'S HIS NAME?
UH, I FORGET... "HOBO" SOME-THING...
HOBO CAPPILETTO?!?
THAT'S THE ONE.
HEY, DID YOU KNOW HIS MANAGER IS MONGREL MOGUL? SMALL WORLD, HUH?
UGH, DON'T REMIND ME...

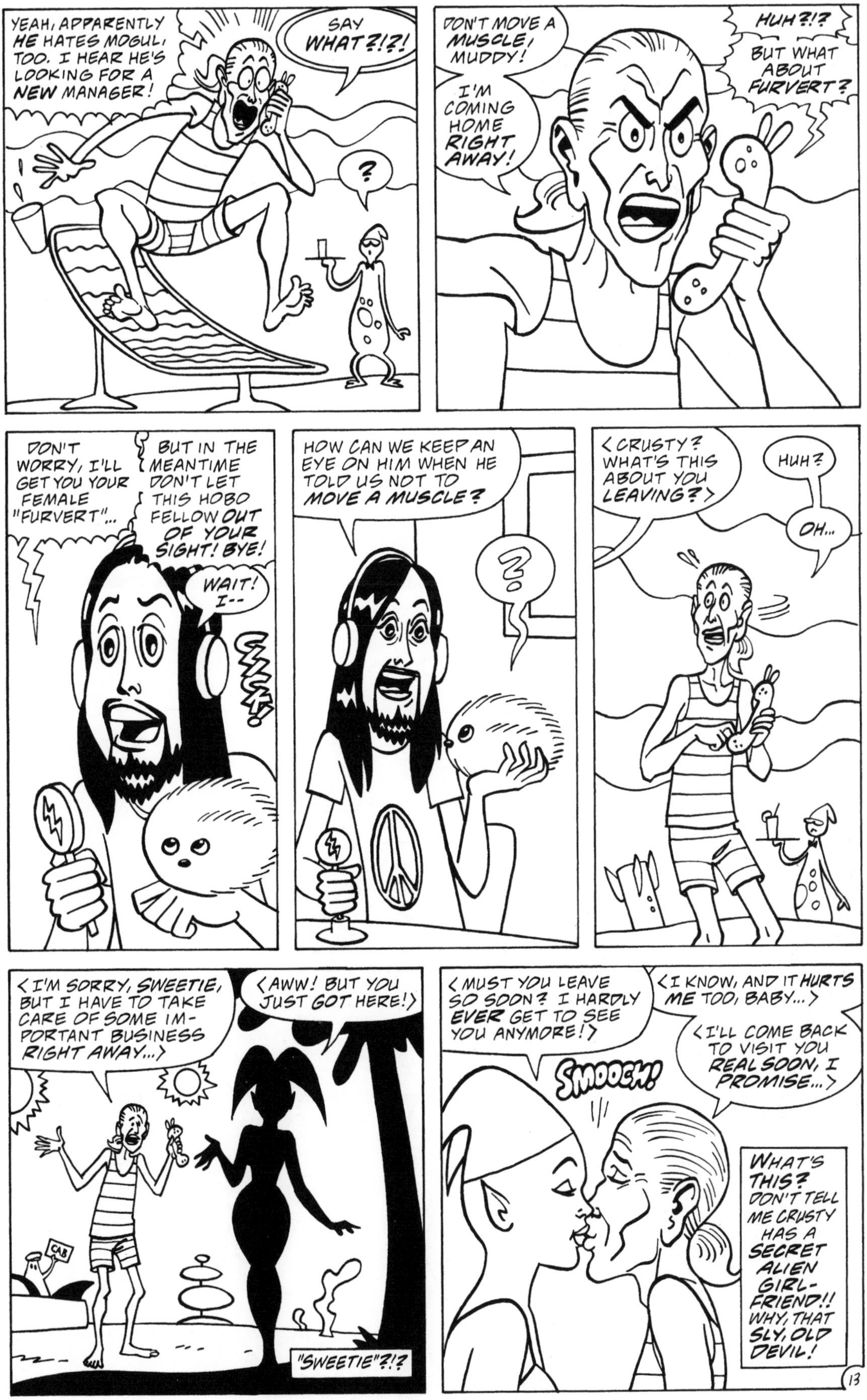
YEAH, APPARENTLY HE HATES MOGUL, TOO. I HEAR HE'S LOOKING FOR A NEW MANAGER!
SAY WHAT?!?!
?
DON'T MOVE A MUSCLE, MUDDY!
I'M COMING HOME RIGHT AWAY!
HUH?!?
BUT WHAT ABOUT FURVERT?
DON'T WORRY, I'LL GET YOU YOUR FEMALE "FURVERT"...
BUT IN THE MEANTIME DON'T LET THIS HOBO FELLOW OUT OF YOUR SIGHT! BYE!
WAIT! I--
CLICK!
HOW CAN WE KEEP AN EYE ON HIM WHEN HE TOLD US NOT TO MOVE A MUSCLE?
?
<CRUSTY? WHAT'S THIS ABOUT YOU LEAVING?>
HUH?
OH...
<I'M SORRY, SWEETIE, BUT I HAVE TO TAKE CARE OF SOME IMPORTANT BUSINESS RIGHT AWAY...>
<AWW! BUT YOU JUST GOT HERE!>
CAB
"SWEETIE"?!?
<MUST YOU LEAVE SO SOON? I HARDLY EVER GET TO SEE YOU ANYMORE!>
<I KNOW, AND IT HURTS ME TOO, BABY...>
<I'LL COME BACK TO VISIT YOU REAL SOON, I PROMISE...>
SMOOCH!
WHAT'S THIS? DON'T TELL ME CRUSTY HAS A SECRET ALIEN GIRL-FRIEND!! WHY, THAT SLY, OLD DEVIL!

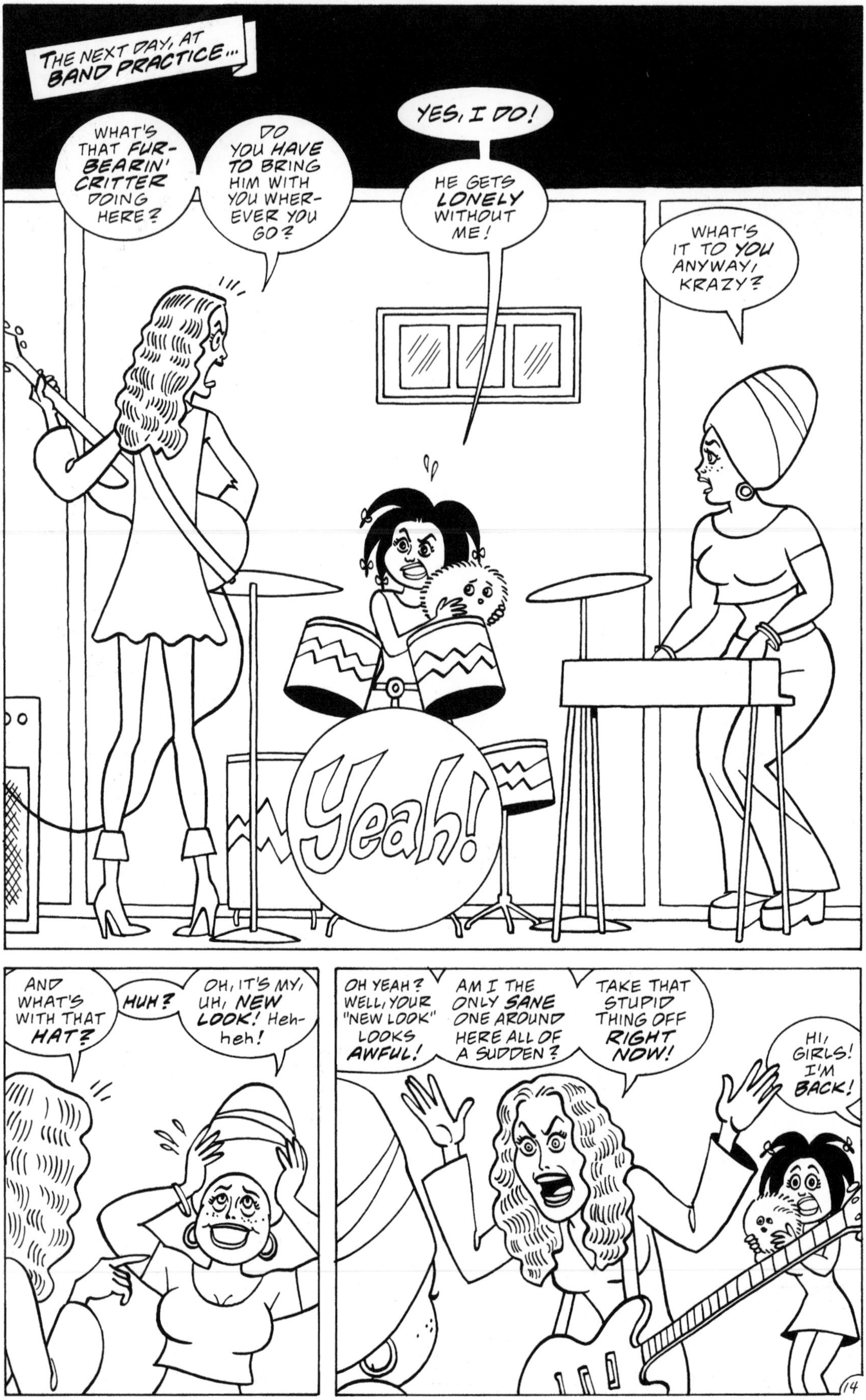

THE NEXT DAY, AT BAND PRACTICE...
WHAT'S THAT FUR-BEARIN' CRITTER DOING HERE?
DO YOU HAVE TO BRING HIM WITH YOU WHEREVER YOU GO?
YES, I DO!
HE GETS LONELY WITHOUT ME!
WHAT'S IT TO YOU ANYWAY, KRAZY?
Yeah!
AND WHAT'S WITH THAT HAT?
HUH?
OH, IT'S MY, UH, NEW LOOK! Heh-heh!
OH YEAH? WELL, YOUR "NEW LOOK" LOOKS AWFUL!
AM I THE ONLY SANE ONE AROUND HERE ALL OF A SUDDEN?
TAKE THAT STUPID THING OFF RIGHT NOW!
HI, GIRLS! I'M BACK!

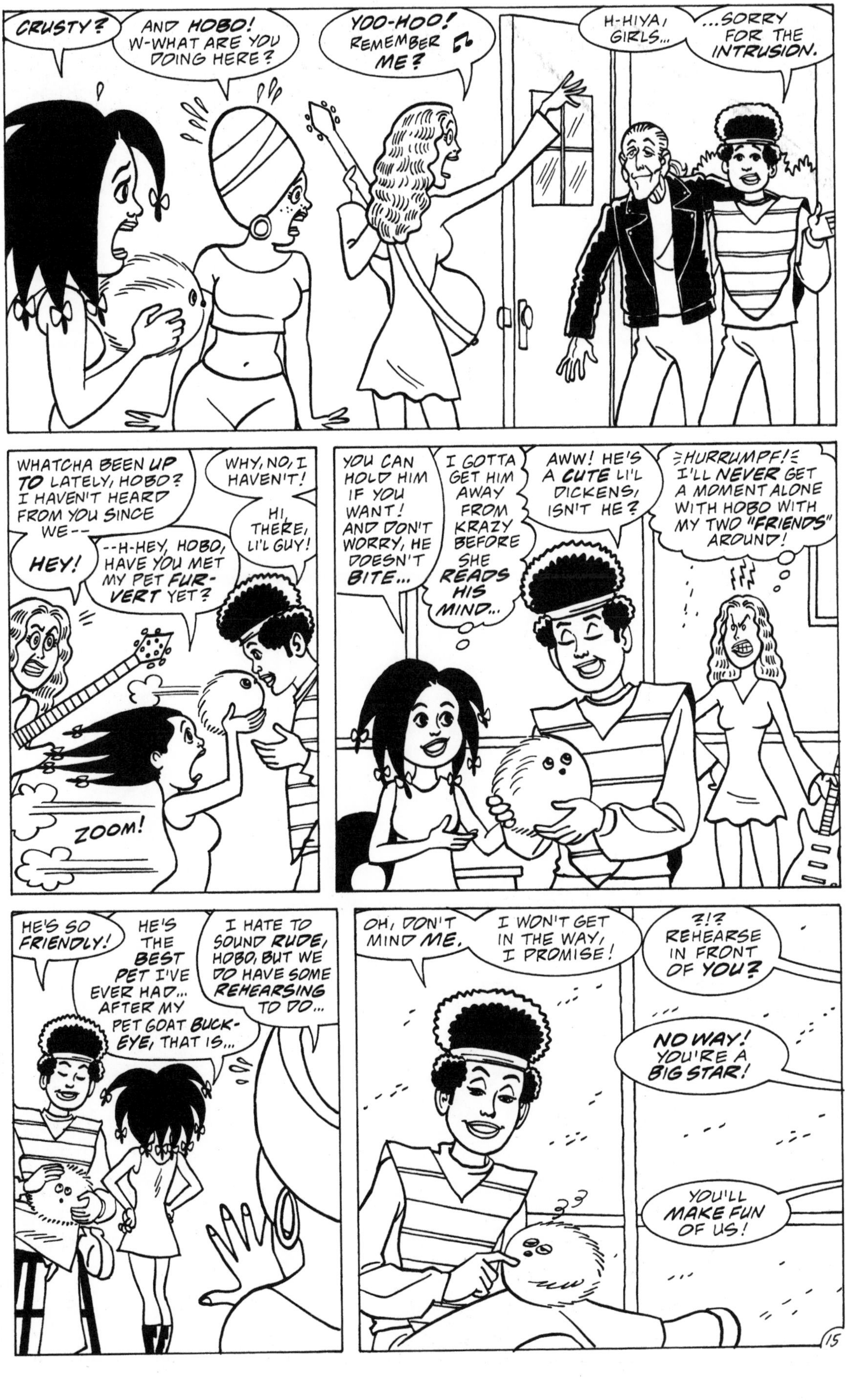
CRUSTY?
AND HOBO! W-WHAT ARE YOU DOING HERE?
YOO-HOO! REMEMBER ME?
H-HIYA, GIRLS...
...SORRY FOR THE INTRUSION.
WHATCHA BEEN UP TO LATELY, HOBO? I HAVEN'T HEARD FROM YOU SINCE WE--
WHY, NO, I HAVEN'T!
HEY!
--H-HEY, HOBO, HAVE YOU MET MY PET FUR-VERT YET?
HI, THERE, LI'L GUY!
ZOOM!
YOU CAN HOLD HIM IF YOU WANT! AND DON'T WORRY, HE DOESN'T BITE...
I GOTTA GET HIM AWAY FROM KRAZY BEFORE SHE READS HIS MIND...
AWW! HE'S A CUTE LI'L DICKENS, ISN'T HE?
HURRUMPF! I'LL NEVER GET A MOMENT ALONE WITH HOBO WITH MY TWO "FRIENDS" AROUND!
HE'S SO FRIENDLY!
HE'S THE BEST PET I'VE EVER HAD... AFTER MY PET GOAT BUCK-EYE, THAT IS...
I HATE TO SOUND RUDE, HOBO, BUT WE DO HAVE SOME REHEARSING TO DO...
OH, DON'T MIND ME.
I WON'T GET IN THE WAY, I PROMISE!
?!? REHEARSE IN FRONT OF YOU?
NO WAY! YOU'RE A BIG STAR!
YOU'LL MAKE FUN OF US!

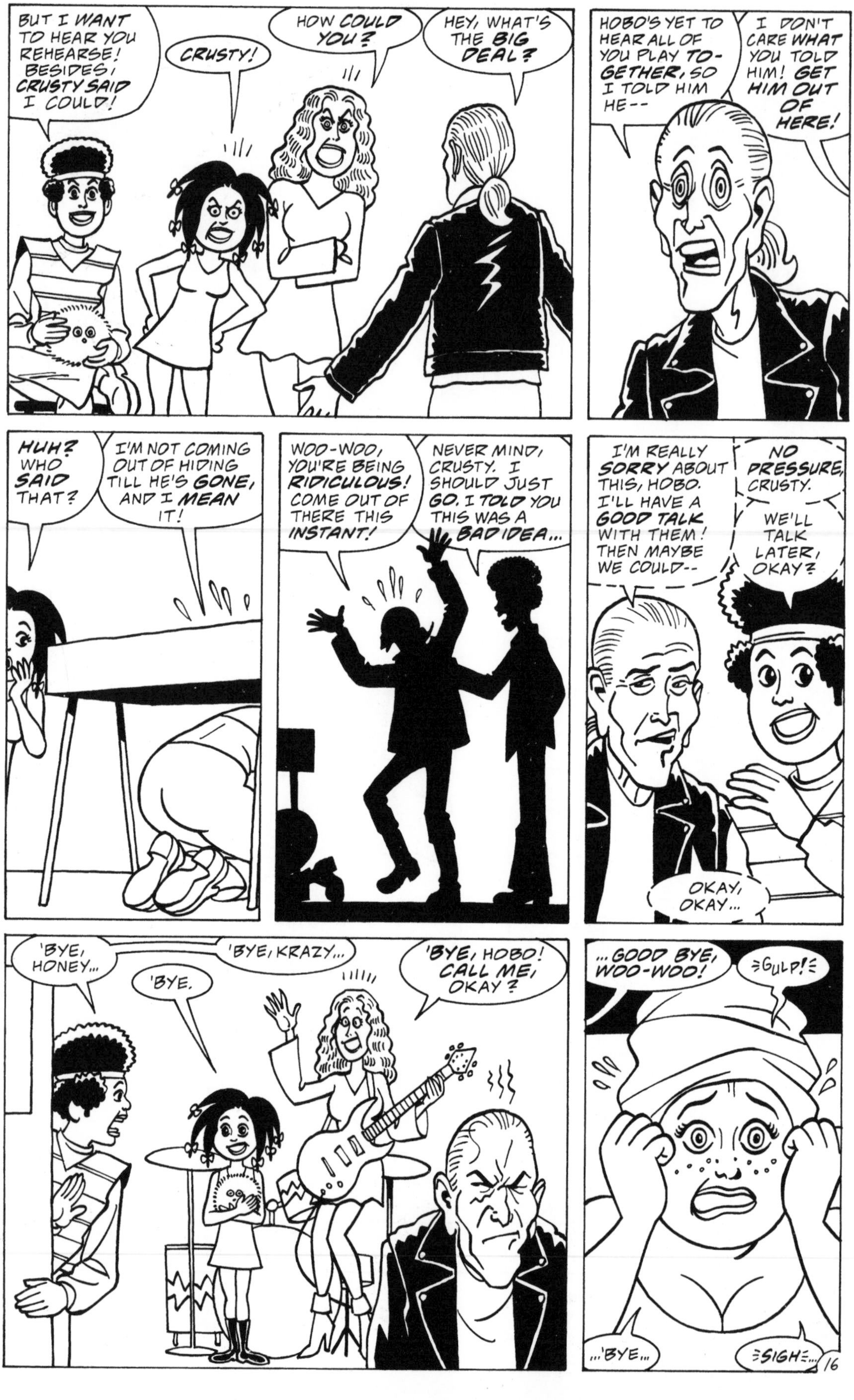
BUT I WANT TO HEAR YOU REHEARSE! BESIDES, CRUSTY SAID I COULD!
CRUSTY!
HOW COULD YOU?
HEY, WHAT'S THE BIG DEAL?
HOBO'S YET TO HEAR ALL OF YOU PLAY TO-GETHER, SO I TOLD HIM HE--
I DON'T CARE WHAT YOU TOLD HIM! GET HIM OUT OF HERE!
HUH? WHO SAID THAT?
I'M NOT COMING OUT OF HIDING TILL HE'S GONE, AND I MEAN IT!
WOO-WOO, YOU'RE BEING RIDICULOUS! COME OUT OF THERE THIS INSTANT!
NEVER MIND, CRUSTY. I SHOULD JUST GO. I TOLD YOU THIS WAS A BAD IDEA...
I'M REALLY SORRY ABOUT THIS, HOBO. I'LL HAVE A GOOD TALK WITH THEM! THEN MAYBE WE COULD--
NO PRESSURE, CRUSTY.
WE'LL TALK LATER, OKAY?
OKAY, OKAY...
'BYE, HONEY...
'BYE, KRAZY...
'BYE.
'BYE, HOBO! CALL ME, OKAY?
...GOOD BYE, WOO-WOO!
GULP!
...'BYE...
SIGH...

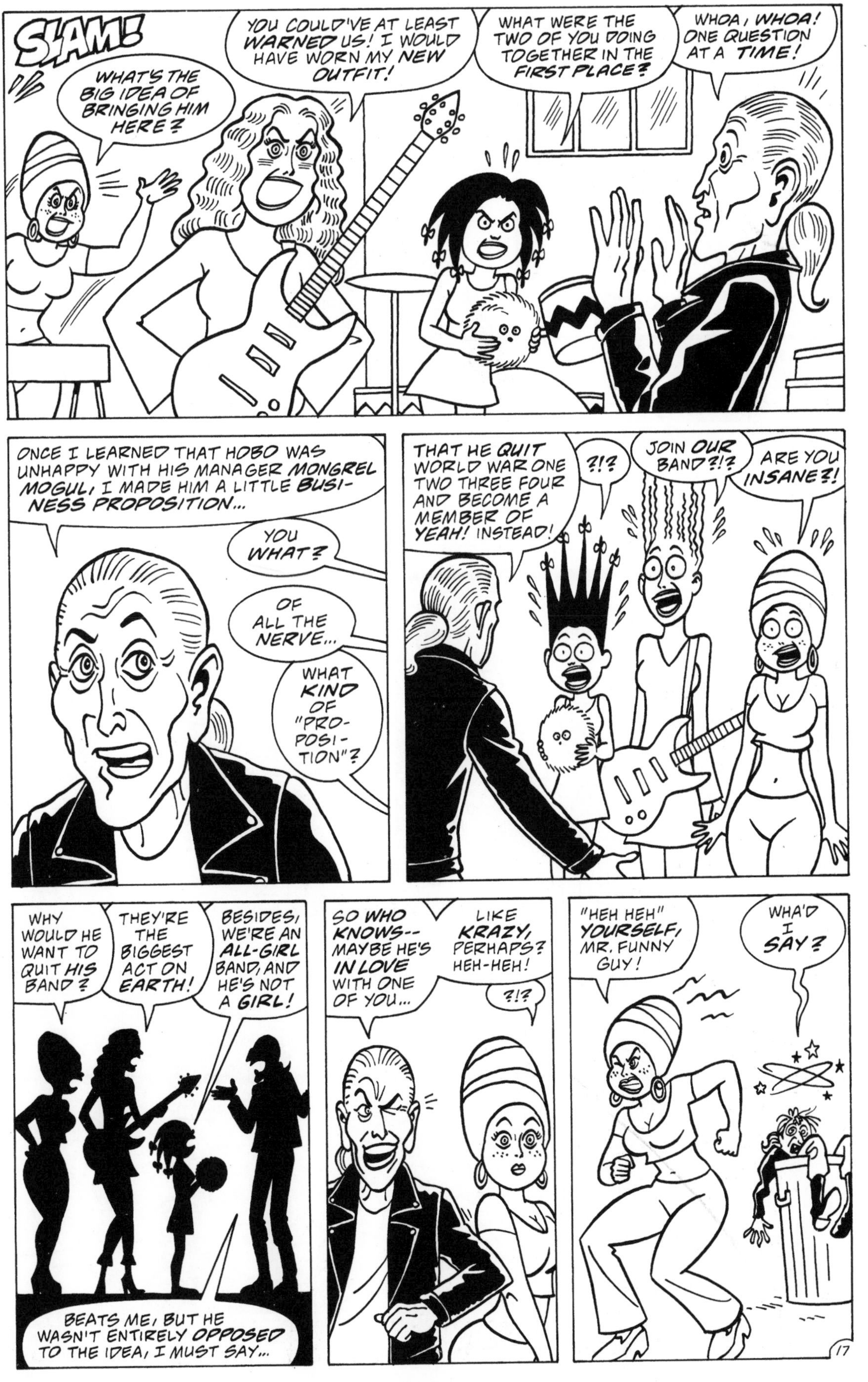
SLAM!
WHAT'S THE BIG IDEA OF BRINGING HIM HERE?
YOU COULD'VE AT LEAST WARNED US! I WOULD HAVE WORN MY NEW OUTFIT!
WHAT WERE THE TWO OF YOU DOING TOGETHER IN THE FIRST PLACE?
WHOA, WHOA! ONE QUESTION AT A TIME!
ONCE I LEARNED THAT HOBO WAS UNHAPPY WITH HIS MANAGER MONGREL MOGUL, I MADE HIM A LITTLE BUSINESS PROPOSITION...
YOU WHAT?
OF ALL THE NERVE...
WHAT KIND OF "PROPOSITION"?
THAT HE QUIT WORLD WAR ONE TWO THREE FOUR AND BECOME A MEMBER OF YEAH! INSTEAD!
?!?
JOIN OUR BAND?!?
ARE YOU INSANE?!
WHY WOULD HE WANT TO QUIT HIS BAND?
THEY'RE THE BIGGEST ACT ON EARTH!
BESIDES, WE'RE AN ALL-GIRL BAND, AND HE'S NOT A GIRL!
BEATS ME, BUT HE WASN'T ENTIRELY OPPOSED TO THE IDEA, I MUST SAY...
SO WHO KNOWS-- MAYBE HE'S IN LOVE WITH ONE OF YOU...
LIKE KRAZY, PERHAPS? HEH-HEH!
?!?
"HEH HEH" YOURSELF, MR. FUNNY GUY!
WHA'D I SAY?

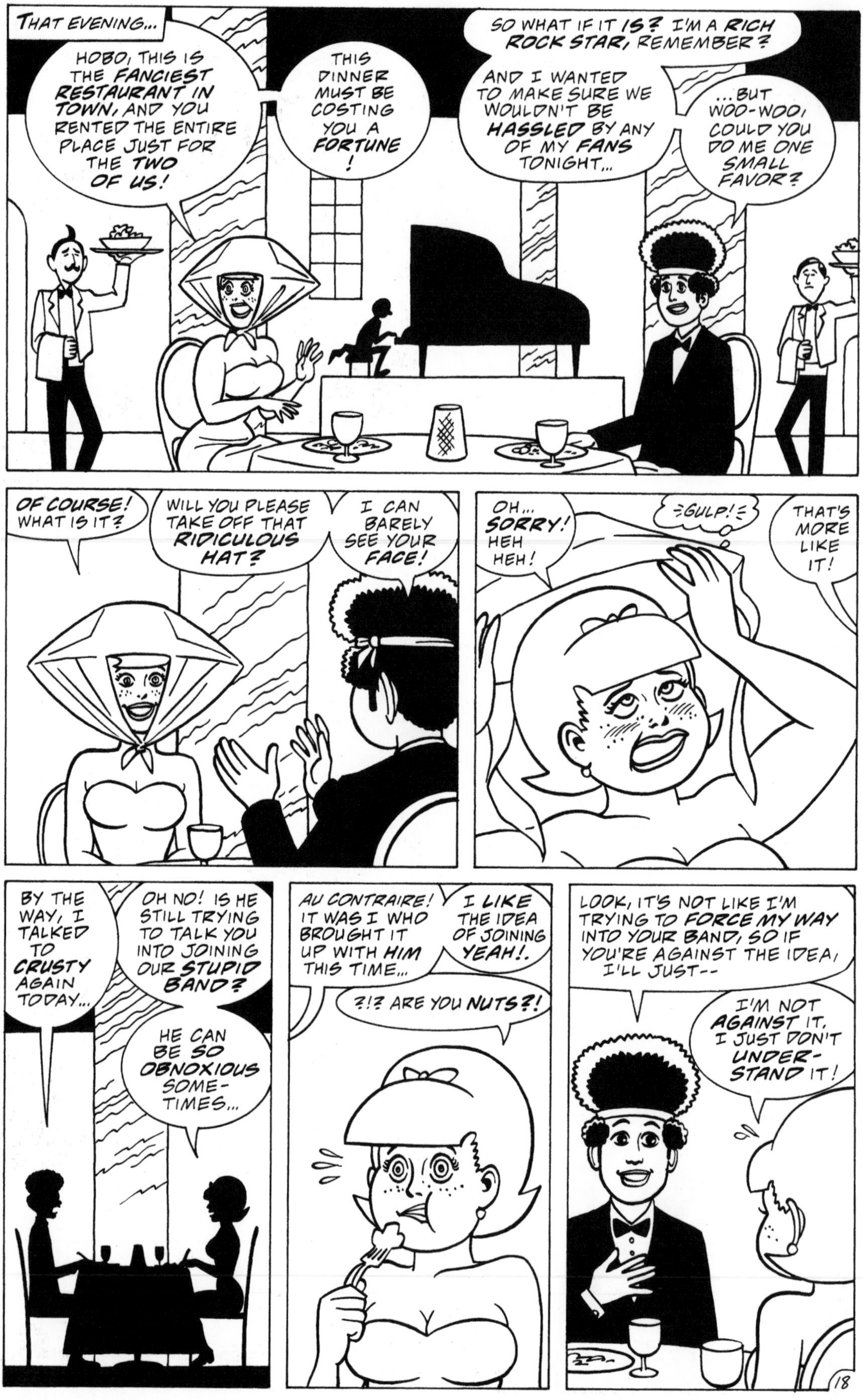
THAT EVENING...
HOBO, THIS IS THE FANCIEST RESTAURANT IN TOWN, AND YOU RENTED THE ENTIRE PLACE JUST FOR THE TWO OF US!
THIS DINNER MUST BE COSTING YOU A FORTUNE!
SO WHAT IF IT IS? I'M A RICH ROCK STAR, REMEMBER?
AND I WANTED TO MAKE SURE WE WOULDN'T BE HASSLED BY ANY OF MY FANS TONIGHT...
...BUT WOO-WOO, COULD YOU DO ME ONE SMALL FAVOR?
OF COURSE! WHAT IS IT?
WILL YOU PLEASE TAKE OFF THAT RIDICULOUS HAT?
I CAN BARELY SEE YOUR FACE!
OH... SORRY! HEH HEH!
GULP!
THAT'S MORE LIKE IT!
BY THE WAY, I TALKED TO CRUSTY AGAIN TODAY...
OH NO! IS HE STILL TRYING TO TALK YOU INTO JOINING OUR STUPID BAND?
HE CAN BE SO OBNOXIOUS SOME-TIMES...
AU CONTRAIRE! IT WAS I WHO BROUGHT IT UP WITH HIM THIS TIME...
I LIKE THE IDEA OF JOINING YEAH!.
?!? ARE YOU NUTS?!
LOOK, IT'S NOT LIKE I'M TRYING TO FORCE MY WAY INTO YOUR BAND, SO IF YOU'RE AGAINST THE IDEA, I'LL JUST--
I'M NOT AGAINST IT, I JUST DON'T UNDER-STAND IT!

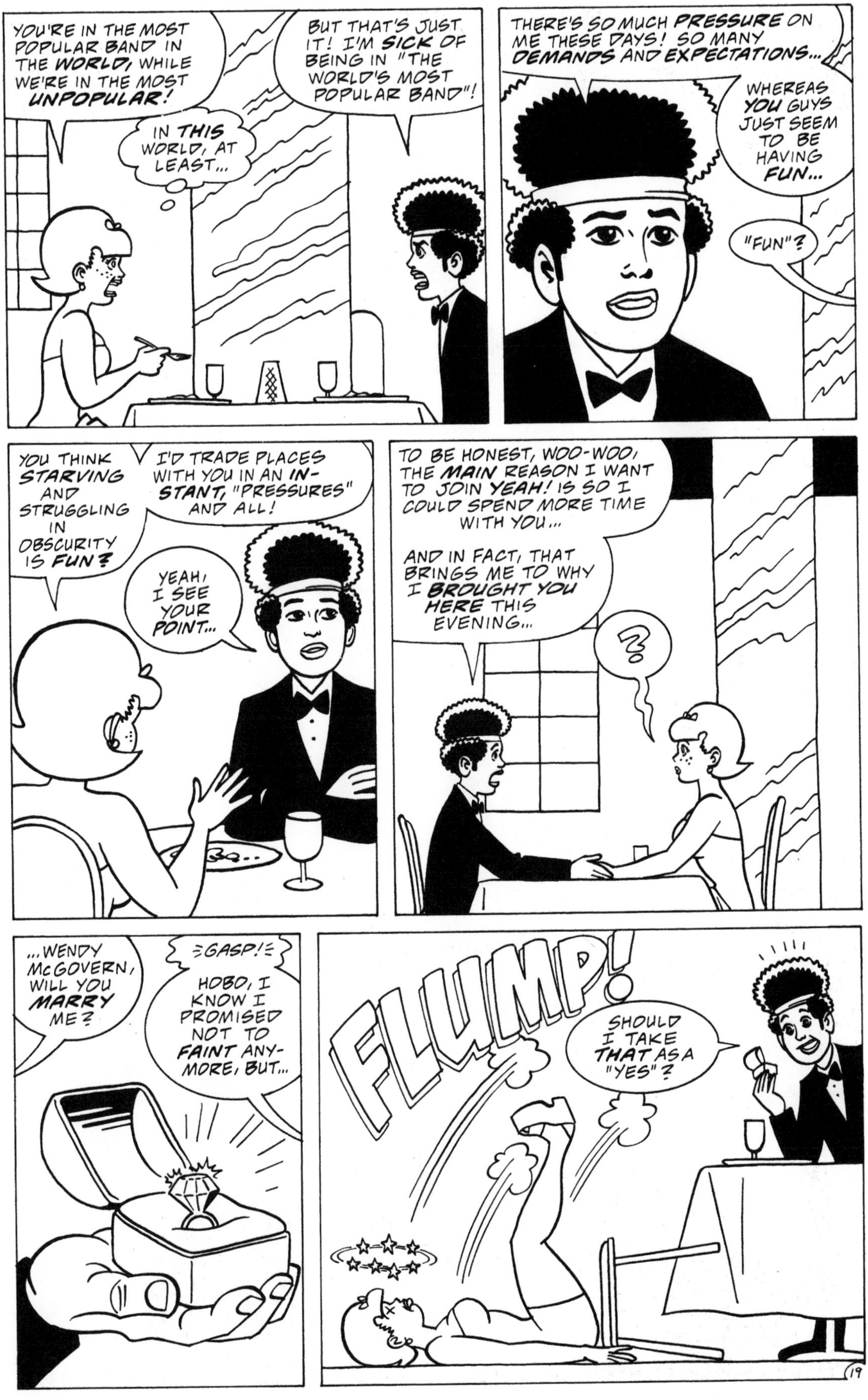

YOU'RE IN THE MOST POPULAR BAND IN THE WORLD, WHILE WE'RE IN THE MOST UNPOPULAR!
IN THIS WORLD, AT LEAST...
BUT THAT'S JUST IT! I'M SICK OF BEING IN "THE WORLD'S MOST POPULAR BAND"!
THERE'S SO MUCH PRESSURE ON ME THESE DAYS! SO MANY DEMANDS AND EXPECTATIONS...
WHEREAS YOU GUYS JUST SEEM TO BE HAVING FUN...
"FUN"?
YOU THINK STARVING AND STRUGGLING IN OBSCURITY IS FUN?
I'D TRADE PLACES WITH YOU IN AN IN-STANT, "PRESSURES" AND ALL!
YEAH, I SEE YOUR POINT...
TO BE HONEST, WOO-WOO, THE MAIN REASON I WANT TO JOIN YEAH! IS SO I COULD SPEND MORE TIME WITH YOU...
AND IN FACT, THAT BRINGS ME TO WHY I BROUGHT YOU HERE THIS EVENING...
?
...WENDY McGOVERN, WILL YOU MARRY ME?
GASP!
HOBO, I KNOW I PROMISED NOT TO FAINT ANY-MORE, BUT...
FLUMP!
SHOULD I TAKE THAT AS A "YES"?

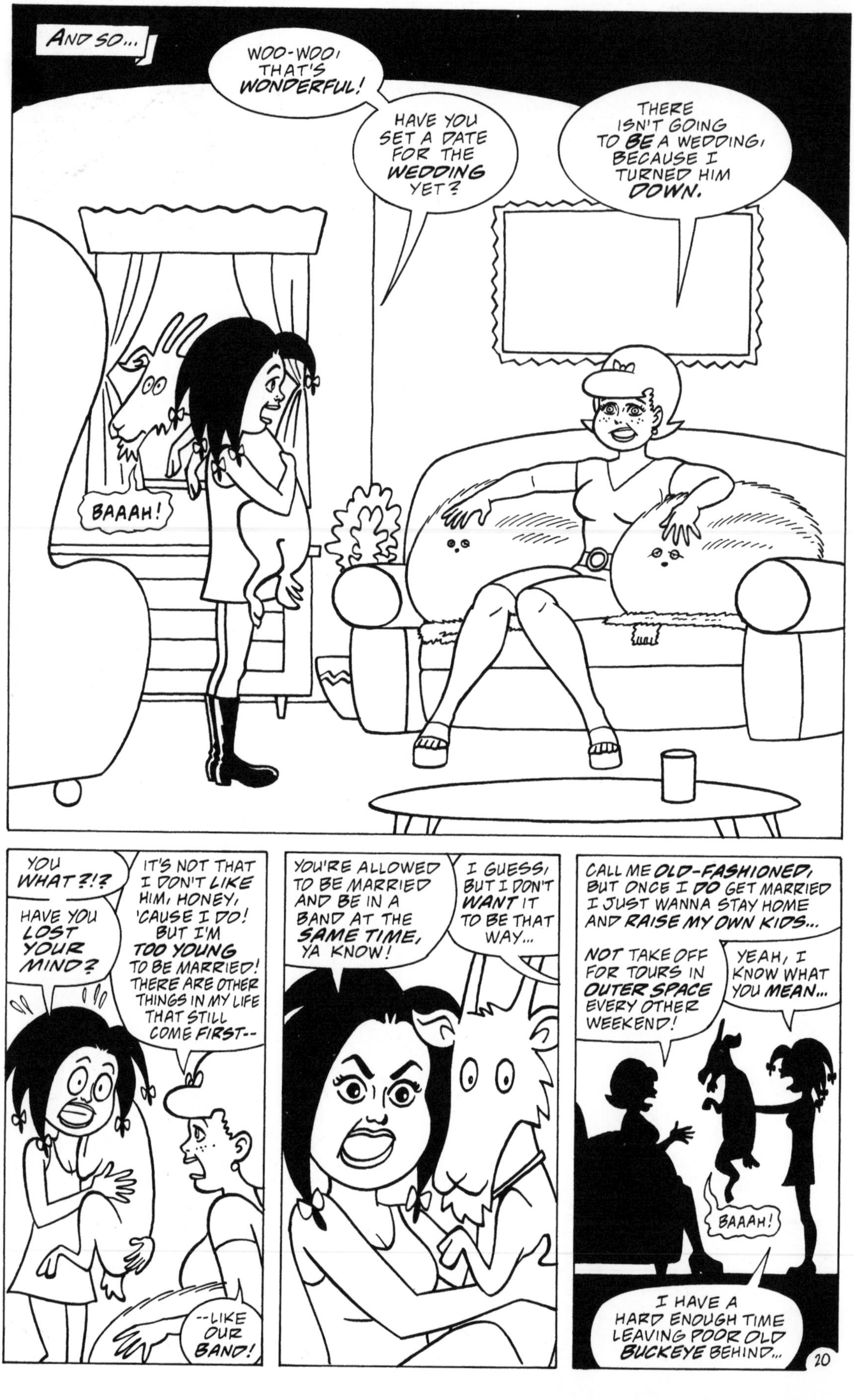
AND SO...
WOO-WOO! THAT'S WONDERFUL!
HAVE YOU SET A DATE FOR THE WEDDING YET?
THERE ISN'T GOING TO BE A WEDDING, BECAUSE I TURNED HIM DOWN.
BAAAH!
YOU WHAT?!?
HAVE YOU LOST YOUR MIND?
IT'S NOT THAT I DON'T LIKE HIM, HONEY, 'CAUSE I DO! BUT I'M TOO YOUNG TO BE MARRIED! THERE ARE OTHER THINGS IN MY LIFE THAT STILL COME FIRST--
--LIKE OUR BAND!
YOU'RE ALLOWED TO BE MARRIED AND BE IN A BAND AT THE SAME TIME, YA KNOW!
I GUESS, BUT I DON'T WANT IT TO BE THAT WAY...
CALL ME OLD-FASHIONED, BUT ONCE I DO GET MARRIED I JUST WANNA STAY HOME AND RAISE MY OWN KIDS...
NOT TAKE OFF FOR TOURS IN OUTER SPACE EVERY OTHER WEEKEND!
YEAH, I KNOW WHAT YOU MEAN...
BAAAH!
I HAVE A HARD ENOUGH TIME LEAVING POOR OLD BUCKEYE BEHIND...

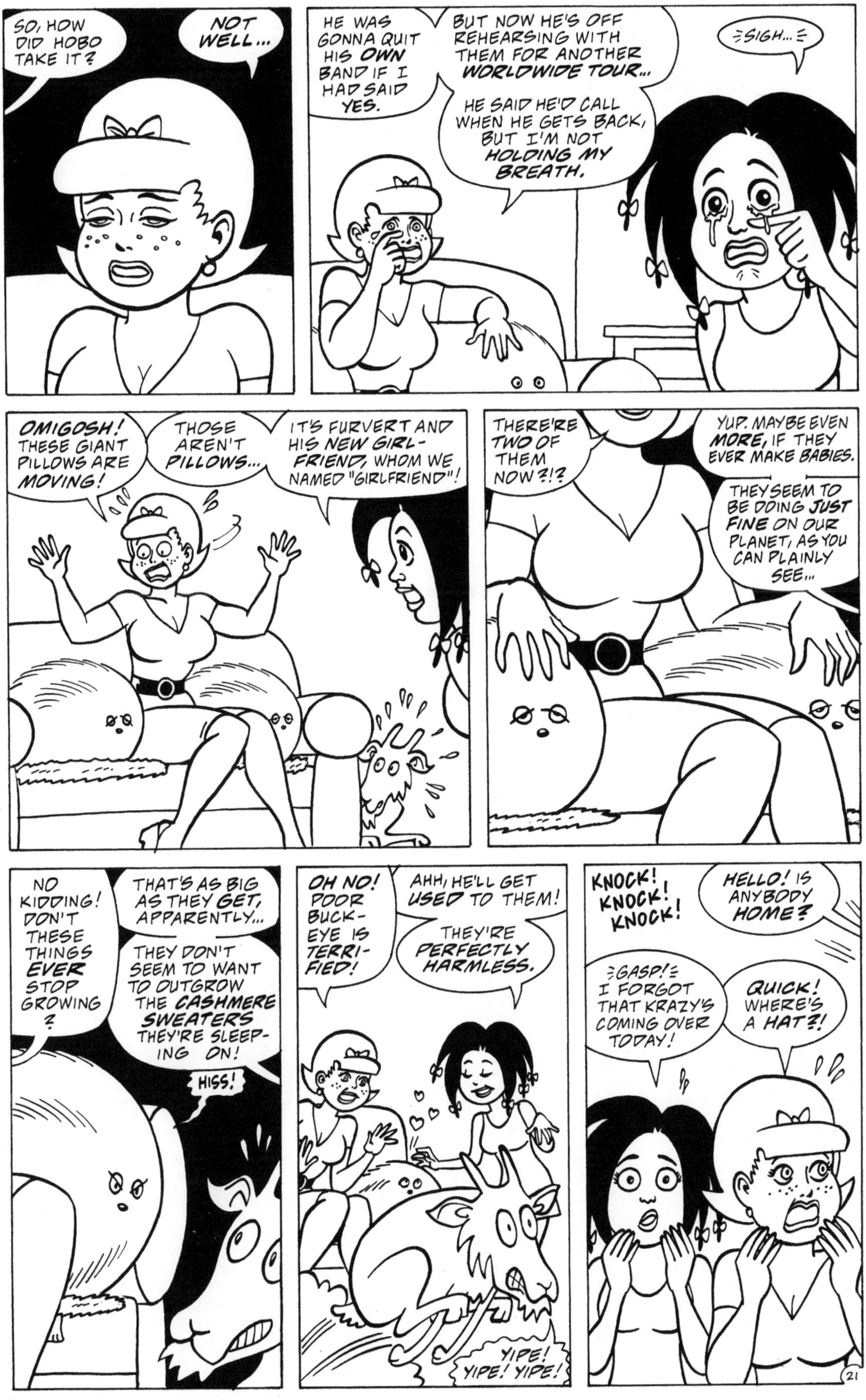

SO, HOW DID HOBO TAKE IT?
NOT WELL...
HE WAS GONNA QUIT HIS OWN BAND IF I HAD SAID YES.
BUT NOW HE'S OFF REHEARSING WITH THEM FOR ANOTHER WORLDWIDE TOUR...
HE SAID HE'D CALL WHEN HE GETS BACK, BUT I'M NOT HOLDING MY BREATH.
SIGH...
OMIGOSH! THESE GIANT PILLOWS ARE MOVING!
THOSE AREN'T PILLOWS...
IT'S FURVERT AND HIS NEW GIRL-FRIEND, WHOM WE NAMED "GIRLFRIEND"!
THERE'RE TWO OF THEM NOW?!?
YUP. MAYBE EVEN MORE, IF THEY EVER MAKE BABIES.
THEY SEEM TO BE DOING JUST FINE ON OUR PLANET, AS YOU CAN PLAINLY SEE...
NO KIDDING! DON'T THESE THINGS EVER STOP GROWING?
THAT'S AS BIG AS THEY GET, APPARENTLY...
THEY DON'T SEEM TO WANT TO OUTGROW THE CASHMERE SWEATERS THEY'RE SLEEP-ING ON!
HISS!
OH NO! POOR BUCK-EYE IS TERRI-FIED!
AHH, HE'LL GET USED TO THEM!
THEY'RE PERFECTLY HARMLESS.
YIPE! YIPE! YIPE!
KNOCK! KNOCK! KNOCK!
HELLO! IS ANYBODY HOME?
GASP! I FORGOT THAT KRAZY'S COMING OVER TODAY!
QUICK! WHERE'S A HAT?!

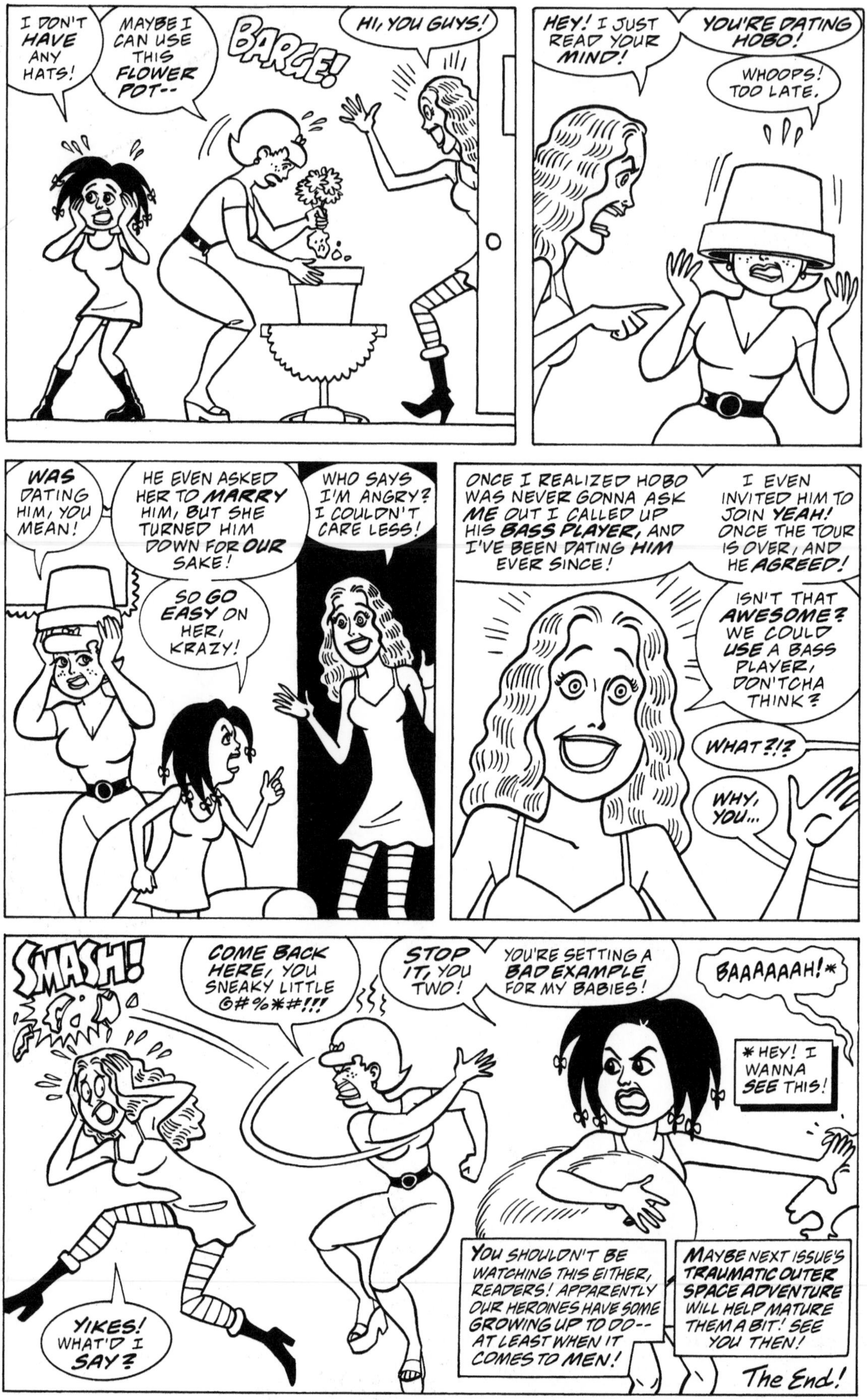
I DON'T HAVE ANY HATS!
MAYBE I CAN USE THIS FLOWER POT--
BARGE!
HI, YOU GUYS!
HEY! I JUST READ YOUR MIND!
YOU'RE DATING HOBO!
WHOOPS! TOO LATE.
WAS DATING HIM, YOU MEAN!
HE EVEN ASKED HER TO MARRY HIM, BUT SHE TURNED HIM DOWN FOR OUR SAKE!
SO GO EASY ON HER, KRAZY!
WHO SAYS I'M ANGRY? I COULDN'T CARE LESS!
ONCE I REALIZED HOBO WAS NEVER GONNA ASK ME OUT I CALLED UP HIS BASS PLAYER, AND I'VE BEEN DATING HIM EVER SINCE!
I EVEN INVITED HIM TO JOIN YEAH! ONCE THE TOUR IS OVER, AND HE AGREED!
ISN'T THAT AWESOME? WE COULD USE A BASS PLAYER, DON'TCHA THINK?
WHAT?!?
WHY, YOU...
SMASH!
COME BACK HERE, YOU SNEAKY LITTLE @#%*#!!!
STOP IT, YOU TWO!
YOU'RE SETTING A BAD EXAMPLE FOR MY BABIES!
BAAAAAAH!*
*HEY! I WANNA SEE THIS!
YIKES! WHAT'D I SAY?
YOU SHOULDN'T BE WATCHING THIS EITHER, READERS! APPARENTLY OUR HEROINES HAVE SOME GROWING UP TO DO-- AT LEAST WHEN IT COMES TO MEN!
MAYBE NEXT ISSUE'S TRAUMATIC OUTER SPACE ADVENTURE WILL HELP MATURE THEM A BIT! SEE YOU THEN!
The End!

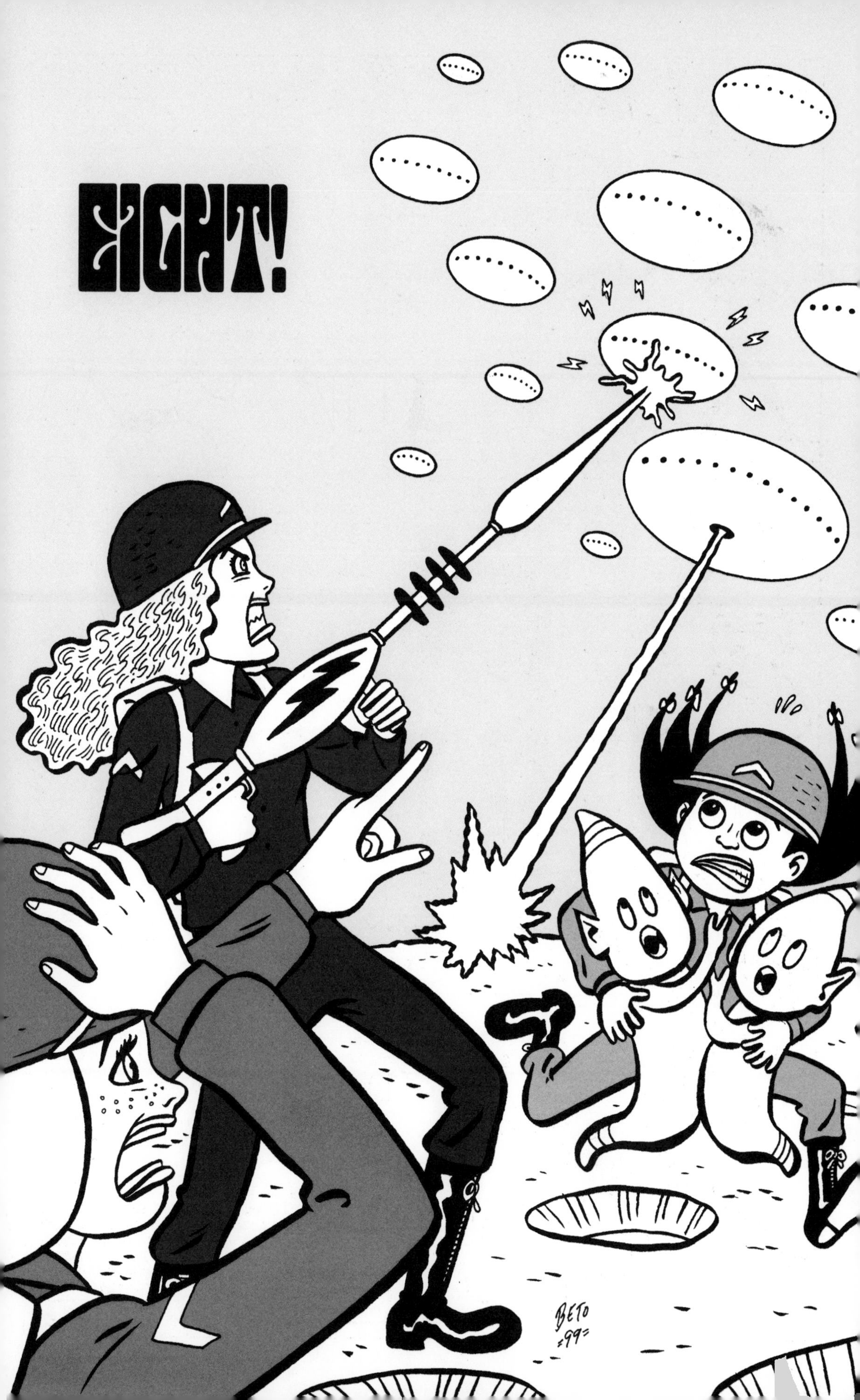
EIGHT!
BETO
=99=

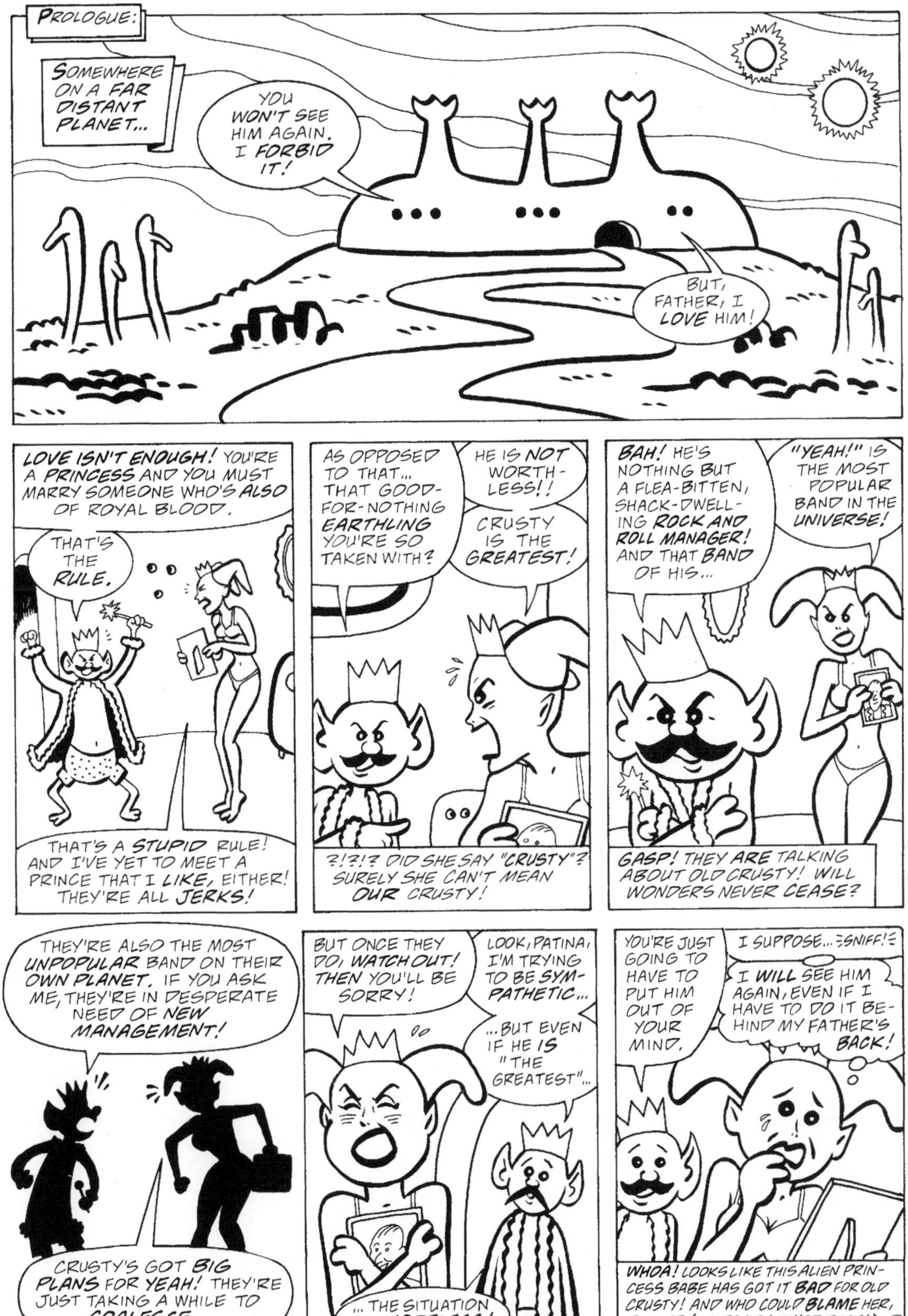
PROLOGUE:
SOMEWHERE ON A FAR DISTANT PLANET...
YOU WON'T SEE HIM AGAIN. I FORBID IT!
BUT, FATHER, I LOVE HIM!
LOVE ISN'T ENOUGH! YOU'RE A PRINCESS AND YOU MUST MARRY SOMEONE WHO'S ALSO OF ROYAL BLOOD.
THAT'S THE RULE.
THAT'S A STUPID RULE! AND I'VE YET TO MEET A PRINCE THAT I LIKE, EITHER! THEY'RE ALL JERKS!
AS OPPOSED TO THAT... THAT GOOD-FOR-NOTHING EARTHLING YOU'RE SO TAKEN WITH?
HE IS NOT WORTHLESS!!
CRUSTY IS THE GREATEST!
?!?!? DID SHE SAY "CRUSTY"? SURELY SHE CAN'T MEAN OUR CRUSTY!
BAH! HE'S NOTHING BUT A FLEA-BITTEN, SHACK-DWELLING ROCK AND ROLL MANAGER! AND THAT BAND OF HIS...
"YEAH!" IS THE MOST POPULAR BAND IN THE UNIVERSE!
GASP! THEY ARE TALKING ABOUT OLD CRUSTY! WILL WONDERS NEVER CEASE?
THEY'RE ALSO THE MOST UNPOPULAR BAND ON THEIR OWN PLANET. IF YOU ASK ME, THEY'RE IN DESPERATE NEED OF NEW MANAGEMENT!
CRUSTY'S GOT BIG PLANS FOR YEAH! THEY'RE JUST TAKING A WHILE TO COALESCE...
BUT ONCE THEY DO, WATCH OUT! THEN YOU'LL BE SORRY!
LOOK, PATINA, I'M TRYING TO BE SYMPATHETIC...
...BUT EVEN IF HE IS "THE GREATEST"...
...THE SITUATION IS HOPELESS!
YOU'RE JUST GOING TO HAVE TO PUT HIM OUT OF YOUR MIND.
I SUPPOSE... SNIFF!
I WILL SEE HIM AGAIN, EVEN IF I HAVE TO DO IT BEHIND MY FATHER'S BACK!
WHOA! LOOKS LIKE THIS ALIEN PRINCESS BABE HAS GOT IT BAD FOR OLD CRUSTY! AND WHO COULD BLAME HER, RIGHT? (ER, DON'T ANSWER THAT!)

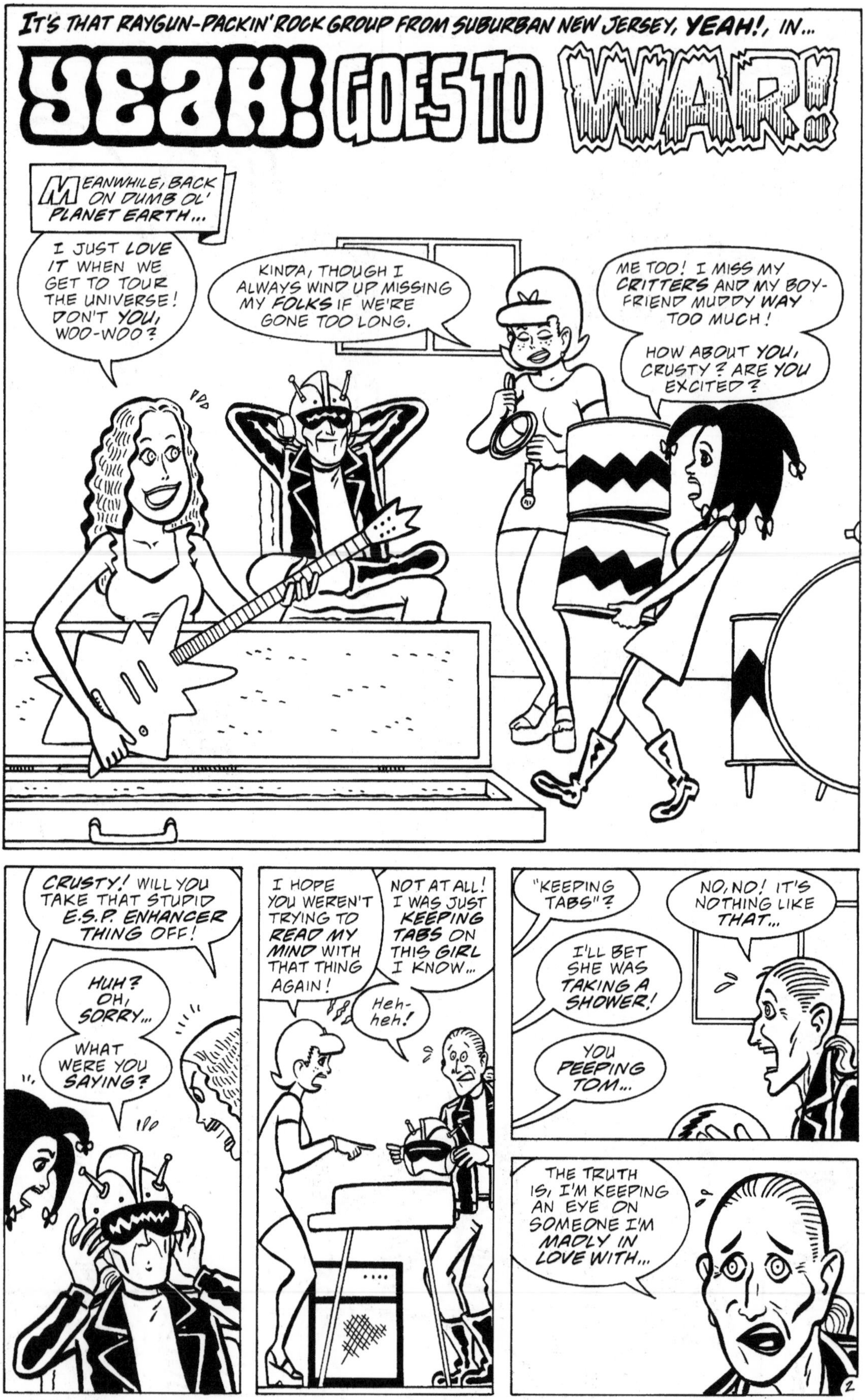
IT'S THAT RAYGUN-PACKIN' ROCK GROUP FROM SUBURBAN NEW JERSEY, YEAH!, IN...
YEAH! GOES TO WAR!
MEANWHILE, BACK ON DUMB OL' PLANET EARTH...
I JUST LOVE IT WHEN WE GET TO TOUR THE UNIVERSE! DON'T YOU, WOO-WOO?
KINDA, THOUGH I ALWAYS WIND UP MISSING MY FOLKS IF WE'RE GONE TOO LONG.
ME TOO! I MISS MY CRITTERS AND MY BOY-FRIEND MUDDY WAY TOO MUCH!
HOW ABOUT YOU, CRUSTY? ARE YOU EXCITED?
CRUSTY! WILL YOU TAKE THAT STUPID E.S.P. ENHANCER THING OFF!
HUH? OH, SORRY...
WHAT WERE YOU SAYING?
I HOPE YOU WEREN'T TRYING TO READ MY MIND WITH THAT THING AGAIN!
NOT AT ALL! I WAS JUST KEEPING TABS ON THIS GIRL I KNOW...
Heh-heh!
"KEEPING TABS"?
I'LL BET SHE WAS TAKING A SHOWER!
YOU PEEPING TOM...
NO, NO! IT'S NOTHING LIKE THAT...
THE TRUTH IS, I'M KEEPING AN EYE ON SOMEONE I'M MADLY IN LOVE WITH...

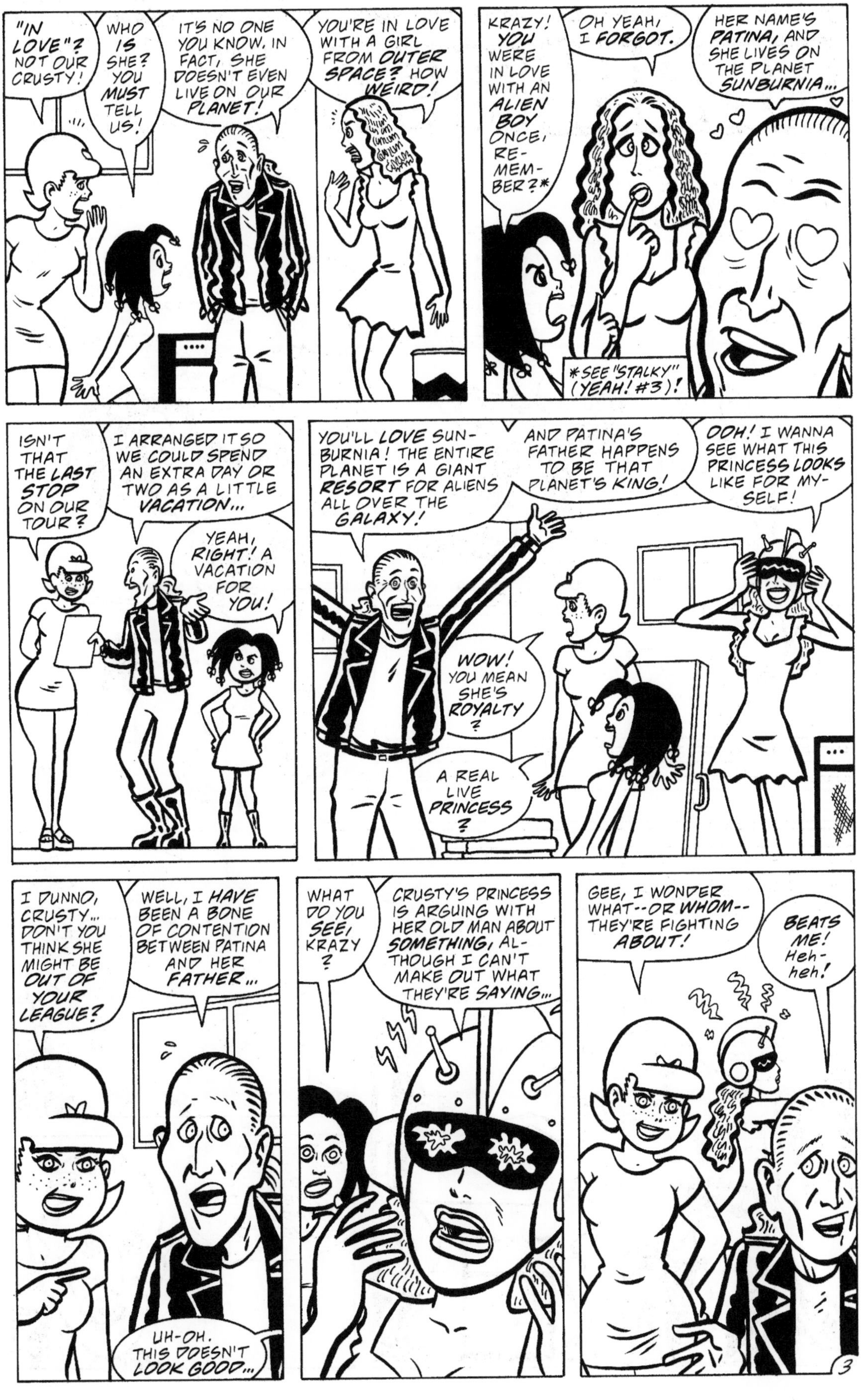
"IN LOVE"? NOT OUR CRUSTY!
WHO IS SHE? YOU MUST TELL US!
IT'S NO ONE YOU KNOW. IN FACT, SHE DOESN'T EVEN LIVE ON OUR PLANET!
YOU'RE IN LOVE WITH A GIRL FROM OUTER SPACE? HOW WEIRD!
KRAZY! YOU WERE IN LOVE WITH AN ALIEN BOY ONCE, RE-MEM-BER?*
OH YEAH, I FORGOT.
HER NAME'S PATINA, AND SHE LIVES ON THE PLANET SUNBURNIA...
*SEE "STALKY" (YEAH! #3)!
ISN'T THAT THE LAST STOP ON OUR TOUR?
I ARRANGED IT SO WE COULD SPEND AN EXTRA DAY OR TWO AS A LITTLE VACATION...
YEAH, RIGHT! A VACATION FOR YOU!
YOU'LL LOVE SUN-BURNIA! THE ENTIRE PLANET IS A GIANT RESORT FOR ALIENS ALL OVER THE GALAXY!
AND PATINA'S FATHER HAPPENS TO BE THAT PLANET'S KING!
OOH! I WANNA SEE WHAT THIS PRINCESS LOOKS LIKE FOR MY-SELF!
WOW! YOU MEAN SHE'S ROYALTY?
A REAL LIVE PRINCESS?
I DUNNO, CRUSTY... DON'T YOU THINK SHE MIGHT BE OUT OF YOUR LEAGUE?
WELL, I HAVE BEEN A BONE OF CONTENTION BETWEEN PATINA AND HER FATHER...
UH-OH. THIS DOESN'T LOOK GOOD...
WHAT DO YOU SEE, KRAZY?
CRUSTY'S PRINCESS IS ARGUING WITH HER OLD MAN ABOUT SOMETHING, AL-THOUGH I CAN'T MAKE OUT WHAT THEY'RE SAYING...
GEE, I WONDER WHAT--OR WHOM--THEY'RE FIGHTING ABOUT!
BEATS ME! Heh-heh!

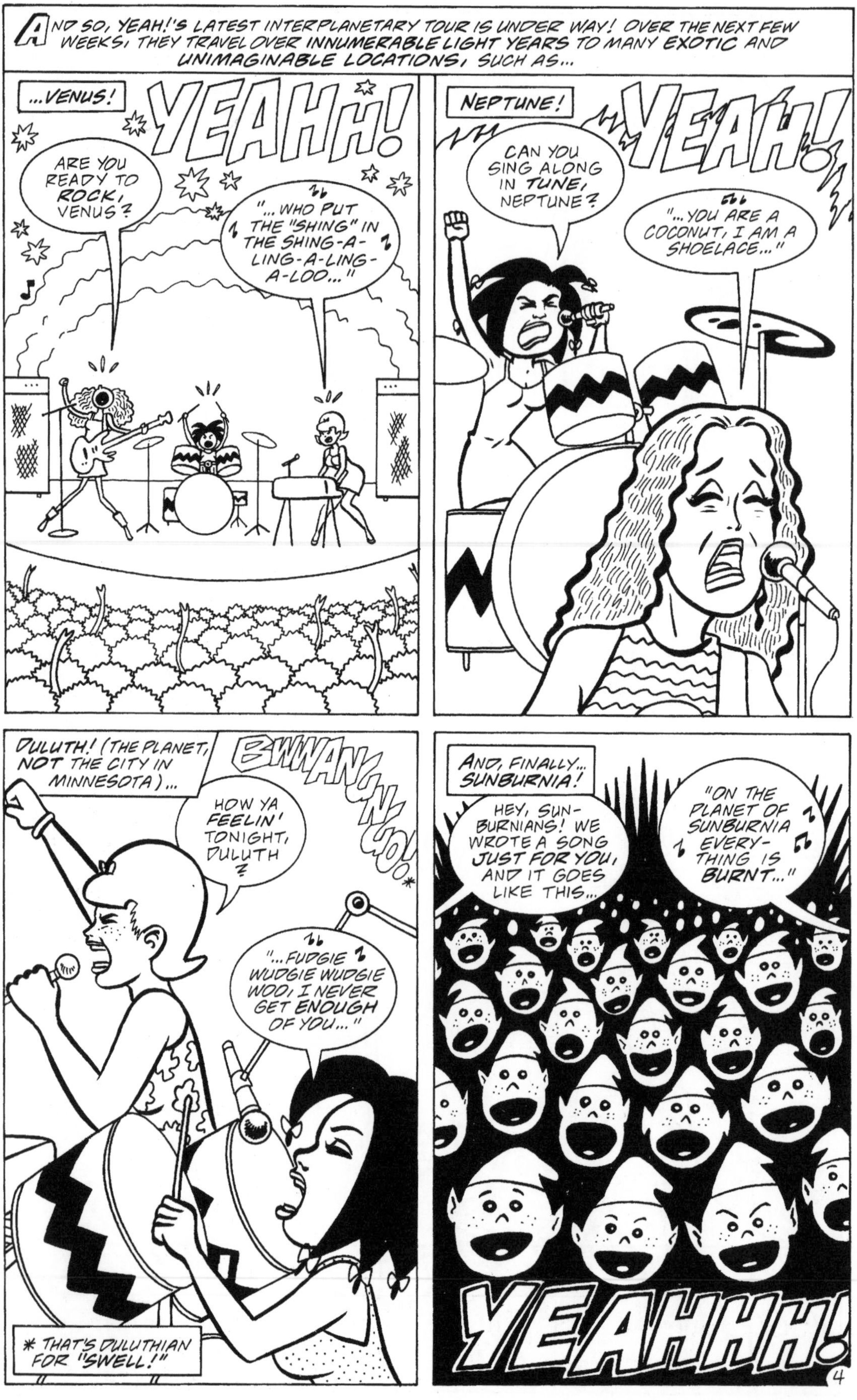

AND SO, YEAH!'S LATEST INTERPLANETARY TOUR IS UNDER WAY! OVER THE NEXT FEW WEEKS, THEY TRAVEL OVER INNUMERABLE LIGHT YEARS TO MANY EXOTIC AND UNIMAGINABLE LOCATIONS, SUCH AS...
...VENUS!
YEAHH!
ARE YOU READY TO ROCK, VENUS?
"...WHO PUT THE "SHING" IN THE SHING-A-LING-A-LING-A-LOO..."
NEPTUNE!
YEAH!
CAN YOU SING ALONG IN TUNE, NEPTUNE?
"...YOU ARE A COCONUT, I AM A SHOELACE..."
DULUTH! (THE PLANET, NOT THE CITY IN MINNESOTA)...
BWWANNNGOO!*
HOW YA FEELIN' TONIGHT, DULUTH?
"...FUDGIE WUDGIE WUDGIE WOO, I NEVER GET ENOUGH OF YOU..."
* THAT'S DULUTHIAN FOR "SWELL!"
AND, FINALLY... SUNBURNIA!
HEY, SUN-BURNIANS! WE WROTE A SONG JUST FOR YOU, AND IT GOES LIKE THIS...
"ON THE PLANET OF SUNBURNIA EVERY-THING IS BURNT..."
YEAHHH!

AFTER THE SHOW...

GOODNESS! THIS PLANET IS HOT!

WELL, NO WONDER... LOOK! IT HAS TWO SUNS!

THAT'S RIGHT! AND TWO SUNS MEANS NO SHADE...

...WHICH IS WHY THIS PLACE IS SO POPULAR WITH SUN WORSHIPPERS!

ICE CREA

BE SURE TO KEEP THOSE SUNGLASSES ON AT ALL TIMES-- AND USE PLENTY OF SUN SCREEN!

ARE YOU KIDDING? I'M GONNA USE GREAT BIG GOBS OF IT!

I'M NOT TAKING ANY CHANCES!

ME NEITHER! I NEED TO PRESERVE MY GHOST-LIKE COMPLEXION!

I DON'T WANNA WIND UP BEET RED LIKE THE NATIVES OF THIS PLANET!

THEY ALL LOOK LIKE DEVILS!

THEY MAY LOOK LIKE "DEVILS," BUT THEY'RE REALLY VERY NICE... AND SPEAKING OF WHICH...

SPLORCH!

...GIRLS, ALLOW ME TO INTRODUCE YOU TO A PERFECT ANGEL NAMED PATINA!

PLEASED TO MEET YOU!

≡GASP!≡ Y-YOU'RE CRUSTY'S GIRLFRIEND?

YYY-- YOU'RE BEAUTIFUL!

AND YOU'RE A REAL LIVE PRINCESS TO BOOT!

WHAT'S IT LIKE, BEING A PRINCESS, HMMM? IS IT, LIKE, TOTALLY GREAT, OR WHAT?

OH, IT'S NOT ALL IT'S CRACKED UP TO BE, BELIEVE ME.

5

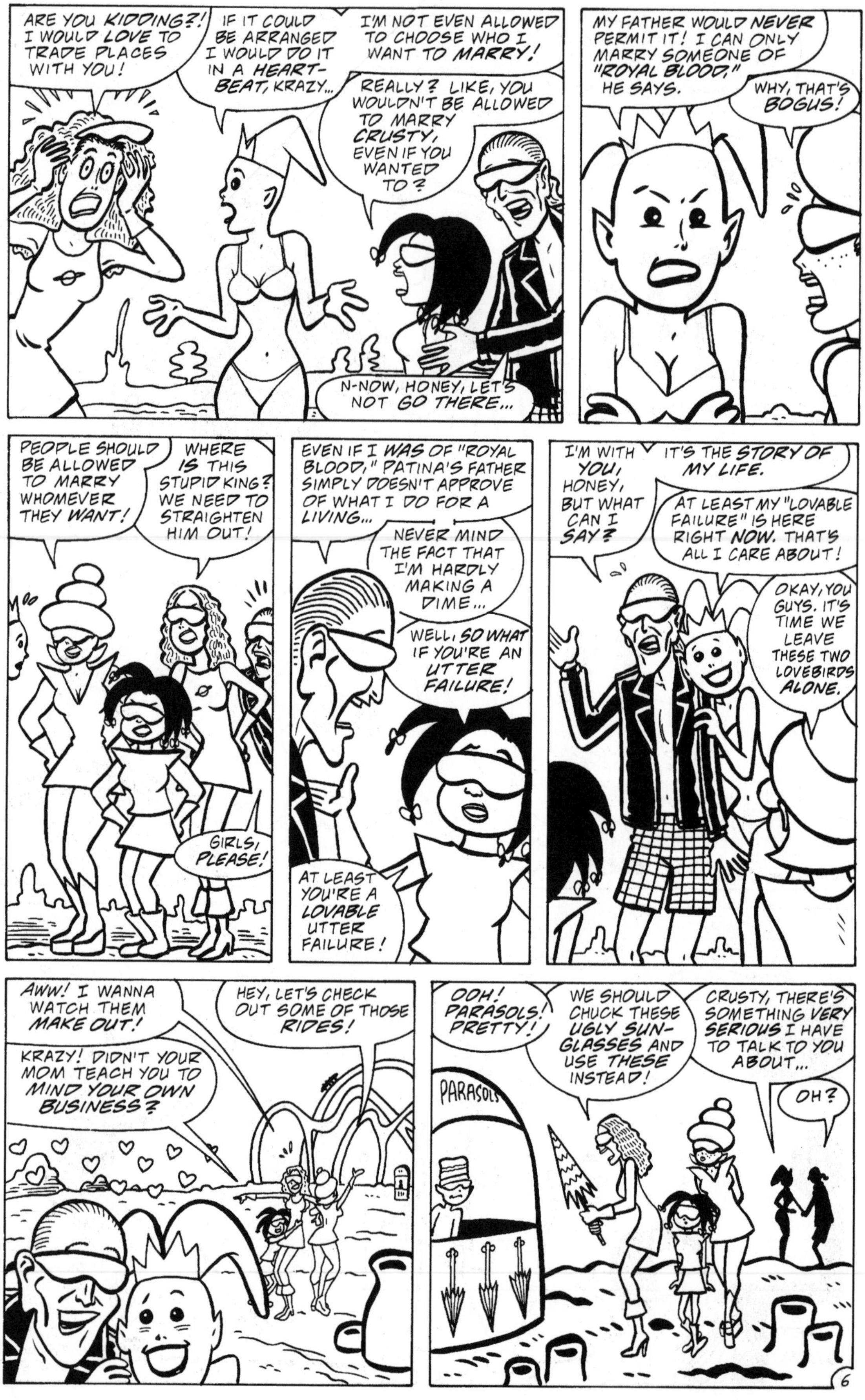
ARE YOU KIDDING?! I WOULD LOVE TO TRADE PLACES WITH YOU!
IF IT COULD BE ARRANGED I WOULD DO IT IN A HEART-BEAT, KRAZY...
I'M NOT EVEN ALLOWED TO CHOOSE WHO I WANT TO MARRY!
REALLY? LIKE, YOU WOULDN'T BE ALLOWED TO MARRY CRUSTY, EVEN IF YOU WANTED TO?
N-NOW, HONEY, LET'S NOT GO THERE...
MY FATHER WOULD NEVER PERMIT IT! I CAN ONLY MARRY SOMEONE OF "ROYAL BLOOD," HE SAYS.
WHY, THAT'S BOGUS!
PEOPLE SHOULD BE ALLOWED TO MARRY WHOMEVER THEY WANT!
WHERE IS THIS STUPID KING? WE NEED TO STRAIGHTEN HIM OUT!
GIRLS, PLEASE!
EVEN IF I WAS OF "ROYAL BLOOD," PATINA'S FATHER SIMPLY DOESN'T APPROVE OF WHAT I DO FOR A LIVING...
NEVER MIND THE FACT THAT I'M HARDLY MAKING A DIME...
WELL, SO WHAT IF YOU'RE AN UTTER FAILURE!
AT LEAST YOU'RE A LOVABLE UTTER FAILURE!
I'M WITH YOU, HONEY, BUT WHAT CAN I SAY?
IT'S THE STORY OF MY LIFE.
AT LEAST MY "LOVABLE FAILURE" IS HERE RIGHT NOW. THAT'S ALL I CARE ABOUT!
OKAY, YOU GUYS. IT'S TIME WE LEAVE THESE TWO LOVEBIRDS ALONE.
AWW! I WANNA WATCH THEM MAKE OUT!
KRAZY! DIDN'T YOUR MOM TEACH YOU TO MIND YOUR OWN BUSINESS?
HEY, LET'S CHECK OUT SOME OF THOSE RIDES!
OOH! PARASOLS! PRETTY!
PARASOLS
WE SHOULD CHUCK THESE UGLY SUN-GLASSES AND USE THESE INSTEAD!
CRUSTY, THERE'S SOMETHING VERY SERIOUS I HAVE TO TALK TO YOU ABOUT...
OH?

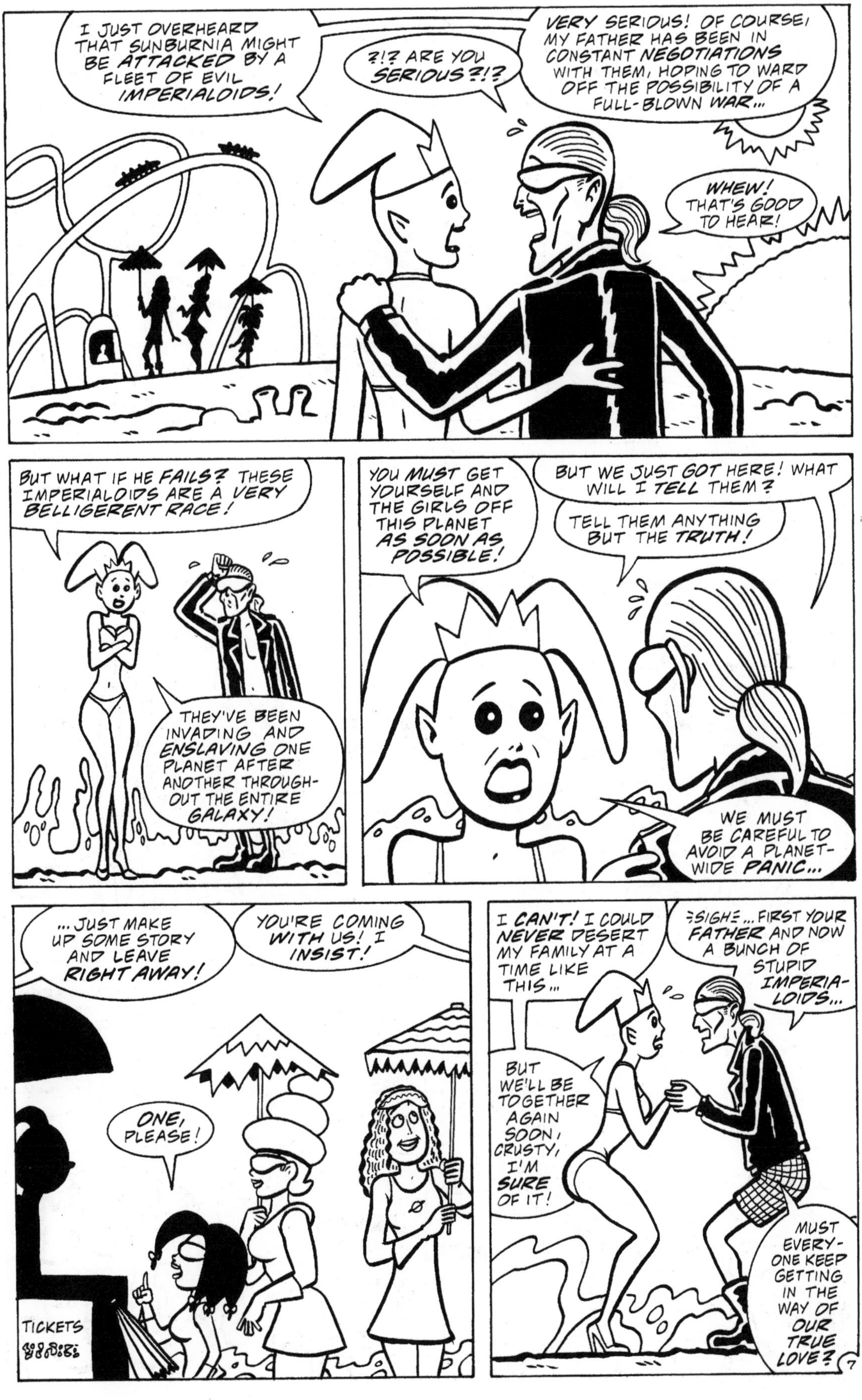
I JUST OVERHEARD THAT SUNBURNIA MIGHT BE ATTACKED BY A FLEET OF EVIL IMPERIALOIDS!
?!? ARE YOU SERIOUS?!?
VERY SERIOUS! OF COURSE, MY FATHER HAS BEEN IN CONSTANT NEGOTIATIONS WITH THEM, HOPING TO WARD OFF THE POSSIBILITY OF A FULL-BLOWN WAR...
WHEW! THAT'S GOOD TO HEAR!
BUT WHAT IF HE FAILS? THESE IMPERIALOIDS ARE A VERY BELLIGERENT RACE!
THEY'VE BEEN INVADING AND ENSLAVING ONE PLANET AFTER ANOTHER THROUGHOUT THE ENTIRE GALAXY!
YOU MUST GET YOURSELF AND THE GIRLS OFF THIS PLANET AS SOON AS POSSIBLE!
BUT WE JUST GOT HERE! WHAT WILL I TELL THEM?
TELL THEM ANYTHING BUT THE TRUTH!
WE MUST BE CAREFUL TO AVOID A PLANET-WIDE PANIC...
...JUST MAKE UP SOME STORY AND LEAVE RIGHT AWAY!
YOU'RE COMING WITH US! I INSIST!
ONE, PLEASE!
TICKETS
I CAN'T! I COULD NEVER DESERT MY FAMILY AT A TIME LIKE THIS...
≈SIGH≈ ...FIRST YOUR FATHER AND NOW A BUNCH OF STUPID IMPERIALOIDS...
BUT WE'LL BE TOGETHER AGAIN SOON, CRUSTY, I'M SURE OF IT!
MUST EVERYONE KEEP GETTING IN THE WAY OF OUR TRUE LOVE?

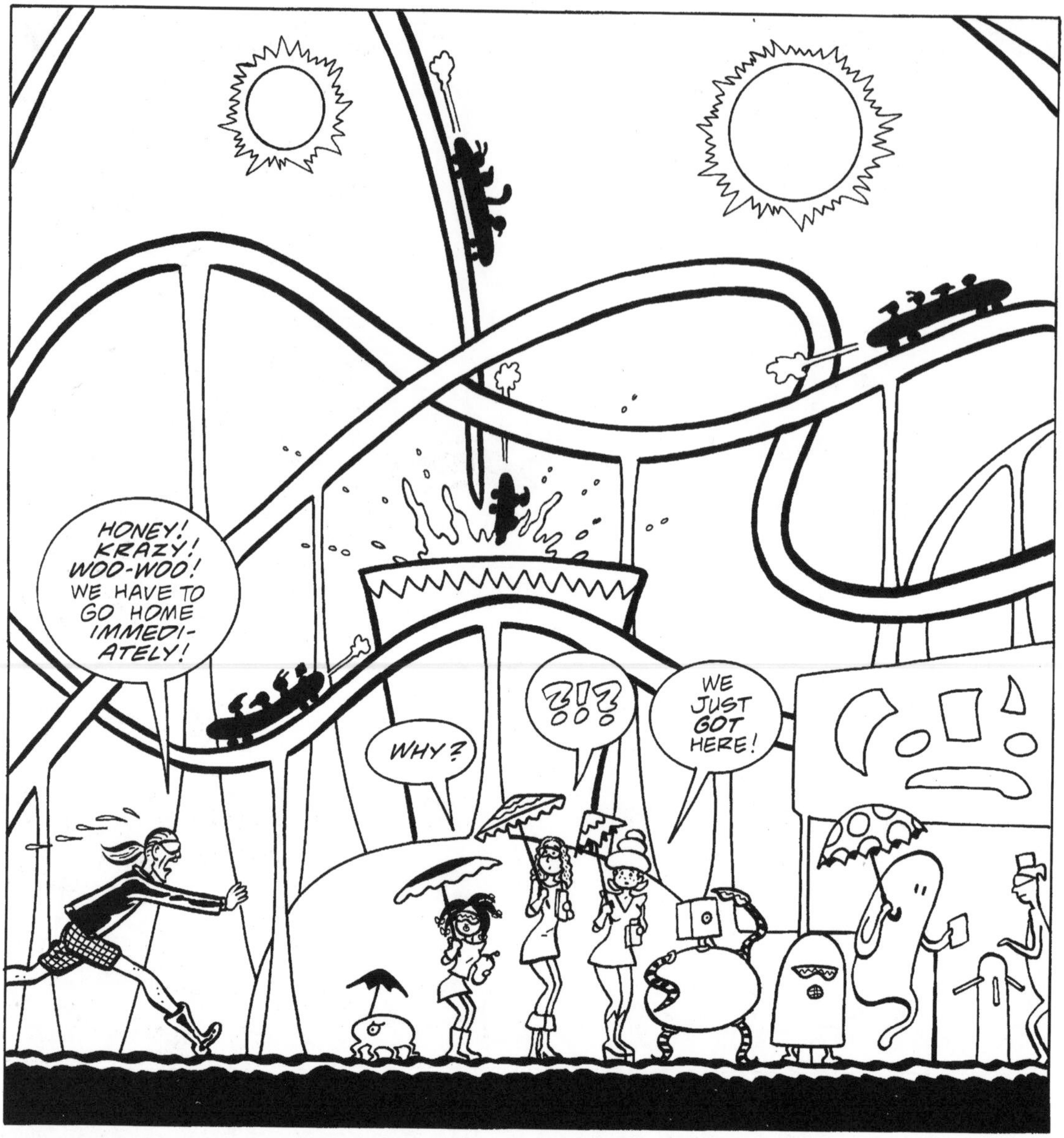
HONEY! KRAZY! WOO-WOO! WE HAVE TO GO HOME IMMEDI-ATELY!
WHY?
?!?
WE JUST GOT HERE!

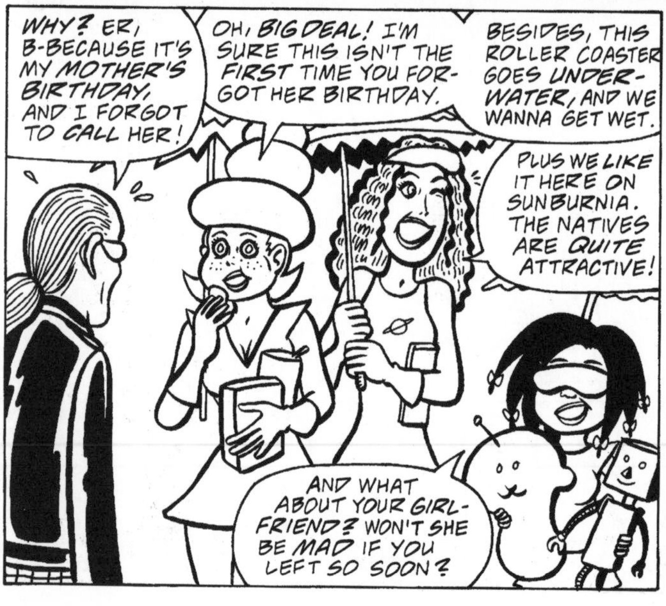
WHY? ER, B-BECAUSE IT'S MY MOTHER'S BIRTHDAY, AND I FORGOT TO CALL HER!
OH, BIG DEAL! I'M SURE THIS ISN'T THE FIRST TIME YOU FOR-GOT HER BIRTHDAY.
BESIDES, THIS ROLLER COASTER GOES UNDER-WATER, AND WE WANNA GET WET.
PLUS WE LIKE IT HERE ON SUNBURNIA. THE NATIVES ARE QUITE ATTRACTIVE!
AND WHAT ABOUT YOUR GIRL-FRIEND? WON'T SHE BE MAD IF YOU LEFT SO SOON?

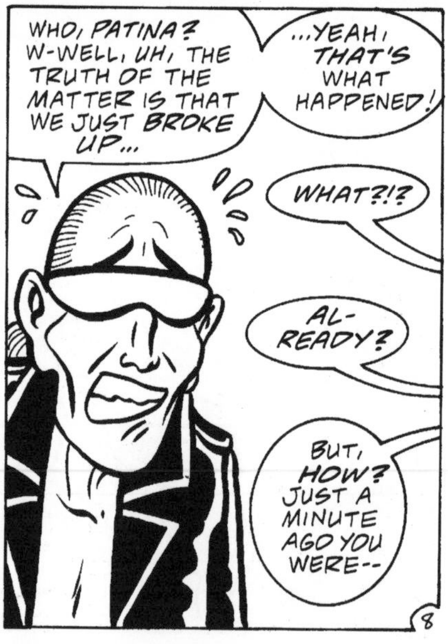
WHO, PATINA? W-WELL, UH, THE TRUTH OF THE MATTER IS THAT WE JUST BROKE UP...
...YEAH, THAT'S WHAT HAPPENED!
WHAT?!?
AL-READY?
BUT, HOW? JUST A MINUTE AGO YOU WERE--

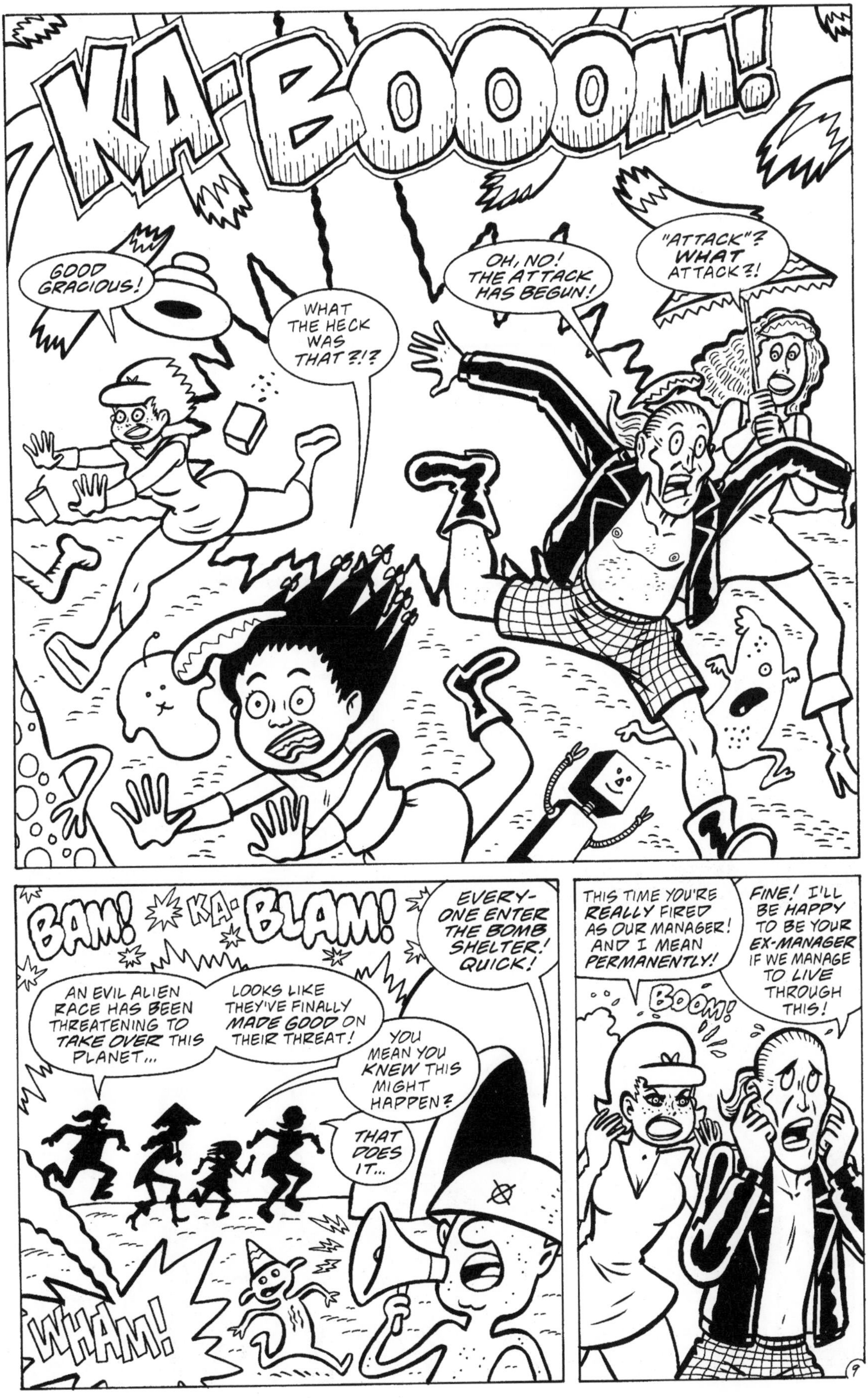
KA-BOOOM!
GOOD GRACIOUS!
WHAT THE HECK WAS THAT?!?
OH, NO! THE ATTACK HAS BEGUN!
"ATTACK"? WHAT ATTACK?!
BAM! KA-BLAM!
AN EVIL ALIEN RACE HAS BEEN THREATENING TO TAKE OVER THIS PLANET...
LOOKS LIKE THEY'VE FINALLY MADE GOOD ON THEIR THREAT!
YOU MEAN YOU KNEW THIS MIGHT HAPPEN?
THAT DOES IT...
EVERY-ONE ENTER THE BOMB SHELTER! QUICK!
WHAM!
THIS TIME YOU'RE REALLY FIRED AS OUR MANAGER! AND I MEAN PERMANENTLY!
FINE! I'LL BE HAPPY TO BE YOUR EX-MANAGER IF WE MANAGE TO LIVE THROUGH THIS!
BOOM!
9

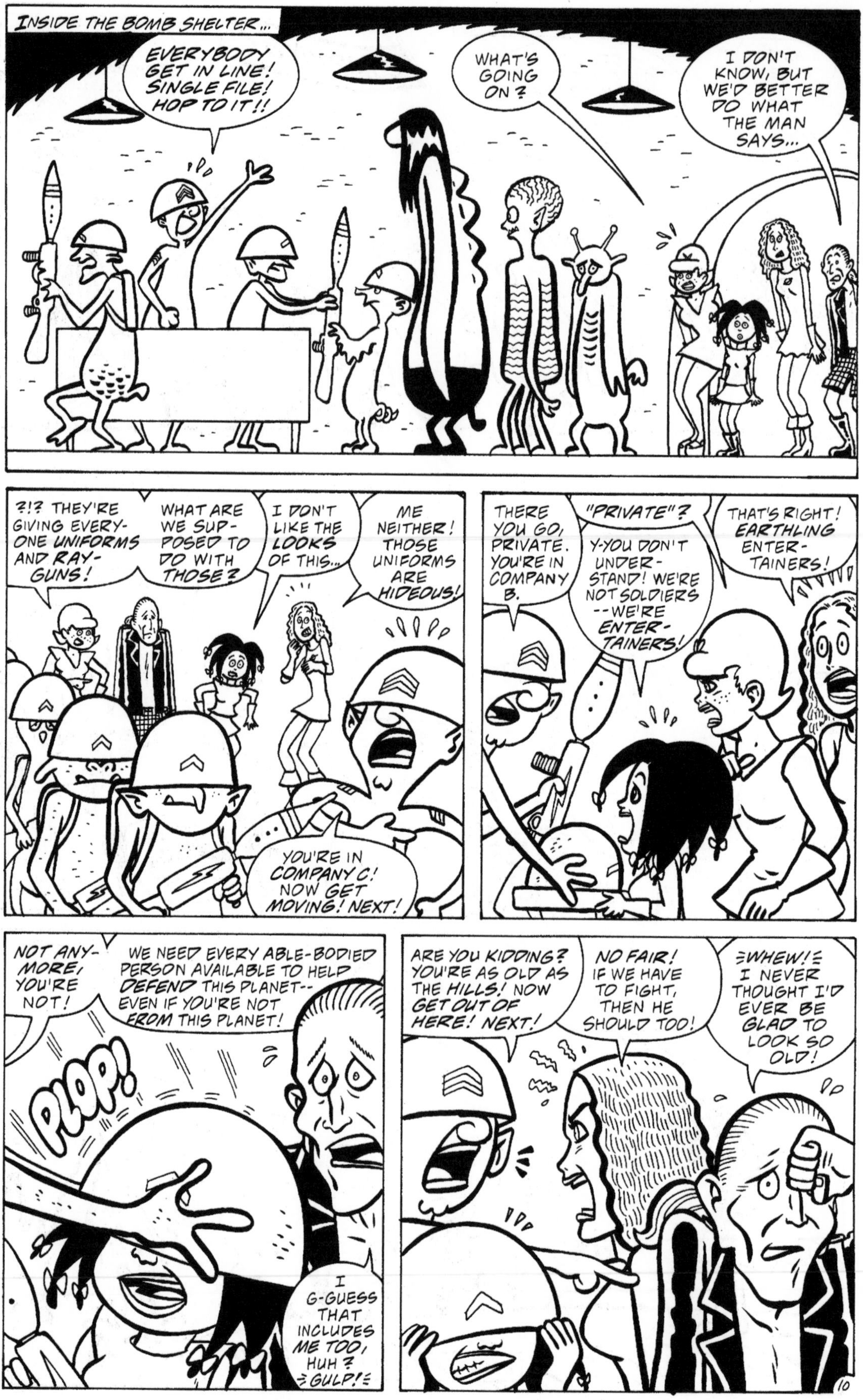
INSIDE THE BOMB SHELTER...
EVERYBODY GET IN LINE! SINGLE FILE! HOP TO IT!!
WHAT'S GOING ON?
I DON'T KNOW, BUT WE'D BETTER DO WHAT THE MAN SAYS...
?!? THEY'RE GIVING EVERYONE UNIFORMS AND RAY-GUNS!
WHAT ARE WE SUPPOSED TO DO WITH THOSE?
I DON'T LIKE THE LOOKS OF THIS...
ME NEITHER! THOSE UNIFORMS ARE HIDEOUS!
YOU'RE IN COMPANY C! NOW GET MOVING! NEXT!
THERE YOU GO, PRIVATE. YOU'RE IN COMPANY B.
"PRIVATE"?
Y-YOU DON'T UNDERSTAND! WE'RE NOT SOLDIERS --WE'RE ENTERTAINERS!
THAT'S RIGHT! EARTHLING ENTERTAINERS!
NOT ANYMORE, YOU'RE NOT!
WE NEED EVERY ABLE-BODIED PERSON AVAILABLE TO HELP DEFEND THIS PLANET-- EVEN IF YOU'RE NOT FROM THIS PLANET!
PLOP!
I G-GUESS THAT INCLUDES ME TOO, HUH? GULP!
ARE YOU KIDDING? YOU'RE AS OLD AS THE HILLS! NOW GET OUT OF HERE! NEXT!
NO FAIR! IF WE HAVE TO FIGHT, THEN HE SHOULD TOO!
WHEW! I NEVER THOUGHT I'D EVER BE GLAD TO LOOK SO OLD!

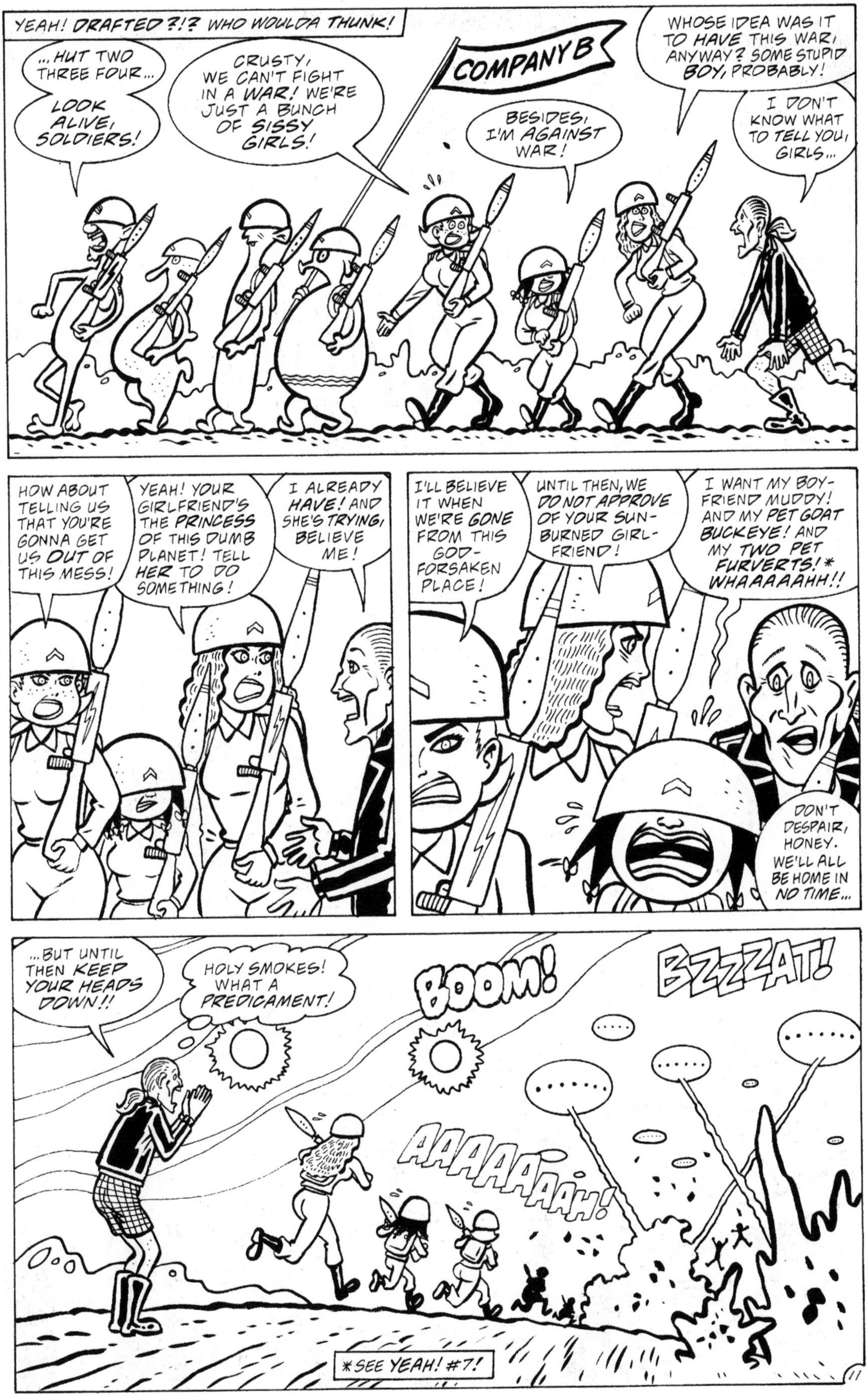

YEAH! DRAFTED?!? WHO WOULDA THUNK!
...HUT TWO THREE FOUR...
LOOK ALIVE, SOLDIERS!
CRUSTY, WE CAN'T FIGHT IN A WAR! WE'RE JUST A BUNCH OF SISSY GIRLS!
COMPANY B
BESIDES, I'M AGAINST WAR!
WHOSE IDEA WAS IT TO HAVE THIS WAR, ANYWAY? SOME STUPID BOY, PROBABLY!
I DON'T KNOW WHAT TO TELL YOU, GIRLS...
HOW ABOUT TELLING US THAT YOU'RE GONNA GET US OUT OF THIS MESS!
YEAH! YOUR GIRLFRIEND'S THE PRINCESS OF THIS DUMB PLANET! TELL HER TO DO SOMETHING!
I ALREADY HAVE! AND SHE'S TRYING, BELIEVE ME!
I'LL BELIEVE IT WHEN WE'RE GONE FROM THIS GOD-FORSAKEN PLACE!
UNTIL THEN, WE DO NOT APPROVE OF YOUR SUN-BURNED GIRL-FRIEND!
I WANT MY BOY-FRIEND MUDDY! AND MY PET GOAT BUCKEYE! AND MY TWO PET FURVERTS! * WHAAAAAAHH!!
DON'T DESPAIR, HONEY. WE'LL ALL BE HOME IN NO TIME...
...BUT UNTIL THEN KEEP YOUR HEADS DOWN!!
HOLY SMOKES! WHAT A PREDICAMENT!
BOOM!
BZZZAT!
AAAAAAAAAH!
*SEE YEAH! #7!

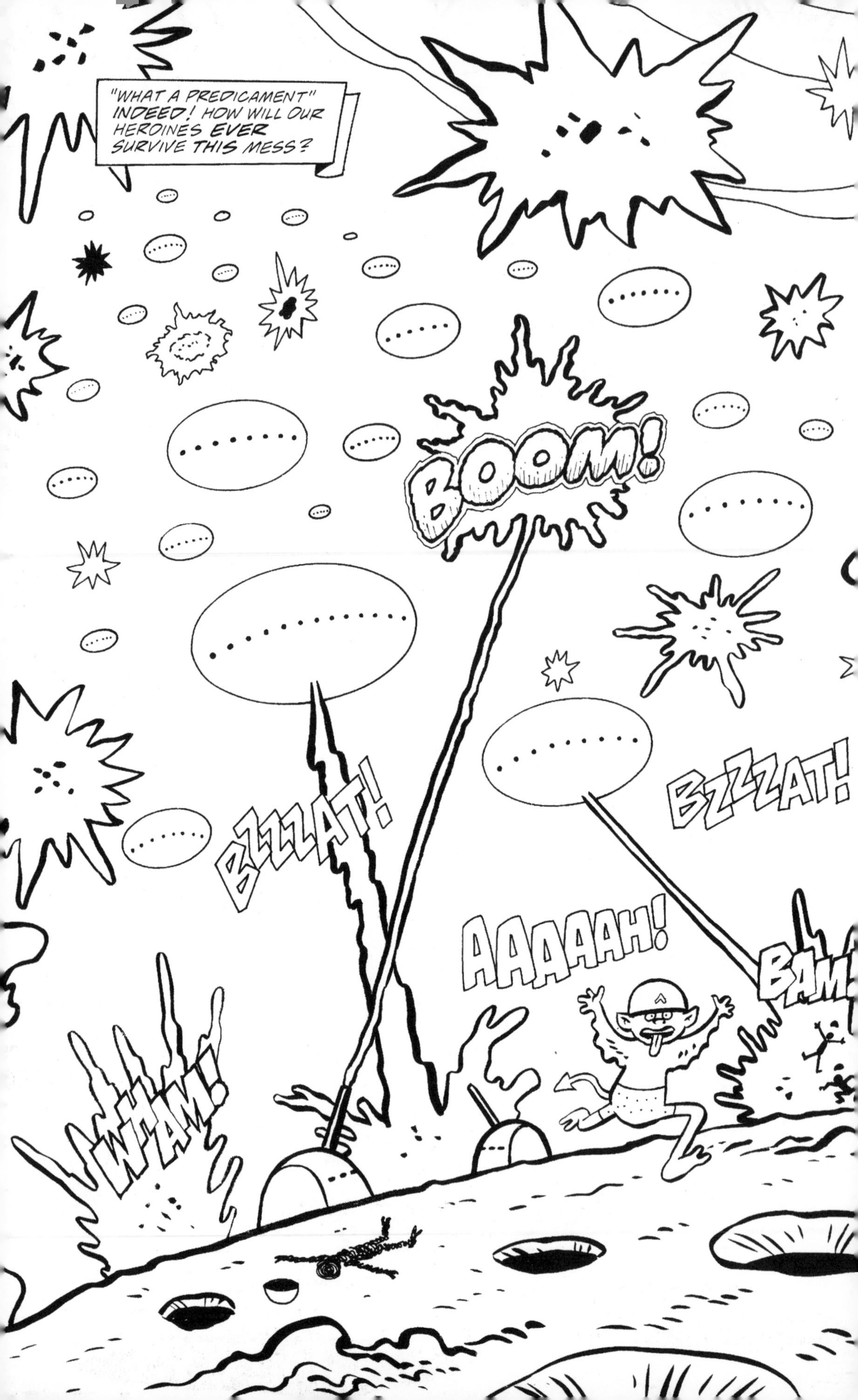
"WHAT A PREDICAMENT" INDEED! HOW WILL OUR HEROINES EVER SURVIVE THIS MESS?
BOOM!
BZZZAT!
BZZZAT!
AAAAAH!
BAM
WHAM!

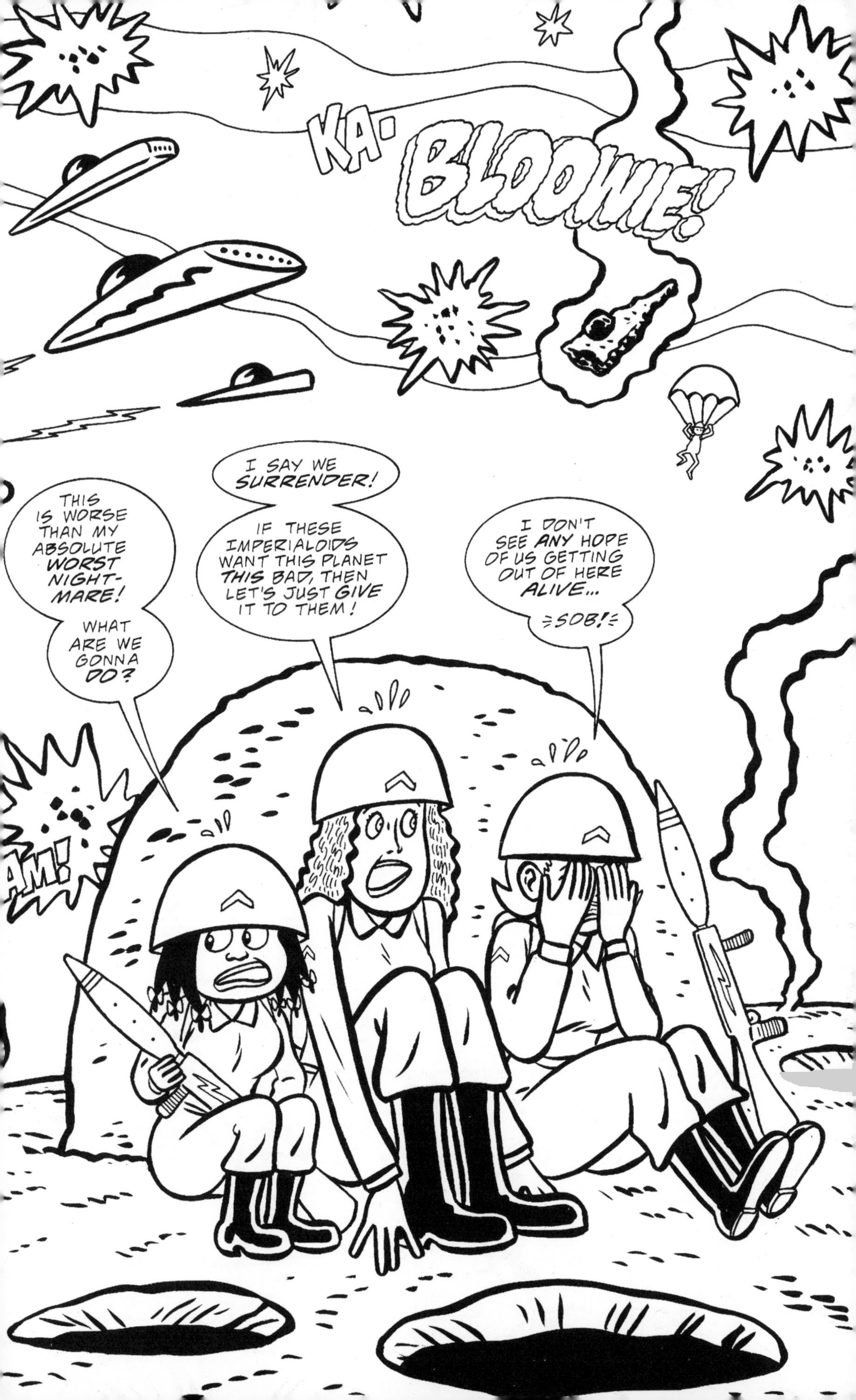
KA-BLOOWIE!
THIS IS WORSE THAN MY ABSOLUTE WORST NIGHT-MARE!
WHAT ARE WE GONNA DO?
I SAY WE SURRENDER!
IF THESE IMPERIALOIDS WANT THIS PLANET THIS BAD, THEN LET'S JUST GIVE IT TO THEM!
I DON'T SEE ANY HOPE OF US GETTING OUT OF HERE ALIVE...
SOB!
AM!

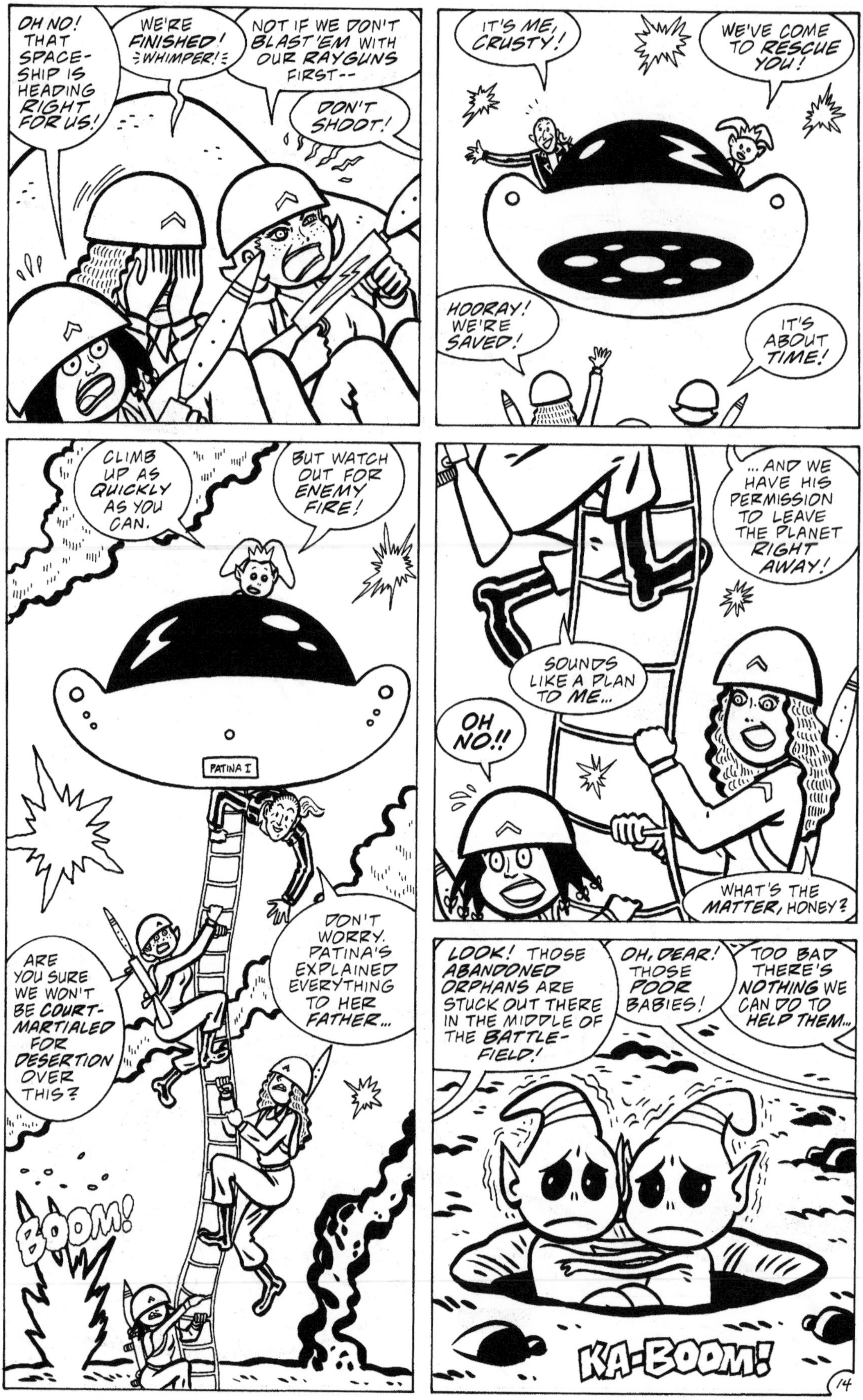
OH NO! THAT SPACE-SHIP IS HEADING RIGHT FOR US!
WE'RE FINISHED! WHIMPER!
NOT IF WE DON'T BLAST 'EM WITH OUR RAYGUNS FIRST--
DON'T SHOOT!
IT'S ME, CRUSTY!
WE'VE COME TO RESCUE YOU!
HOORAY! WE'RE SAVED!
IT'S ABOUT TIME!
CLIMB UP AS QUICKLY AS YOU CAN.
BUT WATCH OUT FOR ENEMY FIRE!
PATINA I
ARE YOU SURE WE WON'T BE COURT-MARTIALED FOR DESERTION OVER THIS?
DON'T WORRY. PATINA'S EXPLAINED EVERYTHING TO HER FATHER...
BOOM!
...AND WE HAVE HIS PERMISSION TO LEAVE THE PLANET RIGHT AWAY!
SOUNDS LIKE A PLAN TO ME...
OH NO!!
WHAT'S THE MATTER, HONEY?
LOOK! THOSE ABANDONED ORPHANS ARE STUCK OUT THERE IN THE MIDDLE OF THE BATTLE-FIELD!
OH, DEAR! THOSE POOR BABIES!
TOO BAD THERE'S NOTHING WE CAN DO TO HELP THEM...
KA-BOOM!

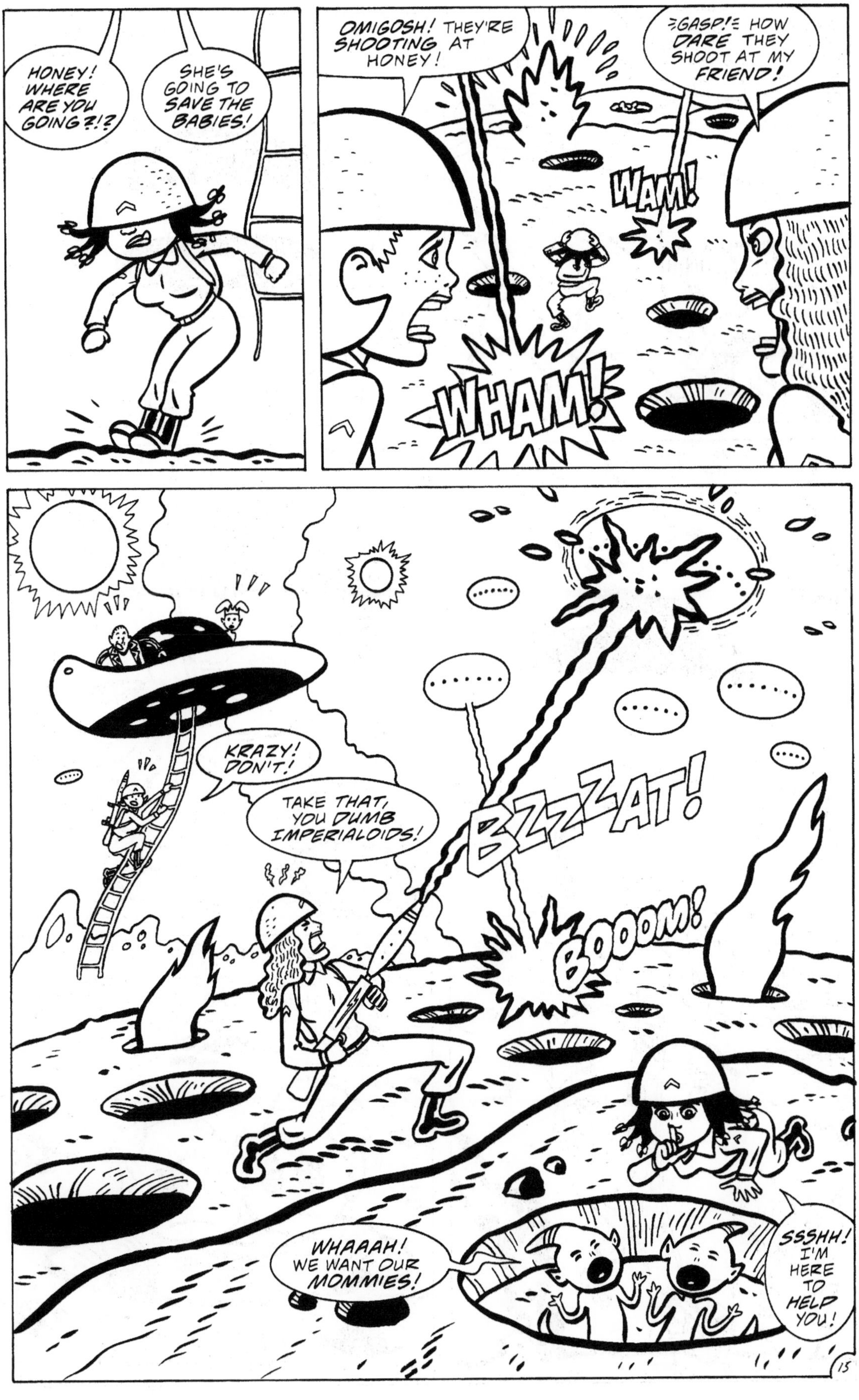

HONEY! WHERE ARE YOU GOING ?!?
SHE'S GOING TO SAVE THE BABIES!
OMIGOSH! THEY'RE SHOOTING AT HONEY!
GASP! HOW DARE THEY SHOOT AT MY FRIEND!
WAM!
WHAM!
KRAZY! DON'T!
TAKE THAT, YOU DUMB IMPERIALOIDS!
BZZZAT!
BOOOM!
WHAAAH! WE WANT OUR MOMMIES!
SSSHH! I'M HERE TO HELP YOU!

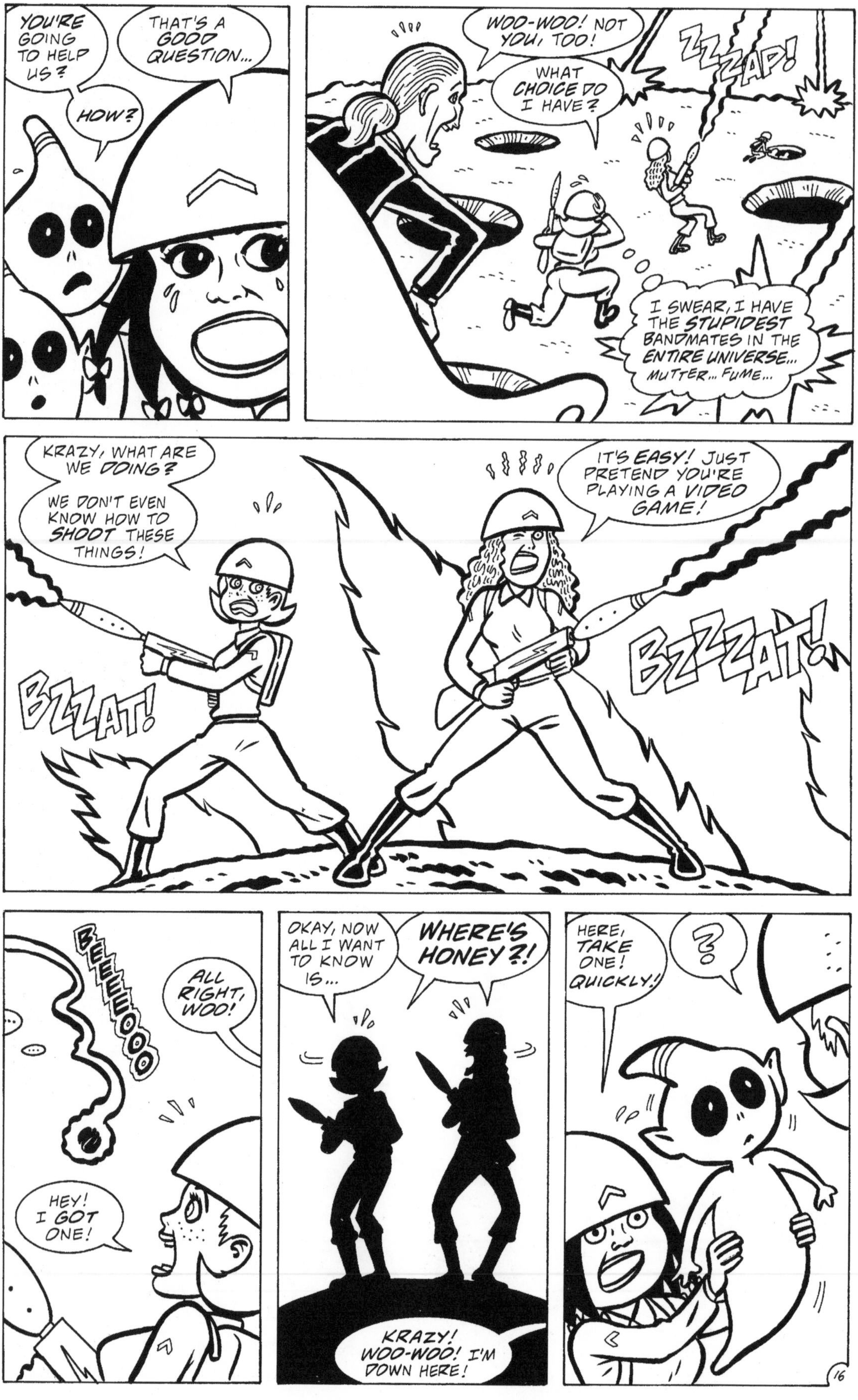
YOU'RE GOING TO HELP US?
THAT'S A GOOD QUESTION...
HOW?
WOO-WOO! NOT YOU, TOO!
WHAT CHOICE DO I HAVE?
ZZZAP!
I SWEAR, I HAVE THE STUPIDEST BANDMATES IN THE ENTIRE UNIVERSE... MUTTER... FUME...
KRAZY, WHAT ARE WE DOING?
WE DON'T EVEN KNOW HOW TO SHOOT THESE THINGS!
IT'S EASY! JUST PRETEND YOU'RE PLAYING A VIDEO GAME!
BZZAT!
BZZZAT!
BEEEEOOO
ALL RIGHT, WOO!
HEY! I GOT ONE!
OKAY, NOW ALL I WANT TO KNOW IS...
WHERE'S HONEY?!
KRAZY! WOO-WOO! I'M DOWN HERE!
HERE, TAKE ONE! QUICKLY!
?

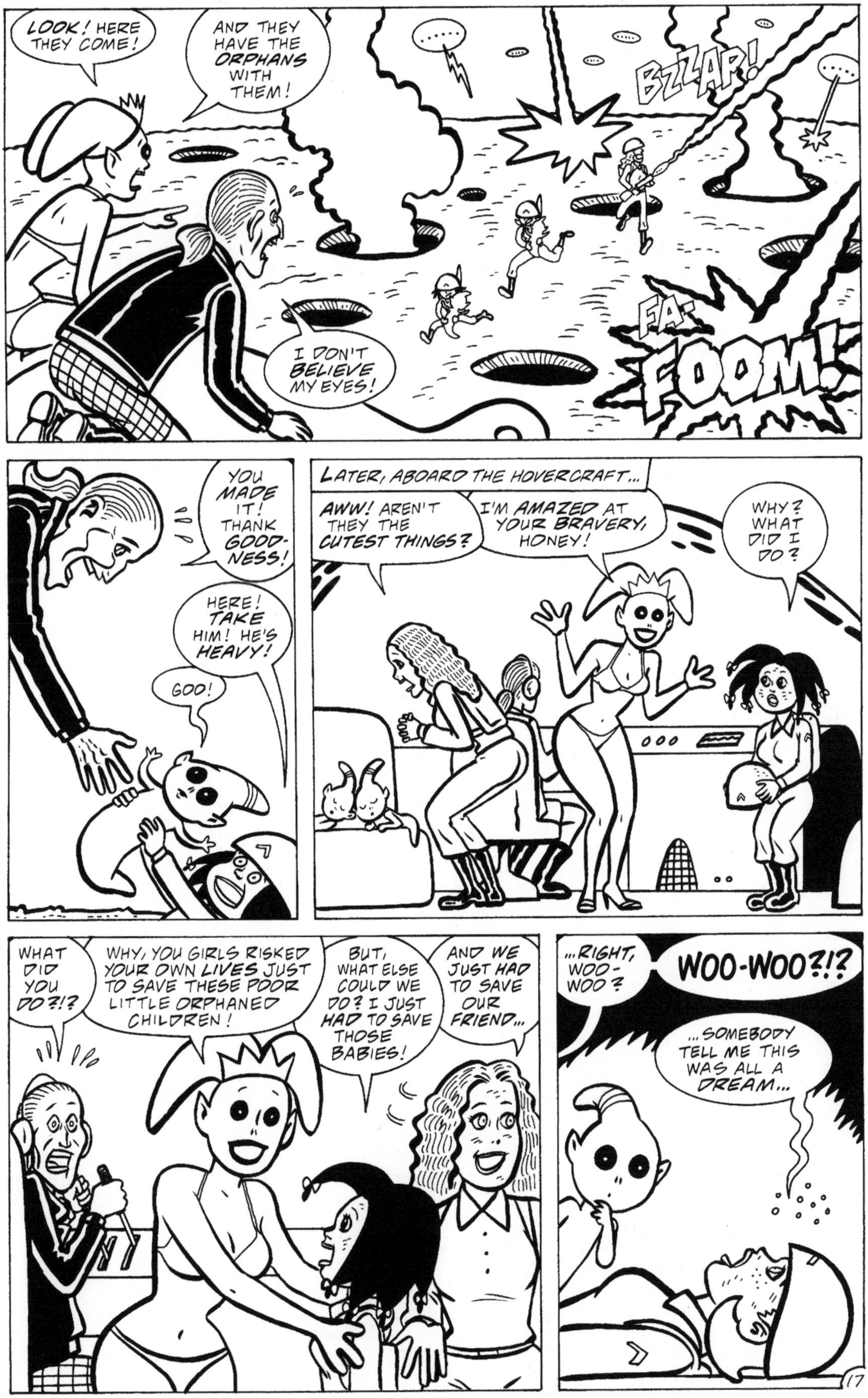
LOOK! HERE THEY COME!
AND THEY HAVE THE ORPHANS WITH THEM!
BZZAP!
I DON'T BELIEVE MY EYES!
FA-FOOM!
YOU MADE IT! THANK GOODNESS!
HERE! TAKE HIM! HE'S HEAVY!
GOO!
LATER, ABOARD THE HOVERCRAFT...
AWW! AREN'T THEY THE CUTEST THINGS?
I'M AMAZED AT YOUR BRAVERY, HONEY!
WHY? WHAT DID I DO?
WHAT DID YOU DO?!?
WHY, YOU GIRLS RISKED YOUR OWN LIVES JUST TO SAVE THESE POOR LITTLE ORPHANED CHILDREN!
BUT, WHAT ELSE COULD WE DO? I JUST HAD TO SAVE THOSE BABIES!
AND WE JUST HAD TO SAVE OUR FRIEND...
...RIGHT, WOO-WOO?
WOO-WOO?!?
...SOMEBODY TELL ME THIS WAS ALL A DREAM...

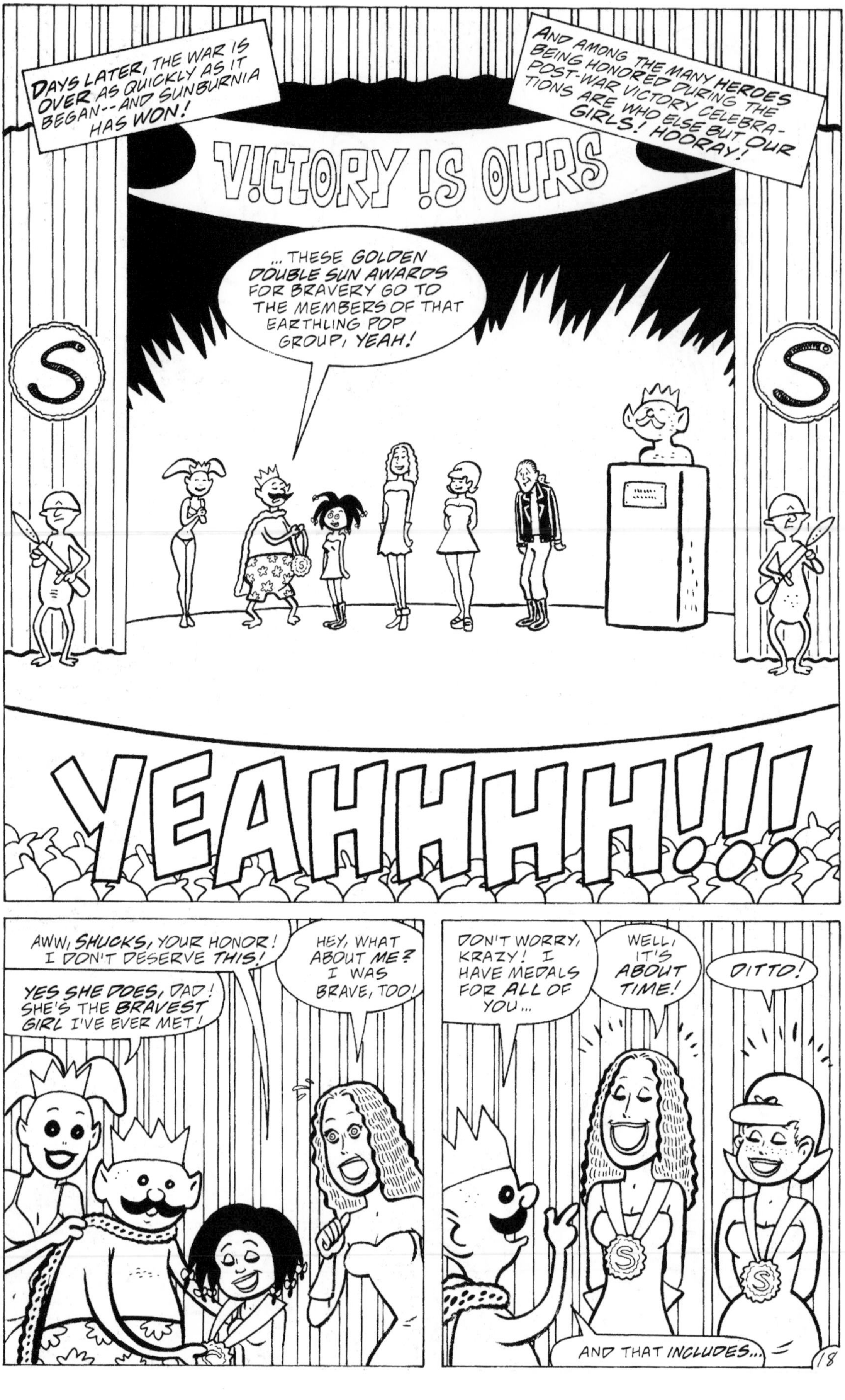
DAYS LATER, THE WAR IS OVER AS QUICKLY AS IT BEGAN--AND SUNBURNIA HAS WON!
AND AMONG THE MANY HEROES BEING HONORED DURING THE POST-WAR VICTORY CELEBRATIONS ARE WHO ELSE BUT OUR GIRLS! HOORAY!
V!CTORY !S OURS
... THESE GOLDEN DOUBLE SUN AWARDS FOR BRAVERY GO TO THE MEMBERS OF THAT EARTHLING POP GROUP, YEAH!
YEAHHHHH!!!
AWW, SHUCKS, YOUR HONOR! I DON'T DESERVE THIS!
YES SHE DOES, DAD! SHE'S THE BRAVEST GIRL I'VE EVER MET!
HEY, WHAT ABOUT ME? I WAS BRAVE, TOO!
DON'T WORRY, KRAZY! I HAVE MEDALS FOR ALL OF YOU...
WELL, IT'S ABOUT TIME!
DITTO!
AND THAT INCLUDES...

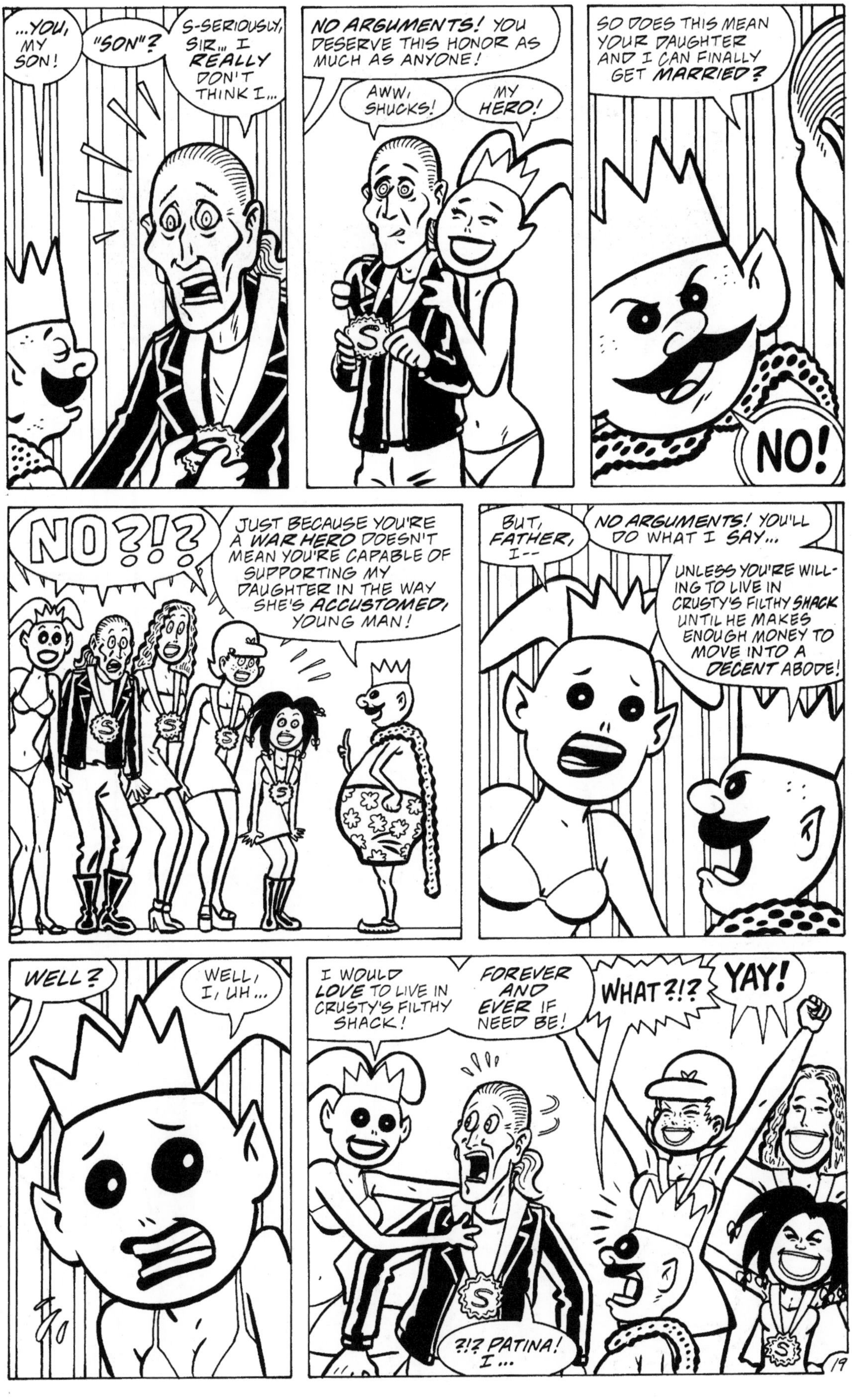
...YOU, MY SON!
"SON"?
S-SERIOUSLY, SIR... I REALLY DON'T THINK I...
NO ARGUMENTS! YOU DESERVE THIS HONOR AS MUCH AS ANYONE!
AWW, SHUCKS!
MY HERO!
SO DOES THIS MEAN YOUR DAUGHTER AND I CAN FINALLY GET MARRIED?
NO!
NO?!?
JUST BECAUSE YOU'RE A WAR HERO DOESN'T MEAN YOU'RE CAPABLE OF SUPPORTING MY DAUGHTER IN THE WAY SHE'S ACCUSTOMED, YOUNG MAN!
BUT, FATHER, I--
NO ARGUMENTS! YOU'LL DO WHAT I SAY...
UNLESS YOU'RE WILLING TO LIVE IN CRUSTY'S FILTHY SHACK UNTIL HE MAKES ENOUGH MONEY TO MOVE INTO A DECENT ABODE!
WELL?
WELL, I, UH...
I WOULD LOVE TO LIVE IN CRUSTY'S FILTHY SHACK!
FOREVER AND EVER IF NEED BE!
WHAT?!?
YAY!
?!? PATINA! I...

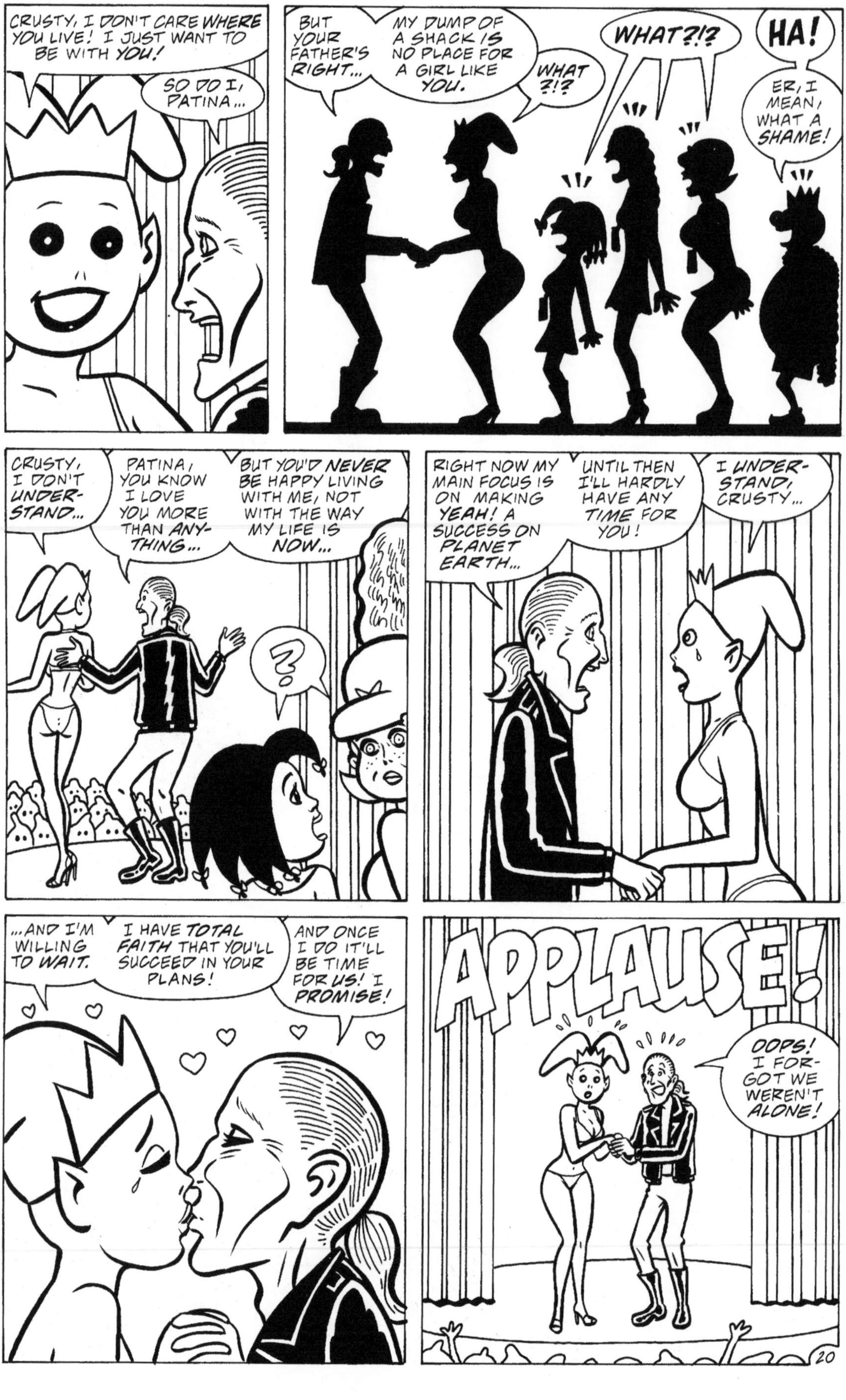
CRUSTY, I DON'T CARE WHERE YOU LIVE! I JUST WANT TO BE WITH YOU!
SO DO I, PATINA...
BUT YOUR FATHER'S RIGHT...
MY DUMP OF A SHACK IS NO PLACE FOR A GIRL LIKE YOU.
WHAT ?!?
WHAT?!?
HA!
ER, I MEAN, WHAT A SHAME!
CRUSTY, I DON'T UNDER-STAND...
PATINA, YOU KNOW I LOVE YOU MORE THAN ANY-THING...
BUT YOU'D NEVER BE HAPPY LIVING WITH ME, NOT WITH THE WAY MY LIFE IS NOW...
?
RIGHT NOW MY MAIN FOCUS IS ON MAKING YEAH! A SUCCESS ON PLANET EARTH...
UNTIL THEN I'LL HARDLY HAVE ANY TIME FOR YOU!
I UNDER-STAND, CRUSTY...
...AND I'M WILLING TO WAIT.
I HAVE TOTAL FAITH THAT YOU'LL SUCCEED IN YOUR PLANS!
AND ONCE I DO IT'LL BE TIME FOR US! I PROMISE!
APPLAUSE!
OOPS! I FOR-GOT WE WEREN'T ALONE!

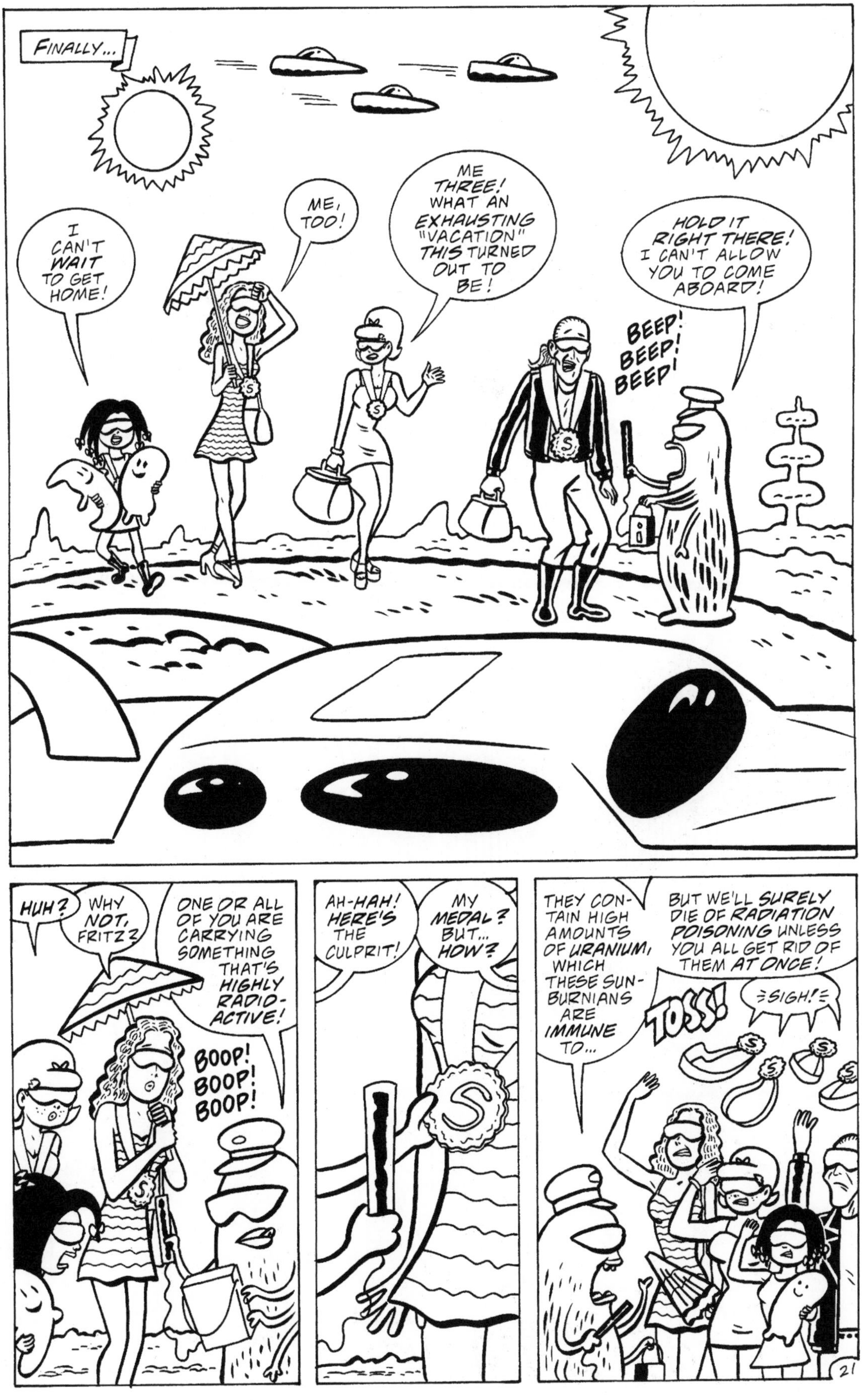
FINALLY...
I CAN'T WAIT TO GET HOME!
ME, TOO!
ME THREE! WHAT AN EXHAUSTING "VACATION" THIS TURNED OUT TO BE!
HOLD IT RIGHT THERE! I CAN'T ALLOW YOU TO COME ABOARD!
BEEP! BEEP! BEEP!
HUH?
WHY NOT, FRITZ?
ONE OR ALL OF YOU ARE CARRYING SOMETHING THAT'S HIGHLY RADIO-ACTIVE!
BOOP! BOOP! BOOP!
AH-HAH! HERE'S THE CULPRIT!
MY MEDAL? BUT... HOW?
THEY CON-TAIN HIGH AMOUNTS OF URANIUM, WHICH THESE SUN-BURNIANS ARE IMMUNE TO...
BUT WE'LL SURELY DIE OF RADIATION POISONING UNLESS YOU ALL GET RID OF THEM AT ONCE!
TOSS!
SIGH!
21

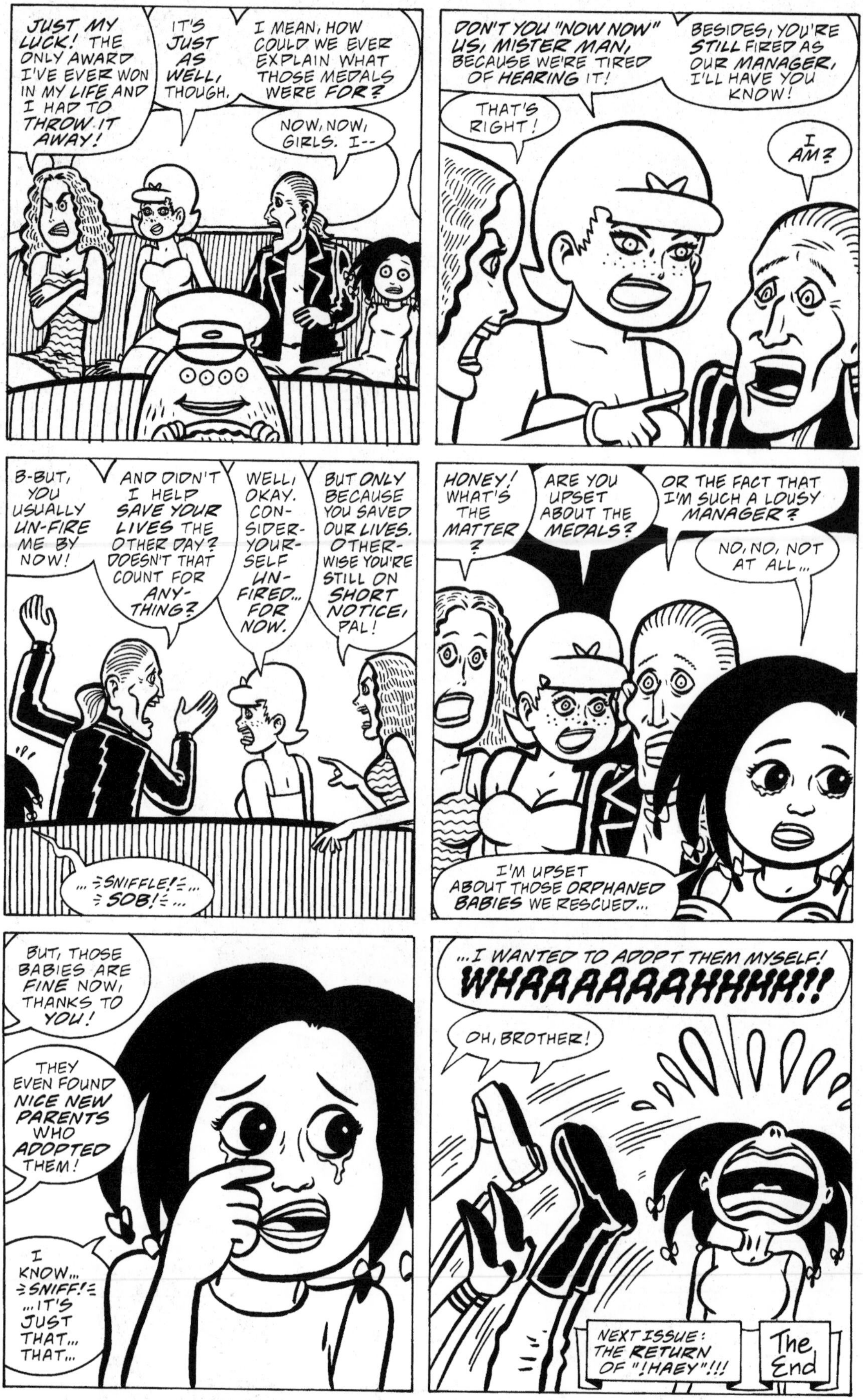
JUST MY LUCK! THE ONLY AWARD I'VE EVER WON IN MY LIFE AND I HAD TO THROW IT AWAY!
IT'S JUST AS WELL, THOUGH.
I MEAN, HOW COULD WE EVER EXPLAIN WHAT THOSE MEDALS WERE FOR?
NOW, NOW, GIRLS. I--
DON'T YOU "NOW NOW" US, MISTER MAN, BECAUSE WE'RE TIRED OF HEARING IT!
BESIDES, YOU'RE STILL FIRED AS OUR MANAGER, I'LL HAVE YOU KNOW!
THAT'S RIGHT!
I AM?
B-BUT, YOU USUALLY UN-FIRE ME BY NOW!
AND DIDN'T I HELP SAVE YOUR LIVES THE OTHER DAY? DOESN'T THAT COUNT FOR ANYTHING?
WELL, OKAY. CONSIDER YOURSELF UN-FIRED... FOR NOW.
BUT ONLY BECAUSE YOU SAVED OUR LIVES. OTHERWISE YOU'RE STILL ON SHORT NOTICE, PAL!
...SNIFFLE!... SOB!...
HONEY! WHAT'S THE MATTER?
ARE YOU UPSET ABOUT THE MEDALS?
OR THE FACT THAT I'M SUCH A LOUSY MANAGER?
NO, NO, NOT AT ALL...
I'M UPSET ABOUT THOSE ORPHANED BABIES WE RESCUED...
BUT, THOSE BABIES ARE FINE NOW, THANKS TO YOU!
THEY EVEN FOUND NICE NEW PARENTS WHO ADOPTED THEM!
I KNOW... SNIFF! ...IT'S JUST THAT... THAT...
...I WANTED TO ADOPT THEM MYSELF! WHAAAAAAAHHHH!!
OH, BROTHER!
NEXT ISSUE: THE RETURN OF "!HAEY"!!!
The End

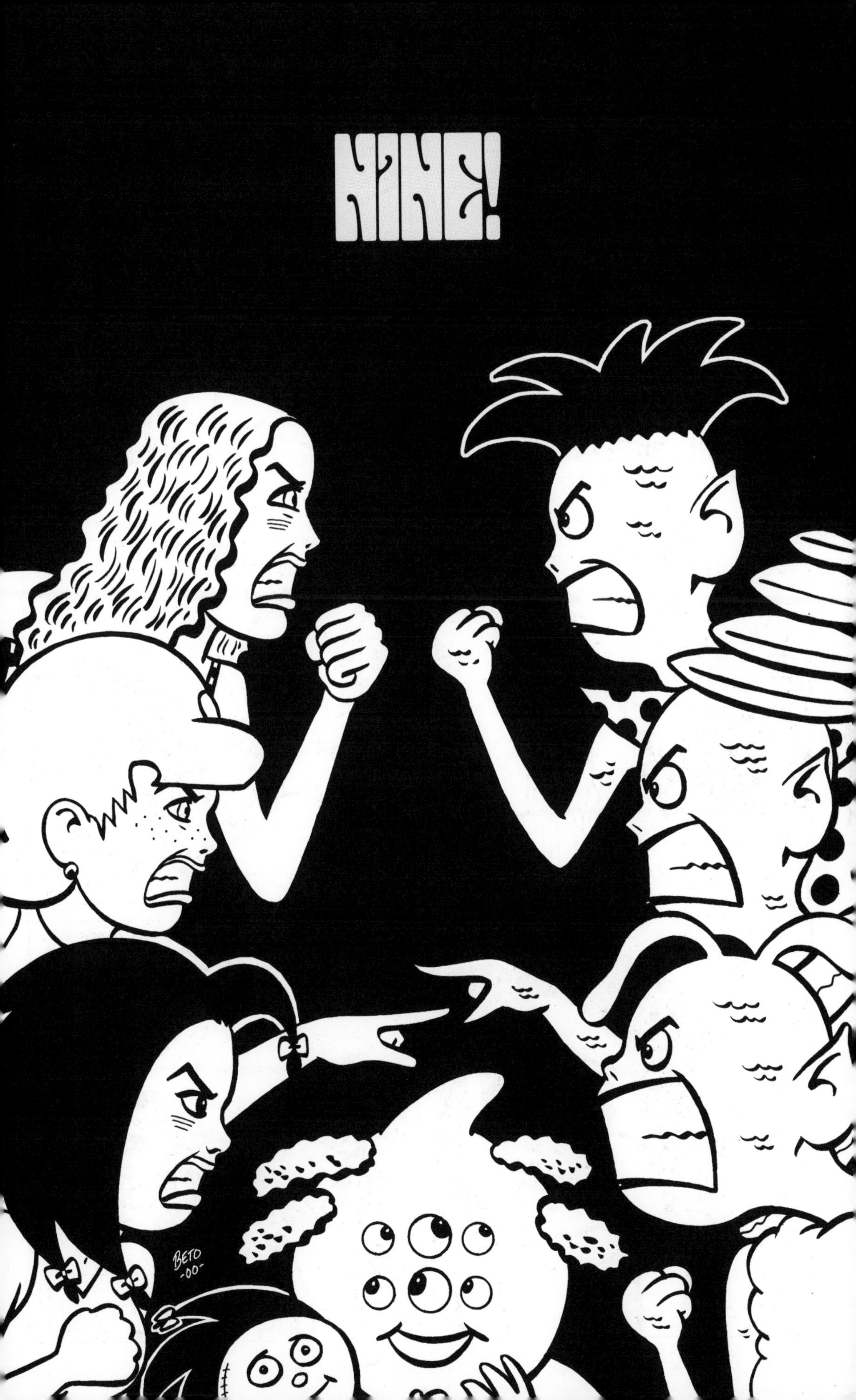
NINE!
BETO
-00-

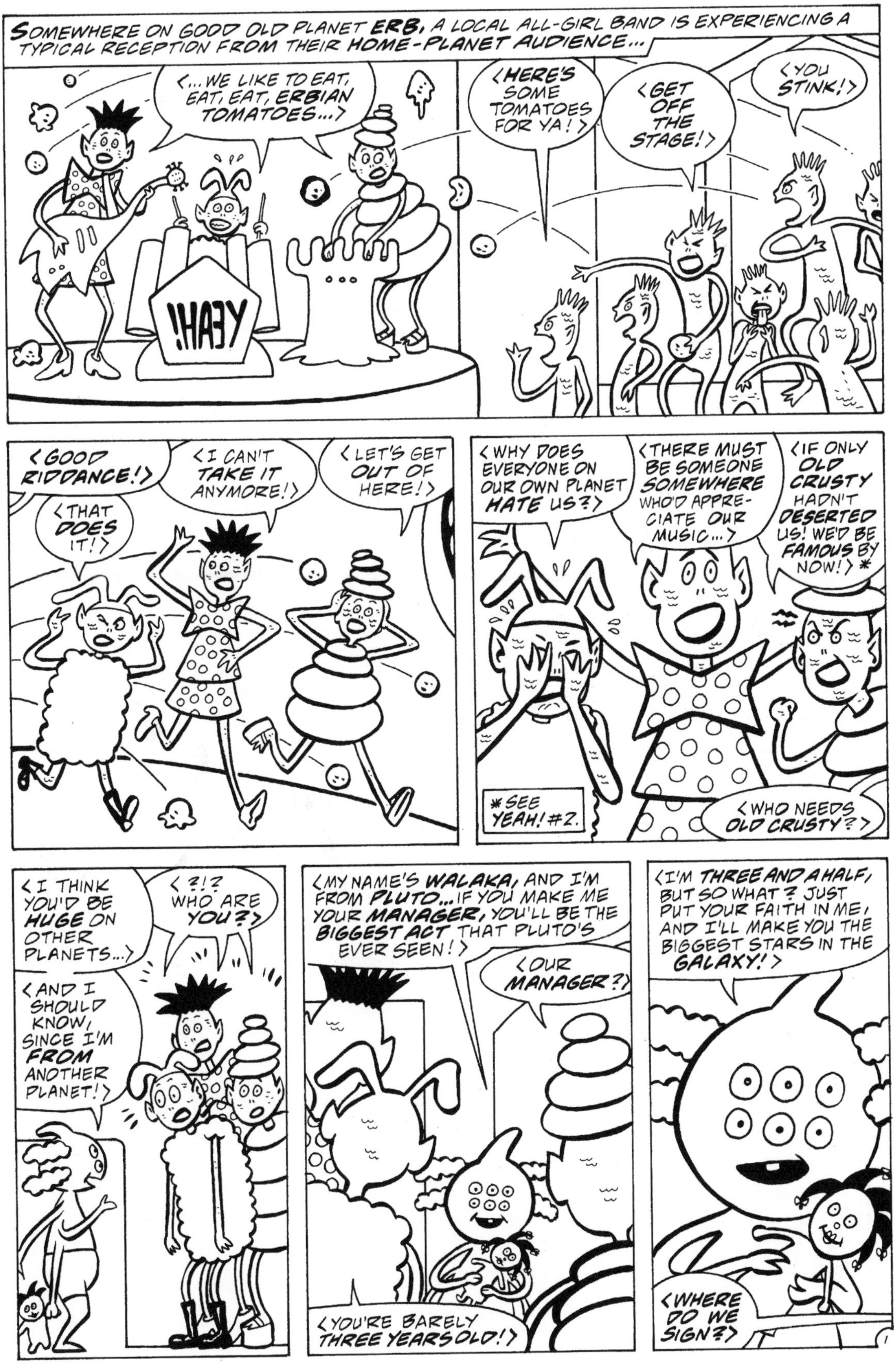
SOMEWHERE ON GOOD OLD PLANET ERB, A LOCAL ALL-GIRL BAND IS EXPERIENCING A TYPICAL RECEPTION FROM THEIR HOME-PLANET AUDIENCE...
<...WE LIKE TO EAT, EAT, EAT, ERBIAN TOMATOES...>
<HERE'S SOME TOMATOES FOR YA!>
<GET OFF THE STAGE!>
<YOU STINK!>
<GOOD RIDDANCE!>
<THAT DOES IT!>
<I CAN'T TAKE IT ANYMORE!>
<LET'S GET OUT OF HERE!>
<WHY DOES EVERYONE ON OUR OWN PLANET HATE US?>
<THERE MUST BE SOMEONE SOMEWHERE WHO'D APPRECIATE OUR MUSIC...>
<IF ONLY OLD CRUSTY HADN'T DESERTED US! WE'D BE FAMOUS BY NOW!> *
*SEE YEAH! #2.
<WHO NEEDS OLD CRUSTY?>
<I THINK YOU'D BE HUGE ON OTHER PLANETS...>
<?!? WHO ARE YOU?>
<AND I SHOULD KNOW, SINCE I'M FROM ANOTHER PLANET!>
<MY NAME'S WALAKA, AND I'M FROM PLUTO... IF YOU MAKE ME YOUR MANAGER, YOU'LL BE THE BIGGEST ACT THAT PLUTO'S EVER SEEN!>
<OUR MANAGER?>
<YOU'RE BARELY THREE YEARS OLD!>
<I'M THREE AND A HALF, BUT SO WHAT? JUST PUT YOUR FAITH IN ME, AND I'LL MAKE YOU THE BIGGEST STARS IN THE GALAXY!>
<WHERE DO WE SIGN?>

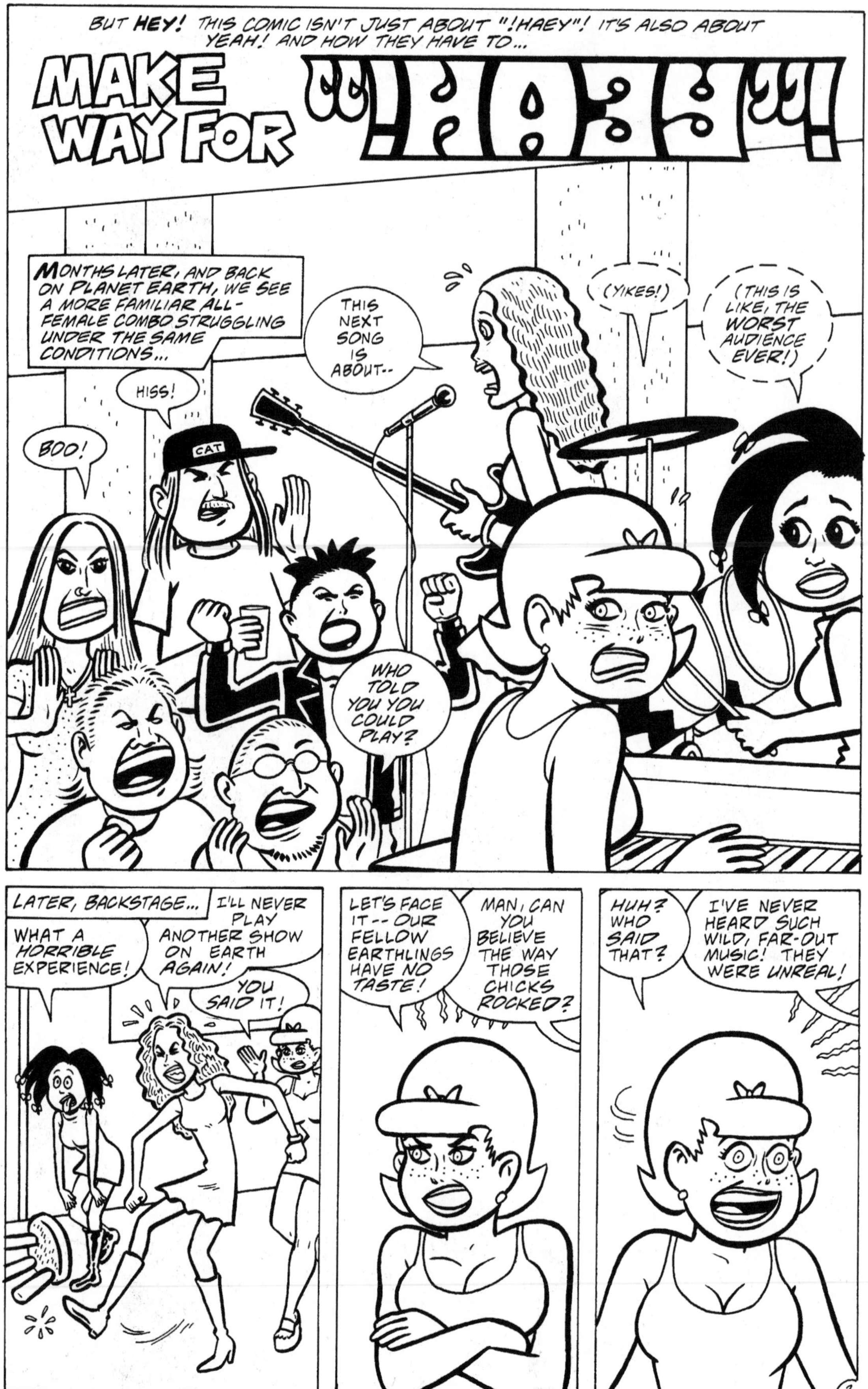

BUT HEY! THIS COMIC ISN'T JUST ABOUT "!HAEY"! IT'S ALSO ABOUT YEAH! AND HOW THEY HAVE TO...
MAKE WAY FOR "!HAEY"!
MONTHS LATER, AND BACK ON PLANET EARTH, WE SEE A MORE FAMILIAR ALL-FEMALE COMBO STRUGGLING UNDER THE SAME CONDITIONS...
THIS NEXT SONG IS ABOUT--
(YIKES!)
(THIS IS LIKE, THE WORST AUDIENCE EVER!)
HISS!
BOO!
CAT
WHO TOLD YOU YOU COULD PLAY?
LATER, BACKSTAGE...
WHAT A HORRIBLE EXPERIENCE!
I'LL NEVER PLAY ANOTHER SHOW ON EARTH AGAIN!
YOU SAID IT!
LET'S FACE IT -- OUR FELLOW EARTHLINGS HAVE NO TASTE!
MAN, CAN YOU BELIEVE THE WAY THOSE CHICKS ROCKED?
HUH? WHO SAID THAT?
I'VE NEVER HEARD SUCH WILD, FAR-OUT MUSIC! THEY WERE UNREAL!

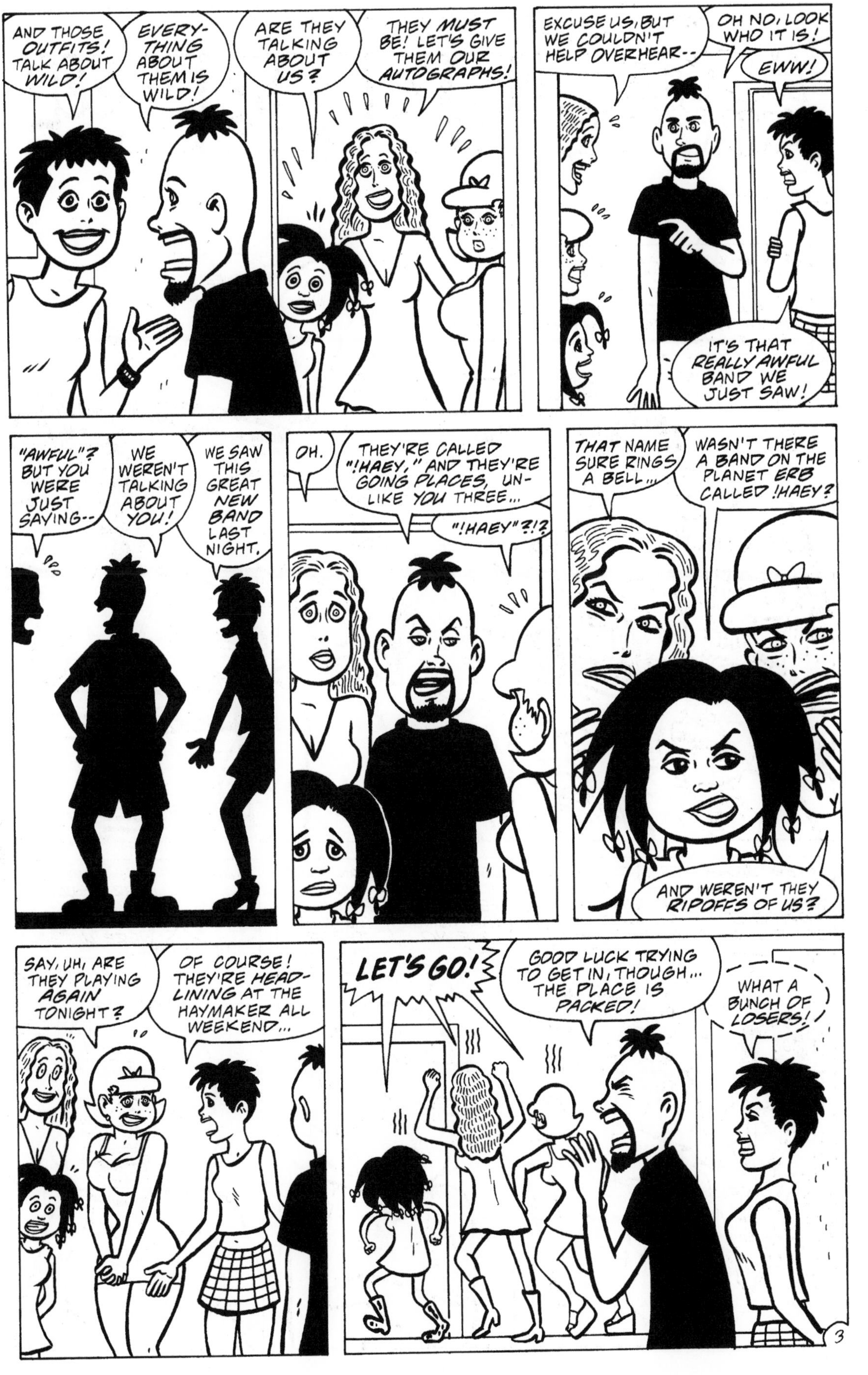

AND THOSE OUTFITS! TALK ABOUT WILD!
EVERYTHING ABOUT THEM IS WILD!
ARE THEY TALKING ABOUT US?
THEY MUST BE! LET'S GIVE THEM OUR AUTOGRAPHS!
EXCUSE US, BUT WE COULDN'T HELP OVERHEAR--
OH NO, LOOK WHO IT IS!
EWW!
IT'S THAT REALLY AWFUL BAND WE JUST SAW!
"AWFUL"? BUT YOU WERE JUST SAYING--
WE WEREN'T TALKING ABOUT YOU!
WE SAW THIS GREAT NEW BAND LAST NIGHT.
OH.
THEY'RE CALLED "!HAEY," AND THEY'RE GOING PLACES, UNLIKE YOU THREE...
"!HAEY"?!?
THAT NAME SURE RINGS A BELL...
WASN'T THERE A BAND ON THE PLANET ERB CALLED !HAEY?
AND WEREN'T THEY RIPOFFS OF US?
SAY, UH, ARE THEY PLAYING AGAIN TONIGHT?
OF COURSE! THEY'RE HEADLINING AT THE HAYMAKER ALL WEEKEND...
LET'S GO!
GOOD LUCK TRYING TO GET IN, THOUGH... THE PLACE IS PACKED!
WHAT A BUNCH OF LOSERS!

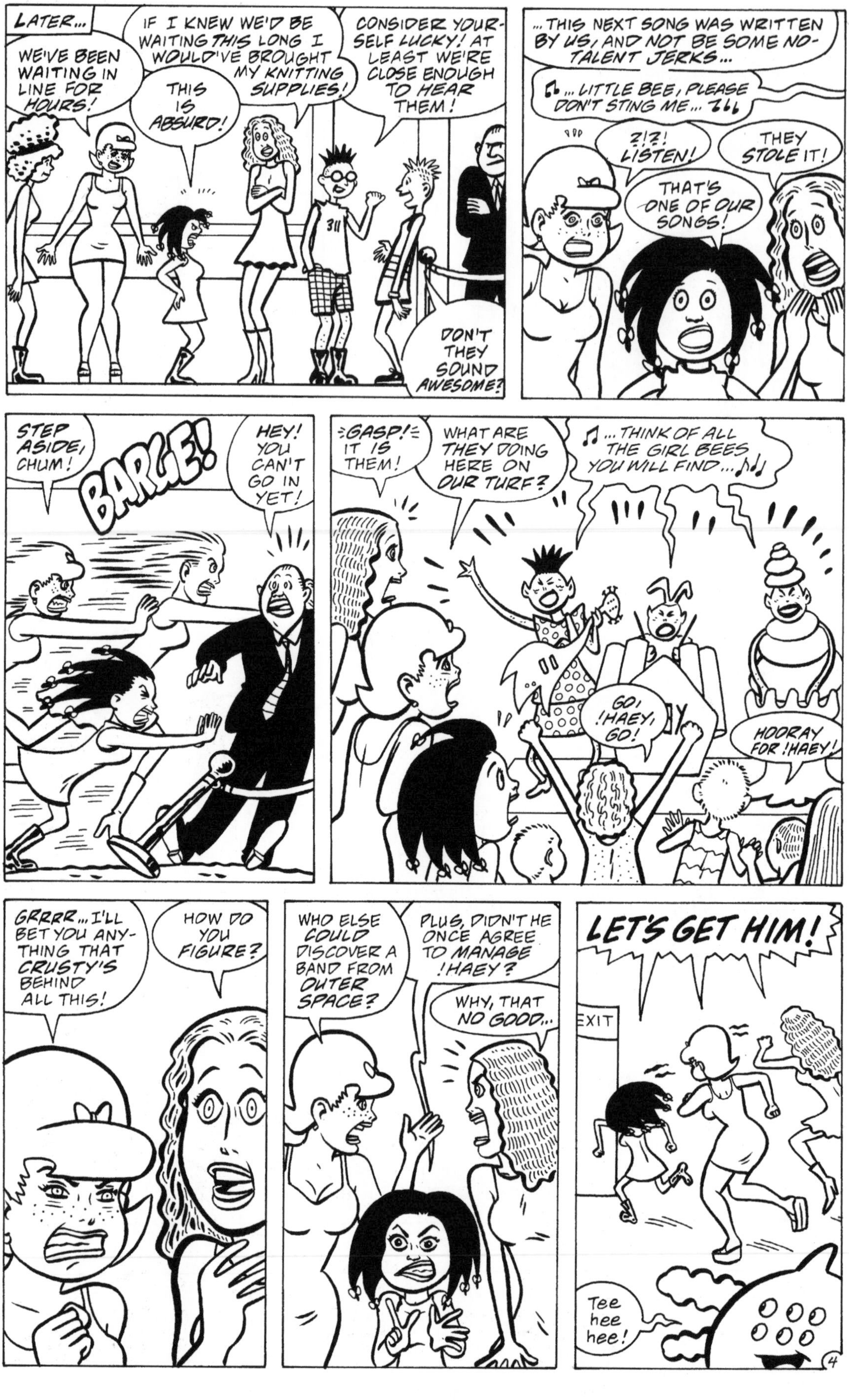
LATER...
WE'VE BEEN WAITING IN LINE FOR HOURS!
IF I KNEW WE'D BE WAITING THIS LONG I WOULD'VE BROUGHT MY KNITTING SUPPLIES!
THIS IS ABSURD!
CONSIDER YOURSELF LUCKY! AT LEAST WE'RE CLOSE ENOUGH TO HEAR THEM!
311
DON'T THEY SOUND AWESOME?
...THIS NEXT SONG WAS WRITTEN BY US, AND NOT BE SOME NO-TALENT JERKS...
... LITTLE BEE, PLEASE DON'T STING ME...
?!?! LISTEN!
THEY STOLE IT!
THAT'S ONE OF OUR SONGS!
STEP ASIDE, CHUM!
BARGE!
HEY! YOU CAN'T GO IN YET!
GASP! IT IS THEM!
WHAT ARE THEY DOING HERE ON OUR TURF?
...THINK OF ALL THE GIRL BEES YOU WILL FIND...
GO, !HAEY, GO!
HOORAY FOR !HAEY!
GRRRR... I'LL BET YOU ANYTHING THAT CRUSTY'S BEHIND ALL THIS!
HOW DO YOU FIGURE?
WHO ELSE COULD DISCOVER A BAND FROM OUTER SPACE?
PLUS, DIDN'T HE ONCE AGREE TO MANAGE !HAEY?
WHY, THAT NO GOOD...
LET'S GET HIM!
EXIT
Tee hee hee!

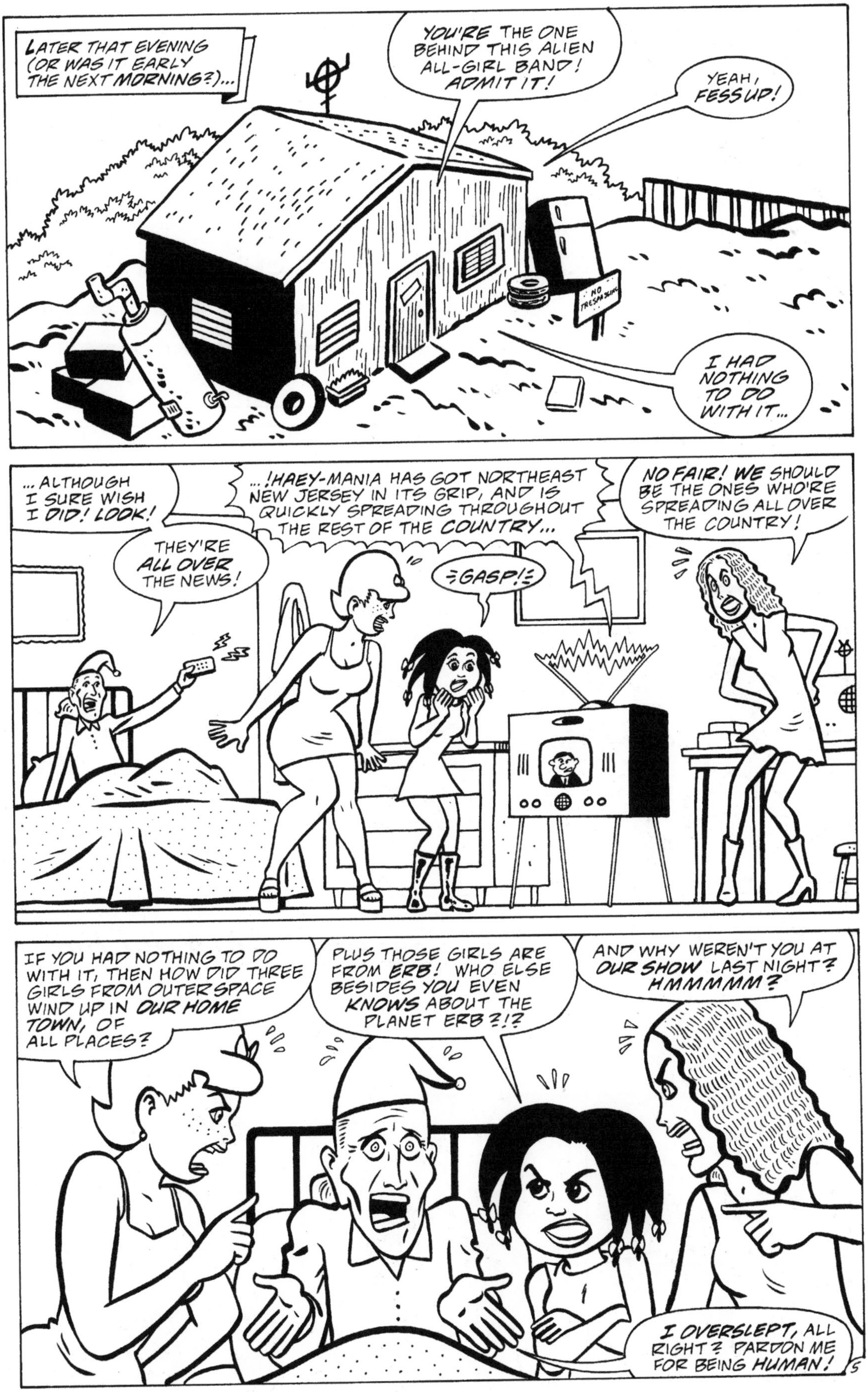
LATER THAT EVENING (OR WAS IT EARLY THE NEXT MORNING?)...
YOU'RE THE ONE BEHIND THIS ALIEN ALL-GIRL BAND! ADMIT IT!
YEAH, FESS UP!
NO TRESPASSING
I HAD NOTHING TO DO WITH IT...
...ALTHOUGH I SURE WISH I DID! LOOK!
THEY'RE ALL OVER THE NEWS!
...!HAEY-MANIA HAS GOT NORTHEAST NEW JERSEY IN ITS GRIP, AND IS QUICKLY SPREADING THROUGHOUT THE REST OF THE COUNTRY...
NO FAIR! WE SHOULD BE THE ONES WHO'RE SPREADING ALL OVER THE COUNTRY!
GASP!
IF YOU HAD NOTHING TO DO WITH IT, THEN HOW DID THREE GIRLS FROM OUTER SPACE WIND UP IN OUR HOME TOWN, OF ALL PLACES?
PLUS THOSE GIRLS ARE FROM ERB! WHO ELSE BESIDES YOU EVEN KNOWS ABOUT THE PLANET ERB?!?
AND WHY WEREN'T YOU AT OUR SHOW LAST NIGHT? HMMMMMM?
I OVERSLEPT, ALL RIGHT? PARDON ME FOR BEING HUMAN!

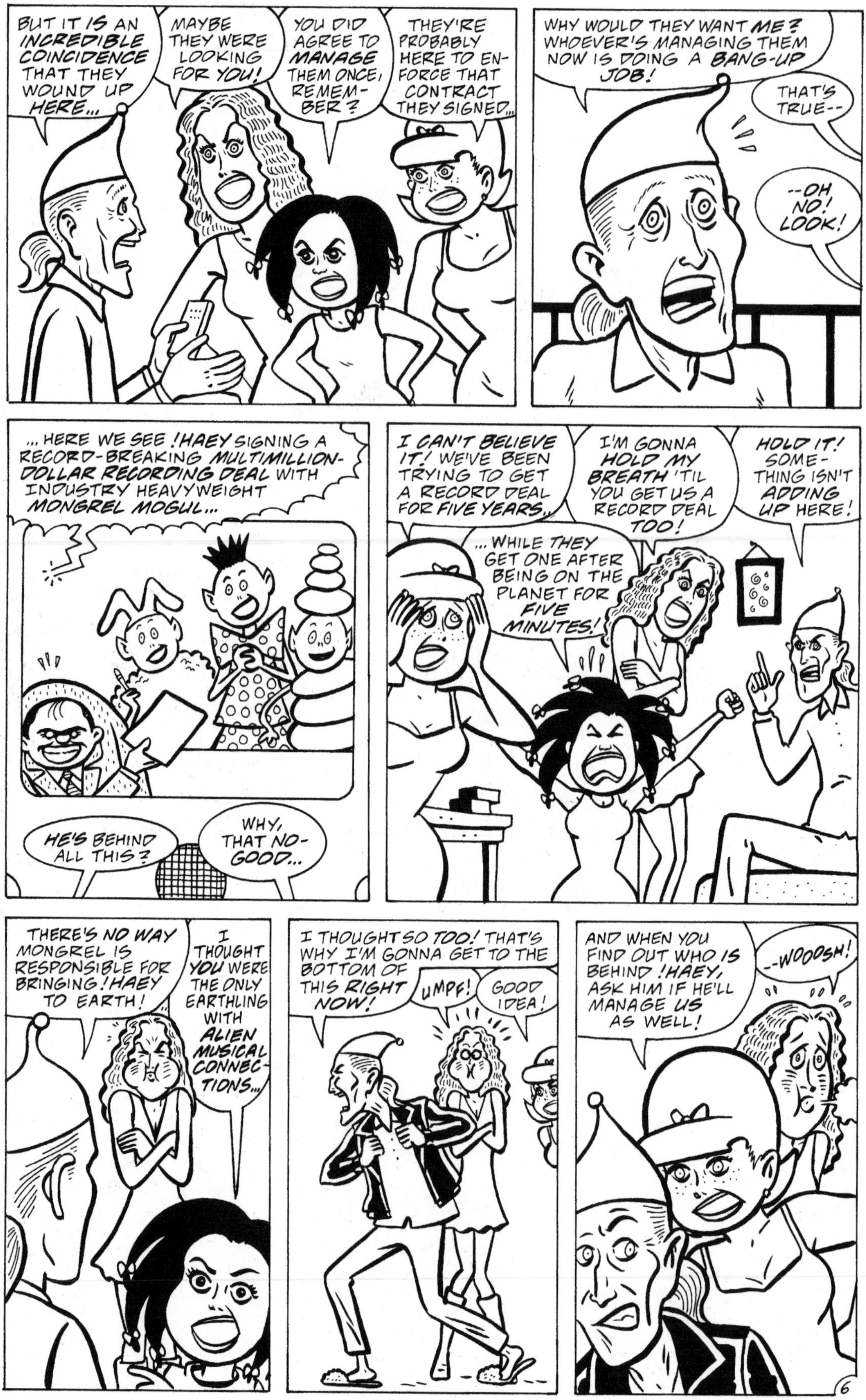

BUT IT IS AN INCREDIBLE COINCIDENCE THAT THEY WOUND UP HERE...
MAYBE THEY WERE LOOKING FOR YOU!
YOU DID AGREE TO MANAGE THEM ONCE, REMEMBER?
THEY'RE PROBABLY HERE TO ENFORCE THAT CONTRACT THEY SIGNED...
WHY WOULD THEY WANT ME? WHOEVER'S MANAGING THEM NOW IS DOING A BANG-UP JOB!
THAT'S TRUE--
--OH NO! LOOK!
...HERE WE SEE !HAEY SIGNING A RECORD-BREAKING MULTIMILLION-DOLLAR RECORDING DEAL WITH INDUSTRY HEAVYWEIGHT MONGREL MOGUL...
HE'S BEHIND ALL THIS?
WHY, THAT NO-GOOD...
I CAN'T BELIEVE IT! WE'VE BEEN TRYING TO GET A RECORD DEAL FOR FIVE YEARS...
...WHILE THEY GET ONE AFTER BEING ON THE PLANET FOR FIVE MINUTES!
I'M GONNA HOLD MY BREATH 'TIL YOU GET US A RECORD DEAL TOO!
HOLD IT! SOMETHING ISN'T ADDING UP HERE!
THERE'S NO WAY MONGREL IS RESPONSIBLE FOR BRINGING !HAEY TO EARTH!
I THOUGHT YOU WERE THE ONLY EARTHLING WITH ALIEN MUSICAL CONNECTIONS...
I THOUGHT SO TOO! THAT'S WHY I'M GONNA GET TO THE BOTTOM OF THIS RIGHT NOW!
UMPF!
GOOD IDEA!
AND WHEN YOU FIND OUT WHO IS BEHIND !HAEY, ASK HIM IF HE'LL MANAGE US AS WELL!
--WOOOSH!

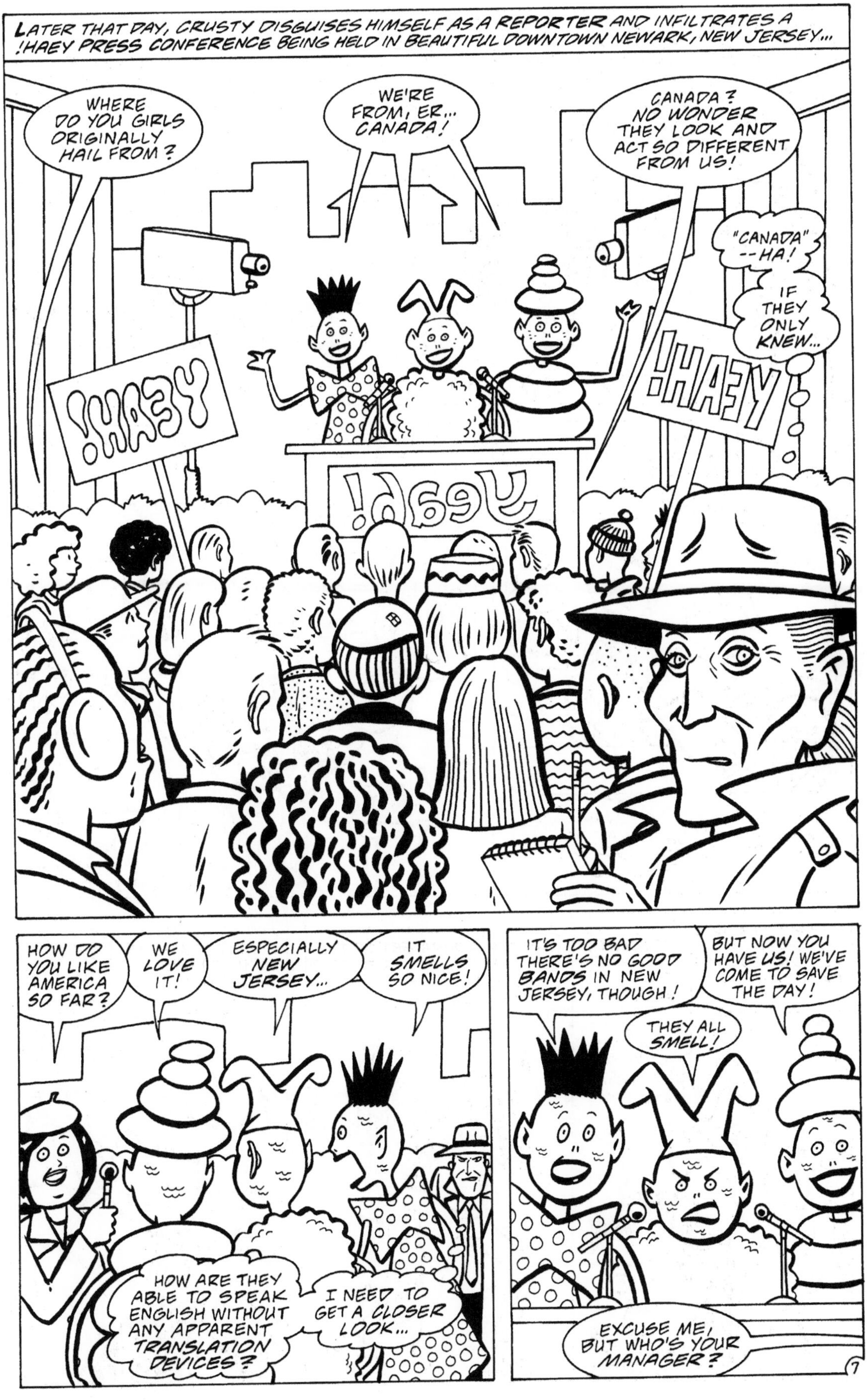
LATER THAT DAY, CRUSTY DISGUISES HIMSELF AS A REPORTER AND INFILTRATES A !HAEY PRESS CONFERENCE BEING HELD IN BEAUTIFUL DOWNTOWN NEWARK, NEW JERSEY...
WHERE DO YOU GIRLS ORIGINALLY HAIL FROM?
WE'RE FROM, ER... CANADA!
CANADA? NO WONDER THEY LOOK AND ACT SO DIFFERENT FROM US!
"CANADA" --HA!
IF THEY ONLY KNEW...
HOW DO YOU LIKE AMERICA SO FAR?
WE LOVE IT!
ESPECIALLY NEW JERSEY...
IT SMELLS SO NICE!
HOW ARE THEY ABLE TO SPEAK ENGLISH WITHOUT ANY APPARENT TRANSLATION DEVICES?
I NEED TO GET A CLOSER LOOK...
IT'S TOO BAD THERE'S NO GOOD BANDS IN NEW JERSEY, THOUGH!
BUT NOW YOU HAVE US! WE'VE COME TO SAVE THE DAY!
THEY ALL SMELL!
EXCUSE ME, BUT WHO'S YOUR MANAGER?

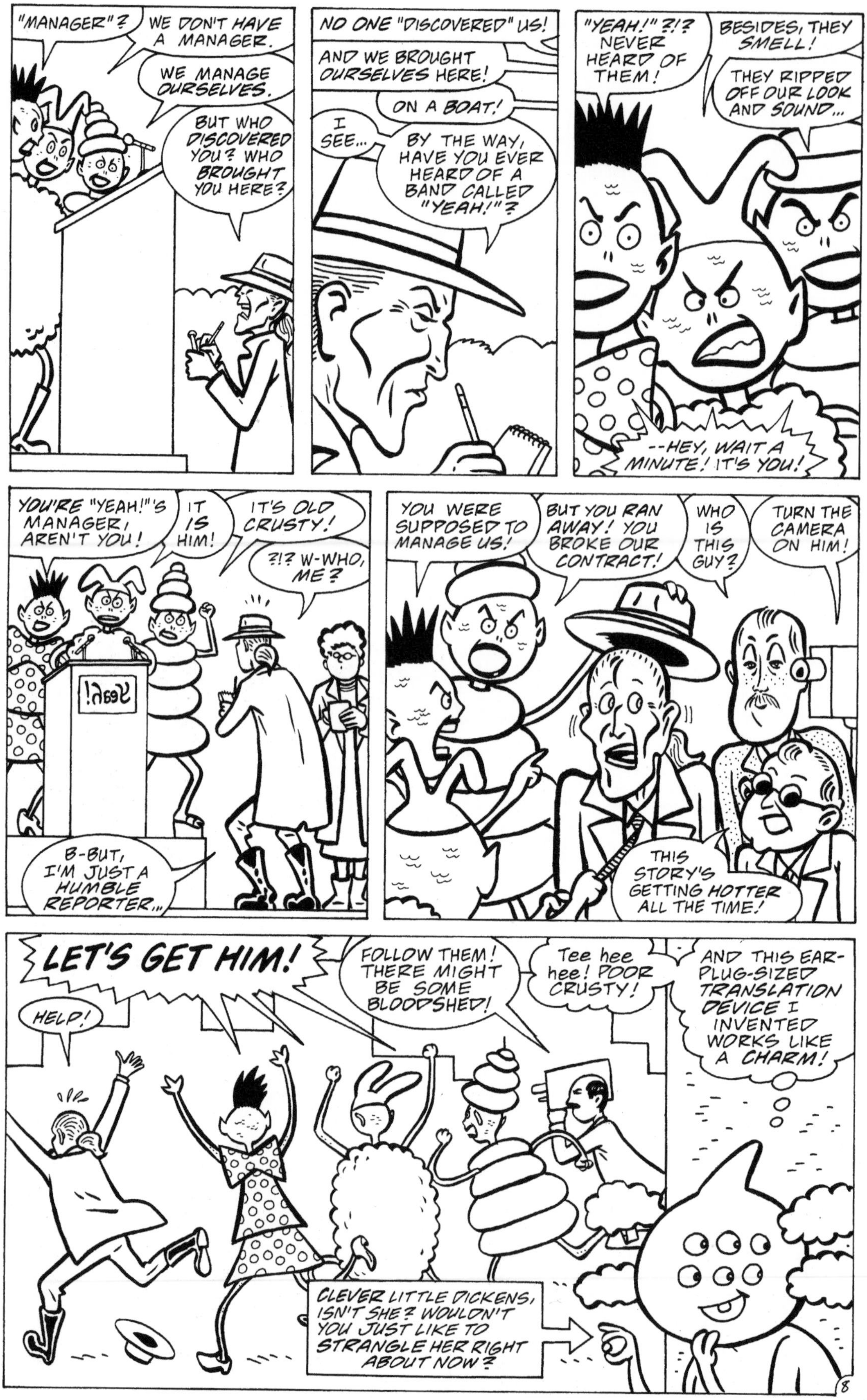

"MANAGER"?
WE DON'T HAVE A MANAGER.
WE MANAGE OURSELVES.
BUT WHO DISCOVERED YOU? WHO BROUGHT YOU HERE?
NO ONE "DISCOVERED" US!
AND WE BROUGHT OURSELVES HERE!
ON A BOAT!
I SEE...
BY THE WAY, HAVE YOU EVER HEARD OF A BAND CALLED "YEAH!"?
"YEAH!"?!? NEVER HEARD OF THEM!
BESIDES, THEY SMELL!
THEY RIPPED OFF OUR LOOK AND SOUND...
--HEY, WAIT A MINUTE! IT'S YOU!
YOU'RE "YEAH!"'S MANAGER, AREN'T YOU!
IT IS HIM!
IT'S OLD CRUSTY!
?!? W-WHO, ME?
B-BUT, I'M JUST A HUMBLE REPORTER...
YOU WERE SUPPOSED TO MANAGE US!
BUT YOU RAN AWAY! YOU BROKE OUR CONTRACT!
WHO IS THIS GUY?
TURN THE CAMERA ON HIM!
THIS STORY'S GETTING HOTTER ALL THE TIME!
LET'S GET HIM!
HELP!
FOLLOW THEM! THERE MIGHT BE SOME BLOODSHED!
Tee hee hee! POOR CRUSTY!
AND THIS EAR-PLUG-SIZED TRANSLATION DEVICE I INVENTED WORKS LIKE A CHARM!
CLEVER LITTLE DICKENS, ISN'T SHE? WOULDN'T YOU JUST LIKE TO STRANGLE HER RIGHT ABOUT NOW?

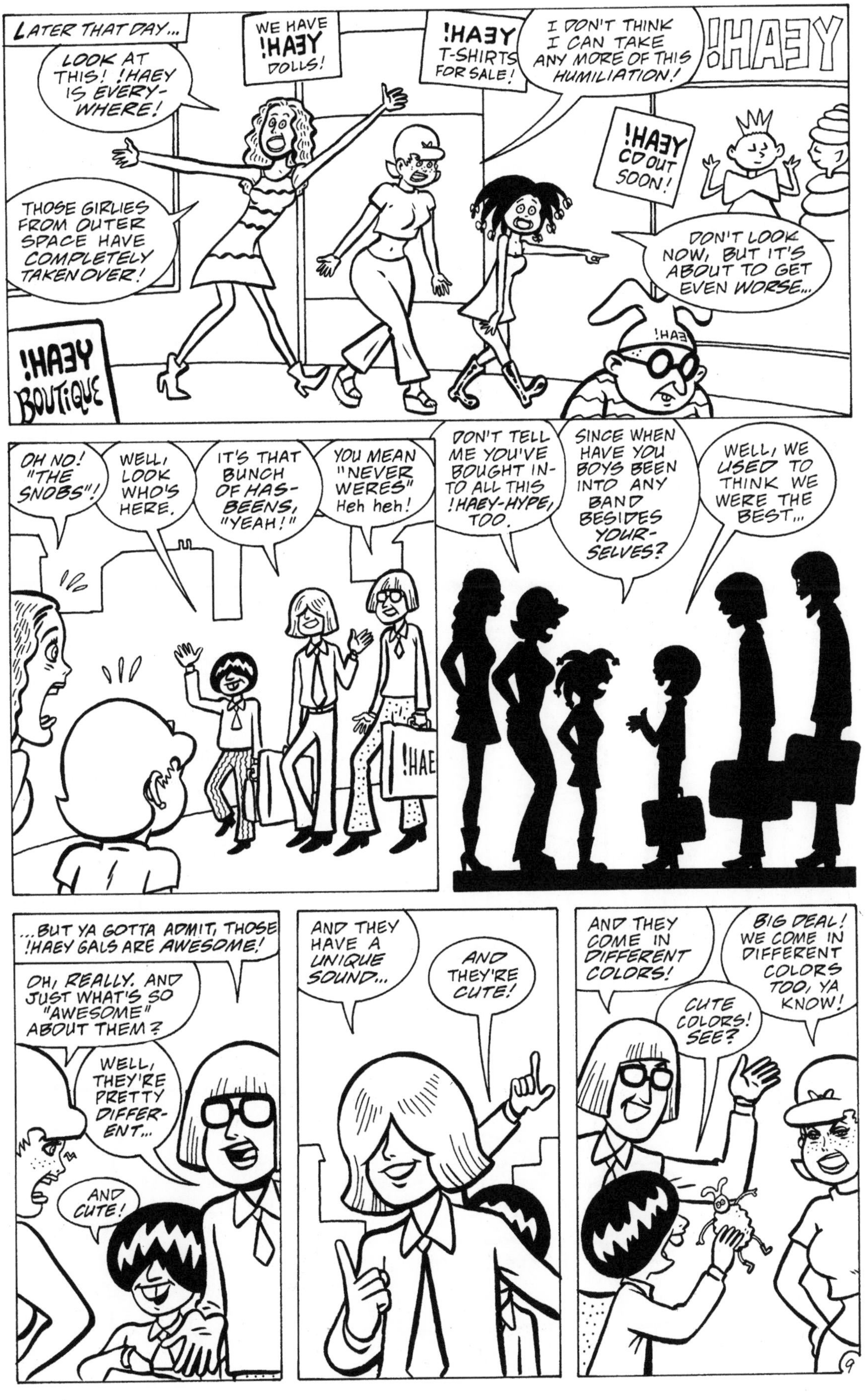
LATER THAT DAY...
LOOK AT THIS! !HAEY IS EVERYWHERE!
WE HAVE !HAEY DOLLS!
!HAEY T-SHIRTS FOR SALE!
I DON'T THINK I CAN TAKE ANY MORE OF THIS HUMILIATION!
YEAH!
THOSE GIRLIES FROM OUTER SPACE HAVE COMPLETELY TAKEN OVER!
!HAEY CD OUT SOON!
DON'T LOOK NOW, BUT IT'S ABOUT TO GET EVEN WORSE...
!HAEY BOUTIQUE
!HAE
OH NO! "THE SNOBS"!
WELL, LOOK WHO'S HERE.
IT'S THAT BUNCH OF HAS-BEENS, "YEAH!"
YOU MEAN "NEVER WERES" Heh heh!
!HAE
DON'T TELL ME YOU'VE BOUGHT IN-TO ALL THIS !HAEY-HYPE, TOO.
SINCE WHEN HAVE YOU BOYS BEEN INTO ANY BAND BESIDES YOURSELVES?
WELL, WE USED TO THINK WE WERE THE BEST...
...BUT YA GOTTA ADMIT, THOSE !HAEY GALS ARE AWESOME!
OH, REALLY. AND JUST WHAT'S SO "AWESOME" ABOUT THEM?
WELL, THEY'RE PRETTY DIFFERENT...
AND CUTE!
AND THEY HAVE A UNIQUE SOUND...
AND THEY'RE CUTE!
AND THEY COME IN DIFFERENT COLORS!
BIG DEAL! WE COME IN DIFFERENT COLORS TOO, YA KNOW!
CUTE COLORS! SEE?

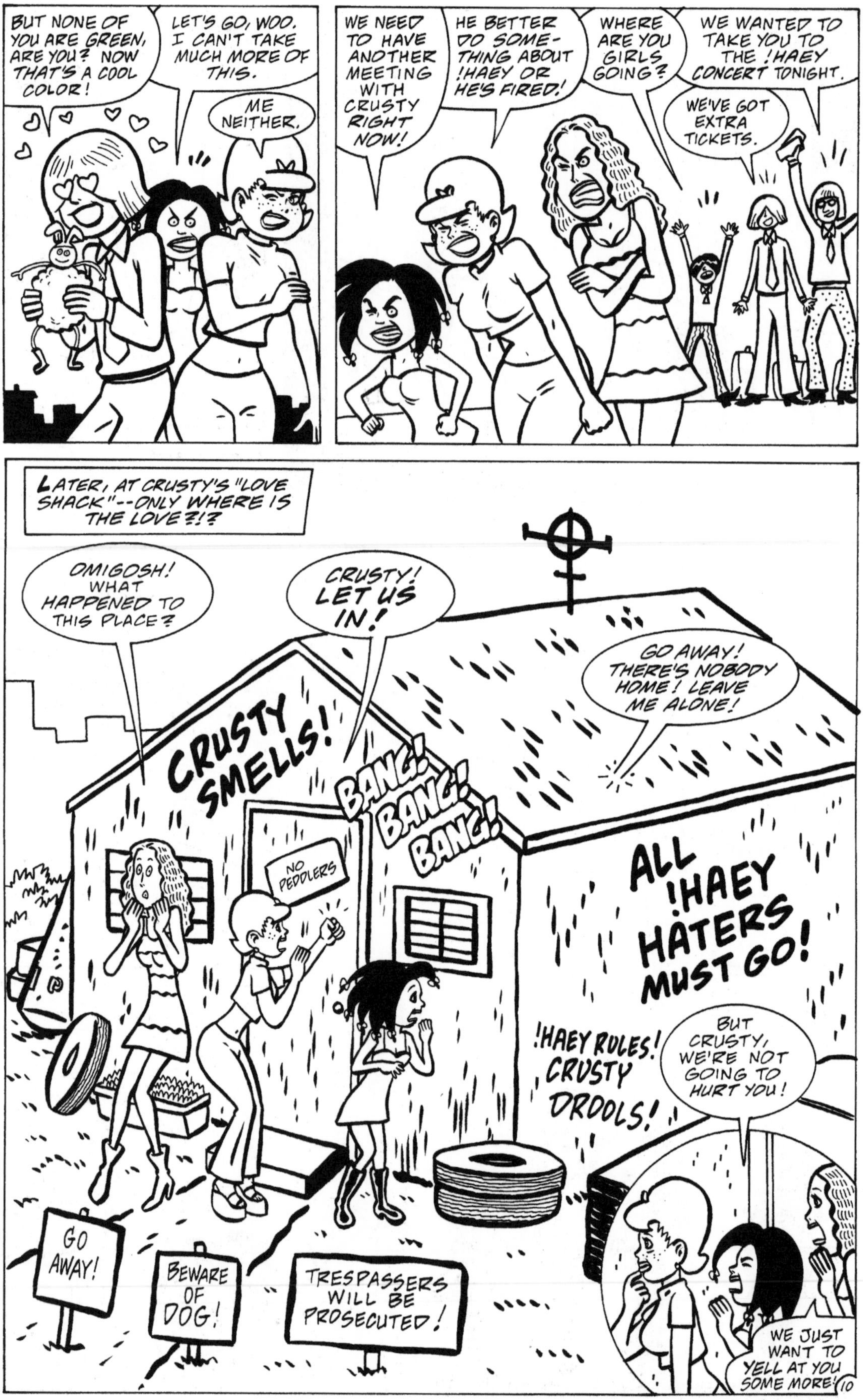

BUT NONE OF YOU ARE GREEN, ARE YOU? NOW THAT'S A COOL COLOR!
LET'S GO, WOO. I CAN'T TAKE MUCH MORE OF THIS.
ME NEITHER.
WE NEED TO HAVE ANOTHER MEETING WITH CRUSTY RIGHT NOW!
HE BETTER DO SOME-THING ABOUT !HAEY OR HE'S FIRED!
WHERE ARE YOU GIRLS GOING?
WE WANTED TO TAKE YOU TO THE !HAEY CONCERT TONIGHT.
WE'VE GOT EXTRA TICKETS.
LATER, AT CRUSTY'S "LOVE SHACK"--ONLY WHERE IS THE LOVE?!?
OMIGOSH! WHAT HAPPENED TO THIS PLACE?
CRUSTY! LET US IN!
GO AWAY! THERE'S NOBODY HOME! LEAVE ME ALONE!
CRUSTY SMELLS!
BANG! BANG! BANG!
NO PEDDLERS
ALL !HAEY HATERS MUST GO!
!HAEY RULES! CRUSTY DROOLS!
BUT CRUSTY, WE'RE NOT GOING TO HURT YOU!
WE JUST WANT TO YELL AT YOU SOME MORE!
GO AWAY!
BEWARE OF DOG!
TRESPASSERS WILL BE PROSECUTED!

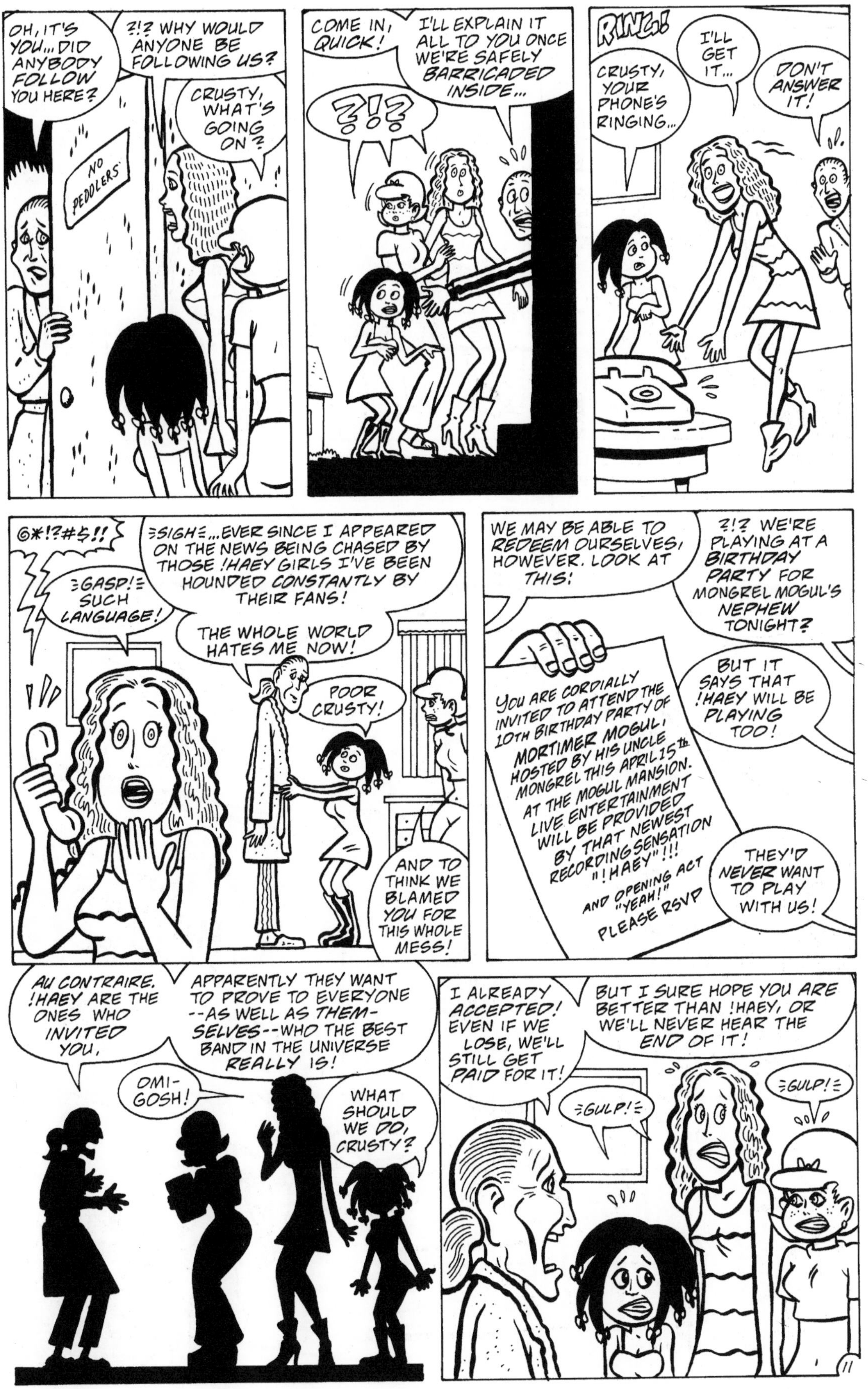
OH, IT'S YOU... DID ANYBODY FOLLOW YOU HERE?
?!? WHY WOULD ANYONE BE FOLLOWING US?
NO PEDDLERS
CRUSTY, WHAT'S GOING ON?
COME IN, QUICK!
I'LL EXPLAIN IT ALL TO YOU ONCE WE'RE SAFELY BARRICADED INSIDE...
?!?
RING!
CRUSTY, YOUR PHONE'S RINGING...
I'LL GET IT...
DON'T ANSWER IT!
@*!?#$!!
=GASP!= SUCH LANGUAGE!
=SIGH=...EVER SINCE I APPEARED ON THE NEWS BEING CHASED BY THOSE !HAEY GIRLS I'VE BEEN HOUNDED CONSTANTLY BY THEIR FANS!
THE WHOLE WORLD HATES ME NOW!
POOR CRUSTY!
AND TO THINK WE BLAMED YOU FOR THIS WHOLE MESS!
WE MAY BE ABLE TO REDEEM OURSELVES, HOWEVER. LOOK AT THIS!
?!? WE'RE PLAYING AT A BIRTHDAY PARTY FOR MONGREL MOGUL'S NEPHEW TONIGHT?
YOU ARE CORDIALLY INVITED TO ATTEND THE 10TH BIRTHDAY PARTY OF MORTIMER MOGUL, HOSTED BY HIS UNCLE MONGREL THIS APRIL 15th AT THE MOGUL MANSION. LIVE ENTERTAINMENT WILL BE PROVIDED BY THAT NEWEST RECORDING SENSATION "!HAEY"!!!
AND OPENING ACT "YEAH!"
PLEASE RSVP
BUT IT SAYS THAT !HAEY WILL BE PLAYING TOO!
THEY'D NEVER WANT TO PLAY WITH US!
AU CONTRAIRE. !HAEY ARE THE ONES WHO INVITED YOU.
APPARENTLY THEY WANT TO PROVE TO EVERYONE --AS WELL AS THEM-SELVES--WHO THE BEST BAND IN THE UNIVERSE REALLY IS!
OMI-GOSH!
WHAT SHOULD WE DO, CRUSTY?
I ALREADY ACCEPTED! EVEN IF WE LOSE, WE'LL STILL GET PAID FOR IT!
BUT I SURE HOPE YOU ARE BETTER THAN !HAEY, OR WE'LL NEVER HEAR THE END OF IT!
=GULP!=
=GULP!=
11

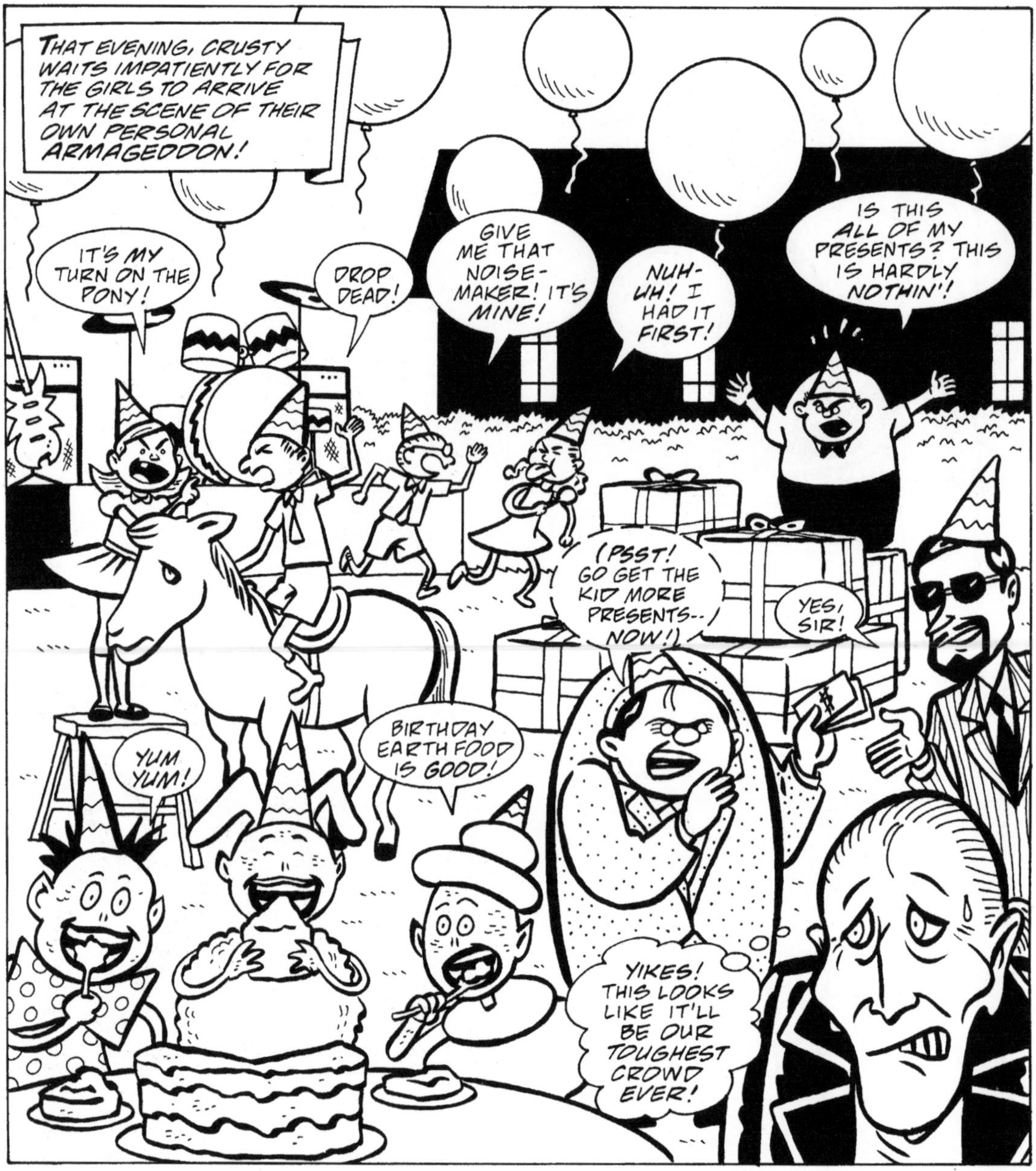
THAT EVENING, CRUSTY WAITS IMPATIENTLY FOR THE GIRLS TO ARRIVE AT THE SCENE OF THEIR OWN PERSONAL ARMAGEDDON!
IT'S MY TURN ON THE PONY!
DROP DEAD!
GIVE ME THAT NOISE-MAKER! IT'S MINE!
NUH-UH! I HAD IT FIRST!
IS THIS ALL OF MY PRESENTS? THIS IS HARDLY NOTHIN'!
(PSST! GO GET THE KID MORE PRESENTS-- NOW!)
YES, SIR!
YUM YUM!
BIRTHDAY EARTH FOOD IS GOOD!
YIKES! THIS LOOKS LIKE IT'LL BE OUR TOUGHEST CROWD EVER!

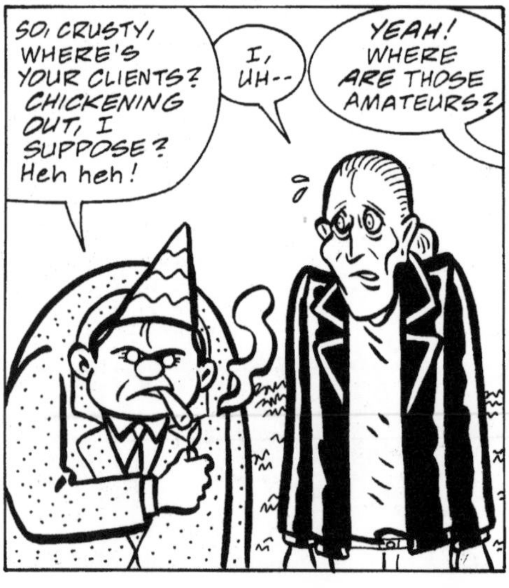
SO, CRUSTY, WHERE'S YOUR CLIENTS? CHICKENING OUT, I SUPPOSE? Heh heh!
I, UH--
YEAH! WHERE ARE THOSE AMATEURS?

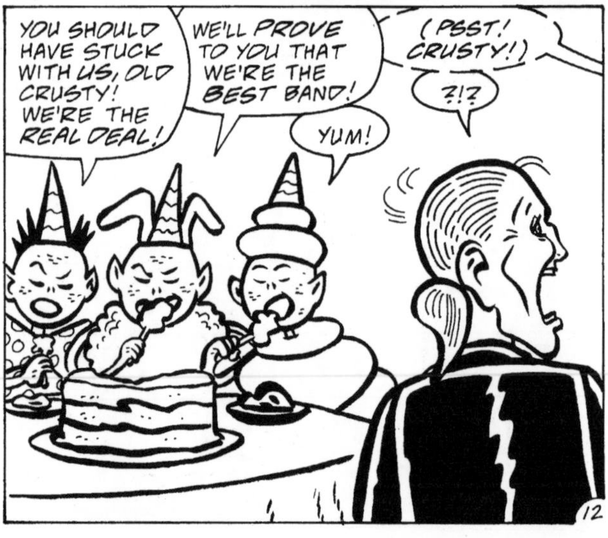
YOU SHOULD HAVE STUCK WITH US, OLD CRUSTY! WE'RE THE REAL DEAL!
WE'LL PROVE TO YOU THAT WE'RE THE BEST BAND!
YUM!
(PSST! CRUSTY!)
?!?

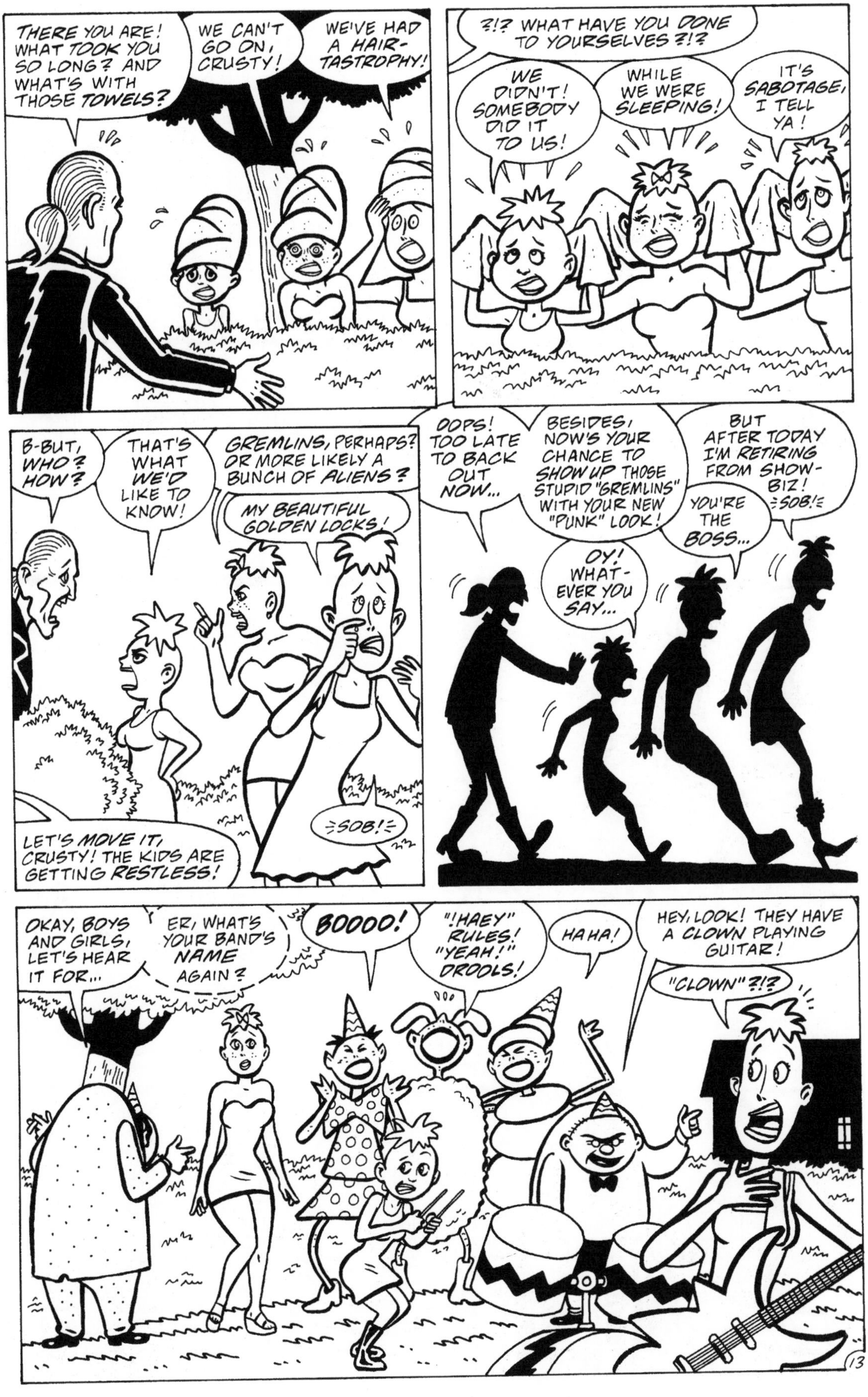
THERE YOU ARE! WHAT TOOK YOU SO LONG? AND WHAT'S WITH THOSE TOWELS?
WE CAN'T GO ON, CRUSTY!
WE'VE HAD A HAIR-TASTROPHY!
?!? WHAT HAVE YOU DONE TO YOURSELVES?!?
WE DIDN'T! SOMEBODY DID IT TO US!
WHILE WE WERE SLEEPING!
IT'S SABOTAGE, I TELL YA!
B-BUT, WHO? HOW?
THAT'S WHAT WE'D LIKE TO KNOW!
GREMLINS, PERHAPS? OR MORE LIKELY A BUNCH OF ALIENS?
MY BEAUTIFUL GOLDEN LOCKS!
=SOB!=
LET'S MOVE IT, CRUSTY! THE KIDS ARE GETTING RESTLESS!
OOPS! TOO LATE TO BACK OUT NOW...
BESIDES, NOW'S YOUR CHANCE TO SHOW UP THOSE STUPID "GREMLINS" WITH YOUR NEW "PUNK" LOOK!
BUT AFTER TODAY I'M RETIRING FROM SHOW-BIZ! =SOB!=
YOU'RE THE BOSS...
OY! WHAT-EVER YOU SAY...
OKAY, BOYS AND GIRLS, LET'S HEAR IT FOR...
ER, WHAT'S YOUR BAND'S NAME AGAIN?
BOOOO!
"!HAEY" RULES! "YEAH!" DROOLS!
HA HA!
HEY, LOOK! THEY HAVE A CLOWN PLAYING GUITAR!
"CLOWN"?!?

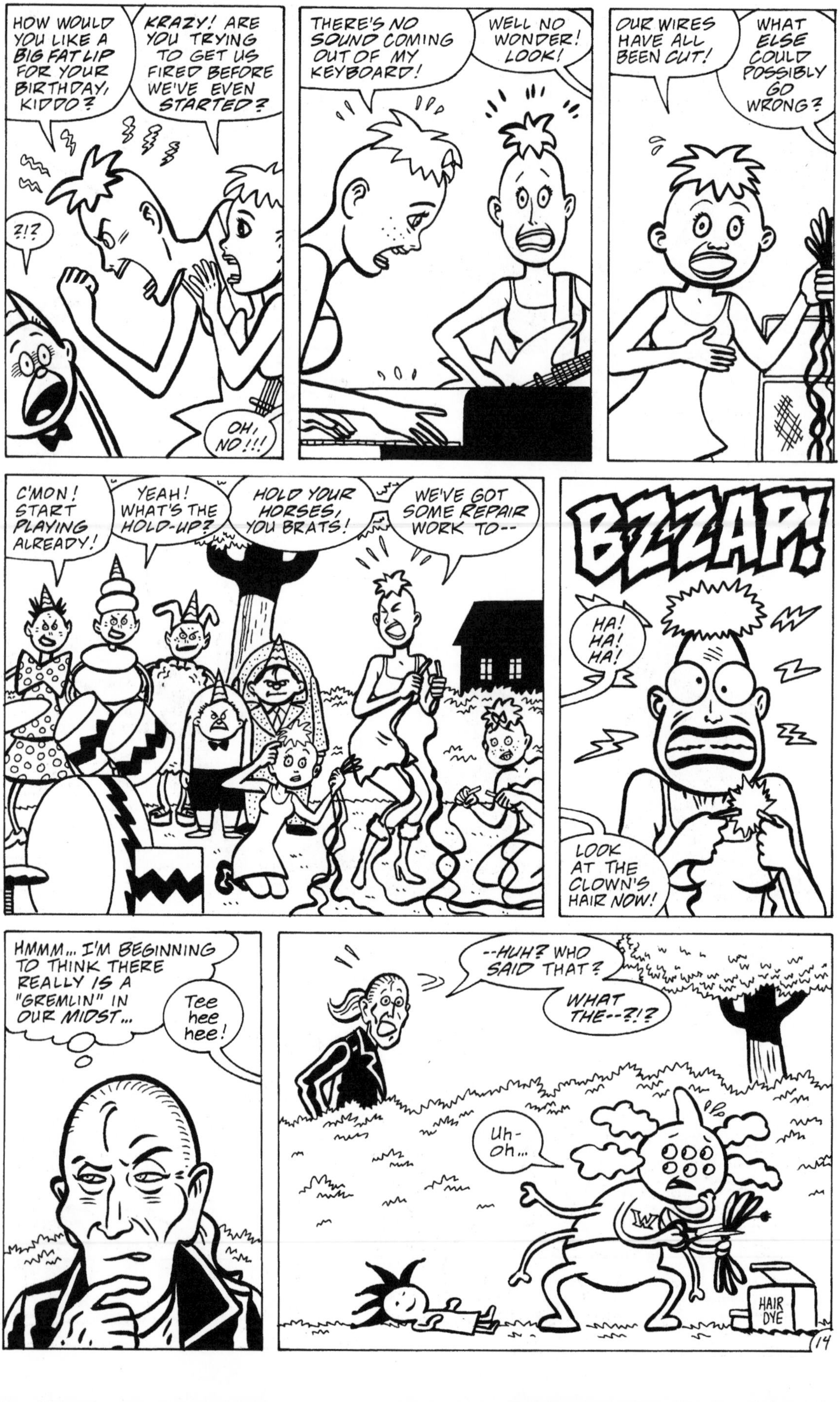
HOW WOULD YOU LIKE A BIG FAT LIP FOR YOUR BIRTHDAY, KIDDO?
KRAZY! ARE YOU TRYING TO GET US FIRED BEFORE WE'VE EVEN STARTED?
?!?
OH, NO!!!
THERE'S NO SOUND COMING OUT OF MY KEYBOARD!
WELL NO WONDER! LOOK!
OUR WIRES HAVE ALL BEEN CUT!
WHAT ELSE COULD POSSIBLY GO WRONG?
C'MON! START PLAYING ALREADY!
YEAH! WHAT'S THE HOLD-UP?
HOLD YOUR HORSES, YOU BRATS!
WE'VE GOT SOME REPAIR WORK TO--
BZZZAP!
HA! HA! HA!
LOOK AT THE CLOWN'S HAIR NOW!
HMMM... I'M BEGINNING TO THINK THERE REALLY IS A "GREMLIN" IN OUR MIDST...
Tee hee hee!
--HUH? WHO SAID THAT?
WHAT THE--?!?
Uh-oh...
HAIR DYE

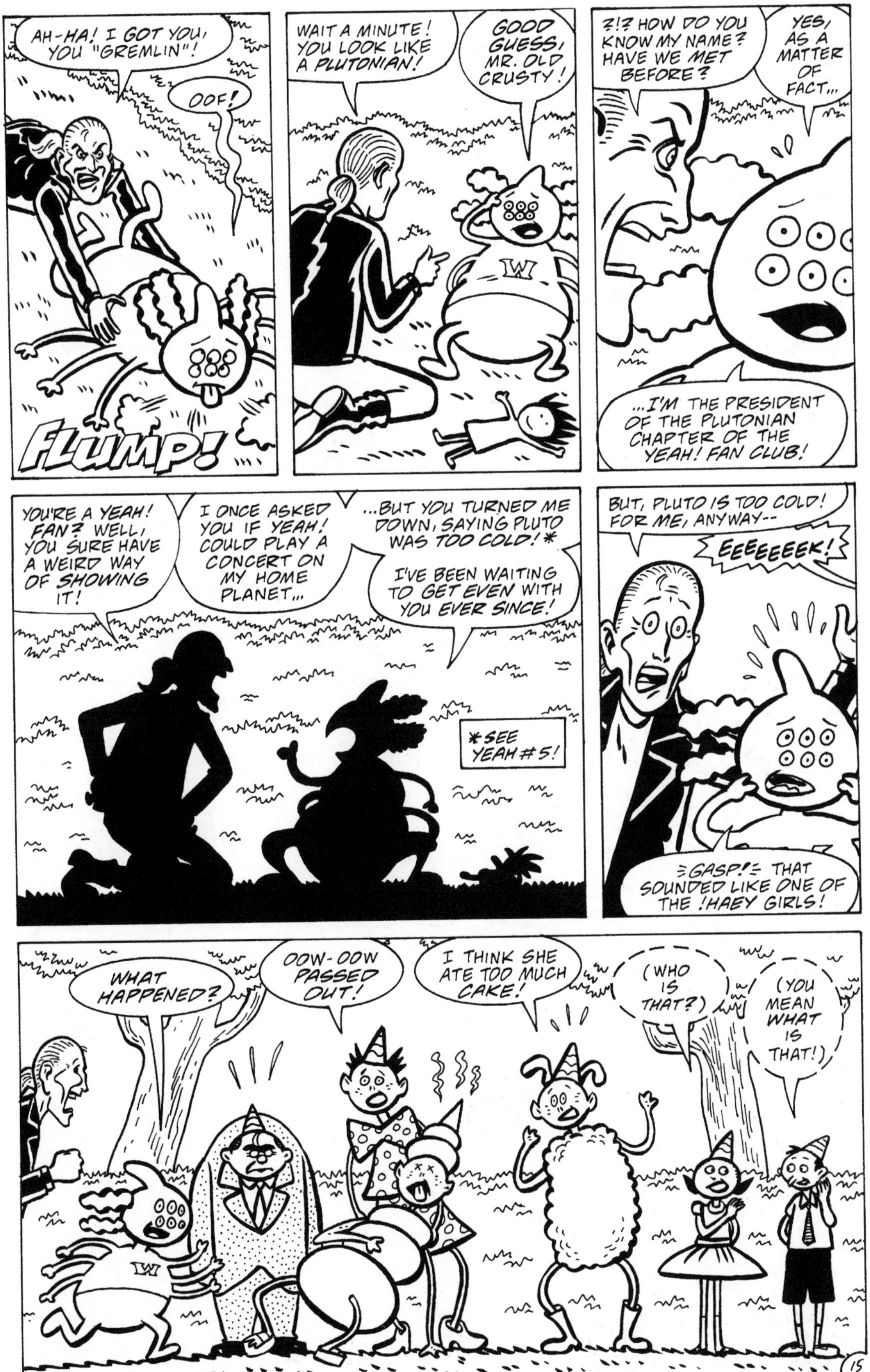
AH-HA! I GOT YOU, YOU "GREMLIN"!
OOF!
FLUMP!
WAIT A MINUTE! YOU LOOK LIKE A PLUTONIAN!
GOOD GUESS, MR. OLD CRUSTY!
?!? HOW DO YOU KNOW MY NAME? HAVE WE MET BEFORE?
YES, AS A MATTER OF FACT...
...I'M THE PRESIDENT OF THE PLUTONIAN CHAPTER OF THE YEAH! FAN CLUB!
YOU'RE A YEAH! FAN? WELL, YOU SURE HAVE A WEIRD WAY OF SHOWING IT!
I ONCE ASKED YOU IF YEAH! COULD PLAY A CONCERT ON MY HOME PLANET...
...BUT YOU TURNED ME DOWN, SAYING PLUTO WAS TOO COLD! *
I'VE BEEN WAITING TO GET EVEN WITH YOU EVER SINCE!
* SEE YEAH #5!
BUT, PLUTO IS TOO COLD! FOR ME, ANYWAY--
EEEEEEEK!
=GASP!= THAT SOUNDED LIKE ONE OF THE !HAEY GIRLS!
WHAT HAPPENED?
OOW-OOW PASSED OUT!
I THINK SHE ATE TOO MUCH CAKE!
(WHO IS THAT?)
(YOU MEAN WHAT IS THAT!)

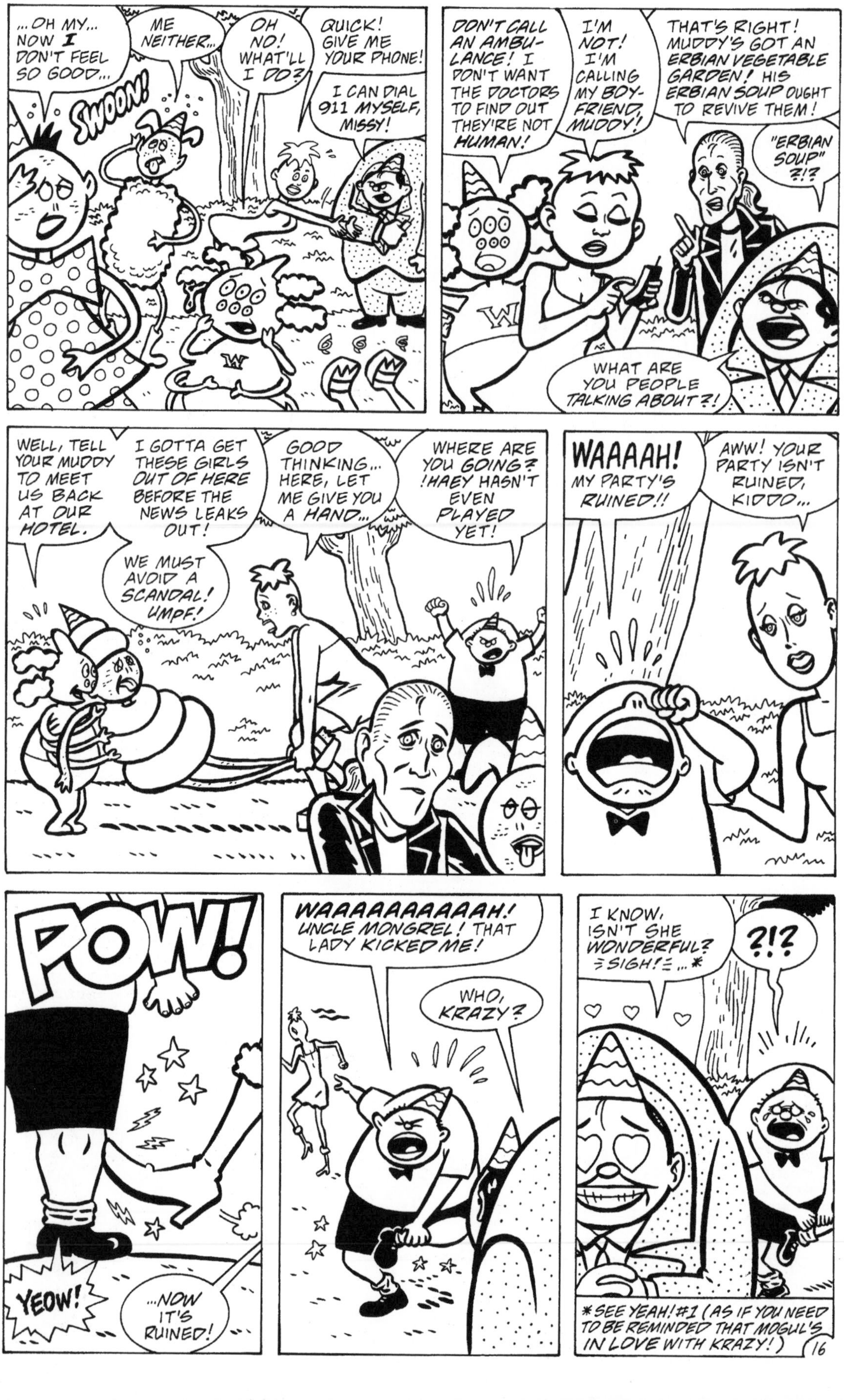
...OH MY... NOW I DON'T FEEL SO GOOD...
SWOON!
ME NEITHER...
OH NO! WHAT'LL I DO?
QUICK! GIVE ME YOUR PHONE!
I CAN DIAL 911 MYSELF, MISSY!
DON'T CALL AN AMBULANCE! I DON'T WANT THE DOCTORS TO FIND OUT THEY'RE NOT HUMAN!
I'M NOT! I'M CALLING MY BOYFRIEND, MUDDY!
THAT'S RIGHT! MUDDY'S GOT AN ERBIAN VEGETABLE GARDEN! HIS ERBIAN SOUP OUGHT TO REVIVE THEM!
"ERBIAN SOUP" ?!?
WHAT ARE YOU PEOPLE TALKING ABOUT?!
WELL, TELL YOUR MUDDY TO MEET US BACK AT OUR HOTEL.
I GOTTA GET THESE GIRLS OUT OF HERE BEFORE THE NEWS LEAKS OUT!
WE MUST AVOID A SCANDAL! UMPF!
GOOD THINKING... HERE, LET ME GIVE YOU A HAND...
WHERE ARE YOU GOING? !HAEY HASN'T EVEN PLAYED YET!
WAAAAH! MY PARTY'S RUINED!!
AWW! YOUR PARTY ISN'T RUINED, KIDDO...
POW!
YEOW!
...NOW IT'S RUINED!
WAAAAAAAAAAH! UNCLE MONGREL! THAT LADY KICKED ME!
WHO, KRAZY?
I KNOW, ISN'T SHE WONDERFUL? SIGH! ...*
?!?
*SEE YEAH! #1 (AS IF YOU NEED TO BE REMINDED THAT MOGUL'S IN LOVE WITH KRAZY!)

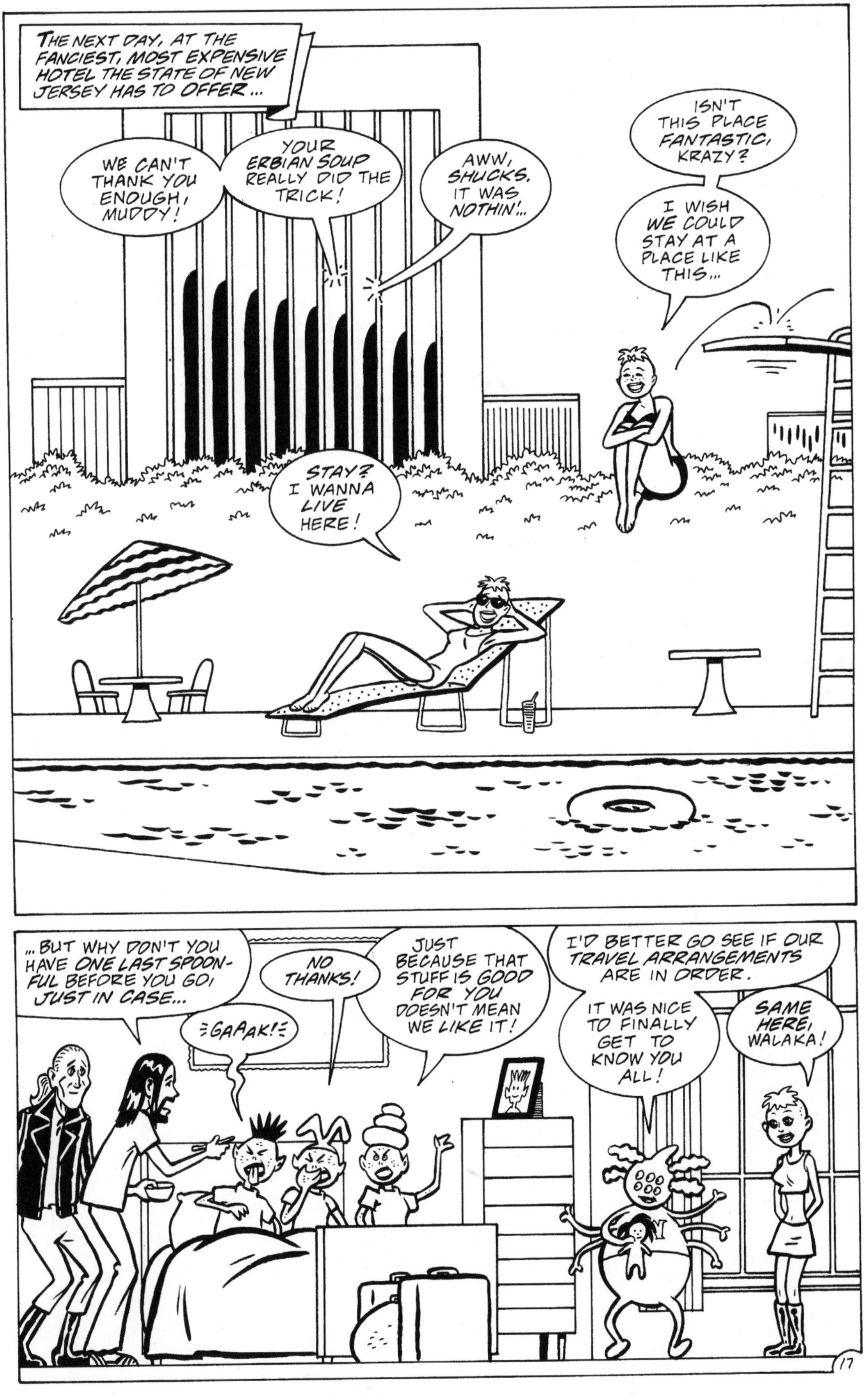
THE NEXT DAY, AT THE FANCIEST, MOST EXPENSIVE HOTEL THE STATE OF NEW JERSEY HAS TO OFFER...
WE CAN'T THANK YOU ENOUGH, MUDDY!
YOUR ERBIAN SOUP REALLY DID THE TRICK!
AWW, SHUCKS. IT WAS NOTHIN'...
ISN'T THIS PLACE FANTASTIC, KRAZY?
I WISH WE COULD STAY AT A PLACE LIKE THIS...
STAY? I WANNA LIVE HERE!
...BUT WHY DON'T YOU HAVE ONE LAST SPOON-FUL BEFORE YOU GO, JUST IN CASE...
GAAAK!
NO THANKS!
JUST BECAUSE THAT STUFF IS GOOD FOR YOU DOESN'T MEAN WE LIKE IT!
I'D BETTER GO SEE IF OUR TRAVEL ARRANGEMENTS ARE IN ORDER.
IT WAS NICE TO FINALLY GET TO KNOW YOU ALL!
SAME HERE, WALAKA!

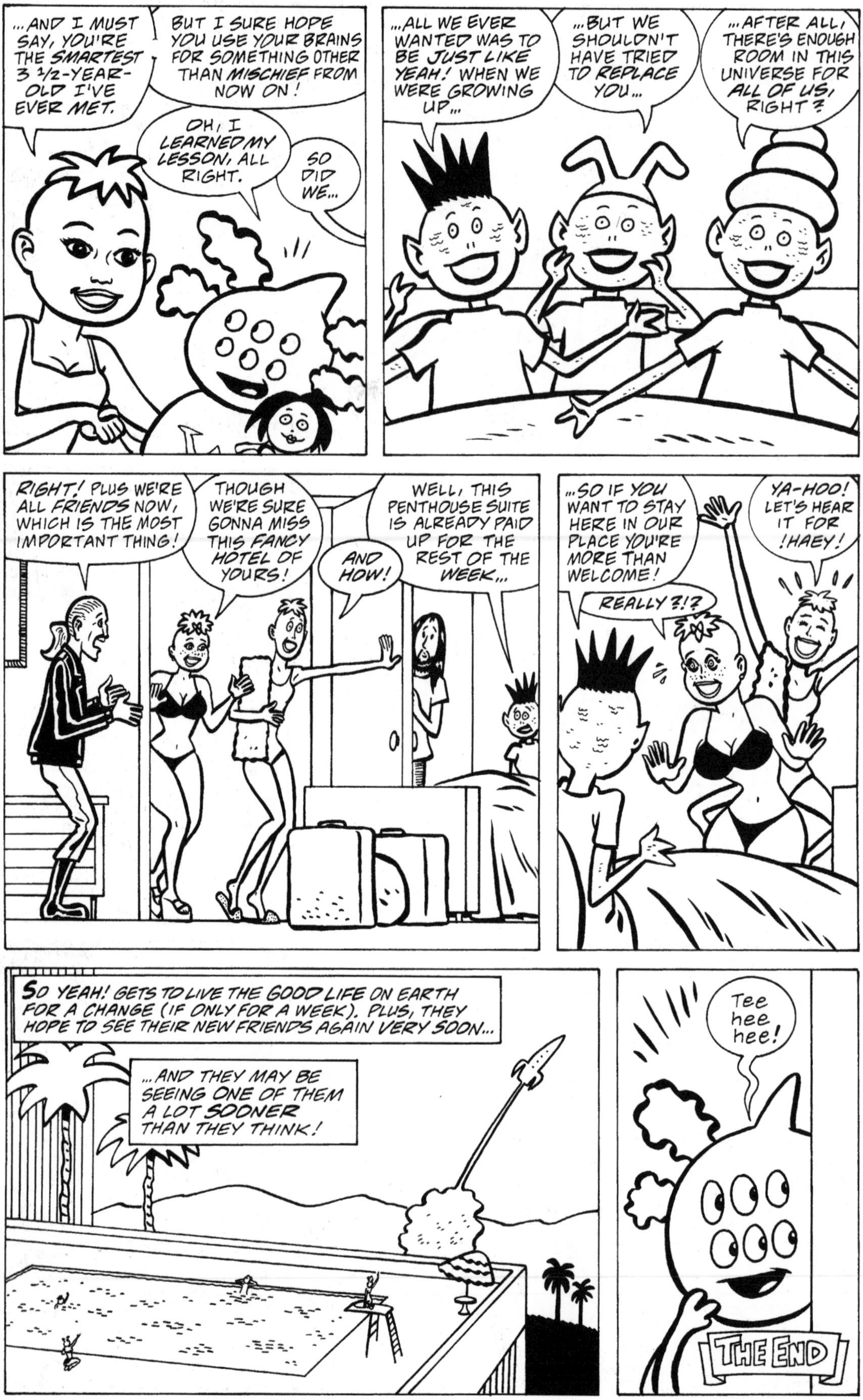
...AND I MUST SAY, YOU'RE THE SMARTEST 3 1/2-YEAR-OLD I'VE EVER MET.
BUT I SURE HOPE YOU USE YOUR BRAINS FOR SOMETHING OTHER THAN MISCHIEF FROM NOW ON!
OH, I LEARNED MY LESSON, ALL RIGHT.
SO DID WE...
...ALL WE EVER WANTED WAS TO BE JUST LIKE YEAH! WHEN WE WERE GROWING UP...
...BUT WE SHOULDN'T HAVE TRIED TO REPLACE YOU...
...AFTER ALL, THERE'S ENOUGH ROOM IN THIS UNIVERSE FOR ALL OF US, RIGHT?
RIGHT! PLUS WE'RE ALL FRIENDS NOW, WHICH IS THE MOST IMPORTANT THING!
THOUGH WE'RE SURE GONNA MISS THIS FANCY HOTEL OF YOURS!
AND HOW!
WELL, THIS PENTHOUSE SUITE IS ALREADY PAID UP FOR THE REST OF THE WEEK...
...SO IF YOU WANT TO STAY HERE IN OUR PLACE YOU'RE MORE THAN WELCOME!
REALLY?!?
YA-HOO! LET'S HEAR IT FOR !HAEY!
SO YEAH! GETS TO LIVE THE GOOD LIFE ON EARTH FOR A CHANGE (IF ONLY FOR A WEEK). PLUS, THEY HOPE TO SEE THEIR NEW FRIENDS AGAIN VERY SOON...
...AND THEY MAY BE SEEING ONE OF THEM A LOT SOONER THAN THEY THINK!
Tee hee hee!
THE END

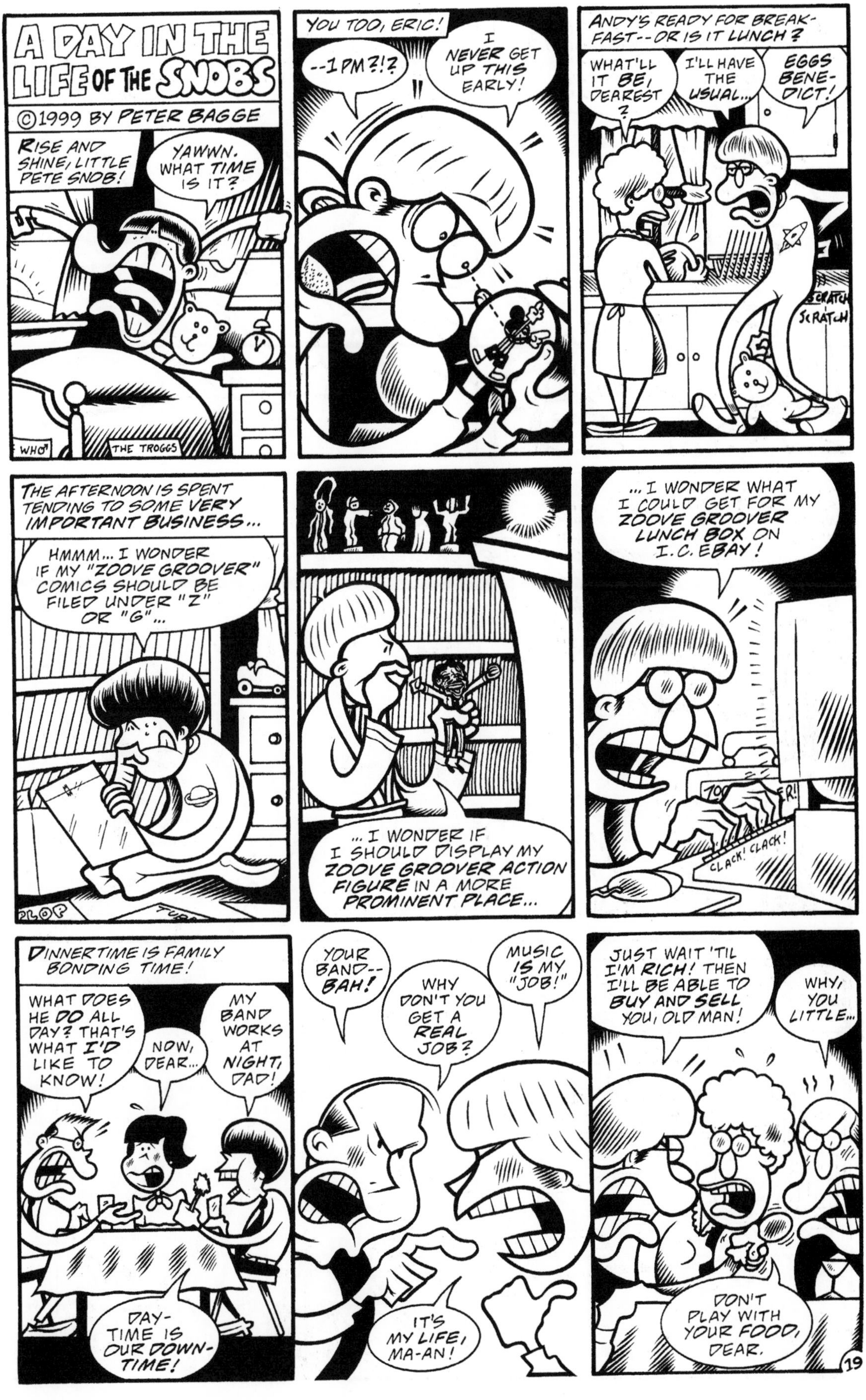

A DAY IN THE LIFE OF THE SNOBS
©1999 BY PETER BAGGE
RISE AND SHINE, LITTLE PETE SNOB!
YAWWN. WHAT TIME IS IT?
WHO
THE TROGGS
YOU TOO, ERIC!
--1 PM?!?
I NEVER GET UP THIS EARLY!
ANDY'S READY FOR BREAKFAST--OR IS IT LUNCH?
WHAT'LL IT BE, DEAREST?
I'LL HAVE THE USUAL...
EGGS BENEDICT!
SCRATCH
SCRATCH
THE AFTERNOON IS SPENT TENDING TO SOME VERY IMPORTANT BUSINESS...
HMMM... I WONDER IF MY "ZOOVE GROOVER" COMICS SHOULD BE FILED UNDER "Z" OR "G"...
PLOP
...I WONDER IF I SHOULD DISPLAY MY ZOOVE GROOVER ACTION FIGURE IN A MORE PROMINENT PLACE...
...I WONDER WHAT I COULD GET FOR MY ZOOVE GROOVER LUNCH BOX ON I.C. EBAY!
CLACK! CLACK!
DINNERTIME IS FAMILY BONDING TIME!
WHAT DOES HE DO ALL DAY? THAT'S WHAT I'D LIKE TO KNOW!
NOW, DEAR...
MY BAND WORKS AT NIGHT, DAD!
DAYTIME IS OUR DOWNTIME!
YOUR BAND--BAH!
WHY DON'T YOU GET A REAL JOB?
MUSIC IS MY "JOB!"
IT'S MY LIFE, MA-AN!
JUST WAIT 'TIL I'M RICH! THEN I'LL BE ABLE TO BUY AND SELL YOU, OLD MAN!
WHY, YOU LITTLE...
DON'T PLAY WITH YOUR FOOD, DEAR.

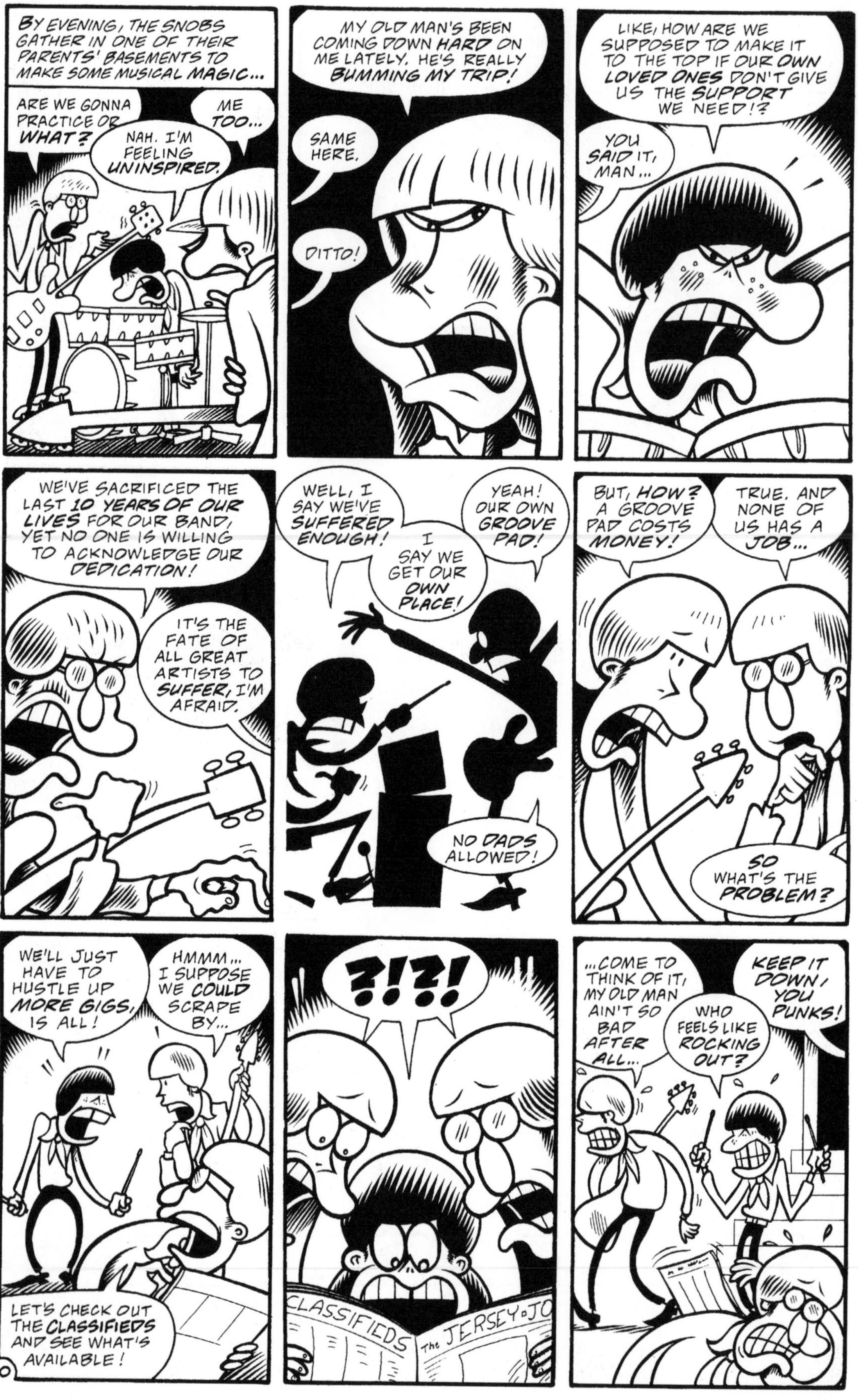

BY EVENING, THE SNOBS GATHER IN ONE OF THEIR PARENTS' BASEMENTS TO MAKE SOME MUSICAL MAGIC...
ARE WE GONNA PRACTICE OR WHAT?
ME TOO...
NAH. I'M FEELING UNINSPIRED.
MY OLD MAN'S BEEN COMING DOWN HARD ON ME LATELY. HE'S REALLY BUMMING MY TRIP!
SAME HERE.
DITTO!
LIKE, HOW ARE WE SUPPOSED TO MAKE IT TO THE TOP IF OUR OWN LOVED ONES DON'T GIVE US THE SUPPORT WE NEED!?
YOU SAID IT, MAN...
WE'VE SACRIFICED THE LAST 10 YEARS OF OUR LIVES FOR OUR BAND, YET NO ONE IS WILLING TO ACKNOWLEDGE OUR DEDICATION!
IT'S THE FATE OF ALL GREAT ARTISTS TO SUFFER, I'M AFRAID.
WELL, I SAY WE'VE SUFFERED ENOUGH!
I SAY WE GET OUR OWN PLACE!
YEAH! OUR OWN GROOVE PAD!
NO DADS ALLOWED!
BUT, HOW? A GROOVE PAD COSTS MONEY!
TRUE. AND NONE OF US HAS A JOB...
SO WHAT'S THE PROBLEM?
WE'LL JUST HAVE TO HUSTLE UP MORE GIGS, IS ALL!
HMMM... I SUPPOSE WE COULD SCRAPE BY...
LET'S CHECK OUT THE CLASSIFIEDS AND SEE WHAT'S AVAILABLE!
?!?!
CLASSIFIEDS
The JERSEY JO
...COME TO THINK OF IT, MY OLD MAN AIN'T SO BAD AFTER ALL...
WHO FEELS LIKE ROCKING OUT?
KEEP IT DOWN, YOU PUNKS!

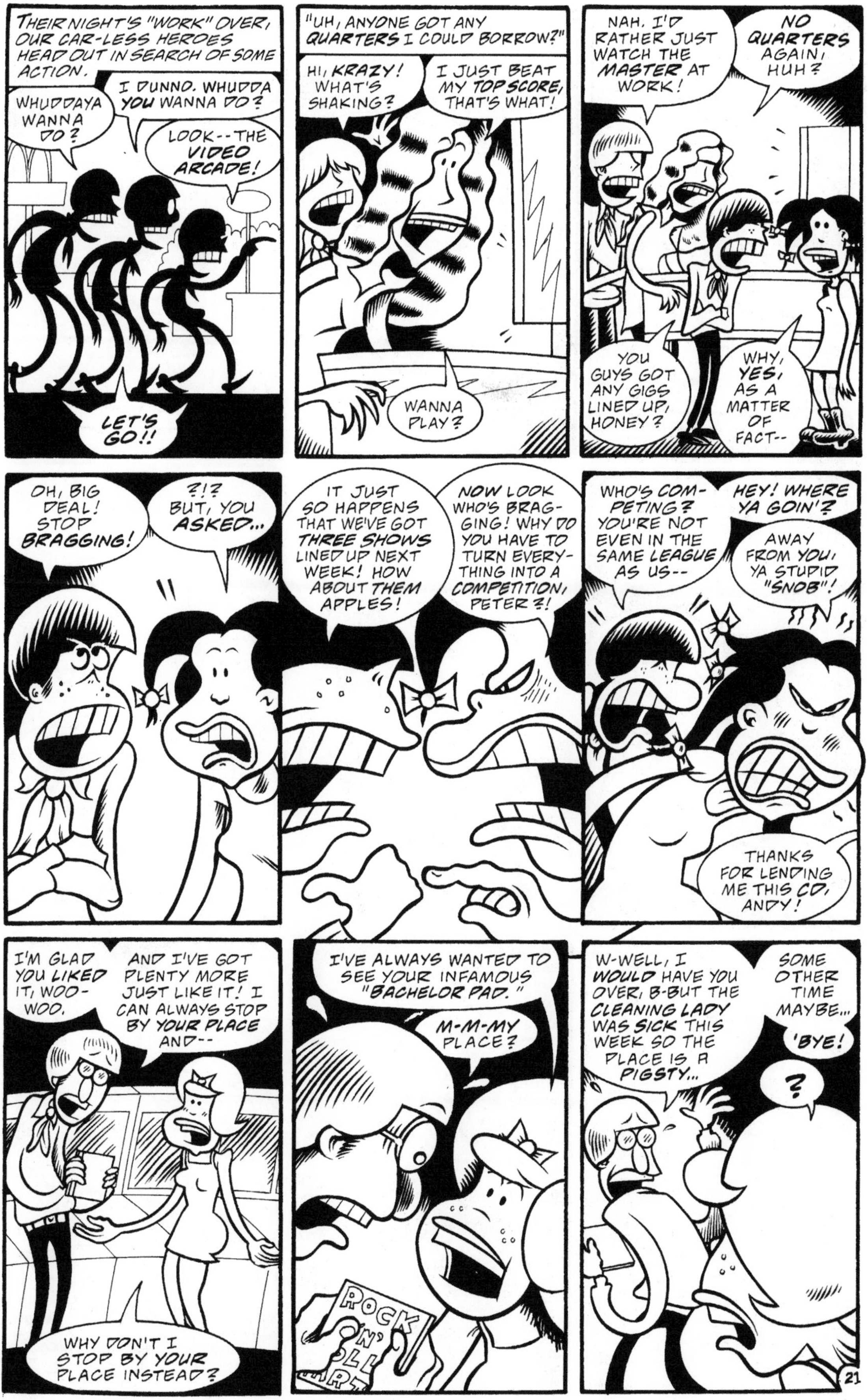

THEIR NIGHT'S "WORK" OVER, OUR CAR-LESS HEROES HEAD OUT IN SEARCH OF SOME ACTION.
WHUDDAYA WANNA DO?
I DUNNO. WHUDDA YOU WANNA DO?
LOOK--THE VIDEO ARCADE!
LET'S GO!!
"UH, ANYONE GOT ANY QUARTERS I COULD BORROW?"
HI, KRAZY! WHAT'S SHAKING?
I JUST BEAT MY TOP SCORE, THAT'S WHAT!
WANNA PLAY?
NAH. I'D RATHER JUST WATCH THE MASTER AT WORK!
NO QUARTERS AGAIN, HUH?
YOU GUYS GOT ANY GIGS LINED UP, HONEY?
WHY, YES, AS A MATTER OF FACT--
OH, BIG DEAL! STOP BRAGGING!
?!? BUT, YOU ASKED...
IT JUST SO HAPPENS THAT WE'VE GOT THREE SHOWS LINED UP NEXT WEEK! HOW ABOUT THEM APPLES!
NOW LOOK WHO'S BRAG-GING! WHY DO YOU HAVE TO TURN EVERY-THING INTO A COMPETITION, PETER?!
WHO'S COM-PETING? YOU'RE NOT EVEN IN THE SAME LEAGUE AS US--
HEY! WHERE YA GOIN'?
AWAY FROM YOU, YA STUPID "SNOB"!
THANKS FOR LENDING ME THIS CD, ANDY!
I'M GLAD YOU LIKED IT, WOO-WOO.
AND I'VE GOT PLENTY MORE JUST LIKE IT! I CAN ALWAYS STOP BY YOUR PLACE AND--
WHY DON'T I STOP BY YOUR PLACE INSTEAD?
I'VE ALWAYS WANTED TO SEE YOUR INFAMOUS "BACHELOR PAD."
M-M-MY PLACE?
ROCK 'N' ROLL
W-WELL, I WOULD HAVE YOU OVER, B-BUT THE CLEANING LADY WAS SICK THIS WEEK SO THE PLACE IS A PIGSTY...
SOME OTHER TIME MAYBE...
'BYE!
?

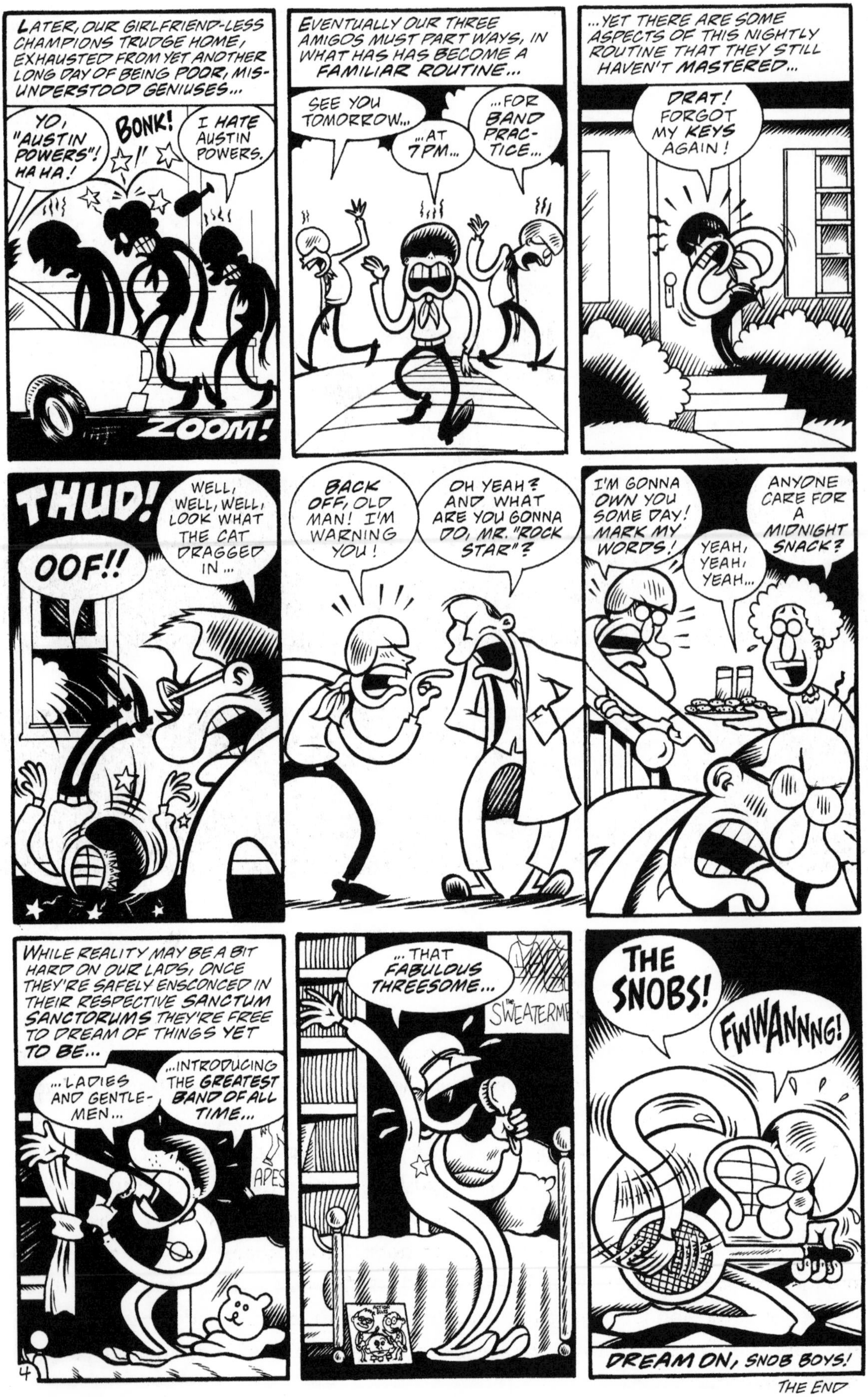
LATER, OUR GIRLFRIEND-LESS CHAMPIONS TRUDGE HOME, EXHAUSTED FROM YET ANOTHER LONG DAY OF BEING POOR, MISUNDERSTOOD GENIUSES...
YO, "AUSTIN POWERS"! HA HA!
BONK!
I HATE AUSTIN POWERS.
ZOOM!
EVENTUALLY OUR THREE AMIGOS MUST PART WAYS, IN WHAT HAS HAS BECOME A FAMILIAR ROUTINE...
SEE YOU TOMORROW...
...AT 7PM...
...FOR BAND PRAC-TICE...
...YET THERE ARE SOME ASPECTS OF THIS NIGHTLY ROUTINE THAT THEY STILL HAVEN'T MASTERED...
DRAT! FORGOT MY KEYS AGAIN!
THUD!
OOF!!
WELL, WELL, WELL, LOOK WHAT THE CAT DRAGGED IN...
BACK OFF, OLD MAN! I'M WARNING YOU!
OH YEAH? AND WHAT ARE YOU GONNA DO, MR. "ROCK STAR"?
I'M GONNA OWN YOU SOME DAY! MARK MY WORDS!
YEAH, YEAH, YEAH...
ANYONE CARE FOR A MIDNIGHT SNACK?
WHILE REALITY MAY BE A BIT HARD ON OUR LADS, ONCE THEY'RE SAFELY ENSCONCED IN THEIR RESPECTIVE SANCTUM SANCTORUMS THEY'RE FREE TO DREAM OF THINGS YET TO BE...
...LADIES AND GENTLE-MEN...
...INTRODUCING THE GREATEST BAND OF ALL TIME...
APES
...THAT FABULOUS THREESOME...
the SWEATERME
THE SNOBS!
FWWANNNG!
DREAM ON, SNOB BOYS!

THE END

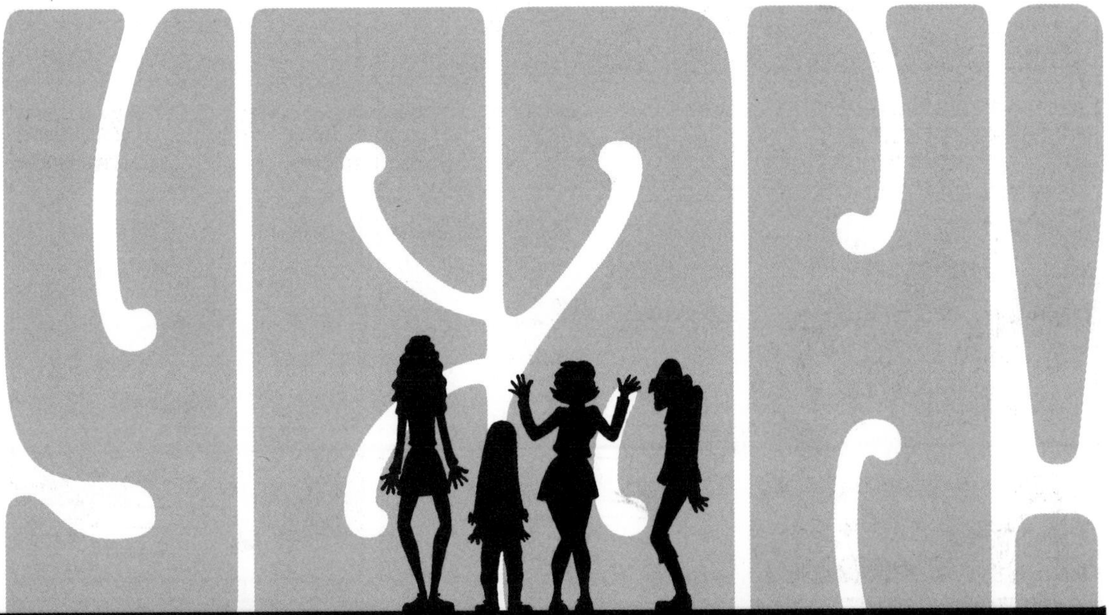
YEAH!

Presenting the band behind the book!

Gary Groth (PUBLISHER) used to publish a rock 'n' roll fanzine but now he listens to stuff like jazz because he's old. Boo! **Kim Thompson** (CO-PUBLISHER, EDITOR) spends most of his time at the office making fun of Gary's musical tastes, even though he's old too and all the "hip" rock he listens to was recorded like, back in the 1980s. Also Lady Gaga. **Eric Reynolds** (ASSOCIATE PUBLISHER, INKER ON THE FINAL YEAH! STORY) is a cartoonist, editor, promoter, rock 'n' roller, and bon vivant. **Alexa Koenings** (DESIGNER OF INTERIOR SPREADS) is currently looking for members to form a post-goth doom-metal band. **Paul Baresh** (PRODUCTION) a.k.a. Paul Diamond Blow rocks out as the lead guitarist and vocalist for the Space Cretins when he's not making Fantagraphics' comics look even more fabulous through his digital wizardry. **Jane Wiedlin** (BACK COVER BLURB WRITER) is a Go-Go (watch for their farewell reunion tour this fall), animal-rights activist, actress, and the co-creator of the comic Lady Robotika. As you can see, all serve the great twin 21st century gods of rock 'n' roll and comics!

Born and raised in the suburbs of New York, **Peter Bagge** (CO-CREATOR, WRITER) soon discovered that the only thing he wanted to do in his life was draw silly cartoons. He so wanted to do this that he even published his own for a while (and this was back in the days where you had to publish actual paper copies, you couldn't just put 'em up on the internet and call it good). Fortunately one day underground comix superstar Robert Crumb saw Pete's work and it made him laugh, and soon Pete was contributing to Crumb's magazine *Weirdo*, which he eventually even got to edit! Meanwhile, Pete started his own magazine *Neat Stuff* for a rinky-dink publisher called Fantagraphics Books, which was followed by a comic called *Hate*, which some have called the best representation of daily life in Seattle among aimless young folks in the "Grunge '90s." These made Pete famous and wealthy (okay, semi-famous and less broke), and he keeps writing and drawing comics to this day, both for Fantagraphics (the now-annual *Hate*) and "real" publishers like Dark Horse Comics and DC Comics (who in fact originally published *Yeah!*): his most recent books are *Bat Boy: The Weekly World News Comic Strips* and *Other Lives* (now in softcover!). Pete lives in Seattle with his wife and cats, and plays in a rock band called Can You Imagine.

California boy **Gilbert Hernandez** (CO-CREATOR, ARTIST), born and raised in Oxnard, was one of six siblings. Their mom was so cool she collected comic books, which is why Gilbert and his brothers and sister were comics fans from an early age, often drawing their own. Like Pete, Gilbert loved comics so much that he actually tried publishing his own (with two of his brothers, Jaime and Mario), something they called *Love and Rockets*. (It was inspired by their love for classic Marvel and DC Comics, the sci-fi comics magazine *Heavy Metal*, and punk rock.) Gary Groth, the grand poo-bah of the rinky-dink publisher Fantagraphics we mentioned above, saw this and told the Brothers he'd take all the hard work of publishing off their hands (also some of the money it would earn, like publishers tend to); they agreed because they'd found out publishing was kind of a pain, and *Love and Rockets* became one of the most acclaimed comics of the last quarter century. (It's true, you can look it up.) *Love and Rockets* continues to this day (like Hate in an "Annual" format), but Gilbert, being a hard-working comics machine, keeps pumping out one great comic after another (his latest is the "graphic novel" *Love From the Shadows*). He lives in Las Vegas with his wife and daughter.